Governing Texas

★★★★★★★★★★★★★★★★★★★★★★★★★★★★★★★★★★★★★★

Governing Texas

3RD EDITION

Anthony Champagne
UNIVERSITY OF TEXAS AT DALLAS

Edward J. Harpham
UNIVERSITY OF TEXAS AT DALLAS

Jason P. Casellas
UNIVERSITY OF HOUSTON

W. W. NORTON & COMPANY

NEW YORK · LONDON

W. W. NORTON & COMPANY has been independent since its founding in 1923, when William Warder Norton and Mary D. Herter Norton first published lectures delivered at the People's Institute, the adult education division of New York City's Cooper Union. The firm soon expanded its program beyond the Institute, publishing books by celebrated academics from America and abroad. By mid-century, the two major pillars of Norton's publishing program—trade books and college texts—were firmly established. In the 1950s, the Norton family transferred control of the company to its employees, and today—with a staff of four hundred and a comparable number of trade, college, and professional titles published each year—W. W. Norton & Company stands as the largest and oldest publishing house owned wholly by its employees.

Editor: Peter Lesser
Assistant Editor: Samantha Held
Project Editor: Christine D'Antonio
Manuscript Editor: Ellen Lohman
Managing Editor, College: Marian Johnson
Managing Editor, College Digital Media: Kim Yi
Production Manager: Ashley Horna
Media Editor: Spencer Richardson-Jones
Associate Media Editor: Michael Jaoui

Media Editorial Assistant: Ariel Eaton
Media Project Editor: Marcus Van Harpen
Marketing Manager, Political Science: Erin Brown
Art Director: Rubina Yeh
Text Design: Tamaye Perry
Photo Editor: Trish Marx
Information Graphics: Kiss Me I'm Polish LLC, New York
Composition: Achorn International, Inc.
Manufacturing: LSC—Kendallville

Permission to use copyrighted material is included in the credits section of this book, which begins on page A43.

Library of Congress Cataloging-in-Publication Data

Names: Champagne, Anthony, author. | Harpham, Edward J., author. | Casellas,
    Jason Paul, 1977- author.
Title: Governing Texas / Anthony Champagne, University of Texas at Dallas,
    Edward J. Harpham, University of Texas at Dallas, Jason P. Casellas,
    University of Houston.
Description: Third edition. | New York : W.W. Norton & Company, [2017] |
    Includes bibliographical references and index.
Identifiers: LCCN 2017004478 | **ISBN 9780393283679** (pbk.)
Subjects: LCSH: Texas—Politics and government.
Classification: LCC JK4816 .C48 2017 | DDC 320.4764—dc23 LC record available at https://lccn.loc.gov/2017004478

W. W. Norton & Company, Inc., 500 Fifth Avenue, New York, NY 10110
wwnorton.com

W. W. Norton & Company Ltd., 15 Carlisle Street, London W1D 3BS

4 5 6 7 8 9 0

Contents in Brief

Contents

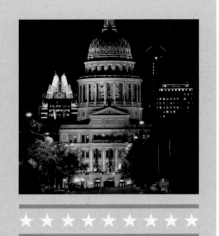

2 • The Texas Constitution   43

3 • Texas in the Federal System   85

4 • Political Parties   111

5 • Campaigns and Elections   143

8 · The Executive Branch   247

11 · Public Finance 361

12 · Public Policy 399

13 • Crime and Corrections Policy   445

★ ★ ★ ★ ★ ★ ★ ★ ★ ★

Preface

OUR GOAL in this text is to offer readers a broad understanding of the factors that are reshaping political processes and institutions in the Lone Star State in the first two decades of the twenty-first century. We are particularly concerned with explaining how the principles underlying constitutional government in Texas are being reworked in the face of new political, economic, and demographic changes. By supplementing our institutional analysis with concrete examples from everyday political life in Texas, we hope to show the reader that politics and government in Texas are not only important to their lives but endlessly fascinating as well.

Features of the Third Edition

Another, related goal of the book is to provide students with extensive pedagogical support throughout each chapter. In every chapter, several features engage students' interest and help them master the learning objectives for the topic.

- **Updated "What Government Does and Why It Matters" chapter introductions** draw students into the chapter by showing them why they should care about the chapter's topic.
- **Chapter Goals** appear at the start of the chapter and then recur at the start of the relevant sections throughout the chapter to create a more focused, active reading experience.
- **NEW Core Objectives are woven into every chapter**, helping students gain proficiency with critical thinking, effective communication, personal and social responsibility, and quantitative reasoning.
- **Updated "Who Are Texans?" infographics** engage visually oriented students with a "statistical snapshot" of the state related to each chapter's topic. Through accompanying quantitative reasoning questions, these features help students grasp the political implications of demographic, political, economic, and regional diversity in Texas. Related exercises in the online coursepacks and slides in the instructor PowerPoints make it easy for instructors to bring these graphics into their online or face-to-face classrooms.
- **Updated "Texas and the Nation" infographics** enable students to compare Texas's government and politics to other states'. Critical thinking questions accompany each "Texas and the Nation" graphic and encourage students to engage deeply with the graphics and draw their own conclusions. Related exercises in the online coursepacks and slides in the PowerPoints make it easy for instructors to bring these graphics into their online or face-to-face classrooms.
- **Revised "You Decide: Voices of Texas" boxes in every chapter** address controversial issues in Texas politics that students care about. These boxes encourage students to think beyond their knee-jerk reactions, consider all sides of the debate, and think about communicating their own effective arguments.

- **NEW "Future of Texas" sections at the end of every chapter** examine how Texas government and politics are likely to change in light of Texas's shifting demographics and economy.
- **Extensive end-of-chapter review sections organized around Chapter Goals** include section outlines, practice quiz questions, and key terms. Students have everything they need to master the material in each section of the chapter.

Revisions to the Third Edition

In the third edition of *Governing Texas*, we have tried to provide students with the most up-to-date account of Texas government and politics. Every chapter was scrutinized with help from dozens of outside reviewers, and we have tried to provide the most current examples and data throughout the text. Highlights of the new edition include:

- Chapter 1 (The Political Culture, People, and Economy of Texas) has been fully updated with the most recent available economic and demographic data. Material has also been added to help students understand the complexity of political culture in Texas and the impact of military bases in the state.
- Chapter 2 (The Texas Constitution) has been updated and refined to include more material on the Texas Founding. Article 1 of the Texas Constitution (the Bill of Rights) has also been included in the appendix with this edition to enhance students' ability to work with original documents while thinking about the role played by the evolving constitution in the state.
- Chapter 3 (Texas in the Federal System) has been rewritten to take into account court decisions that have affected Texas, including recent rulings on the state's voter identification law.
- Chapter 4 (Political Parties) has been updated throughout with particular attention to the growing influence of the Tea Party in state Republican Party politics. The chapter also highlights the role of the Latino community in changing Texas and Democratic Party competition.
- Chapter 5 (Campaigns and Elections) includes a new opener highlighting the mayoral races in San Antonio and Houston, emphasizing why students should care about what happens in elections at the municipal level. This chapter also includes a revamped and updated section on recent changes to electoral practices, including redistricting, voter ID litigation, and *Evenwel v. Abbott*.
- Chapter 6 (Interest Groups and Lobbying) includes many updated examples and stories to highlight the changing role of interest groups in state politics, and devotes considerable attention to recent attempts at ethics reform.
- Chapter 7 (The Legislature) begins with a new opener highlighting Joe Straus's speakership and tensions within the Republican Party. It includes an updated discussion of the two-thirds rule in the State Senate as well as data updated to reflect the changed composition of the legislature.
- Chapter 8 (The Executive Branch) has been significantly rewritten to take into account all the new officials in the Executive Branch. Comparisons are also made between the actions of current officials and those of previous ones—for example, between Governor Perry and Governor Abbott.

- Chapter 9 (The Judiciary) has been updated throughout, with new content added regarding judicial ethics and misconduct.
- Chapter 10 (Local Government) has been significantly rewritten to account for changes in local governments and local officials. Most importantly, discussion of the financial problems facing local governments has been rewritten to make those problems and their causes clearer and easier to understand.
- Chapter 11 (Public Finance) has been fully updated with the data made available to political leaders for the 2017 legislative session. An enhanced discussion of the challenges of both budgetary surpluses and deficits is also included.
- Chapter 12 (Public Policy) has been fully updated. New discussions of the problems facing policy makers in education and health care have been added focusing on the importance of recent court decisions. Explicit linkages have also been made between theories of the policy-making process and the substantive policy areas. A new graphic has been added investigating de facto segregation at the local level in the state.
- Chapter 13 (Crime and Corrections Policy) has been updated so that current developments such as the Sandra Bland case and the Waco Biker case are discussed. New criminal justice reforms, such as the new method for selecting grand juries, are also addressed.

We believe that these changes will assist professors in teaching students the nuts and bolts of Texas government and politics, as well as the broad themes and issues that will shape the Lone Star State in the coming decades.

Resources for Assessment and a Dynamic Classroom Experience

The media package for *Governing Texas,* Third Edition, offers all of the tools needed for effective assessment, targeted self-study, and dynamic classroom presentations— either online or face-to-face. Features include the following.

Norton Coursepacks: Our Content, Your Course
Rachel Bzostek, *University of Texas, Tyler*
Linda Veazey, *Midwestern State University*
Sharon Navarro, *University of Texas, San Antonio*
Ahad Hayaud-Din, *Brookhaven College*

Easily add high-quality Norton digital media to your online, hybrid, or lecture course— all at no cost. Norton Coursepacks work with and leverage your existing Learning Management System, so there's no new system to learn, and access is free and easy. Comprehensive Coursepacks are ready to use, right from the start, but are easy to customize, using the system you already know and understand. Norton Coursepacks include exclusive multimedia content and assessment tools that are not found anywhere else, such as test banks and quizzes, interactive learning tools, and exercises covering chapter objectives and tagged to State Learning Outcomes. Every chapter includes:

- Video exercises to help students retain and apply information through current events

- "Who Are Texans?" and "Texas and the Nation" animated infographics to guide students through interpreting data
- Simulations to get students thinking about how Texas government really works
- **Updated** "You Decide" exercises to help students engage varying views on contemporary issues
- "By the Numbers" exercises to help students practice quantitative skills by exploring key datagraphics from the text

Norton Ebook: Same Great Book, at a Fraction of the Price

Norton ebooks allow students to access the entire book and much more; students can search, highlight, and take notes with ease, as well as collaborate and share their notes with teachers and classmates. The *Governing Texas,* Third Edition, ebook can be viewed on any device—laptop, tablet, phone, even a public computer—and will stay synced between devices.

Lecture PowerPoints

Ronald Vardy, *Wharton County Junior College*

The third edition of *Governing Texas* offers fully customizable lecture slides with clicker questions, teaching ideas, and discussion questions in the instructor-only notes field. "Who Are Texans?" and "Texas and the Nation" slides feature popular infographics and pop quiz questions for the optimal lecture experience.

Art Slides

Photographs and drawn figures from the book are available for classroom use.

Instructor's Manual

Linda Veazey, *Midwestern State University*

The *Instructor's Manual* includes chapter outlines, class activities, and group discussion questions. Each chapter also offers suggested video clips with links and discussion questions.

Test Bank

Sharon Navarro, *University of Texas, San Antonio*

The revised test bank assesses chapter learning goals and Texas Student Learning Outcomes, applies Bloom's Taxonomy across these goals and outcomes, and improves the overall quality and accuracy of our assessment through extensive peer review.

InQuizitive

Guided by an editorial team of experienced teachers, InQuizitive for *Governing Texas* provides formative, adaptive assessment that reinforces reading comprehension with a focus on the key concepts and learning objectives of Texas politics. Guiding feedback helps students understand why their answers were right or wrong and steers them back to the text. Student knowledge is strengthened through questions that compel analysis of Texas politics and government; animated and static infographics; and images, charts, and graphs from this text. Each InQuizitive question is correlated with not only the chapter learning objectives but the state learning objectives for the Texas government course as well.

To learn more about InQuizitive, visit http://books.wwnorton.com/books/inquizitive/overview/.

About the Authors

Over the past 25 years, we have worked together on a number of books that have studied various aspects of government and political life in Texas. We come to the study of Texas politics and government from very different backgrounds.

Anthony Champagne was born in Louisiana as the French surname suggests. His mother's family, however, were pioneer farmers and ranchers in Hopkins County, Texas. It was growing up with Louisiana and Texas connections that gave him a life-long interest in politics. When he moved to the University of Texas at Dallas in 1979, he immediately visited the Sam Rayburn Library in Bonham. Sam Rayburn was one of the Texas's most influential political figures. He was elected to the U.S. House of Representatives in 1912 and served until his death in 1961. During that time, he was chairman of one of the most influential committees of the House, was Majority Leader, Speaker, and Minority Leader of the House. He is responsible for much of the major legislation in the New Deal and for his key role in the politics of the Truman, Eisenhower, and early Kennedy Administrations. A chance meeting at the Sam Rayburn Library with H. G. Dulaney, Sam Rayburn's secretary for 10 years, led to the opportunity to do over 130 oral histories with persons associated with Sam Rayburn. As a result, Champagne was completely hooked on studying Texas politics. He was particularly interested in the transformation of the state from an overwhelmingly Democratic state to a Republican bulwark. And, he was interested in how Texas changed from being a key partner with the national government in the cooperative federalism of the New Deal period to a state whose leaders are frequent critics of national power today. Political change in the state from the Sam Rayburn era to today is a key research focus of his.

Edward Harpham, in contrast, was born in Montreal to second generation Canadian parents who immigrated to the United States soon after his birth. His family's migration over the last 100 years from Sheffield to Toronto (1919) to Delaware (1952) to Texas (1978) and the industries that employed the family (auto service industry, chemical industry, and academia) mirror the demographic changes that have reshaped much of the population movement in the United States and Texas throughout the twentieth century. Trained as a political theorist with a deep interest in political economy, Harpham's move to Texas sparked an interest in how economic changes in the late twentieth century were changing the contours of the state's traditional political life in new and unexpected ways. At the heart of his work lies an abiding interest on the role that ideas play in shaping the growth and development of political institutions and public policies in the modern information age.

Jason Casellas was born in New Orleans and has always had an interest in state and local politics. His grandfather was a professor of Spanish literature at Our Lady of the Lake University in San Antonio. He inspired him to pursue a career as a professor. After graduating from Loyola University in New Orleans, he attended graduate school at Princeton University where he earned a Ph.D. in Politics. His dissertation and book examined Latino representation in state legislatures and Congress, with Texas as one of the key states in his study. Even though he was not born in Texas, he got there as fast as he could. He moved to Texas in 2005 to take an assistant professorship at the University of Texas at Austin, where he continued his immersion in all things Texas. In 2013, he moved not very far to the University of Houston, where he is now an associate professor. Most of his extended family fortuitously reside in all parts of the Houston area. He has continued to teach, research, and comment on Texas politics with a specific expertise in the growing Latino population, and how it might transform the state in the future.

Acknowledgments

WE ARE GRATEFUL for the suggestions that we have received from many thoughtful and experienced government instructors across the state. For their input on the plan and execution of this book, we thank:

Jason Abbott, *Hill College*

Lee Almaguer, *Midland College*

Marcos Arandia, *North Lake College*

Ellen Baik, *University of Texas–Pan American*

Robert Ballinger, *South Texas College*

Annie Johnson Benifield, *Lone Star College–Tomball*

David E. Birch, *Lone Star College–Tomball*

Robin Marshall Bittick, *Sam Houston State University*

Walt Borges, *University of North Texas at Dallas*

Patrick Brandt, *University of Texas at Dallas*

Gary Brown, *Lone Star College–Montgomery*

Lee Brown, *Blinn College*

Jonathan Buckstead, *Austin Community College*

Daniel Bunye, *South Plains College*

James V. Calvi, *West Texas A&M University*

Michael Campenni, *Austin Community College*

Larry Carter, *University of Texas at Arlington*

Max Choudary, *Northeast Lakeview College*

Mark Cichock, *University of Texas at Arlington*

Adrian Clark, *Del Mar College*

Tracy Cook, *Central Texas College*

Cassandra Cookson, *Lee College*

Leland M. Coxe, *University of Texas at Brownsville*

Rosalyn Crain, *Houston Community College–Northwest*

Sandra K. Creech, *Temple College*

Kevin Davis, *North Central Texas College*

Steve Davis, *Lone Star College–Kingwood*

Henry Dietz, *University of Texas at Austin*

Brian K. Dille, *Odessa College*

Douglas Dow, *University of Texas at Dallas*

Jeremy Duff, *Midwestern State University*

David Edwards, *University of Texas at Austin*

Matthew Eshbaugh-Soha, *University of North Texas*

Lou Ann Everett, *Trinity Valley Community College*

Victoria Farrar-Myers, *University of Texas at Arlington*

John P. Flanagan, *Weatherford College*

Ben Fraser, *San Jacinto College*

Joey Fults, *Kilgore College*

Frank J. Garrahan, *Austin Community College*

Will Geisler, *Collin College*

David Garrison, *Collin College*

Mandi Gilligan, *El Centro College*

Shaun M. Gilligan, *Cedar Valley College*

Terry Gilmour, *Midland College*

Randy Givens, *Blinn College*

Donna Godwin, *Trinity Valley Community College*

Elsa Gonzalez, *Texas State Technical College–Harlingen*

Larry Gonzalez, *Houston Community College–Southwest*

Christine Gottemoller, *Del Mar College*

Paul Gottemoller, *Del Mar College*

Kenneth L. Grasso, *Texas State University*

Heidi Jo Green, *Lone Star College–CyFair*

Sara Gubala, *Lamar University*

Yolanda Hake, *South Texas College*

Sabrina Hammel, *Northeast Lakeview College*

Jeff Harmon, *University of Texas at San Antonio*

Tiffany Harper, *Collin College*

Billy Hathorn, *Laredo Community College*

Ahad Hayaud-Din, *Brookhaven College*

Virginia Haysley, *Lone Star College–Tomball*

Tom Heiting, *Odessa College*

John Hitt, *North Lake College*

Kevin Holton, *South Texas College*

Taofang Huang, *University of Texas at Austin*

Casey Hubble, *McLennan Community College*

Gregory Hudspeth, *St. Philip's College*

Glen Hunt, *Austin Community College*

Tammy Johannessen, *Austin Community College*

Doris J. Jones, *Tarrant County College*

Joseph Jozwiak, *Texas A&M Corpus Christi*

Christy Woodward Kaupert, *San Antonio College*

David Kennedy, *Lone Star College–Montgomery*

Edward Korzetz, *Lee College*

Melinda Kovacs, *Sam Houston State University*

Heidi Lange, *Houston Community College–Southwest*

Boyd Lanier, *Lamar University*

James Lantrip, *South Texas College*

David Lektzian, *Texas Tech University*

Raymond Lew, *Houston Community College–Central*

Frank Lewis, *Texas State Technical College–Harlingen*

Bob Little, *Brookhaven College*

Robert Locander, *Lone Star College–North Harris*

Nicholas Long, *St. Edward's University*

George Lyon, *El Paso Community College*

Mitzi Mahoney, *Sam Houston State University*

Lynne Manganaro, *Texas A&M International University*

Sharon Manna, *North Lake College*

Bobby J. Martinez, *Northwest Vista College*

David McClendon, *Tyler Junior College*
Mike McConachie, *Collin College*
Elizabeth McLane, *Wharton County Junior College*
Lindsey McLennan, *Kilgore College*
Phil McMahan, *Collin College*
Eddie Meaders, *University of North Texas*
Gay Michele, *El Centro College*
Tom Miles, *Texas Woman's University; University of North Texas*
Banks Miller, *University of Texas at Dallas*
Eric Miller, *Blinn College–Bryan*
Patrick Moore, *Richland College*
Sherri Mora, *Texas State University–San Marcos*
Dana Morales, *Lone Star College–Montgomery*
Amy Moreland, *Sul Ross State University*
Rick Moser, *Kilgore College*
Mark R. Murray, *South Texas College*
James Myers, *Odessa College*
Sugumaran Narayanan, *Midwestern State University*
Sharon Navarro, *University of Texas at San Antonio*
Jalal Nejad, *Northwest Vista College*
Glynn Newman, *Eastfield College*
Timothy Nokken, *Texas Tech University*
James Norris, *Texas A&M International University*
John Osterman, *San Jacinto College*
Cissie Owen, *Lamar University*
William Parent, *San Jacinto College*
David Putz, *Lone Star College Kingwood*
Himanshin Raizada, *Lamar University*
Prudencio E. Ramirez, *San Jacinto College*
John Raulston, *Kilgore College*
Daniel Regalado, *Odessa College*
Darrial Reynolds, *South Texas College*
Donna Rhea, *Houston Community College–Northwest*
Laurie Robertstad, *Navarro College*
Mario Salas, *University of Texas at San Antonio*

Larry Salazar, *McLennan Community College*
Michael Sanchez, *San Antonio College*
Raymond Sandoval, *Richland College*
Gilbert Schorlemmer, *Blinn College*
Mark Shomaker, *Blinn College*
Dennis Simon, *Southern Methodist University*
Shannon Sinegal, *Temple College*
Steve Slagle, *Texas State Technical College–Harlingen*
Brian William Smith, *St. Edward's University*
Michael Smith, *South Plains College*
Thomas E. Sowers II, *Lamar University*
John Speer, *Houston Community College*
Jeff Stanglin, *Kilgore College*
Jim Startin, *University of Texas at San Antonio*
Andrew Teas, *Houston Community College–Northwest*
Erica C. Terrell, *Richland College*
John Theis, *Lone Star College Kingwood*
Sean Theriault, *University of Texas at Austin*
James Thurmond, *University of Houston*
John Todd, *University of North Texas*
Delaina Toothman, *Texas State University*
Steven Tran, *Houston Community College*
Homer D. Trevino, *McLennan Community College*
Christopher Turner, *Laredo Community College*
Ronald W. Vardy, *University of Houston*
Linda Veazey, *Midwestern State University*
Albert Waite, *Central Texas College*
David Watson, *Sul Ross State University*
Clay Wiegand, *Cisco College*
Geoffrey Willbanks, *University of Texas at Tyler*
Neal Wise, *St. Edward's University*
Kathryn Yates, *Richland College*
Michael Young, *Trinity Valley Community College*
Tyler Young, *Collin College*
Rogerio J. Zapata, *South Texas College*

We thank the following University of Texas at Dallas students for their assistance: Lisa Holmes, Josh Payne, Ali Charania, Alan Roderick, Basel Musharbash, Liza Miadzvedskaya, and Sachi Dave.

At W. W. Norton, Peter Lesser provided editorial guidance throughout the process of developing and publishing the book. Project editor Christine D'Antonio and assistant editor Samantha Held kept everything organized. Copy editor Ellen Lohman helped polish the text. Production manager Ashley Horna made sure we ended up with a high-quality book, right on schedule. Media editor Spencer Richardson-Jones, associate media editor Michael Jaoui, and media editorial assistant Ariel Eaton worked with the authors of accompanying resources to develop useful tools for students and instructors. Our sincere thanks to all of them.

Anthony Champagne
Edward J. Harpham
Jason Casellas
December 2016

Governing Texas

★ ★

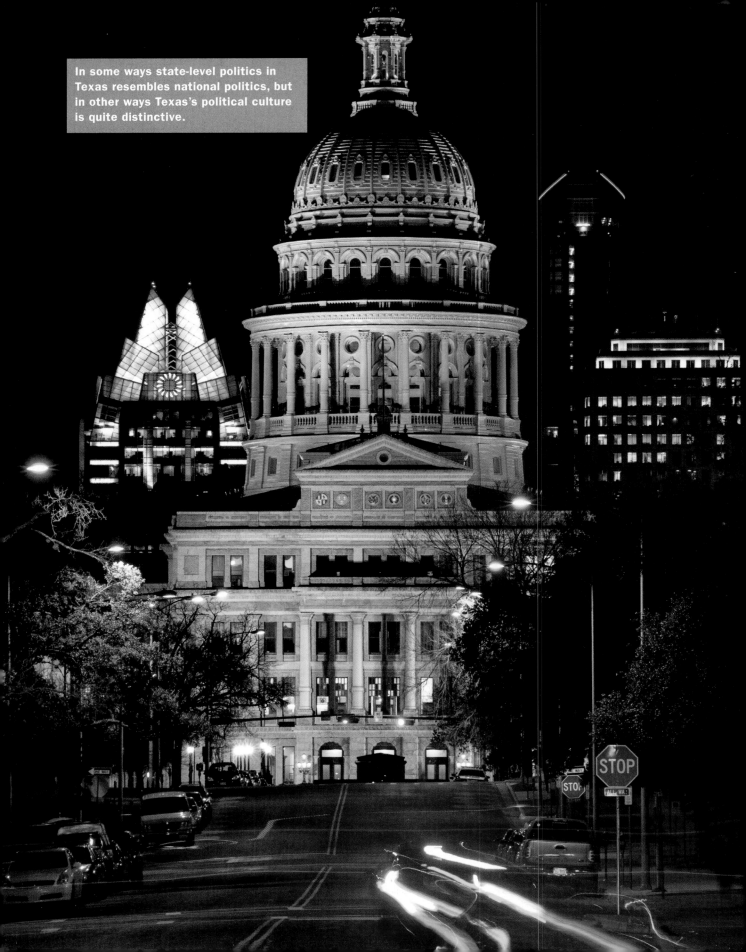

In some ways state-level politics in Texas resembles national politics, but in other ways Texas's political culture is quite distinctive.

1

★ ★ ★ ★ ★

The Political Culture, People, and Economy of Texas

WHY TEXAS'S POLITICAL CULTURE MATTERS In his *Travels with Charley*, John Steinbeck once described Texas as "a state of mind . . . a mystique closely approximating a religion." Americans passionately loved or hated Texas. Steinbeck believed that Texas, despite its vast space, its varying topography, its many cultures and ways of life, had a cohesiveness that may be stronger than in any other part of America. He wrote, "Rich, poor, Panhandle, Gulf, city, country, Texas is the obsession, the proper study and the passionate possession of all Texans."

Certain myths define the obsession that is Texas—and Texans—in the popular imagination. The cowboy who challenges both Native American and Mexican rule, the rancher and farmer who cherish their economic independence, the wildcatter who is willing to risk everything for one more roll of the dice, and the independent entrepreneur who fears the needless intrusion of government into his life—such are the myths about Texans.

These myths extend far into the popular imagination when we think about various politicians who have led the state since its founding: the visionary Stephen F. Austin locked in a Mexican jail after presenting Texas's grievances to the authorities, the military hero Sam Houston who wins the Battle of San Jacinto but is thrown out of office because of his rejection of secession, the irrepressible Ma and Pa Ferguson who both served as governors, and the larger-than-life Lyndon Baines Johnson who began his career as a schoolteacher in Cotulla, Texas, and completed it as a champion of civil rights and the poor.

The reality of Texas today, its people and its leaders, is much more complicated than the Texas of popular myths. Texas is not only the second-largest state in the Union, comprising more than 261,000 square miles; it is also the second most populous. In 2015, Texas is estimated to have a population of almost 27.5 million people, and that population is rapidly growing and becoming more and more diverse. Whites constitute 43.5 percent of the population, while Latinos constitute more than 38.6 percent. Approximately 12.5 percent of the population are African American, and 4.5 percent are Asian. Eighty-five percent of Texans live in urban areas, with many involved in an economy driven by high-tech industry and globalization. More than 27 percent of the population has a bachelor's degree. On the whole, Texans are young, with 26.4 percent under the age of 18 and 10.3 percent over the age of 65.

Throughout this text, we will examine how Texas is changing and creating new myths about the people, politics, and politicians found in the state. We should be careful before we fully accept any of these myths. As in the past, the reality of Texas—its people and its politics—is much more complex than the myths we spin about it. Conservative Republicans may control today's political agenda, but their long-term dominance in politics and government is not certain. Increasing racial and ethnic diversity points to a new Texas, one that looks sharply different from the one in the history books and one that appears to favor Democrats (the party preferred today by most Latinos, African Americans, and recent immigrants). The future of the state and its people will be determined in large part by the struggle between an assertive Republican majority and a Democratic minority trying to regain power as both parties try to address the various political, economic, and demographic challenges facing the state. Moving our understanding of governance and politics beyond the myths about Texas is the goal of this chapter and the book.

CHAPTERGOALS

- Describe the defining characteristics of political culture in Texas (pp. 5–7)
- Explain how Texas's geography has influenced its political culture (pp. 7–10)
- Trace the evolution of Texas's economy (pp. 11–22)
- Explain how the population of Texas has changed over time (pp. 22–30)
- Describe Texas's shift from a rural society to an urban one (pp. 30–38)

Texas Political Culture

Describe the defining characteristics of political culture in Texas

Studies of Texas politics often begin with a discussion of Texas's **political culture**. Though the concept is somewhat open ended, states do often exhibit a distinctive culture that is the "product of their entire history." Presumably the political culture of a state has an effect on how people participate in politics and how individuals and institutions interact.[1] Political scientist Daniel Elazar has created a classification scheme for state political cultures that is used widely. He uses the concepts of moralistic, individualistic, and traditionalistic to describe such cultures. These three state political cultures are contemporary manifestations of the ethnic, socioreligious, and socioeconomic differences that existed among America's original thirteen colonies.[2]

According to Elazar, **moralistic political cultures** were rooted in New England, where Puritans and other religious groups sought to create the Good Society. In such a culture, politics is the concern of everyone, and government is expected to take action to promote the public good and advance the public welfare. Citizen participation in politics is viewed as positive; people are encouraged to pursue the public good in civic activities.

Individualistic political cultures, on the other hand, originated in the middle states, where Americans sought material wealth and personal freedom through commercial activities. A state with an individualistic political culture generally places a low value on citizen participation in politics. Politics is a matter for professionals rather than for citizens, and the role of government is strictly limited. Government's role is to ensure stability so that individuals can pursue their own interests.

Traditionalistic political culture developed initially in the South, reflecting the values of the slave plantation economy (pre-1865) and its successor, the Jim Crow era (1876–1965). Rooted in preindustrial values that emphasize social hierarchy and close interpersonal, often familial, relations among people, traditional culture is concerned with the preservation of tradition and the existing social order. In such states, public participation is limited and government is run by an established **elite**. Public policies disproportionately benefit the interests of those elites.

States can, of course, have cultures that combine these concepts. One book classified California as having a "moralistic individualistic" political culture and New York an "individualistic moralistic" culture. Often, Texas is categorized as having a "traditionalistic individualistic" political culture.[3] Taxes are kept low, and social services are minimized. Political elites, such as business leaders, have a major voice in how the state is run. In spite of the difficulty in measuring the concept of political culture in any empirical way, it is a concept widely regarded as useful in explaining fundamental beliefs about the state and the role of state government.

When considering the political culture of a state, one must recognize that it is not a stagnant thing. Political culture can change over time. Texas is undergoing dramatic changes, including some change in its political culture. It is also difficult to classify the political culture of a state as large and as diverse as Texas in any one category. The liberal cultural norms of urban areas like Houston, Dallas, and Austin often stand in sharp contrast to those found in the conservative suburban and exurban areas of

political culture broadly shared values, beliefs, and attitudes about how the government should function and politics should operate; American political culture emphasizes the values of liberty, equality, and democracy

moralistic political culture the belief that government should be active in promoting the public good and that citizens should participate in politics and civic activities to ensure that good

individualistic political culture the belief that government should limit its role to providing order in society, so that citizens can pursue their economic self-interest

traditionalistic political culture the belief that government should be dominated by political elites and guided by tradition

elite a small group of people that dominates the political process

The seal of Texas reflects the state's individualistic political culture.

these cities. These, too, differ from the political cultures found in south Texas along the border or in the rural Panhandle of west Texas. In fact, Texas has many different political cultures or subcultures within its borders.[4]

To understand the complexity of political culture in Texas today, it is useful to consider three long-lasting patterns in Texas politics and the changes that they are undergoing: the one-party state, the idea of provincialism, and business dominance. We examine these elements of Texas political culture below.

The One-Party State Persists

For over 100 years, Texas was dominated by the Democratic Party. Winning the Democratic Party primary was tantamount to winning the general election. As we will see in later chapters, this pattern no longer holds. During the 1990s substantial competition emerged between the parties for control of the state legislature. Following redistricting in 2002 the Republicans secured a 7-vote majority in the state Senate and a 24-vote majority in the state House. Between 2002 and 2016 all major statewide elected offices were controlled by Republicans. One Court of Criminal Appeals justice switched to the Democratic Party in December 2013 after being elected as a Republican, but was defeated in the November 2016 general elections. The question today is not whether the political culture of Texas will continue to be defined by a powerful Democratic Party, but how that culture will be redefined by two forces: a powerful Republican Party in most suburban, exurban, and rural areas that is growing increasingly conservative and a Democratic Party that controls Texas's most urban areas.

Provincialism Is Declining

provincialism a narrow, limited, and self-interested view of the world often associated with rural values and notions of limited government

A second pattern that once defined Texas political culture is **provincialism**, a narrow view of the world that is often associated with rural values and notions of limited government. The result often was an intolerance of diversity and a notion of the public interest that dismissed social services and expenditures for education. Some of the more popular politicians in Texas have stressed cornpone—a rural rejection of modern urban lifestyles—intolerance, and a narrow worldview rather than policies that might offer advantages to the state as it competes with other states and with other nations. Like the one-party Democratic state, Texas provincialism has faded as a defining feature of the political culture. The growing influence of minorities, women, and gays in state politics, increasing urbanization, and Texas's relevance in the global economy have all undercut Texas's traditional provincialism.

PERSONAL RESPONSIBILITY: WHAT WOULD YOU DO?

- Do you agree with the popular myth that Texas is overly provincial—that is, intolerant, narrow minded, and overly critical of government? Why or why not?

- Do you think Texas needs to be more welcoming of outside interests and ideas? If so, what do you think government and the people could do to foster more open-mindedness in Texas?

Business Dominance Continues

A third, continuing pattern that has helped define Texas's political culture is its longtime dominance by business.

Ties between business and politics have always been close in Texas. Here, Governor Greg Abbott signs a bill prohibiting local government attempts to ban fracking as a way to continue to get oil and natural gas out of the ground.

Labor unions are rare in Texas except in the oil-refinery areas around Beaumont–Port Arthur. Other groups that might offer an alternative to a business perspective, such as consumer interests, are poorly organized and poorly funded. Business groups are major players in Texas politics, in terms of campaign contributions, organized interest groups, and lobbyists.

This chapter will investigate the economic, social, and demographic changes that transformed Texas's political culture during the twentieth century. These changes shook Texas government and politics in the 1990s and have continued to shape them in the second decade of the twenty-first century.

The Land

Explain how Texas's geography has influenced its political culture

Much of Texas's history and political life has been shaped by the relationship forged between its people and the land. When Texas became a republic in 1836, it claimed 216,000,000 acres (approximately 350,000 square miles) of unappropriated land as its own. At its founding, Texas was land rich but money poor, having only $55.68 in its treasury. Texas was the only state, other than the original 13 colonies, to keep control of its public lands when it entered the Union in 1845. Privatizing these public lands was probably the most important ongoing public policy pursued by the state through the Land Office in the nineteenth century. Although Texas turned a large portion of its public lands over to private ownership, it retained ownership of the minerals under some of this land, including land containing oil and natural gas. **Privatization of public property** established the property rules and regulations under which economic development would take place in the state. It also gave the state an ownership of mineral rights that would provide funding for elementary and secondary education as well as higher education for the next 160 years.

Privatization was not the only political issue surrounding land in Texas in the nineteenth century. The exact boundaries of Texas were contentious throughout the 1840s and 1850s. Following the Mexican American War, the Treaty of Guadalupe Hidalgo in 1848 established the Rio Grande as the southern border of the state. Following a threat by Texas to use military force to reassert its land claims in the west, the Compromise of 1850 established Texas's current western borders. In exchange for $10 million in federal bonds, Texas gave up claims to 67,000,000 acres of land in what are now New Mexico, Wyoming, Colorado, Kansas, and Oklahoma. The Compromise of 1850 enabled Texas to pay off the public debts incurred during the Republic and to retain 98,000,000 acres in public lands.[5]

Today, Texas is the second-largest state in size, next to Alaska. To understand the dynamics of political life and governance in Texas demands an appreciation of the vast spaces and topography that define the state.

Perhaps the most distinctive characteristic of Texas's geography is its size. The longest straight-line distance across the state from north to south is 801 miles; the longest east–west distance is 773 miles. To put this into perspective, the north–south distance between New York City and Charleston, South Carolina, is 763 miles, cutting across six different states. The east–west distance from New York City to Chicago is 821 miles, cutting across five different states.

Distances alone do not tell the whole story of the diverse geography found in Texas. There are four distinct physical regions in Texas (Figure 1.1).[6] Their distinctive features have shaped politics in Texas in a number of important ways.

The Gulf Coastal Plains

The Gulf Coastal Plains extend from the Louisiana border and the Gulf of Mexico, along the Rio Grande up to Del Rio, and northward to the line of the Balcones Fault and Escarpment. As one moves westward, the climate becomes increasingly dry. Forests become less frequent as post oak trees dominate the landscape until they too are replaced by the prairies and brushlands of central Texas.

The eastern portion of the Gulf Coastal Plains—so-called east Texas—is characterized by hilly surfaces covered by forests of pine and hardwoods. Almost all of Texas's timber production takes place here. It is also the home of some of Texas's most famous oilfields. To the west is the Blackland Belt. A rolling prairie soil made the Blackland Belt a prime farming area during the late nineteenth and early twentieth centuries. It was a major center of cotton production in Texas. Today, it is the most densely populated area of the state and has a diversified manufacturing base.

The Coastal Prairies around Houston and Beaumont were the center for the post–World War II industrial boom, particularly in the petrochemical industry. Winter vegetable and fruit production plays a major role in the Lower Rio Grande Valley, while livestock is important in the Rio Grande Plain, an area that receives less than

FIGURE 1.1

The Physical Regions of Texas
SOURCE: Dallas Morning News, *Texas Almanac 2000–2001* (Dallas: Dallas Morning News, 1999), p. 55.

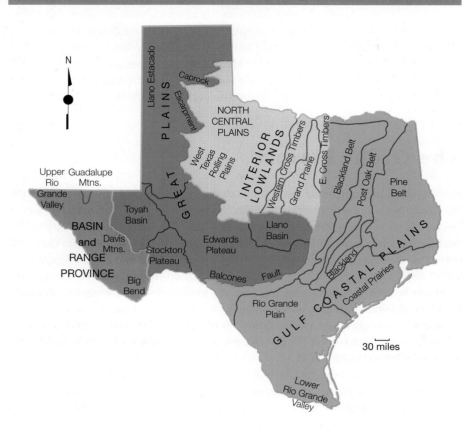

24 inches of rainfall on average every year and during the summer months experiences rapid evaporation.

Texas's political life grew out of the Gulf Coastal Plains. The land grants made available to Americans willing to come to Texas in the first half of the nineteenth century were located here. This region was the foundation of plantation life during the antebellum period when slavery flourished in the state. East Texas was the home of the first oil booms in Texas in the early decades of the twentieth century. The Dallas–Fort Worth area is located in the northwestern part of this region, once a bastion of a small Republican Party. A union movement grew out of the industrialized areas along the coast, providing support to a liberal wing of the Democratic Party. For the most part, though, the Gulf Coastal Plains were dominated by rural conservative values, be they located in the Democratic Party (from 1876 to the early 1990s) or in the Republican Party (from the 1990s to today). Urbanization and suburbanization in Houston and Dallas–Fort Worth have added new dimensions to the political life of this region. Urban areas have become increasingly Democratic, while suburban areas have become more Republican.

The Interior Lowlands

The Interior Lowlands are an extension of the interior lowlands that run down from Canada. They are bordered by the Balcones Escarpment on the east and south and the Caprock Escarpment on the west. Beginning to the west of Fort Worth, the eastern edge of the Interior Lowlands has predominantly an agricultural economy and a rural population. The western portion, meanwhile, rises from 750 to 2,000 feet in elevation. The West Texas Rolling Plains contain much level, cultivable land and are home to a large cattle-raising industry. Many of the state's largest ranches are located here. Like other rural areas of Texas today that have abandoned liberalism and the Democratic Party, this region is dominated by conservative politics and the Republican Party.

The Great Plains

Pushing down into northwest Texas from the Rocky Mountains to the Balcones Fault, the Great Plains define the terrain in much of western Texas, rising from 2,700 feet in the east to more than 4,000 feet along the New Mexico border. The major city on the northern plains is Amarillo. Ranching and petroleum production dominate the economy. The southern plains economy centers on agriculture and cotton production, with Lubbock as the major city. Large-scale irrigation from underwater reservoirs, particularly the Ogallala Aquifer, has played a major role in the economic development of this region. A major concern of policy makers is that pumping out of the aquifer exceeds replenishment, raising questions of the viability of basing future growth on the irrigation practices of the past. We will return to a discussion of the problem of aquifer depletion in Chapter 12.

As in east Texas, conservative political values have a home in the Interior Lowlands and the Great Plains. While representatives from this area have played a major role in the political life of the state over the last 100 years, their power has been ebbing in the face of the population pressures of Texas's expanding urban areas elsewhere.

The Basin and Range Province

The fourth geographic region in Texas is the Basin and Range Province. Here one finds Texas's mountains in the Guadalupe Range along the border with New Mexico, which includes Guadalupe Peak (8,749 feet) and El Capitan (8,085 feet). To the southeast is Big Bend country, so named because the Rio Grande surrounds it on three sides as the river makes its southward swing. Rainfall and population are sparse in this region.

The area running from the Basin and Range Province to the Lower Rio Grande has always had a distinctive political culture, heavily dominated by the fact that Texas and Mexico have been joined at the hip economically and demographically. The population in this region is overwhelmingly Latino. In the late twentieth and early twenty-first centuries, the Border region, including El Paso, McAllen, and Brownsville, has remained a Democratic Party bastion.

Economic Change in Texas

 Trace the evolution of Texas's economy

The famous twentieth-century economist Joseph Schumpeter characterized the capitalist economic system as being a process of "creative destruction."[7] By this he meant that capitalism was an economic system that underwent periodic waves of transformation fueled by technological innovations in production and distribution. These waves of technological transformation were put into place by entrepreneurs who had visions of new ways to produce and distribute goods and services and who were willing to act on those visions. The capitalist process of creative destruction not only creates a new economic and social world; it destroys old ones. The world of railroads, steam, and steel transformed American economic and social life by nationalizing the market and making new opportunities available to businesses and individuals during the late nineteenth century. It also destroyed the local markets that had defined rural American communities since the Founding. The technological innovation tied to gasoline combustion engines, electricity, and radio restructured the American economy again in the 1920s, leaving in its wake a society and an economy that would never be the same.

Schumpeter's theory of creative destruction provides a useful way to think about the economic changes that have shaped and reshaped the Texas economy. Three great waves of technological change have helped define and redefine the Texas political economy over the last 150 years. The first centered on the production of cotton and cattle and their distribution by an extensive railroad system. The second grew out of the oil industry. The third and most recent is tied to the development of the high-tech digital economy.

Cotton

Cotton is one of the oldest crops grown in Texas.[8] Missions in San Antonio in the eighteenth century are reported to have produced several thousand pounds of cotton annually, which were spun and woven by local artisans. Serious cultivation of cotton began in 1821 with the arrival of white Americans. Political independence, statehood, and the ongoing removal of the Native American "threat" in the years before the Civil War promoted the development of the cotton industry. By the mid-nineteenth century, cotton production in Texas soared, placing Texas eighth among the top cotton-producing states in the Union. Although production fell in the years following the Civil War, by 1869 it had begun to pick up again. By 1880, Texas led all states in the production of cotton in most years.

A number of technological breakthroughs further stimulated the cotton industry in Texas. First, in the 1870s barbed wire was introduced, enabling farmers to cordon off their lands and protect their cash crop from grazing cattle. Second, the building of railroads brought Texas farmers into a national market. Finally, a newly designed

During the late nineteenth century, in most years Texas produced more cotton than any other state. But although one-quarter of the cotton produced in the United States still comes from Texas, the importance of the cotton industry to the state's economy has declined since the 1920s. This photo shows land and machinery used to farm cotton.

plow made it easier to dig up the prairie soil and significantly increase farm productivity.

Throughout the 1870s immigrants from the Deep South and Europe flooded the prairies of Texas to farm cotton. Most of these newly arrived Texans became tenant farmers or sharecroppers. Tenants lived on farms owned by landowners, providing their own animals, tools, and seed. They generally received two-thirds of the final value of the cotton grown on the farm, while the landlords received the other third. Another form of tenant farming is sharecropping. Sharecroppers furnished only their labor but received only one-half of the value of the final product. Almost half of the state farmers were tenants by the turn of the century.[9]

Two important consequences resulted from the tenant and sharecropping system. First, it condemned many rural Texans to lives of social and economic dependency. The notorious "croplien" system was developed by landlords and merchants to extend credit to farmers who did not own their land. Under this system, farmers profited from their work only after their debts had been paid or new loans had been made to pay off old debts. The result often was to trap farmers in a debt cycle from which they could not escape. Second, the tenant and sharecropping system helped fuel radical political discontent in rural areas, sparking both the Grange and Populist movements. These movements played a major role in defining the style of Texas politics throughout much of the late nineteenth and early twentieth centuries.

Cotton production cycled up and down as farmers experienced a series of crises and opportunities during the late nineteenth and early twentieth centuries, ranging from destructive boll weevils to an increased demand brought on by World War I to a collapse in prices following the war. The general decline of the cotton culture continued after World War II. The 1930 Census reported that 61 percent of all farmers in Texas were tenant farmers. One-third of these farmers were sharecroppers. These numbers fell throughout the Great Depression and beyond. By 1987 only 12 percent of all farmers were tenants.[10]

Cattle

The history of ranching and the cattle industry parallels that of cotton in many ways.[11] The origins of ranching and the cattle industry extend back to the late seventeenth century, when the Spanish brought livestock to the region to feed their missionaries, soldiers, and civilians. Ranching offered immigrants an attractive alternative to farming during the periods of Mexican and Republic of Texas rule. In the 1830s traffic in cattle was limited to local areas. This began to change as cattle drives and railroads began opening up new markets in the east.

Following the Civil War, the cattle industry took off, expanding throughout the state. As with cotton, the invention of barbed wire helped close off the lands used for grazing. By the end of the nineteenth century, ranch lands had been transformed from open range to fenced pasturing. As a result, conflicts over land often broke out between large and small ranchers, as well as between ranchers and farmers. As cattle raising became a more specialized and efficient business, periodic conflicts broke

Cattle ranching is another of Texas's dominant industries. The most famous ranch in Texas is the King Ranch, shown here in 1950. Currently covering almost 1,300 square miles, it is larger than the state of Rhode Island.

out between employers and employees. Throughout the twentieth century, ranching remained a cyclical industry, struggling when national and international prices collapsed and thriving during upturns in the economy.

Ranching and cotton production remain important industries in the state, although increasingly dominated by big agribusiness companies. Today, Texas normally leads the nation in livestock production. Similarly, it normally leads all other states in cotton production. About 40 percent of the total cotton production in the United States comes from Texas. In 2014 the annual cotton crop was over 6.2 million bales, valued at over $2.1 billion. Most of this production is exported to such places as China, Turkey, and Mexico. Production has fluctuated over the last decade because of the severe drought that plagued parts of the state.[12]

Today, neither cotton production nor ranching drives the Texas political economy. The number of people making a living from agriculture has dropped significantly over the last 50 years as agribusiness has pushed out the family farm and ranch. In 1940, 23 percent of the population worked on farms and ranches. Another 17 percent were suppliers to farms and ranches or helped assemble, process, or distribute agricultural products. Currently, less than 2 percent of the population lives on farms and ranches, with an additional 15 percent of the population providing support, processing, or distribution services to agriculture in Texas.[13]

A new set of technological breakthroughs challenged the nineteenth-century dominance of cotton and cattle in the early twentieth century. These breakthroughs focused not on what grew on the land, but on what lay beneath it.

Oil

Oil was first sighted in the mid-seventeenth century by Spanish explorers.[14] There was no market or demand for the product, and nothing was done to develop this natural resource. Over a century later, encouraged by a growing demand for petroleum products following the Civil War, a scattering of entrepreneurs dug wells, although they were not commercially viable. The first economically significant oil discovery in Texas was in 1894 in Navarro County near Corsicana. By 1898 the state's first oil refinery was operating at the site. Oil production had become economically viable.

What catapulted Texas into the era of oil and gas was the discovery at Spindletop on January 10, 1901. Located three miles south of Beaumont along the Gulf Coast, the Spindletop discovery produced Texas's first oil boom. The success of Spindletop encouraged large numbers of speculators and entrepreneurs to try their luck in the new business. Within three years, three major oilfields had been discovered within 150 miles of Spindletop.

Oil fever spread throughout Texas over the next decade. In north central Texas, major discoveries took place at Brownwood, Petrolia, and Wichita Falls. In the teens major discoveries were made in Wichita County, Limestone County near Mexia, and once again in Navarro County. In 1921 oil was found in the Panhandle, and by the end of the decade major oilfields were being developed all across the state. The biggest oilfield in the state was found in October 1930 in east Texas. As journalist Mary G. Ramos notes, "By the time the East Texas field was developed, Texas's economy was powered not by agriculture, but by petroleum."[15]

The oil and gas industry transformed the social and economic fabric of Texas in a number of important ways. By providing cheap oil and gas, the industry made possible a new industrial revolution in twentieth-century America that was fueled by hydrocarbons. Cheap oil provided a new fuel for transportation and manufacturing. Railroads and steamships were able to convert from coal to oil. Manufacturing plants and farms were able to operate more efficiently with a new, cheap source of energy, encouraging individuals to migrate to cities away from farms. Automobile production was encouraged, as was the building of roads. The Interstate Highway System that was built during the 1950s and 1960s changed fundamentally the transportation patterns that shaped the movements of people and goods in Texas. The triangle formed by I-35 from San Antonio to Dallas–Fort Worth, I-45 from Dallas–Fort Worth to Houston, and I-10 from Houston to San Antonio became the heartland of the Texas economy and the location of an increasing percentage of the state's population.

The oil and gas industry also sparked a rapid industrialization of the Gulf Coast region. Among the companies developing the Gulf Coast oilfields were Gulf Oil, Sun Oil, Magnolia Petroleum, the Texas Company (then Texaco, now Chevron), and Humble Oil (which later became Esso, then Exxon, and finally ExxonMobil). The refineries, pipelines, and export facilities laid the foundations for the large-scale industrialization that would take place along the Gulf Coast in the Houston–Beaumont–Port Arthur region. By 1929 in Harris County, for example, 27 percent of all manufacturing employees worked in refineries. By 1940 the capacity of all the refineries had increased fourfold.[16] The petrochemical industry continued to flourish throughout the 1960s, when demand for its products grew at the rate of 10 percent a year.

One important effect of the oil and gas boom in Texas was the development of a new rhythm to economic life in the state. There had been a natural pace to the economy when it was tied to the production of cotton and cattle. Prices of products could rise and fall, bringing prosperity or gloom to local economies. But there was a bond between the land and the people and the communities that formed around them. Oil and gas, on the other hand, introduced a boom-and-bust mentality that carried over into the communities that sprang up around oil and gas discoveries. Rural areas were often unprepared for the population explosion that followed the discovery of oil or gas. Housing was often inadequate or nonexistent. Schools quickly became overcrowded.

General living conditions were poor as people sought to "make it big." The irony of the oil and gas business was that a major discovery that brought large amounts of new oil and gas to market could lead to a sudden collapse in prices. Prosperous economic times could quickly turn into local depressions. And when particular fields were tapped out, boom towns could quickly become ghost towns.

The oil and gas industry also transformed government and the role that it played in the economy. Following the Civil War, a series of attempts to regulate the railroads had largely failed. In 1890, after considerable controversy fueled by Populist anti-railroad sentiment, a constitutional amendment was passed to create an agency to regulate the railroads, the Texas Railroad Commission. This regulatory agency's powers were extended in 1917 to regulate energy. The Railroad Commission was empowered to see that petroleum pipelines were "common carriers" (that they transported all producers' oil and gas) and to promote well-spacing rules. In an attempt to bring stability to fluctuations in world oil prices brought on by the glut of oil on world markets in the 1930s and to avoid wasteful oil production, the commission won the authority to prorate oil and determine how much every oil well in Texas might produce. Through the late 1960s the Texas Railroad Commission was one of the most important regulatory bodies in the nation. It was also one of the few democratically elected regulatory agencies.

Helping to expand the power of state government in the economy through the Railroad Commission was only one effect of the oil and gas industry in Texas. The oil and gas industry also had an important fiscal effect on state government. Beginning in 1905 the state collected oil production taxes. These rose from $101,403 in 1906 to over $1 million in 1919 and almost $6 million in 1929. For the 2016–17 biennium, it was estimated that oil production taxes, or severance taxes, would contribute $3.9 billion to the state budget, down from $6.75 billion in 2014–15, a decrease of 42.1 percent. Natural gas production taxes in 2016–17 added another $1.9 billion to the state budget, down from $3.18 billion or down 39.8 percent in 2014–15.[17] These numbers have fluctuated in recent years as the price of oil and gasoline has collapsed and then recovered. As we will see in Chapter 11 on public finance in Texas, oil and natural gas production has returned to play an increasingly important role in the state's finances through the severance tax.

Much like the state coffers, higher education in Texas has benefited from the oil and gas industry. What many thought was worthless land at the time had been set aside by the state constitution of 1876 and the state legislature in 1883 to support higher education (the Permanent University Fund). As luck would have it, oil was discovered in the West Texas Permian Basin in 1923 on university land. Soon, 17 wells were producing oil on that land, sparking a building boom at the University of Texas. In 1931 the income of the Permanent University Fund was split between the University of Texas at Austin and Texas A&M University, with the former receiving two-thirds and the latter one-third. In 1984 the income was opened up to all University of Texas and Texas A&M schools. Along with the royalties from other natural resources on university land, oil and gas royalties created one of the largest university endowments in the world. Today, the Permanent University Fund holds title to 2.1 million acres located in 24 counties, primarily in west Texas. In August 2015 the market value of the Permanent University Fund was calculated to be $17.4 billion.[18]

The oil and gas industry had one other effect on life in Texas that is worth noting. Fortunes were made in the industry, and those fortunes paved the way for an expansion of private philanthropy that would have a major influence in shaping Texas's culture. Among the most famous examples of this private philanthropy were the Meadows Foundations, established in 1948 to promote programs in health, education, visual arts, social services, and historical preservation. The Sid W. Richardson Foundation was founded in 1947 and supported health and education programs, as well as the development of the arts in Fort Worth. The Bass Performance Hall, which opened in May 1998, was funded by the Bass brothers, grandnephews of the independent oilman Sid Richardson.

The movement out of the era of oil and gas and into that of high tech was not an easy one. World oil prices rose in 1981 to almost $35 per barrel. At the time, oil-related businesses accounted for 26 percent of the gross state product. From 1971 to 1981 the average rate of economic growth was 4.4 percent. Fueled by a booming oil-based economy and a rapidly increasing population, real estate prices shot up in urban areas such as Houston and Dallas. Projections were made that as oil prices rose, perhaps to $70 or $80 per barrel on the world market, future prosperity was inevitable. Indeed, there was some talk that Texas's oil-driven economy had become recession-proof. Such talk proved to be premature, to say the least.

World oil prices began to collapse in 1982, bottoming out on March 31, 1986, at $10 per barrel. Other sectors of the economy began to suffer as the price of oil fell. Real estate deals fell through, and construction projects slowed and then shut down. Speculators defaulted on their loans, and banks began to fail. Throughout the 1980s, 370 banks went under in Texas. At the same time, the state went through two major recessions, one in 1982 and another in 1986–87. The average annual economic growth slowed to 1.7 percent, the worst since World War II.

Texas emerged from the economic malaise of the 1980s with a transformed state economy. Though remaining an important sector in the economy, the oil and gas business was no longer the primary driving force. By 1992 production of oil had fallen to 642 million barrels worth $11.8 billion. Production continued to fall until 2000 to just under 349 million barrels worth a little over $10 billion. Over 146,000 jobs had been lost in the oil industry throughout the 1980s. By the early 1990s oil accounted for only about 12 percent of the gross state product.

One can trace the rise and decline and rise again of the oil and gas industry in Texas through production figures (see Figure 1.2). Oil production in Texas seemed to peak in 1972, and there were decades of decline in the state's production. New technologies such as horizontal drilling and fracking led to a new boom era of oil and gas production in Texas beginning in 2008 and carrying through 2016. Through March 2016, more than 1.39 million barrels of that daily production came from the Permian Basin region in west Texas. This oilfield may be the second largest in the world. The result of this new oil boom is that today oil (and gas) emerged again as a mainstay of the Texas economy, although it is an economy that is far more diversified than in any earlier era. With the new Texas oil boom came greater resources for the Texas budget. Additionally, with the boom came new demands for vast water supplies—an essential component of the new drilling technology—and new concerns over the effects that those new technologies will have on the environment.[19]

By 2015 there were some dark clouds on the horizon of the oil industry. After hovering around $100 per barrel through mid-2014, the price of oil began a steady decline to around $50 per barrel in mid-2015 before falling below $28 per barrel in early 2016. Not surprising, as the price fell through the second half of 2015, production of oil in Texas went into decline as well. However, by late May 2016, prices began to re-

FIGURE 1.2

Oil Production in Texas

NOTE: Data refer to onshore production in Texas.

SOURCE: Texas Railroad Commission; "Historical Crude Oil Prices," InflationData.com; *Texas Almanac 2015*.

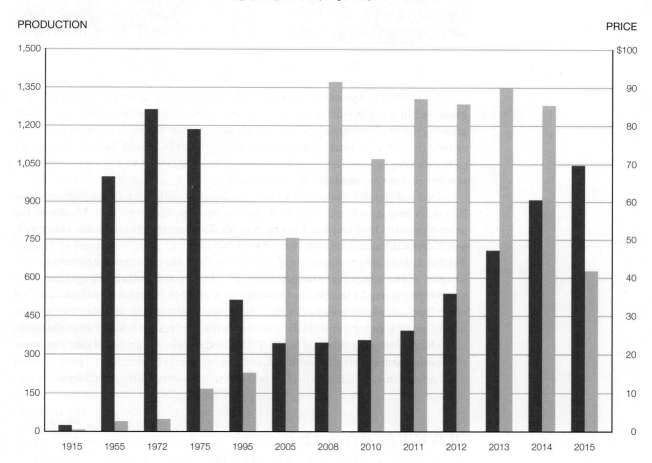

■ Annual production (millions of barrels, left axis)
■ Average price per barrel ($, right axis)

cover, topping $50.00. Whether prices will rise or fall in 2016 and 2017 is uncertain at the time of publication. The long-term impact of the fluctuation of the price of oil and of oil production on the state's economy and budget also is anyone's guess.[20]

High-Tech Industries

By the last decade of the twentieth century, new industries and technologies not based in extraction from the land assumed significant roles in plotting the state's economic future. Among the most important of these was the burgeoning high-tech industry. In contrast to the 1980s, the 1990s were a period of rapid growth. In the 1990s, unlike

In the 1990s, Texas emerged as a leader in high-tech industries. Here, a Texas Instruments employee oversees the production of silicon wafers in the company's Dallas semiconductor plant.

in early periods of speculative booms such as the 1970s, the economy's growth was grounded in a rapidly diversifying economy. At the heart of this boom was a fast-growing manufacturing sector tied to high tech. In the 1990s, Texas went from seventh in the nation in total manufacturing employment to second. By 2013, 15 percent of the state's gross domestic product came from manufacturing. Eight percent of the workforce was employed in manufacturing.[21]

Two metropolitan areas stand out as national centers for the rapidly evolving high-tech industry. The Austin–San Marcos metropolitan area is the home of the computer giant Dell and has become a production center for computer chips, personal computers, and related computer hardware with such companies as Google, Facebook, Flextronics, Apple, Oracle, and IBM. Seven of the area's largest employers are part of the computer or semiconductor industry. The Dallas metropolitan area, particularly north of the city, is the home of a number of important electronic and electronic-equipment companies, including Texas Instruments. Houston has become known worldwide for its medical center and expanding research facilities in the medical field. A 2014 study released by the TechAmerica Foundation found that Texas was the leading tech export state with $45.1 billion in exports in 2012, up 7.3 percent from 2011. Approximately 331,000 jobs in Texas were supported by these tech exports.[22]

NAFTA and the International Economy

Texas's place in national and international markets has been shaped by its central location, its border with Mexico, and its sophisticated transportation infrastructure. There are 306,404 miles of highways in Texas (the most in the nation) along with 45 railroads operating on 10,405 rail miles (the most in the nation). There are 12 deep-water ports in Texas, including the Port of Houston, which was ranked 2nd nationally for total trade and 13th globally for total cargo volume. The Dallas–Fort Worth International Airport and George Bush Intercontinental Airport in Houston ranked high on the list of the world's busiest airports and were major hubs for both national and international travel. Over 6.5 million trucks, 47.8 million personal vehicles, and 22.9 million people crossed the Texas–Mexico border in 2013.[23]

One defining feature of the Texas economy in the 1990s and 2000s was the **North American Free Trade Agreement (NAFTA)**. Signed on December 17, 1992, by Prime Minister Brian Mulroney of Canada, President Carlos Salinas de Gortari of Mexico, and President George H. W. Bush of the United States, NAFTA sought to create a free-trade zone—an area free of customs duties—in North America that was the largest of its kind in the world. Considerable controversy surrounded the passage of NAFTA, with many groups arguing that free trade would hurt U.S. workers and companies because of the cheap labor available in Mexico. An important milestone in the agreement was reached on October 19, 2001, when Mexican trucks were finally allowed to cross over into the United States with goods for U.S. markets. Despite NAFTA provisions, Mexican trucks had been banned in the United States for almost 20 years because of strong labor union opposition and concerns over safety.

Today, NAFTA links approximately 450 million consumers in the United States, Canada, and Mexico with a combined gross domestic product of $19.6 trillion. According to a recent Standard and Poor's study, Mexico has benefited the most from the agreement. But Texas has benefited enormously as well. NAFTA was not the only cause of the diversification of the Texas economy since the 1980s, but it has accelerated that diversification. Along the border, NAFTA has clearly had an impact in stimulating trade and transport across the state and stimulating the production of jobs. For example, Laredo, Texas—the port of entry for 40 percent of U.S.–Mexico truck transport trade—has seen its labor force increase 48 percent between 1994 and 2014, far above the 35 percent state average. International toll bridges alone accounted for 23 percent of Laredo's general fund revenue in 2012.[24]

After more than 20 years, it appears that the trade agreement has had both negative and positive impacts on Texas. A 2011 study by the Economic Policy Institute calculated that almost 683,000 jobs had been lost in the United States because of NAFTA. The study estimated that three-fifths of these jobs were in the manufacturing sector. Over 55,000 of these displaced jobs came from Texas.[25] U.S. workers generally lost their jobs because of the stiffer competition from low-wage businesses in Mexico or because plants had been relocated to Mexico. (Under federal law such workers are entitled to additional unemployment compensation.)

Although there were some losers in the movement toward free trade with Mexico and Canada, there were also big winners. The following statistics from 2013 put the importance of Texas's international trade, particularly with Mexico and Canada, into perspective:[26]

- Texas exports totaled $279.7 billion, up from $207 billion in 2012. Texas exports were 17.7 percent of all U.S. exports.
- The North American market (Mexico and Canada) was the destination for 45.4 percent of these exports.
- Mexico was the top importer of Texas exports at almost $101 billion in 2013, up from $72.7 billion in 2012.
- Canada's imports from Texas totaled $25.9 billion in 2013, up from $18.8 billion in 2010.

The pressing national debate over terrorism and border security has added a new dimension to the debate over NAFTA and global trade in Texas. Most Texas policy makers continue to accept the idea that

North American Free Trade Agreement (NAFTA) trade treaty among the United States, Canada, and Mexico to lower and eliminate tariffs among the three countries

The signing of NAFTA in 1992 created a free-trade zone in North America. Although many Texas workers were adversely affected by the availability of cheaper labor in Mexico, NAFTA appears to have had a beneficial effect on the state's economy as a whole. Here, President George H. W. Bush stands between President Carlos Salinas de Gortari of Mexico and Prime Minister Brian Mulroney of Canada at the signing ceremony.

expanding trade with Mexico and other countries is a good thing. The issue of having a free flow of people across the border, however, is another issue. An increasing number of people, particularly conservative Republicans, now question the benefits to Texas of a porous border. Large numbers of undocumented workers staying in Texas were viewed during the primary campaign and the general election by Donald Trump and other leading Republicans as a burden upon the state's social services. Moreover, fears of Islamic terrorists accompanying Mexicans and other Latin Americans who are seeking work have led to calls for building walls and fences that will make illegal immigration a thing of the past. Conceding that immigration is a national, not a state, issue, numerous Texas politicians have called for a stricter policing of the border by state authorities. It is hard to imagine a new stricter border policy not having negative effects on the trade that has followed from NAFTA and expanding global trade.

For the past 20 years, the information age and the global economy have transformed the Texas economic landscape. It is impossible to say exactly how these forces will continue to change Texas over the next 20 years, or which companies will become the Chevron or ExxonMobils of the information age. We can say, however, that it will be an economy as different from that of the oil and gas era as the oil and gas era was from the era of cotton and cattle.

The Military in Texas

Since annexation, Texas economic development has been closely tied to the establishment of military bases. As population pressures pushed westward, a series of federal forts were built to protect Texans from the Indians. Seizing the federal forts for the Confederacy was one of the first and most important acts of the Texas government following secession. And Texas provided a major military training center during both world wars. Strong leadership in Congress from individuals like Sam Rayburn and Lyndon Johnson in the 1940s brought much-needed jobs and money into the state through the building of one military installation after another (see Figure 1.3).

Today, military installations continue to be important to the economic well-being of certain parts of the state. There are over 173,000 active military, reserve military, and civilian individuals directly employed by the U.S. military living in Texas in 2014. The military, along with the many businesses that help provide consumer services to military members, is big business in Texas. An expanding military stimulates economic growth and employment in Texas. A contracting military does not.

The Great Recession and the "Texas Miracle"

In December 2007 the nation entered what some have called "the Great Recession," a time of chronic economic problems that drew analogies to the Great Depression of the 1930s. A speculative bubble in the housing market fueled by cheap credit and poor business practices culminated in a credit crisis that brought some of America's largest banks and investment houses to their knees. Only the massive intrusion of the Federal Reserve System into credit markets in the fall of 2008 prevented the banking system

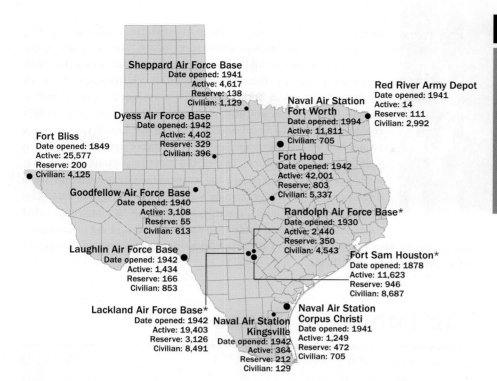

FIGURE 1.3

Major U.S. Military Bases in Texas

*In October 2010, Fort Sam Houston, Lackland Air Force Base, and Randolph Air Force Base were merged into U.S. Air Force 502nd Air Base Wing, Air Education and Training Command.

Sheppard Air Force Base
Date opened: 1941
Active: 4,617
Reserve: 138
Civilian: 1,129

Dyess Air Force Base
Date opened: 1942
Active: 4,402
Reserve: 329
Civilian: 396

Fort Bliss
Date opened: 1849
Active: 25,577
Reserve: 200
Civilian: 4,125

Naval Air Station Fort Worth
Date opened: 1994
Active: 11,811
Civilian: 705

Red River Army Depot
Date opened: 1941
Active: 14
Reserve: 111
Civilian: 2,992

Goodfellow Air Force Base
Date opened: 1940
Active: 3,108
Reserve: 55
Civilian: 613

Fort Hood
Date opened: 1942
Active: 42,001
Reserve: 803
Civilian: 5,337

Randolph Air Force Base*
Date opened: 1930
Active: 2,440
Reserve: 350
Civilian: 4,543

Laughlin Air Force Base
Date opened: 1942
Active: 1,434
Reserve: 166
Civilian: 853

Fort Sam Houston*
Date opened: 1878
Active: 11,623
Reserve: 946
Civilian: 8,687

Lackland Air Force Base*
Date opened: 1942
Active: 19,403
Reserve: 3,126
Civilian: 8,491

Naval Air Station Kingsville
Date opened: 1942
Active: 364
Reserve: 212
Civilian: 129

Naval Air Station Corpus Christi
Date opened: 1941
Active: 1,249
Reserve: 472
Civilian: 705

from melting down. The Federal Reserve reported that between November 2007 and March 2009, 86 percent of American industries cut back production. The GNP (gross national product, the total amount of all goods produced in the United States) dropped 1.7 percent, and household net worth fell $11 trillion or 18 percent during the recession.[27]

Texas was one of the last states to enter the Great Recession and was one of the first to exit. Prior to the recession, Texas employment had peaked at 10.6 million in August 2008. From late 2008 through 2009, 427,600 jobs were lost in Texas to the Great Recession. By November 2011 employment had recovered to prerecession levels. By April 2014 another 829,000 jobs had been added to the Texas economy. The story at the national level was not so rosy. By the summer of 2014 job numbers were only beginning to approach pre–Great Recession levels. Meanwhile the unemployment rate in Texas rose to 8.2 percent and hovered there throughout most of 2010. Unemployment rates began falling in early 2011 and continued to fall for the next two years, dropping from 6.4 percent in March 2013 to 5.2 percent in April 2014.[28]

Many Texas politicians sought to take credit for Texas's performance during and after the Great Recession. Some referred to the "Texas economic miracle." Comparisons were made with big-government, high-tax states like California that suffered severely. Low taxes and low services, pro-business and free market government, an entrepreneurial spirit—all were given credit for the "Texas economic miracle."[29] But the factors that may have helped Texas get by relatively unscathed were likely more straightforward. The housing market declined much less severely in Texas than in the rest of the nation. Prior to the Great Recession, Texas did not experience the

Texas was not hit as hard as other states by the recession that started in 2007 and deepened in 2008. However, some Texans—including these Tea Party protesters—were alarmed by the massive spending involved in the national government's stimulus efforts.

surge in real estate values found in other states like California, Nevada, Florida, and Arizona. While foreclosure rates throughout the country increased sixfold between 2005 and 2009, in Texas they rose only marginally. Texas's banking industry also appeared to have weathered the storm better than its counterparts in other states. Article 16 of the Texas Constitution, as amended in 1997, forbids consumers from using home-equity loans for credit that exceeds 80 percent of the mortgage, and this probably provided a cushion against the credit crunch. Two of the most important factors that may have helped Texas escape the worst of the Great Recession were discussed above: an increasingly diversified economy lubricated by international trade and a resurgent oil and gas industry.[30] A global recession coupled to a prolonged decline in oil and gas prices could undercut the forces that made the "Texas miracle" possible and minimized the impact of the Great Recession in Texas.

The People of Texas

 Explain how the population of Texas has changed over time

The population of Texas has grown rapidly in the last 165 years. In 1850 the population stood at a little more than 210,000 people, more than one-quarter of whom were African American slaves. Texas in 1850 also was an overwhelmingly rural state. Only 4 percent of the population lived in urban areas. By 1900 the population had increased to more than 3 million people, with 83 percent continuing to live in rural areas. The 1980s began as boom years for population growth, with increases running between 2.9 percent and 1.6 percent per year from 1980 through 1986. With the collapse of oil prices, however, population growth slowed significantly between 1987 and 1989 to less than 1 percent.[31] Then, with a recovering economy, population growth surged in the 1990s (see Figure 1.4).

Three factors account for the population growth in Texas: natural increase as a result of the difference between births and deaths; international immigration, particularly from Mexico; and domestic immigration from other states. The makeup of the growth in population shifted in significant ways over the course of the decade. In 1991 almost two-thirds of population growth was accounted for by natural increases. A little more than 20 percent was a result of international immigration, while less than 14 percent resulted from domestic immigration. By 2013 natural increases accounted for only 54 percent of population growth, while international immigration accounted for about 16.8 percent and domestic immigration for about 29.7 percent.[32] In the early decades of the twenty-first century, Texas was being redefined not by native-born Texans but by individuals coming to Texas to share in and contribute to the state's diversified economy. For a deeper understanding of the role that changing demographics have played in Texas's culture and politics, we must look closer at the major racial and ethnic groups that have constituted the population over time.

FIGURE 1.4

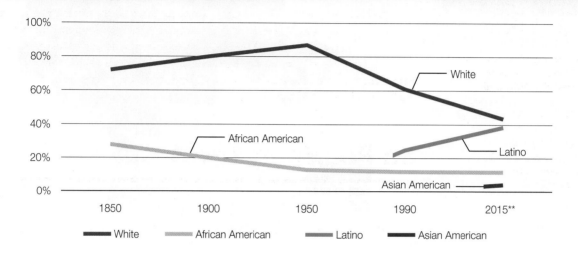

The Changing Face of Texas, 1850–2015

*Latinos were not counted as a separate group until 1990 and were included in the white census count.
**Data for 2015 are estimated based on 2010 census. Percentages are from 2014 estimates.

SOURCES: *Statistical Abstract of the United States: 1994* (Washington, DC: U.S. Department of Commerce, Bureau of the Census, 1994); see also *Texas Almanac* 2014–15 (Denton: Texas State Historical Association, 2014), 15; 2010 U.S. Census. Other editions of the *Texas Almanac* also consulted. These are available online.

Whites

For most of the nineteenth and twentieth centuries, the largest ethnic group was non-Hispanic whites. Whites in Texas comprise a wide range of European ethnic groups, including English, Germans, Scots, Irish, Czechs, and European Jews. The first wave of whites came to Texas before the break with Mexico. Encouraged by **empresarios** such as Moses Austin and his son Stephen F. Austin, who were authorized by the Spanish and later the Mexican leaders to bring people to Texas, these newcomers sought inexpensive land. But they brought along a new set of individualistic attitudes and values about democratic government that paved the way for the Texas Revolution. Following the revolution, a new surge of white immigrants came from the Deep South. Like their predecessors, they sought cheap land. But they brought with them new cultural baggage: slavery. By the time of the American Civil War, this group had come to dominate the political culture of the state. Although most Texas farmers did not own slaves themselves, the vast majority supported the institution as well as secession from the Union.

Defeat in the Civil War shattered temporarily the dominance of the traditional white power structure in the state. By the end of Reconstruction, however, it had reasserted itself, establishing the three patterns that defined Texas politics for the next hundred years: the one-party Democratic state, provincialism, and business dominance.

empresario Spanish word for an individual who promotes, organizes, or helps to finance a particular endeavor

FIGURE 1.5

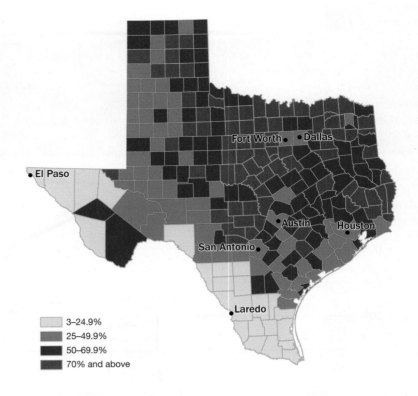

- 3–24.9%
- 25–49.9%
- 50–69.9%
- 70% and above

Whites continued to dominate and define Texas's political culture throughout much of the twentieth century, but by the end of that century much had changed. As a percentage of the population, white population peaked at 74 percent in 1950. This percentage began to fall, reaching 43.5 percent in 2015, and will likely continue to fall (see Figure 1.5).

Numbers alone do not tell the whole story. Whites living in Texas at the end of the twentieth century were not cut from the same cloth as those who had preceded them. A new wave of white immigration into Texas over the past 40 years has redefined the political culture of white Texans. No longer can one assume that a white Texan lives on a farm, holds culturally conservative values, and is firmly tied to the Democratic Party. On the contrary, he or she may be an urbanite or suburbanite who wasn't born in Texas and who votes Republican.

Latinos

The use of the terms *Hispanic* and *Latino* can be confusing. The terms are often used interchangeably to refer to people of Spanish descent or people from Latin America. The U.S. Census generally uses the term *Hispanic* in its databases. We will generally use the term *Latino* to refer to people of Spanish decent or people from Latin America.

Most Latinos in Texas are people of Mexican descent.[33] Prior to independence from Spain, this included people born of Iberian (Spanish) parents as well as mestizos (people of mixed Spanish and Native American ancestry). In the early nineteenth century, approximately 5,000 people of Mexican descent were living in Texas. Although this number fluctuated considerably over the years, by 1850 it was estimated that 14,000 Texans were of Mexican origin. Texas became for many a refuge from the political and economic instability that troubled Mexico from the late 1850s to the 1920s. Despite periodic attempts to curtail the growth of the Mexican American population in Texas, it grew from an estimated 700,000 in 1930 to 1,400,000 in 1960. The 2000 census counted 5.1 million Mexican Americans living in Texas. In 2015 there were 10.6 million Latinos residing in Texas. Texas Latinos constituted over 19 percent of all Latinos in the United States.[34]

Until 1900, Latinos were concentrated in south Texas, constituting a majority along the border with Mexico and in certain border counties of west Texas. During the first few decades of the twentieth century, Latinos migrated to northwest Texas and the Panhandle to work as laborers in the newly emergent cotton economy. Labor segregation limited the opportunities available to many Latinos before World War II. After World War II, however, many Latinos left agricultural work and took jobs in the rapidly growing urban areas of Texas. By the end of the century, Latinos constituted majorities in the cities of San Antonio and El Paso and sizable minorities in Houston, Dallas, Austin, and Fort Worth (see Figure 1.6).

The political status of Latinos in Texas has changed considerably over the past hundred years. In the nineteenth century, numerous obstacles limited their participation in the political life of the state. Voting, particularly among the lower economic classes, was discouraged or tightly controlled. The white-only primary and the **poll tax** actively discouraged voting by Latinos. Only after World War II were Latino politicians able to escape some of the strictures that had been imposed on them by the dominant white political culture of the time. A more tolerant atmosphere in the

poll tax a state-imposed tax on voters as a prerequisite for voting; poll taxes were rendered unconstitutional in national elections by the Twenty-Fourth Amendment, and in state elections by the U.S. Supreme Court in 1966

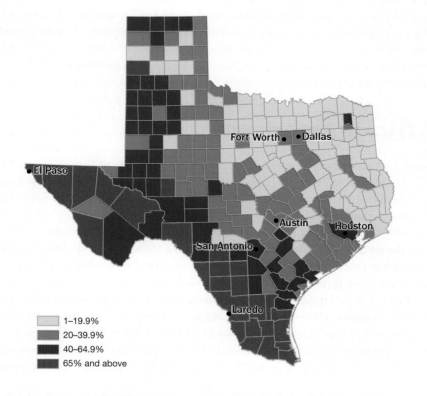

FIGURE 1.6

Latino Population in Texas Counties, 2014

SOURCE: QuickFacts, www.census.gov (accessed 6/21/16).

Legend:
- 1–19.9%
- 20–39.9%
- 40–64.9%
- 65% and above

Most Latinos in Texas are Mexican American. During the first half of the twentieth century, Mexicans immigrated to Texas to work in the emerging cotton industry. Today, Latinos like actor Eva Longoria (center) and Representative Joaquin Castro (right) are influential in politics and important leaders in their chosen professions. Here, they participate in the launch of the Latino Victory Project PAC, founded by Henry R. Muñoz III (left), which supports Latino candidates for public office across the country.

growing urban areas enabled Latino politicians to assume positions of importance in the local political community. In 1956, Henry B. Gonzalez became the first Mexican American to be elected to the Texas Senate in modern times. In the mid-1960s a political movement emerged in the La Raza Unida Party, which sought to confront many of the discriminatory practices that isolated Texas Latinos from the political and economic mainstream. By the 1980s, Latino political leaders were playing a growing role in state politics, and Latino voters were courted heavily by both political parties. The number of Latinos elected to public office rose from 1,466 in 1986 to 2,521 in 2011. In 2013 the National Association of Latino Elected and Appointed Officials reported that 1 Latino served in the U.S. Senate from Texas, 6 Latinos represented Texas in the U.S. House of Representatives, 7 Latinos were in the Texas State Senate, and 40 Latinos were elected to the state legislature. In addition, the association reported that 2,477 Latinos served as local officials in Texas.[35]

African Americans

People of African descent were among the earliest explorers of Texas.[36] Most African Americans, however, entered Texas as slaves. Whites from the upper and lower South brought slaves with them to Texas. At first, antislavery attitudes among Spanish and Mexican authorities kept the slave population down. However, independence from Mexico lifted the restrictions on slavery, creating an incentive for southerners to expand the system of slavery westward. The number of slaves in Texas rose from 5,000 to 58,000 in 1850. By the Civil War (1861–65), over 182,000 slaves lived in Texas, approximately one-third of the state's entire population.

Emancipation for African Americans living in Texas came on June 19, 1865. Emancipation, however, did not bring anything approaching equality. Between 1865 and 1868 a series of Black Codes were passed by the state legislature and various cities that sought to restrict the rights of former slaves. Military occupation and congressional reconstruction opened up new opportunities for former slaves, who supported the radical wing of the Republican Party. Ten African American delegates helped write the Texas Constitution of 1869. Forty-three served as members of the state legislature between 1868 and 1900. The end of Reconstruction and the return to power of the Democratic Party in the mid-1870s reversed much of the progress made by former slaves in the state. In 1900 over 100,000 African Americans voted in Texas elections. By 1903 the number had fallen to under 5,000, largely because of the imposition of the poll tax in 1902 and the passage of an early version of the white-primary law in 1903. In 1923 the legislature explicitly banned blacks from voting in the Democratic primary. Segregation of the races became a guiding principle of public policy, backed by the police power of the state and reinforced by lynching and race riots against African Americans. For all intents and purposes, African Americans had become second-class citizens, disenfranchised by the political system and marginalized by the political culture.

Federal court cases in the 1940s and 1950s offered some hope of relief to African Americans living in Texas. The U.S. Supreme Court decision in *Smith v. Allwright* (1944) outlawed the white primary. *Sweatt v. Painter* (1950) guaranteed African Americans admission to Texas's graduate and professional schools. Finally, *Brown v. Board of Education* (1954) outlawed the segregation of public schools.

Political progress was much slower. The Civil Rights Act of 1964 and the Voting Rights Act of 1965 helped to open up the political system in Texas to African Americans. In 1966 a small number of African American candidates actually began to win political office in the state. In 1972, Barbara Jordan became the first African American woman to be elected to the U.S. House of Representatives from Texas.

Today, the African American population is concentrated in east Texas, where the southern plantation and sharecropping systems were dominant during the nineteenth century. Large numbers of African Americans had also migrated to form sizable minorities in the urban and suburban areas of Houston and Dallas (see Figure 1.7). African American political leaders have come to play major roles in these areas as

As in most former slave states, there was initial resistance to the civil rights movement in Texas. These signs appeared in Fort Worth's Riverside section in September 1956 during a protest over a black family's moving into a previously all-white block of homes.

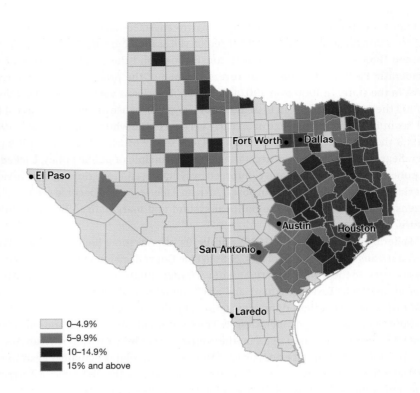

FIGURE 1.7

African American Population in Texas Counties, 2014

SOURCE: QuickFacts, www.census.gov (accessed 6/21/16).

0–4.9%
5–9.9%
10–14.9%
15% and above

members of Congress, the state legislature, and city councils. African Americans were also elected mayors of Houston and Dallas in the late 1990s. The political influence of African Americans in Texas has not been extended to west Texas, where few African Americans live.

Asians

Although considerably smaller than other groups, the Asian population has grown in Texas in recent years. Asians include individuals from a variety of countries, but particularly India, Vietnam, China, Pakistan, Korea, and Japan. In 2015 the U.S. Census Bureau estimated that approximately 1 million Asians resided in Texas, or about 4.5 percent of the state's population.[37] Asians tend to be concentrated in certain urban areas, particularly in west Houston and Fort Bend County, the western and northern suburbs of Dallas, Arlington, and Travis County. Sizable pockets of Asians are also found scattered along the Gulf Coast.[38]

Age

When compared with the rest of the nation, the population of Texas is relatively young. In 2015, 27.3 percent of the population was estimated to be under 18 years old, compared with 24.0 percent nationally. In addition, only 11.5 percent of the population in Texas was 65 years of age or older, compared with 14.5 percent nationally.[39]

TABLE 1.1

	1990	1995	2006	2014
Per Capita Personal Income in Texas and the United States, 1990–2014 (Nominal Nonadjusted Dollars)				
United States	$19,477	$23,076	$36,276	$46,049
Texas	$17,421	$21,033	$34,257	$45,669

SOURCE: U.S. Department of Commerce, Bureau of Economic Analysis.

Having a relatively young population compared with those of other states presents Texas with a variety of problems and opportunities, as we shall see in later chapters.

Poverty and Wealth

Younger populations tend to be poorer, as income and poverty statistics bear out. As noted above, even taking into account the Great Recession (2008–09), the late twentieth and early twenty-first centuries were a period of rapid economic growth in Texas. Despite this growth, Texas continued to lag behind the nation as a whole (see Table 1.1). Per capita income in Texas, however, rose from $17,421 in 1990 to $45,669 in 2014 (see Figure 1.8). Per capita income in Texas metropolitan areas was considerably higher ($41,035 in 2011) when compared with Texas rural areas ($33,621 in 2011).

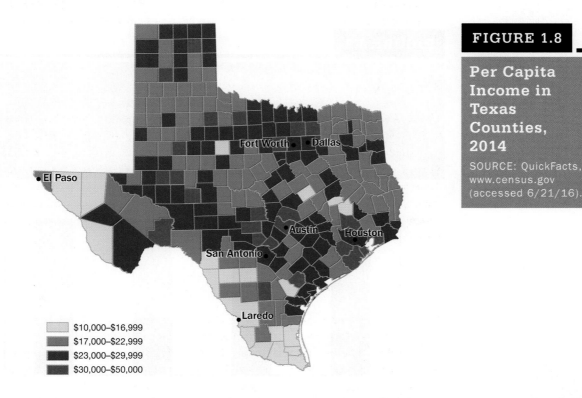

FIGURE 1.8

Per Capita Income in Texas Counties, 2014

SOURCE: QuickFacts, www.census.gov (accessed 6/21/16).

Legend:
- $10,000–$16,999
- $17,000–$22,999
- $23,000–$29,999
- $30,000–$50,000

Interestingly, Sutton County, a lightly populated rural county in southwest Texas, had the highest per capita income of $79,103. This seeming anomaly is explained by the fact that it is rich in oil and natural gas. Starr County, in the southeast corner of the state along the Rio Grande, had the lowest at $19,235. Texas ranked 25th among the states in per capita income, up from 32nd in 1990.

The percentage of the population in Texas living below the poverty level—a level established by the federal government—fell from 15.7 percent to 14.9 percent between 1990 and 2004, rose to 16.9 percent in 2006, and rose to 17.2 percent in 2014. During the same period, the national poverty rate fell from 13.5 percent to 11.7 percent, rose to 13.3 percent in 2006, and rose to 14.8 percent in 2014.[40]

Urbanization

Describe Texas's shift from a rural society to an urban one

urbanization the process by which people move from rural areas to cities

Urbanization is the process by which people move from rural to urban areas. Suburbanization is the process by which people move out of central city areas to surrounding suburban areas. Much of Texas's history is linked to ongoing urbanization. By the first decade of the twenty-first century, this process was largely complete, as 85 percent of the population now reside in urban areas (see Figure 1.9). Suburbanization, however, continues as city populations spill over into surrounding suburban areas.[41]

FIGURE 1.9

Urbanization in Texas, 1850–2010

SOURCE: *Statistical Abstracts of the United States: 1994* (Washington, DC: U.S. Department of Commerce, Bureau of the Census, 1994); Dallas Morning News, *Texas Almanac 2001–2002* (Dallas: Dallas Morning News, 2001); U.S. Department of Agriculture, Economic Research Service, U.S. Census Bureau, "Texas: 2010, Population and Housing Unit Courts, 2010 Census of Population and Housing" (September 2012), p. 16.

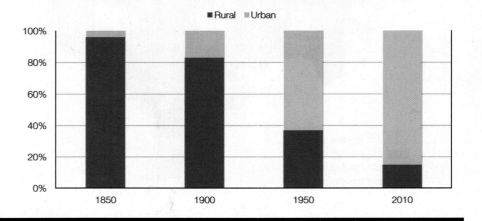

How Is the Texas Population Changing?

The face of Texas is changing rapidly and will continue to change well into the future. The figures below show projections of how the Texas population will change over the next 30 years. The state's population will continue to grow quickly, especially as the number of Latino Texans increases. Further, most of the population growth in the state will happen in metropolitan areas—Dallas–Fort Worth, Houston, San Antonio, and Austin.

Race and Total Population

= 250,000 people

1980

White	66%	Latino	21%
African American	12%	Other	1%

2010

White	45%	Latino	38%
African American	12%	Other	6%

2050

White	28%	Latino	54%
African American	10%	Other	8%

Total population =

1980: 14,229,191   2010: 25,145,561   2050: 41,311,221

Geography (projected population growth from the year 2010, by metropolitan area)

Area	2010	2020		2050	
San Antonio	2,142,508	2,481,286	+16%	3,445,603	+61%
El Paso	804,123	929,478	+16%	1,301,438	+62%
Dallas–Fort Worth	6,426,214	7,445,492	+16%	11,147,784	+73%
Houston	5,920,416	6,934,564	+17%	10,273,617	+74%
Brownsville	406,220	478,974	+18%	729,461	+80%
Austin	1,716,289	2,090,278	+22%	3,338,673	+95%
McAllen	774,769	953,069	+23%	1,589,783	+105%

SOURCES: Texas Demographic Center, demographics.texas.gov; (accessed 6/15/16).

NOTE: Numbers do not always add up to 100 percent due to rounding.

QUANTITATIVE REASONING

- Based on your reading of the data, how many Latinos were added to the state population between 1980 and 2010? How many whites? How is the projected 2050 population different from the population in 2010?

- Given the metropolitan population projections for 2020 and 2050, how might the balance of political power shift over the next 40 years?

Most Texas cities are the result of American settlement and culture.[42] The Spanish influence on urban life in Texas grew out of efforts to extend territorial control northward out of Mexico through a series of presidios (garrisons), missions (churches), and pueblos (towns). The physical organization and planning of the towns reflected this imperial mission. For example, the largest Spanish settlement was San Antonio. It was initially established as a supply depot to missions in east Texas. Later it expanded as missions were established to convert local Native Americans to Christianity and farms were cultivated to feed the local population. By the early nineteenth century, San Antonio's population had reached 2,500. Other smaller settlements were located in east Texas, along the border with French and, later, American territory.

White American influence began with the arrival of Moses Austin in 1820 in San Antonio. Soon, his son Stephen F. Austin followed. The Spanish offered the Austins and other impresarios grants of land to encourage the inflow of Americans into underpopulated regions of Texas. Small towns emerged as administrative units for impresario grants. There were considerably more freedom and dynamism in American urban areas than in Spanish ones. Americans brought with them a host of new interests and ideas that would transform urban life in Texas, including a new language, slavery, Protestantism, and a commitment to free enterprise and democracy. The courthouse became a central feature of many American towns, often located in the center of the town surrounded by shops.

Urbanization has transformed Texas political life. From Reconstruction through the first 50 years of the twentieth century, Texas's political life grew out of its rural-based economy centered on cotton, cattle, oil, and natural gas. Today, urbanization and accompanying suburbanization are the forces driving politics in the state.

The expansion of Texas's urban life initially began along the Gulf Coast and gradually expanded west, particularly along rivers. New technologies transformed the urban landscape of Texas. Dredging technologies helped to stimulate the growth of port cities such as Houston, Galveston, Corpus Christi, and Brownsville. Railroad construction in the second half of the nineteenth century opened up new lands to urban development. In 1880 there were only 11 towns of 4,000 or more people in all of Texas. Following the rapid expansion of the railroads in the 1880s and 1890s, the number rose to 36. By 1910, when the railroad network of 13,110 miles was completed, Texas had 49 towns with a population of 4,000 or more. By 1920, 5 cities—Dallas, El Paso, Fort Worth, Houston, and San Antonio—had populations of more than 50,000. Later technological breakthroughs in transportation, such as cars and air travel, would reinforce the population grid laid out by the railroads.

The Urban Political Economy

Understanding the complexity of the government and politics in Texas today demands having some sense of how Texas's three major metropolitan areas compare with each other (see Table 1.2).

How Does Texas's Population Compare to Other Major States'?

Texas is more diverse than many states in the country, which has important implications for the future of the state's politics. Also, the Texas population has increased dramatically, while some states are not growing as fast. In fact many states in the Midwest such as Ohio and Pennsylvania have seen population declines in recent years.

Racial Diversity

Texas

White	44%
Black	13%
Latino	39%
Asian	4%

California

White	39%
Black	7%
Latino	39%
Asian	14%

Florida

White	56%
Black	17%
Latino	24%
Asian	3%

New York

White	57%
Black	18%
Latino	19%
Asian	9%

Ohio

White	80%
Black	13%
Latino	4%
Asian	2%

Percent Change in Population, 2000-2010

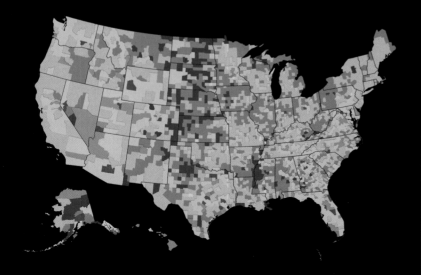

9.7%: overall U.S. change

Gain
- 50% +
- 25.1 to 49%
- 9.7 to 25%
- 0 to 9.6%

- -10 to -0.1%
- **Loss** -50 to -10.1%
- *Data not available*

CRITICAL THINKING

- In what ways are California and Texas similar in terms of demographic makeup? How are they different?

- In what ways will Texas politics change in the future based on its racial and ethnic makeup?

SOURCES: U.S. Census Bureau, QuickFacts 2014, www.census.gov; demography.cpc.unc.edu.

NOTE: Numbers do not always add up to 100 percent. Black Latinos may be counted in both categories.

TABLE 1.2

Race and Ethnic Breakdown of Texas and Its Largest Counties, 2014

	WHITE (%)	BLACK (%)	ASIAN (%)	MULTIPLE RACE (%)	HISPANIC (%)	TOTAL
Texas	43.5 *	12.5	4.5	1.8	38.6	26,956,958
Harris	31.4	19.5	7.0	1.7	41.8	4,441,370
Dallas	31.1	23.1	5.9	1.7	39.3	2,518,638
Tarrant	49.3	16.2	5.3	2.3	27.8	1,945,360
Bexar	29.2	8.3	2.9	2.2	59.3	1,855,866
Travis	49.7	8.9	6.5	2.4	33.9	1,151,145
Collin	60.4	9.6	12.9	2.5	15.1	885,241
El Paso	13.3	4.0	1.3	1.4	81.2	833,487

*Columns may not add to 100 percent as a result of multiple counting. These are estimates projected from the 2014 Census.
SOURCE: 2014 U.S. Census Bureau.

Houston Houston, located in Harris County, is the largest city in Texas and the fourth-largest city in the United States—with a population of 2.1 million—behind New York, Los Angeles, and Chicago. Its consolidated metropolitan area encompasses eight counties, with an estimated population of 6.1 million in 2011. Houston grew by 7.5 percent during the first decade of the twenty-first century.

The city originated in 1836 out of the entrepreneurial dreams of two brothers, Augustus Chapman Allen and John Kirby Allen, who sought to create a "great interior commercial emporium of Texas."[43] The town was named after Sam Houston, the leader of Texas's army during its war of independence from Mexico. Early settlers came from the South, bringing with them the institution of slavery. As a consequence, segregation was built into the social structure from the outset. For the first half of the twentieth century, African Americans were either denied or given limited access to a variety of public services such as parks, schools, buses, restrooms, and restaurants. Although not enforced legally, residential segregation divided the city into a number of distinct racially divided neighborhoods for much of the twentieth century.

In the late nineteenth century, Houston's economic well-being depended on cotton and commerce. Railroads played an integral role in placing Houston at the hub of the Texas economy. The opening of the Houston Ship Channel further enhanced Houston's place in the state economy by helping to turn it into the second or third (depending on whose ranking is used) deep-water port in the United States. But it was oil that fundamentally transformed the Houston area in the twentieth century. Oil refineries opened along the ship channel and a petrochemical industry emerged, making Houston one of the leading energy centers in the world. Today, Houston continues to rank first in the nation in the manufacture of petroleum equipment.

By 1930, Houston had become the largest city in Texas, with a population of around 292,000 people. The population continued to expand throughout the 1940s, 1950s, and 1960s, assisted by a liberal annexation policy that enabled the city to incorporate into itself many of the outlying suburban areas. Although the oil bust in the mid-1980s slowed the city's growth, that growth continued in the early twenty-first century, extending into suburban areas such as Clear Lake City and other urban areas such as Galveston.

Dallas–Fort Worth

Dallas–Fort Worth The Metroplex is an economic region encompassing the cities of Dallas and Fort Worth, as well as a number of other suburban cities, including Arlington (population 383,204), Mesquite (144,416), Garland (235,501), Richardson (108,617), Irving (231,406), Plano (278,480), McKinney (156,767), Carrollton (128,353), Grand Prairie (185,453), Frisco (145,035), and Denton (128,205).[44] The major counties in the area are Dallas, Tarrant, and Collin. The Metroplex is joined together by a number of interlocking highways running north–south and east–west, and a major international airport that is strategically located in the national air system.

Dallas was founded as a trading post in 1841, near where two roads were to be built by the Republic.[45] By the 1850s it had become a retail center servicing the rural areas. By 1870 the population had reached 3,000. The coming of the Houston and Texas Central Railroad in 1871 and the Texas and Pacific Railroad in 1873 made Dallas the first rail crossroads in Texas and transformed forever its place in the state's economy. Markets now beckoned east and north, encouraging entrepreneurs and merchants to set up shop. Cotton became a major cash crop, and the population expanded over threefold to more than 10,000 people in 1880. By the turn of the twentieth century, the city had grown to more than 42,000 people.

As with Houston, the oil economy changed the direction and scope of the city's economic life. With the discovery of oil in east Texas in 1930, Dallas became a major center for petroleum financing. By the end of World War II, the economy had diversified, making Dallas a minor manufacturing center in the nation. In the 1950s and 1960s technology companies such as Ling-Temco-Vought (LTV) and Texas Instruments were added to the industrial mix, transforming Dallas into the third-largest technology center in the nation. The high-tech boom of the 1990s was built from the corporate infrastructure laid down in the 1950s and 1960s. Dallas grew from 844,401 people in 1970 to 1,281,047 in 2014.

Although they are locked together in important ways economically, Dallas and Fort Worth are as different as night and day. Whereas Dallas looks to the east and embodies a more corporate white-collar business culture, Fort Worth looks to the west. It is where the West begins in Texas.

Fort Worth originated as an army post in 1849.[46] By 1853 the post had been abandoned as new forts were located to the west. Although settlers took the fort over, population growth was slow through the early 1870s. The spark that enabled the town to begin to prosper was the rise of the cattle industry. Fort Worth was a convenient place for cowboys to rest on their cattle drives to Kansas. Cattle buyers established headquarters in the city. Gradually, other businesses grew up around these key businesses. Transportation and communication links improved with the establishment of stage lines to the west and railroad lines to the north and east.

By 1900, Fort Worth was served by eight different railroad companies, many of them transporting cattle and cattle-related products to national markets. The two world wars encouraged further economic development in Fort Worth. Over 100,000 troops were trained at Camp Bowie during World War I. World War II brought an important air force base and, along with it, the aviation industry. The Consolidated Vultee Aircraft Corporation, which was later bought by General Dynamics, became

In some areas of Texas, Asian immigrants are a growing force. The signs behind Charles Park, president of the Asian District Development Association of Dallas, at the Asiana Plaza in Dallas attest to the changing demographic landscape of Texas.

Immigration in Texas

Immigration has long been an important part of Texas culture. After the terrorist attacks of September 11, the U.S.–Mexico border tightened considerably. Traditionally, residents in border areas could cross the border easily. With increasing border and security concerns, border crossings become more difficult. The Paso del Norte bridge between El Paso and Ciudad Juarez (shown at left), the busiest cross-border footpath between the United States and Mexico, is one of several official international bridges in the state. One of Texas's ongoing debates is over the most effective ways to ensure border security and respect the diversity of the state's history.

In the 2014 campaign for lieutenant governor, Houston state senator Dan Patrick campaigned on a platform of stopping the "illegal invasion" of immigrants into Texas. Patrick emphasized that the federal government was not enforcing border security by allowing so many immigrants into Texas. He further claimed that lack of border security has brought third world diseases into the state. In his campaign he promised to spend more state money on border security.

Patrick also gained headlines by debating then–San Antonio mayor Julian Castro about immigration reform. Castro accused Patrick of dog whistle politics, that is, appealing to exclusionist and racist rhetoric in order to win the election. Castro argued that there is no "invasion" of immigrants. He said that illegal immigration has dropped from its peak levels and undocumented immigrants are essential to the state's economy. Castro argued that those in the country illegally, especially those in college or serving in the military, should be allowed a path to citizenship.

Patrick disagreed, claiming that those in the country illegally should go to the "back of the line" and wait their turns. He also suggested that granting citizenship to illegal immigrants would only encourage more illegal immigration. Patrick opposed "amnesty," the notion of allowing illegal immigrants the opportunity to eventually become U.S. citizens. More illegal immigration, according to Patrick, will strain the state budget on education and health care. Patrick also opposed in-state tuition for undocumented immigrants. He claimed that citizens should be given the priority and illegal immigrants should not have this benefit.

The debate in Texas mirrors the national debate regarding how best to deal with immigration. There are approximately 11 million undocumented or "illegal" immigrants in the United States, and about 2 million of those immigrants are in Texas, mostly of Latino descent and mostly from Mexico.

Some claim Patrick's views will turn off the growing Latino population because the harsh anti-immigrant rhetoric is perceived as anti-Latino. Patrick maintained that he supports legal immigration and just wants to stop illegal immigration. Castro and others have argued that the United States is a nation of immigrants and there must be a comprehensive way to reform the problem. They say that businesses in Texas greatly benefit from the hard work of undocumented immigrants and as long as jobs are available, immigrants will find a way to make it to the United States despite expensive border security efforts.

COMMUNICATING EFFECTIVELY: YOUR VOICE

- Do you agree with Dan Patrick or Julian Castro? Should illegal immigrants be given a pathway to citizenship or be sent back to their country of origin?

- Is compromise possible on immigration? Are the only two options deportations and amnesty? If you had to suggest a third option, what would it be?

As immigration has changed the demographic profile of Texas, it has also given rise to numerous political debates. Here, protesters for immigration reform rally in San Antonio outside a hotel where former U.S. Speaker of the House John Boehner held a fund-raiser.

the largest manufacturer in the city. Between 1900 and 1950 the population grew from 26,668 to 277,047. In 2014, Fort Worth's population was 812,238. The overall metropolitan area of Dallas–Fort Worth included 6.954 million people in 2014.

San Antonio
San Antonio is located in Bexar County, the fourth-largest county in Texas today. San Antonio grew out of the Spanish presidio San Antonio de Bexar, which was founded in 1718.[47] In 1773 it became the capital of Spanish Texas, with a population of around 2,100 people. Because of the threats posed by Native Americans and Mexicans after the Texas Revolution, the population declined to about 800 people by 1846. On Texas's entry into the Union, however, the population took off, reaching 3,488 in 1850 and 8,235 in 1860. By the Civil War, San Antonio was the largest city in Texas.

Following the Civil War, San Antonio grew rapidly, stimulated by the building of the San Antonio Railroad in 1877. By 1880 the population had grown to more than 20,000 people, mostly white Americans from southern states. The population continued to grow through the first two decades of the twentieth century, reaching 161,000 by 1920. Mexican immigration increased significantly following the Mexican Revolution of 1910 and the building of a city infrastructure that provided paved roads, utilities, water, telephones, and hospitals. By midcentury San Antonio had become a unique blend of Latino, German, and southern Anglo American cultures. Population growth slowed down in the 1930s but picked up again during World War II, reaching over 408,000 in 1950. Major military bases came to dot the landscape around San Antonio. By 1960 the population topped 587,000 people.

Today, San Antonio is Texas's second-largest city. The population of the city was estimated to be 1,436,697 in 2014, and the San Antonio metropolitan area as a whole had a population of 2,234,003, making it the thirty-first-largest metropolitan area in the country. San Antonio's population has become increasingly Latino. In Bexar

County where San Antonio is located, approximately 59.4 percent of the people are Latino, 29.2 percent are white, and 8.3 percent are African American.[48]

Unlike Houston or Dallas, San Antonio lacks high-paying manufacturing jobs, and average metropolitan income is lower than in Houston and Dallas. The economy rests on four legs: national military bases, educational institutions, tourism, and a large medical research complex.

Political Culture and the Future of Texas

In this chapter, we have studied the political culture of Texas and seen how the state has been transformed by economic and demographic shifts over the past hundred years. Three great technological revolutions have reshaped the economic life of the state. Accompanying and fueling these economic revolutions have been ongoing demographic changes, which have redefined who the "typical" Texan is and where this person lives. No longer can it be said that a "typical" Texan is simply an extension of white American culture rooted in southern tradition. No longer does this person reside in a small town, living life close to the land much as his or her ancestors did. Like the economy, the people of Texas have been diversified. Increasing numbers of Latinos from Mexico and whites from other parts of the United States have created a new melting pot of cultures and concerns throughout the state. These cultures have come together in the big metropolitan areas across Texas.

The future of Texas likely will continue to be defined by the economic and demographic changes that we have chronicled in this chapter. A diversifying economy fueled by international trade and a rejuvenated oil and natural gas industry will integrate the state more closely into a burgeoning world economy. Latinos will come to play an increasingly important role in the economic and political life of the state as the Latino population ages and works its way through the educational system. Over the next 30 years, both political parties will have to adjust their expectations and ideologies to meet the demands of an electorate increasingly dominated by young Latino voters.

Use 🐇 INQUIZITIVE to help you study and master this material.

Texas Political Culture

- Describe the defining characteristics of political culture in Texas (pp. 5–7)

Texas political culture can best be characterized as individualistic and traditional. Texans have great pride in their state and have adopted a famous phrase, "Don't mess with Texas," for those external forces wishing to change the state's way of doing things. Texas is a low-tax state with distrust for large government programs. Business plays a major role in defining the political culture of the state.

Key Terms
political culture (p. 5)
moralistic political culture (p. 5)
individualistic political culture (p. 5)
traditionalistic political culture (p. 5)
elite (p. 5)
provincialism (p. 6)

Practice Quiz

1. In terms of area, how does Texas rank among the 50 states?
   a) first
   b) second
   c) third
   d) fifth
   e) seventh

2. *Provincialism* refers to
   a) a narrow view of the world.
   b) a progressive view of the value of diversity.
   c) a pro-business political culture.
   d) an urban society.
   e) a group of counties.

The Land

- Explain how Texas's geography has influenced its political culture (pp. 7–10)

Because of Texas's immense size, the state's topography is diverse, with east Texas's flat lands, west Texas's arid climate, and central Texas's hill country all representing diverse ecosystems and land patterns.

Key Term
privatization of public property (p. 8)

Practice Quiz
3. Which of Texas's physical regions is characterized by the presence of many of the state's largest ranches?
   a) Gulf Coastal Plains
   b) Great Plains
   c) Interior Lowlands
   d) Basin and Range Province
   e) Rio Grande Valley

4. Which of Texas's physical regions is found in the westernmost part of Texas?
   a) Gulf Coastal Plains
   b) Great Plains
   c) Interior Lowlands
   d) Basin and Range Province
   e) Pine Belt

Economic Change in Texas

- Trace the evolution of Texas's economy
  (pp. 11–22)

The Texas economy has undergone a series of technological transformations over the past 100 years. Once, the Texas economy was grounded in cotton and ranching. Oil production came to play an important role in the twentieth century. Today, high technology and international trade play important roles in the state's economy. Texas appears to have weathered the Great Recession better than most other states.

Key Term
North American Free Trade Agreement (NAFTA) (p. 19)

Practice Quiz
5. Creative destruction
   a) destroys both old and new economies.
   • b) creates new economies and destroys old ones.
   c) maintains old economies and creates new ones.
   d) creates and maintains old and new economies.
   e) does not affect economies.

6. Which industry controlled the politics and economy of Texas for most of the twentieth century?
   a) cotton
   b) cattle
   c) railroad
   • d) oil
   e) technology

7. Which of the following statements is true?
   a) Oil production in Texas is less today than it was 10 years ago.
   b) Oil production no longer plays an important role in the state's economy.

   c) Oil has been almost totally drained from Texas oil fields.
   d) The border region has become a major producer of oil in the early twenty-first century.
   • e) Fracking and horizontal drilling have reinvigorated Texas's oil industry.

8. Unlike earlier eras, the Texas economy of the twenty-first century features
   • a) computers, electronics, and other high-tech products.
   b) transportation, oil and natural gas, and banking.
   c) insurance, construction, and banking.
   d) ranching, oil, and tourism.
   e) education, the military, and agriculture.

9. NAFTA refers to
   a) an oil company.
   b) an independent regulatory commission.
   c) an interstate road network.
   d) an interest group.
   • e) an international trade agreement.

10. What is meant by the "Great Recession"?
    a) the post–Vietnam War era in the mid-1970s when housing prices rose
    b) the period of high inflation during the early 1980s
    • c) a time of chronic economic problems beginning in late 2007 that drew analogies to the Great Depression of the 1930s
    d) the time when Democrats lost control of the Texas House for the first time since Reconstruction
    e) a period of high unemployment in the early 1990s

The People of Texas

- Explain how the population of Texas has changed over time (p. 22–30)

Texas demography has changed over the last century. Once dominated by whites, Texas now has a large Latino population that, when coupled with the African American population and other minorities, makes Texas a majority-minority state. Despite considerable overall wealth in Texas, Texans tend to be younger and poorer than the average American.

Key Terms
empresario (p. 23)
poll tax (p. 25)

Practice Quiz
11. Which of the following accounts for most of Texas's population growth today?
    a) immigration
    •b) natural increases as a result of the difference between births and deaths
    c) domestic immigration
    d) NAFTA
    e) movement from rural to urban areas

12. Which of the following is not true?
    a) Latinos are increasing as a percentage of the population in Dallas.
    b) More African Americans live in east Texas than in west Texas.
    •c) San Antonio has a larger white population than Latino.
    d) Houston's largest minority population is Latino.
    e) The Latino population in Texas has grown rapidly in recent decades.

Urbanization

- Describe Texas's shift from a rural society to an urban one (pp. 30–38)

Initially a rural state, Texas has urbanized, with Houston, San Antonio, and Dallas–Fort Worth representing the largest metropolitan areas in the state. This process of urbanization has changed the state's economy from an agricultural powerhouse to a high-tech and innovative economy.

Key Term
urbanization (p. 30)

Practice Quiz
13. *Urbanization* refers to a process in which
    •a) people move from rural to urban areas.
    b) people from the north and west move to Texas.
    c) people move out of urban centers to the suburbs.
    d) people move out of urban centers to rural areas.
    e) minorities assume political control of a city.

14. The three major metropolitan areas in Texas are
    •a) Houston, Dallas–Fort Worth, and San Antonio.
    b) Houston, Dallas–Fort Worth, and El Paso.
    c) El Paso, Houston, and Austin.
    d) San Antonio, El Paso, and Brownsville-Harlingen-McAllen.
    e) San Antonio, El Paso, and Houston.

Amendments to the Texas Constitution originate in the House of Representatives and then go to voters for approval. Here, Texas Speaker of the House Joe Straus strikes the gavel as the Texas House votes to pass a proposed constitutional amendment that would boost spending for roads and bridges.

The Texas Constitution

WHY THE TEXAS CONSTITUTION MATTERS The Texas Constitution is the legal framework within which government works in Texas just as the U.S. Constitution is the legal framework for our national institutions. Perhaps even more than the U.S. Constitution, the Texas Constitution has an immediate and enormous impact on the everyday lives of Texans. There are rights guaranteed to Texans in Article 1 of the Texas Constitution that go far beyond those of the U.S. Constitution, addressing issues related to Texans' private lives. For example, Article 1, Section 7, stipulates that no money will be appropriated or drawn from the treasury that benefits a sect, religious society, or religious seminary. Section 7 clearly lists the conditions that must be met by the state if it wants to take, damage, or destroy the private property of individuals. Section 30 provides a detailed list of the rights that the victims of crime have, including the right to be treated with dignity and privacy in the criminal process and a right to confer with representatives of the prosecutor's office. Section 31—now rendered inoperable by a U.S. Supreme Court decision in 2015—narrowly defines a marriage as consisting "only of the union of one man and one woman." Section 33 guarantees Texans a right to access and use public beaches. One could argue that each of these cases is more a matter of policy preference than of constitutional right. By placing these in the Bill of Rights of the Texas Constitution, particular policy positions take on a protected status. It is more difficult to change a right enshrined in the Texas Constitution than it is to change a policy backed by statutory law.

Given the length and detail of the Texas Constitution, the amendment process assumes a central role in the political process. Every few years, the Texas legislature presents to the voters a list of proposed amendments to the state constitution. There are some important differences between the amending process for the Texas Constitution and that for the U.S. Constitution. For example, voter approval is necessary for the amendments to the Texas Constitution to take effect. Moreover, since 1789 there have been only 27 amendments to the U.S. Constitution but 491 amendments to the Texas Constitution as of 2016. In 2013, 9 amendments were proposed and passed. In 2014, 1 amendment was passed. In 2015, 7 were put before the electorate and approved.

Occasionally, amendments deal with overall structural issues of government. In 1979, for example, an amendment passed giving the governor limited authority to remove appointed statewide officials. In 1995 a constitutional amendment passed that abolished the office of the state treasurer, placing its duties in the Texas Comptroller's Office. In such cases, amendments to the Texas Constitution function like those to the U.S. Constitution. At other times, though, the amendments to the Texas Constitution are a far cry from those to the U.S. Constitution. There are many more amendments to the Texas Constitution that have dealt with technical problems in the constitution, reflecting efforts to clean up specific language in the state constitution that was now out of date. In 2007 an amendment passed that eliminated the county Office of the Inspector of Hides and Animals.[1] The office had been effectively vacated with the passage of a new Agricultural Code that eliminated the office in law.[2] But the constitution needed to be brought up to date with the law. In 2013, Proposition 2 eliminated language relating to a State Medical and Education Board and a State Medical Education Fund, neither of which were operational.

Other amendments to the Texas Constitution grapple with pressing policy matters. Interestingly, the electorate is asked to give its approval of certain policy initiatives directly through the amendment process, something that is inconceivable at the national level. In 2009 amendments were passed protecting private property from certain property takings by the state through eminent domain, establishing a National Research University Fund, and allowing members of emergency service districts to serve for four years. In 2011 amendments were passed allowing the Texas Water Development Board to issue bonds so that loans could be given to local governments for water projects and granting the City of El Paso more borrowing authority. Among the amendments passed in 2013, Proposition 6 provided for the creation of two funds to help finance important water projects in the future. In 2015, Proposition 7 provided for the creation of funds to help finance transportation projects throughout the state. Without the passage of these amendments by the electorate, effective public policy in a variety of areas central to the future of Texas would have ground to a halt. Far more than the U.S. Constitution, the Texas Constitution is involved with the nuts and bolts of public policy and must be taken into account frequently by Texas legislators seeking to address problems in new and innovative ways.

CHAPTER GOALS

- Identify the main functions of state constitutions (pp. 45–47)
- Describe the six Texas constitutions and their role in Texas political life (pp. 47–62)
- Analyze the major provisions of the Texas Constitution today (pp. 62–71)
- Describe modern efforts to change the Texas Constitution (pp. 71–79)

The Role of a State Constitution

Identify the main functions of state constitutions

State **constitutions** perform a number of important functions. They legitimate state political institutions by clearly explaining the source of their power and authority. State constitutions also delegate power, explaining which powers are granted to particular institutions and individuals and how those powers are to be used. They also are responsible for the establishments of local governments, including counties, municipalities, and special purpose districts. They prevent the concentration of political power by providing political mechanisms that check and balance the powers of one political institution or individual officeholder against another. Finally, they define the limits of political power. Through declarations of rights, state constitutions explicitly forbid the intrusion of certain kinds of governmental activities into the lives of individuals.

constitution the legal structure of a government, which establishes its power and authority as well as the limits on that power

The idea of constitutional government in Texas since its first constitution has been heavily indebted to the larger American experience. Five ideas unite the U.S. and Texas constitutional experiences. First, political power in both the United States and Texas is ultimately derived from the people. The Preamble to the U.S. Constitution begins with the clear assertion that it is "We the People of the United States" that ordains and establishes the Constitution. Echoing these sentiments, the Preamble to the Texas Constitution proclaims that "the People of the State of Texas, do ordain and establish this Constitution." In both documents, political power is something that is artificially created through the constitution by a conscious act of the people.

Second, the U.S. and Texas constitutions feature **separation of powers**. The legislative, executive, and judicial branches of government have their own unique powers derived from the people. Each branch has its corresponding duties and obligations.

separation of powers the division of governmental power among several institutions that must cooperate in decision making

Third, the U.S. and Texas constitutions structure political power in such a way that the power of one branch is checked and balanced by the power of the other two branches. The idea of **checks and balances** reflects a common concern among the framers of the U.S. Constitution and the authors of Texas's various constitutions that the intent of writing a constitution was not just to establish effective governing institutions. Its purpose was also to create political institutions that would not tyrannize the very people who established them. In this theory of checks and balances, both the U.S. and Texas constitutions embody the ideas articulated by James Madison in *The Federalist Papers*, nos. 10, 47, and 51. There, Madison argued that one of the most effective ways of preventing **tyranny** (the concentration of power in one branch) was to pit the self-interest of officeholders in one branch against the self-interest of officeholders in the other branches. Good intentions alone would not guarantee liberty in either the United States or Texas. Rather, constitutional means combined with self-interest would ensure that officeholders had an interest in preserving a balance among the different branches of government.

checks and balances the constitutional idea that overlapping power is given to different branches of government to limit the concentration of power in any one branch

tyranny according to James Madison, the concentration of power in any one branch of government

The concern for preventing the emergence of tyranny is also found in a fourth idea that underlies the U.S. and Texas constitutions: the idea of individual rights. Government is explicitly forbidden from violating a number of particular rights that the people possess. Some rights, such as freedom of speech, freedom of assembly, and freedom of religion, are guaranteed by both the U.S. Constitution and the Texas Constitution. Interestingly, the Texas Constitution also guarantees other rights not found in the U.S. Constitution, such as certain victims' rights and the right to have an "efficient system of public free schools." In this the Texas Constitution can be seen as guaranteeing a broader set of rights than the U.S. Constitution.

The final idea embodied in both the U.S. and Texas constitutions is that of **federalism**. Federalism is the division of government into a central government and a series of regional governments (see Chapter 3). Both kinds of government exercise direct authority over individual citizens of the United States and of each particular state. Article IV, Section 4, of the U.S. Constitution guarantees that every state in the Union will have a "Republican Form of Government." Curiously, no attempt is made to explain what exactly a "Republican Form of Government" entails. The Tenth Amendment to the U.S. Constitution also recognizes the importance of the idea of federalism to the American political system. It reads, "The powers not delegated to the United States by the Constitution, nor prohibited by it to the States, are reserved to the States respectively, or to the people." According to the U.S. Constitution, enormous reservoirs of political power are thus derived from the people who reside in the states themselves.

However, some important differences distinguish the constitutional experience of Texas from that of the United States. Most important is the subordinate role that Texas has in the federal system. Article VI of the U.S. Constitution contains the **supremacy clause**, declaring the Constitution and the laws of the United States to be "the supreme Law of the Land." The supremacy clause requires all judges in every state to be bound by the U.S. Constitution, notwithstanding the laws or constitution of their particular state. In matters of disagreement, the U.S. Constitution thus takes precedence over the Texas Constitution.

One of the major issues of the Civil War was how the federal system was to be understood. Was the United States a confederation of autonomous sovereign states that were ultimately independent political entities capable of secession (much like the current European Union)? Was the United States a perpetual union of states that were ultimately in a subordinate relationship to the central government? The results of the war and the ratification of the Fourteenth Amendment in 1868 ultimately resolved this question in terms of the latter. The idea that the United States was a perpetual union composed of subordinate states would have profound implications for constitutional government in Texas throughout the late nineteenth and twentieth centuries. The incorporation of the Bill of Rights through the Fourteenth Amendment, which made much of the Bill of Rights apply to the states, became a dominant theme of constitutional law in the twentieth century. The Fourteenth Amendment effectively placed restrictions on Texas government and public policy that went far beyond those laid out in Texas's own constitution.

Another major difference between the U.S. and Texas constitutions lies in the **necessary and proper clause** of Article I, Section 8, of the U.S. Constitution. Section 8 begins by listing in detail the specific powers granted to Congress by the Constitution. The Founders apparently wanted to limit the scope of national government activities. But Section 8 concludes by granting Congress the power necessary to accomplish its constitutional tasks. The net effect of this clause was to provide a constitutional basis for an enormous expansion of central government activities over the next 200-plus years.

Drafters of Texas's various constitutions generally have been unwilling to grant such an enormous loophole in the exercise of governmental power. Although granting

federalism a system of government in which power is divided, by a constitution, between a central government and regional governments

supremacy clause Article VI of the U.S. Constitution, which states that the Constitution and laws passed by the national government and all treaties are the supreme law of the land and superior to all laws adopted by any state or any subdivision

necessary and proper clause Article I, Section 8, of the U.S. Constitution; it provides Congress with the authority to make all laws "necessary and proper" to carry out its powers

state government the power to accomplish certain tasks, Texas constitutions have generally denied officeholders broad grants of discretionary power to accomplish their goals.

Texas's power to establish local governments has no analogous feature in the U.S. Constitution. States such as Texas are sovereign entities unto themselves deriving power directly from the people in the state through the state constitution. Texas is not created by the U.S. Constitution, although it is subject to it, as we shall see in Chapter 3. Local governments derive their authority directly from the state constitution and the people of Texas, not from the people in their locality. Self-government for local governing bodies in Texas ultimately means self-government by the people of Texas under the state constitution.

The Texas Constitutions: 1836–1876

 Describe the six Texas constitutions and their role in Texas political life

Many myths surround the origins of Texas as a state. Some trumpet its unique origins as an independent republic that fought to attain its own independence from an oppressive regime much like the United States did. Others suggest that Texas has a certain privileged position as a state given the way that it entered the Union or that it reserved for itself a right to break up into separate states or even to leave the Union. To separate the myth from the reality, it is necessary to understand the Founding of Texas out of its war of independence with Mexico and its subsequent constitutional development.

Texas has operated under seven constitutions, one when it was part of a state under the Mexican political regime prior to independence, one as an independent republic, one as a member of the Confederacy, and four as a state in the United States. Each was shaped by historical developments of its time and, following the first constitution, attempted to address the shortcomings of each previous constitution. To understand constitutional government in Texas today demands a clear understanding of the founding of Texas and the specific historical circumstances that gave rise to each constitution. The constitutional regime operating in Texas today is the product of a long course of political and legal development in the state. In this section, we look at historical circumstances that gave rise to Texas's constitutions.

The Texas Founding

Political scientists refer to "the Founding" as that period in American history when the foundational principles of American political life were established, roughly the period of time from the Declaration of Independence in 1776 through the ratification of the Constitution (1790) and the Bill of Rights (1791). Texas has a founding period, but one that is much longer and more convoluted.

On the face of it, Texas's road to independence appears to mirror that of the United States. Like the United States, Texas had a period of discontent with the governing regime that culminated in a Declaration of Independence. This document cataloged grievances against Mexico and announced the establishment of a new Republic of Texas. But whereas Britain was a stable and powerful empire in the mid-eighteenth century, Mexico was not. Mexico had only recently freed itself from Spain and was experiencing a lengthy period of domestic turmoil. In addition, while the American colonies had been effective self-governing entities before the Declaration of Independence, Texas was not. The Texas Founding encompassed a number of phases of constitutional government. These phases stretched from 1836 when Texas declared itself an independent republic to 1876 when reconstruction after the Civil War came to an end and a new (Texas's current) state constitution was put into place.

The Constitution of Coahuila y Tejas, 1827 Despite the growing fears of American expansionism following the Louisiana Purchase, in 1803 Spanish Texas was still sparsely populated. In 1804 the population of Spanish Texas was estimated to be 3,605. In 1811, Juan Bautista de las Casas launched the first revolt against Spanish rule in San Antonio. The so-called Casas Revolt was successfully put down by the summer of 1811. The next year, a second challenge to Spanish rule took place along the border between Texas and the United States. After capturing Nacogdoches, La Bahia, and San Antonio, rebel forces under José Bernardo Gutiérrez de Lara issued a declaration of independence from New Spain and drafted a constitution. By 1813, however, this revolt had also been put down, and bloody reprisals had depopulated the state. Texas remained part of New Spain until the Mexican War of Independence.[3]

The Mexican War of Independence grew out of a series of revolts against Spanish rule during the Napoleonic Wars. Burdened by debts brought on by a crippling war with France, Spain sought to extract more wealth from its colonies. The forced abdication of Ferdinand VII in favor of Napoleon's brother Joseph in 1808 and an intensifying economic crisis in New Spain in 1809 and 1810 undermined the legitimacy of Spanish rule. Revolts broke out in Guanajuato and spread throughout Mexico and its Texas province. Although these rebellions were initially put down by royalist forces loyal to Spain, by 1820 local revolts and guerrilla actions had helped to weaken continued royal rule from Spain. On August 24, 1821, Mexico was formally granted independence by Spain.

Being part of Mexico, the first federal constitution that Texas operated under was the Mexican Constitution. At the national level, there were two houses of Congress in Mexico. The lower house was composed of deputies serving two-year terms. In the upper house, senators served four-year terms and were selected by state legislatures. The president and vice president were elected for four-year terms by the legislative bodies of the states. There was a supreme court, composed of 11 judges, and an attorney general. Although the Mexican Constitution mandated separate legislative, executive, and judicial branches, no attempt was made to define the scope of states' rights in the Mexican confederation. Local affairs remained independent of the central government. Although the Mexican Constitution embodied many of the ideas found in the U.S. Constitution, there was one important difference: Catholicism was established as the state religion and was supported financially by the state.[4]

Under the Mexican Constitution of 1824, the state of Coahuila and the sparsely populated province of Texas were combined into the state of Coahuila y Tejas. Saltillo,

The speech bubbles in the cartoon read (left to right):

"Slandered as she is, let him that is without sin, cast the first stone at her!"

"Welcome, sister. Your Valor has won you liberty and independence, and you have fairly won the right to be identified with the land of the brave, and the home of the free."

"Shall the slanders that have been urged against your sister, sever those whose blood flows from the same fountain?"

"Stand back, Madam Texas! For we are more holy than thou! Do you think we will have anything to do with gamblers, horse-racers, and licentious profligates?"

"Softly, Softly friend Harry. Thou hast mentioned the very reason that we cannot Vote for thee!"

DALLAS.   POLK.   TEXAS.   CLAY.   QUAKER.

This 1844 cartoon satirized congressional opposition to the annexation of Texas. Personified as a beautiful young woman, Texas is holding a cornucopia filled with flowers. Though James K. Polk, elected to the presidency in 1844, welcomes Texas, the Whig Party leader Senator Henry Clay, with arms folded, warns, "Stand back, Madam Texas! For we are more holy than thou! Do you think we will have anything to do with gamblers, horse-racers, and licentious profligates?"

Mexico, was the capital. More than two years were spent drafting a constitution for the new state. It was finally published on March 11, 1827.

The state of Coahuila y Tejas was formally divided into three separate districts, with Texas composing the District of Bexar. Legislative power for the state was placed in a **unicameral** legislature composed of 12 deputies elected by the people. The people of the District of Bexar (Texas) elected 2 of these. Along with wide-ranging legislative powers, the legislature was also empowered to elect state officials when no majority emerged from the popular vote, to serve as a grand jury in political and military matters, and to regulate the army and militia. Executive power was vested in a governor and a vice governor, each elected by the people for a four-year term. Judicial power was placed in state courts. The Constitution of 1827 formally guaranteed citizens the right to liberty, security, property, and equality. Language in the Constitution of 1827 also supported efforts to curtail the spread of slavery, an institution of vital importance to planters who were immigrating from the American South. The legislature was ordered to promote education and freedom of the press. As in the Mexican federal constitution, Catholicism was the established state religion.[5]

Political instability in Mexico in the late 1820s and early 1830s largely undercut the provisions and protections of both the federal and state constitutions under which Texans lived. But they were important to political debate at the time as discontent against the central government built up. At least in the early stages of the Texas rebellion against Mexico, many Texans could, and did, see themselves as defending these constitutions and most of the political principles that they represented. The turn away from defending the Mexican Constitution of 1824 and the state constitution of 1827 to articulating a new constitutional regime relying more on American political and cultural values was a fundamental step on the road to independence for Texas.

unicameral comprising one body or house, as in a one-house legislature

The Constitution of the Republic of Texas, 1836

Texas's break with Mexico was in large part a constitutional crisis that culminated in separation. Americans had come to Texas for a variety of reasons. Some, like Stephen F. Austin, had come to Texas in the service of the Mexican state as *empresarios*, individuals whose goal was to encourage immigration into Texas from America through the distribution of land made available by the Mexican government. They saw themselves as Mexican citizens working with the constitutional regime of 1827. There were other American immigrants who came to Texas as part of America's move westward. They were far less committed to integrating themselves into the Mexican political community. For these people, independence from Mexico either as an independent Republic or as part of the United States was the ultimate political objective.

Recognizing the dangers to Mexican authority by Americans coming into Texas, Mexican officials made various attempts to limit the influx of new American immigrants. These restrictions, along with other grievances, led to growing discontent among Texans over their place in the Mexican federal system. Ultimately, Texans called for political conventions in 1832 and 1833 to discuss new constitutional forms of government. Along with demands for a more liberal immigration policy for people from the United States and for the establishment of English- and Spanish-speaking primary schools, calls for separate statehood for Texas emerged from the conventions. The 1833 convention actually drafted a constitution for this newly proposed state modeled on the Massachusetts Constitution of 1780. Stephen F. Austin's attempt to bring the proposed constitution to the attention of the central government in Mexico City led to his imprisonment, which in turn pushed Texas closer to open rebellion against the central Mexican government.

On November 7, 1835, a declaration was adopted by a meeting of state political leaders at San Felipe, which stated the reasons Texans were beginning to take up arms against the Mexican government. The declaration proclaimed that Texas was rising up in defense of its rights and liberties as well as the republican principles articulated in the Mexican Constitution of 1824. It was one thing to call for a defense of republican principles under the Mexican Constitution of 1824; it was something else to call for separation from Mexico; and it was something else again to advocate separation from Mexico followed by union with the United States. In the end, the declaration was but a prelude to the formal Texas Declaration of Independence that emerged out of the Convention of 1836 held at Washington-on-the-Brazos.

Of the 59 delegates attending the Convention of 1836, only 10 had lived in Texas prior to 1830. Two had arrived as late as 1836. Thirty-nine of the delegates were from southern slave states, 6 were from the border state of Kentucky, 7 were from northern states, 3 were from Mexico (including 2 born in Texas), and 4 were from other English-speaking lands.[6] The final products of the convention—the Texas Declaration of Independence and the Constitution of 1836—reflected the interests and values of these participants.

In their own Declaration of Independence, delegates to the convention proclaimed that the federal constitutional regime they had been invited to live under by the rulers of Mexico had been replaced by a military tyranny that combined a "despotism of the sword and the priesthood." Echoing the American Declaration of Independence, they presented a long list of grievances against the central government, including the failure to provide freedom of religion, a system of public education, and trial by jury.

The Texas Declaration of Independence Like the Founders during the American Revolution, leaders of the Texas Revolution felt they needed to justify their actions in print. Written by George C. Childress and adopted by the general convention at Washington-on-the-Brazos on March 2, 1836, the Texas Declaration of Independence stated why it was necessary to separate from Mexico and create an independent republic (see Appendix, pp. A1–A3). Not surprisingly, the document draws heavily on the ideas of John Locke and Thomas Jefferson for inspiration. The description of the role of the government, "to protect the lives, liberty, and property of the people," repeated verbatim Locke's litany of the primary reasons for establishing government. Like Jefferson's Declaration, Texas's declaration catalogs a list of grievances against the Mexican regime. According to Texas's declaration, the existing government had abdicated its duties to protect the governed and had broken the trustee relationship that binds a people to those in authority. By dissolving civil society into its original elements, the government had forced the people to assert their inalienable right of self-preservation and to take political affairs into their own hands again. The "melancholy conclusion" of Texas's declaration echoed ideas that Locke and Jefferson would have understood well: any government that stripped a people of their liberty was unacceptable to those raised on principles of self-government. Self-preservation demanded "eternal political separation" from the very state (Mexico) that had invited them to settle in Texas (see Figure 2.1).

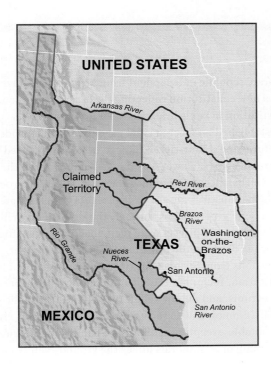

FIGURE 2.1

The Republic of Texas 1836–45

This map shows the Republic of Texas with its large claimed territory. Texas's current boundaries were not established until 1850. Even then, minor controversies persisted along the Red River.

The Texas Declaration of Independence was written by George C. Childress and adopted at the Convention of 1836. Childress modeled the document on the American Declaration of Independence (see Appendix).

UNANIMOUS

DECLARATION OF INDEPENDENCE,

BY THE

DELEGATES OF THE PEOPLE OF TEXAS,

IN GENERAL CONVENTION,

AT THE TOWN OF WASHINGTON,

ON THE SECOND DAY OF MARCH, 1836.

bicameral having a legislative assembly composed of two chambers or houses

After declaring Texas a separate republic independent from Mexico, the convention proceeded to draft and pass a new constitution reflecting these republican sentiments. Resembling the U.S. Constitution in being brief and flexible (fewer than 6,500 words), the 1836 Constitution established an elected chief executive with considerable powers, a **bicameral** legislature, and a four-tiered judicial system composed of justice, county, district, and supreme courts.[7] Power was divided among these three branches, and a system of checks and balances was put into place. Complicated procedures were included for amending the constitution, and a bill of rights was elaborated.

The values of American democracy percolated through the document. White male suffrage was guaranteed. Ministers and priests were ineligible for public office. Checks and balances were established between the three branches of government.

A number of important provisions from Spanish-Mexican law were adapted for the Texas Republic in the constitution, including the idea of community property, homestead exemptions and protections, and debtor relief. By 1840, the Republic of Texas adopted the rules of English Common Law to replace Spanish Law in most civil and criminal matters, with one notable exception. Following Spanish and Mexican law, Texas initially retained ownership of all minerals under the ground even as land grants gave individual ownership to the land itself. Until the Constitution of 1866, a consensus existed that the best model for developing the state and its mineral resources was through direct state ownership of all mineral rights. Under the constitutions of 1866, 1869, and 1876, a new model was adopted granting ownership of mineral rights to the private individuals who owned the land under which minerals were found. Some claims to mineral rights were kept, largely in western parts of the state to fund public schools and higher education. But the new idea was that private entrepreneurs would do a better job developing the state's natural resources than state actors. The complicated history of mineral rights and oil and gas law (as well as the entire oil and natural gas industry) in the nineteenth and twentieth centuries follows directly from the decisions made in later constitutions to replace the original mineral rights provisions of the constitutions of 1836, 1845, and 1861.

One of the most important aspects of the Constitution of 1836, at least from the perspective of newly immigrated Americans from the South, was the defense of slavery as an institution. The Constitution of Coahuila y Tejas of 1827 had challenged, albeit unsuccessfully, the existence of slavery as an institution. Although the 1836 Constitution of the Republic of Texas outlawed the importation of slaves from Africa, it guaranteed that slaveholders could keep their property and that new slaveholding immigrants could bring their slaves into Texas with them. The results of this constitutional protection were monumental. In 1836, Texas had a population of 38,470, including 5,000 slaves. By 1850 the slave population had grown to 58,161, over one-quarter of the state's population. By 1860 there were more than 182,566 slaves, accounting for more than 30 percent of the state's population.[8] The Constitution of 1836 not only saved slavery as an institution in Texas but also provided the protections needed for slavery to flourish.

Writing a constitution is one thing; putting it into effect is another. Only after the Battle of San Jacinto, where on April 21 Sam Houston's force of 900 men overran the 1,300-man force of Santa Anna and captured general and dictator Santa Anna himself, did Texas really become an independent state with a working constitution. Many questioned whether the Lone Star Republic would survive given the dismal state of its finances, an army that couldn't protect rather audacious land claims to the west and the south, a hostile Mexico that only reluctantly accepted Texas's secession, and a United States that appeared to be unwilling to bring Texas into the Union.[9] Annexation to the United States in 1845 ended such questions and brought into being a new constitution, this time a state constitution that would operate within the framework of the U.S. Constitution.

The Texas State Constitution of 1845

The next phase of Texas's Founding took place from 1845 to 1861. Although the 1836 Constitution called for annexation by the United States, Texas remained an independent republic for nine years. There were concerns in the United States that if Texas were admitted to the Union, it would be as a slave state. Texas's admission to the Union could alter the delicate balance between slave and free states and further divide the nation over the sensitive subject of slavery. Additionally, it was feared that annexation by the United States would lead to war with Mexico. The defeated Mexican general and dictator Santa Anna had repudiated the Treaty of Velasco, which had

The lowering of the Republic flag marked Texas's annexation to the Union on March 1, 1845. A state constitution was drafted shortly thereafter to reflect Texas's new role.

ended the war between Texas and Mexico. Still claiming Texas as part of its territory, Mexico undoubtedly would have gone to war to protect what it felt to be rightfully its own.

Hesitation over admitting Texas to the Union was overcome by the mid-1840s. On March 1, 1845, the U.S. Congress approved a resolution that brought Texas into the Union as a state (see Appendix, pp. A5–A6). The annexation resolution had a number of interesting provisions. First, the Republic of Texas ceded to the United States all military armaments, bases, and facilities pertaining to public defense. Second, Texas retained a right to all "its vacant and unappropriated lands" as well as to its public debts. This was no small matter, because Texas claimed an enormous amount of land that extended far beyond its present state boundaries. The boundary issues were not resolved until Congress passed the Compromise of 1850, which, among other things, established Texas's boundaries in exchange for a payment from the federal government where some of the funds were used to pay Texas's debts. Finally, Texas was given permission to break up into four additional states when population proved adequate.

On July 4, 1845, Anson Jones, fourth and final president of the Republic of Texas, called a convention in Austin to draft a state constitution. Drafters of the constitution relied heavily on the Constitution of 1836, although the final document ended up being almost twice as long. The familiar doctrines of separation of powers, checks and balances, and individual rights defined the basic design of government.

Under the Constitution of 1845, the legislature would be composed of two houses. The House of Representatives would have between 45 and 90 members, elected for two-year terms. Members were required to be at least 21 years of age. The Senate would be composed of between 19 and 33 members, elected for four-year terms. Half of the Senate would be elected every two years. As in the U.S. Constitution, revenue bills would originate in the House. Executive vetoes could be overturned by a two-thirds vote of each house. In a separate article on education, the legislature was ordered to establish a public school system and to set aside lands to support a Permanent School

Fund. Another interesting power granted to the legislature was the power to select the treasurer and comptroller in a joint session.

This constitution provided for an elected governor and lieutenant governor. The governor's term was set at two years. He could serve only four years as governor in any six-year period. Among the executive powers granted to the governor were the powers to convene and adjourn the legislature, to veto legislation, to grant pardons and reprieves, and to command the state militia. The governor also had the power to appoint the attorney general, secretary of state, and district and supreme court judges, subject to the approval of the Senate.

The Constitution of 1845 established a judicial branch consisting of a supreme court composed of three judges, district courts, and lower courts deemed necessary by the legislature. Judges on the higher courts were to be appointed to six-year terms and could be removed from office subject to a two-thirds vote of both houses of the legislature.

Amending the Constitution of 1845 was difficult. After being proposed by a two-thirds vote of each house, amendments had to be approved by a majority of the voters. In the next legislature, another two-thirds vote of each house was necessary for ratification. Only one amendment was ever made to the Constitution of 1845. In 1850, an amendment was added to provide for the election of state officials who were originally appointed by the governor or by the legislature.[10]

This constitution retained some of the unusual provisions from the annexation resolution. Texas could divide itself into as many as five states and was responsible for paying its own foreign debt. It would retain title to its public lands, which could be sold to pay its debt. There was even a provision allowing Texas to fly its flag at the same height as the U.S. flag.

The Constitution of 1861: Texas Joins the Confederacy

The issue of slavery had delayed Texas's admission into the United States for nine years, until 1845. Northerners rightly feared that admission of Texas into the Union would intensify southern efforts to extend the slave system westward and would destroy the tenuous balance of power between slave and free states that had been established under the Missouri Compromise. While slavery made it difficult for Texas to get into the Union in 1848, slavery drove Texas from the Union in 1861. By 1860 slavery had become a vital institution to the Texas economy. Concentrated in east Texas and along the Gulf Coast, slaves had come to constitute 30 percent of the population. However, in large sections of the state, particularly in the north and west, the economy was based on ranching or corn and wheat production rather than cotton. There, slavery was virtually nonexistent. The question of whether Texas should secede was a controversial one that divided the state along regional and ethnic as well as party lines.

Pressure to secede mounted following the presidential election of Abraham Lincoln in November 1860. A staunch Unionist, Governor Sam Houston refused to convene a special session of the legislature to discuss secession (see Appendix, pp. A7–A8). Seeking to bypass Houston, a number of influential political leaders in the state, including the chief justice of the Texas Supreme Court, called for a special convention in January 1861 to consider secession. Giving in to the pressure, Houston

This image shows what the Texas State capitol looked like in the 1850s. It burned in 1881. Texas's first constitution after joining the Union as a state was ratified in 1845. It lasted until 1861 when Texas seceded from the Union along with other southern states.

called a special session of the legislature in the hopes of undercutting the upcoming secession convention. The legislature, however, had other ideas, validating the call for the convention and turning its chambers over to the convention.

Lawyers and slaveholders dominated the secession convention. Lawyers composed 40 percent of the delegates; slaveholders composed 70 percent. The Texas Ordinance of Secession, produced by the convention on February 2, 1861, reflected this proslavery membership (see Appendix, pp. A9–A10). In striking language, it proclaimed that the northern states had broken faith with Texas, particularly regarding the institution of slavery. Northerners had violated the very laws and constitution of the federal Union by appealing to a "higher law" that trampled on the rights of Texans. In language that people living in the twenty-first century find hard to understand, the Ordinance of Secession proclaimed,

> We hold as undeniable truths that the governments of the various States, and of the confederacy itself, were established exclusively by the white race, for themselves and their posterity; that the African race had no agency in their establishment; that they were rightfully held and regarded as an inferior and dependent race, and in that condition only could their existence in this country be rendered beneficial and tolerable.[11]

Texas voters approved secession from the Union on February 23, 1861. The secession convention reconvened to enact a new constitution to guide the state as it entered the **Confederacy**. There were surprisingly few changes in the final document. This constitution was similar to the Constitution of 1845 except that references to the United States of America were replaced with references to the Confederate States of America. Public officials had to declare allegiance to the Confederacy, and slavery and states' rights were defended. A clause in the 1845 Constitution that provided for the possible emancipation of slaves was eliminated, and freeing slaves was declared illegal. But for the most part, the document accepted the existing constitutional framework. Controversial proposals, such as resuming the African slave trade, were rejected. The move out of the Union into the Confederacy may have been a radical one, but the new constitution was conservative insofar as it reaffirmed the existing constitutional order in the state.[12]

Confederacy the Confederate States of America, those southern states that seceded from the United States in late 1860 and 1861 and argued that the power of the states was more important than the power of the central government

The Constitution of 1866: Texas Rejoins the Union

Defeat in the Civil War led to the institution of another state constitution in 1866. The provisional governor, pro-Union Andrew Jackson Hamilton, called a constitutional convention on November 15, 1865, a little over six months after the surrender of Lee's army in Virginia. Delegates were elected on January 8, 1866, and the convention was held February 7. Under the provisions of President Andrew Johnson's "Presidential Reconstruction," few former secessionists were excluded from voting. As a result, the convention was dominated by former secessionists, many who had held commissions in the Confederate army.

A number of actions were taken to bring the state into compliance with President Andrew Johnson's policy of Reconstruction, so-called **Presidential Reconstruction**. These included the rejection of the right to secession (see Appendix, p. A11), a repudiation of the war debt incurred by the state, and an acceptance of the abolition of slavery. The convention granted freedmen fundamental rights to their persons and property and gave them the right to sue and be sued as well as the right to contract with others. However, it did not extend suffrage to former slaves, and they were banned from holding public office. The various amendments to the Constitution of 1861 passed by the convention came to be known as the Constitution of 1866.

Presidential Reconstruction a reconstruction plan for reintegrating former confederate states back into the Union and freeing the slaves that placed mild demands upon the existing white power structure

As in the two previous constitutions, the size of the House was set between 45 and 90, and that of the Senate between 19 and 33. Terms of office remained the same as under the 1845 and 1861 constitutions, although salaries were increased. Reapportionment was to be based on the number of white male citizens, who would be counted in a census every 10 years.

The governor's salary was also increased, and the term was extended to 4 years, with a limit of 8 years in any 12-year period. The governor was also granted, for the first time, a line-item veto on appropriations. The comptroller and the treasurer were to be elected by the voters for 4-year terms.

Under the new constitution, the state supreme court was expanded from three to five judges and terms were increased to 10 years. Their salaries also were increased. The chief justice was to be selected from the five judges on the supreme court. District court judges were to be elected for 8-year terms, and the attorney general for a 4-year term.

Voters ratified the Constitution of 1866 in June in a relatively close referendum, 28,119 to 23,400. The close vote was attributed to a widespread unhappiness with the increase in salaries of the various state officers.[13] But there were problems facing the Constitution of 1866. Many pro-unionists who had been driven from the state during the war rejected the constitution, arguing it was the product of a convention dominated by former secessionists. They appealed to the increasingly Radical Republican Congress in Washington, D.C., for redress, arguing that former secessionists should be disenfranchised and forbidden from holding office. Elections were held in Texas, and a legislative session met under the provisions of the Constitution of 1866. New laws were passed by the legislature, including the Black Codes, which limited the social, political, and economic status of African Americans in Texas. In response, Radical Republicans in Washington passed the Congressional Reconstruction Acts of 1867.

The Reconstruction Constitution of 1869

Republicans in Congress had come to see the initial efforts of reintegrating Texas and other southern states back into the Union as a failure. Under the direction of Congress, General Winfield Scott, the commander of the Texas and Louisiana military district, summarily dismissed most state officials elected to office under the 1866 Constitution and called for a new convention to write a new constitution in Texas in 1868. This time, however, former secessionists would be banned from voting or holding office. Against limited Democratic opposition, **Radical Republicans** easily won the vote for a convention by 44,689 to 11,440. Of the 90 delegates to the convention, only 6 had served in the previous constitutional convention. Ten were African American. The vast majority represented the interests of various wings in the Republican Party. The convention was a rancorous affair as delegates argued over a wide range of issues, including railroad charters, lawlessness in the state, and whether laws passed during the war years were legal. In the final days of the convention, delegates finally got down to the constitutional matters and the problems of accepting the Thirteenth and Fourteenth Amendments. Although delegates never completed their task of reworking the Constitution of 1866, their efforts were published under orders by military officials, without being submitted to the voters, and became the Constitution of 1869.

A number of features of the Constitution of 1869 stand out.[14] The U.S. Constitution was declared to be the supreme law of the land. Slavery was forbidden, and African Americans were given the right to vote. Fourteenth Amendment guarantees of equality before the law were recognized. Additionally, the constitution altered the relationship among the three branches of government.

The House of Representatives was set at 90 and the Senate at 30 members. Senatorial terms were extended to six years, with one-third of the seats to be elected every biennium. Legislative sessions were to be held annually.

The most critical changes were in the executive branch and the courts. The powers of the governor were vastly expanded. Among other things, the governor was given wide-ranging appointment powers that included the power to appoint judges. The state supreme court was reduced from five to three judges. The term of supreme court judges was also lowered to nine years, with one new judge to be appointed every three years. Salaries for state officials were increased.

Underlying and fueling the debate over the Constitution of 1869 was another deeper constitutional debate about the meaning of the Secession Ordinance of 1861, the Constitution of 1861, and the Texas government that had functioned under the Confederacy. From the perspective of the U.S. Constitution, had Texas ever "left the union"? Was the Constitution of 1861 "illegal"? And what about the laws that had been passed by the legislature under the powers granted by the 1861 Constitution? Were they the law of the land, or did they have no legal force at all? Were all laws that had been written and all contracts that had been made during the period of rebellion "null and void"? This debate came to an end with the U.S. Supreme Court decision *Texas v. White et al.* (1869). Here, the court ruled that Texas had never left the Union, which was "perpetual, and as indissoluble as the union between the original states." The Ordinance of Succession of 1861 and all acts of the legislature that gave effect to that ordinance were considered to be "null" (see Appendix, pp. A11–A12).

TABLE 2.1

The Changing Texas Constitutions, 1845–1876

The common perception of major constitutional provisions is that they are fixed in time and never to be changed. In Texas, however, constitutional changes are commonplace.

	1836	1845	1861	1866	1869	1876
LEGISLATURE						
Session frequency	annual	biennial	biennial	annual	annual	biennial
House term length	1 year	2 years	2 years	2 years	2 years	2 years
Senate term length	3 years	4 years	4 years	4 years	6 years	4 years
SUPREME COURT						
Size	*	3	3	5	3**	3[†]
Term length	4 years	6 years	6 years	10 years	9 years	6 years
Method of selection	elected[††]	appointed[†]	elected	elected	appointed	elected
GOVERNOR						
Term length	2 years	2 years	2 years	4 years	4 years	2 years[††]

* Chief justice and district judges acting as associate judges. The constitution provides for 3–8 district judges.
** Increased to 5 in 1874 by constitutional amendment.
[†] Amended. Currently 9 members.
[††] Elected by joint ballot by the Texas congress.
[†] Election made selection method in 1850 by constitutional amendment.
[††] Amended. Currently 4 years.

A Republican affiliated with the Radical faction of the party and a former Union general, Edmund Davis, governed under this constitution. Davis had vast authority, since the constitution had centralized power in the executive while reducing local governmental control. Varying interpretations exist of the government provided by Davis, though the popular perception at the time was that Davis presided over a corrupt, extravagant administration that eventually turned to the state police and the militia to attempt to maintain its regime. Closer to the truth may be the fact that Davis sought to maintain his rule by relying on former slaves who had become a bulwark of the Republican Party in the state and by limiting the reintegration of former Confederates back into state politics.

In 1872 the Democrats regained control of the state government, and in 1873 the Democrat Richard Coke was elected governor. Davis attempted to maintain control over the governor's office by having his handpicked supreme court invalidate Coke's election. Davis refused to give up his office and surrounded himself with state police in the capitol. However, when Democrats slipped past guards and gathered upstairs in the capitol to organize a government, Davis was unable to obtain federal troops to retain him in office. Democrats were able to form a government, and Davis left office.

The Constitution of 1876

The final phase of Texas's Founding takes place with the passage of the Constitution of 1876. To prevent another government such as Davis's, efforts were made to write a new constitution. In 1874 a constitution was proposed and later rejected by a sitting legislature.[15] Finally, in 1875 a new constitutional convention was called. Three delegates were selected by popular vote from each of the 30 senatorial districts. The final composition of the convention included 75 white Democrats and 15 Republicans, 6 of whom were African American. Not one of the elected delegates had participated in the constitutional convention of 1868–69. Forty of the delegates were farmers, and 40 were members of the **Grange**, a militant farming organization that had emerged to improve the plight of farmers.

Grange a militant farmers' movement of the late nineteenth century that fought for improved conditions for farmers

The document that emerged from this convention, the Constitution of 1876, is still the basis for Texas government today. In an era of agriculture when prices and incomes were low and when little was demanded or expected from government, much in the 1876 Constitution made sense. However, one might question whether a constitution designed primarily by white males for whites in a rural agrarian society—and for the purpose of keeping the likes of Edmund Davis from ever controlling the state again—is the best foundation for government in the modern era.

The framers were committed to a constitution with four major themes. First, they wanted strong popular control of state government. Second, they believed that a

The example of Edmund Davis's reign motivated the revision of executive branch power in the Constitution of 1876. The framers of that constitution sought popular control of state government in order to limit the appointment powers of the governor as provided by the Constitution of 1869.

constitution should seriously limit the power of state government. Third, they sought economy in government. Fourth, the framers sought to promote agrarian interests, particularly those of small farmers, who formed the basis of support for the Grange movement.

Popular control of state government meant that the governor's vast appointment powers were limited by making judges and other public officials subject to election. But popular control of the government did not mean that all the electorate voted. When the framers of the 1876 Constitution thought of popular control of state government, they thought of control by white males.

In the effort to limit the powers of state government, the constitution placed great restrictions on the actions of government, restrictions that could be modified only through a complex constitutional amendment process. Executive authority was diffused among numerous officeholders, rather than concentrated in the hands of the governor. Although subsequently changed by constitutional amendment, an initial provision further limited gubernatorial power by setting a two-year term limit for the office. The legislature was part-time, ordinarily sitting for a proscribed time period every other year. This was in contrast to the 1869 Constitution, which provided that the legislature meet in annual sessions.

Economy in government was accomplished in several ways. The constitution restricted the extent of government debt and of government's power to tax. In addition, there were limits on the salaries of state officials, especially those of legislators. A major economic depression had begun in 1873, and many Texans were experiencing economic hardship. One way money was saved was by decentralizing public education. Schools were segregated, and compulsory education laws were eliminated. By having local control over education, white landowners could avoid paying taxes for the education of African American students.

Texas at that time was an agricultural state. Wishing to protect agrarian interests, the framers wrote provisions protecting homesteads and restricting institutions that were perceived to be harmful to farmers, such as banks and railroads. Greater responsibility was placed on local instead of state officials. There were also detailed regulations on railroad competition, freight and passenger rates, and railroad construction incentives.

The Constitution of 1876 broke with the more activist government model laid out by the two reconstruction constitutions of 1866 and 1869. The debates of the Constitutional Convention of 1875 drew attention to the fact that Texas was undergoing rapid change. New social and economic conditions, particularly the aggregation of capital in "immense railroad systems," gave rise to new social and political problems. These, in turn, demanded the institution of new restrictions on the powers of state government to prevent corruption. Ironically, a new constitution with new provisions that restricted the activities of government became the bulwark of a conservative white social and political order in the state throughout the late nineteenth and early twentieth centuries (see Governor Richard Coke's Inaugural Address in 1876, Appendix, p. A13).

Even in its earliest stages, the Texas Constitution of 1876 was a lengthy, rigid, and detailed document, and purposely so. Regulations curtailing government power were

SOCIAL RESPONSIBILITY: GET INVOLVED

- Considering the history of Texas constitutions, why does the state constitution place so many limits on state government?

- What changes could be made to the constitution to increase its effectiveness? What could you do to make your suggestions known?

TABLE 2.2

A Constitutional Timeline, 1836–1876

DATE	MAJOR FEATURES
1836 The Constitution of the Republic of Texas following the revolution	• Adopted U.S. Constitution as a working model, including separation of powers, checks and balances, bill of rights. • Rejected Catholicism as state religion. • Defended slavery.
1845 The first Constitution of the State of Texas after annexation by the United States.	• Affirmed many of the institutional features of the U.S. Constitution and the 1836 Constitution of Texas. • Difficult amendment process. • Texas retained ownership of all public lands and minerals under these lands.
1861 The constitution following secession from the Union.	• Affirmed broad features of the 1845 Constitution. • Radical defense of slavery as an institution. • A conservative defense of existing white-dominated political and economic system.
1866 Embodied values of Presidential Reconstruction. Suspended by military rule under Radical Reconstruction.	• Affirmed broad institutional features of the 1845 and 1861 constitutions. • Reflected values of former secessionists. • Accepted results of Civil War and an end to slavery. • Rejected equality before the law or the franchise for former slaves.
1869 The product of Radical Reconstruction. Never completed and went into effect without approval by the people.	• Affirmed U.S. Constitution as the "Supreme Law of the Land." • Affirmed 13th Amendment (ending slavery) and the 14th Amendment (granting equality under the law and due process to all former slaves). • Powers of governor greatly expanded. • Salaries of state officials increased.
1876 Texas's current constitution. Amended 491 times.	• Backs away from radical features of reconstruction including the acceptance of the dominance of the national government over the state. • Reflects a break with activist constitutions of 1869. • Promotes traditional agrarian interests like the Grange in Texas. • Promotes values of "economy" and "efficiency." • Powers of governor and legislature are curtailed. • Provides for election of judges. • Provides for future regulation of railroads.

placed not in statutes where they could easily be reversed, but in the body of the constitution. The goal of this design was to ensure that the Radical Republicans and Edmund Davis would never again be able to reign and spend in Texas. They, of course, never did, although over the years the constitution became an increasingly unwieldy document (see Tables 2.1 and 2.2).

The Constitution of Texas Today

Analyze the major provisions of the Texas Constitution today

The U.S. Constitution has two great virtues: brevity and flexibility. Neither of these virtues can be said to characterize the Texas Constitution. The U.S. Constitution is

TABLE 2.3

The Texas Constitution: An Overview

Article 1: The Bill of Rights

Article 2: Separation of Powers in State Government

Article 3: The State Legislature

Article 4: The Plural Executive

Article 5: The Judicial Department

Article 6: Suffrage

Article 7: Public Education

Article 8: Taxation and State Revenues

Articles 9 and 11: Local Government, Including Counties and Municipal Corporations

Article 10: Empowering the State to Regulate Railroads and to Create the Texas Railroad Commission

Article 12: Empowering the State to Create General Laws for Corporations

Article 13: Concerning Spanish and Mexican Land Titles, Now Deleted from the Constitution

Article 14: Creates the General Land Office to Deal with Registering Land Titles

Article 15: Impeachment Provisions

Article 16: General Provisions Covering a Wide Range of Topics

Article 17: Amendment Procedures

limited to 7 short articles and 27 amendments, and takes up only 8 pages of the *World Almanac*. Much in the federal document is left unsaid, allowing lawmaking to be accomplished by statute. In contrast, in 2016 the Texas Constitution contained 16 articles (Table 2.3; another article that concerned Spanish and Mexican land titles was deleted from the constitution in 1969). Six hundred and seventy-three amendments have been proposed by the legislature. Four hundred and ninety-one have been approved by the electorate, while 179 have been defeated. Curiously, three amendments were proposed by the legislature, but for obscure historical reasons never voted on by the electorate.[16] Many of the articles are lengthy, complex affairs, taking up over 67 pages of text in one edition of the *Texas Almanac*. But it is not just the length that differentiates the two constitutions. There is a difference in tone. The Texas Constitution reflects the writers' fears of what government could do if the principle of **limited government** was not clearly established.

In addition to its severe limits on executive power, the Texas Constitution also addresses a number of specific policy problems directly in the text, turning what might appear to be matters of public policy into issues of constitutional authority. By granting a variety of boards and districts a special place in the constitution, the framers set out additional checks and balances that make it difficult for governors to exercise power effectively. Quite unintentionally, the Texas Constitution became a place where special interests could promote and protect their own agendas, even in the face of considerable political opposition.

limited government a principle of constitutional government; a government whose powers are defined and limited by a constitution

The contrasts in character between the federal and Texas constitutions are a direct reflection of the differences in their framers' underlying goals. The U.S. Constitution was written to overcome the liabilities of the Articles of Confederation and create a government that could act effectively in the public welfare in a variety of policy areas. The Texas Constitution was written to prevent the expansion of governmental authority and the return of a system of political power that was perceived as acting against the interests of the people.

The Preamble

The preamble to the Texas Constitution is surprisingly short: "Humbly invoking the blessings of Almighty God, the people of the State of Texas do ordain and establish this Constitution." This brevity is more than made up for in what follows.

Article 1: Bill of Rights

Article I of the U.S. Constitution establishes and delegates power to the legislative branch of government. One of the overriding concerns of the Founders was to create a legislature that could act effectively in public affairs. What came to be known as the Bill of Rights—the first 10 amendments to the Constitution—was added after the original Constitution was drafted and approved.

In contrast, the Texas Constitution puts its Bill of Rights up front as Article 1, well before any discussion of the legislature, the executive, or the courts. From the beginning, the purpose of the Texas Constitution was not simply to create a set of institutions that could wield political power. It was to limit the way political power is used and to prevent it from being abused.

Section 1 of the Bill of Rights proclaims that "Texas is a free and independent State, subject only to the Constitution of the United States, and the maintenance of our free institutions and the perpetuity of the Union depend upon the preservation of local self-government, unimpaired to all the States." On the face of it, this proclamation would seem to be relatively noncontroversial, as it appears to accept the Constitution of the United States and the perpetuity of the Union. Put into proper historical context, however, it meant something very different. The Constitution of 1869, written under the watchful eyes of Radical Republicans in Texas and in the U.S. Congress, had rejected the "heresies of nullification and secession" and explicitly acknowledged that the U.S. Constitution was "the supreme law of the land" and that the Texas Constitution was "subject to national authority." Article 1, Section 1—the product of a constitutional convention in 1876 that was hostile to many of the efforts of Reconstruction—concedes two very different things: (1) that Texas is free and independent "subject" to the U.S. Constitution and (2) that free and perpetual institutions depend upon local self-government that is "unimpaired." No mention is made of the supremacy of the U.S. Constitution over the state constitution. The idea of a "perpetual union" is made to depend upon "the preservation of self-government," meaning an independent and autonomous state government freed from an intrusive national authority. Texas may have lost the Civil War, but Article 1, Section 1, claims autonomy to the state from outside forces that would have surprised many politicians outside the state. Such sentiments continue to resonate throughout parts of Texas today.

The Texas Bill of Rights embodies certain ideas captured in earlier state constitutions and the U.S. Bill of Rights. All "free men" are declared to have free and equal rights that cannot be denied or abridged because of sex, race, color, creed, or national origin. Freedom of religious worship is guaranteed, and there will be no religious test for office. Liberty of speech and liberty of the press are guaranteed. Individuals are protected from unreasonable search and seizure, from excessive bail, from bills of attainder and ex post facto laws, and from double jeopardy. Article 1 also guarantees an individual a right to trial by jury and the right to bear arms "in the lawful defense of himself or the State; but the Legislature shall have the power, by law, to regulate the wearing of arms, with a view to prevent crime" (Article 1, Section 23).

Article 1 also contains some ideas that move beyond those guaranteed by the first 10 amendments to the U.S. Constitution. The right to **republican government**, something clearly stated in the main body of the U.S. Constitution but not in the U.S. Bill of Rights, is powerfully articulated in the first two sections of Article 1. According to Article 1 of the Texas Constitution, all political power is inherent in the people, and the people of Texas have at all times the "inalienable right to alter, reform or abolish their government in such manner as they may think expedient" (Article 1, Section 2).

republican government a representative democracy, a system of government in which power is derived from the people

The differences between the Texas Bill of Rights and the U.S. Bill of Rights are not simply matters of where best to articulate a philosophy of republican government. They also involve very concrete matters of public policy. Section 26 in the Texas Bill of Rights, for example, forbids monopolies that are contrary to the public interest, and states that the law of primogeniture and entail (a law designed to keep large landed properties together by restricting inheritance to the firstborn) will never be in effect in the state. Although monopolies remain a public concern today, primogeniture and entail are not. Section 11 in the Texas Bill of Rights grapples with the complicated issue of bail and under what specific circumstances an individual can be denied bail. Significantly, Section 11 has been the subject of three major constitutional revisions: in 1955, 1977, and 1993. Section 30, adopted in 1989, provides a long list of the "rights of crime victims," including the right to be treated fairly and with dignity, the right to be protected from the accused, and the right to restitution. Although these are important matters of public policy for Texas today, they could hardly be considered proper material for the U.S. Constitution.

Article 2: The Powers of Government

Like the U.S. Constitution, Article 2 divides the power of government in Texas into three distinct branches: the legislative, the executive, and the judicial. It also stipulates that no one in any one branch shall be attached to either of the other branches, except where explicitly permitted (as in the case of the lieutenant governor's role in the Senate). The article—one short paragraph of text—assures that a version of the separation of powers doctrine found in the U.S. Constitution will be embodied in Texas institutions.

Article 3: Legislative Department

Article 2 is one of the shortest articles in the Texas Constitution. Article 3 is the longest, comprising almost one-third of the text. Like Article I of the U.S. Constitution, Article 3 of the Texas Constitution vests legislative power in two houses: a Senate of 31 members and a House of Representatives of no more than 150 members. It stipulates the terms of office and qualifications. House members serve two-year terms, whereas senators serve four-year terms, half being elected every two years. House members must be citizens of the United States, must be at least 21 years of age, and must have resided in the state for two years and in their district for one year. Senators must be citizens of the United States, must be at least 26 years old, and must have resided in the state for five years and in their districts for one year. In addition, Article 3 provides for the selection of officers in both houses of the legislature, states when and for how long the legislature shall meet (Section 5), and explains how the legislative proceedings will be conducted (Sections 29–41) and how representative districts will be apportioned (Sections 25, 26, and 28).

Like Article 1, Texas's Bill of Rights, Article 3 moves well beyond the U.S. Constitution, putting limits on what the legislature can do. For example, it puts limits on legislators' salaries and makes it difficult to increase those salaries. Article 3 also creates a bipartisan Texas Ethics Commission whose job, among other things, is to recommend salary increases for members of the legislature and to set per diem rates for legislators and the lieutenant governor. Article 3, Section 49a, also subjects the legislature to the actions of the comptroller of public accounts, whose duty is to prepare a report prior to the legislative session on the financial condition of the state treasury and to provide estimates of future expenditures by the state. This provision of the Texas Constitution effectively limits the state legislature to the financial calculations and endorsements of the comptroller, a check on the legislature all but unimaginable to the writers of the U.S. Constitution.

Putting constraints on certain legislative actions is only part of the story. The largest portion of Article 3 (Sections 47–64) is dedicated to addressing a variety of policy problems, including lotteries, emergency service districts, the problem of debt creation, problems surrounding the Veterans' Land Board and the Texas Water Development Board, Texas park development, the creation of a state medical education board, and even the establishment of an economic development fund in support of the now defunct superconducting supercollider.

Article 4: Executive Department

Article II of the U.S. Constitution concentrates executive power in the presidency. The desire was to create a more effective and more responsible executive than had been possible under the Articles of Confederation. The Texas Constitution lists a number of offices in the executive, legislative, and judicial branches, which are specified in Table 2.4. Article 4 of the Texas Constitution states that the executive shall consist of six distinct offices: the governor, who serves as the chief executive; the lieutenant governor, who serves as the president of the Senate; the secretary of state, who keeps the official seals of the state; the comptroller of public accounts; the commissioner of

TABLE 2.4

Major Constitutional Officers in Texas

LEGISLATIVE (ARTICLE 3)

OFFICE/POSITION	ELECTED BY/APPOINTED BY	DUTIES
Speaker of the House	Elected by House members	Leads the House
President Pro Tempore of the Senate	Elected by Senate members. Most senior member of the Senate from either party.	Leads Senate in absence of the lieutenant governor

EXECUTIVE (ARTICLE 4)

Governor	Elected by Texas voters for 4-year term	Chief executive of the state
Lieutenant Governor	Elected by Texas voters for 4-year term	Acts as governor in absence of governor and presides over Senate
Secretary of State	Appointed by the governor by and with advice and consent of Senate	Chief election officer of Texas
Comptroller of Public Accounts	Elected by Texas voters	Chief steward of state finances
Commissioner of the General Land Office	Elected by Texas voters	Manages state assets, investments, and mineral rights from state lands and serves as chair for numerous state boards and commissions
Attorney General	Elected by Texas voters	Represents the state in cases where the state is a party

JUDICIAL (ARTICLE 5)

Justice of Supreme Court	9 positions elected by Texas voters for 6-year terms	Decides on civil cases reaching Texas Supreme Court
Judge of Court of Criminal Appeals	9 positions elected by Texas voters for 6-year terms	Decides on criminal cases reaching Texas court of criminal appeals
Justice of the Court of Appeal	80 justices in 14 courts of appeal elected by Texas voters for 6-year terms from multimember districts	Decides on cases reaching Texas court of appeal
District Court Judge	456 district court judges elected by Texas voters for 4-year terms from a mixture of multi- and single-member districts	Decides on cases in Texas district court

Other county-level court officials are also elected for 4-year terms on a county or precinct basis. Municipal court judges are usually appointed.

OTHER IMPORTANT OFFICES

Texas Railroad Commissioner (Article 13, Section 30)	3 officers elected by Texas voters for 6-year overlapping terms	Regulates the oil and gas industry, gas utilities, pipeline safety, and surface coal and uranium mining (no longer regulates railroads)
State Board of Education Member (Article 7)	15 members elected by Texas voters from single-member districts for 4-year terms	Makes statewide policies for public schools
Agricultural Commissioner (office established under Agricultural Code, not the constitution)	Elected by Texas voters to a 4-year term	Regulates state agriculture and administers state agriculture policy

the General Land Office; and the attorney general, who acts as the state's chief legal officer. With the exception of the secretary of state, who is appointed by the governor and approved by the Senate, all other offices are elected by qualified voters every four years. Besides creating a **plural executive**, Article 4 guarantees its members will have independent political bases in the electorate. This provides an additional check against any concentration of powers in the hands of any one person.

Article 5: Judicial Department

Article III of the U.S. Constitution succinctly provides for a Supreme Court and empowers Congress to create any necessary lower courts. Nothing could be further from the detailed discussion of the state courts found in Article 5 of the Texas Constitution. Besides creating one supreme court to hear civil cases and one court of criminal appeals to hear criminal cases, Article 5 provides for such lesser courts as courts of appeal, district courts, commissioner's courts, and justice of the peace courts, and empowers the legislature to establish other courts as deemed necessary. It also goes into such details as the retirement and compensation of judges, the jurisdictions of the various courts, and the duties of judges; it states what to do in the case of court vacancies; and it includes a series of discussions on particular issues involving the lower courts.

An even greater difference between the federal Constitution and the Texas Constitution is the crucial role the latter gives to elections. Federal judges are appointed by the executive and approved by the Senate. In Texas, the people elect state judges. Nine supreme court and nine court of criminal appeals judges are elected at large in the state. Lower court positions are elected by voters in their relevant geographic locations. Much like the U.S. Constitution, the Texas Constitution seeks to create an independent judiciary that can check and balance the other two branches of government. But it seeks an additional check as well. It wants the people to watch over the courts.

Article 6: Suffrage

Article 6 contains a short but detailed discussion about who may vote in Texas. It also empowers the legislature to enact laws regulating voter registration and the selection of electors for president and vice president.

Article 7: Education

The concerns found in the Texas Declaration of Independence over the need for public schools to promote a republican form of government are directly addressed in Article 7, which declares, "A general diffusion of knowledge [is] essential to the preservation of the liberties and rights of the people." Section 1 makes it a duty of the state legislature to support and maintain "an efficient system of public free schools." The Texas Supreme Court's interpretation of this provision as applying to school funding in the state has led to political battles over school finance for 40 years. Sections 2–8 provide for their funding and the creation of a State Board of Education to oversee the operations of elementary and secondary education in the state. State universities are the subject of over half of Article 7, where detailed discussions of the funding and operations of particular state institutions are put directly into the text.

Article 8: Taxation and Revenue

The complex issue of taxation is the subject of Article 8. Once again we find a highly detailed account of several important policy issues built directly into the text of the constitution. One of the most controversial sections of the Texas Constitution centers on the issue of the income tax. Section 1 enables the legislature to tax the income of individuals and businesses. This power, however, is subject to Section 24, which was passed by the 73rd Legislature in 1993. Section 24 requires that the registered voters in the state approve a personal income tax and that the proceeds from this tax be dedicated to education and tax relief. As with other portions of the constitution, the net effect of these provisions is to curtail severely what the state legislature can do and how it is to do it. If Section 24 of Article 8 is any indication, the public fear of unresponsive and potentially tyrannical government is as alive today as it was in 1876.

Articles 9 and 11: Local Government

These articles provide highly detailed discussions of the creation, organization, and operation of counties and municipal corporations.

Articles 10, 12, 13, and 14

These heavily revised articles deal with a series of specific topics: the railroads (10), private corporations (12), Spanish and Mexican land titles (13), and public lands (14). Article 10 empowers the state to regulate railroads and to establish the Railroad Commission. Article 12 empowers the state to create general laws creating private corporations and protecting the public and individual stockholders. Article 13, now entirely deleted from the constitution, dealt with the nineteenth-century issue of Spanish and Mexican land titles. Article 14 created a General Land Office to deal with the registration of land titles.

Article 15: Impeachment

Impeachment is, in the U.S. Constitution, one of the major checks Congress holds against both the executive and judicial branches of government. The House of Representatives holds the power to impeach an individual; the Senate is responsible for conducting trials. A two-thirds vote in the Senate following impeachment by the House leads to the removal of an individual from office.

impeachment under the Texas Constitution, the formal charge by the House of Representatives that leads to trial in the Senate and possible removal of a state official

A similar process is provided for in Article 15 of the Texas Constitution. The House has the power to impeach. The Senate has the power to try the governor, lieutenant governor, attorney general, land-office commissioner, and comptroller, as well as judges of the supreme court, the courts of appeal, and district courts. Conviction requires a two-thirds vote of the senators present. In contrast to the U.S. Constitution, the Texas Constitution rules that all officers against whom articles of impeachment are proffered are suspended from their office. The governor is empowered to appoint a person to fill the vacancy until the decision on impeachment is reached.

Despite these similarities to the impeachment procedures in the U.S. Constitution, the Texas Constitution has its own caveats. Most notably, the Texas Constitution does not explicitly define impeachable offenses in terms of "Treason, Bribery, or other high Crimes and Misdemeanors," as the U.S. Constitution does. The House and Senate (and the courts) decide what constitutes an impeachable offense.[17] In addition, the supreme court has original jurisdiction to hear and determine whether district court judges are competent to discharge their judicial duties. The governor may also remove judges of the supreme court, courts of appeal, and district courts when requested by the two-thirds vote of each legislature. Significantly, the reasons for removing a judge in this case need not rise to the level of an impeachable offense, but need only involve a "willful neglect of duty, incompetence, habitual drunkenness, oppression in office, or other reasonable cause" (Article 15, Section 8). The barriers to removing a judge by political means are thus, at least on paper, much lower in Texas than in national government.

In 1980, Section 9 was added to Article 15, providing a new way to remove officials appointed by the governor. With the advice and consent of two-thirds of the members of the Senate present, a governor may remove an appointed public official. If the legislature is not in session, the governor is empowered to call a special two-day session to consider the proposed removal.

Article 16: General Provisions

Article 16 is one of the lengthiest in the Texas Constitution and has no parallel in the U.S. Constitution. It is literally a catchall article tackling a variety of issues ranging from official oaths of office to community property to banking corporations and stock laws to the election of the Texas Railroad Commission to the state retirement systems. Here, perhaps more than anywhere else, we see the complexity and confusion of the philosophy reflected in the Texas Constitution.

Article 17: Amending the Constitution

Like the U.S. Constitution, the Texas Constitution explicitly delineates how it can be amended. Essentially, amendments undergo a four-stage process: First, the legislature must meet in either regular or special session and propose amendments. Second, these amendments must be approved by a two-thirds vote of all the members elected to each house. Third, a brief statement explaining the amendments must be published twice in each recognized newspaper in the state that meets the publication requirements for official state notices. Finally, the amendments must be approved by a majority of the state voters.

Recent Attempts to Rewrite the Texas Constitution

 Describe modern efforts to change the Texas Constitution

Given the difficulty of amending the state constitution, a surprising number of amendments have been proposed since 1876. A considerable number of these have been turned down in the popular vote. As Table 2.5 shows, demands for amending the Constitution have intensified in recent years, as legislators have dealt with the problem of making changes in public policy while being constrained by an unwieldy constitutional document.

TABLE 2.5

Amending the Texas Constitution
The Constitution of Texas has been amended 491 times since its inception in 1876.

YEARS	NUMBER PROPOSED	NUMBER ADOPTED
1876–1900	31	17
1901–20	56	21
1921–40	71	47
1941–60	78	59
1961–80	151	98
1981–2000	180	148
2001–10	79	77
2011	10	7
2013	9	9
2014	1	1
2015	7	7
Total	673	491

SOURCE: Texas Legislative Council and Texas Secretary of State.

Sharpstown and the Failed Constitutional Reforms of 1974

Land developer Frank Sharp was convicted of violating federal banking and security laws in 1972. The Sharpstown scandal rocked Texas politics and led to calls for constitutional reform.

A drive to rewrite the Texas Constitution grew out of a major stock fraud that broke in the early 1970s, involving the Sharpstown State Bank and the National Bankers Life Insurance Corporation. Following the 1970 elections, which had been dominated, as generally was the case, by the conservative wing of the Democratic Party, a suit filed in Dallas federal court by the Securities and Exchange Commission alleged that a number of influential Democrats, including Governor Preston Smith, the state Democratic chairman and state banking board member Elmer Baum, Speaker of the House Gus Mutscher, and others, had been bribed. By the fall of 1971 Mutscher and two of his associates had been indicted. On March 15, 1972, they were convicted and sentenced to five years' probation.

The convictions fueled a firestorm in the state to "throw the rascals out." During the 1972 elections, "reform" candidates dominated the Democratic primary and the general election. The conservative rancher-banker Dolph Briscoe became governor, but only by a plurality, making him the first governor in the history of the state not to receive a majority of the popular vote. Other reform-minded candidates such as Lieutenant Governor William P. Hobby, Jr., and Attorney General John Hill were successful. When the smoke cleared, half of the House seats were occupied by new members, and the Senate had witnessed a higher-than-normal rate of turnover. The elections had one other outcome: an amendment was passed empowering the legislature to sit as a constitutional convention whose task would be to rewrite the constitution.[18]

The constitutional convention met on January 8, 1974, in Austin. The idea was for the convention to draft a new constitution that would then be presented to state voters for ratification. Originally scheduled to last 90 days, the convention was extended to 150 days. Even so, it did not have enough time. Bitter politics, coupled with the intense demands of highly mobilized special interests, made it impossible to reach the necessary agreement. In the end, proponents of a new constitution failed to achieve a two-thirds majority by three votes (118 to 62, with 1 abstention).

The movement to rewrite the constitution did not die at the convention. During the next session of the legislature, eight constitutional amendments were passed that effectively would have rewritten the constitution through the normal amendment process. Each proposal, however, was turned down by the electorate in a special election on November 4, 1975. The Constitution of 1876 remained alive, if not well.

Recent Amendments

In the 2015 constitutional amendment elections, voters were asked to consider seven proposed amendments. All the amendments passed, although only approximately 11.34 percent of registered voters bothered to vote, up from 8.55 percent in the 2013

Which State Has the Longest Constitution?

State Constitution Length (estimated)

- < 19,999 words
- 20,000–39,999 words
- 40,000–59,999 words
- 60,000–79,999 words
- > 79,999 words

VERMONT
8,565 words
Shortest

ALABAMA
388,882 words
Longest

TEXAS
86,936 words
Second longest

The Texas Constitution is the second-longest state constitution in the United States. The framers of the Texas Constitution gave the state government very specific powers so that the government could not use ambiguity to expand its powers. As a result, the Texas Constitution requires frequent amendments to address situations not covered specifically in the original constitution. The Texas Constitution has been amended 484 times as of 2015, fourth most of any state.

SOURCE: Book of the States, 2015. Council of State Governments. Data for 2015 compiled by the authors.

Amendments Added to Constitution

- < 75 amendments
- 75–149 amendments
- 150–224 amendments
- 225–300 amendments
- > 300 amendments

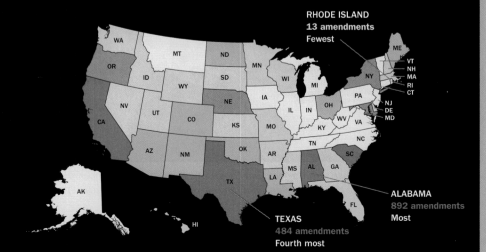

RHODE ISLAND
13 amendments
Fewest

ALABAMA
892 amendments
Most

TEXAS
484 amendments
Fourth most

CRITICAL THINKING

- After examining the two maps, do you see any relationship between the length of a state constitution and the number of amendments to the constitution? Why do you think that there might be such a relationship in some states?

- Do different regions in the country seem to favor short rather than long state constitutions? What factors might account for such similarities?

constitutional amendment elections. Despite the increase, one thing that is clear about elections that deal with constitutional amendments is that voting participation is invariably low. "Who Are Texans?" compares the percentage turnout of registered voters in November special elections on constitutional amendments with the percentage turnout in presidential elections (which tend to produce the highest turnout). There are two likely reasons for the low voter turnout in constitutional amendment elections: (1) Constitutional amendment elections are usually held in "off" years when there are no elections with candidates on the ballot. Because of this, the political parties take a less active role in getting out the vote, and there are no candidates to generate voter turnout. As a result, advertising campaigns to get out the vote are frequently limited only to the activities of interest groups that support or oppose the issues on the ballot. (2) Many of the amendments are relatively insignificant to most voters.

Most of the 2015 proposed constitutional amendments listed in Table 2.6 were uncontroversial. Such was not the case in 2011 when 3 of the 10 amendments presented to the voters were turned down. The controversial ones were those that the Tea Party and other antitax groups saw as increasing the financial burden on Texans. For example, Proposition 4 was defeated because it would have expanded the ability of counties to issue bonds to finance the development of unproductive areas where those bonds were to be repaid with property tax revenues. Critics of the proposal argued that it would clear the way for new toll roads. Proposition 7 was defeated because it would have given El Paso new borrowing authority. Proposition 8 passed the legislature with bipartisan support. It would have given property owners the opportunity to opt out of agricultural or wildlife conservation property tax exemptions in favor of

Amendments to the state constitution affect many areas of Texans' lives. The amendments passed in 2015 included one providing additional funds available for transportation projects throughout the state.

Who Votes in Texas Elections Amending the Constitution?

Turnout of Registered Voters in Texas Constitutional Amendment Elections Compared with Presidential Elections*

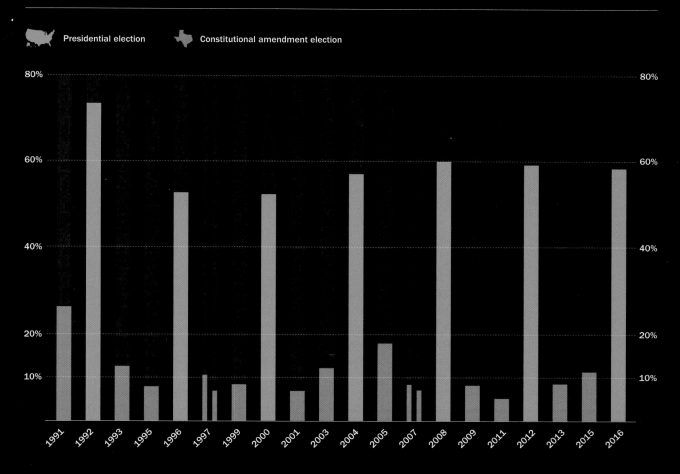

Presidential election   Constitutional amendment election

Since 1983, Texans have voted to amend the state's constitution dozens of times. Turnout in these elections is always low, even when well-publicized amendments are on the ballot. For example, in 2005, 17 percent of registered voters voted on Proposition 2, which banned same-sex marriage in the state.

* 1997 elections in August and November; 2007 elections in May and November.

SOURCE: Texas Secretary of State, www.sos.state.tx.us/ (accessed 3/18/16).

QUANTITATIVE REASONING

- What is the difference between participation rates in presidential elections and constitutional amendment elections? What might account for this difference?

- What could be done to increase turnout in constitutional amendment elections?

TABLE 2.6

Passed Constitutional Amendments, 2015

Proposition 1 The constitutional amendment increasing the amount of the residence homestead exemption from ad valorem taxation for public school purposes from $15,000 to $25,000, providing for a reduction of the limitation on the total amount of ad valorem taxes that may be imposed for those purposes on the homestead of an elderly or disabled person to reflect the increased exemption amount, authorizing the legislature to prohibit a political subdivision that has adopted an optional residence homestead exemption from ad valorem taxation from reducing the amount of or repealing the exemption, and prohibiting the enactment of a law that imposes a transfer tax on a transaction that conveys fee simple title to real property. (Passed 86.4%)

Proposition 2 The constitutional amendment authorizing the legislature to provide for an exemption from ad valorem taxation of all or part of the market value of the residence homestead of the surviving spouse of a 100 percent or totally disabled veteran who died before the law authorizing a residence homestead exemption for such a veteran took effect. (Passed 91.4%)

Proposition 3 The constitutional amendment repealing the requirement that state officers elected by voters statewide reside in the state capital. (Passed 66.1%)

Proposition 4 The constitutional amendment authorizing the legislature to permit professional sports team charitable foundations to conduct charitable raffles. (Passed 69.4%)

Proposition 5 The constitutional amendment to authorize counties with a population of 7,500 or less to perform private road construction and maintenance. (Passed 82.7%)

Proposition 6 The constitutional amendment recognizing the right of the people to hunt, fish, and harvest wildlife subject to laws that promote wildlife conservation. (Passed 81.1%)

Proposition 7 The constitutional amendment dedicating certain sales and use tax revenue and motor vehicle sales, use, and rental tax revenue to the state highway fund to provide funding for nontolled roads and the reduction of certain transportation-related debt. (Passed 83.2%)

water conservation property tax exemptions. The Tea Party successfully opposed the proposition on the grounds that it would shift the tax burden to others.[19] While the Tea Party and other antitax groups could not defeat all of the propositions they opposed, low voter turnout enabled them to exert a significant influence. Indeed, their defeat of three proposals broke the modern pattern in which amendments are routinely approved. For example, between 2001 and 2010, 77 of 79 proposed amendments were approved.

Participation in the 2005 constitutional amendment election may appear to be abnormally high (see "Who Are Texans?" p. 75). Most of the 2005 proposed constitutional amendments were, like the previously discussed propositions, of significance only to a narrow group of people. For example, one of the nine proposed amendments provided for clearing land titles in Upshur and Smith counties. Another authorized the legislature to provide for a six-year term for a board member of a regional mobility authority. Yet the turnout in this election was much higher than is typically seen in constitutional amendment elections. The reason was Proposition 2, which defined marriage in Texas as the union

PERSONAL RESPONSIBILITY: WHAT WOULD YOU DO?

- Do you think that more people should participate in constitutional amendment elections? Why or why not?

- What do you think groups or political parties should do to increase turnout for constitutional amendment elections?

Proposition 2 and Same-Sex Marriage

Recent controversy over same-sex marriage highlights the tensions that emerge between the federal and the Texas constitutions.

In November 2005, Texans went to the polls to vote on Proposition 2 to amend the Texas Constitution, a measure aimed at prohibiting same-sex marriages in the state. Supporters of Proposition 2 wanted the ban on such marriages enshrined in the state constitution in order to prevent any future legislation supporting gay and lesbian marriages. The measure passed with nearly 76 percent of Texans voting in support of the proposition.

In *Obergefell v. Hodges* (2015), the U.S. Supreme Court ruled 5–4 that marriage was a fundamental right guaranteed to same-sex couples by the due process clause and the equal protection clause of the Fourteenth Amendment of the Constitution. Writing for the majority, Justice Kennedy explained the Supreme Court opinion clearly: "The Court now holds that same-sex couples may exercise the fundamental right to marry. No longer may this liberty be denied them." Although Texas was not one of the states considered in the *Obergefell* case, the ruling clearly applied to Texas.

One would have thought that the *Obergefell* decisions would have ended debate over same-sex marriage in Texas, superseding the provisions put into the Texas Constitution. But a few public officials sought to undercut the full effect of the U.S. Supreme Court ruling. In June, 2015, Hood County Clerk Katie Lang said that she would refuse to issue same-sex marriage licenses because of her religious faith. Backtracking after a public furor broke out, she later agreed to allow staff members to issue the licenses. Attorney General Ken Paxton, a bitter opponent of same-sex marriage, advised county clerks in Texas that they could refuse marriage licenses to same-sex couples on religious grounds. According to Paxton, "Justices of the peace retain religious freedoms, and may claim that the government cannot force them to conduct same-sex wedding ceremonies over their religious objections." Threatened with a contempt citation from a federal judge, Paxton backed off, maintaining that he himself was not enforcing the laws that impeded gay marriage rights, only advising others about what courses of action could be pursued by public officials in Texas.

Paxton's "advisory" opinion and Metzger's refusal to marry same-sex couples in his court raise interesting questions. Should the personal religious values of a

public official allow them to not enforce the law? Should lawmakers bring the Texas Constitution in line with the *Windsor* and *Obergefell* cases by deleting the Proposition 2 provisions? Should new provisions be added that protect the religious beliefs of state officials in the performance of their duties while upholding the principles of the U.S. Constitution?

COMMUNICATING EFFECTIVELY: YOUR VOICE

- Is Proposition 2 a violation of the equal protection clause of the U.S. Constitution? Should it be deleted from the Texas Constitution?

- If you were writing a letter to the editor about this issue, what arguments would you make either in support of Paxton or in disagreement with him? How would you answer, or support, those who ask that they be allowed to listen to their "religious consciences" and not perform the duties for which they were elected?

Protesters gather outside the Hood County Court in support of County Clerk Katie Lang, who denied marriage licenses to same-sex couples after the Supreme Court ruling in Obergefell v. Hodges *(2016) on the grounds that being required to do so would abridge her freedom of religion.*

of one man and one woman. The proposition also prohibited the state or any political subdivision of the state from creating or recognizing any legal status identical to or similar to marriage. The proposition generated a strongly favorable vote—1,723,782 in favor versus 536,913 against. Unlike Proposition 12 in 2003, this was not an economic battle involving interests concerned with tort law; rather, this was an issue pitting social conservatives against those more sympathetic to gay rights. The strength of the social conservative vote in the state was, of course, remarkable, since the amendment carried by more than a 3-to-1 margin. Many churches and religious organizations strongly supported the proposed amendment. Their activities probably generated the relatively high voter turnout. The proposition was unusual in that people felt it was important to their lives because it affected their value systems. Although it is doubtful the amendment was necessary to support the traditional concept of marriage and although the ambiguity of the provision rejecting any legal status similar to marriage is disturbing, a significant part of the voting population apparently believed that it was important to vote their moral values, even if the proposal was largely symbolic.

Although most constitutional amendments are not of great importance, there are some notable exceptions. Table 2.7 identifies some of those amendments that, like Proposition 12 in 2003 or Proposition 2 in 2005, have had great significance in the public policy of the state.

TABLE 2.7

Some Important Constitutional Amendments

In 1894, Texans strongly supported an amendment providing for the election of railroad commissioners. In later years, when Texas became a major oil producer, the railroad commission gained the authority to regulate oil production and became the most powerful elected regulatory agency in the country.

In 1902, Texans by a huge majority backed an amendment "requiring all persons subject to a poll tax to have paid a poll tax and to hold a receipt for same before they offer to vote at any election in this state, and fixing the time of payment of said tax." The poll tax required a payment of money prior to voting. The effect was to reduce the size of the electorate, limiting the opportunity of those with lower incomes to vote.

In 1919, the same year the national Prohibition Amendment was ratified, Texas ratified a state prohibition amendment.

In 1935, Texans repealed statewide prohibition. In its place was a local option whereby local communities chose whether alcohol would be sold in those communities. This was two years after repeal of national Prohibition.

In 1954, Texans passed an amendment requiring women to serve on juries. Previous to that, women were exempt on the grounds that they were needed at home as the center of home life.

In 1966, Texans repealed the poll tax as a voting requirement in the face of pressures from the U.S. Supreme Court and from a national constitutional amendment that eliminated the poll tax in national elections.

In 1972, Texans overwhelmingly passed a constitutional amendment "to provide that equality under the law shall not be denied or abridged because of sex, race, color, creed or national origin." This amendment was primarily seen as an equal rights amendment banning sex discrimination, since federal civil rights statutes largely dealt with discrimination on other grounds. It was the state version of a proposed sexual equal rights amendment that was never ratified and made part of the U.S. Constitution.

In 2003 a constitutional amendment promoting the tort reform agenda passed that placed limitations on lawsuits. In "civil lawsuits against doctors and health care providers, and other actions," the legislature was authorized "to determine limitations on non-economic damages."

In 2005 a constitutional amendment was passed "providing that marriage in this state consists only of the union of one man and one woman and prohibiting this state or a political subdivision of this state from creating or recognizing any legal status identical or similar to marriage." The amendment was passed in response to the movement toward the recognition of civil unions and same-sex marriage in some states.

In 2009, Texans supported an amendment establishing "the national research university fund to enable emerging research universities in this state to achieve national prominence as major research universities." The amendment was a recognition that the Texas economy would benefit by the development of nationally recognized research universities in the state.

In 2009, in reaction to a U.S. Supreme Court decision involving eminent domain—the taking of private property for public use—that was seen as unsympathetic to property rights, Texans passed an amendment "to prohibit the taking, damaging, or destroying of private property for public use unless the action is for the ownership, use, and enjoyment of the property by the State, a political subdivision of the State, the public at large, or entities granted the power of eminent domain under law or for the elimination of urban blight on a particular parcel of property, but not for certain economic development or enhancements of tax revenue purpose."

★ ★

The Constitution and the Future of Texas

In this chapter, we explored the Texas Founding and the story of constitutional government in Texas. We analyzed the seven constitutions under which Texas has been governed and explained the similarities and differences between the U.S. Constitution and Texas's current constitution (the Constitution of 1876). We also discussed attempts over the past 30 years to replace this constitution with a new one, and the many constitutional issues that face Texas today.

It has been decades since there was any serious effort to change the Texas Constitution in any way other than by adding to its numerous amendments. This pattern likely will continue: more and more amendments will be added to an already lengthy and cumbersome document. Many of these amendments will address technical problems often related to the operations of various state agencies and local governments. Some may create additional funding sources for major state initiatives as we have seen recently in water and transportation policy. Other amendments might be adopted in response to such controversial social issues as abortion or the free exercise of religion. As in the past, the constitution and its amendments will reflect the values and goals of the people of Texas and the political system that the people have put into place through the constitution.

Use 🐰 INQUIZITIVE to help you study and master this material.

The Role of a State Constitution

• Identify the main functions of state constitutions (pp. 45–47)

The state constitution is the governing document of the state much in the same way the U.S. Constitution sets up the framework for the nation as a whole. Many of the ideas found in the U.S. Constitution are also found in Texas's constitutions, including republican government, separation of powers, checks and balances, and individual rights.

Key Terms
constitution (p. 45)
separation of powers (p. 45)
checks and balances (p. 45)
tyranny (p. 45)
federalism (p. 46)
supremacy clause (p. 46)
necessary and proper clause (p. 46)

Practice Quiz
1. Which idea is contained in both the U.S. and Texas constitutions?
   a) separation of powers
   b) Keynesianism
   c) laissez-faire economics
   d) *Rebus sic stantibus*
   e) none of the above

2. Which of the following is *not* an important function of a state constitution?
   a) prevents the concentration of political power
   b) delegates power to individuals and institutions
   c) prevents government from intruding in the lives of businesses and individuals
   d) legitimizes political institutions
   e) limits application of the U.S. Constitution

3. Which part of the U.S. Constitution reserves power to the states?
   a) Article I
   b) Article VI
   c) First Amendment
   d) Tenth Amendment
   e) Nineteenth Amendment

4. Under the U.S. Constitution, the government of Texas is most limited by
   a) Article IV of the U.S. Constitution.
   b) the implied-powers clause and the Tenth Amendment of the U.S. Constitution.
   c) the Fourteenth Amendment of the U.S. Constitution.
   d) all of the above equally
   e) none of the above

The Texas Constitutions: 1836–1876

> • Describe the six Texas constitutions and their
>   role in Texas political life (pp. 47–62)

Texas has had six constitutions reflecting the concerns of the historical periods in which they were written. The Civil War and Reconstruction played a major role in shaping Texans' attitudes toward the dangers of strong state government. The Constitution of 1876 sought to limit the powers that had been wielded under the previous constitution by Republican governor Edmund Davis. It remains, though much amended, the existing state constitution of Texas.

Key Terms
unicameral (p. 49)
bicameral (p. 52)
Confederacy (p. 56)
Presidential Reconstruction (p. 57)
Radical Republicans (p. 58)
Grange (p. 60)

Practice Quiz
5. The Constitution of 1861
  a) generally accepted the existing constitutional framework.
  b) guided Texas's entry into the Confederate States of America.
  c) supported slavery.
  d) defended states' rights.
  e) all of the above

6. A unique feature of the Constitution of 1869 was that
  a) it explicitly rejected the power of the federal government in Texas.
  b) fewer than 1 percent of voters opposed it.
  c) it was less than four pages long.
  d) it was published before being submitted to the voters.
  e) it is considered the best of Texas's constitutions.

7. A new Texas Constitution was written
  a) during the Reconstruction period.
  b) when the Compromise of 1850 was adopted.
  c) at the start of World War I.
  d) in 1999.
  e) none of the above

8. The present Texas Constitution
  a) is well organized and well written.
  b) is considered to be one of the best of the 50 state constitutions.
  c) delegates a great deal of power to the governor.
  d) severely limits the power of the governor and other state officials.
  e) all of the above

9. The Constitution of 1876 was a reaction to the Reconstruction Constitution of 1869 because
  a) the 1869 Constitution was too short.
  b) the 1869 Constitution forbade slavery.
  c) the 1869 Constitution increased state officials' salaries.
  d) the 1869 Constitution was seen as giving the governor too much power.
  e) none of the above

10. When the framers of the Constitution of 1876 wrote of "the people," they meant
  a) all adult citizens of Texas.
  b) all adult male citizens of Texas.
  c) all men and women over the age of 21.
  d) all citizens except carpetbaggers and scalawags.
  e) none of the above

The Constitution of Texas Today

Today's Texas Constitution is lengthy and includes over 400 amendments. It limits the power of state government and tries to prevent the concentration of power in the hands of one person.

Key Terms
limited government (p. 63)
republican government (p. 65)
plural executive (p. 68)
impeachment (p. 69)

Practice Quiz
11. Article 1 of the Texas Constitution
   a) contains the Texas Bill of Rights.
   b) renounces the use of the death penalty.
   c) rejects the U.S. Constitution's Bill of Rights.

   d) recognizes the supremacy of the national government.
   e) accepts the principle of rapprochement.

12. The Texas Bill of Rights
   a) guarantees some rights not found in the U.S. Bill of Rights.
   b) duplicates the U.S. Bill of Rights.
   c) is unusual, since state constitutions generally do not have Bills of Rights.
   d) guarantees gay marriage.
   e) outlaws abortion.

13. The Texas Constitution requires that Texas judges
   a) be appointed by the governor.
   b) be a member of the Republican Party.
   c) be senior lawyers.
   d) be elected by the people.
   e) cannot receive campaign contributions.

Recent Attempts to Rewrite the Texas Constitution

Recent attempts to rewrite the Texas Constitution have been unsuccessful. Amendments continue to be the easiest way to modify the document.

Practice Quiz
14. A new constitution for Texas
   a) is likely to be ratified in 2018.
   b) is scheduled for a vote in 2020.
   c) has a 50–50 chance of being ratified in 2018.
   d) has a very small chance of being written and ratified in the near future.
   e) none of the above

15. Voter turnout for constitutional amendment elections could be improved if
   a) they were held at the same time as presidential elections.
   b) there were more voter awareness of the proposed amendments.
   c) the amendments involved significant issues for voters.
   d) all of the above
   e) none of the above

The relationship between the state and federal governments has remained a key issue in Texas. Recently, Governor Greg Abbott called for a U.S. constitutional convention to amend the Constitution and strengthen the powers of states versus those of the national government.

RESTORING THE RULE OF LAW
WITH STATES LEADING THE WAY

BY GOVERNOR GREG ABBOTT

Texas in the Federal System

WHY FEDERALISM MATTERS The issue of federalism has been a fundamental political concern since the nation's founding, and it continues to be a major political issue in Texas. Former governor Rick Perry was a major advocate of state power and a critic of the power of the national government. In a speech in November 2014, Perry explained his views: "One of the ideas that has returned to the fore of the conversation, to the forefront of people's minds, if you will, is the proper place of states within our federal system. Indeed, we have spent the last six years challenging edicts out of Washington that amount to federal control of our classrooms, our healthcare, and our environment and our economy. Washington's assault on state sovereignty and individual freedom is a well-documented assault on the Constitution and, in particular, the Tenth Amendment.[1]

Governor Greg Abbott has taken the states' rights argument a giant step further than Perry by calling for a constitutional convention to pass nine new constitutional amendments that would limit national governmental power. Essentially, his position is that it is necessary to amend the Constitution in order to save it. Abbott claims,

> Indeed, the entire structure of the Constitution was premised on the idea that the States would be stronger than the national government. . . . And the Anti-Federalists principal complaint with the Constitution was premised on their fear that it would turn the States into "useless and burdensome" relics. Madison passionately rebutted those concerns by insisting that the States would remain the most powerful and important organs of American government. If only we had heeded Madison's solutions to the Anti-Federalists' concerns, our Nation would not be mired in this constitutional conundrum today. But over the last 227 years, in fits and starts, through baby steps and giant leaps, our government lost its way; it left the Constitution in its rearview; and it pushed States into the roadside ditch.[2]

To strengthen the states and weaken the power of the national government, Abbott would like to require a balanced budget. He would also like to prevent Congress from regulating activities occurring within a state—an amendment that would likely prevent federal regulation of gun use and marriage. Among the other proposed amendments would be a requirement that federal laws and U.S. Supreme Court decisions could be overridden by two-thirds of the states. Abbott would also require that there be a seven-justice supermajority for the Supreme Court to invalidate a state or national law.[3]

➡

Abbott's proposal for a convention, while unlikely to be adopted, is one of the most comprehensive proposals for change that has been offered by Texans unhappy with the exercise of national governmental power by the Obama administration. For the time being, however, rather than in a constitutional convention, the issues of federalism are fought out in the federal courts where Texas (and other states) is involved in litigation involving immigration policy, voter ID, affirmative action, and environmental legislation.

CHAPTER GOALS

- Understand the foundations of the U.S. federal system (pp. 87–92)
- Trace the major changes in national and state power over time (pp. 92–96)
- Describe the sources of, and tensions between, national and state power (pp. 96–106)

The Roots of American Federalism

Federalism is a system of government in which power is divided between a central government and regional governments. At its core is decentralization of government, and in the United States, the balance in the powers of the states and national government has been the subject of intense political dispute since the American Revolution. States have always done much of the routine governance in the United States. State laws provide the regulations for birth, death, marriage, divorce, and most crime and punishment. Most commercial law is regulated by the states, and states manage education, prisons, highways, welfare, environmental issues, corporations, and professions. Many of the political conflicts in the nation have been fought over the proper roles of states versus the national government. These conflicts include disputes over the states' rights to leave the Union, the power of government to regulate business, the implementation of political reforms, and responses to problems of race, poverty, and abortion.

Roughly 40 percent of the world's population lives in countries that are organized around a federal principle where there is a national government and regional governments, each of which has the authority to maintain order, make laws, spend money, and provide services. Federalist countries include the United States, Argentina, Australia, Austria, Belgium, Brazil, Canada, Ethiopia, Germany, India, Mexico, Nigeria, Spain, and Switzerland. The European Union may be developing into a federalist system as well. Federalism exists because it is a method for bringing together smaller units to achieve larger goals—primarily the fostering of commerce and improving military security. In

federalism a system of government in which power is divided between a central government and regional governments

In recent years, some Texans have called for a decentralized system of government. Some have looked back to the Republic of Texas as an ideal.

India, Belgium, and Spain, for example, federalism has been used to hold together nations that have serious geographical, ethnic, or cultural divisions. In these countries, the regional governments represent ethnic or religious minorities and have unique powers of self-governance. This is different from the United States, where all states have equal legal standing and authority. In other federal systems, the national government consciously attempts to redistribute the country's wealth to the poorest regions, something not done in the United States. Additionally, federalism in the United States has proven enormously flexible in comparison with other federal nations. Federalism in America has adapted to vast changes in the geographic size of America, to large increases in its population, and to changes in the racial, religious, and ethnic background of its population. It has also adapted to vast economic changes in the nation.[4]

The Constitutional Roots of Federalism

Immediately following the United States' independence from Britain, the Articles of Confederation gave states the primary role in governance, and the national government was small and had limited powers. The relative weakness of the national government meant that the states functioned as nearly independent entities rather than as one nation. In the mid-1780s, the diversity of the states and their self-serving policies appeared to be splitting the new nation apart. An economic decline in the 1780s worsened the divisions in the country. Daniel Shays led a rebellion of Massachusetts debtors who attacked towns and burned courthouses. The new nation seemed on the precipice of revolt. George Washington criticized the state governments for the new nation's problems, saying the states' pursuit of narrow self-interest was making "the situation of this great country weak, inefficient and disgraceful."

It was hard for the national government under the Articles of Confederation to act. The Confederation Congress had limited powers, and the rules allowed a few states—in some cases a single state—to block congressional action. It took 9 states (out of 13) to enact any defense or economic policy. The Congress could not tax; it had to request money from the state governments and it could not compel payment by the states. There was no executive or court system under the Confederation. The Confederation could not defend the nation because it could not pay for an army or a navy. By 1786 the Congress was broke because states were not paying their share of expenses for the national government. Even though a majority of the states supported the Congress's efforts to tax imports, individual states objected and killed these tax proposals. Moreover, the Articles of Confederation could not be easily amended because a unanimous vote of the states was required for amendment.[5]

By 1786 it was becoming clear that something had to be done to increase the power of the national government. A meeting was held in Annapolis, Maryland, in 1786 that called for a convention of states to meet in Philadelphia the following year to "render the constitution of the Federal Government adequate to the exigencies of the Union." That led to the Constitutional Convention in 1787, where 55 delegates met and designed the new U.S. Constitution.[6]

Under the U.S. Constitution, a federal system was created in which the national government was **sovereign**, deriving its power directly from the American people.

sovereign possessing supreme political authority within a geographic area

During the American Revolution, the lack of a strong central government made it difficult for the United States to fund a strong military, as exemplified by terrible conditions for the troops at Valley Forge.

Individual states were also sovereign, deriving their power from the people in their state through their state constitutions.[7] The immediate effect of the Constitution was to increase national power and to delegate to the national government distinctive powers and responsibilities such as national defense and foreign policy. State governments also had separate powers and responsibilities, such as protecting public safety. Local governments were created by state governments, and their powers are granted (and can be revoked) by state governments. Rather than being a part of a federal system, local governments were the creations of states, and continue to be so today (see Chapter 10).

State interests were protected under the new Constitution in a variety of ways, and one of the most important was that each state would get equal representation in the Senate. At the time, state legislatures chose the U.S. senators from that state, and so the senators were agents of state interests in the national government. States also retained their power to tax and to maintain a militia, and they had commercial powers, for example, the power to regulate commerce within states. The national government had taxing authority, military powers, and commercial authority such as the power to regulate commerce between states. And it had flexible powers that could be expanded in the future through Congress's constitutional power, "To make all Laws which shall be necessary and proper for carrying into Execution the foregoing Powers, and all other Powers vested by this Constitution In the Government of the United States."[8]

The Tenth Amendment In the debates over ratification of the Constitution, there was great concern that the national government had been made too powerful and that, if ratified, the Constitution would foster a centralized tyranny that would destroy the rights of the people and the states. In an effort to alleviate these concerns, the Bill of Rights was added to the Constitution in the form of the first ten amendments. The Tenth Amendment, commonly called the States' Rights Amendment, states, "The powers not delegated to the United States by the Constitution, nor prohibited by it to the States, are reserved to the States respectively, or to the people." Although James Madison personally did not believe that the Tenth Amendment was necessary, Madison urged that it be adopted. The problem with the amendment is that it does not delineate national and state powers, and rather than settle conflicts over federalism, the amendment has been a source of conflict over the meaning of federalism.[9]

Federalism in Early America

Controversy over the exact nature of the federal system divided Americans in the late 1820s and '30s. During the Nullification Crisis in 1833, South Carolina tried to assert the right to veto (or nullify) national legislation passed by Congress. John C. Calhoun argued that a strong national government was a threat to the sovereignty of states, and argued for a system along the lines of the original Articles of Confederation. President Andrew Jackson responded by threatening to use military force in support of federal law. South Carolina backed down.

Although the national government had imposed its will successfully during the Nullification Crisis, the question of the exact relationship between the central government and individual states was still open. In spite of the forces of decentralization, most notably coming from the South, the Supreme Court under Chief Justice John Marshall (1801–35)—a Federalist and an appointee of President John Adams—issued a number of important opinions that promoted national power at the expense of state power. In *McCulloch v. Maryland* (1819), for example, one issue was whether Congress had the power to incorporate the Second Bank of the United States. If Congress did have the power to incorporate the bank, the second issue was whether Maryland could tax the bank. Writing for a unanimous court, Marshall noted that Article I, Section 8, of the Constitution enumerated the powers of Congress. Nowhere in Article I, Section 8, is specifically found the power to incorporate a bank. However, Article I, Section 8, also contains a provision that Congress has the power "To make all Laws which shall be necessary and proper for carrying into Execution the foregoing powers, and all other Powers vested by this Constitution in the Government of the United States." A Bank of the United States could be a means to accomplish some of those enumerated powers, such as carrying out the power to borrow money. As a result, Congress did have the implied power to incorporate the bank, as the "necessary and proper" clause of Article I, Section 8, provided a source of implied powers for the national government. Marshall further noted in his opinion that unlike the Articles of Confederation, there was no provision of the U.S. Constitution that excluded the recognition of implied powers. He even made the case that the Tenth Amendment recognized that Congress had implied powers because it said "The powers not delegated to the United States" rather than "The powers not *expressly* delegated to the United States." Marshall also wrote that the states did not have the power to tax the Second Bank of the United States. For the states to have that taxing power, he argued, would transfer the supremacy of the national government to the states. It was a vastly important decision favoring national power at the expense of state powers.[10]

Gibbons v. Ogden (1824) was another major Marshall Court decision that expanded national power. The case dealt with a dispute over the operation of steamboats in New York waters. Robert Fulton and Robert Livingston obtained a monopoly from New York to operate steamboats in its waters, and they granted a license to Aaron Ogden to operate steamboats between New Jersey and New York. Thomas Gibbons obtained a license from the national government to operate steamboats between New Jersey and New York, and Ogden went to New York courts to get an injunction against Gibbons. Marshall wrote that one of the powers of Congress in Article I, Section 8, was the "power to regulate commerce with foreign nations, and among the several states."[11] Ogden argued that power was limited to the interchange of commodities and did not include navigation, but Marshall broadly defined commerce to include navigation

A major power of the national government is the power to regulate interstate commerce. Gibbons v. Ogden (1824) was a key case that expanded national power. It held that Congress had the power to regulate interstate commerce, like shipping between New York and New Jersey, pictured here.

and wrote that interstate commerce "cannot stop at the external boundary line of each state, but may be introduced into the interior." While the completely internal commerce of a state could be considered reserved to the states for regulation, if commerce was not completely internal to a state, it was interstate commerce and could be regulated by Congress, as the regulation of interstate commerce "does not stop at the jurisdictional lines of the several states."[12] This decision, providing a broad definition of interstate commerce, was to be the primary source of the most important regulatory power of Congress: the power to regulate interstate commerce.

Marshall was consistent in deciding cases to expand the power of the national government and weaken the power of states. However, Marshall was unwilling to make the Bill of Rights apply to the states as well as the national government. That would take the ratification of the Fourteenth Amendment in 1868. In Marshall's time, it was clear that the Bill of Rights was not a restriction on the powers of states; it was intended to limit the powers of the national government.

The Constitution was created out of a fear of disunity. Seventy-five years after the ratification of the Constitution, an observer of the American experiment with federalism would have concluded that it was a failure. America faced a massive rebellion and a war that was immensely bloody.[13] Texas played a major part in the tensions between the North and the South that threatened the Union when Texas sought and was ultimately admitted to the Union as a slave state. Only sixteen years after its admission to the Union, Texas seceded and joined the Confederacy. With secession of southern states came the Civil War, which was, in part, a struggle over the meaning of the federal system and the proper relationship between the national and the state governments. Southern states, including Texas, feared that a national government controlled by northern states would move to end slavery, an institution that the southern states felt was essential to their social, political, and economic way of life. They saw the creation of the Confederacy as a movement back to the older confederation system embodied in the Articles of Confederation where the central government in Richmond was weak and the individual states were strong. This vision of a confederation effectively came to a close with General Lee's surrender at the Appomattox Court House.

In 1869 the Supreme Court in the case *Texas v. White* resolved the debate over whether states can secede from the Union. The case dealt with the legality of a bond sale sponsored by Texas that had occurred under the Confederate government of Texas. In rejecting the legality of the sale of bonds, Chief Justice Salmon Chase authored the opinion which said that the Constitution "in all its provisions, looks to an

The United States and Texas flags that fly in front of many government buildings in Texas (including Dallas's city hall, pictured here) reflect the nature of federalism. Both the national government and the state government are sovereign. The third flag is the flag of the city of Dallas.

indestructible Union, composed of indestructible states." Secession was void and Texas had remained a state during the Civil War. Texas had not had a lawful government during the Confederacy, and so the bond sale was void. Additionally, the Union had a right to provide Texas with a republican form of government. The national government could create a government in Texas after the war where no legitimate government existed because Article IV, Section 4, of the Constitution provided, "The United States shall guarantee to every State in this Union a Republican Form of Government."[14]

Dual Federalism

 Trace the major changes in national and state power over time

Reconstruction the period after the Civil War when much of the South was under military occupation

dual federalism the system of government that prevailed in the United States from 1789 to 1937, in which most fundamental governmental powers were strictly separated between the federal and state governments

Following the end of **Reconstruction** and into the early twentieth century, the court further embraced **dual federalism**. The national government was relatively small in comparison to the states and states did most of the governing. The national government's role was more or less limited to providing for national defense and foreign policy and assisting in the development of commerce. Citizens' daily lives were chiefly affected by their state governments, not the national government.

Prior to the late 1930s the Supreme Court was using dual federalism to strike down regulation of the economy by the national government. Congress's power to regulate interstate commerce was narrowly defined so that it could only ban the shipment of harmful goods in interstate commerce and could only regulate the distribution of goods in interstate commerce but not the production of goods. This meant, for example, that Congress was powerless to forbid the distribution of the products of child labor in interstate

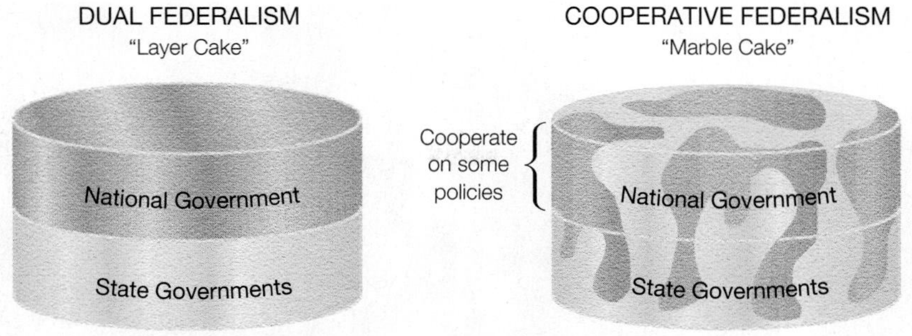

DUAL FEDERALISM
"Layer Cake"

COOPERATIVE FEDERALISM
"Marble Cake"

Cooperate on some policies

National Government

State Governments

National Government

State Governments

FIGURE 3.1

Dual versus Cooperative Federalism

In layer-cake federalism, the responsibilities of the national government and state governments are clearly separated. In marble-cake federalism, national policies, state policies, and local policies overlap in many areas.

commerce, and it could not regulate the aspects of the manufacture of goods such as monopolies on production of goods or working conditions in factories.

This system of dual federalism was described by political scientist Morton Grodzins as **layer-cake federalism** (see Figure 3.1). Like the layers on a cake, the powers of the national government and state governments were largely separate and, one might add, the layer that was the national government's powers and responsibilities was smaller than was the layer that represented the powers and responsibilities of state governments.[15] Under layer-cake federalism, there were still clear limits to the sovereignty of states. States could not nullify national legislation, nor could they secede from the Union. But states had a major role to play in governance that was quite distinct from the role of the federal government.

Dual federalism had tremendous effects on issues relating to both economic regulations and civil rights in Texas. For example, the power to regulate the oil industry was a state power. The Railroad Commission of Texas established rules that, among other things, limited the number of oil wells that could be drilled on a particular amount of land, and it limited the amount of oil that could be pumped from those wells. Such regulations were seen as a matter for state regulation rather than national regulation until the discovery of the East Texas Oil Field, which then was the largest oil field in the world. As a result of this oil discovery, such overproduction of oil occurred that national legislation was needed to prevent an interstate market in oil produced in violation of state regulations. Dual federalism was also used to prevent national intervention into acts of racial violence. Enforcement of criminal laws was seen as a state matter. Texas did pass an anti-lynching law in 1897 that was used to prevent some lynchings of persons by authorizing the governor to call out the state guard. Nevertheless, Texas and other states were remarkably ineffective in preventing lynching. It is hard to identify the precise number of people who were lynched, but the Equal Justice Initiative has identified 3,959 lynchings between 1877 and 1950 whose purpose was to enforce racial separation and segregation laws. Of those, 376 occurred in Texas.[16] It was only in the 1960s that national laws began to be used to successfully prosecute these crimes.

layer-cake federalism a way of describing the system of dual federalism in which there is a division of responsibilities between the state and the national governments

Marble-Cake Federalism

With the presidency of Franklin Roosevelt—when America faced the Great Depression and then World War II—the relationship between the national government

During the 1930s, Texans were affected by unemployment and drought that had led to massive poverty across the state. The federal government stepped in to help, employing people in public works projects. Here, people make copper utensils for a Texas hospital.

marble-cake federalism a way of describing federalism where the boundaries between the national government and state governments have become blurred

cooperative federalism a type of federalism existing since the New Deal era in which grants-in-aid have been used to encourage states and localities (without commanding them) to pursue nationally defined goals; also known as *intergovernmental cooperation*

categorical grants congressionally appropriated grants to states and localities on the condition that expenditures be limited to a problem or group specified by law

and the states changed dramatically. Federalism changed to what has been called **marble-cake federalism**, where the boundaries between the national government and the states became blurred. The initial form of marble-cake federalism was **cooperative federalism**, where national and state governments worked together to provide services—often with joint funding of programs or state administration of programs mostly funded by the national government. In fighting the Great Depression, Roosevelt pursued a variety of such programs. The Social Security Act of 1935, for instance, changed the existing federal system in a number of fundamental ways. First, it put into place a national insurance program for the elderly (now known as Social Security) where individuals in all states were assessed a payroll tax on their wages. Upon retirement, "participants" were to receive a pension check. Second, the act put into place a series of state-federal programs to address particular social problems, including unemployment insurance, aid to dependent children, aid to the blind and disabled, and aid to impoverished elderly people. The basic model for these programs was that the federal government would make money available to states that established their own programs in these areas, provided they met specific administrative guidelines. Although the federal dollars came with these strings attached, the programs were state run and could differ from state to state. This type of funding system was common in the early days of cooperative federalism. The grants using this model were called **categorical grants**.

During the New Deal period, the idea was abandoned that the Tenth Amendment was a barrier to national power and that the national government could not involve itself in areas that were reserved only to the states. As the Supreme Court case *Wickard v. Filburn* (1942) suggested, the regulatory power of the national government under the interstate commerce clause was so broad that there seemed no boundaries on national power.[17]

In the 1960s during President Lyndon B. Johnson's Great Society, new programs were added to the Social Security Act. Medicare was established to provide health insurance for the elderly, paid for through a payroll tax on current workers. Medicaid was added to provide health care funding for individuals enrolled in the state-federal Aid to Families with Dependent Children (AFDC) program. Medicaid's funding and administration were based on the same state-federal principles as AFDC and unemployment insurance: the federal government provided funding for approved state programs. Federalism

Federal Funds to Texas versus Other States

Many factors affect how much federal funding a state recieves. Federal money can go directly to individuals, such as Social Security or Medicare. Federal money can also go to the states, which then decide how best to use the funds to benefit their constituents, such as for highway funding. In the graph below, we can compare how much federal money Texas and Texans receive compared to California, Florida, New York, and Ohio.

Federal Funds Received by States, 2003–2015

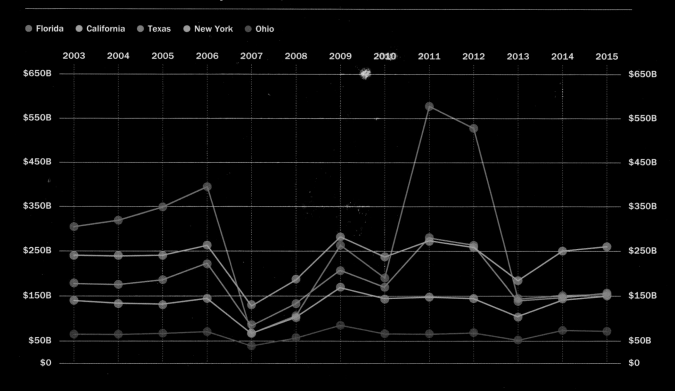

● Florida   ● California   ● Texas   ● New York   ● Ohio

Federal Funding as a Percentage of State Revenue, 2015

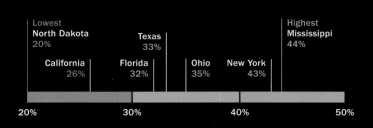

| Lowest North Dakota 20% | California 26% | Texas 33% | Florida 32% | Ohio 35% | New York 43% | Highest Mississippi 44% |

20%   30%   40%   50%

SOURCES: "Spending Map," USA Spending.gov, www.usaspending.gov (accessed 3/29/16); John S. Klerman, "2015's States Most and Least Dependent on the Federal Government," WalletHub, wallethub.com (accessed 3/29/16).

CRITICAL THINKING

- What might explain why certain states receive more funding than others at different time periods?

- Florida and Texas received about the same amount of federal funding in 2015, even though the population of Texas is much larger. Why do you suppose Florida receives proportionally more federal funds than Texas?

continued to evolve with the passage of civil rights legislation in the 1950s and '60s, when the role of the national government was expanded to protect the rights of minorities. In the process, the national government was often thrown into conflict with southern states such as Texas that persisted in trying to maintain a segregated society.

President Richard M. Nixon briefly tried a somewhat different version of federalism that he called **New Federalism**. In an attempt to reduce federal control, Nixon introduced a funding mechanism called **block grants**, which allowed the states considerable leeway in spending their federal dollars. In the 1980s, President Ronald Reagan adopted Nixon's New Federalism as his own, and block grants became an important part of state-federal cooperation.

New Federalism's biggest success, however, was during President Bill Clinton's administration when, in 1996, major reforms were passed in welfare programs that gave the states a significant decision-making role. By the 1990s, liberals and conservatives were in agreement that welfare in America was broken. Replacing the state-federal system with a system of grants tied to federal regulations and guidelines lay at the heart of the Clinton welfare reforms, the most important since the New Deal.

New Federalism the attempts by Presidents Nixon and Reagan to return power to the states through block grants

block grants federal grants that allow states considerable discretion on how funds are spent

Coercive Federalism: Texas and the Federal Government

Describe the sources of, and tensions between, national and state power

coercive federalism federal policies that force states to change their policies to achieve national goals

unfunded mandates federal requirements that states or local governments pay the costs of federal policies

preemption where the national government imposes its priorities and prevents the state from acting in a particular field

In recent years some national actions have been described as **coercive federalism**, where federal regulations are used to force states to change their policies to meet national goals. Until the 2012 Supreme Court decision involving the Affordable Care Act (commonly called Obamacare) struck down the provision, states were threatened with the loss of all Medicaid funding if they did not expand their Medicaid coverage to comply with the legislation. Perhaps most disturbing for states are the federal **unfunded mandates**, which are the federal requirements that the state (or local) governments pay the costs of federal policies.[18] For example, the federal Americans with Disabilities Act requires that street curbs be accessible to wheelchairs, but the federal government does not pay for the curbs. That cost is passed on to state and local governments. Along with unfunded mandates, federal **preemption** is another aspect of coercive federalism. Preemption is where Congress passes laws and, through the supremacy clause of the Constitution in Article VI of the Constitution, which states, "This Constitution and the Laws of the United States which shall be made In Pursuance thereof; . . . shall be the supreme Law of the Land," Congress can pass laws that impose national priorities upon the states. The U.S. Conference of Mayors identified 10 federal mandates that cost cities about 11 percent of their budgets.[19] The National Association of Counties has identified 12 federal mandates that cost counties about 12 percent of their budgets.[20]

How Do Federal Funds Flow to Texas?

Federal grants provide states with money for programs that range from Medicaid and school lunches to tuberculosis control and immunization programs. As the chart below indicates, federal grants make up a majority of the money the state of Texas spends on health care and a large share of the money spent on natural resources, education, and general government.

2014–2015 Texas Budget

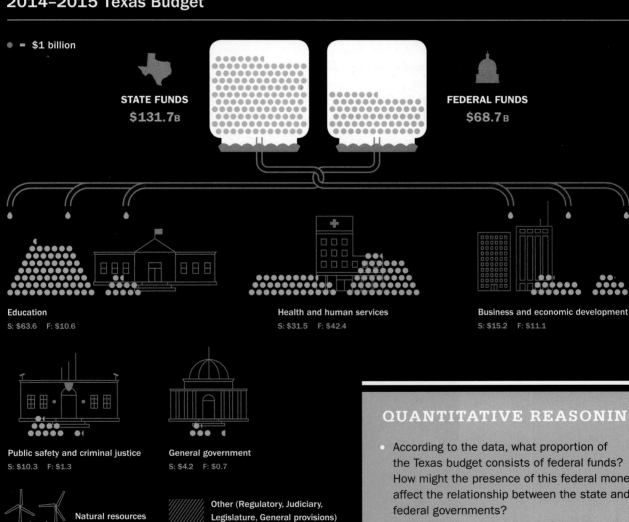

● = $1 billion

STATE FUNDS
$131.7B

FEDERAL FUNDS
$68.7B

Education
S: $63.6   F: $10.6

Health and human services
S: $31.5   F: $42.4

Business and economic development
S: $15.2   F: $11.1

Public safety and criminal justice
S: $10.3   F: $1.3

General government
S: $4.2   F: $0.7

Natural resources
S: $4.2   F: $2.6

Other (Regulatory, Judiciary, Legislature, General provisions)
S: $2.7   F: $0.04

SOURCE: Legislative Budget Board, "Fiscal Size-Up 2014–15 Biennium," pp. 2, 6.

QUANTITATIVE REASONING

- According to the data, what proportion of the Texas budget consists of federal funds? How might the presence of this federal money affect the relationship between the state and federal governments?

- Suppose federal funds for health and human services were eliminated. How might Texas reallocate state funds to avoid drastically reducing these services?

The States Respond

**SOCIAL RESPONSIBILITY:
GET INVOLVED**

- Do you think the federal government should be allowed to impose "unfunded mandates" on the states?

- What state issues, if any, do you feel the federal government should be involved in? Why these and not others?

States have begun to fight back against modern federalism. State officials in Mississippi, Oregon, and Texas vowed to reject attempts by the federal government to impose new gun laws.[21] Numerous sheriffs from around the country claimed that if new federal gun laws were passed, they would not enforce them. Similarly, several state leaders have been highly critical of the Affordable Care Act and have refused to initiate the health insurance exchanges under the act. State leaders have also been critical of the federal government's efforts to enforce immigration laws. A number of states, including Texas, have been involved in numerous lawsuits against the federal government. Much of this litigation and criticism of the federal government reflects the rebellion against modern federalism. As then attorney general Greg Abbott put it in defending his office's lawsuits against the federal government, "when Texas challenges the federal government, it's about more than money. It's about principles—fundamental principles enshrined in the Constitution and recently reaffirmed by the U.S. Supreme Court when it said: 'The national government possesses only limited powers; the states and the people retain the remainder. The independent power of the states serves as a check on the power of the federal government.' Defending the constitutional principles that have made the United States truly exceptional: That's priceless."[22]

As coercive federalism became more common, concerns were expressed in the last few decades of the twentieth century, particularly among conservative Republicans, that the central state was becoming too strong in the federal system. Not surprisingly, the Supreme Court rethought its doctrines on federalism still again. The effort to rethink the federal system is evident in Supreme Court decisions beginning in the

Gun control is a key federalism issue. Here, protesters demonstrate in front of the Texas state capitol in support of Second Amendment rights.

1990s. Although not dramatic reinterpretations of constitutional law, the court's rulings did begin to place limits on Congress's ability to legislate under the interstate commerce power, and it resurrected the Tenth Amendment as a protection for the rights of states.

The court returned to the Tenth Amendment—the so-called states' rights amendment—some of the strength that it had lost during the New Deal era. *Printz v. United States* (1997) challenged a provision of the 1993 Brady Handgun Violence Prevention Act. The Brady Act required the attorney general to establish by the end of November 1998 a national database for instant background checks on anyone buying a handgun. Until the database could be finalized, the act required local law enforcement officials to verify that no handguns were sold to unqualified persons. Sheriffs in Montana and Arizona claimed that this provision was unconstitutional on the grounds that the federal government did not have the authority to command state and local officials to administer a federal program. The Supreme Court agreed that the law infringed on the rights of states, writing, "The Federal Government may neither issue directives requiring the States to address particular problems, nor command the States' officers, or those of their political subdivisions, to administer or enforce a federal regulatory program."[23]

Major U.S. Constitutional and Statutory Restrictions on the States

The Thirteenth, Fourteenth, and Fifteenth amendments to the Constitution were ratified in the aftermath of the Civil War. The Thirteenth Amendment banned slavery and was important after the Civil War in ending slavery as a basis of the southern economy. It was the other Civil War amendments, the Fourteenth and Fifteenth amendments, that even today have had a dramatic effect on the nature of federalism because the Fourteenth and Fifteenth amendments provide the basis for the major constitutional and statutory restrictions on the powers of states.

The Equal Protection Clause

With few exceptions, in the nineteenth century the equal protection clause offered little promise of being a U.S. constitutional restriction on the states. The importance of the equal protection clause as a restriction on the states began to increase early in the twentieth century. That was due to two developments: (1) the incorporation of the Bill of Rights and (2) the use of the equal protection clause in the 14th Amendment to combat racial discrimination. The incorporation of the Bill of Rights meant that the court selected some rights in the Bill of Rights as fundamental—so essential to the concept of ordered liberty that those rights were incorporated in (held to be part of) the "liberty" that was guaranteed in the language of the Fourteenth Amendment to the U.S. Constitution that stated that "nor shall any State deprive any person of life, *liberty* [emphasis added], or property, without due process of law." More and more rights were selected by the court to be fundamental rights that were held to apply to the states. Most recently, in 2010 the court held that the Second Amendment right to "keep and bear arms" applied to the states.[24] There are now very few rights in the

Heman Sweatt (right) walks with a white student at the University of Texas. Sweatt refused to attend a separate, all-black law school.

"separate but equal" an interpretation of the equal protection clause of the Fourteenth Amendment that held that states could segregate races as long as equal facilities were provided; it was overturned in 1954

Bill of Rights that have not been held to be fundamental. In the 1930s the court began to chip away at state laws promoting racial discrimination. In 1950 a Texas case heralded the end of segregated higher education. H. M. Sweatt was denied admission to the University of Texas Law School because he was black. He refused to attend a black law school that had been set up by Texas to provide what Texas claimed to be a separate but equal education for black Texans seeking a legal education. Texas claimed that having an all-white University of Texas Law School and a separate all-black law school provided separate but equal educations for black and white law students, which complied with the interpretation of the equal protection clause by the Supreme Court in *Plessy v. Ferguson* (1896) when it upheld state-required racially segregated train cars in Louisiana. Sweatt's argument was that the black law school was not equal to the University of Texas Law School but was inferior and, therefore, to require him to go to the black law school would deny him the equal protection of the laws. The Supreme Court agreed with Sweatt, pointing out that there were vast differences in the facilities as well as differences in the prestige of the schools, the reputation of the faculty, the experience of the administration, and the influence of the alumni. While the court stopped just short of declaring the doctrine of "separate but equal" to be unconstitutional, after *Sweatt*, it was hard to see how the doctrine could survive.[25] The doctrine did not survive. In 1954, in *Brown v. Board of Education of Topeka*, the Supreme Court unanimously held that segregated public schools were inherently unequal.[26] The doctrine of **"separate but equal"** was dead, though there was opposition to the decision in many states including Texas that would delay for decades the end of legally created segregation in public schools.

State Regulation of Voting

The Voting Rights Act was passed under Congress's authority under the Fifteenth Amendment to legislate to protect the right to vote where that right was denied or restricted on the basis of race or color. Section 4 of the act provided a coverage formula that defined the jurisdictions covered under the act, and Section 5 of the act required that federal officials—initially the U.S. Department of Justice—approve or preclear any changes in voting in jurisdictions that are defined in the law. Those jurisdictions included Texas. Voting changes that must be precleared included such things as the establishment of voter identification laws, redistricting political boundaries, and changes in the times or locations of polling places. Texas had been required to preclear since 1975, and as in other covered jurisdictions, state officials have chafed over the need to secure federal approval for the changes they wished to make in voting in the state. That is why an Alabama case decided by the U.S. Supreme Court in the summer of 2013 is so important to Texas

Voting Rights and Redistricting

In 1965, President Lyndon Johnson made history by signing the Voting Rights Act into law. The purpose of the legislation was to eliminate racial discrimination in voting. A somewhat controversial element of the law was Section 5, which required states covered under that provision, including Texas, to have any changes to voting procedures approved by the Department of Justice or a federal court in the District of Columbia. The rationale behind what is termed "preclearance" was to ensure that the federal government would have oversight over voting laws in states that have had histories of excluding racial minorities from the political process.

The Voting Rights Act has been renewed periodically since 1965. During that time, the Department of Justice has challenged many states, including Texas, and required them to redraw legislative districts in order to comply with the Voting Rights Act. In recent years, there has been a backlash against the Voting Rights Act by many state governments, including Texas. In 2013, Attorney General Greg Abbott challenged the Department of Justice by claiming that preclearance was a violation of Texas state sovereignty. Abbott argued that the federal government singled out Texas for preclearance and that it is not fair to make some states, but not others, comply with the law. He argued that in 2013 there is no longer a question of voter discrimination in Texas and that all states should be treated equally. He also claimed that the Voting Rights Act exceeded the bounds of federal authority. He cited the Tenth Amendment to the U.S. Constitution, which reserves powers to the states that are not specifically enumerated to the federal government in the Constitution.

While the U.S. Supreme Court did not agree with Abbott's arguments in full, it did deliver a ruling striking down portions of the Voting Rights Act that establish a formula used to determine which states are subject to Section 5 preclearance. By the court's striking down the formula, preclearance has been suspended for now. It is uncertain today that Congress will pass a new and constitutional formula. Civil rights groups are alarmed that without the protection of preclearance, Texas and other states will design legislative districts that will dilute the influence of minority voters and prevent them from electing candidates of their choice.

Part of the conundrum is that in Texas most minorities are members of the Democratic Party, and during redistricting parties attempt to maximize their influence in elections. Republicans claim that they are not discriminating against minorities, but against Democrats, which is perfectly acceptable and legal. However, when most minorities are Democrats, how do we know the true source of the discrimination? The courts have been reluctant to give a definitive answer, but part of the challenge is distinguishing racial discrimination (which is illegal) from political discrimination (which is legal). If it turns out that Democratic minorities are packed into heavily concentrated districts, the influence of minorities in Texas politics may be diluted as a practical matter. However one feels about the politics, Texas's redrawing of the boundaries of these districts has, absent the preclearance requirement, become far easier for the state.

COMMUNICATING EFFECTIVELY: YOUR VOICE

- Does preclearance violate the Tenth Amendment and give the federal government too much power, or is it a necessary check on the states to make sure that minorities are not discriminated against?

- What are ways that Texas and the federal government can compromise on how best to ensure the rights of minorities in the electoral process?

and to federalism. The case, *Shelby County, Ala. v. Holder* (2013), involved a challenge to Congress's decision to reauthorize the Voting Rights Act. Shelby County, Alabama, claimed that the act went beyond Congress's power to pass the law under the authority of the Fifteenth Amendment and that the law placed "substantial federalism costs" on the covered jurisdictions, costs that were so great that the Tenth Amendment rights of the states were violated. Shelby County as a political unit of the state of Alabama had been covered by the preclearance requirement since 1965. It viewed the act as outdated and as trying to remedy racial discrimination in voting that was far in the past. Texas filed an amicus curiae or "friend of the court" brief in the Supreme Court litigation. (Such a brief is sometimes filed by states, groups, or individuals with a strong interest in the outcome of the case but who are not the parties to the litigation.) Texas's brief supported Shelby County's claim that Section 5 of the Voting Rights Act went beyond Congress's powers to pass laws under the Fifteenth Amendment and placed substantial enough costs on federalism that there was a violation of the Tenth Amendment. Texas's brief noted that the act was based on voting conditions in Texas in 1975. Unlike 1975, however, Texas now has bilingual ballots, and in every federal election between 1996 and 2004, African Americans in Texas registered and voted at higher rates than whites, while Latinos in Texas registered to vote at higher rates between 1980 and 2002 than Latinos in jurisdictions not covered by Section 5. The remainder of the Texas amicus brief is essentially an argument that substantial costs to federalism are created by the preclearance requirement, and the evidence used is that preclearance has prevented the implementation of Texas's voter identification law where a voter must provide an identification—a Texas driver's license, an election identification certificate, a personal identification card issued by the state, a U.S. military identification with a photo of the prospective voter, a U.S. citizenship certificate with a photo of the prospective voter, a U.S. passport, or a Texas concealed handgun license.[27] The Texas brief argued,

> For nearly two years, the Civil Rights Division of the Department of Justice has used every weapon in its arsenal to thwart the implementation of a law that the Court has recognized as a legitimate and constitutional fraud-prevention measure. Because of section 5, the State of Texas still is unable to implement its voter-identification law—a law that Indiana and non-covered jurisdictions may enact and enforce without any interference from federal authorities.[28]

In late June 2013 the court issued its blockbuster 5–4 decision striking down the formula for determining the states covered under the Section 5 preclearance requirement. Holding that the formula for determining coverage under the act was based on decades-old data, the court held that Shelby County was correct in its position that the data used to determine if a jurisdiction was covered were too outdated to be valid. Congress could, of course, draft another formula to cover jurisdictions under the act, but that formula must be based on current voting conditions. The court emphasized two important points about the federal system: (1) all states enjoy equal sovereignty, and (2) under the Tenth Amendment, states have broad power to regulate elections. Only exceptional conditions, such as the racial discrimination in voting at the time of the initial passage of the 1965 Voting Rights Act, justified intrusion on the powers and the equality of states. The court's view was that the outdated data that determined which jurisdictions were covered under the act did not provide sufficient evidence of those exceptional conditions that justified current intrusion into state powers over voting and thus, absent a valid formula to determine which states must go through a preclearance procedure, no state had to undergo preclearance.[29] Given this decision, Texas no longer has to obtain preclearance to change aspects of its system of elections. However, under Section 2 of the Voting Rights Act it is still possible to sue a state in federal court if the voting procedure change negatively affects minority voters. That is what happened in *Veasey v. Abbott*, where a federal district court in Corpus Christi, Texas, found that the voter identification requirement had a purpose to discriminate against minorities, was in effect a poll tax, and had a disparate impact on minority voters. The district court decision was appealed to the federal court of appeals, which heard the case in a 3-judge panel. The court agreed in part with the district court's decision. It sent the case back to the district court for further evidence on whether the voter identification requirement had a discriminatory purpose.

In order to prove that the law had a disparate impact on minorities and thus violated the Voting Rights Act, plaintiffs' lawyers presented statistical evidence to the court prepared by expert witnesses. In the district court case, the plaintiffs' experts included a prominent political scientist, Stephen Ansolabehere of Harvard University, who found that Latino and African American registered voters were 195 percent and 305 percent more likely than whites to lack the required voter identification. Such evidence was quite damning for the state's defense of the voter ID law because it provided support for the argument that there is a racially disparate impact in the implementation of the law. Perhaps even more destructive of the state's case was that even the expert witness for the state, in evidence the district court found to suffer from severe methodological problems, found that 4 percent of eligible white voters lacked the required voter identification, but that 5.3 percent of eligible African American voters did and 6.9 percent of eligible Latino voters.[30] In a 9-to-6 decision, the court of appeals held that the law had a racially discriminatory effect on those without identification and sent the case back to the district court to develop a remedy for this discrimination. As a result of this decision, Texas reached an agreement which allowed voters without the required identification to vote in the November 2016 election if they signed a statement saying they were unable to reasonably procure the required identification and if they provided alternative identification such as a voter registration certificate, a birth certificate, a utility bill, bank statement, or government document with their name and address (such as a government check).

Flexibility for States under the Constitution

Although there are restrictions on the states imposed by the Fourteenth Amendment and by statutes passed under the authority of the Fifteenth Amendment, states do have some leeway to expand rights of their citizens through a concept known as **independent state grounds**. State constitutions can provide greater constitutional guarantees to a state's citizens than the U.S. Constitution. Independent state grounds are a characteristic of federalism in that states are free to add to the rights guaranteed at the national level. Some states, such as Massachusetts, have relied on their state constitutions to invalidate laws against same-sex marriage.[31] Under the U.S.

independent state grounds allow states, usually under the state constitution, to expand rights beyond those provided by the U.S. Constitution

Constitution, Texas's very inequitable property tax–based system for funding public education was held to be constitutional. The U.S. Supreme Court held that education was not a fundamental right and so Texas only needed a rational justification—that is, local control of schools—in order for the funding system to be upheld.[32] However, in *Edgewood v. Kirby* (1989), the Texas Supreme Court relied on the Texas Constitution to strike down the school funding system. The court held, "Whether the legislature acts directly or enlists local government to help meet its obligation, the end product must still be what the [Texas] constitution commands—i.e., an efficient system of public free schools throughout the state."[33]

In the 1970s there was a major effort to gain ratification of an Equal Rights Amendment to the U.S. Constitution. If ratified, the key part of the amendment would have stated, "Equality of rights under the law shall not be denied or abridged by the United States or by any state on account of sex." Although that amendment to the U.S. Constitution was never ratified, in 1972 Texas adopted its version of the Equal Rights Amendment, which is Article 1, Section 3a, of the Texas Constitution: "Equality under the law shall not be denied or abridged because of sex, race, color, creed, or national origin." U.S. Supreme Court decisions have provided major protection against sex discrimination under the equal protection clause of the Fourteenth Amendment to the U.S. Constitution; however, it is the Texas Constitution, rather than the U.S. Constitution, that contains an explicit ban.

Texas and the Obama Administration

There was a great deal of tension between Texas's political leadership and the Obama administration over national power, which Texas leaders believe was expanded during the Obama administration at the expense of the states. In fact, Texas sued the Obama administration 46 times. Texas's legal expense for 35 of those suits was about $5.1 million. The suits were over a variety of issues, including air quality regulations, business regulation, climate change, education, health care, immigration, natural resources, voting, and gay marriage.[34] It is likely that Texas will be less litigious with the Trump administration given that Texas's leadership shares the same party affiliation and many of the same political values as President Trump.

Immigration Among the most important of these cases is Texas's challenge to President Obama's executive orders on immigration policy. When it became clear that Congress would not pass comprehensive immigration reform, President Obama announced a new policy for undocumented immigrants who met two criteria: (1) they must have children who are U.S. citizens or lawful permanent residents, and (2) they must have been in the United States at least since January 2010. If they met these criteria, they would be allowed to stay in the country for three years and work legally. This policy could have allowed as many as 4,000,000 people to remain in the United States. Texas and 25 other states went to court to try to block this policy, and the federal trial court issued an order to keep the policy from going into effect. A federal appeals court upheld the decision of the trial court, and the case was then appealed to the U.S. Supreme Court in *United States v. Texas*.[35] The Supreme Court tied 4–4 in the case, which means that the appeals court's decision upholding the trial court's invalidation of the policy stands. While a number of issues were presented by the case, Texas claimed that President Obama's decision would increase costs for the state for services ranging from driver's licenses to education, and Attorney General Paxton argued that the new policy, known as Deferred Action for Parents of Americans and Lawful Permanent Residents (DAPA), was "a crucial change in the Nation's immigration law and policy—and this is precisely why it could be created only by Congress, rather than unilaterally imposed by the Executive." In contrast, the Obama administration argued its actions were within presidential authority and that if the lower court decision was not overturned, it would allow states to "frustrate the federal government's enforcement of the Nation's immigration laws."[36]

Redistricting In 2016 the Supreme Court decided a case where the national government and Texas were partly on the same side in asserting that states have the power to use total population as the metric in drawing legislative district lines. Texas and the national government differed in that Texas argued that states were free to choose a metric other than total population if they so desired, whereas the national government argued that the appropriate metric was total population. The case is *Evenwel v. Abbott*, which challenged the way the Texas state senate is districted. In districting the state senate, the Texas legislature apportioned the districts to achieve a relatively equal number of individuals in each district based on the total population in the districts. Deviation from the ideal of equal population in each senate district in the state was 8.04 percent, which is well within the range accepted by the U.S. Supreme Court. However, the plaintiffs in *Evenwel* wanted the eligible voters in the state to be evenly distributed among the senate districts rather than the distribution to be based on total population. The plaintiffs argued that it was possible for the Texas legislature to adopt a senate map containing 31 districts of equal total population even if 30 of the senate districts contained only one eligible voter and the 31st district contained every other eligible voter in the state. Thus, the question presented by *Evenwel* to the Supreme Court was, Does the Supreme Court's requirement that legislative districts be drawn on the basis of one person, one vote protect the right of eligible voters to have an equal vote?

The case had huge political implications because a decision favoring the plaintiffs would not only reduce the political power of Latinos; it would also reduce the political influence of the state's most urban areas where many noncitizens live. Additionally, the case raised a major issue of federalism. States have usually decided how to count population for districting purposes. Indeed, the three-judge district court that initially decided against the plaintiffs in *Evenwel* did so largely in deference to the state's power to draw district lines.[37] From the perspective of the lower court, then, the issue is one of federalism where absent discrimination by the state, the state can choose whatever population counting metric it wishes without interference from the federal government. The *Evenwel* plaintiffs, on the other hand, have argued that the state is not free to choose a metric that weakens the political power of voters in districts with fewer numbers of noncitizens because that, argue the plaintiffs, is a federal constitutional violation of equal protection of the law. Few cases had the potential to change the distribution of power in a state between Latinos and whites, between Democrats and Republicans, between urban and non-urban areas, and between the state and national governments as did *Evenwel*.[38] When the court decided *Evenwel* in April 2016, it held that states were free to use total population as the metric for drawing political districts. Important for future redistricting, however, the court did not address Texas's claim that states were free to use any reasonable metric to draw district lines, including total voters.

Federalism and the Future of Texas

One of the most intriguing political questions is whether the new generation of leadership in Texas will be successful in creating a new relationship between the states and the national government. We have seen that federalism has significantly changed over time, and there is no reason to believe that federalism will not continue to evolve.

Leading Texans are now wishing to return greater power to the states. They argue the national government is too distant, controlling, expensive, and unresponsive. National Democrats have a philosophical inclination to look to the national government for solutions to problems; Texas Republicans prefer to look to the state for solutions. The effect of this difference is, of course, a dispute over federalism. This country originated in a dispute over national versus state power, and these battles have continued throughout U.S. history. The intensity of the disagreement over federalism will, however, vary depending on which political party controls state governments, Congress, and the White House. It is likely, for example, that the Trump administration will more closely share the views of Texas's leadership regarding federalism and so, for the time being, tensions between the state and national government will lessen.

Use 🐰 INQUIZITIVE to help you study and master this material.

The Roots of American Federalism

> • Understand the foundations of the U.S. federal system (pp. 87–92)

Along with many other countries, the American system of government has divided power between national and regional or state governments. That division of power has varied over time, and America's notion of federalism has evolved through a number of forms.

Key Terms
federalism (p. 87)
sovereign (p. 88)

Practice Quiz

1. *Federalism* refers to
   a) a system of government where cities are strong.
   b) a system of government where executive power is grounded in a committee of governors.
   • c) a system of government where there is a national government as well as a number of regional governments.
   d) a system of government dominated by business interests.
   e) a system of government with strong parliaments.

2. The Articles of Confederation
   a) were a loose confederation of independent states that operated in the 1820s.
   b) were never accepted by a majority of the states.
   • c) derived their power directly from the state governments.
   d) replaced the U.S. Constitution of 1787.
   e) outlawed ineffective state constitutions.

3. The relationship between the states and the national government
   a) has been a matter of continuing controversy throughout the nation's history.
   b) was finally settled when the Articles of Confederation were rejected in favor of the U.S. Constitution.
   c) was resolved for all time by the Civil War.
   d) was resolved by Article I, Section 8, of the U.S. Constitution.
   e) was not a problem in a federal system.

4. The Supreme Court under John Marshall expanded national power partly through
   a) rejecting the Articles of Confederation.
   • b) expanding the meaning of interstate commerce.
   c) expanding Congress's war-making powers.
   d) ignoring the Tenth Amendment.
   e) increasing the powers of the president.

5. Prior to the ratification of the Fourteenth Amendment, the Bill of Rights
   a) applied only to states.
   • b) applied only to the national government.
   c) applied to states and the national government.
   d) was essential in protecting individual rights.
   e) was applied only in extreme cases of rights violations.

6. *McCulloch v. Maryland* (1819) was important
   • a) in establishing that the national government had implied powers.
   b) in establishing that state governments had implied powers.
   c) in showing that the state and national governments could cooperate.
   d) in preventing national banks from operating.
   e) in destroying corrupt state banking systems.

Dual Federalism

- Trace the major changes in national and state power over time (pp. 92–96)

American federalism has gone through major changes over the history of the country. In the late nineteenth century there was a strict division between the powers of the state and the powers of the national government. That division was called *dual federalism* or *layer-cake federalism*. During Franklin Roosevelt's New Deal, federalism was dramatically redefined and there was greater involvement of the national government in all areas of American life. Cooperative federalism or marble-cake federalism became the new approach to state and national relationships. In recent times, many believe federalism has taken a new form and has become coercive, where the national government compels states to act in ways that achieve national priorities.

Key Terms
Reconstruction (p. 92)
dual federalism (p. 92)
layer-cake federalism (p. 93)
marble-cake federalism (p. 94)
cooperative federalism (p. 94)
categorical grants (p. 94)
New Federalism (p. 96)
block grants (p. 96)

Practice Quiz

7. *Dual federalism*
   a) refers to a system of government where states do most of the governing.
   b) existed in the United States following World War II.
   c) rejected the idea that states were sovereign political entities.
   d) is the idea that there are two branches to the national legislature.
   e) drained all power from state governments.

8. Layer-cake federalism switched to marble-cake federalism
   a) after the Civil War.
   b) during World War I.
   c) during the New Deal.
   d) after the fall of the Soviet Union.
   e) because of President Ronald Reagan's efforts.

9. The use of categorical grants was a way of promoting
   a) cooperative federalism.
   b) dual federalism.
   c) coercive federalism.
   d) bipartisan federalism.
   e) civil rights.

Coercive Federalism: Texas and the Federal Government

- Describe the sources of, and tensions between, national and state power (pp. 96–106)

The incorporation of much of the Bill of Rights has limited the power of state governments by making them subject to restrictions under the U.S. Constitution. Additionally, the preemption doctrine has allowed the national government to prohibit state legislation in certain fields. An important constitutional provision that limits state action is the Fourteenth Amendment, particularly the equal protection clause of that amendment, which prohibits discriminatory actions by state governments. Until recently, a number of jurisdictions—including Texas—were limited by the 1965 Voting Rights Act in the legislation they could pass involving the electoral process, although a recent U.S. Supreme Court decision has made it possible for Texas to pass controversial voter identification legislation. Finally, while state governments cannot reduce the rights guaranteed by the U.S. Constitution, they can expand those guarantees under the concept of independent state grounds.

Key Terms

coercive federalism (p. 96)
unfunded mandates (p. 96)
preemption (p. 96)
"separate but equal" (p. 100)
independent state grounds (p. 103)

Practice Quiz

10. Hostility to modern federalism is partly a result of
   a) dual federalism.
   b) funded mandates.
   c) unfunded mandates.
   d) Tenth Amendment interpretations.
   e) high taxes.

11. States must adhere to most of the provisions of the Bill of Rights because of a process known as
   a) inclusion of the Bill of Rights.
   b) incorporation of the Bill of Rights.
   c) expansion of the Bill of Rights.
   d) ratification of the Bill of Rights.
   e) the Sanford dictum.

12. The equal protection clause of the Fourteenth Amendment
   a) makes it difficult for states to discriminate against minorities.
   b) is rarely used by federal courts.
   c) ensures that states will continue to have a republican form of government.
   d) mandates the right to vote for all adult citizens.
   e) requires all states to have an equal number of senators.

13. Independent state grounds
   a) allow states to provide fewer state constitutional protections.
   b) allow states to provide more state constitutional protections than does the U.S. Constitution.
   c) allow states to remain independent of the national government.
   d) prevent the national government from overriding the Tenth Amendment rights of states.
   e) limit the power of the national government to pass economic regulations.

14. The national government can preempt state laws because
   a) the national government is weaker than any state.
   b) the Tenth Amendment to the Constitution specifically allows state laws to be overridden by federal laws.
   c) the supremacy clause of the Constitution makes national laws supreme over state laws.
   d) the Sanford dictum established preemption.
   e) the main reason the Constitution was adopted was so that state laws could be preempted.

15. The Voting Rights Act
   a) ensured the right to vote for women.
   b) ensured the right to vote for 18-year-olds.
   c) approved photo ID requirements for voters.
   d) required that voters know how to read and write.
   e) was the major law providing the right to vote for African Americans.

Democrats dominated Texas politics for nearly a century, but today the Republican Party is dominant. Can Democrats turn Texas blue again? How do party politics affect Texans?

Political Parties

WHY POLITICAL PARTIES MATTER Congressman Gene Green is a white Democrat who represents the 29th congressional district in Texas. This district is composed of north Houston, Pasadena, and swaths of east and southeast Houston. Green was first elected to the district in 1992 and has been re-elected ever since. The district was created by the Texas legislature following the 1990 Census as a majority-Latino district with the intention of facilitating the election of a Latino to Congress. However, the district has never had a Latino representative.

Former Harris County sheriff Adrian Garcia, a Democrat like Green, announced after his failed mayoral bid that it was time for Green to go. In addition to some policy differences, Garcia has announced that it is time for a Latino to represent a district that is over two-thirds Latino. It is a heavily Democratic district in a state that is heavily Republican, so the winner of the Democratic primary is virtually assured victory in the general election.

Garcia also campaigned against Green on some policy differences. For example, Garcia claimed that Green has voted in favor of oil and gas companies and against environmental regulations. Garcia also claimed that Green's voting record on LGBT rights was too conservative for the district. Green defended his record of bringing jobs and development to the district and touted his endorsement of major Latino elected officials in the district, including the district's Latino state representatives and other elected officials. In addition, the Congressional Hispanic Caucus (CHC) also indirectly endorsed Green through its Political Action Committee. This is noteworthy because the caucus is composed of Democratic Latino members of Congress, and one of its major goals is to help elect more Latinos to Congress. Green had a strong working relationship with members of the CHC and other Latino members of Congress from Texas such as Filemon Vela of Brownsville, who also endorsed his re-election bid. The power of incumbency prevailed on Election Day when Gene Green defeated Garcia in the Democratic primary.

This race demonstrates a couple of important facts about parties in Texas. All too often, we hear about Texas as being a solidly Republican state, but important and consequential Democrats serve Texas in Washington. The major cities of Houston, Austin, El Paso, San Antonio, and Dallas–Fort Worth send Democratic representatives to Washington, so we should look beyond statewide offices and examine these races as well as other local races. Internal division within parties is present not only in the Republican Party with the Tea Party faction and the mainstream business faction but also to a certain extent within the

Democratic Party. Because the Democratic Party is not as successful in state-wide races, some of these divisions are overlooked. As the Democratic Party in Texas becomes more Latino, we might see more races pitting Latino candidates against white or African American incumbents, all within the Democratic Party.

It is important to understand political parties and their structure because knowledge of the rules in government is essential to advancing public policy. Because parties play such a large role in government processes, we must know how parties are organized, how candidates are selected, and how partisanship influences public policy. This chapter will address the history of political parties in Texas, the current party system, and what the future holds for the party system in the state, including some answers to the much-talked-about question of "when Texas will turn blue."

CHAPTERGOALS

- Describe the main functions and structure of state party organizations (pp. 113–24)
- Trace the evolution of the party system in Texas (pp. 125–32)
- Analyze how ideological divisions and demographic change affect Texas political parties (pp. 132–38)

The Roles and Structure of Political Parties in Texas

 Describe the main functions of state party organizations

Political parties can be looked at from a number of perspectives. In the narrowest sense, a political party refers to an organization of people established to win elections. This can include people holding or running for office who identify formally with the party. It can also refer to the professionals and volunteers who actively work for the election of their party's candidates. In a broader sense, a political party can refer to those people in the electorate who identify with a particular party and vote for that party's candidates on a regular basis.

Political parties help candidates win elections and assist voters in making their electoral choices. Perhaps the most important function of parties in Texas is that they provide a label under which candidates can run and with which voters can identify. Because Texas elects large numbers of officeholders, it is unlikely that voters will be familiar with the views or the qualifications of every candidate. However, Texas voters overwhelmingly identify with or lean toward either the Republican Party or the Democratic Party.[1] Those voters use the party affiliation of the candidates as a way to decide for whom to vote. Thus, for many voters, without other information, the party label becomes the standard they apply in casting a ballot for a candidate. Voters often use the party label as a cue to the ideology of candidates. A voter may assume that, for example, a Republican candidate is a "conservative" and may vote for or against that candidate because of the ideology that a party affiliation implies.[2]

Parties to some extent help in raising money for candidates' campaigns and in assisting candidates with legal requirements and training for a campaign. They sometimes recruit candidates for political races, although in Texas any candidate may run in a party primary, and if victorious in the primary will become the party nominee. Parties also assist in "getting out the vote" for candidates through phone banks, door-to-door contacts, and other efforts.

Once a candidate is elected to office, party affiliation helps in organizing the government. Governors will usually appoint people who are members of their own party. Increasingly, the Texas legislature is divided by party. Public officials may also feel a greater sense of loyalty and cooperation toward other public officials of their party. After all, they often campaign together and make appearances at the same political events, and their fortunes often rise and fall together based on the popularity of the party. In that sense, the banding together of officeholders with the same party affiliation provides voters an opportunity to hold the party accountable for its policies or its failures.

Texas Parties in the National Context

As the political parties have become more polarized nationwide and in Texas, voters have elected fewer moderates to office. This has had the result of creating more

One of the most important functions of political parties is to select candidates to run for office under the party label. The Republican Party of Texas officially announced its candidates for office at its 2014 convention in Fort Worth.

friction in government, including gridlock and stalemate in Congress and in the Texas legislature. States differ in terms of the strength of the political parties, and in Texas the dominant Republican Party has its own internal divisions. In neighboring Louisiana, the parties in the legislature are relatively weak. In the Louisiana legislature, even though the majority party controls committee assignments, chairs of committees sometimes include a mix of Democrats and Republicans. This has historically also been true in Texas. The current speaker of the Texas House, Joe Straus from San Antonio, is considered a moderate Republican and owes his election to the speakership to many Democrats in the legislature who voted to elect him speaker. In recognition of their support, Straus made some Democrats committee chairs. This would never happen in the U.S. Congress, as parties are much more salient in national politics. In Congress, the majority party gives leadership positions like committee chairs only to its own loyal party members. As the Republican Party has moved further to the right, however, this tradition will likely change as it already has in the state senate when Dan Patrick took over as lieutenant governor. Among his campaign promises was to end the previous lieutenant governor's practice of appointing Democrats as committee chairs.

Why might parties at the state level have less power? Tip O'Neill, the former Speaker of the U.S. House, used to say that "all politics is local," and this certainly rings true in Texas. Local issues are usually not ideological in nature. They often deal with who is most effective at creating jobs and providing public works projects within the district. Voters in state races are therefore likely to be influenced by these concerns in addition to hot-button issues such as abortion and same-sex marriage. This means that partisanship is not always a major concern in running the everyday business of the state. To be sure, ideological issues might matter in certain state-level elections during some election years. **Partisan polarization**, which is the degree to which Republicans have become more conservative and Democrats have become more liberal, is beginning to become more pronounced in the Texas legislature. Partisan polarization in politics means that it is increasingly difficult for politicians to compromise on important policy issues. Compromise is often considered a sign of weakness and caving in to the other side.

partisan polarization the degree to which Republicans have become more conservative and Democrats have become more liberal

Party politics in Texas is similar to party politics in some other southern states, but there are important differences. Other southern states have had historically larger African American populations than Texas. As we will discuss later, African Americans are generally loyal Democrats. They constitute nearly 30 percent of the population in Mississippi and Louisiana, for example. In Texas, African Americans are concentrated in east Texas and in the major urban areas, and represent only 12 percent of the state's population. Another major difference between Texas and some other southern states is Texas's large Latino population, which currently is estimated at 39 percent of the state's population. Like African Americans, Latinos tend to be Democrats, but not to the same degree.

To a certain extent, Texas is similar to New Mexico, Arizona, and Colorado in terms of its large Latino population. In contrast with the Latino population in Arizona, however, Tejanos (Texans of Mexican descent) are more likely to have resided in the state for generations. In Arizona, the Sonora Desert region is the largest gateway for Mexican immigration, and new immigrants in Arizona exhibit political behavior that differs from that of their Tejano counterparts in many ways. For example, new immigrants are even more likely than Tejanos to identify as Democrats and to see the Democratic Party as more supportive of immigrant rights.

Public Attitudes about Parties

Texans, like many other Americans, are increasingly identifying as independent. However, in practice many self-identified independents lean toward either Democratic or Republican affiliation. What is the source of these political leanings? The process of **political socialization** occurs throughout our early years, when our parents, religious leaders, teachers, and others influence our partisan identifications. Although this can change over time for many people, we often retain the same political beliefs as those of our parents. We are also profoundly shaped by our surrounding environment. Texas has a long history of state pride, independence, and conservatism. People growing up in the state are accustomed to these values and thus incorporate them into their political ideologies and partisan preferences. Visitors to the state are often surprised at how much state pride exists. For example, the very notion of a state pledge of allegiance recited by many schoolchildren is a practice that surprises people from other states.

political socialization the introduction of individuals into the political culture; learning the underlying beliefs and values on which the political system is based

How does partisan affiliation affect Texas voters? According to a May 2012 *Texas Tribune* poll, 56 percent of respondents cited party affiliation as either very or somewhat important when deciding for whom to vote. Party identification acts as an important cue that signals candidates' political views. For the most part, when we see an "R" or a "D" next to a candidate's name, we make certain assumptions about the positions the candidate takes. Of course, other characteristics of candidates matter too; in the same poll, voters also cited the candidate's record, issue positions, and character as important considerations in their voting choices.[3]

In Texas, the Republican Party has complete control of state government, and voters continue to re-elect Republicans to all levels of government. This does not mean that there is no competition within the Republican Party, however. Republican primaries often pit conservatives against moderates. An example of this was the Republican lieutenant gubernatorial primary between Lieutenant Governor David Dewhurst and state senator Dan Patrick in 2014. Patrick positioned himself to the right of Dewhurst and defeated him in the primary.

At the conservative end of the spectrum, the Tea Party movement is particularly strong in Texas. In a November 2015 *Texas Tribune* poll, 17 percent of respondents said that they would vote for a Tea Party candidate if the movement organized as a third party. When asked about the Tea Party's influence on the state Republican Party, respondents were split: 34 percent felt that the Tea Party had too much influence, 19 percent thought their degree of influence was about right, and 26 percent thought that they had too little influence.[4] According to a 2014 *Texas Tribune* poll, roughly 40 percent of voters in Texas would support a generic Democratic candidate for Congress, while 53 percent would support a generic Republican candidate for Congress.[5] This leaves a substantial remainder of "swing" voters who ultimately decide elections. Since their control of state government gives Republicans a built-in advantage, it is increasingly difficult for Democrats to win statewide.

The Contemporary Republican Party in Texas

Texas Republicans are currently experiencing a major division within the party. Established pro-business Republicans have dominated state politics in recent years, but the Tea Party movement has begun to influence state legislative races as well as major statewide races.

Consider the lieutenant governor's race in 2014. The Republican candidate, Lieutenant Governor David Dewhurst, had the endorsement of Governor Rick Perry and many of the state's political leaders. However, state senator Dan Patrick, a darling of the Tea Party movement, posed a significant challenge to Dewhurst, especially in terms of grassroots support. Patrick was one of several Republicans who challenged Dewhurst because they sensed a weak candidate who lost the U.S. Senate primary in 2012 to now senator Ted Cruz. Patrick ran to the right of Dewhurst and all the other candidates, especially on his immigration positions. In a debate in early 2014, he called for an end to the "invasion" of illegal immigrants from the southern border. In a low-turnout primary in early March 2014, Patrick forced Dewhurst into a runoff by winning a plurality of 41 percent versus Dewhurst's 28 percent. In the runoff primary, Patrick overwhelmed Dewhurst, receiving 65 percent of the vote compared to 35 percent for Dewhurst. It was remarkable that an incumbent lieutenant governor would be defeated in his own party primary, but Patrick successfully positioned himself to the right of Dewhurst in an increasingly conservative party.

Patrick ran ads criticizing Dewhurst for being too moderate, a label that would be seen negatively in a typical Republican primary. Patrick took a page from Cruz's playbook by criticizing Dewhurst for being an insider and state government official with endorsements from the state's political establishment. Patrick went on to win the general election over Democrat Leticia Van de Putte, a Latina state senator from San Antonio, with 58 percent of the vote.

Texas Republicans currently hold all of the major statewide elected offices. The governor, lieutenant governor, comptroller, attorney general, all members of the state

supreme court, and the railroad commissioners are all Republicans. Texas Democrats have attempted to recruit challengers for these offices but have come up short. As the lieutenant governor's race demonstrates, the major competition for important state-wide offices occurs during the Republican primary, much in the same way the Democratic primary used to fulfill this role when Texas was a Democratic state.

The Republican Party in Texas has not always been so powerful. Prior to 1994, Democrats held many statewide offices in Texas. Ann Richards, the state's last Democratic governor, was a proud liberal, as was former U.S. senator Ralph Yarborough, who championed the Bilingual Education Act in 1968. However, few pundits seriously thought that the Democratic candidate for the U.S. Senate seat in 2014 had a realistic chance of winning the general election in November. This is a remarkable change from only 10 years prior, when Democrat Ron Kirk was seen by Democrats as a more formidable candidate for statewide office, even though on Election Day he lost to Senator John Cornyn by double digits.

The Contemporary Democratic Party in Texas

Texas Democrats have been relegated to minority status in the state since the early 2000s. Democrats controlled the Texas House until 2002. The only other southern state with a Democratic-controlled body is the Kentucky State House. In Louisiana and West Virginia, for example, Democrats control the governorship, but in presidential elections, the states often vote Republican. Before 1994, Texas exhibited similar voting patterns, but now Republicans are elected to all statewide offices at the state and federal levels.

Most Texas Democrats today would be classified as liberal. The party's base is made up of African Americans, Latinos, and white liberals in urban areas. Most white liberals are located in Austin, Houston, Dallas, and San Antonio and have often moved to Texas from other parts of the country. This coalition, however, is currently not large enough to win many elections in statewide races. Most whites in the state have settled into the Republican Party, and because whites turn out to vote at much higher rates than Latinos, who are the fastest-growing minority group in the state, Republicans have won recent elections. Democrats hope to mobilize Latinos, who constitute nearly 40 percent of the state's population, to encourage them to vote. Sixty-nine percent of Texas Latinos are American citizens by birth, but a large proportion of these are under age 18 and cannot vote. Moreover, voter turnout rates among Texas Latinos are lower than the rates among their Anglo counterparts. It will require extensive efforts to register and bring Latino voters to the polls in force to change this.

No Democrat has won Texas in a presidential race since Jimmy Carter in 1976. In 2016, Republican presidential candidate Donald Trump won 52 percent of the vote in Texas, while Hillary Clinton won just 43 percent. Democratic candidates have also fared poorly in recent U.S. Senate races. For example, in the 2012 election to replace retiring senator Kay Bailey Hutchison, Ted Cruz, the Republican nominee, won the office easily.

This does not mean that Texas Democrats do not have influence in certain localities. In Travis County, the home of Austin, Democrats dominate city government. Other major cities, including Houston and San Antonio, have Democratic mayors and city councils. However, this influence does not extend to statewide elections. When Democrat Bill White, the former mayor of Houston, ran for governor in 2010, he lost to Rick Perry.

Eight of the eleven Democrats representing Texas in the U.S. Congress are either Latino or African American. The first African American woman elected to Congress from Texas was Barbara Jordan, who played a major role in the investigation of Richard Nixon during the Watergate scandal. Her legacy remains strong among African Americans in Texas. Lloyd Doggett of Austin, Beto O'Rourke of El Paso, and Gene Green of Houston are the only white Democrats representing Texas in Congress. This suggests that the majority of Texas Democrats are minorities, and, with the growth of the minority population in the state, the party makeup will become more minority and less white. This demographic change in Texas makes the state more similar to its southern neighbors. In the Deep South, the Democratic Party is mostly an African American party. This is not true in the Northeast and on the West Coast, where White Democrats are a larger proportion of the electorate.

Gene Green of Houston has represented a majority Latino district since 1993. In 2016, he fought off a serious challenge by Harris County sheriff Adrian Garcia in the Democratic primary.

Democratic and Republican Party Organization

Although many Texans proclaim that they are "registered Republicans" or "registered Democrats," Texas does not have a system of party registration. Registered voters may vote in either the Democratic or Republican primary. When they do vote in a primary, their voter registration card will be stamped "Democrat" or "Republican" to prevent them from voting in the other primary as well.

One of the most important functions of political parties is to select candidates to run for office under the party label. Today that is done through primary elections. If

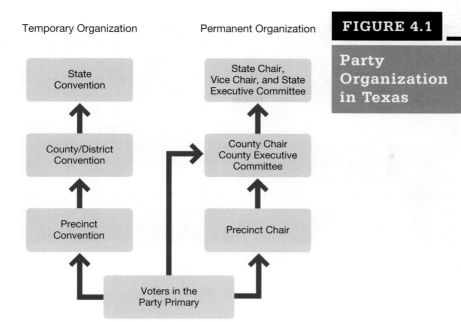

Temporary Organization | Permanent Organization

FIGURE 4.1

Party Organization in Texas

State Convention

State Chair, Vice Chair, and State Executive Committee

County/District Convention

County Chair County Executive Committee

Precinct Convention

Precinct Chair

Voters in the Party Primary

precinct the most basic level of political organization at the local level

precinct chair the local party official, elected in the party's primary election, who heads the precinct convention and serves on the party's county executive committee

county executive committee the party group, made up of a party's county chair and precinct chairs, that is responsible for running a county's primary elections and planning county conventions

county chair the county party official who heads the county executive committee

state executive committee the committee responsible for governing a party's activities throughout the state

state chair and **vice chair** the top two state-level leaders in the party

precinct convention a meeting held by a political party to select delegates for the county convention and to submit resolutions to the party's state platform; precinct conventions are held on the day of the party's primary election and are open to anyone who voted in that election

county convention a meeting held by a political party following its precinct conventions, for the purpose of electing delegates to its state convention

several candidates are running for the party nomination in a primary election, it may be that none receive a majority vote. In that case, the party will hold a runoff election to determine who will be nominated. Primaries were not always used to select the party nominee. During the nineteenth century, candidates were nominated at party conventions, but early in the twentieth century the state moved to the primary as a way to select candidates.

To understand how the parties are organized, think first in terms of the permanent organization of the party and then in terms of the temporary (campaign) organization (see Figure 4.1). In each election **precinct**, a **precinct chair** will be elected in the party primary. The precinct chair will head the precinct convention and will also serve on the party's **county executive committee**. In the primary, the **county chair** will also be elected. The county chair will head the county executive committee, which is composed of the chair and the precinct chairs. The main responsibility of the county executive committee is to run the county primary and plan the county conventions. There may be other district committees as well for political divisions that do not correspond to the county lines.

At the state level, there is a **state executive committee**, which includes a **state chair** and **vice chair**. These officers are selected every two years at the state party conventions. The state executive committee accepts filings by candidates for statewide office. It helps raise funds for the party, and it helps establish party policy. Both the Democratic and Republican parties also employ professional staff to run day-to-day operations and to assist with special problems that affect the party.

The temporary organization of the party includes the **precinct conventions**. The main role of the precinct conventions is to select delegates to the **county convention** and possibly to submit resolutions that may eventually become part of the party platform.

Delegates chosen by the precinct convention then go to the county conventions (or in urban areas, to district conventions). These conventions will elect delegates to

Political parties in Texas are organized at the precinct level, the county level, and the state level. This photo shows members of the Harris County Republican Party organization in Houston.

state convention a party meeting held every two years for the purpose of nominating candidates for statewide office, adopting a platform, electing the party's leadership, and in presidential election years selecting delegates for the national convention and choosing presidential electors

the **state convention**. Both the Democratic and Republican parties hold state conventions every other year. These conventions certify the nominees of the party for statewide office; adopt a platform; and elect a chair, a vice chair, and a state executive committee. In presidential election years, the state conventions select delegates for the national party conventions, elect delegates for the national party committee, and choose presidential electors, who, if the party's choice for president carries the state in the election, will formally cast the state's electoral votes for the president in the electoral college.

Conflict occurs not only between political parties but also within the parties. Battles for control of a state party have often been fought in Texas politics, where rival ideological and other interest groups have struggled to control precinct, county, and state conventions and to elect their candidates for precinct chair, county chair, and state executive committee. In the 1950s struggles for control of the Democratic Party between liberals and conservatives were fierce. There have also been calmer times in Texas politics, when involvement in the parties has been minimal and battles have been few. Sometimes, apathy has been so great that precinct conventions have been sparsely attended and offices such as precinct chair have gone unfilled.

Third Parties in Texas

In Texas, as in many other states, the two major parties have made it difficult for third parties to gain power. In essence, both parties agree that a third competitor is not a net positive for either party. Third-party candidates rarely win elections in Texas. In general, third-party candidates are also seen as inevitable losers at the ballot box, and voters would prefer to "go with the winner."

In Texas, third parties have emerged at certain points in history, mainly because of a particular issue. In the late nineteenth century, two farmers movements—the Grange and the Populist movements—provided alternatives to the two major political parties in various elections. In 1948 racial integration became an issue when the

How Republican Is Texas?

The South has become a solidly Republican region, and Texas is no exception to this. Indeed, former President Clinton official Paul Begala, a native Texan, once called the state "South Carolina on steroids." Since the 1960s, South Carolina has been a reliable Republican state in presidential elections. On the other hand, California has become a solidly Democratic state since the 1990s largely due to its growing Latino population and its relatively high population of white liberals. How does Texas compare with other key states on political partisanship?

Percentage of Residents Who Identify as Republicans*

Wyoming	Utah	Idaho	South Dakota	North Dakota	Alabama	Alaska	Oklahoma	Kansas
59.6%	56.0%	55.8%	51.9%	51.6%	51.4%	50.7%	49.3%	48.0%

South Carolina	Nebraska	Montana	Tennessee	New Hampshire	West Virginia	Missouri	Arkansas	Kentucky
47.9%	47.9%	47.6%	46.4%	46.4%	45.7%	45.5%	45.4%	45.0%

Indiana	Mississippi	Georgia	Nevada	Wisconsin	Colorado	Texas	Iowa	Louisiana
44.2%	44.0%	43.7%	43.5%	43.3%	43.0%	42.9%	42.9%	42.7%

Maine	Virginia	Minnesota	Ohio	Pennsylvania	Arizona	North Carolina	Florida	Delaware
42.5%	42.5%	42.4%	42.0%	41.6%	41.4%	41.3%	40.7%	39.3%

Oregon	Michigan	Washington	Connecticut	New Mexico	New Jersey	Illinois	Maryland	California
39.2%	38.7%	37.5%	36.8%	36.5%	36.3%	36.0%	34.9%	32.6%

Massachusetts	New York	Hawaii	Vermont	Rhode Island
32.2%	31.5%	30.8%	30.2%	28.9%

* Or who identify as independents but say they lean Republican.

SOURCE: 2015 Gallup Organization.

CRITICAL THINKING

- How does Texas compare with other states in terms of partisanship?

- How might demographic change, especially the growing Latino population, change Texas's political preferences?

Dixiecrats conservative Democrats who abandoned the national Democratic Party in the 1948 presidential election

La Raza Unida political party formed in Texas in order to bring attention to the concerns of Mexican Americans

States' Rights Party, or **Dixiecrats**, rallied behind segregationist Strom Thurmond for president instead of Democratic Party candidate Harry Truman. Interestingly, while Thurmond carried some states, he did not carry Texas, which voted for Truman. Segregation became a third-party issue again in 1968 when Alabama governor George Wallace ran as a third-party candidate against the liberal Democratic candidate Hubert Humphrey. Echoing the success of Dixiecrat Thurmond, Wallace carried a number of southern states but failed to win Texas, which supported Humphrey. Much of Humphrey's support can be attributed to the lingering popularity of President Johnson in the state.

The civil rights movement in the 1960s planted the seeds for an independent Latino movement named **La Raza Unida**, meaning "united race." José Ángel Gutiérrez led the party at its inception, which was concentrated in Zavala County. La Raza Unida developed into a third party in Texas and was able to win races in Crystal City and other small towns in south Texas. The party was able to do this by taking advantage of nonpartisan elections in many cities and towns. Even today, many cities, such as Austin, conduct nonpartisan elections. This does not mean that the candidates running for office do not belong to political parties. It just means that their party affiliation is not listed on the ballot. Reformers in many cities pushed for this so that voters would vote on the basis of candidate qualifications rather than by political party. La Raza Unida won many of these races in Zavala County and other surrounding counties, so that at one point, the party was able to take control of some city councils, school boards, and even the top city job of mayor. By 1972 the party nearly cost Democrat Dolph Briscoe the governorship because of the candidacy of Ramsey Muñiz. While this movement ultimately faded away, as most third-party movements do, it marked the growing influence of Latinos in the state.

In recent years, the Libertarian Party in Texas has emerged as a third-party alternative to the two major political parties. While running candidates for a wide range of offices across the state, the Libertarian Party has not been successful at the polls and had little impact on Election Day. For the most part, it has been a party of protest in which people dissatisfied with politics in the state can express their discontent at the polls. Libertarians believe in limited government and can be considered fiscal conservatives and social liberals. Former U.S. representative Ron Paul of Lake Jackson, nominally a Republican, ran for president in 1988 as a Libertarian, and his isolationist views on foreign policy in particular are quite distinct from those of other Republicans. Libertarians are particularly active in some of the major cities, including Austin. While they do not win very many elections, they can influence politics in other ways. For example, the major parties may adopt some of the positions promoted by Libertarians (or members of other minor parties) in order to win their support in runoff elections.

The most recent case involving a significant threat to the major-party candidates was the 2006 election for governor. Rick Perry was seen as a vulnerable incumbent, especially during a year that was not particularly favorable for Republicans. Democrat Chris Bell, a former Houston member of Congress, won the Democratic nomination, but two major independent candidates also ran for governor. They were former comptroller Carole Keeton Strayhorn from Austin and musician and humorist Kinky Friedman, whose catchy slogan was "Why the hell not?" When all the ballots were counted, Perry was re-elected governor with 39 percent of the vote. While it is not clear that a two-way race between Bell and Perry would have ensured a Bell victory,

Independent candidates face considerable challenges in elections. Although the musician and writer Kinky Friedman's 2006 candidacy for governor attracted major media attention, Friedman received only 12.4 percent of the vote.

the candidacies of Strayhorn and Friedman damaged whatever mandate Perry could claim from a victory without a majority.

Why don't people vote for third parties? In general elections, Texas employs what is known as a **"first past the post," single-member district** electoral system. Under a first past the post system, only the candidate who wins the plurality of votes, that is, the most votes, is elected. According to **Duverger's Law**, this type of voting system tends to favor a two-party system because a vote for a third-party candidate generally does not result in a win. Consider the 2006 governor's race in which Perry won with less than an outright majority. Although Friedman and Strayhorn made a good showing for third-party candidates, they still only received 12.4 percent and 18.1 percent of the vote, respectively. Even if a runoff election had occurred, it would have been between the top two vote getters, Perry and Bell. This is not to say that a vote for a third-party candidate is "wasted," because major-party candidates as well as the parties themselves can often be responsive to voters who might have voted for a third-party candidate. Winning candidates often run in future elections and would like to appeal to constituents who might not have supported them in the past.

In contrast, some other countries use a system of **proportional representation** that encourages third-party voting because even if a party wins only 10 percent of the vote in an election, it will still win 10 percent of the seats in the legislature or other representative body. Voters in these countries are therefore more likely to vote for third and minor parties, because they will almost certainly be able to elect at least one of these candidates.

Many American voters believe that their votes would be wasted if they voted for a third-party candidate. This expectation is rational, as the history of elections shows that

"first past the post" an election rule that states that the winner is the candidate who receives a plurality of the votes

single-member district an electorate that is allowed to elect only one representative for each district

Duverger's Law the observation that in a single-member district system of electing representatives, a two-party system will emerge

proportional representation a multimember district system that allows each political party representation in proportion to its percentage of the total vote

PERSONAL RESPONSIBILITY: WHAT WOULD YOU DO?

- Do you think Texas should make it easier for minor parties to gain political power? Why?

- What changes would you make in order to improve the visibility and power of minor parties?

a Republican or Democrat will almost always win. Most voters logically decide that it makes more sense to vote for the major-party candidate whose ideology is closest to their own.

The Tea Party Movement in Texas

The **Tea Party movement** has become prominent nationwide and in Texas. Tea Party advocates have had a great deal of influence in Texas mainly because of their libertarian antitax message, which resonates with many Texans. The implications of these antitax policies in Texas mean less funding for K–12 and higher education and fewer social services, such as children's health care programs.

Tea Party organizers have not yet sought to run a third-party candidate in elections, however. Instead, they have tried to influence Republican primary elections (see Figure 4.2). They believe that they can have more influence in state politics if they become a force to be reckoned with within the Republican Party. Undoubtedly, this is a wise strategy given the history of defeat for third parties, not only in the state but nationwide. Tea Party groups have focused their efforts on key statewide races. They have campaigned against incumbents, such as Speaker Straus of San Antonio, whom they deem to be too moderate. While the Tea Party has had some success in defeating incumbents and nominating preferred candidates, it remains to be seen whether the movement will be co-opted by the Republican Party or be an independent influence. Dan Patrick's victory in the lieutenant governor's race in 2014 seemed to suggest that the Tea Party movement has been co-opted by the Republican Party.

ON TO THE RUNOFF!
Konni
Burton
for Texas State Senate
Vote: May 27

The Tea Party has had a strong influence on the Republican Party. Tea Party leader Konni Burton got the Republican nomination for Wendy Davis's state senate seat in Fort Worth, and won the general election in 2014.

Tea Party movement a political movement that advocates lower government spending, lower taxes, and limited government

Parties and the Media

Traditionally, parties relied on newspapers, television, and radio to disseminate their messages to voters, fund-raise, and mobilize. However, in the new digital media age, parties have established active presences in social media platforms, such as Facebook, Twitter, and Snapchat. Parties hire digital media professionals to monitor social media and respond to criticisms, publicize the other party's faults, and advertise for their candidates.

Social media are also an important fundraising tool. In the digital age, it is less costly to solicit campaign contributions. Before the Internet, parties relied on snail mail and phone calls to raise money, but now parties can blast emails and post on social media to raise funds, which can be done easily over the Internet.

Parties use the media for voter mobilization as well. Parties can urge their supporters who follow them on Facebook or Twitter to turn out to vote. They can also encourage their friends to pass on these messages. The Texas Democratic Party website (txdemo crats.org) and the Texas Republican Party website (texasgop.org) provide Texans an opportunity to learn more about party positions, contribute money, volunteer, and make inquiries.

FIGURE 4.2

Tea Party Support in Texas

SOURCE: Texas Politics Project at the University of Texas at Austin.

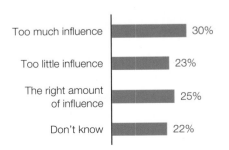

How would you rate the Tea Party's influence in the Republican Party?

Too much influence	30%
Too little influence	23%
The right amount of influence	25%
Don't know	22%

Texas's History as a One-Party State

Trace the evolution of the party system in Texas

In order to understand the present partisan environment in Texas, let us look at the history of partisanship in Texas since the end of the Civil War. With the defeat of the Republican governor Edmund J. Davis in 1873, Texas entered a period of Democratic dominance that would last for over a century. Often the Republican Party would not contest major state offices, and other parties, such as the Populist or People's Party, though having some influence for brief periods, did not have staying power. In general elections, it was a foregone conclusion that the Democratic nominee would win. If there was a meaningful election contest, it was in the Democratic Party primary.

Republicans tended to have a limited role in Texas politics. Most commonly, people remained Republicans in the hope of gaining political patronage (usually local postmaster or rural mail carrier positions) when Republican presidents were in office. Some Republicans were businesspeople unhappy with the liberal policies of Democratic presidents such as Franklin Delano Roosevelt or Harry Truman. However, the Republican Party was not a threat to Democratic dominance in the state. Indeed, Republicans interested in patronage from the national government may have had an incentive to keep the Republican Party small, as the fewer the Republicans, the less the competition for patronage positions. When the father of the late senator Lloyd Bentsen first moved to the Rio Grande Valley, he visited with R. B. Creager, who was then state chairman of the Republican Party. Lloyd Bentsen, Sr., told Creager that he wanted to get involved in the Republican Party because his father had been a devoted Republican in South Dakota. Rather than welcoming Bentsen into the Republican Party, Creager told Bentsen, "You go back to Mission [Texas] and join the Democratic Party, because what's best for Texas is for every state in the union to have a two-party system and for Texas to be a one-party state. When you have a one-party state, your men stay in Congress longer and build up seniority."[6]

In 1952 and 1956, however, the Democratic governor Allan Shivers led a movement often known as the **Shivercrat movement**, which presaged a dramatic change in party alignments a quarter century later. Governor Shivers was a conservative Democrat and widely regarded as one of the most able Texas governors of the twentieth century. He supported the candidacy of the Republican Dwight Eisenhower for the presidency against the Democratic nominee, Adlai Stevenson. Stevenson opposed the Texas position on the Tidelands, offshore lands claimed by both Texas and the national government, which were believed to contain oil. Additionally, Stevenson was much more liberal than Shivers, and Eisenhower was a famous and popular hero of World War II. Governor Shivers not only supported Eisenhower for the presidency; he and all statewide officeholders except the agriculture commissioner, John White, ran on the ballot as Democrats *and* Republicans. It was an act of party disloyalty condemned by loyal Democrats such as Speaker of the U.S. House of Representatives Sam Rayburn, and it led to much tension in the Democratic Party between liberal and conservative Democrats as well as between party loyalists and the Shivercrats.

Shivercrat movement a movement led by the Texas governor Allan Shivers during the 1950s in which conservative Democrats in Texas supported Republican candidate Dwight Eisenhower for the presidency because many of those conservative Democrats believed that the national Democratic Party had become too liberal

Though Democrats dominated Texas politics for decades, presidential Republicanism grew when Democrats supported Republican presidential candidate Dwight Eisenhower, who ran for president in 1952 and 1956. Here, Eisenhower is seen campaigning in Lubbock.

presidential Republicanism
a voting pattern in which conservatives vote Democratic for state offices but Republican for presidential candidates

The Shivercrat movement sent a strong message that many conservative Democrats were philosophically opposed to the national Democratic Party and although they were unwilling to embrace the Republican Party fully, they found the Republican Party more compatible with their views. A pattern in voting known as **presidential Republicanism** was strengthening, whereby conservative Texas voters would vote Democratic for state offices but vote Republican for presidential candidates. With the Shivercrat movement, those conservatives were more numerous and more closely aligned with the Republican Party. To be sure, the fact that some Democratic voters supported the Republican candidate did not mean that the state would vote Republican during every presidential election. As the "Who Are Texans?" graphic shows, the fortunes of Republican presidential candidates fluctuated between 1944 and 2016. Nevertheless, presidential Republicanism would persist in Texas and other southern states until Republicans began to get elected in state and local races in the 1990s and beyond.

Still, in state elections from 1874 to 1994 the Democratic Party was overwhelmingly the dominant party. There might be pockets of the state where Republicans showed strength. Traditionally, in the post–Civil War era, the "German counties" in the Texas Hill Country, which were settled by German immigrants, showed Republican leanings. Dallas County, whose voters were influenced by a powerful group of conservative businesspeople and a conservative newspaper, the *Dallas Morning News*, showed early Republican strength, electing a very conservative Republican congressperson in the 1950s. However, for the most part, the Democratic Party was so dominant in state elections that the Republican Party did not field opponents to the Democratic nominees.

During this era, the Democratic Party was an umbrella party that held a variety of groups and interests. Liberals and conservatives belonged to the party, as did members of labor unions, businesspeople, farmers, and city dwellers. Often liberals and conservatives within the party battled for control of the party and its offices. But when liberals and conservatives were not engaged in periodic intraparty battles, struggles that occurred with considerable regularity, what political organization existed tended to be based on personal ties and personal popularity of individual candidates.

Until about the 1940s, Texas politics was often chaotic and confused. By about the mid-1940s, however, a split between liberals and conservatives developed in the Democratic Party that focused on New Deal economic policies and civil rights measures. This liberal-conservative split became a characteristic division within the Democratic Party, and liberals and conservatives battled in the party primaries. Between the mid-1940s and the mid-1970s, the victor in these primary squabbles would then go on to win the general election. However, by the late 1970s the winner of the Democratic primary had to face a significant conservative challenge from Republicans in the general election.[7]

The Era of Conservative Democrats

After Reconstruction and through the mid-twentieth century, conservative Democrats were in control of state government. These Democratic officeholders were conservative on fiscal and racial issues and exerted a powerful influence in the region as well as in Congress. This may seem hard to fathom in today's political environment, where Democrats are seen as liberal and Republicans as conservative. But recall that

When Did Texas Become Republican?

The Republican Party is the dominant party in Texas. However, this is a fairly recent development. Before the 1970s, Texans were less likely than the rest of the nation to support Republican presidential candidates. And it was only in the 1990s and the early 2000s that Republicans came to hold a majority of seats in the Texas delegation to the U.S. House and in the Texas legislature.

Republican Share of the Presidential Vote

■ Texas   ■ National

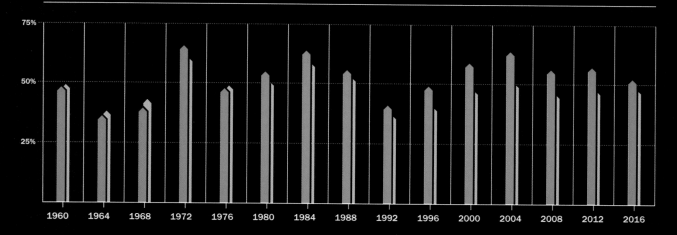

75%
50%
25%

1960 1964 1968 1972 1976 1980 1984 1988 1992 1996 2000 2004 2008 2012 2016

Republican Share of Offices Held

SOURCES: First figure: 1960–2004 data from the CQ Elections and Voting Collection. 2008 data from the Associated Press. Second figure: 1986–2002 data from Republican Party of Texas. 2004–16 data calculated by author from election results archived at the Texas Secretary of State.

Texas statewide offices
4%   100%

Texas House
37%   63%

Texas Senate
19%   65%

Texas delegation to U.S. House
37%   69%

1986 1990 1994 1998 2002 2006 2010 2014 2017

QUANTITATIVE REASONING

- Based on these data, how has the Republican share of the presidential vote in Texas changed compared to the rest of the nation? Why?

- Describe the trend in the growth of the Republican Party in Texas according to the data shown here. What factors might have shaped this trend? Do you think it will continue in the future?

the Republican Party was initially started in Illinois as an antislavery party. Conservative Democrats in the early to mid-twentieth century were not particularly favorable to policies that would make it easier for African Americans to vote or participate in civic life in an equal manner. Many southern Democrats were elected to Congress and gained seniority there, where Democrats were usually in control. Northern Democrats, however, had always been more liberal than their southern counterparts and did not like the growing influence of the South on policy matters in Washington.

In the many contests between conservative Democrats and liberal Democrats within Texas when the Democratic Party was the only game in town, the conservatives usually won because of the sheer fact that there were more conservatives than liberals in the state. However, some liberals did emerge, such as U.S. senator Ralph Yarborough, and to some extent, President Lyndon B. Johnson. Even though the two men were political adversaries, they both held progressive views, unlike many of their white Texas counterparts. U.S. senator Lloyd Bentsen, who served the state during the 1980s, became the vice-presidential candidate for Michael Dukakis in 1988 but was unable to win the state for his running mate. Instead, Republican George H. W. Bush, who had moved to Texas from Connecticut, carried the state and the general election. The Reagan Revolution had reached Texas, and from that point on, the Democratic Party in the state shrank to become the minority party.

The Growth of the Republican Party

One of the most important developments in Texas politics has been the growth of the Republican Party (see Figure 4.3). This growth can be seen along three interrelated dimensions: in terms of those who identify with the Republican Party, those who vote for Republican Party candidates in primaries and the general election, and those Republicans who have been elected to office.

In the 1950s more than 60 percent of Texans identified with the Democratic Party and fewer than 10 percent identified themselves as Republicans. The remainder considered themselves independents. In the 1960s, Republican identification in Texas rose above 10 percent, Democratic identification remained above 60 percent, and identification as independents dropped slightly. The 1970s saw a decline in Democratic affiliation and an increase in Republican affiliation. Both patterns accelerated during the 1980s.[8] In 2016, Gallup reported that 37 percent of Texans identified themselves as Democratic or leaning Democratic and 43 percent identified as Republican or leaning Republican. A 2016 Gallup poll study identified Texas as leaning Republican.[9] There is, however, clearly a difference between poll responses and election results where Texas has been and remains strongly Republican. Interestingly, when one considers competition between the two parties in terms of actual voters in the primaries or the general election, a different story emerges. Among actual voters in both primaries and general elections, Texas has become a strongly Republican state

FIGURE 4.3

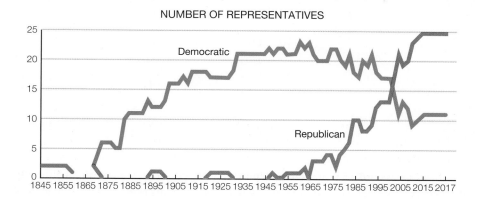

Party Composition of the Texas Delegation to the U.S. House of Representatives, 1845–2017

NOTE: Third-party data are not included.

SOURCE: Texas Politics Project at the University of Texas at Austin.

NUMBER OF REPRESENTATIVES

over the last decade. This conclusion is confirmed when one considers the number of Republican officeholders in the state.

In the first quarter of the twentieth century, the Republican Party was only a token party. In the state legislature, for example, Republicans never held more than one seat in the Texas Senate and never more than two seats in the Texas House from 1903 to 1927. From 1927 to 1951 there were no Republicans in the Texas legislature, and then a lone Republican was elected from Dallas to serve only one term in the Texas House. It was another decade before Republicans were again elected to the legislature, when 2 served in the Texas House. Then in 1962, 6 Republicans were elected to the House from Dallas County and 1 from Midland County. By 1963 there were 10 Republicans in the Texas House and none in the Texas Senate.[10]

As Table 4.1 shows, as late as 1974 there were very few Republican officeholders in the entire state of Texas. One of those officeholders was U.S. senator John Tower, and there were 2 Texas Republicans in the U.S. House of Representatives. No Republicans were elected to state office in statewide elections. There were only 3 Republicans in the Texas Senate and only 16 Republicans in the Texas House of Representatives. Ronald Reagan's election as president in 1980 marked a significant change in how Texans began to vote not only in presidential elections but also in state elections. The Reagan era ushered in a period when conservative Democrats began to switch to the Republican Party in record numbers. This switch became more evident at the end of the Reagan and Bush years when Texas became a Republican state not only in presidential races but also in state races. In 2016 both U.S. senators from Texas were Republican and 25 Texas members of the U.S. House of Representatives were Republican. A majority of the Texas Senate, 20 of the 31 members, and the Texas House of Representatives, 94 of the 150 members, was Republican.

TABLE 4.1

Growth of the Republican Party in Texas

YEAR	U.S. SENATE	OTHER STATEWIDE	U.S. HOUSE	TEXAS SENATE	TEXAS HOUSE	TOTAL
1974	1	0	2	3	16	22
1980	1	1	5	7	35	49
1990	1	6	8	8	57	80
2000	2	27	13	16	72	130
2010	2	27	23	19	101	172
2012	2	27	24	19	95	167
2014	2	27	25	20	98	172
2016	2	27	25	20	94	168

It was a record of remarkable Republican growth and Democratic decline. By 1999 every statewide elected official was Republican. (This remained true in 2016 as well.) That included the governor, lieutenant governor, attorney general, comptroller, land commissioner, agriculture commissioner, all three members of the Texas Railroad Commission, and all nine members of both the Texas Supreme Court and the Texas Court of Criminal Appeals. Only 20 years earlier, William Clements was the first statewide official elected as a Republican since Reconstruction.

The Disappearance of Conservative Democrats

Blue Dog Democrats another name for conservative Democrats, mostly from the South

Conservative Democrats, also known as **Blue Dog Democrats**, are becoming an endangered species in Texas and in the rest of the South. Such Democrats never left the party they grew up in, and they have become marginalized in the national party because of their social conservatism. Many of these Democrats are opposed to abortion and same-sex marriage while supportive of gun rights. These positions put them at odds with the prevailing consensus in the Democratic Party. Some of the few conservative Democrats elected to Congress in recent years even refused to support Nancy Pelosi of San Francisco as their party leader because of their divergence from her more liberal views.

By 2012 all of the conservative Democrats elected to represent Texas in the U.S. Congress had retired, switched parties, or lost their elections. For example, former congressperson Chet Edwards was a conservative Democrat who represented Crawford, the home of former president George W. Bush. In the 2010 elections, Edwards lost his bid for re-election to Republican Bill Flores, a businessman. Congressperson Ralph Hall of Rockwall switched to the Republican Party in 2004 after spending many years as a conservative Democrat. He switched parties in order to have more

Should the Tea Party Movement Launch a Third Party?

In Texas, all state legislators and members of the executive branch are members of one of the two major political parties: the Democratic Party or the Republican Party. In Texas history, several third-party movements have appeared but diminished over time as the major political parties absorb the sentiments behind these movements. As discussed in this chapter, the state parties hold primary elections in order to determine who their candidates will be for the general election. However, in recent years, the Tea Party has had an increasingly important role in state politics since its emergence during the early years of the Obama administration. Should the Tea Party attempt to change the Republican Party or create an independent political movement?

Voters are not necessarily limited to choosing between the two major parties. For example, third-party presidential candidate Gary Johnson, representing the Libertarian Party, appeared on the ballot in all 50 states in 2012. However, general election ballot access is difficult in Texas because of laws passed by the legislature. This results in many elections between candidates of the two major political parties.[a] The Tea Party has pushed for more conservative policies and antitax sentiment within the Republican Party as well as in independent bids.

Tea Party advocates have challenged moderate Republicans at all levels of state government arguing that they were insufficiently conservative and unwilling to push major reforms. Some of these Tea Party–backed candidates have been successful winning Republican primaries. The most prominent cases are U.S. senator Ted Cruz and state senator Dan Patrick's defeat of moderate establishment Republican lieutenant governor David Dewhurst in 2013 and 2015, respectively. In other statewide races, Tea Party–backed Republicans performed very well, including Attorney General Ken Paxton's defeat of moderate candidate Dan Branch in 2015. With these Tea Party successes, one argument is that "if you can't beat them, join them," and this is what the Tea Party has been able to accomplish. Knowing that third-party runs are difficult, some argue that the Tea Party can and should just try to take over the Republican Party in the state. They also argue that launching a third party would divide the conservative vote, making it easier for Democrats to win and thus making matters even worse.

Other more extreme Tea Party advocates claim that the Republican Party is still composed of too many "RINOs" (Republicans in Name Only) who are not interested in or committed to fundamental change. They

argue that the Tea Party should split from the Republican Party and launch as a third-party. They point to moderate Republican House Speaker Joe Straus of San Antonio, who has remained in office because of moderate Republicans and Democrats. They argue that as more Texans identify as independent and become frustrated with two major political parties, the Tea Party stands to benefit from this dissatisfaction.

COMMUNICATING EFFECTIVELY: YOUR VOICE

- What features of electoral law might help or hinder the Tea Party if it decides to break away and run independently of the Republican Party?

- If you were advising the Tea Party on how to maximize its power and influence, would you tell Tea Party members to stay with the Republican Party or launch their own? What arguments would you make to the Tea Party leadership?

Recent elections have continued the trend toward greater strength of Republicans in Texas. Some conservative Democrats—like Representative Henry Cuellar of Laredo, pictured here—continue to serve in Congress.

influence in Congress's governing party, although just two years later, the Democrats retook control of the U.S. House. In 2014, Hall decided to run for re-election despite his 91-year-old age. Hall lost in a runoff with Tea Party–backed attorney John Ratcliffe. The seat is strongly Republican, and Ratcliffe was elected to the seat.

The biggest losses for conservative Democrats came following the 2003 redistricting cycle, spearheaded by Tom DeLay. As House majority leader, DeLay wanted to take advantage of the new Republican majority in the state legislature in order to redraw congressional districts, which he thought were too favorable to Democrats. Although controversial, DeLay was able to succeed in organizing a dramatic redistricting session, which put many conservative Democrats from Texas at risk of losing their seats.

After this episode, two Texas Democrats, Representatives Charles Stenholm and Max Sandlin, lost their seats to Republicans. Another Democrat, Jim Turner, decided not to seek re-election in his newly configured district in east Texas. Redistricting has left liberal Lloyd Doggett of Austin as the only white Democrat representing a majority white congressional district in Texas. Gene Green of Houston and Beto O'Rourke of El Paso represent majority-Latino districts.

The pattern we observe in Congress is also present at the state legislative level. Of the 55 Democrats in the Texas House of Representatives in 2013, 11 were considered conservative in research conducted by Mark Jones of Rice University. This is relative to other Democrats, not Republicans. The most conservative Democrat in the Texas House is still more liberal than the most liberal Republican.[11] In the 2015 legislative session, however, Allan Ritter of Nederland, who was one of the 12 conservative Democrats, switched to the Republican Party.

In today's political environment, the influence of conservative Democrats and liberal Republicans is very limited. At the national level and in Texas, conservatives are disproportionately members of the Republican Party and liberals are members of the Democratic Party. In many races, there are a shrinking number of truly independent voters who can swing elections. Often, both parties attempt to mobilize their own bases instead of trying to reach these swing voters.

Texas Party Politics Today

Analyze how ideological divisions and demographic change affect Texas political parties

Both the Democrats and the Republicans have factions within the party, and these factions emphasize different issues. For example, the Democratic Party in Texas has a large Latino base, which is very interested in the issue of immigration. The Republican Party has a strong and growing Tea Party contingent, which is making the party more antitax and fiscally conservative. In this section, we will examine some of these conflicts both between and within the major parties.

Party Unity and Disunity

All groups have opposing factions within them, and political parties are no exception. When a party becomes dominant in a state, these factional battles become particularly important because the stakes are higher for the factions of the dominant party.

When the Democratic Party was the dominant party in Texas, factional battles were common between liberals and conservatives in the party. These conflicts in the Democratic Party were especially notable during the 1950s, as we saw in the struggles between the pro-Eisenhower conservative Democrats, led by Allan Shivers, and the pro-Stevenson liberal and loyalist Democrats, led by Sam Rayburn, Lyndon Johnson, and Ralph Yarborough. Now that the Republican Party is the dominant party in Texas, major factional battles have occurred for control of that party. One faction is the religious right. This group includes religious conservatives who are especially concerned with social issues such as abortion, prayer in public schools and at school events, the teaching of evolution in public schools, and the perceived decline in family values. The other major segment of the party is composed of economic conservatives. This group is primarily concerned with reduced government spending, lower taxes, and greater emphasis on free enterprise. At the end of the day, however, these factions often end up supporting their party candidate in the general election.

Starting in the 2006 primary, some Republicans, including two of the party's largest contributors in Texas, believed that some Republicans in the Texas House were too moderate and spent money to try to defeat them.[12] At least six Republican incumbents were aided by last-minute contributions from a political action committee that poured about $300,000 into their campaigns to help protect them from Republican challengers. Nevertheless, two of the six incumbents were defeated and one was thrown into a runoff.[13] The 2014 primary battle between Lieutenant Governor David Dewhurst and Senator Dan Patrick shows that the ideological tensions in the Republican Party continue between what is essentially a conservative faction and an even more conservative faction. The latter faction has been identified with the Tea Party movement. Tea Party favorite U.S. senator Ted Cruz now has protégés: Dan Patrick in the lieutenant governor's position and Ken Paxton as attorney general. Governor Greg Abbott also supported Senator Ted Cruz in his primary bid for the presidency in 2016. A number of the newly elected members of the state legislature are also Tea Party favorites.

To maintain its political strength, the Republican Party has to keep these factional disputes within the party. When Senator Kay Bailey Hutchison challenged Governor Rick Perry in the primary, some of Perry's appointees endorsed Hutchison. Afterward, they were asked to step down from their appointive positions. These were seen as examples of the rift that emerged between two wings of the Republican Party. For years, the Democratic Party battles between its liberal and conservative wings were kept inside the party because there was no rival party to which one of the factions could go. Eventually the Republican Party emerged as a home where many conservative Democrats felt comfortable. Conceivably, the factional disputes in the Republican Party could lead one of the factions—the more moderate Republicans—to move to the Democratic Party.

Urban, Rural, and Suburban Influences on Partisanship

As in the rest of the country, one of the major divides in political party affiliation is rural versus urban. Today's large suburban populations must be added to this equation. The growth of suburban enclaves around major cities such as the Dallas–Fort Worth metroplex, Houston, and San Antonio has profoundly changed politics. Prior to the growth of suburbia, people lived either in cities or in rural areas. Rural residents were often cattle ranchers or farmers. As cattle raising and farming became more mechanized and large companies displaced local farmers, it became less profitable to run family farms. Many rural residents relocated to urban areas to work in banks, oil companies, or other industries.

During the 1950s the federal government embarked on a major project to connect cities through an interstate highway system. One consequence of this system was that it made it easier for workers to travel to and from urban areas. For those who wanted to escape urban congestion, it became easier to move to the outskirts of the city and travel by car to their jobs. While mass transit facilitated suburban commuting in other parts of the country, in Texas, taxpayers were unwilling to fund these infrastructure investments.

Texas's interstate highway system encouraged the process of "white flight," the mass exodus of more affluent whites from urban areas to suburban areas. This left urban areas with eroding tax bases and remaining poor minority populations, who did not have the luxury of purchasing automobiles to commute between city and suburb.

The political result of this changing demographic is that cities have become more Democratic, even in Texas, where the urban strongholds of Austin, Dallas, El Paso, and Houston deliver the most Democratic votes in the state. Rural areas have remained solidly conservative and have become Republican in Texas, and suburban areas can best be described as hybrid areas with pockets of Republicans and Democrats depending on the specific area and local issues. An important exception is the Rio Grande Valley, which has large rural areas with Democratic dominance. However, voter turnout in the valley is substantially lower than in other parts of the state.

Another consequence is that voters tend to settle in places with like-minded people so that cities tend to attract more Democrats, and suburban and rural areas tend to attract more Republicans. This reinforces the political proclivities already established in such communities. A recent book, *Our Patchwork Nation*, by Dante Chinni and James Gimpel explores this phenomenon nationwide, arguing that different communities have distinct political characteristics.[14]

The tensions introduced by suburbanization are clearly seen in Dallas County over the last decade. As Dallas County has urbanized and the suburbs have extended to adjoining counties, Dallas County has been transformed into an urban, Democratic county. In the media coverage of the 2000 presidential election, one small judicial race in Dallas County was almost overlooked. Only one puzzled article on the race's results appeared in the *Dallas Morning News*.[15] A three-time Republican judge, Bill Rhea, won re-election against a first-time Democratic candidate, Mary Ann Huey. That should have been no surprise. By the late 1980s the only Democrat who could win a judicial race in Dallas County was Ron Chapman, a Democratic judge who happened to share the name of the most popular disk jockey in the county.[16] In the early 1980s

there had been a wholesale rush of incumbent Democratic judges to the Republican Party. Although varying explanations were given by the party switchers, perhaps the most honest and straightforward was by Judge Richard Mays: "My political philosophy about general things has nothing to do with me [*sic*] being a judge. . . . That's not the reason I'm switching parties. The reason I'm switching is that to be a judge in Dallas County you need to be a Republican." With Mays's switch in August 1985, 32 of the 36 district judges in Dallas County were Republicans, though none were Republicans before 1978.[17] It would, of course, not take long until all judges in Dallas County were Republican.[18]

So what was remarkable about that one district court race between a Democratic challenger and a longtime Republican incumbent, other than the fact that a Democrat had the temerity to challenge an incumbent in a Republican bastion such as Dallas County? Out of 560,558 votes cast, only 4,150 votes separated the two candidates. In other words, a three-term Republican judge with no scandal or other controversy surrounding his name won with only 50.3 percent of the vote. It is no wonder that the judge commented, "I'm thrilled to be serving again and duly humbled by the vote count."[19] Even more astounding, Judge Rhea's Democratic opponent, Mary Ann Huey, had run with no money, no political experience, and no support from the legal community. She ran in the same year that George W. Bush was the presidential nominee, with no other Democratic judicial candidates on the ballot at the county level, and with little more than audacity on her side.

Judge Rhea's humbling experience, of course, was not caused by his judicial performance but rather by demographic changes. The Republican base in Dallas County has moved to places such as Collin, Denton, and Rockwall counties. That suburban growth has changed those traditionally Democratic counties into Republican counties but has left the old Republican base—Dallas—with a larger African American and an even larger Latino population and has returned it to the Democratic column that it left a little more than 20 years ago.

In the 2004 elections, George W. Bush carried Dallas County by fewer than 10,000 votes (50.72 percent), and Dallas County elected Democrats as sheriff and four countywide elected judges. The 2006 elections in Dallas County were truly a watershed in the county's politics. A Democrat was elected county judge, a Democrat was elected district attorney, and all 42 Democrats who ran for Dallas County judgeships were elected. Democrats continued their sweep of countywide elections in 2008, 2010, 2012, and 2016.

In 2008, Harris County also dramatically shifted to the Democratic column, electing a large number of Democrats to county office. It seemed to be following in Dallas County's footsteps. However, the 2010 elections moved Harris County back into the Republican column, and in 2012, Harris County was a virtual tie between Obama and Romney. In 2016, Hillary Clinton won Harris County by double digits, and Democrats swept the countywide races.

African Americans in Texas Political Parties

In Texas, African Americans are a smaller percentage of the population than in neighboring Louisiana. Approximately 12 percent of the Texas state population is African American—roughly the same percentage as in the total U.S. population—and most of that population is concentrated in east Texas as well as in the major cities of Houston, Dallas, San Antonio, and Austin. Depending on the election, the vast majority of African Americans cast their votes for Democrats. This is not unusual, as African Americans in other parts of the country are similarly loyal to the Democratic Party.

The influence of African Americans in the Democratic Party in Texas is high not only because they tend to vote Democratic more than Republican but because they participate in elections more than other ethnic groups. During the 2014 statewide elections, 35.3 percent of African Americans turned out to vote. Only 22.4 percent of Hispanics turned out to vote that same year, while 35.2 percent of whites turned out. See Table 4.2.

This is not to say that all African Americans are Democrats. Former railroad commissioner Michael Williams became the first black Republican to be elected to the

TABLE 4.2

Turnout by Race: 2012 Presidential Year versus 2014 Statewide Election Year

	NUMBER OF ELIGIBLE VOTERS IN 2012 (IN MILLIONS)	TURNOUT OF ELIGIBLE VOTERS IN 2014 STATEWIDE ELECTION YEAR (%)	TURNOUT OF ELIGIBLE VOTERS IN 2012 PRESIDENTIAL YEAR (%)	DIFFERENCE BETWEEN 2012 AND 2014 (%)
White*	8.33	35.2	60.9	25.7
African American	2.00	35.3	63.1	27.8
Asian	0.57	17.9	42.4	24.5
Hispanic	4.38	22.4	38.8	16.4
Total	15.4	30.2	53.8	23.6

*White does not include whites who identify as Hispanic.
SOURCE: U.S. Census Bureau, "Voting and Registration in the Election of November 2014—Detailed Tables."

statewide post. The former Texas Supreme Court chief justice Wallace Jefferson is also an African American Republican and was elected by voters to his position. Other than Williams and Jefferson, only two other African Americans have been elected to statewide office in recent years.

African Americans have been elected mayors of important cities in Texas. Democrat Lee Brown became Houston's first African American mayor in 1997, and Democrat Ron Kirk became Dallas's first African American mayor in 1995. In 2002, Kirk ran for the U.S. Senate but lost to white Republican John Cornyn. In 2015, Houston elected its second African American mayor, former state representative Sylvester Turner, to replace term-limited Annise Parker. In 2014, African American Ivy Taylor was elected San Antonio mayor after Julian Castro left the seat to serve in President Obama's administration.

Latinos in Texas Political Parties

In the 2014 gubernatorial election, Republican Greg Abbott ran television ads in English and Spanish with his Latina mother-in-law's endorsement. Abbott made no secret that if he were elected governor, Texas would have a Latina first lady. Abbott's appeal to Latino voters in this way highlights at the very least the growing importance of this electorate.

Just twelve years prior to Abbott's election, Democrats attempted to break the lock that the Republicans had on statewide offices by putting forward a "Dream Team" with Tony Sanchez, a wealthy Latino businessman from Laredo who had been an appointee of Republican governor Rick Perry and had a record of not participating in many elections, running for governor alongside Ron Kirk running for the U.S. Senate and John Sharp (a former state comptroller and white conservative Democrat) running for lieutenant governor. The idea was to mobilize minority voters to vote for the Democratic ticket while holding traditional white voters. The strategy failed dismally as Sanchez lost to the Republican candidate Perry (40 percent to 58 percent), Kirk lost to the Republican Cornyn (43 percent to 55 percent), and Sharp lost to the Republican Dewhurst (46 percent to 52 percent). Especially disappointing because Sanchez was the first Latino major party nominee for governor, Latino voter turnout was only 32.8 percent. The Democratic "Dream Team" became a nightmare. Sanchez had money and spent it with abandon, but he was a poor campaigner who could not even mobilize the Latino vote.

Additionally, Democrats didn't anticipate the grassroots get-out-the-vote effort put forth by the Republicans. Republican straight-ticket voting in key urban and suburban counties across the state appeared to have outdistanced Democratic straight-ticket voting. Further, it appeared that negative campaigning, particularly directed at Tony Sanchez, may have undercut support for the Democratic ticket among traditional white conservative voters.[20]

The 2010 election has been described as a Republican tsunami running throughout the nation. Texas experienced this wave in three important ways. First, four Democratic incumbent U.S. congresspeople were defeated. Second, Republicans maintained their monopoly over statewide elected offices. Third, Republicans gained 22 seats in the Texas House. A conservative majority reasserted itself in Texas politics. Since the 2010 elections, two Latino members of the state house have switched parties. Aaron

Peña of Edinburg and Jose Lozano of Kingsville became Republicans, although redistricting led Peña to retire from politics in January 2013.

Despite the final results of the 2008 and 2010 elections, few commentators were willing to dismiss the growing importance of the Latino vote in the state. One indication of that importance is that in 2010 it was estimated that Hispanics constituted about 20 percent of the registered voters in Texas.[21]

However, Latinos have not fully realized their potential voting strength. Table 4.2 shows Latino voting population figures and turnout rates in comparison with those of other racial and ethnic groups in the state in 2012 (a presidential year) and 2010 (a statewide election year). This is an issue that we will explore in more depth in Chapter 5. For now, we should note that Latino voters have a significantly lower turnout rate than that of whites and African Americans in both presidential years and statewide election years. Moreover, there are a large number of Latinos living in Texas—perhaps around 2 million—who are not citizens, some of whom are documented residents and many others who are not, who are not eligible to vote.[22] Such facts will likely depress the electoral power of the Latino population in Texas political parties in the short and medium runs. It should be remembered, however, that many of the children of these noncitizens will be Americans by being born in the United States and thus eligible to vote. Few would be surprised if a life spent living and being educated in the United States led to higher turnout rates among younger Latinos in the future. The full impact of the Latino demographic surge on political parties may not be felt until the next generation comes of age.[23]

Political Parties and the Future of Texas

We often think of conflict in politics between the Democratic and Republican parties, especially in government. While this is certainly true, conflict can also occur within political parties among different factions. These factions usually compromise to support their candidates during the general election. Political parties therefore provide a structure through which candidates strive to win office.

One of the most striking developments in Texas politics over the past 20 to 25 years is that though one-party dominance persists, control of government has moved from near-total Democratic to near-total Republican control (in 2016 every statewide elected officeholder in Texas was a Republican). This change was fueled by many factors, including the disappearance of conservative Democrats and the sorting of conservatives into the Republican Party and liberals into the Democratic Party. Like other southern states, Texas has long been very socially conservative and religious. The Republican Party became the conservative party while Democrats became the liberal party and Texas has remained solidly conservative and Republican. What would it take for Democrats to regain even some significant power in the state? There are three factors to watch as partisan politics in Texas evolves: divisiveness within parties, people from outside of Texas moving in, and the effort put forth by the Democratic Party itself.

Internal divisions within the Republican Party can provide Democrats an opportunity to capitalize on what voters might perceive as dysfunction and extreme policies. If more Tea Party–backed Republicans are elected statewide and move further and further to the right, a centrist Democrat can run and possibly win. This is not impossible. Neighboring state Louisiana elected a moderate to conservative Democrat as governor in 2015 by capitalizing on the state Republican Party's move to the right and a weak Republican candidate.

While Texas is becoming more diverse and is now a majority-minority state, it is also seeing a major influx of residents from other states. Many of these individuals are themselves conservatives who are attracted to the state's low taxes and low regulation policies. If these individuals vote at higher rates than others, then this will complicate efforts by the Democratic Party to make inroads.

Finally, the Democratic Party has to make efforts to appeal to Texans by adopting policies that are mainstream and not too far to the left. To some extent, Wendy Davis tried to do this on the issue of guns, but her reputation as a defender of abortion rights overshadowed her other policy positions. The group Battleground Texas attempted to mobilize Democrats in Texas during Wendy Davis's campaign for governor in 2014, but Davis lost resoundingly to Greg Abbott. The failure of Battleground to even move the needle ever more slightly to Democrats might give pause to Democratic donors who might instead choose to invest their resources in swing states. In early 2016, discussion about tapping former San Antonio mayor and Secretary of Housing and Urban Development Julian Castro as a possible running mate for Hillary Clinton led some to believe that this might mobilize Latino voters not only in Texas but nationwide. Even Castro's presence on the Democratic ticket, however, would probably not have moved Texas into the Democratic column in 2016. Even though Texas is becoming more diverse, it remains strongly dominated by the Republican Party at least for the foreseeable future.

Clearly, a lot has to happen for Democratic power in Texas to increase. Right now, this seems unlikely. But in 1950, the same was being said about Republicans. We will see what the future holds.

Use 🐰 INQUIZITIVE to help you study and master this material.

The Roles and Structure of Political Parties in Texas

- Describe the main functions of state party organizations (pp. 113–24)

In Texas, political parties serve as brand labels for voters to determine whom to vote for in elections that have little or no publicity. Texas political parties also have conventions and committees that help their members organize and mobilize in elections.

Key Terms
partisan polarization (p. 114)
political socialization (p. 115)
precinct (p. 119)
precinct chair (p. 119)
county executive committee (p. 119)
county chair (p. 119)
state executive committee (p. 119)
state chair and vice chair (p. 119)
precinct convention (p. 119)
county convention (p. 119)
state convention (p. 120)
Dixiecrats (p. 122)
La Raza Unida Party (p. 122)
"first past the post" (p. 123)
single-member district (p. 123)
Duverger's Law (p. 123)
proportional representation (p. 123)
Tea Party movement (p. 124)

Practice Quiz
1. Providing a label that helps voters identify those seeking office is an important function of
   a) the state
   b) political parties
   c) interest groups
   d) regional and subregional governments
   e) the president

2. The process by which political parties become more distant from each other in terms of ideology is
   a) partisan convergence
   b) partisan polarization
   c) partisan conventions
   d) partisan equilibrium
   e) partisan deliverance

3. All of the following groups constitute the Democratic Party base in Texas *except*
   a) business leaders
   b) Latinos
   c) African Americans
   d) white liberals
   e) urban residents

4. Which minority group is the fastest growing in Texas?
   a) African Americans
   b) Latinos
   c) Asian Americans
   d) Native Americans
   e) All are growing equally

5. In the state of Texas, the highest level of temporary party organization is the
   a) state convention
   b) state executive committee
   c) governor's convention
   d) civil executive committee
   e) speaker's committee

6. Which of the following third parties and movements had the most success in winning elections in post–World War II Texas?
   a) La Raza Unida Party
   b) the Dixiecrats
   c) the Green Party
   d) the Kinky Friedman movement
   e) the Constitution Party

Texas's History as a One-Party State

> • Trace the evolution of the party system in Texas (pp. 125–32)

Texas has traditionally been a one-party state, meaning that one party has been in control of state politics for a long time. In the post–Civil War period, the Democrats held power in the state, but since 1994 the Republicans have won every statewide election and consequently dominate state politics.

Key Terms

Shivercrat movement (p. 125)
presidential Republicanism (p. 126)
Blue Dog Democrats (p. 130)

Practice Quiz

7. The Shivercrat movement was
   a) a group of conservative Democrats in Texas who supported Eisenhower for president.
   b) a group of liberal Democrats who supported equal rights for all Americans.
   c) a group of conservative Republicans who rejected the Obama administration.
   d) a group of liberal Republicans who rejected the Bush administration.
   e) a group of Libertarians.

8. In Texas, the Republican Party became the dominant party in
   a) the 1950s.
   b) the 1960s.
   c) the 1970s.
   d) the 1980s.
   e) the 1990s.

9. Blue Dog Democrats were
   a) northeastern Democrats with conservative views.
   b) southern Democrats with liberal views.
   c) southern Democrats with conservative views.
   d) northern Democrats with liberal views.
   e) western Democrats with liberal views.

10. Presidential Republicanism refers to which of the following?
    a) Texans voting for Republican local candidates
    b) Texans voting for Republican presidents and Democrats for state offices
    c) Texans voting for Republican presidents and Republicans for state offices
    d) Texans voting for Democratic local candidates
    e) Texans voting for third-party candidates at all levels

Texas Party Politics Today

> • Analyze how ideological divisions and demographic change affect Texas political parties (pp. 132–38)

Texas is a diverse state with divisions between north and south and east and west. Latinos currently constitute nearly 40 percent of the state's population and currently favor the Democratic Party, although their registration and turnout rates are lower than those of the other major demographic groups.

Practice Quiz

11. Which of the following is *not* true?
    a) Cities in Texas have become more Democratic.
    b) Cities in Texas are dominated by third parties.
    c) Rural areas of Texas are solidly Republican.
    d) Texas suburbs contain pockets of both Democrats and Republicans.
    e) Democrats dominate elections in Dallas County.

12. African Americans in Texas
    a) tend to cast their votes for Democrats.
    b) are a large part of the Republican base.
    c) vote mainly for independent candidates.
    d) constitute less than 10 percent of the population.
    e) split their votes evenly between the Democratic and Republican parties.

In 2015, two cities in Texas elected new mayors. Sylvester Turner, a longtime state representative, became Houston's second elected African American mayor. In San Antonio, Ivy Taylor, pictured here, became the city's first African American mayor.

Campaigns and Elections

WHY CAMPAIGNS AND ELECTIONS MATTER Two of the largest cities in Texas, Houston and San Antonio, held municipal elections to elect new mayors in 2015. In Houston, the mayoral race initially drew a large field of candidates to replace outgoing mayor Annise Parker, who made national headlines when she became the first openly gay mayor of the fourth-largest city in the country. The top two vote getters were state representative Sylvester Turner, a Democrat who led the field with 32 percent of the vote, and businessman Bill King, an independent who had previously identified as a Republican and followed with 26 percent of the vote.

In the December runoff election between the two candidates, Turner campaigned on a platform to reform city finances, address the city's infrastructure problem, promote economic development, and pay attention to the city's poor and underserved. Turner received the support of the city's unions and the Democratic Party establishment. King's campaign platform was one of fiscal conservatism. He opposed lifting the city revenue cap because of the possibility that this would lead to higher property taxes for Houstonians. Turner did not campaign for higher property taxes, but left open the possibility of raising them in order to address city needs. King also ran to reform the city's pension system. He argued that current benefit plans strained the city budget by guaranteeing city workers retirement benefits that the city could not afford. In a hotly contested election, Turner defeated King by a narrow margin of 51 to 49 percent.

In San Antonio, the race for mayor featured former state senator Leticia Van de Putte, a Latina Democrat who lost to Dan Patrick in the lieutenant governor's race in 2014, and Ivy Taylor, an independent African American city council member. Taylor had been appointed temporary mayor when her predecessor, Julian Castro, became secretary of Housing and Urban Development in the Obama administration.

Van de Putte's campaign focused on the city's infrastructure, such as roads, bridges, and parks, and economic development. She promised not to raise the city's property taxes. Taylor emphasized the city's workforce and economic development. In the election Taylor and Van de Putte appealed to different segments of the electorate. Taylor accused Van de Putte of putting her partisan Democratic agenda ahead of the city's needs. Taylor appealed to conservative voters in the city by promising to be fiscally conservative and by reminding voters of her opposition to an equal rights amendment aimed at preventing discrimination against the LGBT community. Van de Putte received the endorsement of the city's police and fire unions, which were embroiled in tense contract negotiations with Taylor while she was temporary mayor.

And like Houston, San Antonio also had to face the issue of city workers' pensions. On Election Day, Taylor narrowly defeated Van de Putte. This was an upset, as San Antonio, which is heavily Latino, has traditionally elected Democratic mayors.

Why should it matter who is mayor? Mayors often have important national stature, and sometimes become cabinet secretaries or move on to statewide offices. The mayor has the power to set the local political agenda, veto municipal legislation, and influence public policy in the city. If King were elected in Houston, he would have focused on different issues than Turner. In San Antonio, Ivy Taylor's election will lead the city in a different direction with a focus on economic development and more business-friendly policies. As these contests show, all elections matter for public policy in Texas. Elections to the city council, school board, state legislature, governor, and more all make huge differences in our lives. Education funding, health care policy, taxes, and environmental policy all hang in the balance.

CHAPTER GOALS

- Describe the types of elections held in Texas and how they work (pp. 145–48)

- Explain how the rules for voting affect turnout among different groups of Texans (pp. 148–64)

- Present the main features of election campaigns in Texas (pp. 164–73)

Features of Elections in Texas

Describe the types of elections held in Texas and how they work

Elections are the most important vehicles by which the people express themselves in the democratic process in Texas. At the national level, elections are limited to the selection of the president and vice president (via the electoral college) and members of Congress. In Texas, however, voters select candidates for various offices in all three statewide branches of government (the legislature, executive, and judiciary) and in numerous local elections. Texans also vote for changes to the state constitution, which can alter public policy in the state. In theory, such elections are meant to enable the people to exercise some direct control over each branch. In practice, however, one-party dominance and low levels of voter participation have often told a different story, leaving the government exposed to special interests and big money.

Elections are the mechanisms people use to select leaders, authorize actions by government, and borrow money on behalf of government. In Texas, there are a multitude of elections: primary elections, general elections, city elections, school board elections, special elections, elections for community college boards and the governing boards for many special districts, and bond elections for city, county, and state governments.

Primary Elections

Primary elections are the first elections held in an electoral cycle. In Texas, they are generally held on the second Tuesday in March of even-numbered years. Primary elections determine the party's nominees for the general election. They are conducted by the political party and funded jointly by the party and the state. Essentially, parties collect filing fees from those seeking nomination and use these funds to pay for their share of holding the primary election.

The Democratic and Republican parties conduct primaries in nearly all of Texas's 254 counties. Within each county, voters cast ballots in precincts. The number of voting precincts varies depending on the population of the county. Less-populated counties such as Loving and Kennedy have as few as 6 precincts, whereas Harris County contains more than 1,000 voting precincts.

Republicans seeking their party's nomination file papers and pay a filing fee to the Republican Party. Likewise, Democrats file papers and pay a filing fee to the Democratic Party. If several Republicans (or Democrats) seek the office of governor, they will campaign against each other and one will be chosen to run in the general election. Winning the primary election requires an absolute majority. The party's nominees must have more votes than all opponents combined. If no candidate receives an absolute majority, there is a **runoff primary** between the two candidates receiving the most votes. Voters who participate in the Republican Party primary cannot vote in a Democratic runoff; likewise, anyone who voted in the Democratic Party primary cannot

primary election a ballot vote in which citizens select a party's nominee for the general election

runoff primary a second primary election held between the two candidates who received the most votes in the first primary election if no candidate in the first primary election had received a majority vote in a Republican runoff. However, those who voted in neither the Democratic nor Republican primary can vote in either the Republican or Democratic runoff primary.

An **open primary** allows any registered voter to cast a ballot in either, but not both, primaries. There are no party restrictions. One can consider oneself a Republican and vote in the Democratic primary or can leave home intending to vote in the Democratic primary, change one's mind, and vote in the Republican primary.

The Texas Constitution and election laws call the Texas system a **closed primary**, because one must declare one's party affiliation before voting, but in practice it is an open primary. Before receiving a primary ballot, the voter signs a roll sheet indicating eligibility to vote and pledging to support the party's candidates. By signing the roll sheet, the voter makes a declaration of party affiliation prior to voting. However, because the voter declares a party affiliation only a few moments prior to voting in the primary, the primary is closed only in the narrowest sense of the term. These declarations in no way bind a voter to support the party's candidates in future elections. Many other states have true closed primaries in that only registered party members can vote in these elections. Each state decides how it will run primary elections.

open primary a primary election in which any registered voter can participate in the contest, regardless of party affiliation

closed primary a primary election in which only registered members of a particular political party can vote

General Election

general election the election in which voters cast ballots to select public officials

The **general election** is held the first Tuesday following the first Monday in November of even-numbered years. The Democratic Party's nominee runs against the nominee of the Republican Party. It is possible that independent and minor-party candidates will also appear on the general election ballot.

Major state officials (governor, lieutenant governor, comptroller of public accounts, attorney general, and so on) are elected in nonpresidential election years. This arrangement seeks to prevent popular presidential candidates from influencing the outcomes of Texas races. For example, it is possible that a popular Republican presidential candidate might draw more than the usual number of Republican votes, and an unusually large Republican presidential vote might swing the election for statewide candidates running under the Republican banner. Likewise, it prevents an uncommonly popular statewide candidate from influencing the presidential election. If statewide elections were held in presidential election years, a Democratic candidate for governor, for example, might influence Texas's presidential voting by increasing the number of votes for Democratic candidates in general.

General elections are held in November to select national and state officeholders. Members of city councils, school boards, and other local government entities are also selected by general elections; however, these elections usually take place outside the traditional early November time period. In many cases, this means very low voter turnout. For example, in the San Antonio municipal elections in June 2015, there was a low turnout of only 14.12 percent of the city's registered voters. Leaders in some parts of the state have proposed moving municipal elections to November in the future to encourage a larger proportion of voters to participate. In Houston's mayoral race in November 2015, the turnout was much higher at 27.5 percent of the city's registered voters due to an open mayoral race and a controversial ordinance on the ballot that drove voters to the polls.

Some blame the relatively low voter turnout for Texas elections on the frequency of elections and the large number of candidates. Also, state officials are not elected in presidential election years, when voter participation tends to be highest.

Special Elections

In Texas, **special elections** are used to fill vacancies in office, to give approval to borrow money, or to ratify or reject amendments to the Texas Constitution. The dates for special elections are specified by the Texas legislature. If a Texas state senator resigns, for example, the governor will call a special election to fill the vacancy.

Texas laws require voter approval before any governmental agency in Texas can borrow money and assume long-term debt. If the local school district wants to borrow money to build a new high school and repair three elementary schools, a special election must be held. During the election, voters decide whether they will allow the school board to borrow the money.

The legislature proposes amendments to the Texas Constitution, and the voters in a special election ratify them.

special election an election that is not held on a regularly scheduled basis; in Texas, a special election is called to fill a vacancy in office, to give approval for the state government to borrow money, or to ratify amendments to the Texas Constitution

Running as an Independent

It is unusual for a candidate to run for office in Texas as an independent. One reason is that there are substantial requirements for getting one's name on the ballot. Additionally, an independent candidate lacks the political support of party organizations and the advantage of having a party label on the ballot. In 2006, Texas had two independent candidates for governor: Kinky Friedman and former Austin mayor Carole Keeton Strayhorn, the state comptroller, who had been elected to that office as a Republican.

Both candidates were obviously hoping that an independent candidacy would attract the votes of Democrats who believed that a Democratic candidate for governor could not win in Texas. They also were hoping to get substantial votes from Republicans disaffected with the policies and performance of the Republican governor, Rick Perry. Strayhorn, in particular, seemed to have strong appeal to Democrats who usually contributed large sums to Democratic nominees. One study of Strayhorn's contributions from July through December of 2005, for example, found that 52 percent of her campaign funds were from people who had given exclusively or almost exclusively to Democrats over the previous five years.[1]

Each state decides its own requirements for getting on the ballot. Some states make it easier for independents to get on the ballot, but the process in Texas is relatively difficult. For Friedman and Strayhorn to get on the ballot, for example, they had to meet the following requirements:

1. The candidates must obtain signatures on a petition from registered voters. The signatures must equal 1 percent of the total votes in the last governor's race. This meant that Friedman and Strayhorn each had to obtain 45,540 signatures.
2. The signatures must come from registered voters who did not participate in any political party primary election.
3. Signature collection cannot begin until the day after the last primary election. In 2006 this was March 8.
4. Voters may sign only one candidate's petition. If they sign both, only the first signature provided will count.[2]

The two major political parties don't agree on much, but they do agree on keeping third-party competitors out. Making it difficult for independents to get their names on the ballot helps ensure that the two major political parties will continue to dominate politics in the state well into the future. Elections may be open in Texas, but they work through the dominant political parties, helping to solidify their control over the political process and the major political offices in the state. The electoral performances of Friedman and Strayhorn also point to the difficulties of independent candidacy in that both of these candidates received only a small fraction of the overall vote.

Participation in Texas Elections

 Explain how the rules for voting affect turnout among different groups of Texans

When we think of political participation, we often think of voting. This is the most basic and fundamental duty citizens have in a democracy. Other forms of political participation include signing petitions, protesting, and writing letters to the newspaper and elected officials, some of which we will discuss in this chapter and others we will discuss in later chapters. Here, we begin by examining the history of voting in the state and the regulations and procedures surrounding voting rights. Issues include who can vote, how easy it is to register to vote, and why so few Texans vote.

The Rules: Who Can Vote?

"The franchise" refers to the act of voting or the right to vote. For much of the period of one-party Democratic control that began in the late nineteenth century, there were restrictions on the franchise.

Early Restrictions on the Franchise Women were allowed to vote in primaries and party conventions in Texas in 1918 and obtained the right to vote in all elections as a result of the **Nineteenth Amendment** to the U.S. Constitution in 1920. However, some of the most influential politicians in the state were opposed to the franchise for women. Joseph Weldon Bailey, for example, who had been Democratic leader in the U.S. House of Representatives and later the informal Democratic leader in the U.S. Senate, was an eloquent opponent of women's **suffrage**, arguing that women could not vote because they could not perform the three basic duties of citizenship: jury service, *posse comitatus* service (citizens who are deputized to deal with an emergency), and military service. He believed that women's morals dictated their beliefs and women would force their beliefs on men. The result, he felt, would be prohibition of alcohol.[3] Tinie Wells, the wife of Jim Wells, perhaps the most influential south Texas political leader of his day, was also an important and influential spokesperson for the anti–women's suffrage movement.[4] Governor "Farmer Jim" Ferguson was another opponent of women's suffrage, but when he was impeached, his successor, William P. Hobby, proved a key supporter of women's right to vote. It was Governor Hobby who called the legislature into special session in 1919 to consider the Nineteenth Amendment. Thus Texas became the ninth state and the first state in the South to ratify the women's suffrage amendment.[5]

> **Nineteenth Amendment** ratified in 1919, amendment guaranteeing women the right to vote
>
> **suffrage** the right to vote

Minorities had an even tougher time gaining access to the ballot in Texas. In the early part of the twentieth century, powerful political bosses had economic power and personal influence over Latino voters. They used this power to support national politicians such as John Nance Garner. Garner represented a huge part of south Texas, which stretched from Laredo to Corpus Christi and then north almost to San Antonio. A lifelong Democrat, he began his service in the House of Representatives in 1903 and served until 1933. From 1931 to 1933, he was Speaker of the U.S. House of Representatives, and from 1933 to 1941, he was vice president of the United States. He is most famous for his quip that the vice presidency was not worth more than a bucket of warm spit. Garner was the first Speaker from Texas and the first vice president from Texas. His south Texas political base was secured by votes that were controlled by the south Texas political bosses.[6]

One restriction on voting that affected poor people in general during this era was the **poll tax**. Enacted in 1902, it required voters to pay a tax, presumably to cover the costs of elections by the end of January in an election that took place in early November. That tax was usually between $1.50 and $1.75. It was a small sum, but it had to be paid in advance of the election, and in the first third of the century the tax could be one, two, or even more days' wages for a farm worker. Thus, it tended to disenfranchise poorer people.

> **poll tax** a state-imposed tax on voters as a prerequisite for voting; poll taxes were rendered unconstitutional in national elections by the Twenty-Fourth Amendment, and in state elections by the Supreme Court in 1966

The south Texas political bosses used the poll tax to great advantage. They would purchase large numbers of poll tax receipts and provide those receipts to their supporters, who often depended on the bosses for jobs and other economic, legal, and political assistance and who therefore would vote as the bosses wanted.

Although the poll tax was made illegal in federal elections in 1964 by the passage of the Twenty-Fourth Amendment to the U.S. Constitution, it remained legal in state elections in Texas until 1966, when it was held unconstitutional.[7] After the elimination of the poll tax, Texas continued to require **early registration** for voting—registration more than nine months before the general election. Early registration was required on a yearly basis. This requirement effectively prevented migrant workers

> **early registration** the requirement that a voter register long before the general election; in effect in Texas until 1971

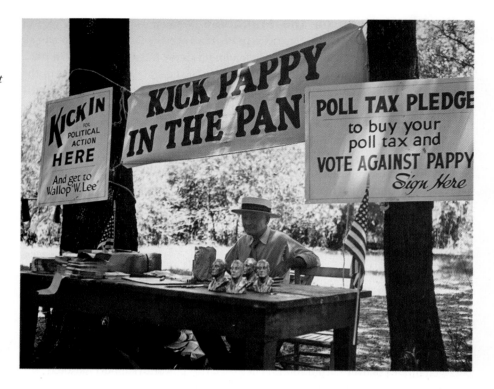

Participation in elections in Texas is low relative to that in other states. In the past, there were restrictions on the franchise. One such restriction that discouraged poor people from voting was the poll tax, which remained legal in Texas until 1966. Here, voters are asked to pay the poll tax and then vote against Pappy O'Daniel.

from voting. These provisions lasted until 1971, when they were voided by the federal courts.[8] Texas even prohibited anyone who was not a property owner from voting in revenue bond and tax elections until the practice was stopped by federal courts in 1975.[9] Texas also required an unusually long period of residency. Until 1970 voters had to have lived in the state for at least one year and to have lived in the county for at least six months prior to voting. This was another restriction on the franchise that was struck down by the federal courts.[10]

white primary primary election in which only white voters are eligible to participate

The most oppressive restriction on the franchise, however, was designed to minimize the political strength of African American voters. It was the **white primary**. This practice came under scrutiny by federal courts numerous times in the 21 years between 1923 and 1944; yet each time, the Texas legislature and state parties found a way to maintain the white primary and exclude black voters. In 1923 the Texas legislature flatly prohibited African Americans from voting in the Democratic primary. Since Texas was a one-party state at this time the effect, of course, was to prevent African Americans from participating in the only "real" election contests. Texas was able to do this because of a 1921 U.S. Supreme Court decision, *Newberry v. United States*, which dealt with a federal campaign-expenditures law. In interpreting the law, the Court stated that the primary election was "in no real sense part of the manner of holding the election."[11] This cleared the way for southern states, including Texas, to discriminate against African Americans in the primaries.

In 1927, however, the Supreme Court struck down the Texas white primary law, claiming that the legal ban on black participation was a violation of the equal protection clause of the Constitution.[12] In response, the Texas legislature passed another law that authorized the political parties, through their state executive committees, to determine the qualifications for voting in the primaries. That law, of course, allowed

They have appealed the 2015 ruling to the full Appellate Court. Since other states have similar legal challenges, the Supreme Court might ultimately decide on the constitutionality of voter ID laws. After a court order in August 2016, Texas agreed to weaken its voter ID law so that more forms of ID would be accepted at the vote (see Chapter 3). The "You Decide" section takes a closer look at this issue.

Qualifications to Vote Today

Meeting the qualifications to register to vote in Texas is relatively easy today. A voter must be

1. eighteen years of age.
2. a U.S. citizen.
3. a resident of Texas for 30 days.
4. a resident of the county for 30 days.

To be eligible to vote, one must be a registered voter for 30 days preceding the election and a resident of the voting precinct on the day of the election. Two groups of citizens cannot vote even if they meet all the preceding qualifications: felons who have not completed their sentences and those judged by a court to be mentally incompetent.

According to the Texas secretary of state, 73.8 percent of the state's voting age-population (14.2 million citizens) was registered to vote in 2016.[19] The **motor voter law**,[20] which allows individuals to register to vote when applying for or renewing driver's licenses, is one factor in increased registration. Public schools distribute voter registration cards as students turn 18. Cooperative efforts between the secretary of state's office and corporations also increase the number of registered voters. Most colleges and universities also have registration drives to encourage young people to register to vote.

Following the November 2014 election, a Census Bureau survey found that registration rates among citizens varied across racial and ethnic lines. Latino eligible voters registered at a 46.2 percent rate, well below that of blacks (60.7 percent) and whites (59.3 percent).[21]

motor voter law a national act, passed in 1993, that requires states to allow people to register to vote when applying for a driver's license

Early Voting

Early voting is a procedure that increases the polling period from 12 hours on Election Day to an additional two weeks prior to the election. The legislature has allowed early voting in an effort to increase participation. It is designed for those who have trouble getting to the polls between 7 A.M. and 7 P.M. on Election Day. For most elections, early voting commences on the 17th day before the elections and ends four days prior to Election Day.

Voting early is basically the same as voting on Election Day. An individual appears at one of the designated polling places, presents appropriate identification, and receives and casts a ballot. Early voting has at best only modestly increased voting participation.

Predictions that Democrats would benefit from early voting did not hold true after Texas moved strongly into the Republican column. Republican candidates for the highest office on the ballot get a much larger proportion of early votes than do the Democratic candidates. In 2016, for example, 53 percent of the early votes for president in Texas were cast for Donald Trump, compared with 43 percent of the early votes for Hillary Clinton. In 7 of the 10 elections examined, however, Republicans got a slightly smaller proportion of overall votes (votes cast in early voting plus Election Day voting) than early votes. And in 6 of the 10 elections, Democrats got a slightly

early voting a procedure that allows voters to cast ballots during the two-week period before the regularly scheduled election date

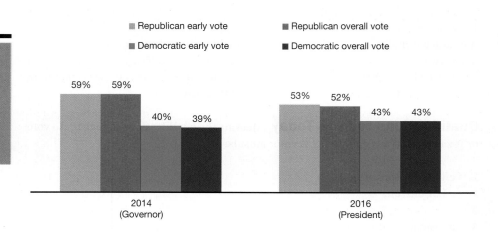

FIGURE 5.1

Early Voting and Overall Voting by Party in Texas

SOURCE: Texas Secretary of State.

■ Republican early vote   ■ Republican overall vote
■ Democratic early vote   ■ Democratic overall vote

2014 (Governor): 59%, 59%, 40%, 39%

2016 (President): 53%, 52%, 43%, 43%

larger proportion of overall votes than early votes. This suggests that early voting has been a bit more beneficial to Republicans than to Democrats, although the advantage has been very slight (Figure 5.1).

Contemporary Barriers to Voting

While the days of poll taxes are over, there are still barriers to voting in contemporary Texas. For example, in many cities, council members are elected at large, meaning that there are no individual districts for the city. Consider a city that has 10 city council seats and is 20 percent African American, 25 percent Latino, and 55 percent white. In at-large races, the white majority could theoretically capture all of the city's 10 council seats. If the city had a single-member district system, there would be a distinct possibility that at least 4 of the seats would be held by minorities. Austin had an at-large system of electing city council members but changed its system in 2014 in order to provide for better geographic and racial representation.

Other tactics for preventing certain groups from voting include reducing the number of polling places in certain areas, the presence of broken voting machines, misleading information provided to voters, and voter intimidation. While such practices are becoming less frequent, there are still reports of them in every contested election.

Redistricting: Where Do People Vote?

reapportionment process that takes place every 10 years to determine how many congressional seats each state will receive, depending on population shifts

redistricting the process of redrawing election districts and redistributing legislative representatives in the Texas House, Texas Senate, and U.S. House; this process usually happens every 10 years to reflect shifts in population or in response to legal challenges in existing districts

Every 10 years, the U.S. Census is charged with counting how many people live in the United States. The process of **reapportionment** involves recalculating how many congressional districts each state will receive based on the state's population. For example, Texas gained four new congressional seats following the 2010 Census because of the explosive population growth of the state. Since the House of Representatives is capped at 435 members, other states had to lose some of their congressional seats. States such as New York lost congressional seats because their populations had increased more slowly during the previous 10 years. The state legislature is tasked with drawing new congressional districts at least every 10 years to comply with the new overall number of seats allowed.

In 2011 the Texas legislature drew new congressional districts (Figure 5.2A), a process called **redistricting**. This is a blatantly political procedure because the majority party uses it to retain power by creating as many friendly districts as it can.

Voter Identification Laws

In 2011 the Texas legislature passed a law that requires all voters to produce photo identification when they present themselves to vote in an election. Prior to the law, Texans could present a voter registration certificate, which does not carry a photograph. Under the new law, not all forms of photo identification are considered valid for voting purposes. For example, state-issued concealed weapons permits are allowed, but student identification cards are not. A voter who shows up to the polls without appropriate photo identification may cast a provisional ballot, but must return to the registrar's office with photo identification within six days to make his or her vote count.

Supporters of the law argue that requiring photo identification is necessary to ensure the integrity of the election system and assure Texans that their elections are free from fraud. They claim that fraud is often undetected and difficult to prosecute, so the absence of high rates of voter fraud prosecution does not mean that it is a problem that should be ignored. Supporters believe that having the potential of penalties for breaking the law will deter any attempts to commit fraud. Former governor Rick Perry noted that the law "makes sense" since one needs to show photo identification to board airplanes, conduct official business, and perform transactions with banks and other organizations.[a] Those in favor of the law also point to public opinion polls showing that the majority of Texans support the simple proposition that you must show photo identification to prove who you are in order to vote.

Opponents of the law claim that the measure is not really about preserving the integrity of the electoral system but is meant to minimize Democratic turnout in order to help the state Republican Party keep its hold on power. Those who oppose the law claim that it puts an undue burden on populations who are less likely to possess photo identification (and who often vote for Democrats), such as elderly, disabled, minority, and poor voters, by making them go through additional steps to vote. Lubbock county commissioner Gilbert Flores noted that the bill's goal is to "weaken and deter the Hispanic vote."[b]

The law does provide for free photo identification, but in some rural areas, opponents argue, the nearest Department of Public Safety office is far away and not easily accessible. In addition, opponents suggest that the law is in essence a solution in search of a problem, pointing to studies that show there is no real problem concerning voter fraud in Texas.

The question remains whether voter identification laws are on balance positive or negative. There are legitimate arguments for and against the legislation, but one thing is clear: Republicans strongly support the measure and Democrats have attempted to stop the measure. This fact alone suggests that Republicans believe they will

electorally benefit from the law, while Democrats believe they will be harmed. In Wisconsin and North Carolina, federal judges agreed with challengers to these states' voter ID laws and declared them unconstitutional because of social science evidence suggesting that minorities were adversely affected by the new requirements. However, backers of the Texas law point to data showing that turnout in the November 2013 election was nearly double that of previous elections without the voter ID requirement, including in heavily Hispanic counties. This suggests, they argue, that the law did not adversely affect minority turnout. As of the November 2016 election, the Texas voter identification law has been somewhat softened by a federal court. Voters who did not have an authorized identification were allowed to vote, but they had to sign an affidavit indicating a reasonable impediment to obtaining an approved identification card. It is possible that a higher court will revisit Texas's voter identification law in future cases. Should voter IDs be required for voting in Texas elections? You decide.

COMMUNICATING EFFECTIVELY: YOUR VOICE

- Do the arguments for the voter identification legislation outweigh the arguments against it?

- Do you think a student ID should be accepted for voting? Write a brief letter to the editor of your school or local paper arguing your position.

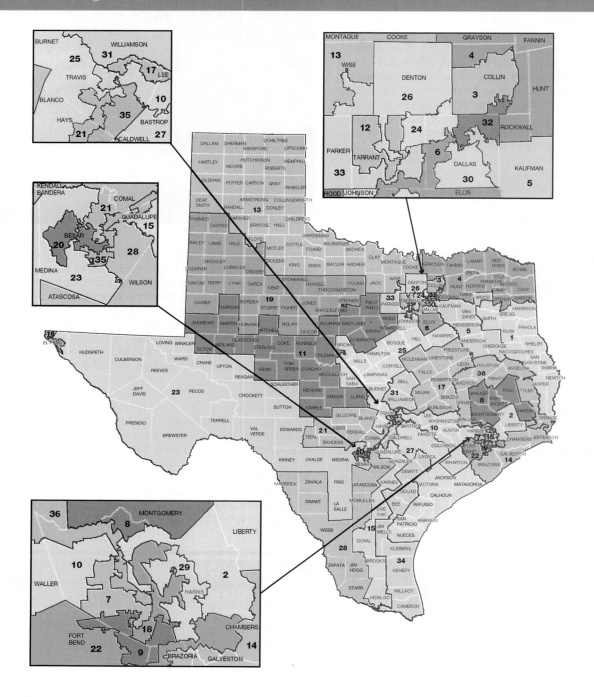

FIGURE 5.2A

Texas U.S. Congressional District Maps: Legislature Plan

The district map drawn by the Republican majority in the Texas legislature in 2011 was designed to help Republicans win as many U.S. House seats as possible. However, Latino leaders complained that the plan didn't create more Latino-majority districts.

SOURCE: Texas Legislative Council.

FIGURE 5.2B

Texas U.S. Congressional District Maps: Court Plan

By comparing the court-approved plan above with the Republican legislature's plan at left, we can see district lines were changed to comply with the Voting Rights Act. Note significant differences in the urban areas as well as in east Texas.

SOURCE: Texas Legislative Council.

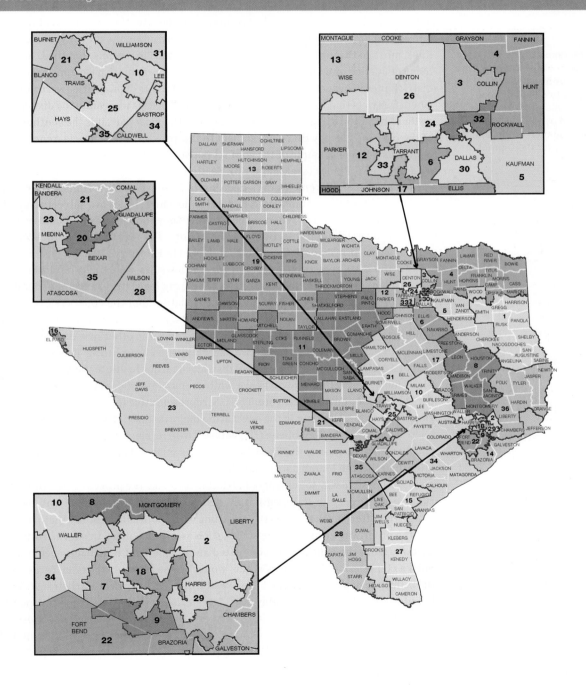

The Republicans in charge of the legislature attempted to draw as many Republican-voting districts as possible. If Democrats had been in control, they would have tried to maximize their number of seats as well. Because more than 67 percent of the population growth in Texas was a result of Latino immigration and birth rates among native-born Latinos and foreign-born Latinos, Latino leaders in the state wanted at least two of the new seats to be majority Latino. Most Latino-majority districts in the state tend not to elect Republicans, which put the Republican-led legislature in a bind.

Until a 2013 U.S. Supreme Court decision, the terms by which Texas must comply with the Voting Rights Act further complicated the situation. Section 5 of the act required that any changes to election procedures, including the drawing of new district lines, must go through the process of **preclearance**. This means that the U.S. Department of Justice or a District of Columbia federal court must have approved the new district lines in order to make sure that the voting rights of minorities were not diminished. Districts that have been created to help minorities win cannot be dismantled in order to benefit a particular political party. For the most part, it is the southern states of the old Confederacy that were subject to this provision. The preclearance requirement was but one example of the conflict between Texas and the federal government on a number of issues (see Chapter 3). Section 5 is no longer applicable to Texas because of the U.S. Supreme Court's decision in *Shelby County v. Holder,* in which the Court ruled that the formula used to determine which states are subject to preclearance is unconstitutional. When asked whether they thought Texas should be subject to federal oversight of its elections, 41 percent of respondents said yes and 47 percent responded no in a *Texas Tribune* poll conducted in February 2013.[22]

In the 2011 redistricting round, several lawsuits were filed by different parties challenging the districts created by the Texas legislature, and the federal court stepped in (Figure 5.2B). Ultimately, the legislature and the court created one new congressional district with a majority Latino population that stretched from Bexar County to Travis County along Interstate 35. The three other new districts were designed to elect Republicans. This was accomplished by splitting Travis County, the seat of Austin, into five congressional districts in order to dilute the Democratic vote. Since most Travis County voters are white Democrats, there are no protections under the law for diluting their vote. The U.S. representative for Austin, Democrat Lloyd Doggett, was forced to run in the new Latino majority district, since the other four districts were majority Republican (Doggett still won re-election). Because of the federal court's lengthy process, the Texas primary was pushed back to May 29, 2012, much later than the late March date originally scheduled.

One possible way to reform redistricting is to take the process away from the legislature. In Texas, the state legislature decides how the district lines will be drawn, and critics often say that this is the only time when politicians choose their voters and not the other way around. Some states, such as Arizona, have taken the responsibility away from the legislature and created an independent redistricting commission. Such a commission, supporters argue, would create fairer districts in Texas without the influence of politicians who have a vested interest in protecting their seats and political parties. According to a May 2011 *Texas Tribune* poll, 40 percent of respondents voiced support in principle for such a system, while 30 percent were opposed, and 30 percent were unsure of the plan.[23] Changing the system of redistricting will be challenging because legislators of both parties greatly benefit from the ability to influence how district lines are drawn.

preclearance provision under Section 5 of the Voting Rights Act of 1965 requiring any changes to election procedures or district lines to be approved by the U.S. Department of Justice or the U.S. District Court for the District of Columbia

In the court case *Evenwel v. Abbott* (2015), plaintiffs sued the State of Texas claiming that using total number of residents to create state legislative districts violated the principle of one person, one vote and the equal protection clause of the Fourteenth Amendment. Plaintiffs argued that the state should use registered or eligible voters to draw legislative districts. Voters living in districts with high numbers of undocumented immigrants, children, and/or prisoners claimed that their votes were diluted compared to those of voters living in other districts. The Supreme Court ruled that states were justified in using total population rather than voting eligible population in drawing legislative districts.

Turnout: Who Votes?

In most elections, fewer than 50 percent of U.S. citizens vote.[24] Even fewer Texans exercise their right to vote, especially young people. Texas ranks last in the nation in voter participation. Figure 5.3 provides data on the abysmal turnout of registered voters in the various types of recent Texas elections. Considering the ease of registration and the ability to vote early, voter participation should be higher. Why do so few Texans vote?

A more detailed analysis reveals several factors that may contribute to low participation rates:

1. low levels of educational attainment
2. low per capita income
3. high rate of poverty
4. location in the South
5. young population
6. traditionalistic and individualistic political culture
7. candidate-centered elections and little party competition
8. lack of media attention to substantive political issues
9. large numbers of undocumented residents and felons

FIGURE 5.3

Turnout by Registered Voters in Texas Elections

SOURCE: Texas Secretary of State Division of Elections.

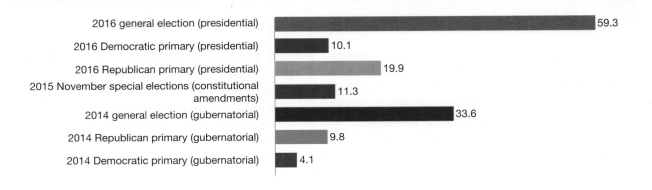

Election	Turnout
2016 general election (presidential)	59.3
2016 Democratic primary (presidential)	10.1
2016 Republican primary (presidential)	19.9
2015 November special elections (constitutional amendments)	11.3
2014 general election (gubernatorial)	33.6
2014 Republican primary (gubernatorial)	9.8
2014 Democratic primary (gubernatorial)	4.1

In 2016 only 59.3 percent of registered voters cast ballots in the Texas presidential election.

Education and income appear to be the two most important factors in determining whether someone votes, and this is often referred to as socio-economic status (SES). In Texas, low levels of education and high levels of poverty are both the strongest predictors of low voter participation. While college students and other young adults were mobilized by President Obama's election in 2008 and 2012, the fact remains that voter turnout among this demographic is low. In addition, the average age of Texans is less than the national average, and young people vote in smaller numbers; this may also contribute to Texas's low turnout rate.

In the southern states that composed the Confederacy, individuals participate in smaller numbers than in other parts of the United States. Texas was part of the Confederacy, and its level of participation is consistent with lower levels of voting in the South. That said, Texas differs from most other southern states with its large Latino population, many of whom, perhaps up to 2.0 million, are not eligible to vote because either they are not registered or they are undocumented residents in the state. As the children born and educated in America of these residents reach voting age, it is likely that registration rates and voting rates among Latinos will increase. For now, however, they remain lower than those for whites or blacks.

There are several possible explanations for low voter participation in Texas. In keeping with the Texas tradition of decentralized government, there are so many elections in Texas and so many candidates for office that voters are simply overloaded with elections and candidates. Note that as shown in Figure 5.3 (and discussed in Chapter 2), voter participation was much higher in the general election than in the special constitutional election. If there were fewer elections, the ballot might be longer, but voter turnout would likely be higher, because more voters would be attracted to at least some races or issues on the ballot. Additionally, the practice of having elections in nonpresidential election years decreases voter turnout because the highest voter participation tends to occur for presidential elections. A third problem is that most elections in Texas involve very low-visibility offices. Voters likely know little about the candidates for these positions or the offices themselves, and such a lack of knowledge would naturally discourage voter participation. Efforts have been made in a number of states, most notably Washington, to increase voter knowledge by having the state provide biographical information about the candidates to voters, but Texas makes little effort to enhance voter knowledge of candidates. Independent groups such as the League of Women Voters often provide voter guides, but only readers of newspapers or those who actively seek these voter guides benefit from this information. Finally, some suggest that the new voter identification law will reduce voter turnout even more.

Racial and Ethnic Variations in Voting and Participation

While Texas is a state with a larger percentage of minorities than non-Hispanic whites, this does not mean that the majority of the state's voters are minorities. For example, in the November 2014 elections, Latinos comprised only about 17 percent of the Texas electorate.[25] As a result of a variety of factors, including

PERSONAL RESPONSIBILITY: WHAT WOULD YOU DO?

- Voter participation in Texas is among the lowest in the nation. What accounts for the state's low levels of participation? Do you think things would be better if voter turnout was higher?

- What can you do to increase voter participation in the short term? In the long term?

Who Votes in Texas Statewide Elections?

Voter Turnout by Race, 2014

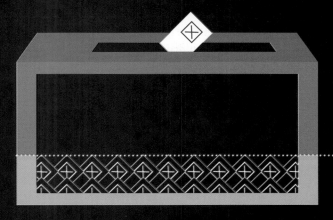

Texas is now a majority-minority state. This means that the nonwhite population exceeds the white population. However, this does not mean that the majority of the state's voters are nonwhite. It is still the case that the Latino population is underrepresented compared with their population on the state's voter rolls.

Texas totals

Citizen voting-age population
16,844,000

Total voter turnout*
34.6%

White voter turnout
● 10% voter turnout

Citizen voting-age population 13,693,000
35.2%

Latino voter turnout

Citizen voting-age population 4,878,000
22.4%

African American voter turnout

Citizen voting-age population 2,198,000
35.3%

Asian American voter turnout

Citizen voting-age population 565,000
18.0%

* % of citizen voting-age population who voted in 2014.

NOTE: Totals for citizen voting-age population sum to more than the Texas population because some voters are counted as both white and Latino.

SOURCES: Noncitizen data from U.S. Census Bureau, Current Population Survey. Racial group data from American Community Survey, U.S. Census Bureau. Turnout data from U.S. Census Bureau.

QUANTITATIVE REASONING

- Some argue that minorities do not turn out to vote in Texas elections. Based on the data provided, is this true? How might you respond to such a statement?

- Based on the voter turnout data in the graph, what can you conclude about racial and ethnic differences in voter turnout?

the large undocumented population consisting of mostly Latinos from Mexico and Latin America and the lower rate of voter turnout for Latino citizens, non-Hispanic whites wield considerable influence in the state electorate.

Because most African Americans and Latinos tend to vote for Democrats and non-Hispanic whites tend to vote for Republicans, the balance of power in most state elections currently tilts toward Republicans. Democrats hope that as more Latinos become citizens, they will register and turn out to vote, but these hopes have yet to fully materialize.

The Importance of the Republican Primary

Table 5.1 shows how important the Republican primary has become in statewide elections. That is because the winner of the Republican primary, in this era of Republican dominance in the state, will be the winner of a statewide election. For example,

TABLE 5.1

Percentage of Registered Voters and Voting-Age Population Voting in the Republican Primaries

YEAR	REGISTERED VOTERS	PERCENTAGE OF REGISTERED VOTERS VOTING IN REPUBLICAN PRIMARIES	PERCENTAGE OF VOTING-AGE POPULATION VOTING IN REPUBLICAN PRIMARIES
2016	14,238,436	19.89%	14.80%
2014	13,601,324	9.98	7.18
2012	13,065,425	11.09	7.93
2010	13,023,358	11.40	8.00
2008	12,752,417	10.68	7.68
2006	12,722,671	5.15	3.94
2004	12,264,663	5.60	4.27
2002	12,218,164	5.09	4.01
2000	11,612,761	9.70	7.78
1998	11,159,845	5.35	4.24
1996	9,698,506	10.52	7.44
1994	9,041,906	6.16	4.26

How Did Texans Vote in 2016?

Race	Pop.%	= Clinton	= Trump	Clinton	Trump

National

Race	Pop.%	Clinton	Trump
White	61.1%	37%	58%
Black	13.3%	88%	8%
Latino	17.6%	65%	29%
Asian	5.6%	65%	29%
Other	4.0%	56%	37%

Texas

Race	Pop.%	Clinton	Trump
White	43.0%	26%	69%
Black	12.5%	85%	11%
Latino	38.8%	61%	34%
Asian	4.7%	73%	27%
Other			

Note: Data on other groups were not available from Texas exit polls.

California

Race	Pop.%	Clinton	Trump
White	38.0%	50%	45%
Black	6.5%	88%	9%
Latino	38.8%	71%	24%
Asian	14.7%	73%	17%
Other			

Note: Data on other groups were not available from California exit polls.

As expected, Republican presidential candidate Donald J. Trump carried Texas on Election Day and won the state's 38 electoral votes. However, Democratic presidential candidate Hillary Clinton outperformed Barack Obama, as the margin of victory was much closer in 2016 than in either 2008 or 2012. Racial divisions persisted between the parties, with Clinton winning large majorities of African American, Latino, and Asian voters.

SOURCE: 2016 CNN exit poll data.

CRITICAL THINKING

- Looking at the data, how does the national vote compare to California and Texas?

- Why do you think Latinos were more supportive of Trump in Texas than they were nationally?

11.09 percent of registered voters and only 7.93 percent of the voting-age population in Texas voted in the Republican primary in 2012, but the winner of that primary has since the 1990s become the victor in statewide elections. Of course, many of the Republican primaries for statewide offices are contested, and to be successful in winning office all that is needed is a majority of the vote in the primary. In the 2012 elections, theoretically a person could win statewide office with the votes of less than 5.546 percent of the registered voters in the state, assuming those voters cast ballots in the Republican primary.

Campaigns

Present the main features of election campaigns in Texas

Political campaigns are efforts of candidates to win support of the voters. The goal of the campaign is to attain sufficient support to win the primary election in March and the general election in November. Some campaigns last a year or more; however, the more accepted practice is to limit the campaign to a few months before the election.

Candidates: Who Runs?

Candidates from all walks of life run for office in Texas. Business people, lawyers, stay-at-home mothers, teachers, retirees, and more have all run for office in Texas. As the prestige of the office increases, candidates tend to have more political experience. Career paths for Texan officeholders usually begin with a run for a local office such as school board or city council. Many then decide to run for state representative, then state senator. Candidates for U.S. Congress usually have had prior political experience. For example, U.S. representative Randy Weber (R-Friendswood) previously served as a state representative.

Incumbents have the advantage in most races. Since there are no term limits in the Texas legislature, some members have served for many years. For example, Representative Tom Craddick (R-Midland) will have served in the legislature for 48 years once his term ends in 2017. Challengers to incumbents often fail to win, and many wait until a retirement in order to run for a seat.

Money

Campaigns involve attempts to reach the voters through print and electronic media, the mail, door-to-door campaigning, speeches to large and small groups, coffee hours, and telephone solicitation. Costs are enormous.

In the 2014 gubernatorial race, Greg Abbott spent $47 million to Wendy Davis's $36 million. For all statewide offices, Republican campaign contributions over-

TABLE 5.2

Money Raised by All Candidates in Texas, 2014*

OFFICE	DEMOCRATIC ($)	REPUBLICAN ($)	THIRD-PARTY ($)
Governor	$12,297,956	$82,539,241	$83,152
Judicial	8,355,127	15,347,602	3
Other statewide	2,668,590	39,302,189	9,395
House	15,818,016	49,747,747	62,273
Senate	5,847,622	23,123,190	9,284

*Listed by political party.
SOURCE: Calculated from Institute on Money in State Politics.

whelmed Democratic campaign contributions. Total contributions in state house and state senate races were also far greater for Republicans than for Democrats. There is no question, then, that money is important for candidate success in Texas. Candidates must continually raise money by hosting fund-raisers with donors, making phone calls to potential donors, and setting up websites that make it easy for ordinary citizens to contribute (see Tables 5.2 and 5.3).

Candidates who run in Texas for federal office, such as the U.S. Congress, are subject to federal campaign finance laws, which are stricter than state laws and which impose limits for campaign contributions. (Recently, though, the federal laws have been greatly weakened by U.S. Supreme Court decisions that have held parts of the federal laws to restrict free speech.) Candidates for state offices are subject to state laws enacted in 1991 when the Texas Ethics Commission (TEC) was established. State candidates and lobbyists must file quarterly reports with the TEC, but with the exception of judicial campaigns there are no limits to campaign contributions for state races. The state imposes a moratorium on contributions to state legislators just prior to the beginning of a legislative session.

Payments for media ads account for the greatest expense in most campaigns. In metropolitan areas, television, radio, and print advertising are very costly. Full-page ads in metropolitan newspapers can cost as much as $40,000. Candidates for metropolitan districts in the Texas House of Representatives and Texas Senate need to reach only a small portion of the population, but they are forced to purchase ads in media sources that go to hundreds of thousands of people not represented. In rural areas, any individual ad is relatively inexpensive. However, candidates must advertise in dozens of small newspapers and radio stations, and the costs add up.

Outside Groups

Interest groups have become much more of a factor in state elections in Texas. For example, Empower Texans, a group backed by Michael Quinn Sullivan, spent millions of dollars in state legislative Republican primaries to oust backers of Speaker Joe Straus, whom they considered insufficiently conservative. While they were unable to unseat

TABLE 5.3

Campaign Contributions in Statewide Executive Offices: Texas General Elections 2014

OFFICE	CANDIDATE	DOLLARS CONTRIBUTED	PERCENTAGE OF VOTE
Governor	Greg Abbott (R)	$47,463,245	59.3%
	Wendy Davis (D)	4,034,095	38.9
Lieutenant governor	Dan Patrick (R)	18,278,278	58.1
	Leticia Van de Putte (D)	8,263,861	38.7
Agriculture commissioner	Sid Miller (R)	837,917	58.6
	Jim Hogan (D)	0	36.8
Attorney general	Ken Paxton (R)	8,337,345	58.8
	Sam Houston (D)	596,153	38.0
Comptroller	Glenn Hegar (R)	5,047,917	58.4
	Mike Collier (D)	1,561,942	38.7
Land commissioner	George P. Bush (R)	5,287,154	60.7
	John Cook (D)	77,246	35.3
Railroad commissioner	Ryan Sitton (R)	4,070,984	58.3
	Steve Brown (D)	73,789	36.5

Straus in the March 2016 primary, they were able to help oust some of Straus's lieutenants in the legislature, including state representative Debbie Riddle (R-Tomball).

Other outside groups have had important roles to play in shaping public policy in the state. For example, the Texas Association of Business and the Texas Public Policy Foundation have been very influential in advancing conservative legislation. These groups have helped sway Governor Abbott and other Republican officials to pass laws that expand school vouchers, lower taxes, and reduce regulation in the state economy. Because state legislators and other statewide officials are subject to limited campaign regulations, the growth of outside groups in Texas politics will no doubt continue.

Parties

In some places in the United States, the parties have a major role in the running of political campaigns. That is not the case in Texas. Here the candidates have the major responsibility for campaign strategy, for running their campaigns, and for raising money. At times, party leaders will try to recruit individuals to run for office, especially if no candidates volunteer to seek an office or if the candidates appear to be weak ones. For the most part, the benefit of the party to a candidate in Texas is that the party provides the party label under which the candidate runs. That "Democratic" or "Republican" label is, of course, important to candidates because many voters use the party label in casting their votes, especially for low-visibility races. The party also contains numerous activists whom the candidate can tap for campaign tasks such as manning phone banks, preparing mailings, and posting campaign ads. Additionally, the party does provide some support for the candidate, most commonly through campaigns to get out the vote for the party's candidates. Campaigning in Texas, however, is generally left up to the candidate, and in that effort, the parties take a secondary role.

Name recognition is essential for candidates, and parties can help build it. Incumbents hold a distinct advantage in name recognition. Officeholders have many ways to achieve name visibility. They can mail out news releases, send newsletters to their constituents, appear on radio talk shows, and give speeches to civic clubs. Newspaper coverage and local television news coverage of the politician can increase name recognition. Challengers have a more difficult time getting this crucial name visibility, although new media sources such as Facebook and Twitter accounts can help both incumbents and challengers gain name recognition, especially among young people.

The case of William R. Clements illustrates the importance of name recognition. In 1978, William R. Clements was a political unknown. He spent thousands of dollars of his own fortune to gain name recognition. He leased hundreds of billboards throughout the state. Each had a blue background with white letters proclaiming "CLEMENTS." In the print media, early ads bore the simple message, "ELECT CLEMENTS." The unprecedented scale of this advertising effort made Clements's name better known among the voters in Texas. This, in turn, stimulated interest in his campaign's message. Clements won the race for governor, becoming the first Republican to hold that office in Texas since the end of Reconstruction.

Strategy

Even more important, the campaigns must be well designed and well executed. A slipup in a well-funded campaign can do great harm, as Greg Abbott discovered in his campaign for governor. While Abbott has made efforts to appeal to the Latino vote, his campaign received criticism when in February 2014 he referred to law enforcement tactics in the border region as resembling "third world country practices that erode the social fabric of our communities." A journalist for the *Monitor*, a newspaper in the Rio Grande Valley, called on Abbott to apologize for his comments. Abbott refused to apologize, saying his comments were not directed at Latinos, but rather at the lack of border security in south Texas. Abbott sought to repair his relationship with Latino voters by emphasizing his Latina wife as the imminent first Latina first lady of Texas. While this slipup did not cost him the election (he received 44 percent of the Latino vote—a healthy number for a Republican candidate), it still raised larger questions about the state's Republican Party and its relationship with the growing Latino vote.[26]

Some impressive but limited evidence indicates that television can be a very valuable tool for a Texas political candidate. On four occasions in the 1990s Republican supreme court candidates were challenged in the primary by candidates with little, if any, organized support and minimal funding. Yet the insurgent candidates all showed great strength in areas where the established candidates did not run television ads. Of course, there may be additional explanations for the strength of established

Candidates for statewide office in Texas routinely spend hundreds of thousands, if not millions, of dollars on their campaigns. Though much money goes to television advertising, candidates also spend time meeting voters one-on-one, as Republican attorney general candidate Ken Paxton does here at Joe Allen's Pit Bar-B-Que in Abilene.

candidates in areas where ads were shown. Perhaps the candidates worked harder in those areas or were better organized. And in some areas, candidates may have had stronger name recognition than their opponents.[27]

None of the insurgent candidates had the resources to run television ads; only the established candidates did, and only in some media markets. It was the support the established candidates received in the areas where they ran television ads that led to their victories. It is important to note that since the data all relate to the Republican primary, the effect of the political party label is controlled. If we compare the percentage difference in votes for established candidates in areas where television ads were run with votes in areas where no ads were run, the difference is remarkable: established candidates received between 12 percent and 18.5 percent more votes in media markets where they bought television time.[28]

Given the myriad factors that may explain electoral success, we should beware of imputing victory in these judicial races solely to television ads. On the other hand, the general pattern of high margins of victory in areas where television was used is so powerful that the role of television advertising cannot be ignored.

Important Issues in Texas Campaigns

The open gubernatorial seat in 2014 pitted Greg Abbott against Wendy Davis. With the state's economic challenges of the mid-2000s largely in the rearview mirror, both candidates fought hard to distinguish themselves on issues. Davis had become prominent because of her filibuster of an antiabortion bill in 2011, but she wanted to expand her policy portfolio beyond this one issue. Abbott had distinguished himself as attorney general of Texas by challenging the Obama administration on a host of policy issues, including the Affordable Care Act, the Voting Rights Act, and gun rights.

Education policy became an important issue in the 2014 elections when Greg Abbott proposed expanding programs for pre-kindergarten. Wendy Davis had already proposed a plan that would increase funding for this program, but Abbott criticized Davis's plan for not including measures to monitor whether the programs were working. Davis countered by accusing Abbott of hypocrisy by defending cuts to pre-kindergarten programs in his capacity as the state's attorney general. The tenor of the education debate in 2014 is a far cry from the debates in 2010, when the debate revolved around mitigating drastic budget cuts to education in the face of a budget shortfall.

The gubernatorial campaign also highlighted issues that were not typical in previous races. Equal pay for equal work became a major issue in April 2014 when the *San Antonio Express-News* revealed that female assistant attorneys general in Abbott's office were paid approximately $6,000 less on average than their male counterparts. Abbott responded by asserting that the reason for the discrepancy was that the male employees were on average more experienced. Wendy Davis pressed Abbott on whether he would support her bill guaranteeing equal pay for equal work in Texas. Abbott claimed that he supported equal pay for equal work but not her bill because of his belief that a new law was not necessary. It did not help Abbott that his surrogates fumbled some of their explanations as to why Abbott opposed the legislation. For example, Abbott supporter and Red State Women PAC chair Cari Christman claimed women were "too busy" to think about equal pay for equal work and Texas GOP chair Beth Cubriel stated that the reason women are paid less than men is because men "are better negotiators."[29] These issues have no doubt become more prominent because of Wendy Davis's presence in the gubernatorial race as the first female Democratic Party candidate for governor since Ann Richards.

Gun rights continues to be a salient issue in Texas, especially regarding recent debates about whether firearms should be allowed on college campuses. Texas also has a concealed carry law allowing licensed individuals to carry concealed firearms throughout the state with some exceptions such as bars. As of January 1, 2016, Texas allows permit holders open carry of personal firearms in most public places, although individual businesses can choose whether to allow this. Even Democrats in Texas do not take positions at odds with the pro-gun sentiment in the state. Wendy Davis surprised many when she announced that she would back a bill allowing Texans to carry unconcealed pistols on their waists. Of course, Abbott also supports the legislation, but he criticized Davis for her support of allowing private individuals and businesses to block individuals from carrying pistols on their property. He also accused Davis of wanting to enact more restrictions on gun owners and compared her to former New York City mayor Michael Bloomberg, a strong gun control advocate. The National Rifle Association, the nation's leading pro-gun lobbying group, gave Abbott an A and Davis a D on their gun control policies.

Immigration policy also became a very salient issue in all of the statewide races. Republican candidates for all major elective offices pledged to enact strict border security measures and spend state resources on keeping illegal immigrants out of the state. This emphasis on immigration is a marked change from the 1990s when then-governor Bush appealed to the Latino vote in the state. For example, Republican candidate for agriculture commissioner Eric Opiela ran a television ad where he appeared on a farm next to a barbed wire fence announcing that illegal immigrants need to go to the back of the line and that there should be no amnesty for illegal immigrants. He lost the Republican primary with only 17 percent of the vote. More notorious, however, in his positions on immigration was lieutenant gubernatorial candidate Dan Patrick, who said in a debate that he wanted to stop the "invasion" of illegal immigrants to Texas. Patrick challenged Lieutenant Governor David Dewhurst from the right by arguing that Dewhurst was not sufficiently conservative on this issue. Land commissioner Jerry Patterson, another candidate for lieutenant governor, accused Patrick of hypocrisy by revealing that Patrick had knowingly hired an undocumented immigrant for his sports bar business back in the 1990s. Patrick denied that he knew the individual in question was in the country illegally, but it did not seem to hurt Patrick's candidacy, as he was easily elected lieutenant governor in 2014.

Tax policy also became a state issue, especially in the comptroller's race between Senator Glenn Hegar (R-Katy) and Mike Collier (D-Houston). Collier, a certified public accountant, ran campaign ads claiming that Hegar wanted to abolish the state property tax and increase sales taxes. Since Texas does not have a state income tax, property taxes are somewhat higher than in other states. The state relies on property taxes to fund public education and sales taxes for other state spending. Sales taxes in Texas usually average 8.25 percent on most items, with the exception of medicine and groceries. Increasing sales taxes often disproportionately affects lower-income Texans, since a higher percentage of their income is spent on purchasing goods and services. Hegar ran a campaign touting his conservative credentials and his desire for lower taxes in general, and was ultimately elected comptroller of public accounts in the November election.

Though the issues above seem to be important, in recent statewide elections the distinguishing feature of the campaigns has been the lack of emphasis on state issues. Instead, Republicans have run against President Obama, his administration, Hillary Clinton, and the national Democratic Party, all of which are very unpopular among Republican voters. A *Texas Tribune* survey conducted in February 2016 showed that 50 percent of Texans disapproved of Barack Obama's job as president. Likewise, Democratic candidates in Texas, in attempting to attract support from moderate Republican voters, tried to distance themselves from President Obama and his policies. Perhaps surprisingly, Hillary Clinton performed considerably better in the 2016 election in Texas than Obama did in 2012.

One of the more interesting developments in 2016 was the effort by Tea Party groups to mount challenges to establishment Republicans in the state legislature. The Speaker, Joe Straus (R–San Antonio), spent nearly $4 million to defend his seat in the legislature against a challenge by a Tea Party Republican. Even some Texan members of Congress, including U.S. representative Kevin Brady (R–The Woodlands), were challenged by a Tea Party–backed candidate even though Brady was recently elevated to the position of chair of the House Ways and Means Committee, the powerful tax-writing committee in Congress. Although Brady survived his challenge, other Texas Republicans are wary of not being perceived as sufficiently conservative for fear of attracting a Tea Party challenge. After the 2016 elections, Republicans lost five seats in the State House but retained a solid majority in the chamber.

Public Opinion Differences on Issues Public opinion on issues varies according to race and ethnicity. In a book titled *Divided by Color*, Donald Kinder and Lynn Sanders show that the views of African Americans and whites are remark-

Immigration is a major issue in Texas elections. Democrats and Republicans have called for reform, but their approaches differ strongly.

ably different on issues ranging from the death penalty to affirmative action.[30] For example, according to a November 2013 *Texas Tribune* survey, 76 percent of whites supported the death penalty, while 60 percent of African Americans supported the death penalty. Significantly more African Americans, however, believe that the death penalty is often implemented for innocent citizens. In the same survey, 31 percent of African Americans believed the death penalty was implemented for innocent citizens "a great deal of the time" compared with 9 percent of whites.[31] In most cases, African Americans are more liberal than whites on political issues.

One issue with remarkable convergence on public opinion between blacks and whites is same-sex marriage. In Texas, according to a June 2013 *Texas Tribune* survey, 33 percent of African Americans, 38 percent of whites, and 45 percent of Latinos supported same-sex marriage.[32] This is one reason why Texas is one of several states that were able to pass a state constitutional amendment defining marriage in the state as between one man and one woman. While the gulf in public opinion is more pronounced between African Americans and whites compared to Latinos and whites, even the latter two groups differ on attitudes about public policy, especially the role of government.

Consider the issue of immigration policy. Most Latinos surveyed in Texas support the DREAM Act, a policy that would allow undocumented students who serve in the military or graduate from college to become citizens. According to a February 2014 *Texas Tribune* poll, 54 percent of whites in Texas strongly oppose this policy, especially the version that allows college graduates to become citizens.[33] For conservatives, this amounts to an unacceptable form of amnesty for illegal immigrants. In contrast, a minority of Latinos (33 percent) strongly oppose the DREAM Act. Whites are also more likely than Latinos to support restrictive immigration policies, although African Americans are just as likely to support such immigration policies.

Regarding education policy, Latinos in Texas are more likely to support a greater role for government in public education. In general, Latinos view education as a more important policy issue than their white counterparts. This could be for several reasons. First, Latinos are generally poorer and less educated than the majority white population and correctly see educational attainment as a key to success. Second, many Latinos are immigrants who view education as the ticket to the American Dream. Finally, Latinos have the highest high school dropout rates, and this reality has important ramifications for social, political, and economic advancement.

One related issue area with a significant divide in opinion between whites and Latinos is bilingual education. Most Latinos in Texas support the use of bilingual education—instruction in English and Spanish until students can transition to full English instruction. On the other hand, most Anglos oppose this policy and support total immersion in English. A May 2010 *Texas Tribune* poll shows that 55 percent of white Texans strongly supported ending bilingual education, while only 22 percent of Latinos supported this position. Forty-four percent of Latinos strongly opposed ending bilingual education, while only 15 percent of whites strongly opposed ending bilingual education.[34] This policy, along with attitudes about an English Only law for Texas, is one of the most polarized by ethnicity in the state.

Media

Campaigns in Texas are covered mostly by local and statewide media. One of the more thorough statewide media outlets covering Texas politics is the *Texas Tribune* founded in 2009. Based out of Austin, the *Tribune* is a one-stop shop for all things Texas politics, including data, campaign news, legislature updates, and coverage of statewide issues.

Of course, the major large city newspapers, including the *Houston Chronicle*, the *Dallas Morning News*, the *San Antonio Express-News*, the *El Paso Times*, and the *Austin American Statesman* cover state politics and campaigns extensively, especially local races in their respective reader areas. (See Table 5.4.) More importantly, they endorse candidates in primaries and general elections. These endorsements often carry important weight especially in down ballot races for local offices such as school board or a city council, which do not attract significant attention from voters.

Television stations also play an important role in covering races by hosting programs and events aimed at informing the public. In Houston, Channel 2 KPRC hosts a weekly show called *Houston Newsmakers*. Hosted by Khambrell Marshall, this show often has political guests, hosts debates, and informs the public on local issues. Channel 13 KTRK in Houston hosts a public affairs show called *Viva Houston* aimed at the local Hispanic market and informing them of local political issues.

TABLE 5.4

Circulation of Texas's Top Five Daily Newspapers

Dallas Morning News	413,480
Houston Chronicle	370,961
Fort Worth Star-Telegram	173,833
San Antonio Express-News	146,463
Austin American Statesman	132,873

SOURCE: www.cision.com (accessed 4/11/16).

Local PBS stations in Houston, Dallas, and Austin also host programs, inviting guests to be informed of local campaigns and elections.

Candidates make efforts to advertise their campaigns through newspaper ads, meeting with newspaper editorial boards for endorsements, appearance on television shows, and any other means possible. Running a campaign can be expensive, and any opportunity for free airtime to increase name recognition can go a long way, especially in down ballot races. In 2014 the Center for Public Integrity published a report indicating that nearly $39 million was spent by candidates and other organizations on political ads in Texas, second only to Pennsylvania in terms of total dollars spent that year. Social media are transforming campaigns in Texas as they have transformed them across the nation. Many, if not most, Texas candidates for all offices use Facebook and Twitter to push campaign messages, attack or defend themselves from opponents, and stay in touch with supporters and donors.

Campaigns, Elections, and the Future of Texas

Elections in Texas are essential to the state's functioning democracy. Although Republicans have been winning statewide elections, the growing Latino population and increased diversification of the state may eventually change this. Wendy Davis had hoped to capitalize on the changing demographics of the state in her bid for governor in 2014 but could not overcome countervailing winds against her candidacy, including the state's entrenched conservatism and the national tilt in favor of Republicans.

Campaigns—especially statewide campaigns—are very expensive. For the most part, the candidates themselves must raise the money necessary to win an election. Gubernatorial campaigns can cost $40 million or more. One effect of the high cost of campaigns in Texas is that candidates are often wealthy individuals willing to use their own money in their campaigns. Wealthy individuals, however, will not always prevail at the ballot box. Consider former lieutenant governor David Dewhurst. His bruising loss to Senator Ted Cruz in the state Republican primary for a U.S. Senate seat in 2012 left him vulnerable in his bid for re-election as lieutenant governor. Insurgent senator Dan Patrick challenged Dewhurst from the right, forced him into a runoff, and defeated him in the primary. Dewhurst had invested millions of his own money in the Senate primary but still lost.

Although Texas once tried to restrict the franchise, primarily by limiting the right to vote through poll taxes and white primaries, in recent years it has tried to expand the franchise through the motor voter law and through early voting. Yet voter participation in Texas is the lowest in the nation. Overall, voter turnout in 2014 was only 33.4 percent of eligible voters, which was less than the turnout in 2010. Turnout in the 2016 presidential election was only 51.1 percent of the eligible voters, up slightly from 49.6 percent in 2012. That is probably because of the demographics of Texas voters and Texas's political culture, but it may also be a result of the scheduling of elections in Texas, the vast number of elections, and the large number of low-visibility candidates for office. It also remains to be seen whether the state's new voter identification law will have an impact on voter turnout in the state, as critics contend that this law will have the effect of suppressing the vote of minorities in the state.

One of the biggest factors that could affect Texas elections is the state's changing demographics. As we have discussed elsewhere in the text, the proportion of Latino voters in Texas is growing and the proportion of white voters is shrinking. While not as strongly Democratic as African Americans, Latinos in Texas are more likely to identify as Democrats. If this demographic trend continues, and if more Latinos register to vote and participate in state elections, Texas may once again become a competitive two-party state.

Use ɫ INQUIZITIVE to help you study and master this material.

Features of Elections in Texas

- Describe the types of elections held in Texas and how they work (pp. 145–48)

Texas allows all registered voters the choice to vote in one party primary during an election season. Should a candidate not receive a majority of votes in a primary, a runoff is held to determine who the party nominee will be. The general election ultimately decides who is elected to office.

Key Terms

primary election (p. 145)
runoff primary (p. 145)
open primary (p. 146)
closed primary (p. 146)
general election (p. 146)
special election (p. 147)

Practice Quiz

1. In a primary election,
   a) voters choose all local officials who will hold office in the following year.
   b) voters select federal officials for office.
   c) voters select their party's candidate for a general election.
   d) voters choose third-party candidates.
   e) voters cast ballots on proposed constitutional amendments.

2. Which of the following is *not* a type of election found in Texas?
   a) general
   b) primary
   c) distinguished
   d) special
   e) runoff primary

3. Officially, Texas has a
   a) joint primary.
   b) extended primary.
   c) open primary.
   d) closed primary.
   e) Jaybird primary.

4. The first Tuesday following the first Monday in November of even-numbered years is the day for which election?
   a) primary election
   b) runoff primary
   c) runoff for the general election
   d) secondary election
   e) general election

5. When are gubernatorial elections held?
   a) during presidential election years
   b) during odd-numbered years
   c) during even-numbered years that are not presidential election years
   d) every year
   e) every six months

Participation in Texas Elections

• Explain how the rules for voting affect turnout among different groups of Texans (pp. 148–64)

Participation in Texas elections varies by election. Turnout is lowest in party primaries, followed by elections when a presidential candidate is not on the ballot. Latinos and those of lower socioeconomic status are also less likely to vote in state elections.

Key Terms
Nineteenth Amendment (p. 149)
suffrage (p. 149)
poll tax (p. 149)
early registration (p. 149)
white primary (p. 150)
Jaybird Party (p. 151)
Voting Rights Act of 1965 (p. 152)
motor voter law (p. 153)
early voting (p. 153)
reapportionment (p. 154)
redistricting (p. 154)
preclearance (p. 158)

Practice Quiz
6. Which of the following is true?
   a) Poll taxes are legal.
   b) Women acquired the right to vote in the original 1876 Texas Constitution.
   c) The poll tax restricted the participation of poor people in the general election.
   d) You do not have to be a resident of Texas to vote in Texas.
   e) Latinos vote at higher rates than African Americans.

7. Who has benefited the most from early voting?
   a) Republicans
   b) Democrats
   c) All parties have benefited equally.
   d) Independents
   e) Greens

8. The procedure by which certain states, such as Texas, are required to obtain approval every time they make changes to districts is called
   a) redistricting.
   b) reapportionment.
   c) preclearance.
   d) external validation.
   e) judicial review.

9. The two most important factors in determining whether someone will vote are
   a) income and education.
   b) education and family history of voting.
   c) income and gender.
   d) party membership and gender.
   e) ethnicity and race.

10. In which of the following elections is voter turnout the highest?
   a) presidential elections
   b) gubernatorial general elections
   c) city elections
   d) runoff elections
   e) off-year congressional elections

Campaigns

- Present the main features of election campaigns in Texas (pp. 164–73)

Because of Texas's size, statewide campaigns can be expensive. There are several major media markets, which makes television advertising very expensive. Grassroots efforts to mobilize voters are also costly because of the large territory. This means wealthy candidates are often on the ballot.

Practice Quiz

11. The most costly item for most political campaigns is
   a) travel.
   b) security.
   c) fund-raising.
   d) media.
   e) food.

12. Who is the first Republican to become Texas governor since Reconstruction?
   a) William Clements
   b) Rick Perry
   c) George W. Bush
   d) Ann Richards
   e) Kinky Friedman

13. One distinguishing feature of the 2014 campaign in Texas was
   a) the increased presence of third-party candidates.
   b) the lack of emphasis on education policy.
   c) the candidates' focus on equal pay for equal work.
   d) the unusually low levels of money spent on media ads.
   e) the candidates' focus on welfare reforms.

14. Prior to running for re-election as a lieutenant governor, David Dewhurst unsuccessfully ran for which office?
   a) state senate
   b) U.S. Senate
   c) U.S. House of Representatives
   d) governor
   e) attorney general

Dineen Majcher (right) was frustrated with the emphasis her daughter's school placed on standardized testing. She took action by helping to create an interest group and challenging Texas's education policies.

Interest Groups and Lobbying

WHY INTEREST GROUPS MATTER Dineen Majcher had had enough. A lawyer and mother of an incoming ninth grader in a prestigious Austin high school, she couldn't believe what she was hearing. Fifteen percent of her daughter's final grade in history would come from a new mandated statewide test, one that the teacher had never seen. This struck her as unfair and unreasonable. How could students prepare for such a test? Why 15 percent of the grade? She went first to the principal to protest, but to no avail. This was after all a mandated state test, part of a 30-year effort of the education reformers to bring testing and accountability to all elementary and secondary schools across the state. So Majcher raised the ante, getting the Austin School Board to request a waiver from the State Board of Education from the "15 percent rule." The request was denied. Raising the ante again, Majcher signed up to testify at legislative committee hearings that had been called for January 2012. During the hearings Majcher met others from across Texas who were also dissatisfied with the testing movement that had dominated educational policy for over 30 years. Together these individuals established an interest group called Texans Advocating for Meaningful Student Assessment, or TAMSA. The group became known in the legislature as "Mothers Against Drunk Testing."

The goals of TAMSA were clearly articulated on its website: "to improve public education in Texas through the use of meaningful and effective student assessments that allow for more productive classroom instruction and more efficient use of public funds." On their face, these goals might seem to be relatively uncontroversial. In fact, however, they were questioning the philosophy of educational reform that had dominated the state for almost three decades.

TAMSA enabled people to join together and seek policy change in a number of ways: first, by providing like-minded individuals an organizational structure for discussing problems and offering solutions; second, by providing a vehicle for working with other organizations like the Texas Association of School Administrators, who were also concerned with testing; third, by raising money to help pay for their efforts; and fourth, by educating the public and policy makers alike about the problems of testing across the elementary and secondary curriculum. TAMSA spearheaded the drive to change public policy regarding testing in the state. What had begun as a protest about unfair testing was morphing into an interest group with a clear political object.

Since the early 1980s, testing was seen to be one of the best ways to ensure accountability by identifying schools that worked and those that didn't. Support for reform through testing and accountability came from a variety of sources inside and outside the legislature. Leading legislators from both parties, leaders at the Texas Education Agency, and business leaders came to believe statewide testing was a key to higher performance. George W. Bush identified testing as a central part of his plan for educational reform in Texas in the '90s and placed testing at the heart of his "No Child Left Behind" initiatives when he was president in the early 2000s. Key business interests, including the Texas Association of Business, supported expanded testing, seeing the tests as a way to ratchet up the quality of poorly performing schools across the state. Not surprisingly, the businesses involved in creating the tests also came to support the tests. As the debates over reform were proceeding in the legislature, Pearson publishers had a five-year contract with the state that was estimated to be worth $462 million. Testing itself had become big business with big interests seeking protection in the state legislature.

Given the interests supporting testing and decades-old accountability initiatives, few thought at the beginning of the 2013 legislative session that change was in the wind. But it was. New legislators open to new ideas about reform were chairing the educational committees in both the House and the Senate. Entrenched interests in educational reform had lost their ability to control the agenda. On a paltry budget of under $100,000, drawing upon inexpensive social media and relying on the expertise of a few key members, TAMSA played a major role in getting the legislature to rethink what educational reform meant. In response to the efforts of TAMSA and other like-minded groups and individuals, the legislature dropped the number of end-of-year course exams from 15 to 5.

The story of Dineen Majcher and TAMSA highlights how interest groups matter in Texas politics. Interest groups provide support for existing policies in many areas of public policy, support legislators in their electoral campaigns, and help to articulate ideas from which policies can be crafted. Texas politics can be understood only with a clear understanding of the role that interest groups play in elections and in the legislative process.[1]

CHAPTER GOALS

- Define interest groups, and describe the major ways they try to influence Texas government (pp. 181–92)

- Describe the role of PACs in Texas elections (pp. 192–201)

- Explain how ordinary individuals can influence Texas government (pp. 201–3)

Interest Groups in the Political Process

Define interest groups, and describe the major ways they try to influence Texas government

It is probably true that all of us have political interests, goals, or objectives that can be achieved with governmental intervention. Many of us, however, will never act to achieve those goals. A few of us may speak privately to a legislator or other official. Some of us will join with others to try to convince the government to help us achieve our interests. When we do that, we have formed an **interest group**.

In Texas, as elsewhere, interest groups assume a variety of forms. There are a wide range of interests active in national, state, and local politics that form into interest groups, including those concerned with business, labor, agriculture, the professions such as law, medicine, and accounting, government affairs such as state employees, cities, and universities, and public interest advocates such as the Sierra Club. Interest groups can be set up to serve the interests of a small number of people concerned with one particular interest, such as getting a road built in a county. They can also be established to serve the interests of a group of people with broader interests, such as those interested in reforming the school system by promoting vouchers, charter schools, home schooling, or better testing. Some interests are established to represent the common interests of various business or labor groups in the state, such as those of the real estate industry or chemical workers unions. An interest group is a "peak association" when it is an interest group organized as an umbrella organization that seeks to coordinate the various activities of member groups in a number of targeted areas.

interest group an organization established to influence the government's programs and policies

Resources and Strategies of Interest Groups

Political scientists have identified various resources that interest groups are able to mobilize in politics. First, interest groups have members. Groups can become influential because of whom they represent. The Texas Medical Association and the Texas Bar Association are excellent examples of groups representing influential people across Texas. Some people and industries clearly are more important to legislators than others. But numbers matter, too. Politicians who ignore the concerns of broad-based evangelical groups in discussions of abortion or marriage do so at their own peril. Second, and perhaps more important than the first, interest groups have the ability to raise money. Clearly, it is advantageous to have access to a few deep-pocketed individuals when trying to raise money in support of a particular cause. But in the age of the Internet, it is also useful for there to be large numbers of members who are willing to give, if only a little.

Third, interest groups possess information about their membership and about the problems that concern their membership. In recent years, interest groups have begun to mine large databases of people who might be interested in particular policies or issues. Such information can become a valuable resource for politicians seeking to raise money or to promote a particular policy objective. Interest groups also offer advice on the best ways to address the concerns of their membership. Interest groups clearly are motivated by their self-interest, and the positions they present to legislators reflect this interest. The first drafts of bills introduced into the House or Senate often come from interest groups seeking to promote their own particular perspective. A fourth resource, one closely related to the third, is credibility. Providing information to a policy maker is important. But this must be good information if, over the longer run, an interest group or its representatives are to be taken seriously. Bad information about a problem or the concerns of a group's members can undercut an interest group's effectiveness quickly.

The resources that are available to interest groups are the foundation upon which various strategies are developed by interest groups to promote their concerns. Among the strategies that we will explore in this chapter are (1) explicit political strategies such as grassroots organizing, get-out-the-vote and electioneering campaigns, and campaign financing; (2) legislative strategies such as lobbying and testifying before legislative committees; (3) public awareness strategies such as drafting policy reports, writing editorials, and conducting educational campaigns in various public forums; and (4) supporting litigation that challenges existing policies in court. As we will see, the strategies that are adopted by various interest groups largely depend on the resources available to them at the time.

Interest Groups and Democratic Politics

The rights to associate with others and to petition government lie at the heart of the rights guaranteed by the U.S. and Texas constitutions. These constitutional rights have helped to make the United States and Texas into what political scientists call a "pluralistic society" where individuals organize into groups to serve common interests and compete with one another for power and influence. In *Federalist 10*, an essay written in defense of the U.S. Constitution in 1787, James Madison discussed how a large republic comprising many interests competing with one another in the political arena could work to protect individuals from the abusive power of any one powerful interest. Drawing upon Madison for inspiration, later pluralist writers in the twentieth century would argue that groups could check and balance one another in the political process, much like different branches of government checked and balanced one another in constitutional government. Having a common interest is one thing. Organizing that common interest into an effective group that can act to promote that interest is quite something else.

In his seminal book *The Logic of Collective Action*, Mancur Olson analyzed a collective action problem that lies at the heart of interest-group politics: people have an interest in organizing into an interest group that effectively represents their interests in politics. But people also have an interest in getting someone else to pay for that group's organizational costs. This is the **free rider problem**. If everyone acts as a free rider, some organizations do not form to represent particular interests in politics.

free rider problem the incentive to benefit from others' work without making a contribution, which leads individuals in a collective action situation to refuse to work together

Ironically, the larger the common interest, the more difficult it may be to overcome the free rider problem and create effective interest groups. According to Olson's theory, a small group of insurance companies are more likely to form a powerful interest group to affect health care policy than the millions of poor people who lack quality health care. Similarly, business interests are more likely to form a common front in politics than consumers because it is easier for the business interests to overcome the costs of collective action, that is, the costs of acting together as an organized interest group.[2]

Interest groups engage in a number of activities to overcome the free rider problem. Sometimes, they offer people particular incentives to join a group. These selective benefits often cover a wide range of activities, from a subscription to a magazine, to access to special information on the Internet, to invitations to special conferences, to special discounts. For example, AAA (the American Automobile Association) organizes for road and vehicle safety and provides members with roadside assistance and travel discounts—strong incentives to join.

Interest groups also can provide people with symbolic benefits, such as listing individuals' names as sponsors of an organization or offering free buttons, hats, or T-shirts showing their support to the ongoing activities of the organization. The purpose of such activities is to strengthen the commitment an individual has to an interest group and to overcome the free rider problem.

One of the most important lessons to be drawn from the logic of collective action is that some interests do not get represented easily in the political process. Upper-class business interests are more likely to be represented than lower-class minority interests. A second lesson is that it is very difficult, even rare, for interest groups to emerge that protect the broad interests of large numbers of people or any vaguely defined public interest. Significantly, when such groups do emerge, as with the Grange or Prohibition movement in the nineteenth and early twentieth centuries, they can come to wield considerable power. Nevertheless, in the push and pull of everyday politics in Texas, it is more likely for narrowly targeted interests to organize effectively in defense of their interests than it is for the public as a whole to organize. Even the above-mentioned "public interest groups" are not so much advancing the public good as a whole (whatever that may be) than advocating for the views that certain individuals have about the public good.

Olson's theory provides an explanation of why it has often been claimed that business-oriented interest groups dominate the Texas legislature. Using campaign contributions, political pressure, and sometimes corruption, "the Lobby," as pro-business groups were called, was once purported to run Texas government. Some of the most influential business leaders of the state belonged to the "8F Crowd." At the Lamar Hotel in Houston, 8F was the number on a suite of rooms where George R. Brown held court. Brown was a founder of Brown and Root, one of the world's largest construction firms and until April 2007 part of the even larger Halliburton Company. He met regularly with other fabulously wealthy Texans such as Jesse Jones of Texas Commerce Bank and Tenneco, Gus Wortham of American General Insurance, and James

PERSONAL RESPONSIBILITY: WHAT WOULD YOU DO?

- Do you think that business interests should have such a profound effect on Texas government and politics? Why or why not?

- Why do business interests have such a strong voice in Texas government and politics? If you were advising an environmental group on opposing business interests, what tactics would you suggest they take?

Elkins of the Vinson and Elkins law firm and First City National Bank. These men socialized together and worked together to promote their political interests. For 40 years they were considered the king makers in Texas politics who determined much of the important policy of state government.[3]

The 8F Crowd was, of course, an interest group—an elite, wealthy, powerful, pro-business interest group. Although the 8F Crowd is long gone from the Texas political scene, much of what it did is still done in Texas politics by other interest groups, though no modern-day group is ascribed the influence that was allegedly held by the 8F Crowd.

Nevertheless, Texas is known as a state that has long had powerful interest groups. During the Texas Constitutional Convention of 1875, an interest group played an important role. That was the Grange, a powerful farmers' organization, of which many of the constitution's framers were members. As Chapter 2 indicated, the Constitution of 1876 reflected many of the values of Grange members. It was a document for rural Texas that was pro–small farmer and opposed to a powerful state government.

With the development of a strong oil and gas industry in Texas in the first half of the twentieth century, the oil industry began playing an important role in state politics. With major oil companies such as ExxonMobil with headquarters in Texas and employing millions of the state's residents, their interests are well represented in the state legislature. While the oil and gas industry is very important, the state's economy has also become more diversified in recent years. Interest groups representing other industries such as telecommunications and high-tech companies in the Austin area have also influenced legislation.

Interest Groups and Policy Makers

Interest groups want something from policy makers: they want policy that is beneficial for their groups. On the other hand, policy makers benefit from developing relationships with interest groups. From those groups, the policy maker gains information, since the interest groups can provide substantial expertise in areas that are their special concern. Additionally, interest groups can provide campaign funds to the policy maker. In a state as large as Texas, with numerous media markets and with some party competition, considerable campaign funds are necessary to run and win elections. For example, in the 2014 gubernatorial race, according to the media project at Wesleyan University, interest groups favoring Democrat Wendy Davis spent $2.6 million in ads in Texas, while interest groups favoring Republican Greg Abbott spent $5.2 million in ads. An interest group can help raise money from its membership for a candidate sympathetic to the interest group's goals. Also, interest groups can supply votes to the policy maker. They can assist in mobilizing their own groups, and they can supply campaign workers to distribute campaign leaflets and to operate phone banks to get out the vote. Interest groups can also publicize issues through press conferences, press releases, publications, conferences, and hearings and even by filing lawsuits. Finally, interest groups can engage in research and education programs. It has become increasingly common for interest groups to engage in public education programs by running advertisements in the Texas media explaining why their particular approaches to a public policy problem would be more beneficial to Texans in general.

Unlike a private citizen interested in and involved in politics, larger or better-funded interest groups have the advantages of time, money, expertise, and continuity. Although concerned citizens do have an impact on public policy in Texas, organized and well-funded interest groups have an advantage in affecting the policy process. It is difficult for a concerned citizen from Houston to spend time in Austin developing relationships with policy makers and trying to convince those policy makers to support public policies that are compatible with the individual's goals. On the other hand, if that individual joins with like-minded people to create an organized interest group, the group may have a greater likelihood of achieving policy goals. It might be possible to fund an office in Austin with a staff that could monitor events in state government on a daily basis and develop relationships with key policy makers. Additionally, although some individuals in Texas do have the money to provide substantial campaign support to policy makers, even those individuals can get more "bang for the buck" if they join with others in **bundling** their funds into a larger contribution from the interest group. The creation of an organized interest group also allows for the development of a staff. The staff can gain in-depth knowledge of an area of policy far greater than could be gained by most individuals working alone. Also, an individual may be intensely concerned with an issue in one legislative session but may find it difficult to sustain that interest over a period of many legislative sessions. The larger, better-funded, more successful organized interest groups have continuity. They are in Austin developing relationships with policy makers and presenting the views of the organization day in and day out, year in and year out. The result is that legislators and other policy makers can develop long-standing relationships with the interest groups and the groups' representatives in Austin.

bundling the interest-group practice of combining campaign contributions from several sources into one larger contribution from the group, so as to increase the group's impact on the candidate

Consider the role of Raise Your Hand Texas, founded by Charles Butt of the HEB Grocery store chain located throughout Texas and parts of Northern Mexico. Raise Your Hand Texas is an interest group aimed at stopping school vouchers in Texas and promoting public education. In the 2013 legislative session, legislators were particularly influenced by the group. When Representative Ken King (R-Canadian) introduced a bill regarding education on the House floor, Representative Abel Herrero (D-Corpus Christi) asked his colleagues whether Raise Your Hand Texas had taken a position on his bill.[4] At that point, one of his colleagues showed Herrero a text message showing that the interest group had supported the bill during the committee stage of the process. This is but one example of how an interest group can have important influence over legislators.[5]

Types of Interest Groups and Lobbyists

Interest groups strive to influence public opinion, to make their views known to policy makers, and to elect and support policy makers who are friendly to their points of view. To accomplish these goals, interest groups usually maintain **lobbyists** in Austin who try to gain access to policy makers and communicate their objectives to them. There are several different types of lobbyists. Some interest groups have full-time staffs in Austin whose members work as lobbyists. One form of interest group is, of course, a corporation, and companies often have government relations departments that lobby for the companies' interests. Lobbyists may be employed by an interest group to deal with one issue, or they may be employed by an interest group on

lobbyist an individual employed by an interest group who tries to influence governmental decisions on behalf of that group

a regular basis. Some lobbyists represent only one client; others will represent large numbers of clients. All lobbyists, however, must be able to reach and communicate with policy makers. Corporate interest groups tend to use either government relations departments or law firms to represent their interests in Austin. Often industries have broad interests that need representation. For example, an insurance company may have one specific interest it wishes to have represented. However, the insurance industry as a whole also has a wide range of issues that need representation, and thus it will form an industrywide interest group.

Interest groups may also represent professional groups. One of the most influential professional groups in Austin is the Texas Medical Association, which represents the interests of doctors. Other professional groups represent accountants, chiropractors, opticians, dentists, lawyers, and teachers.

That teachers are an important interest group suggests still another type of interest group—public-employee interest groups. Public school teachers may be the largest and most effective of these groups, but firefighters, police officers, and even justices of the peace and constables all are represented in Austin.

Some interest groups are formed with a single issue in mind, as the introduction to this chapter illustrates. For example, an interest group may be concerned about the regulation of abortion or school vouchers or tort reform or the environment. Other interest groups are concerned with multiple issues that affect the groups. Public school teachers, for example, are concerned about job security, qualifications of teachers, health insurance, pensions, salaries, and other matters that affect the lives of their members.

Civil rights groups such as the National Association for the Advancement of Colored People, the League of United Latin American Citizens, and the Mexican American Legal Defense and Education Fund are concerned about civil rights issues affecting the lives primarily of African Americans and Latinos. Interestingly, not only do these groups often try to influence public opinion and the legislature, but they have had notable success in representing their groups' interests through litigation, especially in the federal courts.

Other public interest groups try to promote consumer, environmental, and general public issues. Examples of these groups are Public Citizen, the Sierra Club, and Common Cause. Groups such as the Sierra Club work to promote environmental interests, whereas groups such as Public Citizen and Common Cause tend to have broader interests and work to promote more open government. These groups rarely have much funding, but they often can provide policy makers with information and expertise. In addition, they can mobilize their membership to support or oppose bills, and they can publicize matters that are important to their goals.

Getting Access to Policy Makers

In order to communicate the goals of their interest groups to policy makers, lobbyists must first gain access to those policy makers. Gaining access to policy makers, of course, imposes on the time of legislators, so lobbyists will often spend significant sums entertaining them. That entertainment is one of the most criticized aspects of lobbying. But from the lobbyists' perspective, entertainment is an important tool for reaching policy makers and putting them in a congenial frame of mind. Entertainment by lobbyists can involve expensive dinners, golf, and other activities. For example, lobbyists for Texas Utilities (TXU) bought a $300 saddle for one state representative and a $200 bench for another. TXU lobbyists also treated a state senator to a trip to the Masters golf tournament and picked up the dinner tab as well. One House member received a gun as a gift, another received a jacket, and several got "deer-processing" costs paid for by these lobbyists.[6]

When former representative Lon Burnam (D–Fort Worth) proposed legislation to regulate consumer versions of "stun guns," the lobbyist for TASER International as a joke gave Burnam a gift of a pink "stun gun" valued at more than $150. The "stun gun" was, of course, a minor expenditure.[7] Others are much more lavish. When Governor Abbott was attorney general, he received gifts ranging from hunting trips to college football tickets.[8]

In the 2015 legislative session, lobbyists spent more than $1.8 million on food and meals alone, with an additional $331,000 in entertainment and gifts for lawmakers and others in state government.[9]

Texas lawmakers receive only $600 per month plus $190 a day when on legislative business, but lawmakers are permitted to use campaign contributions for expenses associated with holding office. This allows interest groups to fund significant lavish benefits for lawmakers. For example, about one-third of the spending of north Texas lawmakers—about $3.4 million of roughly $10 million in 2007–09—has gone to fund things other than campaign expenditures. Senator Florence Shapiro has used her contributions to fund a car lease for a Mercedes Benz and to pay for conference stays at the Ritz-Carlton in Palm Beach, the Venetian in Las Vegas, and the Hay-Adams in Washington, D.C. Thirty-six north Texas lawmakers spent nearly $560,000 on travel and entertainment, $470,000 on Austin living expenses, and $290,000 on food.[10]

Some interest groups focus on a single issue, such as abortion. When Texas passed a law requiring women to undergo a sonogram 24 hours before having an abortion, antiabortion groups applauded the measure, but some women's groups protested against it.

In 2013 there were 1,704 registered lobbyists in Texas.[11] This is a decrease from the 1,836 registered lobbyists in 2011. An analysis that was done of the lobbying reports in 2013 found these lobbyists had 2,932 clients.[12] Because of the loose nature of the Texas reporting laws, it is unclear what these lobbyists were paid, but it was as much as $349 million in 2013.[13] Thirty-three of them reported maximum lobbying incomes of at least $1.5 million.[14]

Sometimes lobbyists have long-standing personal ties to policy makers, and those bonds can be invaluable to the lobbyists' clients. When lobbyist Andrea McWilliams celebrated her 40th birthday in California's wine country, six Texas lawmakers traveled to California for the party including the chair of the House Appropriations Committee and the chair of the Senate Public Education Committee. In McWilliams's case, the personal ties to these lawmakers were probably strengthened by the fact that she and her clients had contributed more than $206,000 to the campaigns of the six lawmakers over the past several years.[15] McWilliams was the highest-paid lobbyist with the largest number of clients in the 2013 legislative session and the largest revenue of $4.5 million.[16]

Access to policy makers may also be gained by building support for an issue among their constituents. Constituents may be encouraged, for example, to write or call legislators about a bill and offer their opinions. Essentially, the interest group tries to mobilize interested voters to get involved in the political process on behalf of the group's goals.

Lobbying and Government's "Revolving Door" One important way of gaining access to those in government is to employ former officials as lobbyists. A lobbyist who is a former legislator often has friends in the legislature and can use that friendship to gain access. Additionally, a former legislator often is in an exceptionally good position to understand the personal relationships and informal power centers that must be contacted to accomplish a legislative objective. As a result, some of the best-paid lobbyists in Austin are former Texas state officials and often are former legislators.

In 2010, 65 registered lobbyists were former legislators. What they have in common is knowledge of "how to pass bills, to kill them, whom to talk to, which clerks are friendly, whose birthdays are coming up—all inside stuff that makes the government machine whir."[17] Other especially valuable lobbyists have been former committee clerks for major committees and chiefs of staff of members who were on major committees.[18] Ten recently retired lawmakers were lobbyists in the 2009 legislative session. The 10 had a total of 68 lobbying contracts allowing them to generate between $2,025,000 and $3,890,000 in fees. In 2013, former senator Tommy Williams of the Woodlands, who was chairman of the Budget Committee, took a $300,000 per year job with the Texas A&M System after he left office. While not officially a "lobbyist," one of his duties is to advocate for the Texas A&M System in Austin. One gets a sense of the value of these ex-legislators-turned-lobbyists from the explanation Representative Jim Pitts gave for sponsoring an amendment that was pushed by an AT&T lobbyist and former legislator, Pat Heggerty.

SOCIAL RESPONSIBILITY: GET INVOLVED

- If you were to start an interest group in Texas, on what issue would you focus?

- How would you (1) attract members and (2) influence policy makers?

Andrea McWilliams is one of Texas's highest-paid and most successful lobbyists.

The amendment would have forced the state to pay for rerouting phone lines for road projects. Said Representative Pitts of the amendment, "I was just trying to help Pat out."[19] The amendment later failed to pass. In 2013, 12 additional defeated or recently retired legislators became lobbyists. They reported up to $2,130,000 in income from 49 clients.[20]

It is not only former legislators who can move on to successful lobbying careers. Forty Rick Perry aides either had left the administration to become lobbyists or have joined the administration after having been lobbyists. Some have moved back and forth from administration to lobbying in a revolving door fashion. Five of Perry's closest campaign aides have been lobbyists. Two of his ex-aides became lobbyists who headed pro-Perry PACs.[21]

One former-legislator-turned-lobbyist who reversed course and went back into the legislature is Todd Hunter. Hunter had served in the legislature from 1989 to 1997. An active lobbyist as late as 2007, he was elected to the Texas House in 2008.[22] Jerry Patterson, Texas land commissioner, was a state senator, became a lobbyist, and was able to move to his statewide office with little criticism of his role as a lobbyist. However, David Sibley, a state senator who became a lobbyist and then tried to regain his old position, caught tremendous political flak for this decision and, to a considerable degree, lost the Republican primary because of that career choice.[23] The issue of lobbying by former officials and their staffs is a significant one, as there is concern that policy decisions may be made with an eye toward future lucrative lobbying jobs.

Texas has only weak laws dealing with lobbying by former government officials. A former member of the governing body or a former executive head of a regulatory agency cannot lobby the agency for two years after leaving office. Senior employees or former officers of Texas regulatory agencies cannot ever lobby a governmental entity on matters they were involved in when employed by the government. However, there are no legal restrictions on lobbying by a former governor, former lieutenant governor, former legislator, or any former aides to these officials.[24] In the most recent legislative session, Governor Abbott pledged action on ethics reform to address the problem of former legislators lobbying. Senator Van Taylor (R-Plano) introduced a Senate bill that would impose a two-year ban before an outgoing legislator could lobby her former colleagues. The bill passed the Senate and a similar bill passed the House, but Governor Abbott vetoed ethics reform legislation, claiming that the bill was not meaningful and included too many loopholes, including a provision to allow legislators to avoid reporting requirements by listing their assets and financial information under their spouse's name.[25]

What Lobbyists Do with Access   The public perception of lobbying may be that interested groups bring bags of money to members of the legislature in exchange for their votes on important bills. The reality is much more complex, and far less underhanded. Once lobbyists obtain access to policy makers, they provide information that may be useful. For example, they may explain how a bill benefits a legislator's district, or how it benefits the state, or how it is perceived as being unfair. Since the staffs of Texas legislators are small, lobbyists perform useful functions by explaining what numerous bills are intended to do. They may even write bills to be introduced by friendly legislators or write amendments to bills. Almost certainly, if a bill affects the interests of a lobbyist's client and reaches a point in the process where hearings are held on the bill, the lobbyist will arrange for testimony to be given at the hearing explaining the interest group's viewpoint on the proposed legislation.

Lobbyists do not limit their activities to the legislative process, of course. Rules proposed by the bureaucracy or the courts can affect the interests of lobbyists' clients. Lobbyists will testify at hearings on rules and try to provide information to administrators in face-to-face meetings as well.

Corruption   There is always a concern that lobbyists may corrupt policy makers by bribing them in order to accomplish the interest groups' policy objectives. Early in the twentieth century, Sam Rayburn, later a famed U.S. congressperson and Speaker of the House, served in the Texas House of Representatives for six years. At that time, he was especially concerned with corruption and refused to accept free meals and entertainment from lobbyists. He called some of his fellow legislators "steak men." By that he meant that the legislators would sell their votes on a bill for a steak dinner at the Driskill Hotel in Austin. "Steak men" (and women) may still exist in Texas politics, but for the most part, lobbyists provide information, campaign contributions, and political support (or opposition) rather than bribes. Still, corruption occurs, as is illustrated by the indictments of the mayor and all but one city council member in Crystal City, Texas, for accepting $12,000 in bribes from a businessman wanting a lucrative city contract.[26]

In 1989, "Bo" Pilgrim, a large poultry producer, distributed $10,000 checks to state senators in the capitol while he was lobbying them on workers' compensation reform. Perhaps even more troubling, some senators accepted the checks until media attention forced them to reconsider. Yet this practice of offering $10,000 while asking for a senator to vote on a specific bill was not illegal under state law. A year later, the Speaker of the Texas House of Representatives, "Gib" Lewis, got in trouble for his close relationship with a law firm that specialized in collecting delinquent taxes

Should Former Legislators Be Lobbyists?

Lobbyists come from different backgrounds. Most are lawyers and many have not held elected office. However, in Washington, D.C., as well as Austin, the number of former legislators engaging in lobbying activities has grown substantially. This is happening so often now that a new term, *revolving door*, has emerged to describe former legislators taking high-paying jobs lobbying their former colleagues. An article in the *Dallas Morning News* estimated that in one legislative session, former legislators earned up to a collective $1.7 million in salaries.[a]

It is not surprising that interest groups such as corporations or labor unions would want to hire former legislators as lobbyists. Former legislators have cultivated relationships with their colleagues as well as with staff members. They can easily arrange meetings for their clients with important government leaders. Lobbying firms see former legislators as strong investments because of their ability to influence legislation.

Former legislators defend taking lobbying jobs by claiming that they have a right to make a living. Texas legislators make only $7,200 per year, and their experience should not go to waste once they leave office. They are uniquely suited to advise their clients because of their knowledge and expertise in legislative politics. They are also employed not only to influence the legislature but also to educate them about the concerns of their clients, who are constituents as well. As long as reporting requirements exist so that the public knows whom they are lobbying for, then there are no ethical or moral issues with this practice. Former legislator and now lobbyist Cliff Johnson defends his experience by suggesting, "You have to hire somebody to get through the administrative minefield."[b] Lobbying firms will naturally gravitate toward hiring individuals who know the legislative process and are able to best represent them.

On the other hand, opponents of the revolving door claim that this practice is unethical and should be curtailed. Legislators are public servants who should not personally profit from their time in office. Representative Donna Howard (D-Austin) has proposed a moratorium so that legislators should have to wait a period of time before they lobby. Senator Jane Nelson (R-Flower Mound) expressed her opposition to the revolving door in this way: "It just doesn't feel right. I don't want people questioning: Is she filing that bill because she hopes to cash in on that at some point in the future? I would rather be boiled in oil."[c] Governor Abbott and Lieutenant Governor Patrick have also proposed ethics reform

in the legislature addressing the issue of the revolving door. A proposal to enact a two-session "cooling off" period before legislators could lobby failed in the 2015 legislative session, despite the efforts of state senator Van Taylor (R-Plano, shown above) and others. Ten states currently have revolving door laws, but Texas will have to wait until the next legislative session to even consider these bills to limit the practice.

COMMUNICATING EFFECTIVELY: YOUR VOICE

- Do you agree or disagree that former legislators lobbying their former colleagues is unethical? Why?

- Should Texas enact laws to limit the ability of legislators to lobby? If so, what specific provisions should Texas enact and why?

for local governments. In 1991, Speaker Lewis was indicted for receipt of an illegal gift from the law firm. Ultimately, Lewis plea-bargained and received a minor penalty. The result of these scandals, however, was legislation that created a state ethics commission. The legislation imposed additional lobbying reporting requirements and restrictions on speaking fees that interest groups paid legislators and pleasure trips that lobbyists provided. By no means was the law a major regulation of or restriction on lobbying practices, but it did put some limits on lobbying behavior.

Who Represents Ordinary Texans?

Another problem with lobbying was well described by the director of a public-interest lobby, Craig McDonald: "Legislators are rubbing shoulders with . . . lobbyists, almost all of whom hustle for business interests. While corporate interests dominate our legislative process, there is virtually no counterbalancing lobby to represent ordinary Texans. Nowhere on the list of Texas's biggest lobby spenders will you find a single group dedicated to the interests of consumers, the environment or human services. No wonder these citizen interests repeatedly get steamrolled in Austin."[27]

The "Who Are Texans?" graphic looks at campaign contributions to Texas legislators. Although the categories are very broad, it is clear that business interests dominate in Texas government. Of course, many issues considered by Texas government may pit one business interest against another, and sometimes a business or professional organization may find itself aligned with consumer interests. For example, the Texas Trial Lawyers Association, an organization of plaintiffs' lawyers in Texas, frequently allies with consumer interests. Many of the clients of these lawyers are consumers who sue large businesses. The interests of these lawyers and their clients are especially close, since the lawyers are paid on a contingent fee basis, which means they don't receive payment unless their clients receive payment. It is also the case that lobbying is not all there is to the representation of interests in Austin. Interest groups without money may still mobilize their members in order to accomplish their objectives, or they may influence public opinion.

Still, there is no question that money does help in politics. In this battle of mostly business interests, there may not be an objective voice, or at least a voice for the public interest, that reaches the ears of legislators.

Another Side to Lobbying

 Describe the role of PACs in Texas elections

Lobbyists in Texas represent mostly business interests, and they are active in trying to gain access to government officials and inform them of the legislative desires of their clients. But interest groups are not simply information channels between business and government. They also promote the political interests of elected officials who support their viewpoints and oppose the interests of those who do not. One major way that interest groups engage in this activity is by making campaign contributions. Interest groups may encourage individual members to make contributions to candidates, or they may collect funds from their members, bundling those funds as a donation from the interest group. When this is done, the interest group creates a **political action committee (PAC)** to make the contribution.

There are numerous reasons for forming a PAC. A candidate is more likely to notice a substantial contribution from a PAC than many small contributions from individual members of an interest group. Additionally, the lobbyist who delivers a substantial PAC check to a candidate can more likely gain political access than can a lobbyist who simply asks interest-group members to mail individual checks. The PAC becomes a way for the interest group to send a message to the candidate that its members care strongly enough about their agenda that they are prepared to back those goals with money. In some cases, a PAC can even serve as an intermediary to provide money to candidates that the PAC's members might not want to support publicly.

PACs may give money directly to the candidate, or they may engage in **issue advocacy** that supports the candidate but is independent of the candidate's control. The candidate does not report these independent expenditures on contribution disclosure statements. PACs may also spend money to support an issue rather than a specific candidate or to support such activities as "get-out-the-vote" campaigns. In 2012, there were 1,364 active PACs in Texas that cumulatively spent $126,367,460. Texans for Lawsuit Reform was the state's largest PAC in 2012, spending $7,824,875 helping candidates who supported tort reform limiting liabilities of corporations and professions.[28] Tort reform is an effort by business and professional interests to cap awards by juries and make it harder for individuals to sue businesses and doctors for malpractice.

Campaign contributions can be, to a considerable degree, divided in terms of the economic interests represented by the contributors. The "Who Are Texans?" graphic in this chapter shows that the largest contributor was the finance, insurance, and real estate sector. This sector is a major part of the Texas economy and is subject to significant state regulation. That is also true of general business, energy and natural resources, construction, and health care. In contrast to business, political parties, agriculture, and even candidates providing funds to their own campaigns, labor represents a small amount of campaign spending.

political action committee (PAC) a private group that raises and distributes funds for use in election campaigns

issue advocacy independent spending by individuals or interest groups on a campaign issue but not directly tied to a particular candidate

Getting Out the Vote

Getting out the vote on Election Day is an important and difficult task. Both the Republican and Democratic parties spend much time and money making sure that their voters get to the polls and vote for their candidates. In recent years, get-out-the-vote efforts by both parties have involved mining so-called big databases to identify people who are likely to vote for their candidates, calling them on the phone, and visiting them at home. Battleground Texas is the latest attempt by the Democratic Party to identify potential Democratic voters, to make them familiar with Democratic positions and candidates, and to get them to vote. Similar efforts have been made by the Republican Party in recent years, particularly those identifying with the Tea Party movement.

Get-out-the-vote initiatives also can be an important part of interest-group activity. The most successful get-out-the-vote campaign run by an interest group was that conducted by the Texas Medical Association in 1988, which sought to elect its slate of candidates to the Texas Supreme Court. Physicians were encouraged to give to TEXPAC, the medical association PAC. They were also encouraged to make individual contributions to certain candidates. Additionally, physicians were given slate cards with recommended candidates, literature endorsing candidates, and even expensively produced videotapes. They were asked not only to encourage families and friends to vote for the candidates endorsed by the medical association but also to encourage their patients to vote for them. The effort by the medical association was remarkable for its fund-raising success and for its reaching and mobilizing the grass roots.[29]

Most efforts by interest groups, however, are far less sophisticated. Generally, interest groups' PACs simply provide resources for the candidates to get out the vote. Unfortunately for the interest groups, sometimes they misjudge the political viability of the candidates they support. Backing an unsuccessful candidate results in a waste of the interest group's funds and the likely alienation of the winning candidate. In the 2010 primary campaign, Texans for Lawsuit Reform, the pro-business and pro–tort reform interest group that has had spectacular successes in forwarding its agenda over the past 15 years, suffered a remarkable failure. Although it had contributed $602,290 to 28 candidates, 53 percent of this money was spent on 4 incumbent candidates who lost their primaries, and another 28 percent of their money was spent on 3 candidates— 2 of them incumbents—who were forced into a runoff election. Obviously, Texans for Lawsuit Reform thought these candidates were important for achieving its agenda, but it is questionable how desirable it is for an interest group to pump huge amounts of money into the campaigns of incumbent candidates who do not have the political strength to win even in their party's primary. And the high degree of financial support for candidates can be hurtful to the candidate. In one of these races, the winning candidate's main issue was that the defeated incumbent had received money from an organization known for giving huge sums to Republican candidates. This, contended the winner, was proof that the incumbent Democrat was not a real Democrat but a Republican with a Democratic label.[30]

Nevertheless, Texans for Lawsuit Reform scored impressive victories in the 2012 general election. It gave more than $250,000 to Republican Donna Campbell to defeat moderate Republican state senator Jeff Wentworth and $463,393 to Republican James White to keep his seat.[31]

Defeating Opponents

Generally, incumbents have a huge advantage over challengers in an election. Since they are officeholders, they usually have greater name recognition than challengers, and it is easy for incumbents to get publicity by holding town hall meetings, by announcing the relocation of new businesses to the district, or simply by attending community events. Additionally, they usually have an established network of supporters who helped them get into office at least once previously.

Because of the incumbency advantage, it is far safer for interest groups to try to work with incumbents than challengers. Campaign money, for example, overwhelmingly goes to incumbents. In the 2014 campaign for the Texas legislature, incumbents

Which Interest Groups Contribute the Most?

Interest groups try to achieve favorable policies not only by lobbying members of the Texas legislature directly but also by influencing who becomes members of the legislature in the first place by donating to the election campaigns of favored candidates. The chart below breaks down contributions from employees of different industries by party in 2014.

Contributions to Texas Legislature Candidates, 2014

 = $1,000,000   Contributions to Democrats   Contributions to Republicans

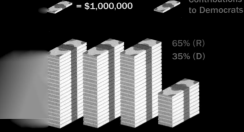

Finance, insurance, and real estate
$68,449,883
65% (R)
35% (D)

Labor
$59,745,893
18% (R)
82% (D)

General business
$54,573,566
68% (R)
32% (D)

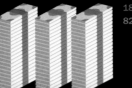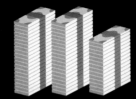

Health
$52,123,643
61% (R)
39% (D)

Lawyers and lobbyists
$37,643,736
51% (R)
49% (D)

Energy and natural resources
$35,023,592
70% (R)
30% (D)

Construction
$18,297,785
74% (R)
26% (D)

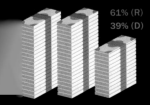

Communications and electronics
$17,631,798
57% (R)
43% (D)

Agriculture
$16,285,284
76% (R)
24% (D)

Transportation
$14,065,546
67% (R)
33% (D)

Defense
$291,826
71% (R)
29% (D)

QUANTITATIVE REASONING

- Which group contributes the highest percentage of contributions to Democrats? Republicans? Why might these groups provide strong support to a particular party?

- Which group provides the lowest total dollar amount to candidates of either political party? Why do you think this group provides less than other groups?

SOURCE: National Institution on State Money in Politics Industry Influence, www.followthemoney.org (accessed 3/10/16).

FIGURE 6.1

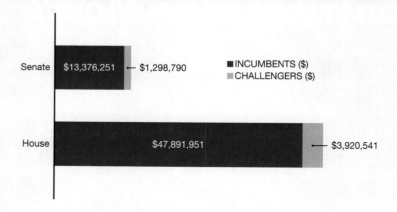

Dollars Contributed to Incumbents and Challengers for the Texas Legislature, 2014

SOURCE: National Institute on Money in State Politics.

raised more than 10 times the amount raised by challengers (see Figure 6.1). Incumbents win elections to an overwhelming degree. Some of the campaign contributions to incumbent legislators are spectacularly large. Speaker Joe Straus, for example, received $8,429,380 in contributions in 2015—no doubt in recognition that as Speaker he was in a position to advance or hinder much legislation. In the Texas Senate in 2012, incumbent Wendy Davis faced a tough Republican challenger but outraised the challenger with $4,310,971 in contributions compared to her Republican opponent's $3,340,325.[32]

Of course, sometimes an interest group does not want to help a candidate or even pressure a candidate; it wants to defeat that candidate. This can be a risky strategy because if the candidate wins, then the interest group will be faced with not only an unfriendly public official but also one displeased with the interest group for its opposition. When that happens, the interest group will often "get well" or "get on the late train." This means that the interest group will make a substantial political contribution to the winning candidate whom it formerly opposed. Often, winning candidates have significant campaign debts after a grueling election battle, and they appreciate the late contributions of former enemies, which are offered as a way of making amends.

Although "late-train" contributions may improve the relationship between officials and interest groups, usually candidates reserve a special loyalty for those supporters who backed them early. Without support at the very beginning of a campaign, it is hard for a candidate to build an organization and get the support necessary to make a decent campaign start. That is why early supporters are so valuable. The best lobbyists start early in trying to develop relationships with candidates and with new

Registered Lobbyists: How Does Texas Compare?

While we often associate lobbyists with Washington, DC, the reality is that lobbyists are active at all levels of policy making. Some states, such as Texas, are larger and more populated, so it stands to reason that more lobbyists are active in those states and have a higher degree of impact on businesses and labor. The chart below compares Texas with five other states in terms of the number of registered lobbyists and the lobbyists per 100,000 people. The map compares all states in terms of how many lobbyists per 100,000 people are actively persuading government officials.

Number of Lobbyists in Selected States

● Registered lobbyists   ● Lobbyists per 100,000 people

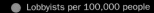

	New York	Ohio	Alabama	Florida	Texas	California
Registered lobbyists	5,061	1,581	636	2,222	1,850	2,059
Lobbyists per 100,000 people	37	18	18	16	11	8
Voting eligible pop.	13,553,426	8,701,243	3,588,783	13,914,216	16,675,420	24,440,416

Lobbyists per Capita, Nationwide

Lobbyists per 100,000 people   ● < 15   ● 15–24.9   ● 25–34.9   ● 35–45   ● > 45

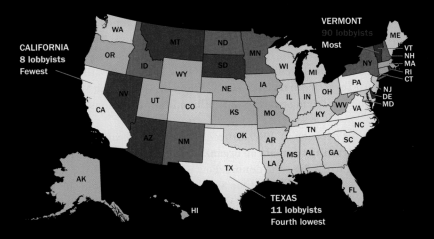

VERMONT
90 lobbyists
Most

CALIFORNIA
8 lobbyists
Fewest

TEXAS
11 lobbyists
Fourth lowest

NOTE: Data for Vermont, Nebraska, and Illinois are from 2014, the most recent year for which data are available.

SOURCES: Population data from www.electproject.org/2014g; lobbyist data from www.followthemoney.org/lobbyist-link.

CRITICAL THINKING

- How does Texas compare with other states regarding the total number of lobbyists and the number of lobbyists per capita? Do you think Texas has too many, too few, or just the right number of lobbyists?

- Looking at the map, what can you conclude about the most populated states and the number of lobbyists per capita? Which states go against the norm? Why might this be?

legislators. One national PAC, EMILY's List (EMILY stands for Early Money Is Like Yeast), is funded by women and provides early campaign contributions to female candidates. Legislators remember who was with them at the beginning of their political careers—and this can be immensely beneficial to the lobby that cultivated that early relationship.[33]

Sometimes PACs give to both candidates as a way to avoid alienating either one, though the possibility remains that such dual giving will wind up alienating both. At other times, interest groups simply don't care if they alienate a candidate. The 2010 Democratic primary election between state representatives Tara Rios Ybarra and Jose Manuel Lozano highlighted the lines that can clearly separate interest groups during a campaign. Texans for Lawsuit Reform contributed $256,610 to Ybarra, which was 56 percent of her campaign funds. Ybarra lost to Lozano, who was backed by trial lawyers who were not the least bit sympathetic to the goals of Texans for Lawsuit Reform.[34]

An extraordinary battle occurred in the 2012 Republican primary where Texans for Lawsuit Reform backed railroad commissioner Elizabeth Ames Jones in her challenge to Republican state senator Jeff Wentworth. Wentworth served nearly five years in the Texas House before being elected to the state senate in 1992. He appeared to be well established and unbeatable. An early poll showed him with a large lead. But although Wentworth supported 21 of 23 bills considered by Texans for Lawsuit Reform to be "major" legislation, he angered the interest group by criticizing a 2003 constitutional amendment that limited the amounts patients could receive in medical malpractice suits. He also voted against a bill that reduced the amount of money coastal homeowners could receive after hurricanes. While Wentworth was defeated, it was not by Jones, but by Donna Campbell, who had Tea Party backing. Nevertheless, Wentworth blamed his defeat on the "mammoth $2 million–plus negative campaign launched against me by Texans for Lawsuit Reform."[35] The defeat no doubt sent a message to Republican lawmakers that they had better not cross Texans for Lawsuit Reform.

When an interest group is convinced that it cannot work with a public official, the interest group may undertake an all-out effort to defeat that official. But spending money by no means guarantees success. Dr. James Leininger is one of the biggest contributors to Republican candidates. In the 2006 election cycle, he gave over $5 million to Republican candidates in Texas, either through individual contributions or by giving to PACs that then made contributions. Leininger and some of the PACs he supports are strong supporters of school vouchers. Much of this money backed challengers to Republican incumbents who were unfavorable to vouchers. The effort was unsuccessful and the result, according to Texans for Public Justice, was a legislature "even less receptive to vouchers than its predecessor. While Leininger is still an active donor to Republicans in Texas, more recently Houston Texans Owner Bob McNair has also been active in donations, giving nearly $3.55 million in contributions during the 2014 election cycle."[36]

A U.S. Supreme Court decision in 2009, *Citizens United v. Federal Election Commission*, created the opportunity to create an organization that opposed powerful incumbents without having to disclose the donors. Few wealthy Texans proved willing to openly fund political attacks on Speaker Joe Straus and his allies, but in the 2012 election cycle, Empower Texans moved several hundred thousand dollars through its nonprofit organization and thus avoided having to disclose its political contributors. Most of this money was spent on a number of House races with the biggest ex-

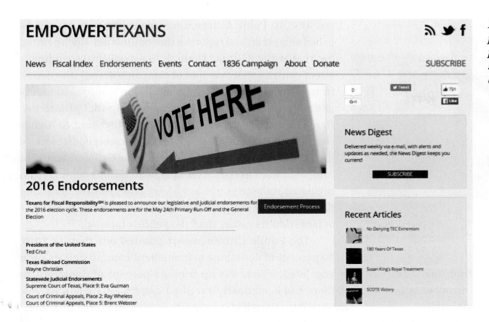

Empower Texans is a powerful political action committee that provides money to candidates, sometimes from undisclosed donors.

penditures going to failed challenges to Speaker Straus and to Representative Lance Gooden. The nonprofits spent about $290,000 on mailers, about $40,000 on Internet ads, and about $18,000 on robo-calls. Another nonprofit that does not have to report donors is the Texas Organizing Project, which spent a bit more than $234,000 mostly supporting then–Harris County sheriff Adrian Garcia and 14 other local candidates along with the Texas House campaign of Mary Ann Perez. These new funding structures where donors do not have to be reported are known as sources of **dark money**.[37]

dark money political money where the donors of the money do not have to be disclosed

Interest-Group Capture

Interest groups can sometimes have such influence over an agency of government that it is said that the interest group has "captured" that agency—meaning that the agency primarily serves the objectives of the interest group. Interest groups can develop long-term relationships with the agencies that regulate the industries that they represent in a number of ways. For example, interest groups can donate money to the election or re-election of agency officials who must seek election to their office. Subject to certain ethics rules, industries can also hire former agency officials to work for them as lobbyists. The closer the connection between the agency and the industry, the more complete is the capture.

Such **interest-group capture** may have occurred with the Texas Railroad Commission. The Railroad Commission has the primary responsibility for regulating the oil and natural gas industry, pipelines, and coal and uranium surface-mining operations. The commission is run by three statewide elected officials who serve staggered six-year terms. Although one unsuccessful candidate for the commission included railroad safety in his campaign platform, the Railroad Commission's name is long outdated and has nothing to do with railroads.[38]

interest-group capture government agency that serves the objectives of the interests that the agency is supposed to regulate

The Texas Railroad Commission regulates Texas's oil and gas drilling (pictured above). Some say that this commission has been captured by those special interests, which sometimes advocates controversial procedures like fracking.

In 2010, Public Citizen, a consumer advocacy group, published a highly critical report on the commission which pointed out that at the Railroad Commission, "political spending is out of control, well over half of campaign donations coming from the very industries the commission is supposed to regulate. Real or perceived, this creates a conflict of interest. Railroad commissioner is seen as a springboard to higher elected office in the state, giving influence-peddlers more incentive to curry favor and sitting commissioners to amass campaign war chests. . . . Campaign donations coming from regulated industries present a very real problem, inserting the probability that regulatory decisions are made in favor of large donors rather than the public's interest."[39]

The Public Citizen report pointed out that by 2010, 80 percent of donations to incumbent commissioners were from the industries they regulated, which was up from 45 percent of donations to incumbents in 2001, and there had been nearly a tenfold increase in donations. Additionally, the size of individual donations had increased—in 2000, 80 percent of donations were $1,000 or more; in 2010, 92 percent of donations were $1,000 or more.[40] In the 2012 election an incumbent, Barry Smitherman, received $5,144,683 in campaign contributions, with the oil and gas industry being the largest group to make contributions. In a race for an open seat, Christi Craddick won with $2,850,158 in contributions, again with the oil and gas industry being the largest business/industrial group to make contributions.[41] In the 2016 Republican primary for seats on the Railroad Commission, three candidates proposed banning donations from people or organizations that have business before the commission. These three candidates, however, raised very little funds for their campaigns, and lost their primaries.[42] Of course, that so many contributions should come from the oil and gas industry should not be surprising, since the commission is the main regulatory agency for oil and gas and other industries do not have the concerns about the commission's work that would cause those industries to make major contributions. And groups such as environmental groups do not have the resources to compete with the oil and gas industry in backing environmental candidates.

The staff of the Sunset Advisory Commission prepared a report in 2012 that attempted to deal with some of the concerns that the Texas Railroad Commission had been captured by the oil and gas industry. Among other things, the report recommended that the commission's name be changed to realistically reflect its contemporary duties: the Texas Energy Resources Commission. It also recommended that solicitation and receipt of campaign contributions by commissioners or candidates seeking the office be limited to the one- and one-half-year time frame around the election rather than having full-time fund-raising throughout the six-year term of office. It recommended that commissioners be banned from knowingly accepting contributions from those with contested cases before the commission, and it recommended that commissioners must resign their office if they become candidates for another elected office. There was also a recommendation that independent hearing examiners be used in contested cases involving oil and gas.[43]

House Speaker Pro Tem Dennis Bonnen was especially concerned that two sitting railroad commissioners had recently run for the U.S. Senate while retaining their offices and raising money from the oil and gas industry. While the efforts to reform the commission were publicly endorsed by the railroad commissioners, Bonnen claimed the commissioners were privately lobbying to weaken the proposals. The reform proposals failed in the 2013 legislature.[44]

Individuals as Lobbyists

Explain how ordinary individuals can influence Texas government

Sometimes ordinary individuals can have a remarkable impact on public policy, although interest groups clearly have an advantage in influencing the legislative process. Nevertheless, as we saw at the beginning of the chapter in the case of Dineen Majcher and school testing, a persistent individual with a well-reasoned argument can make a difference. For example, Tyrus Burks lost his wife and two children in a late-night electrical fire in West Dallas. Burks did not awaken in time to save them because he is deaf and did not hear the audible smoke alarm. Texas's state property code required the installation of audible smoke alarms but not visual alarms. In 2009, Burks became an advocate for a bill that would require property managers to buy and install visual smoke alarms if hearing-impaired tenants requested them and to put the alarms in visible locations such as bedrooms. Supported by state senator Royce West, the Sephra Burks Law, named for Tyrus's wife, who was also deaf, went into effect at the start of 2010. Tyrus Burks was an active lobbyist for the bill and gave legislative testimony in support of it with the aid of a sign language interpreter.

Occasionally, ordinary individuals can have a direct influence on policy. Tyrus Burks (right) lobbied the legislature to require landlords to buy and install visual smoke alarms for hearing impaired tenants who requested them.

Burks's efforts benefited from the support of the Texas Apartment Association, a major interest group representing apartment property interests, who backed the bill. Burks's story was tragic and his argument was compelling. It would have been difficult for opposition to emerge against such a proposal. Still, his efforts resulted in a major victory for the deaf, who are protected by such a law requiring visual smoke alarms in only three other states and the District of Columbia.[45] Burks's achievement demonstrates that individuals can, at least sometimes, be successful lobbyists.

The problem is that relatively few Texans are engaged in the neighborhood, in their community, or in politics, and thus much lobbying is left to organized interest groups with professional lobbyists. Table 6.1 provides a number of measures of civic engagement, and all show Texas is considerably lower than the national average on these measures. Texas is near the bottom of the nation in terms of measures of social connectedness that would lead to civic involvement such as discussing politics with friends or family, group involvement, frequent communication with friends and family, and even trust in all or most of the people in the neighborhood. Nor in comparison

TABLE 6.1

Measures of Texas Civic Health

	PERCENTAGE OF TEXANS AGREEING (%)	NATIONAL AVERAGE (%)	RANKING OF TEXAS AMONG THE STATES
Contacted or visited public official	9%	12%	49
Discuss politics with friends or family a few times a week or more	26	29	44
Communicate with friends and family frequently	78	79	41
Trust all or most people in the neighborhood	50	57	47
Donate $25 or more to charitable or religious organizations	47	52	43
Group involvement	38	39	37
Volunteer activity	25	27	42
Registered to vote	62	65	42
Voting	36	45	50

SOURCE: Regina Lawrence, Deborah Wise, and Emily Einsohn, *Texas Civic Health Index* (Austin: Annette Strauss Institute for Civic Life, 2013).

with the rest of the nation are Texans involved in volunteer activity or charitable donations. Texans tend not to contact or visit their public officials, register to vote, or vote. With such low levels of civic engagement, individual effects on the Texas political process are likely to be low.[46]

Interestingly, while 52 percent of Texans in one survey claimed they were very interested in politics and public affairs and 37 percent said they were somewhat interested, Texas has the lowest proportion of actual voters of any state. Texans give all sorts of reasons for not voting, the most common reason being that Texans claim they are too busy or that work conflicts with voting and the next most common reason being that they either are not interested or believe their vote does not matter.[47] Of course, Texas's low levels of voting participation—the lowest level in the country—means that organized interest groups fill the void in political activity and can wield vast influence in the state's political process.

Interest Groups and the Future of Texas

Interest groups play an important role in Texas politics even though Texas is no longer a one-party state with limited economic development. Even with two major political parties and a diverse economy, Texas politics cannot be understood without also examining the role of interest groups.

Though no single interest group or coalition of interest groups dominates Texas politics, by far most lobbyists represent business interests, and the bulk of PAC money comes from business interests. Often, of course, businesses are pitted against one another in the political process. Also, public interest, civil rights, consumer, and environmental groups may still be successful by mobilizing public opinion and influencing the media. However, there are only a few interest groups that offer alternatives to business perspectives on policy issues. Less frequently, ordinary individuals are able to influence public policy. Although they tend to be at a disadvantage in terms of money and other resources, dedicated individuals with a compelling argument sometimes succeed in lobbying for specific legislation. This is especially true when they are pursuing goals that do not put them in conflict with well-organized and well-funded interest groups.

The influence of interest groups in Texas shows no signs of diminishing. As long as federal law and state law allow donations and the creation of PACs and other groups, we will see the strong influence of interest groups not only in Austin but also in Washington. Texas is a pro-business state, and the Texas Association of Business will continue to be a dominant interest group representing the concerns of corporations and other entrepreneurs in Austin. At times, however, business interests might conflict with other conservative groups, especially on the issue of immigration. Business leaders have often welcomed more immigrants because of the low-cost labor they provide. While the state is limited in what it can do to curtail immigration, the election of Lieutenant Governor Dan Patrick and his emphasis on curtailing immigration might pose a counternarrative to business interest groups. As Texas becomes more diverse and more immigrants settle in the state, the response by different interest groups will be something to watch.

Use 🐰 INQUIZITIVE to help you study and master this material.

Interest Groups in the Political Process

- Define interest groups, and describe the major ways they try to influence Texas government (pp. 181–92)

Interest groups in Texas are organizations of interested citizens who band together to influence public policy. Lobbyists are hired to cultivate relationships with legislators and convince them of their clients' interests. The goal of lobbyists is to gain access to policy makers to persuade them to support the positions of the interest group.

Key Terms
interest group (p. 181)
free rider problem (p. 182)
bundling (p. 185)
lobbyist (p. 185)

Practice Quiz
1. The "8F Crowd"
    a) was a group of legislators who failed the eighth grade.
    b) was a group of extremely wealthy Texans who met in Suite 8F of the Lamar Hotel in Houston and controlled Texas politics for 40 years.
    c) were 25 legislators who boycotted the eighth session of the legislature in order to prevent the legislators from taking any action because it lacked a quorum.
    d) was made up of eight lobbyists who were close friends of the governor.
    e) were the eight most powerful officials in the state who met in Suite F of the Austin State Office Building.

2. Interest groups provide public officials with all the following except
    a) information.
    b) money.
    c) media coverage.
    d) votes.
    e) committee assignments.

3. The goals of interest groups include all except
    a) electing people to office in order to support the groups' goals.
    b) influencing those who control government.
    c) educating the public and members about issues of importance to the group.
    d) providing campaign funds for favored candidates.
    e) maintaining a heterogeneous membership.

4. Interest groups have an advantage over individuals in influencing policy because interest groups usually have
    a) more time to influence officials.
    b) greater expertise than individuals.
    c) more money to influence elections.
    d) more staff.
    e) all of the above

5. When interest groups combine small contributions from many sources to form one large contribution, it is called
    a) bundling.
    b) compacting.
    c) cracking.
    d) polling.
    e) packing.

6. The most important thing interest groups need to be effective is
    a) the support of a majority of Texans.
    b) office space in Austin.
    c) a variety of issues on which to lobby.
    d) a large, paid staff.
    e) access to politicians.

7. Trial lawyers are which type of interest group?
   a) professional group
   b) public employee group
   c) single-issue group
   d) consumer group
   e) business group

8. Interest groups often hire former legislators as lobbyists to
   a) gain greater access to current legislators.
   b) benefit from the policy expertise of former legislators.

   c) benefit from the personal "insider" knowledge of the former legislator.
   d) all of the above
   e) none of the above

9. Lobbyists are
   a) all corrupt.
   b) all unethical.
   c) important sources of information for legislators.
   d) harmful to the democratic process.
   e) never retired legislators.

Another Side to Lobbying

- Describe the role of PACs in Texas elections (pp. 192–201)

Political action committees (PACs) are private groups that raise and distribute funds for election campaigns. Interest groups play a major role in getting out the vote. Interest-group money can play a major role in defeating as well as electing candidates.

Key Terms
political action committee (PAC) (p. 193)
issue advocacy (p. 193)
dark money (p. 199)
interest-group capture (p. 199)

Practice Quiz
10. In Texas, the most powerful interest groups represent which interests?
    a) consumer
    b) civil rights
    c) business
    d) owners of oil wells
    e) public employee

11. PACs are used to
    a) stir the public's interest in politics.
    b) raise money from individuals, which is then bundled and given to candidates.
    c) create media campaigns to influence the course of government.
    d) create grassroots campaigns.
    e) all of the above

12. One of the most important grassroots tactics of interest groups is
    a) to gain support from all the mayors of towns in a district.
    b) to get out the vote.
    c) to form political alliances with executive and legislative leaders.
    d) to lobby the judicial branch of national and state government.
    e) to interpret the needs of their members.

13. *Dark money* refers to
   a) money that is illegally donated to politicians for their re-election.
   b) money that cannot be used to pay typical campaign expenditures.
   c) vouchers that candidates can use to fund their campaigns.
   d) donated money that does not have to be reported by a campaign.
   e) money that is printed on special dark green paper specifically formulated for campaigns.

14. *Capture theory* refers to the idea that
   a) interest groups are controlled by politicians.
   b) through long-term relationships, government interests come to serve the objectives of an interest group.
   c) politicians work for the public good by controlling special interests.
   d) labor unions are controlled by business.
   e) business interests are captured by labor unions.

Individuals as Lobbyists

- Explain how ordinary individuals can influence Texas government (pp. 201–3)

Citizens can lobby their legislators by calling, writing, or visiting their offices. Industries and well-financed interests can afford professional lobbyists to try to influence legislation, but legislators will listen to individual citizens, especially if they join together in large numbers.

Practice Quiz

15. Individuals have the best chance to influence public policy when they
   a) are not opposed by organized interest groups.
   b) are polite.
   c) entertain legislators.
   d) vote.
   e) live in Austin.

Representative and Speaker of the Texas House Joe Straus (R-San Antonio) celebrates his victory in the 2016 Republican Primary. Straus faced challenges from Tea Party–backed candidates who thought Straus was not conservative enough.

The Legislature

WHY THE TEXAS LEGISLATURE MATTERS Joe Straus from San Antonio is not your typical Texas Republican. A Jewish American in a state and party dominated by evangelical Christians, Straus does not fit your typical profile of a Republican state legislator. Even more surprising is the fact that Straus is Speaker of the State House of Representatives—the most powerful position in the legislature. Straus was first elected Speaker in 2009, ousting longtime Speaker Tom Craddick, a conservative from Midland who alienated many members of his party. Straus owed his election to all of the Democrats from the House as well as sixteen Republicans who joined forces to elect him.

Ever since his election as speaker in 2009, Tea Party conservatives have had a target on Straus's back. He was challenged in 2015 by a more conservative member of the House, Representative Scott Turner, an African American endorsed by the Tea Party. In the race for Speaker, Turner garnered 19 votes in the 150-member House, but his challenge was indicative of discontent by the more conservative members of the legislature. Turner decided not to seek re-election to his Frisco-area seat in 2015. Straus has also faced primary opposition in his own district from Tea Party–backed candidates. He has managed to survive these challenges despite well-funded efforts. In the run-up to the 2016 primary on March 1, Joe Straus faced the toughest challenge yet to his seat in the Texas legislature. Straus attracted two more conservative opponents in his race, Jeff Judson and Sheila Bean. Judson was the better-funded challenger who raised $660,000. Sensing the possibility of defeat, Straus spent nearly $4 million to keep his seat, a huge amount for a state legislative race. The problem for Straus is that conservative PACs joined in to help defeat Straus and support Judson. For example, Young Conservatives of Texas and other Tea Party groups spent money on ads attacking Straus for his purportedly liberal positions on immigration and gay rights.

Why does it matter who is Speaker of the Texas House? Being the head of the most powerful branch of state government brings much power. The Speaker has a huge influence on what gets voted on in the legislature. And the Speaker appoints chairs of committees and otherwise sets the agenda. To the chagrin of Tea Party Republicans, Straus has appointed some Democrats as committee chairs. This Democratic and moderate Republican coalition, however, is fragile as moderate Republicans retire or lose their primaries to more conservative challengers. Should this coalition break, Republicans will undoubtedly elect a more conservative legislator as speaker, thus solidifying the hold of the Tea Party on Texas government.

We have already seen changes in the State Senate when Lieutenant Governor David Dewhurst lost to Dan Patrick. The lieutenant governor is president of the state senate and has the power to appoint committee chairs and set the legislative agenda. Patrick criticized Dewhurst for appointing Democrats as committee chairs and vowed to return the Senate to more conservative rule when he took office. Indeed, he has already replaced the infamous two-thirds rule, which required the agreement of a supermajority of senators to conduct business. Now, a simple majority can conduct business, thus locking out all of the Democratic senators.

The Texas legislature has become more and more like the U.S. Congress in terms of political polarization and partisan division. When Democrat Bob Bullock was lieutenant governor during the late 1990s, he worked with then–Republican governor George W. Bush in a bipartisan fashion. Today, the legislature is completely controlled by Republicans, who are themselves internally divided between the establishment and the Tea Party faction. Straus is hanging on as the last establishment Republican in control of one side of the Texas legislature. His ability to stay in his position might become precarious given the seeming takeover of the state Republican party by the Tea Party faction. A Tea Party speaker would herald a more conservative direction in the House as well as the elimination of the little bipartisanship that exists with regard to some Democratic committee chairs and some cooperation that Straus must employ with Democrats who helped elect him.

CHAPTER GOALS

- Describe the organization and basic rules of the legislature (pp. 211–16)
- Outline the legislative and nonlegislative powers of the legislature (pp. 216–19)
- Trace the process through which law is made in Texas (pp. 219–30)
- Analyze how party leadership and partisanship affect power in the legislature (pp. 230–37)
- Explain the politics of redistricting (pp. 237–40)

Structure of the Texas Legislature

Describe the organization and basic rules of the legislature

The Texas state legislature is the most important representative institution in the state. Members share many of the duties and responsibilities that are taken up at the national level by members of the U.S. Congress. Like members of the U.S. Congress, the members of the Texas House and Senate are responsible for bringing the interests and concerns of their constituencies directly into the democratic political processes. But the important constitutional and institutional differences between the U.S. Congress and the Texas state legislature must be taken into account if we are to understand the role that the state legislature plays in democracy in Texas.

Bicameralism

Like the U.S. Congress and all the states except Nebraska, Texas has a **bicameral** legislature, with two chambers: the Texas House of Representatives and the Texas Senate. The Texas legislature's 150 House members and 31 senators meet in regular session for 140 days every odd-numbered year. Senators serve four-year terms, and House members serve for two years. Each represents a single-member district. Each member of the Texas House represents approximately 168,000 people. Each senator represents over 811,000 constituents. A state senator now represents more people than does a member of the U.S. House of Representatives. Elections are held in November of even-numbered years, and senators and House members take office in January of odd-numbered years.

Bicameralism creates interesting dynamics in a legislature. For one thing, it means that before a law is passed, it will be voted on by two deliberative bodies representing different constituencies. In 2009, for example, the Texas Senate passed legislation to allow college students and faculty with concealed handgun licenses to carry their firearms on campus. That legislation, however, was killed in the Texas House of Representatives.[1] In 2011 the Texas Senate again passed a bill with an amendment allowing guns on campus. In the Texas House, the bill had support from a majority of members. However, the bill failed in the House because of a successful parliamentary objection that the gun amendment was not germane to the bill it amended, which dealt with scholarships.[2] In 2013 the National Rifle Association–backed bill allowing guns on campus passed the House, but the bill died in the Texas Senate when it failed to get the two-thirds vote needed in the Senate for the bill to be brought to the floor for discussion and a vote.[3] If a bill cannot be killed in one house, it can be killed or modified in the other body. Eventually, this bill to allow holders of concealed handgun licenses to carry firearms on campus was passed in 2015, and led to resistance, especially at the University of Texas at Austin.

One effect of bicameralism in Texas is that the author of a bill in one house that has been amended in the other body has the option of accepting or rejecting the

bicameral having a legislative assembly composed of two chambers or houses

Before becoming law in Texas, a bill must pass in both houses of the legislature. In 2013 the legislature passed a law forbidding guns on college campuses unless specifically authorized by the campus.

amendment. If the author accepts the amendment, the bill moves forward; if the author rejects the amendment, the bill is killed.

Bicameralism allows a member of one legislative body to retaliate against a member of either body for not cooperating on desired legislation. A "local and consent" calendar in the House is usually reserved for uncontroversial bills or bills limited to a localized problem. In order for a bill to be passed from that calendar, it has to pass without the objection of any member of the House. That requirement provides a perfect opportunity for members to retaliate against other members for perceived slights.[4]

Sessions of the Legislature

Not all state legislatures meet for the same time periods. Some state legislatures meet every year like the U.S. Congress. Texas's legislature generally meets every other year unless the governor calls it to meet between regular sessions.

regular session the 140-day period, occurring only in odd-numbered years, during which the Texas legislature meets to consider and pass bills

biennial occurring every two years

Regular Sessions The Texas Constitution specifies that **regular sessions** of the Texas legislature be held for 140 days in odd-numbered years. The **biennial** legislative sessions have their origin in the nineteenth-century idea that legislative service is a part-time job and a belief that short, biennial sessions would limit the power of the legislature. For a few years, legislators were encouraged to end their work early by being paid for only 120 days of service.

Thousands of bills and resolutions are introduced into the legislature during a regular session, and the 140-day limitation places a considerable restriction on the legislature's ability to deal with this workload. In the 2015 regular legislative session, for example, 6,276 bills were introduced and 1,322 passed. If resolutions are included as well as bills, 11,356 were introduced and 6,083 were passed. The governor vetoed 42 of the bills passed by the legislature.[5] Hundreds of bills pass in the last hours of a legislative session, most with little or no debate. More die in the end-of-session crush of business because there isn't time to consider them.

special session a legislative session called by the governor that addresses an agenda set by him or her and that lasts no longer than 30 days

Special Sessions If the legislature does not complete its agenda before the end of the legislative session or if problems arise between regular sessions, the governor may call a **special session**. Special sessions last no more than 30 days, but there is no limit to the number of special sessions a governor can call, and the governor sets their agenda. Texas has averaged one special session a year since 1876, although years may go by with no special session, whereas in some years there may be three or four sessions.

The ability to call and set the agenda of a special session provides the governor with control over which issues are discussed and what bills are passed. In many instances, the governor, the Speaker of the Texas House, the lieutenant governor, and various committee chairs will meet to decide what will be done to solve the problem at hand. Once the leaders address the issue and develop solutions, the governor calls the special session.

Once the session begins, the governor can open it to different issues. At times, the governor bargains for a legislator's vote in return for adding to the special session agenda an issue of importance to that legislator. In 2003, Governor Perry called three special sessions of the legislature to address congressional redistricting. In 2004 a fourth special session was called to address school finance. In 2005, in addition to the regular session, two special sessions addressed school finance. There was also a special session in 2006, 2009, and 2011. In 2013 two special sessions were called to deal with Texas abortion laws.

Between legislative sessions, members serve on interim committees that may require a few days of their time each month. Legislators are also frequently called on to present programs to schools, colleges, and civic clubs. They supervise the staff of their district offices and address the needs of their constituents. Special sessions, interim committee meetings, speeches, and constituent services require long hours with little remuneration. Many members devote more than 40 hours a week to legislative business in addition to maintaining their full-time jobs.

When Texas was a rural, predominantly agricultural state, biennial sessions worked well; however, Texas has moved beyond this description. In the twenty-first century, Texas is a modern state with more than 80 percent of its population living in metropolitan areas. Population growth continues at a rapid rate. The state's gross domestic product exceeds that of many nations. Part-time legislators serving biennial 140-day sessions may not work well anymore in allowing the state to respond quickly and effectively to problems that arise.

Membership

There are 150 Texas House districts and 31 Texas Senate districts. One senator or one member of the House represents each district. This is called representation by **single-member districts**. Districts must be roughly equal in population. House districts each contain about 165,000 people, while Senate districts contain about 800,000. Some districts are geographically small, like House district 137, which is one of 29 districts in Harris County in the Houston metropolitan area. Some districts are large; House district 74 covers 12 counties in West Texas.

single-member district a district in which one official is elected rather than multiple officials

The constitutional requirements for becoming a member of the Texas legislature are minimal. A senator must be a U.S. citizen, a qualified voter, and a resident of the state for at least five years and of the district for at least one year. Additionally, the senator must be at least 26 years of age. Members of the House must be at least 21, U.S. citizens, qualified voters, and residents of the state for two years and of the district for one year. These requirements are in keeping with the political philosophy of those who wrote the Constitution of 1876. They believed holding public office required little or no formal training and should be open to most citizens.

In Texas, the typical legislator is white, male, Protestant, college educated, and affluent and has a professional or business occupation. These characteristics do not mean that others cannot be elected to the state legislature, but they do indicate that individuals with most of these informal characteristics have a distinct advantage. Members of the legislature must have jobs that allow them the flexibility to campaign for office and to work in the legislature for 140 days every other year, as well as in special legislative sessions and meetings of committees when the legislature is not in session. Thus, about one-third of the members of the legislature are attorneys. The legal profession is one of the few careers that pays well and offers the flexibility a legislator needs. Lawyers who serve in the legislature may even gain increased legal business either from interests with legislative concerns or because of the enhanced visibility of a lawyer-legislator.[6]

Republicans control both houses of the Texas legislature. In 2017 there were 11 Democrats and 20 Republicans in the Texas Senate and 56 Democrats and 94 Republicans in the Texas House of Representatives.

Legislators in Texas cannot expect to live on their legislative salaries. In keeping with the Texas constitutional tradition of a low-cost, part-time legislature, Texas representatives receive a salary of only $7,200 per year. Legislators also receive a payment of $190 a day when the legislature is in session. When the legislature is not in session, legislators may claim up to 12 days per month of **per diem** pay if they are in Austin on official business, or 16 days if they are committee chairs. The legislators themselves determine what qualifies as official business. It is common to pay expenses from officeholder expense accounts and to pocket the per diem so that it becomes a salary supplement. Legislative retirement pensions are very generous. The pension is tied to district judges' salaries, which are $140,000 a year. That salary is multiplied by the years of service of the legislator times 2.3 percent. A legislator who has served 10 years thus would qualify for a pension of $32,200 per year. A legislator serving 20 years would qualify for a pension of $64,400 per year. Lawmakers are eligible for pensions with at least 8 years of service. With 8 years of service, the lawmaker can start collecting a pension at age 60. With 10 years of service, a lawmaker can start collecting at age 50.[7]

Originally, per diem rates were set by the Texas Constitution, and a constitutional amendment was necessary to change this. In 1991, Texans adopted an amendment allowing the Texas Ethics Commission to propose changes in legislative salaries, which then require voter approval. At the start of each regular session, the Ethics Commission sets the legislative per diem. In the 2011 session, with major belt-tightening throughout state government, the legislature asked the Texas Ethics Commission to reduce its scheduled per diem of $168 a day to $150.[8] One Texas legislator found a way to increase his income by billing both the state and his campaign funds for his travel expenses. Representative Joe Driver of Garland pled guilty to a third-degree felony for double billing thousands of dollars in expenses. His conviction raises questions about how closely legislators' expenses are monitored.[9] During one of the 2013 special legislative sessions, which lasted 30 days, 147 Texas lawmakers collected their $150 per diem for the entire time even though a number of them did not attend the session and even though the House and Senate actually met only a few days. Eight senators and 26 House members gave written notice that they did not wish to receive the per diem when they were not in Austin.[10] The commission recommended a per diem increase to $190 in 2015.

"Who Are Texans: Who Are the Members of the Texas Legislature?" shows the proportions of minorities and women serving in the legislature. Although those numbers have increased over the years, they are not in proportion to their population in Texas. Civil rights laws have increased voting by minorities, and those laws provide protection for minority political districts, though the 2013 decision of the U.S. Supreme Court overturning part of the Voting Rights Act may lead to reduced legal protection for minority districts. Thus, more minority officeholders have been elected and, as the Hispanic population in Texas increases, additional Latino legislators will be elected. Women have also had an increased role in

per diem daily payment to a public official engaged in state business

Although the "typical" member of the Texas state legislature is white and male, women and minority groups have increased their representation in recent years. For example, state representative and entrepreneur Helen Giddings has become an influential member of the House Business and Industry and Appropriations committees.

Who Are the Members of the Texas Legislature?

The Texas legislature is designed to be a representative body, which looks and sounds like the state as a whole. How well does the legislature represent Texas? In many ways, the legislature does not look like Texas. The state is evenly split between men and women, while the legislature is four-fifths male. While the state has no ethnic majority in its population, more than two-thirds of Texas legislators are white. Perhaps the biggest differences, though, relate to socioeconomic status. Over half of the members of the legislature hold graduate degrees, while only 9 percent of the population does.

Gender

	Texas pop.	Texas House	Texas Senate
Female	50%	24%	26%
Male	50%	76%	74%

Key

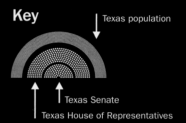

Texas population

Texas Senate

Texas House of Representatives

SOURCES: For Texas legislature, numbers calculated by author based on data from the Directory of Elected Officials of the Texas Tribune, www.texastribune.org/directory. State demographic data calculated from the U.S. Census Bureau American Community Survey, www.census.gov (accessed 11/10/16).

Race

	Texas pop.	Texas House	Texas Senate
White	43%	66%	70%
African American	13%	12%	7%
Latino	39%	20%	23%
Asian	5%	2%	0%

Education*

	Texas pop.	Texas House	Texas Senate
< HS diploma	19%	0%	0%
High school grad.	48%	7%	3%
Associate's degree	17%	3%	0%
Bachelor's degree	7%	53%	39%
Graduate degree	9%	37%	58%

QUANTITATIVE REASONING

- How much do you think the racial, gender, and socio-economic makeup of the Texas legislature matters to the type of laws that the legislature passes? If the legislature had more people of color, more women, or more middle-class members, would it pass different policies?

- Why do you think that members of the Texas legislature come from the more educated, higher socioeconomic groups? Does the structure of the Texas legislature encourage or discourage people from particular occupations to run?

Occupation*

- Business
- Attorney
- Community service
- Health care
- Education
- Other

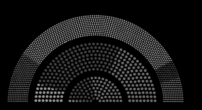

Texas House

35% 30% 5% 25% 4% 1%

Texas Senate

39% 23% 13% 23% 3%

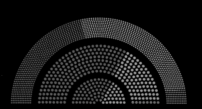

* Education and occupation data are from the 2015 session of the Texas legislature.

politics, especially since the 1970s, and as a result, it is likely that additional women will be elected to legislative office.

Powers of the Legislature

Outline the legislative and nonlegislative powers of the legislature

The Texas legislature sets public policy by passing bills, but it also supervises the state bureaucracy through the budgetary process and the Sunset Act, an act that provides for the review and, when deemed appropriate, the termination of state agencies. This supervision is achieved using legislative and nonlegislative powers. Legislative powers consist of passing bills and resolutions. Nonlegislative powers are those functions falling outside the lawmaking function.

Legislative Powers

bill a proposed law that has been sponsored by a member of the legislature and submitted to the clerk of the House or Senate

local bill a bill affecting only units of local government, such as a city, county, or special district

special bill a bill that gives an individual or corporation a special exemption from state law

general bill a bill that applies to all people and/or property in the state

resolution an expression of opinion on an issue by a legislative body

concurrent resolution a resolution of interest to both chambers of the legislature and which must pass both the House and Senate and generally be signed by the governor

Bills Revenue bills must begin in the House of Representatives. All other bills may start in either the House or the Senate. For decades, a **bill** would be introduced in either the House or the Senate and work its way through the legislative process in that chamber. A bill introduced in the Senate would be passed by the Senate prior to going to the House. Today, it is customary for a bill to be introduced in the House and the same bill, a companion bill, to be introduced in the Senate at the same time. This simultaneous consideration of bills saves time in the legislature.

There are three classifications of bills in the Texas legislature: (1) local bills, (2) special bills, and (3) general bills. **Local bills** affect only units of local government such as a city, a county, special districts, or more than one city in a county. A local bill, for example, might allow a county to create a sports authority or to establish a community college. **Special bills** give individuals or corporations an exemption from state law. A special bill could grant compensation to an individual wrongly convicted and sentenced to prison. **General bills** apply to all people and/or property in the state. General bills define criminal behavior; establish standards for divorce, child custody, or bankruptcy; and address other matters affecting people and property throughout the state. There is great variation among legislators in terms of the number of bills sponsored. In the 2015 regular session of the legislature, for example, Senator Judith Zaffirini sponsored 371 bills, whereas Senator Eddie Lucio introduced 274. Representative James White sponsored 486 bills, and Representative Drew Springer sponsored 300.[11]

Resolutions There are three types of **resolutions** in the Texas legislature: (1) concurrent resolutions, (2) joint resolutions, and (3) simple resolutions. **Concurrent resolutions** must pass both the House and Senate, and they require the governor's signature. These resolutions involve issues of interest to both chambers. They may request information from a state agency or call on Congress for some action. Senate

A Full-Time or Part-Time Legislature?

The Texas legislature is a part-time, citizen legislature. It meets only once every two years for 140 days. Members of the Texas House are elected for two-year terms and are paid $7,200 per year.

It is interesting to contrast the Texas legislature with a professional legislature, such as New York's. The New York legislature is considered professional because legislators are committed to being full-time representatives; they meet year-round, and members are paid $79,500 per year. Members of Congress serve year-round.

Former governor Rick Perry campaigned for president on adapting the Texas model to the U.S. Congress. Perry argued that the Founders intended a "citizen" Congress similar to the one in Texas, with members serving for only a few terms and retaining their regular employment in the private sector. As far back as 2007, Perry remarked, "When you have a full-time legislature, they just feel pretty inclined to be doing something. So they are going to dream up new laws, new regulations and new statutes—and generally all of those cost money."[a] This vision also fits with the principle of limited government—the principle that Congress or the legislature really should have a small role and the more they are in session, the more temptations they have to engage in corrupt practices and to pass laws restricting liberties.

Opponents argue that the Texas model is not one that should be adopted for the U.S. Congress or other legislatures. Legislators are not any less prone to corruption under the Texas model. Under either model, lobbyists attempt to influence policy makers, and the fact that legislators have private-sector jobs does not minimize this possibility. Meeting once every two years reduces the time to deliberate and make sensible policies. In Texas, critics argue that the legislative session is rushed, and legislators rely too heavily on staff who work year-round and are more familiar with the ins and outs of policy making. Former Houston-area congressman Chris Bell also warns that state legislators are more susceptible to corruption because "unless they're retired or independently wealthy, [legislators are] in a tough spot. There aren't a whole lot of jobs that lend themselves to a legislator's schedule, so those in office become prime targets [for lobbyists]."[b] The rush of completing the legislation necessary to govern the state often leaves important issues unresolved, leading to the need for more special sessions. Members who are not independently wealthy are unable to legislate effectively because they cannot just leave their jobs for

140 days at a time every two years. All of these factors result in a less productive legislature.

Your vision of the proper role of government will likely affect where you come down on this issue. Liberals, who prefer an active government, would probably prefer a full-time legislature that actively addresses social problems. Conservatives, who are not supporters of government activity in the economy, are more likely to support a minimal role for legislators so that citizens are free to make their own choices without governmental interference.

Why should citizens care about this issue? The political process matters, and how legislative institutions are designed makes a difference in terms of policy outcomes.

COMMUNICATING EFFECTIVELY: YOUR VOICE

- Are you more convinced by the arguments for a part-time legislature or those for a full-time legislature? What are the advantages and disadvantages of each approach?

- What sorts of compromises are possible between Texas's 140-day session and a full-time approach?

Concurrent Resolution 6 might, for example, call on Congress to propose an amendment requiring a balanced federal budget.

joint resolution a resolution, commonly a proposed amendment to the Texas Constitution or ratification of an amendment to the U.S. Constitution, that must pass both the House and Senate but that does not require the governor's signature

Joint resolutions require passage in both the House and Senate but do not require the governor's signature. The most common use of joint resolutions is to propose amendments to the Texas Constitution or to ratify amendments to the U.S. Constitution. Resolutions that propose amendments to the Texas Constitution require a two-thirds vote of the membership of both houses of the state legislature. Ratification of amendments to the U.S. Constitution requires a majority vote in both the Texas House and Senate.

simple resolution a resolution that concerns only the Texas House or Senate, such as the adoption of a rule or the appointment of an employee, and that does not require the governor's signature

Simple resolutions concern only the Texas House or the Senate, and they do not require the governor's signature. They are used to adopt rules, to request opinions from the attorney general, to appoint employees to office in the House or Senate, or to honor outstanding achievements by Texas residents. For example, a House or Senate resolution could recognize the achievements of a Nobel Prize winner or the San Jacinto College baseball program for accomplishments in the National Junior College Athletic Association.

Resolutions of honor or recognition are acted on without debate and without requiring members to read the resolution. Such resolutions are mostly symbolic acts that are designed to promote goodwill with voters. However, at times these simple symbolic acts can go terribly wrong. A Fort Worth doctor was twice honored by the Texas House of Representatives as the "doctor of the day." It was then reported, to the embarrassment of the House and the legislators who introduced him to the House, that the doctor was a registered sex offender who had been convicted of having a sexual relationship with a 17-year-old female patient.[12]

Nonlegislative Powers

Nonlegislative powers include the power to serve constituents, electoral powers, investigative powers, directive and supervisory powers, and judicial powers. The functions of these powers fall outside the scope of passing bills and resolutions; however, the passage of legislation may be necessary to exercise these powers.

constituent a person living in the district from which an official is elected

Legislators have the power to get things done for or in the name of **constituents**. Efforts on behalf of constituents may involve legislative activity, such as introducing a bill or voting on a resolution. Often, however, working on behalf of constituents involves nonlegislative activity, such as arranging an appointment for a constituent with a government agency that regulates some aspect of the constituent's life, writing a letter of recommendation for a constituent, or giving a speech to a civic group in the legislator's district.

electoral power the legislature's mandated role in counting returns in the elections for governor and lieutenant governor

Electoral powers of the legislature consist of formally counting returns in the elections for governor and lieutenant governor. This is accomplished during a joint session of the legislature when it is organized for the regular session.

investigative power the power, exercised by the House, the Senate, or both chambers jointly, to investigate problems facing the state

Investigative powers can be exercised by the House of Representatives, by the Senate, or jointly by both bodies. The legislature can undertake to investigate problems facing the state, the integrity of a state agency, or almost anything else it wishes. A special investigative committee is established by a simple resolution creating the committee, establishing the jurisdiction of the committee, and explaining the need for the investigation. If the special committee is formed in the House, the Speaker appoints the members of the committee. The lieutenant governor appoints members for special committees in the Senate. The Speaker and the lieutenant governor share appointments if it is a joint investigation.

Directive and supervisory powers enable the legislature to have considerable control over the executive branch of government. The legislature determines the size of the appropriation each agency has to spend for the next two years. The amount of money an agency has determines how well it can carry out its goals and objectives. A review of each agency of state government takes place every 12 years.

Judicial powers include the ability of the House to impeach members of the executive and judicial branches of state government. On **impeachment**, a trial takes place in the Senate. A majority vote of the House is required to bring charges, and a two-thirds vote of senators attending is necessary to convict an individual of the impeachment charges. Unlike the U.S. Constitution, the Texas Constitution does not explicitly define what constitutes an impeachable offense. This will be determined by the House and Senate in the impeachment process itself.[13]

Each body can compel attendance at regular and special sessions. More than once, Texas Rangers have handcuffed absent members and brought them to the legislature. On rare occasions, a chamber will punish nonmembers who disrupt proceedings by imprisoning them for up to 48 hours. The House and Senate judge the qualifications of members and can expel a member for cause.

How a Bill Becomes a Law in Texas

 Trace the process through which law is made in Texas

Anyone can write a bill, but only members of the legislature can introduce a bill. Bills may be written by members of the executive branch, by lobbyists, by constituents, or by local governmental entities. Legislators may also write bills, often with the help of a legislative staff expert in drafting legislation. There are, of course, innumerable reasons for drafting and introducing a bill.

Revenue bills must start in the House of Representatives. Other bills can start in either the House or Senate. Figure 7.1 shows the flow of a bill from the time it is introduced in the Texas House of Representatives to final passage and submission to the governor. A bill introduced in the Senate would follow the same procedure in reverse. Examining this figure suggests that the process of how a bill becomes law is long, detailed, and cumbersome. However, when the process is distilled to its basic parts, there are only six steps in how a bill becomes law. For a bill that starts in the House these steps are (1) **introduction**, (2) **referral**, (3) **consideration by standing committee**, and (4) **floor action**. Steps (1) through (4) are repeated in the Senate. Step (5) is action by a **conference committee** and approval by both houses, and finally, step (6) is action by the governor.

directive and supervisory power the legislature's power over the executive branch; for example, the legislature determines the size of appropriations for state agencies

judicial power the power of the House to impeach and of the Senate to convict members of the executive and judicial branches of state government

impeachment according to the Texas Constitution, the formal charge by the House of Representatives that leads to a trial in the Senate and possibly to the removal of a state official

introduction the first step in the legislative process, during which a member of the legislature gets an idea for a bill and files a copy of it with the clerk of the House or secretary of the Senate

referral the second step in the legislative process, during which a bill is assigned to the appropriate standing committee by the Speaker (for House bills) or the lieutenant governor (for Senate bills)

consideration by standing committee the third step in the legislative process, during which a bill is killed, amended, or heard by a standing committee

floor action the fourth step in the legislative process, during which a bill referred by a standing committee is scheduled for floor debate by the Calendars Committee

conference committee a joint committee created to work out a compromise on House and Senate versions of a piece of legislation

FIGURE 7.1

How a Bill Becomes a Law in Texas

Passing legislation in Texas is a complicated process. There are many points along the way where a bill can die.

SOURCE: This graphic was created for the February 2013 Issue of *Texas Co-op Power* magazine, a publication of Texas Electric Cooperatives.

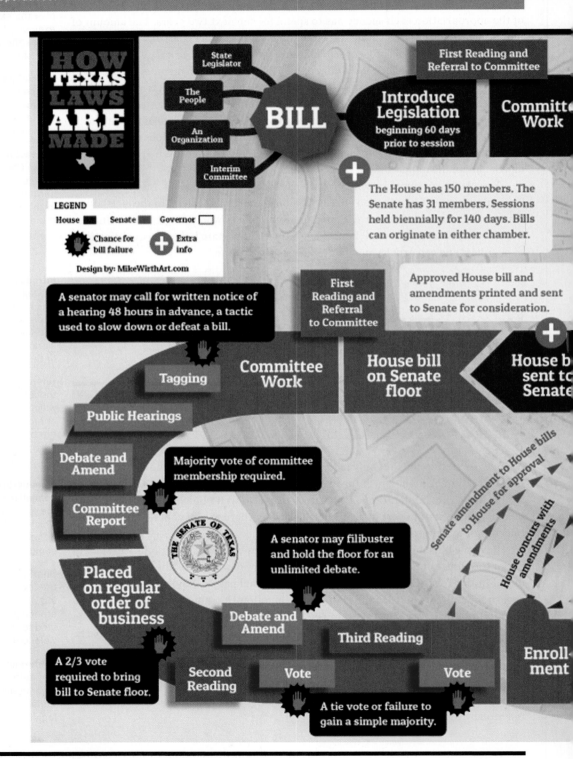

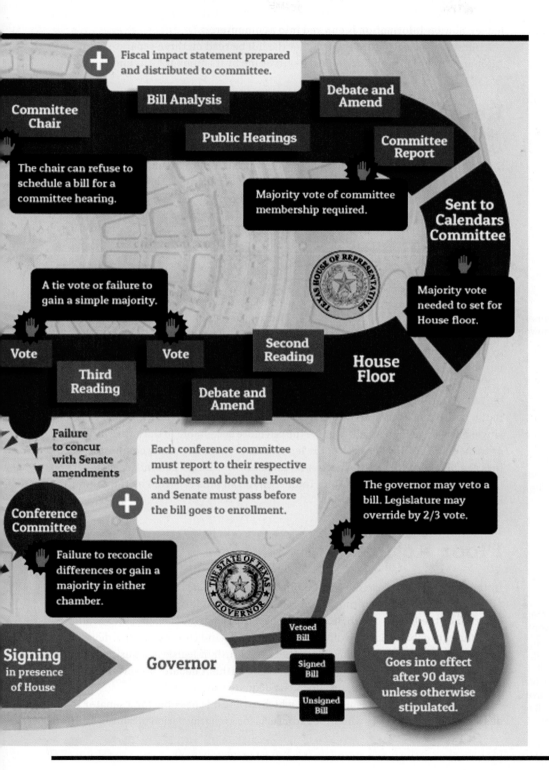

Fiscal impact statement prepared and distributed to committee.

Bill Analysis

Debate and Amend

Committee Chair

Public Hearings

Committee Report

The chair can refuse to schedule a bill for a committee hearing.

Majority vote of committee membership required.

Sent to Calendars Committee

A tie vote or failure to gain a simple majority.

Majority vote needed to set for House floor.

Vote

Vote

Second Reading

Third Reading

House Floor

Debate and Amend

Failure to concur with Senate amendments

Each conference committee must report to their respective chambers and both the House and Senate must pass before the bill goes to enrollment.

The governor may veto a bill. Legislature may override by 2/3 vote.

Conference Committee

Failure to reconcile differences or gain a majority in either chamber.

Signing in presence of House

Governor

Vetoed Bill

Signed Bill

Unsigned Bill

LAW
Goes into effect after 90 days unless otherwise stipulated.

Introduction in the House

A legislator introduces a bill by placing copies of the bill with the clerk of the House. In the Senate, the secretary of the Senate receives the bill. The clerk or secretary numbers the bill and enrolls it by recording its number, title, caption, and sponsor in a ledger. Similar information is entered into a computer.

Rules of the legislature require that the bill be read on three separate occasions. After enrollment, the bill is read for the first time by its number, title, and caption.

Referral

After undergoing first reading, the bill is assigned to a standing committee by the Speaker. In the Senate, the lieutenant governor assigns it to a committee. Since committees in the Texas legislature have overlapping jurisdictions, the Speaker and lieutenant governor can assign a bill to a friendly committee or an unfriendly one. The committee to which a bill is assigned can determine whether the bill survives or dies in committee.

Committee Action

standing committee a permanent committee with the power to propose and write legislation that covers a particular subject, such as finance or agriculture

pigeonholing a step in the legislative process during which a bill is killed by the chair of the standing committee to which it was referred, as a result of his or her setting the bill aside and not bringing it before the committee

Every bill introduced in the Texas legislature is assigned to a **standing committee**, and the vast majority of bills die in committee. The chair of the committee kills most by pigeonholing. **Pigeonholing** means that the committee chair sets the bill aside and never brings it before the committee.

Standing committees are considered the "workhorses" of the legislature (see Table 7.1). If the bill does not die, it most likely is amended. Few bills leave the committee in the same form as they arrived. Parts of several bills can also be combined to form a single bill. Changes are made to make the bill more acceptable to the entire legislature or to meet the political desires of the leadership or members of the committee. Hearings can take place to allow experts and the public to educate committee members on the good and bad points of the bill. In the Senate, all bills reported by the committee must have a public hearing.

Floor Action

filibuster a tactic used by members of the Senate to prevent action on legislation they oppose by continuously holding the floor and speaking until the majority backs down. Once given the floor, senators have unlimited time to speak as long as they follow Senate rules

In the House, bills referred by a standing committee go next to the Calendars Committee, which, after consulting the Speaker, schedules bills for debate. The Speaker determines the length of debate in the House. Customarily, each member is allowed 10 minutes of debate. Early in the session when the agenda is not crowded, debate may last longer. Later in the session when there is a crush of legislative business, debate will be more limited. Some bills will be voted on without debate; however, important or controversial bills are usually allocated adequate time.

Debate in the Senate is unlimited, which means it is possible for a senator to **filibuster**. A filibuster occurs when a senator talks for a lengthy period of time in an effort

TABLE 7.1

Standing Committees of the Texas Senate and House (85th Legislature), 2017

SENATE STANDING COMMITTEES

Administration	Finance	Nominations
Agriculture, Rural Affairs & Homeland Security	Health & Human Services	State Affairs
Business & Commerce	Health & Human Services	Transportation
Criminal Justice	Intergovernmental Relations	Veteran Affairs & Military Installations
Education	Natural Resources & Economic Development	

HOUSE STANDING COMMITTEES

Agriculture & Livestock	General Investigating & Ethics	Natural Resources
Appropriations	Government Efficiency and Reform	Pensions
Business & Industry	Higher Education	Public Education
Calendars	Homeland Security & Public Safety	Public Health
Corrections	House Administration	Redistricting
County Affairs	Human Services	Rules & Resolutions
Criminal Jurisprudence	Insurance	Special Purpose Districts
Culture, Recreation & Tourism	International Trade & Intergovernmental Affairs	State Affairs
Defense & Veterans' Affairs	Investments & Financial Services	Technology
Economic & Small Business Development	Judiciary & Civil Jurisprudence	Transportation
Elections	Land & Resource Management	Urban Affairs
Energy Resources	Licensing & Administrative Procedures	Ways & Means
Environmental Regulation	Local & Consent Calendars	

to kill a bill or to obtain amendments or other compromises. There are certain rules that apply to the filibuster in the Texas Senate that are quite different from those in the U.S. Senate. There is no eating or drinking during a filibuster. Senators must stand at their desks and may not lean, sit, or use their desk or chair in any way. Remarks must be confined to the issue under consideration. Finally, one must speak in an audible voice.

In the past 72 years, there have been more than 100 filibusters. The longest filibuster was in 1977 by Senator Bill Meier, who spoke for 43 hours. Given the time constraints under which the Texas legislature operates, even the threat of a filibuster may be sufficient to kill or force changes in a bill. In 2013 former state senator

Former state senator Wendy Davis, shown here during her filibuster of a Republican bill aimed at restricting abortion, later ran for governor in 2015 and lost to Greg Abbott.

Wendy Davis (D–Fort Worth) garnered headlines for her nearly 24-hour filibuster against a controversial bill requiring sonograms for women who wanted abortions. She became famous nationwide for this filibuster and later won the Democratic gubernatorial nomination but lost to Republican Greg Abbott.

Another tactic used in both the House and the Senate to prevent or delay passage of a bill is called "chubbing." Here, one or more members debate bills at length to slow down the legislative process. Like the filibuster, this is a particularly effective tactic as the legislative session draws to a close.

Sponsors of a bill are expected to gather sufficient votes to pass the bill. In fact, before the Calendars Committee schedules the bill for floor debate, sponsors often assure the committee that they have enough votes to pass the bill.

The Texas Senate has a rule that bills generally shall be considered according to the "regular order of business." This means that bills and resolutions are considered on the second reading and listed in the order in which the committee report was received by the secretary of the Senate. Bills and resolutions are considered on the third reading in the order in which they were passed on the second reading. In order to conduct business, especially when dealing with legislation that is controversial, this "regular order" blocks consideration of legislation because it can be considered only if the Senate suspends this rule requiring consideration in order. Until the 2015 legislative session, a two-thirds vote was required to suspend the rules. Thus, for all practical purposes, legislation in the Senate had to have two-thirds support to pass rather than a simple majority. Lieutenant Governor Dan Patrick campaigned successfully to rid the Senate of the two-thirds rule. As a conservative, he observed that the rule had previously been used by the Democratic minority to block conservative legislation.

Conference Committee

Bills must pass the House and Senate in exactly the same form. If the bill is different in any way, it is sent to a conference committee. Conference committees have 10 members: 5 members from the House appointed by the Speaker, and 5 members from the Senate appointed by the lieutenant governor.

Senate rules require that two members of the standing committee that considered the bill must be appointed. Unless specifically instructed, the conference committee cannot change parts of the bill that are the same. Changes are made and compromises reached only on parts of the bill that differ.

Once a compromise is reached, the report of the conference committee goes to the House and Senate. It can be debated in each chamber, but the report cannot be changed. It must be either accepted or rejected as is. If either chamber fails to approve the report of the conference committee, the bill is dead. Although it is possible for the conference committee to try a second time to reach a compromise, it is unusual for conference committees to do so.

If the report is accepted in both chambers of the legislature, a final copy of the bill is prepared. The Speaker of the House, the clerk of the House, the president of the Senate (lieutenant governor), and the secretary of the Senate sign the bill. Signatures of

How Representative Is the Texas Legislature Compared with Other States?

	Texas	California	Florida	New York	Ohio
Gender	Female 20% / Male 80%	Female 26% / Male 74%	Female 25% / Male 75%	Female 25% / Male 75%	Female 25% / Male 75%
Race	Latino 23% / African American 10%	Latino 19% / African American 9%	Latino 13% / African American 16%	Latino 8% / African American 15%	Latino 2% / African American 11%
Education level	H.S. diploma 2% / Bachelor's degree 39% / Graduate degree 54%	H.S. diploma 0% / Bachelor's degree 44% / Graduate degree 44%	H.S. diploma 4% / Bachelor's degree 33% / Graduate degree 51%	H.S. diploma 2% / Bachelor's degree 27% / Graduate degree 58%	H.S. diploma 3% / Bachelor's degree 41% / Graduate degree 44%

The Texas legislature is predominately white and male, even though the state population has become more diverse. The Latino and African American populations in Texas combine to form nearly half of the state's residents, although this is not reflected in the legislature. How does Texas compare with other states on the representation of women, minorities, and educational attainment?

CRITICAL THINKING

- How does Texas compare with the other states in the chart regarding the racial and ethnic composition of the legislature? What might explain any differences?

- How representative are the five legislatures presented in terms of educational level? How is Texas similar to or different from the other states in this regard?

SOURCE: National Conference of State Legislators, www.ncsl.org/research/about-state-legislatures (accessed 5/18/16).

Before a law is passed in Texas, it is voted on by the two chambers of the legislature—the House and the Senate. Here, state senators Dan Patrick (left) and Robert Nichols cast votes on a 2013 transportation bill. Raising one finger means "yes" and raising two fingers means "no."

the Speaker and lieutenant governor are required by Article 3, Section 38, of the Texas Constitution. The next stop is the governor's desk.

The Governor

veto according to the Texas Constitution, the governor's power to turn down legislation; can be overridden by a two-thirds vote of both the House and Senate

It is the governor's responsibility to sign or **veto** legislation. During the first 130 days of a regular session, the governor has 10 days from the time a bill arrives on his or her desk to sign or veto the legislation. If the governor neither signs nor vetoes the bill in the 10 days, it becomes law without the governor's signature. In the last 10 days of a session, the governor has 20 days from the time the bill arrives on his or her desk to sign or veto the legislation. Again, if the governor does neither, it becomes law without the governor's signature. Unlike the U.S. president, who may sometimes kill a bill without signing it through what is called a "pocket veto," the Texas governor does not have this power.

The governor's veto can be overridden by a two-thirds vote of both the House and Senate. Anytime the governor vetoes a bill, he or she attaches a message explaining why it was vetoed. It is then returned to the chamber that originated the bill. If the presiding officer elects to allow a vote to override the veto, a vote is scheduled. Only two vetoes have been overridden in more than 70 years.

Many bills arrive on the governor's desk in the last few days of a session. Almost all important or controversial bills reach the governor in the waning moments of a session. If the governor wants to veto a bill that comes to him or her from day 131 to day 140, the governor simply waits until the legislature adjourns to exercise the veto. The governor's veto cannot be overridden because the legislature has adjourned. Vetoing legislation after legislative adjournment is called a **post-adjournment veto**, or a strong veto, since the legislature has no opportunity to overturn the veto. The post-adjournment veto provides the governor with an excellent bargaining tool, since the governor can threaten a veto unless changes are made in a bill. Table 7.2 provides the total number of vetoes by Texas governors since 1991.

post-adjournment veto a veto of a bill that occurs after the legislature adjourns, thus preventing the legislature from overriding it

line-item veto the power of the executive to veto specific provisions (lines) of an appropriations bill passed by the legislature

The governor also has a **line-item veto** that allows him or her to sign a bill and draw lines through specific items, deleting them from the bill. Except for the items that the governor has deleted, the bill becomes law. In Texas, the line-item veto applies only to the state's omnibus appropriations bill. Governor Abbott used the line-item veto in 2015 to cut $295 million, or 0.1 percent, from the state budget. Some of these cuts included a new Department of Motor Vehicles building in Austin, a new parking garage for a state office building in Houston, and state annual dues to the Southern Regional Education Board, which supports Common Core.

Other Ways in Which the Governor Influences Legislation

Message power is the governor's ability to communicate with the legislature. Early in each session, the governor delivers a State of the State message that is similar to the president's State of the Union message. In this address, the governor puts forth a vision for Texas and what legislation will accomplish that vision. If the governor chooses to submit an executive budget, a letter stating why this budget should be adopted accompanies it.

Periodically, the governor will visit with legislators to gain their vote on a bill. A personal visit can be persuasive, but increasingly, it is members of the governor's paid staff who are sent on these legislative visits. Like lobbyists for corporations and interest groups, the governor's representatives use their skills to encourage passage of bills the governor favors and to kill bills the governor opposes. However, there is a problem with this practice. The Texas Constitution forbids use of tax dollars to influence the legislature, and the governor's staff is, of course, paid through tax dollars. The governor's representatives avoid this ban by claiming they are simply providing needed information to

TABLE 7.2

Total Number of Vetoes by Texas Governors, 1991–2015

YEAR	GOVERNOR	TOTAL VETOES
2015	Abbott	42
2013	Perry	26
2011	Perry	25
2009	Perry	38
2007	Perry	54
2005	Perry	19
2003	Perry	48
2001	Perry	82*
1999	Bush	33
1997	Bush	37
1995	Bush	25
1993	Richards	26
1991	Richards	36

*Record number of vetoes by a Texas governor.
SOURCES: Texas Legislature, "Legislative Statistics," July 10, 2013; Legislative Reference Library of Texas, "Bill Statistics."

Greg Abbott, shown here addressing the Texas legislature, was elected governor in 2015. He previously served as the state's attorney general.

the legislators. One should not underestimate the informal power that the governor has to influence legislation.

Additional Players in the Legislative Process

In addition to the legislators and the governor, there are others involved in the lawmaking process during both regular and special sessions. One official, the comptroller of public accounts, has direct involvement in the legislative process, while other players are involved indirectly.

The Comptroller of Public Accounts
The comptroller of public accounts issues revenue estimates to inform the legislature of the amount of money it can spend in the next two years. Texas's operating budgets must balance. The Texas Constitution forbids borrowing money to conduct the daily operations of government. The estimate provided by the comptroller sets the limit on state spending. If the legislature wants to spend more than the comptroller estimates, it must enhance revenue—that is, increase taxes and fees.

The comptroller's estimates can be political in nature. The comptroller can provide a low revenue estimate and tell the legislature that the estimate will remain low until it passes bills the comptroller wants. On passage of those bills, the comptroller can revise the estimate to increase the spending limit and allow the legislature to complete its business.

The Media
The media can determine issues of importance by the selection of stories they cover. If the media cover more stories on crime, crime and criminal justice issues will move toward the top of the legislature's agenda. A media focus on corporate fraud, rising homeowners' insurance rates, alcohol-related traffic deaths, or poor performance by Texas public school students will increase legislative attention to these issues.

The media can influence the legislative agenda through the stories that they cover. Accordingly, legislators try to attract media attention that will support their positions. Here, Speaker Joe Straus speaks at a press conference.

The media inform the public about the issues the legislature is considering and about the job the legislature is doing during the session. Media coverage of the legislature provides the public with needed information on what is going on in Austin. Stories portraying the legislature as modern, efficient, and hardworking provide the public with a positive image of the legislature, whereas stories about legislators sleeping at their desks or killing legislation on technicalities provide a negative image.

Legislators also use social media, such as Twitter, Facebook, and Instagram, to communicate their messages. While some legislators do their own tweeting or postings, some allow their staffs to update their social media profiles. Legislators must be careful about this in case mistakes are made. For example, when state senator Dan Patrick was running for lieutenant governor in 2014, he accidentally tweeted "Marriage=One

Man and One Man," shocking supporters who had assumed he was for traditional marriage. While he quickly deleted the tweet and updated it to "Marriage=One Man and One Woman," media outlets reported this blunder.

More often, legislators use social media to get their messages out to their constituents. They advertise their positions and take credit for sponsoring bills. Followers on Twitter or fans on Facebook can then retweet or share legislators' concerns, which in turn helps them set an image for their constituents.

The Courts

Federal and state courts influence the legislative agenda. In recent years, the courts' scrutiny has included the prison system, the state's treatment of patients in state mental hospitals, the funding of public education, and equality of funding for colleges and universities in South Texas. The ability to rule acts of the legislature and actions of state agencies unconstitutional gives courts significant power over issues the legislature addresses. To a remarkable degree, state and federal courts have issued decisions that have forced the Texas legislature to act in areas that the legislature would have preferred to avoid—largely because action required a significant expenditure of money. For example, many recent legislative actions directed toward criminal justice and public education are responses to court rulings.

Lobbyists and Interest Groups

During a regular session, roughly 1,800 individuals register as lobbyists and attempt to influence the legislature. A lobbyist's responsibility is to convince legislators to support the interest the lobbyist represents. Lobbyists want legislators' votes on bills. At the least, they desire access to legislators.

Interest groups in Texas have been actively involved in supporting legislation as well as stopping legislation they do not support. The Texas Association of Business is a very active interest group lobbying legislators to support their policies of lower taxes and regulations. Its leader, Bill Hammond, a former legislator, is one of the most influential policy makers in Austin. Other interest groups, such as the Texas Alliance for Life, have been very successful in passing abortion restrictions in the Texas legislature in recent years. Its leader, Joe Pojman, has been a powerful presence lobbying Texas legislators and most recently has led the effort to defund Planned Parenthood from the state budget. These are but two examples of the most powerful interest groups in Texas, but there are many more interest groups that employ lobbyists to influence and educate legislators in Austin as well as in Washington, D.C.

The Public

Individuals can influence legislators. Legislators are evaluated at each election. If the people believe their elected officials are representing them well, legislators are re-elected. A legislator who fails to live up to expectations might not be re-elected.

The public and interest groups may also influence the legislature. During a special session in which the legislature dealt with tax reduction, these Houston-area realtors and others demonstrated in favor of property tax relief.

The public can serve as lobbyists. Letters, email, or telephone calls urging representatives or senators to vote a certain way constitute a lobbying effort. In many instances, the public will write to legislators when the media publicize a particular issue, or an interest group will make it easier for members to write to their legislators. Members of the public can also write legislation, but must convince at least one legislator to sponsor it and introduce it for consideration by the legislature.

Some legislators can also commission public opinion polls, especially right before an election. While most of the time the purpose of the poll is to find out where they stand in their districts, some polls will ascertain how the public feels on important issues facing the district. The legislator can then choose to emphasize certain issues in the election. If, for example, the legislator does not personally place a high priority on a particular issue such as immigration, but polls show a majority of his constituents do, then he will choose to emphasize this issue in his campaign.

Power and Partisanship in the Legislature

Analyze how party leadership and partisanship affect power in the legislature

Among the most powerful political figures in Texas are the leaders of the House and Senate. They play a key role in structuring the committees of the legislature, setting the state's political agenda, and passing or defeating bills.

Leadership

Speaker the chief presiding officer of the House of Representatives; the Speaker is the most important party and House leader, and can influence the legislative agenda, the fate of individual pieces of legislation, and members' positions within the House

lieutenant governor a state-wide elected official who is the presiding officer of the Senate; the lieutenant governor is one of the most important officials in state government and has significant control over legislation in the state Senate

The **Speaker** of the Texas House of Representatives and the lieutenant governor are two of the most powerful political figures in the state. Republican representative Joe Straus of San Antonio is currently the Speaker of the House. In November 2014, Dan Patrick was elected **lieutenant governor** and leads the Senate. The Texas House and Senate endow both officials with considerable control over the legislative process. It is fair to say that either of them can usually kill legislation they oppose, and often they have the power to pass legislation they support.

Members of the House elect the Speaker at the beginning of the regular session. Additionally, at the start of each regular session, members of the House adopt rules that give the Speaker institutional powers sufficient to control the work of the House. Speakers usually are the dominant figures in the Texas House and wield vast power.

One of the most interesting developments in modern times in the Texas legislature was the turmoil surrounding the 2002–08 speakership of Republican Tom Craddick. Craddick first challenged the Democratic Speaker "Pete" Laney and ultimately displaced Laney when the Republicans gained control of the House. Craddick worked

The Speaker of the House is one of the most powerful people in Texas politics. In 2009, Tom Craddick (left) was replaced as Speaker by Joe Straus (right). Despite being criticized by conservatives, Straus has been able to hold onto his position as Speaker.

to redistrict Texas congressional districts so as to increase substantially the number of Republicans in the Texas congressional delegation. As Speaker, Craddick was accused of micromanaging the House, of taking discretion away from committee chairs, and of insisting that members support his views on key issues even when contrary to the desires of their constituents. Republicans also lost seats in the Texas House between 2004 and 2006—a loss blamed in part on Craddick's leadership. The result was an open rebellion against Craddick, who was able to retain his position in the 2007 session only by resorting to a questionable parliamentary maneuver: he refused to recognize a motion to "vacate the chair," which would have caused a vote on his fate as Speaker.[14] It is doubtful that such dissension over a Speaker had occurred since Ira Evans was removed as Speaker in 1871.[15] In 2009, Craddick lost his speakership to Joe Straus, a Republican from San Antonio, who was elected Speaker by a coalition of anti-Craddick Republicans and Democrats. Straus has faced opposition in every legislative session from conservatives who saw him as too moderate and as too favorable to Democrats, but Straus has been able to retain his position as Speaker.

The lieutenant governor is elected statewide to a four-year term. His or her major responsibility is to serve as president of the Senate and to preside over the Senate. Unlike the Speaker, the lieutenant governor is not a member of the Senate, simply its presiding officer, who may vote only to break a tie.

At the start of each regular session, senators adopt rules that the Senate will follow for the next two years. Article 22 of the Senate Rules requires a vote of two-thirds of the members present to suspend any rule of the Senate unless the rules specify a different majority. The rules also establish the office of president pro tempore of the Senate, who is a member elected by the Senate to perform the duties of lieutenant governor in the absence or disability of the lieutenant governor. These rules also give the lieutenant governor enormous control of the work of the Senate. Among those powers granted to the lieutenant governor under the rules are

- the power to decide all questions of order on the Senate floor (subject to appeal from members)
- the power to recognize members on the floor
- the power to break a tie on a particular vote

- the power to refer bills to committees
- the power to appoint members to standing committees, subcommittees, special committees, and conference committees

Centralizing Power: Sources of the Leadership's Power

The operation of the Texas legislature is significantly different from that of the U.S. Congress. In the U.S. Congress, the leader of the president's party in the House and the Senate is the president's spokesperson in that house of Congress. Additionally, the level of partisanship is high. Committee appointments are made in such a way that the majority party controls every committee, and chairs of those committees are always members of the majority party. Each house of Congress has majority party leadership and minority party leadership. Such divisions do not exist in the Texas legislature. No member of the Texas legislature is formally known as the governor's spokesperson.

Because the governor has no leader in the legislature, the membership does not owe allegiance to party leaders in the legislature, and leadership and power have become centralized in the Speaker and lieutenant governor. The Speaker and lieutenant governor can make appointments with limited regard for party affiliation, thus ensuring that members will be loyal to them rather than to the party. The Texas legislature is not organized along party lines the way the U.S. Congress is. Committee assignments and committee chairmanship appointments cross party lines so that in the Texas House, for example, where the majority party is now Republican, a Democrat may chair an important committee and successfully sponsor important legislation. The bipartisan appointment of committee chairs, however, may be a declining tradition.

Certain factors may undermine the state legislature's tradition of nonpartisan politics. Most of the powers of the Speaker and of the lieutenant governor are granted by the rules that each chamber's membership votes on at the beginning of the legislative session. The powers of the Speaker and of the lieutenant governor could potentially be greatly reduced if the members of the legislature so chose. One could, for example, imagine a future Republican Senate that would reduce the powers of the lieutenant governor over the Texas Senate if a Democrat were elected lieutenant governor.

The Republican congressional redistricting bill in 2003 led to abandonment of the two-thirds rule for that bill so that redistricting that was beneficial to Republicans could be passed. That bill would have been impossible to pass without changes in the rules that allowed passage by majority vote. In the 2009 special session of the legislature, the Texas Senate was able to pass a highly partisan bill that required voters to show identification. This occurred solely because the two-thirds rule is not used in special sessions.[16] It was not until 2011, when the Texas Senate again abandoned the two-thirds rule, that the voter identification bill became law. The restrictions

PERSONAL RESPONSIBILITY: WHAT WOULD YOU DO?

- Who are the most important leaders in the Texas legislature? What are their powers?

- If you were the Speaker or the lieutenant governor, would you appoint committee chairs from the opposite party? Why or why not? What would be the likely consequences of your decision?

on abortion that were passed in the second special session of the 2013 legislature were passed because it was a special session in which the two-thirds rule in the Texas Senate is not used.

As the Texas Senate has become more partisan, it is not surprising that Lieutenant Governor Dan Patrick was able to successfully change Senate rules to abolish the two-thirds rule in 2015. To be sure, prior to the formal elimination of the two-thirds rule, Republicans waived Senate rules to pass partisan legislation. Republicans did not want to rely on luring a single Democratic senator in order to pass their legislation.

The structure of the Texas legislature and the lack of formal lines of gubernatorial authority in the legislature are very important in centralizing power in the hands of the Speaker and the lieutenant governor. However, these officials have other important sources of power as well. One of those powers—a power especially important in the Texas House—is the power of **recognition**. The Senate rule allowing unlimited debate decreases the lieutenant governor's power in this area. In the House, the Speaker controls legislative debate, including who speaks and how long debate will last. On occasion, the Speaker ignores or skips a member seeking recognition to speak. This is a signal to other members of the House that this individual has fallen from the Speaker's good graces. That ability to pick and choose among those desiring to speak on the House floor, however, allows the Speaker to structure the debate and to affect the outcome of legislation.

recognition the power to control floor debate by recognizing who can speak before the House and Senate

As mentioned earlier, the Senate has a rule that for votes to be taken on bills, the bills must be taken in order, or for a bill to be taken out of order, there must be a three-fifths vote. Given the vast powers of the lieutenant governor, on issues that are important to him, he can usually control the votes of at least one-third of the membership. Thus, if a bill is opposed by the lieutenant governor, he or she can frequently prevent it from being taken out of order for consideration.

One of the most important sources of power for the Speaker and the lieutenant governor is the committee assignment power. The committees on which legislators serve are important to individual members and to the presiding officer. For members, assignments to powerful committees increase their prestige in the legislature. Committee assignment also affects how well constituents are represented. Assigning members to standing committees is one of the most important duties of the lieutenant governor and the Speaker.

The Speaker and the lieutenant governor have major roles in appointing the membership of committees, appointing chairs of committees, and setting the legislative agenda. Party affiliation and seniority are of only moderate importance in committee assignments. The most important factor in committee assignments is the members' relationships with the presiding officer. In order to maintain control over the legislature, the Speaker and lieutenant governor use their committee assignment powers to appoint members who are loyal to them and who support their legislative agendas. When chairs and vice chairs of important committees are appointed, usually only the most loyal friends and allies of the Speaker and lieutenant governor are chosen. In 2013, 6 of the 18 standing committee chairs in the Senate were Democrats. Thirteen of the 38 standing committee chairs in the House were Democrats. Speaker Straus has stated that one issue important to him when appointing chairs and members of committees is to ensure that the committees "reflect the geographic and demographic diversity of Texas."[17]

At the beginning of every legislative session, members of the House are asked to submit a list of committees on which they would like to serve. The Speaker then assigns committee memberships with consideration given to the House members' seniority, their leadership skills, and their interest in particular issues. Chairs and other leadership positions are often given to more senior members with leadership skills and interests in the areas over which their committee has jurisdiction.[18] As we have discussed, Straus, a Republican, was initially elected Speaker with Democratic votes in a successful challenge to the then Republican Speaker Tom Craddick's leadership. As Table 7.3 shows, since being elected Speaker, Straus has named Democrats to the chairs of standing committees of the House roughly in proportion to their numbers in the House. Of course, some committees are more important than others, but in a purely partisan legislative body, no Democrats would be appointed chair of a committee by a Republican Speaker.

During his tenure as Republican lieutenant governor, David Dewhurst was in a far different position from Speaker Straus. Straus was elected from a House district like all other members and then was elected to the Speaker's office by the membership of the House; Dewhurst was elected to preside over the Texas Senate in a statewide election. Nevertheless, like Straus, as Tables 7.3 and 7.4 show, Dewhurst maintained a practice of appointing Democrats to chair Senate standing committees roughly in proportion to the number of Democrats overall in the Texas Senate.

Not only do the Speaker and the lieutenant governor have vast committee assignment powers, but committees in the Texas legislature also have overlapping jurisdiction. Although each bill must be assigned to a committee, it can be assigned to more than one committee. Since the Speaker and the lieutenant governor assign bills to committees in their respective chambers, they use the bill assignment power to influence the fate of the bill. They can, for example, assign bills they oppose to committees they believe hostile to the bill and those they support to committees they believe will favor the bill.

TABLE 7.3

Partisanship of House Committee Chair Appointments

	2009		2011		2013		2015	
Speaker	Straus		Straus		Straus		Straus	
	DEM.	REP.	DEM.	REP.	DEM.	REP.	DEM.	REP.
Standing committees	14	20	11	25	13	24	13	25
Select committees	1	5	0	3	1	3	1	4
Joint committee	—	—	0	1	0	1	0	3
Democratic House committee chairs (%)	38%		28		33		13	
Democrats in House (%)	49%		33		37		34	

NOTE: We are indebted to Sachi Dave for her work on this table.
SOURCES: Legislative Reference Library and *Texas Tribune*.

TABLE 7.4

Partisanship of Senate Committee Chair Appointments

	2005		2007		2009		2011		2013*		2015		2017**	
Lieutenant Governor	Dewhurst		Dewhurst		Dewhurst		Dewhurst		Dewhurst		Patrick		Patrick	
	DEM.	REP.	DEM.	REP.	DEM.	REP.	DEM.	REP.	DEM.	REP	DEM.	REP.	DEM.	REP.
Standing committees	5	10	11	20	6	12	7	12	7	11	2	12	2	12
Select committees	0	3	5	10	0	2	1	1	0	2	0	4	0	4
Democratic Senate committee chairs (%)	28%		35		30		38		35		11		11	
Democrats in Senate	39%		35		39		39		37		35		35	

NOTE: We are indebted to Sachi Dave for her work on this table.
*As a result of the death of a Democratic senator, there were only 30 senators during this session.
**Subject to change.
SOURCES: Legislative Reference Library and *Texas Tribune*.

Since bills must pass the House and Senate in exactly the same form, the Speaker and the lieutenant governor can exercise still another important influence on policy through their power to appoint conference committees. As we have seen, if any differences exist in a bill passed by both the House and the Senate, the bill goes to a conference committee that works out the differences in the House and Senate versions. By appointing the conference committee members, the Speaker and lieutenant governor can affect the language and even the fate of the bill.

Partisan Voting in the Texas Legislature

Between 1876 and 1980, the Democratic Party controlled both houses of the Texas legislature. The last 20 years of the twentieth century saw the growth of the Republican Party in both the House and the Senate, culminating in the Republican seizure of power in both houses in 2004. As conservative Republicans replaced conservative Democrats, particularly from rural and suburban districts, more traditional ideological splits appeared along partisan lines. When Representative Straus initially gained the speakership in 2011 with liberal Democratic and moderate Republican votes, some observers felt that the partisan rhetoric might be muted. As more conservative Republicans were elected in his second term and moderate Republicans either retired or were defeated, partisan divisions appeared with a vengeance. Ideological differences between Democrats and Republicans now play a major role in legislative politics (see Figure 7.2).

It is possible to show that increasing gulf between Democrats and Republicans by using roll-call votes cast by members of the Texas House over time. If one categorizes the votes along the dimension of liberalism-conservatism such that a score of −1.00 is extreme liberal and a score of 1.00 is extreme conservative, the average score of Republicans in the Texas House in 1973 was 0.44. The average score for Democrats was 0.01. In 2009 the average Republican score was 0.67, a significant movement toward increased conservatism. In contrast, the Democrats in the Texas House became increasingly liberal. In 2009 the Democratic score was −0.34. More recent data by Mark Jones of Rice University show the widening gulf between Democrats and Republicans on how they cast roll call votes. The most liberal Republican in the state House is Sarah Davis (R-Houston) and the most conservative Democrat is Ryan Guillen (D–Rio Grande City). Jones's data show, however, that the most liberal Republican is still more conservative than the most conservative Democrat.[19]

Another indication of the partisan gap between Democrats and Republicans in the Texas House is that in 1973, 37 percent of Democratic House members were more

FIGURE 7.2

Ideological Differences in the Texas House of Representatives

Ideological differences between state legislators have grown in recent years. This graphic illustrates how ideology scores of Texas legislators have diverged over time.

SOURCE: Boris Shor and Nolan McCarty, "Aggregate State Legislator Shor-McCarty Ideology Data, June 2015 update," Harvard Dataverse, V1.

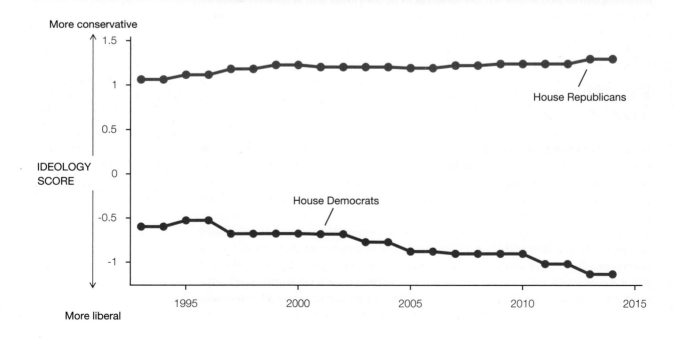

conservative than the most liberal Republican in the House. In 1995 only 4 percent of Democratic House members were more conservative than the most liberal Republican. Since 1999 there has been no Democrat in the House who has been more conservative than the most liberal Republican.[20] In a recent study of the 2015 Texas House, political scientist Mark Jones found that every Democrat was more liberal than any Republican.[21] Jones found the same pattern in the Texas Senate.[22] The ideological gap that exists between Democrats and Republicans makes it harder for common ground across party lines to be identified and to produce a policy consensus. In that sense, the Texas legislature is becoming more like the U.S. Congress. As sociologist Paul Starr has pointed out regarding the U.S. Congress,

> Traditionally, political parties in the United States have been broad coalitions that overlapped each other ideologically. The Republicans had included liberals . . . and the Democrats had included conservatives. But by 2009, the ideological alignment of the parties was nearly complete. . . . The growing ideological divergence between the two parties made cooperation between them more difficult.[23]

That pattern Starr saw in the U.S. Congress is now seen in the Texas legislature. With it we are seeing the end of the cooperation between Democrats and Republicans in Austin.

Redistricting

 Explain the politics of redistricting

As we discussed earlier, the Texas legislature is divided into single-member districts. The makeup of the population in each district has a profound effect on who wins each seat in the legislature. A district might have more Republicans, or more Latinos, or more wealthy people. All of these factor into who is likely to win election to the legislature. Because of the stake involved, one of the most controversial and partisan issues is **redistricting**—the redrawing of district lines for the Texas House, the Texas Senate, and the U.S. House of Representatives, which must be done at least every 10 years, after the federal census.

Although redistricting can be more frequent, at least after each census the legislature draws new boundaries for each Texas House and Senate district. Newly drawn districts for the Texas House and Senate must contain an almost equal number of people in order to ensure equal representation. That requirement guarantees that each person's vote counts the same whether the vote is cast in Houston, Big Lake, El Paso, Presidio, Brownsville, or Commerce.

For much of the first half of the twentieth century, Texas and other states failed to draw new boundaries, and even after U.S. Supreme Court decisions, Texas did not do so willingly. Not until the U.S. Supreme Court's decisions in *Baker v. Carr* (1962) and *Reynolds v. Sims* (1964), compelling the legislature to draw new districts, were boundaries drawn that represented the population fairly.[24] These and subsequent decisions meant that Texas had to draw legislative districts of roughly equal populations—a

redistricting the process of redrawing election districts and redistributing legislative representatives in the Texas House, Texas Senate, and U.S. House; this usually happens every 10 years to reflect shifts in population or in response to legal challenges in existing districts

one-person, one-vote principle
the principle that all districts should have roughly equal populations

concept known as the **one-person, one-vote principle**. This principle was challenged in a Supreme Court case emanating from Texas (*Evenwel v. Abbott*) in which two Texas residents sued, claiming that districts should be drawn based on registered or eligible voters rather than total population. Plaintiffs argued that their votes were diluted because they lived in a state legislative district with a smaller proportion of nonvoting residents. The Court disagreed and sided with Texas that the historical practice of using total population to draw legislative districts was consistent with the Constitution.

Congressional redistricting is also a responsibility of the legislature. Once the U.S. Congress apportions itself, the Texas legislature divides Texas into the appropriate number of congressional districts. According to the 1964 Supreme Court case *Wesberry v. Sanders*, each state's U.S. House districts must be roughly equal in population.[25] Depending on how the districts are drawn, the representation of the two political parties in the U.S. House of Representatives can be significantly changed. Indeed, reapportionment and redistricting can so change the division of the parties that control of the U.S. House of Representatives can be affected. Thus, maneuvering over redistricting is highly partisan.

If the legislature fails to redistrict at the first regular session after the census, the task falls to the Legislative Redistricting Board (LRB). The LRB has five members: the lieutenant governor, the Speaker of the House, the attorney general, the commissioner of the General Land Office, and the comptroller of public accounts.

When the legislature adjourns without redistricting, the LRB convenes. The LRB must meet within 90 days of legislative adjournment and complete its responsibilities within another 60 days. Even here, the influence of the Speaker and the lieutenant governor is clearly visible.

Texas redistricting plans must comply with the federal Voting Rights Act, although the U.S. Supreme Court has recently weakened that law. A federal court can temporarily redraw district lines if a redistricting violates this law by disadvantaging minority voters.

Partisan differences in the state legislature resulted in the failure to pass a redistricting plan in 2001 during its regular session, transferring the responsibility to the Republican-dominated LRB. On a split vote, the board developed redistricting plans that appeared to favor the Republican Party. The board's decision, in turn, was appealed to the federal courts. A three-judge panel, composed of two Democrats and one Republican, approved the lines drawn for the state senate, noting that the U.S. Justice Department had determined that the plan did not violate the Voting Rights Act. However, the court modified the board's plan for the House, arguing that the Department of Justice had rejected the plan because it was seen as diluting Hispanic voting strength in three areas of the state. The court felt that its role in the entire redistricting process was constrained. In their decision, the judges commented that "federal courts have a limited role in considering challenges to pre-cleared, legislatively adopted redistricting plans."[26]

The final plan approved by the court appeared to be a great victory for the Republican Party. Twenty-seven incumbent Democrats found themselves placed in districts with other Democratic incumbents. Four Democrats who chaired key committees announced that they would not seek re-election. Many observers felt that redistricting would make the Republicans the majority party in the House and would maintain their majority status in the Senate.

In 2006 the U.S. Supreme Court upheld most of the new boundaries drawn in the Republicans' controversial redistricting but found that some of the redrawn districts failed to protect minority voting rights. Here, Governor Perry displays the new redistricting map. The new map drawn by Republicans after the 2010 census again went to federal courts.

And many doubted that the Speaker of the House, Democrat Pete Laney, would be able to mobilize the votes needed for re-election to the speakership in the next session. After the 2002 elections, these observers were proven correct.[27]

Power and Partisanship in the Redistricting Battle

Republican control of the Texas House and Senate in 2002 heralded more than simply a shift in party control of the legislature. With Republican control came a significant decline in the harmonious, bipartisan spirit that had largely governed the Texas legislature. The Republican leadership, especially House Speaker Tom Craddick, chose to govern in a more partisan fashion. Additionally, a number of Democrats in the House who saw their power slipping away chose a rebellious course. They worked to make Craddick's speakership a difficult one, obstructing Republican legislative efforts as much as possible.

This new partisan tension in the Texas legislature rose to a fever pitch in 2003 when Republicans, with the support of the Republican majority leader Tom DeLay, sought to alter the Texas congressional districts for partisan advantage. The Republican goal was to increase Republican representation in the Texas congressional delegation and, in so doing, help ensure a continuing Republican majority in the U.S. House of Representatives. The Republican effort was unconventional in that it occurred in midcycle—that is, it was the second redistricting after the 2000 census. As a rule, redistricting occurs only once after each decennial census, although there is no legal requirement that this be the case.

After the 2000 census, the Texas legislature could not agree on redistricting, and a federal court devised a plan. The 2000 congressional redistricting gave the Democrats an advantage. With control of the state legislature, however, Republicans argued that the existing redistricting plan was unsatisfactory because it reflected a Democratic majority that no longer existed. Republicans wanted a plan that more clearly reflected Republican voting in Texas.[28] In 2000, Democrats won 17 congressional seats and Republicans won 13, even though Republicans won 59 percent of votes in the state and Democrats received only 40 percent. In 2002, Democrats got only 41 percent of the statewide vote, but they won 17 seats to 15 for the Republicans. In fact, since 1996, Republicans had never received less than 55 percent of the statewide vote, and Democrats never won more than 44 percent, yet Republicans were a minority in the Texas congressional delegation. With the new redistricting plan in 2004, Republicans got 58 percent of the statewide vote and elected 21 members of Congress from Texas. Democrats got 41 percent of the statewide vote and elected 11 members of Congress from Texas.[29]

The Republican congressional redistricting plan was not enacted without political turmoil, however. At the end of 2003, 51 Democrats from the state legislature walked out and gathered in Ardmore, Oklahoma, where the Texas state police did not have jurisdiction to bring them back to the state capitol. The result was that a quorum could not be reached to pass the plan. The Democratic legislators did not return to Austin until redistricting was taken off the agenda. A special legislative session was called to deal with redistricting, but the bill did not pass. In a second special session

Although the Texas legislature is not as susceptible to partisan squabbling as the U.S. Congress, flare-ups between the Democrats and Republicans do occur. For example, in this photo, Texas House Democrats celebrate their return to Texas in May 2003, after spending four days in Ardmore, Oklahoma, to kill a GOP-produced congressional redistricting plan.

dealing with redistricting, 11 of the 12 Democratic members of the Senate fled to Albuquerque in order to prevent a Senate vote. Finally, a third special session produced a plan that passed both houses of the legislature.[30]

Most notable about the 2004 redistricting was that seven incumbent congressional Democrats were targeted for defeat. A lawsuit that challenged the redistricting on the grounds that it diluted minority votes stressed that the Democrats had been elected with minority support. The lawsuit also pointed out that these seven Democrats either had been paired so that they had to run against another incumbent or had been given a more Republican district.[31] A case before the U.S. Supreme Court challenged the extremely partisan gerrymandering of the Texas redistricting, its reduction of the strength of minority voters, and its use of the now outdated 2000 census. The Court did find that there had been a reduction in the strength of minority voters. However, the extremely partisan gerrymander and the mid-decennial redistricting using the 2000 census were upheld. For the most part, Republicans were successful in reshaping the partisan composition of the Texas delegation to the U.S. House of Representatives. However, the 2006 election led to Democratic control of the U.S. House and to a Texas congressional delegation with vastly weakened power because of the loss of key Democrats in the redistricting.[32]

The 2010 census led to another round of redistricting for the Texas legislature and the U.S. House of Representatives. The overwhelmingly Republican legislature designed a redistricting plan strongly favorable to Republicans, but the plan ran afoul of a federal court, which held that minority voting rights were violated. The court ordered a redistricting plan that was more favorable to Democrats. Redistricting has seemingly become a perpetual issue before the Texas legislature. In 2013 the Texas legislature again voted on redistricting for the Texas House, the Texas Senate, and Texas's U.S. congressional districts. The legislature basically accepted the districting done by the federal courts prior to the 2012 elections, although there are legal challenges to the Texas House and the congressional district lines on the grounds that insufficient recognition of minority interests was given in developing the 2012 districts.[33]

The Legislature and the Future of Texas

The Texas legislature has undergone great changes and continues to do so. Perhaps the most significant change has been increasing partisanship. The Texas legislature is less partisan than the U.S. Congress, but the Texas party divide was especially notable under Speaker Tom Craddick, during the redistricting battles, and during the battles over a voter identification law in 2009 and 2011. Straus's bipartisan election as Speaker in 2009 was indicative of a desire to calm down some of the partisanship in the House that had risen during the Craddick years. Tea Party supporters such as Lieutenant Governor Dan Patrick, however, may be moving the legislature back into a more partisan direction.

The end of the two-thirds rule in the Texas Senate also heralds a new era of partisanship. The two-thirds rule required members of both parties to work together to pass legislation. Now that only a majority is needed, partisanship and rancor will probably increase in the Texas Senate.

The Texas legislature seems in some ways like an archaic institution. Unless there are special sessions, it meets once every two years and is a part-time body with very limited compensation for its members. The structure of the legislature, however, has survived since the 1876 Constitution, and there seems little likelihood that the structure will soon change.

Especially notable regarding the legislature is the vast power held by the Speaker and the lieutenant governor. The 1876 Constitution showed its distrust of a powerful governor, and the result is that in Texas the governor must share political influence with two other major powers in Texas government—the Speaker and the lieutenant governor, over whom the governor exerts no formal control. Still, the revolt against Speaker Craddick does remind us that it is perilous for the Speaker to try to exert so much power that he becomes subject to rebuke from a constituency whose views he ultimately must reflect—the views of a majority of the members of the Texas House.

STUDY GUIDE

Use 🐰 INQUIZITIVE to help you study and master this material.

Structure of the Texas Legislature

> • Describe the organization and basic rules of the legislature (pp. 211–16)

The Texas legislature is bicameral. The leader of the House is the Speaker, and the lieutenant governor presides over the Texas Senate. Although the typical member of the legislature is white and male, women and minorities have increased their representation in recent years.

Key Terms
bicameral (p. 211)
regular session (p. 212)
biennial (p. 212)
special session (p. 212)
single-member district (p. 213)
per diem (p. 214)

Practice Quiz

1. There are _____ members of the Texas Senate, and state senators serve a _____ -year term.
   a) 31/4
   b) 100/6
   c) 150/2
   d) 300/6
   e) 435/2

2. Texas House members differ from Texas Senate members because
   a) House members represent smaller districts and are subject to more frequent elections.
   b) House members represent people, and senators represent counties.
   c) House members are elected from single-member districts and senators from multimember districts.
   d) House members have term limits, and senators do not have term limits.
   e) House members must live in the state for 10 years before standing for election, and senators do not have a residency requirement.

3. The Texas legislature meets in regular session
   a) 90 days every year.
   b) 180 days every year.
   c) 140 days each odd-numbered year and 60 days each even-numbered year.
   d) 140 days each odd-numbered year.
   e) 180 days each even-numbered year.

4. The agenda for a special session of the Texas legislature is set by the
   a) lieutenant governor and the Speaker of the House.
   b) governor.
   c) Texas Supreme Court.
   d) chair of the joint committee on special sessions.
   e) agenda-setting committee.

Powers of the Legislature

> • Outline the legislative and nonlegislative powers of the legislature (pp. 216–19)

The Texas legislature passes bills and resolutions and supervises the state bureaucracy through the budgetary process and sunset legislation.

Key Terms

bill (p. 216)
local bill (p. 216)
special bill (p. 216)
general bill (p. 216)
resolution (p. 216)
concurrent resolution (p. 216)
joint resolution (p. 218)
simple resolution (p. 218)
constituent (p. 218)
electoral power (p. 218)
investigative power (p. 218)
directive and supervisory power (p. 219)
judicial power (p. 219)
impeachment (p. 219)

Practice Quiz

5. The Texas legislature does not pass this type of bill or resolution:
- **a)** local bill
- **b)** special bill
- **c)** joint resolution
- **d)** concurrent resolution
- **e)** holiday resolution

6. Texas legislators do not
- **a)** provide assistance to constituents.
- **b)** investigate wrongdoing by federal agencies.
- **c)** investigate wrongdoing in state agencies.
- **d)** pass bills and resolutions.
- **e)** count election returns for governor and lieutenant governor.

How a Bill Becomes a Law in Texas

- Trace the process through which law is made in Texas (pp. 219–30)

The process of a how a bill becomes a law is similar to that at the federal level. A key difference is the governor's use of the line-item veto by which the governor can eliminate individual appropriations or line items in the state budget. Additionally, the lieutenant governor and the Speaker of the Texas House have exceptionally strong powers. The committee system plays a major role in shaping the legislative process.

Key Terms

introduction (p. 219)
referral (p. 219)
consideration by standing committee (p. 219)
floor action (p. 219)
conference committee (p. 219)
standing committee (p. 222)
pigeonholing (p. 222)
filibuster (p. 222)
veto (p. 226)
post-adjournment veto (p. 226)
line-item veto (p. 226)

Practice Quiz

7. If a bill fails to pass the Texas House and Texas Senate in exactly the same form, the bill
- **a)** dies.
- **b)** is returned to the standing committee in the House or Senate that originally considered the bill.
- **c)** is sent to a conference committee.
- **d)** is sent to the governor, who decides which version of the bill will be signed.
- **e)** becomes a law.

8. The _____ provides the governor with a powerful tool with which to bargain with the legislature.
- **a)** ability to introduce five bills in a regular session
- **b)** post-adjournment veto
- **c)** pocket veto
- **d)** message power
- **e)** initiative

9. Which state official, in large part, determines the total amount of money the legislature may appropriate?
- **a)** governor
- **b)** lieutenant governor
- **c)** treasurer
- **d)** comptroller of public accounts
- **e)** attorney general

Power and Partisanship in the Legislature

> • Analyze how party leadership and partisanship affect power in the legislature (pp. 230–37)

The Speaker of the House and the lieutenant governor are the most important actors in the legislature. Together they help to centralize power in the legislature, and they facilitate or prevent the passage of legislation. The legislature has become increasingly partisan.

Key Terms

Speaker (p. 230)
lieutenant governor (p. 230)
recognition (p. 233)

Practice Quiz

10. The two most powerful political figures in the Texas legislature are the
    a) governor and the lieutenant governor.
    b) governor and the attorney general.
    c) Speaker of the House and the governor.
    d) Speaker of the House and the lieutenant governor.
    e) chairs of the finance committee in each house.

11. The Speaker of the Texas House is chosen
    a) in a statewide election.
    b) in a party-line vote by members of the Texas House.
    c) by a majority of the members of the House, whether Democrat or Republican.
    d) by seniority in the House.
    e) by lot.

12. The lieutenant governor is the presiding officer of
    a) the Texas Senate.
    b) the governor's cabinet.
    c) the Texas legislature.
    d) the Legislative Conference committees.
    e) the Treasury.

13. The chairs of the Texas House committees are
    a) of the same party as the Speaker.
    b) selected on the basis of seniority.
    c) chosen because of their experience.
    d) both Democrats and Republicans.
    e) independents.

14. The ability of the lieutenant governor and the Speaker of the House to control the final outcome of legislation comes from their power to
    a) appoint members of conference committees.
    b) refuse to approve the work of standing committees.
    c) exercise the legislative line-item veto.
    d) change up to three lines in any bill.
    e) control floor debate.

15. In recent years, the Texas legislature has
    a) become more partisan.
    b) become less partisan.
    c) become more experienced in lawmaking.
    d) been more inclined to let the governor make policy.
    e) been more respectful of county officials.

Redistricting

- Explain the politics of redistricting (pp. 237–40)

One of the most partisan activities of the legislature involves redrawing of district lines for the Texas House of Representatives and the Texas Senate. New districts must be drawn at least every 10 years to reflect changes in the population of the state. This process of redistricting provides the opportunities for the dominant political party to create districts for their partisan advantage. While there are some legal and constitutional restrictions on redistricting, generally as long as the districts reflect equal populations and racial or ethnic minorities are not disadvantaged, legislators have great freedom in drawing district boundaries.

Key Terms
redistricting (p. 237)
one-person, one-vote principle (p. 238)

Practice Quiz

16. An important issue for the legislature at least every 10 years is
    a) adopting a budget.
    b) deciding the order of succession to the office of governor.
    c) impeaching the lieutenant governor.
    d) redistricting.
    e) electing the president.

17. Legislative districts in Texas
    a) are created by a nonpartisan commission.
    b) are designed to benefit partisan interests.
    c) are voted on in a special election.
    d) are created in a cooperative effort between the two parties.
    e) are designed by the Center for Legislative Districts every 10 years.

Although the governor is the most visible leader in Texas politics, Texas governors have fewer powers than governors in many other states. Greg Abbott, elected in 2014, succeeded one of the more powerful governors in Texas history, Rick Perry. Does Abbott use the power of the governor's office like Perry did?

The Executive Branch

WHY THE EXECUTIVE BRANCH MATTERS The late lieutenant governor of Texas Bob Bullock said that he did not want to be governor because he claimed that all a Texas governor did was cut ribbons. Bullock was a remarkably powerful and effective lieutenant governor, and he gave weight to the view that real power in Texas was not in the governor's office, but in the lieutenant governor's office. As one reporter put it, "Before Perry, half the stories about the doings in the state Capitol were either about the inherent weakness of the governor's office or the ancient lore about how the lieutenant governor holds the state's most powerful office."[1] After all, in Texas the governor has no cabinet, and although the governor appoints people to the various boards and commissions that run state agencies, only a third of board members come up for appointment every two years, and they cannot easily be fired.

While the governor's office may appear to be weak in terms of the formal powers granted by the constitution, particularly when compared to that in other states, Texas governors can come to possess considerable power. Brian McCall, a former legislator and author of a book on the Texas executive, claims that there were Texas governors who have been real powers in the state and did not just let the state be run by the lieutenant governor, or the legislature and its leadership, or other powerful elected officials such as the attorney general or the comptroller. In spite of McCall's research, the myth persists that Texas governors are mere figureheads.[2]

How does Governor Greg Abbott wield the power of the governorship? If Abbott needs a model of a powerful Texas governor, he need not look further than his predecessor, Rick Perry. In 1998, Perry was elected lieutenant governor, and in December 2000, upon the resignation of Governor George W. Bush to become president of the United States, Rick Perry assumed the governorship. He was elected to full terms as governor in 2002, 2006, and 2010. Perry was the longest-serving governor in Texas history. He was nominated by President Trump to be secretary of the Department of Energy, a department he once promised to dismantle if he were elected president.

Perry had failures—the best known were his failed presidential campaigns in 2012 and 2016. However, Perry exerted control over state government in a way that no other Texas governor has. He was the only governor who appointed every member of the boards and commissions that run Texas government. He used the veto power to punish political opponents in the legislature, and he successfully advocated a social agenda that greatly limited access to abortion. He successfully pushed a pro-business agenda that includes tort reform, low taxes, and business-friendly regulation. He claimed that he caused Texas to weather the Great Recession better than other states and to be a job-creating state.[3] Greg Abbott, Perry's successor, will need time to be able to mobilize the limited constitutional power of the office of the governor as effectively as Perry did.

Though Abbott is fairly new to the job of governor, he has emphasized his successes in his first two years: promoting early childhood education, investing in state universities to attract nationally recognized researchers, investing more in roads, and spending $800 million more on border security. He has done this while providing tax relief with a state budget that is below the state's spending limit.[4] And, while a newspaper consortium that fact checks political claims noted that he has failed to keep most of his campaign promises,[5] he was promoted by some conservatives as a potential vice presidential candidate.

Abbott's popularity with conservatives is largely due to his hostility, as Texas attorney general, toward the Obama administration. Abbott jokingly described what he did as, "I wake up in the morning, I go into the office, I sue Barack Obama, and I go home." In that position, he filed numerous lawsuits against the national government over issues ranging from clean air regulations to the Affordable Care Act. As governor, he has continued that disdain for the national government by ordering the Texas National Guard to keep an eye on a U.S. military training operation in the state, has ordered state agencies to stop accepting Syrian refugees, and has called for a constitutional convention to amend the Constitution so the states can take back power from the national government.[6] To date, Abbott's primary impact has been as an adversary of the national government. He will likely need to find a different role with respect to the new Trump administration. He still needs time to develop a more solid record as governor, and it still remains to be seen if he can break into national politics more successfully than his predecessor Rick Perry. One thing that Perry and Abbott show, however, is that Texas governors do matter.

CHAPTER GOALS

- Describe the powers of the Texas governor and the limits of the governor's power (pp. 249–67)

- Identify the other elected officials who make up Texas's plural executive (pp. 267–76)

- Explain the roles played by boards, commissions, and regulatory agencies (pp. 276–83)

The Governor

Describe the powers of the Texas governor and the limits of the governor's power

At the national level, the president represents and is responsible to the people as a whole. The president is the spokesperson for the government and the people in national and international affairs. Throughout the twentieth century, various presidents parlayed the powers granted them by the U.S. Constitution into what some commentators call the "imperial presidency." The governorship in Texas is not an analogous imperial one. Compared with the president, the governor of Texas is weak. Executive power in Texas is divided among a number of separately elected officials, all of whom are elected by and responsible to the people as a whole. This plural executive has important implications for democratic life in the Lone Star State.

Texas generally scores quite low in scales that compare the power of Texas governors with that of governors in other states. In a study done by Professors Thad Beyle and Margaret Ferguson, Texas tied with four other states for a ranking of 39th among the states in the overall institutional powers of the governor.[7] The *2015 Book of the States* examined the formal powers of the office of governors throughout the United States and noted that the Texas governor, unlike governors of 30 states, has to share responsibility with others for budget making. Twelve states give them the power to item veto all bills; the Texas governor only has the line item veto on appropriations bills, although five governors have no line item veto powers. Texas governors do have considerable power to have their vetoes upheld by the legislature since a supermajority is required to override a veto. In 9 states, only a majority is required to override a veto. Texas is one of only 14 states where the governor cannot reorganize government without approval of the legislature.[8]

To understand the restrictions placed on the office, it is necessary to remember that the Constitution of 1876 was a reaction to the Reconstruction government that existed in Texas following the Civil War. During Reconstruction, the governor was very powerful, and many regarded state government as oppressive and corrupt. When a new constitution was drafted at the end of the Reconstruction era, Texans did their best to ensure that no state official had extensive power. The Texas Constitution of 1876 placed strict limits on the governor's ability to control the people appointed to office and almost eliminated the possibility that appointees to office could be removed. Power was further fragmented among other officeholders, who are collectively known as the plural executive. Each of these officeholders is elected and has separate and distinct responsibilities. Members of major state boards, such as the Railroad Commission and the State Board of Education, are also elected and are largely outside the control of the governor.

Governors who are successful in pushing their programs through the legislature and seeing them implemented by the bureaucracy are able to use the limited formal powers available to them, exercise their personal political power, exploit the prestige of the office of governor, and marshal various special interests to their cause. Former state representative Brian McCall has written about the modern Texas governorship, arguing that Texas governors can be quite powerful in spite of the weaknesses

George W. Bush was governor of Texas from 1995 until he was elected president of the United States in 2000. Here, Bush is seen campaigning for re-election as governor in 1998. Like Rick Perry, Bush was able to achieve a number of his political goals as governor, despite the limited powers of the office.

of the office that are inherent in the Texas Constitution. He points out that governors who develop a collaborative relationship with the legislature can realize many of their goals if they are flexible, have a vision, are willing to motivate others to achieve that vision, and will work cooperatively with the legislature. McCall notes that when former governor Allan Shivers was asked about the weak governorship of Texas, he responded, "I never thought it was weak. I had all the power I needed."[9] McCall, in stressing that capable individuals could parlay the Texas governorship into a position of power, noted that only the governor has the power to call special sessions of the legislature. The governor can pardon criminals and can permit fugitives to be extradited to other states. The governor appoints people to state governing boards and commissions. Only the governor can declare martial law. Only the governor can veto acts or specific appropriations passed by the legislature. Through the traditional State of the State address delivered at the beginning of every legislative session, the governor can outline state priorities and convince others of the importance of those priorities. The governor can be a major persuasive force in mobilizing interest groups, editorial boards of newspapers, and opinion leaders to support his or her agenda.

Not all governors have the personal skills to turn the office into a powerful one. Some have been unable to develop a collaborative relationship with the legislature. Others have not had the interest or the ability to develop their own vision and political agenda. Still others have been unable to accomplish their goals because of economic downturns that have limited their resources. However, McCall argues that modern governors such as John Connally, Ann Richards, and George Bush have had the persuasive skills that have enabled them to achieve major political objectives in spite of the constitutional limitations on the powers of the office.[10]

Still, even many successful governors have not acted as if the job is a demanding one. George W. Bush, according to McCall, would typically arrive at the office by eight in the morning, leave for a run and a workout at 11:40 AM, return at 1:30 PM, and play video golf or computer solitaire until 3 PM.[11] Governor Perry was so detached from the operation of state government that he did not receive a full briefing on the raid on a polygamist cult that put 400 children in protective custody and involved a half-dozen state agencies and 1,000 state personnel until five days after the event. One review of Governor Perry's schedule during the first four months of the 2011 legislative session

How Much Power Does the Texas Governor Have?

Budget-Making Power

Full responsibility — California ★★★ | Shared responsibility — New York ★★★, Illinois ★★★, Florida ★★★, Texas ★★★

Line-Item Veto

All bills — New York ★★★, Illinois ★★★ | Appropriations bills only — California ★★★, Florida ★★★, Texas ★★★

Power to Reorganize State Government

Yes — California ★★★, Illinois ★★★, Florida ★★★ | No — New York ★★★, Texas ★★★

Term Limits

Yes — California ★★★, Florida ★★★ | No — New York ★★★, Illinois ★★★, Texas ★★★

Power Sharing

California | Texas (2) | Florida/Illinois (3) | New York (4)

1   2   3   4   5

(1 = governor shares more power with other elected officials; 5 = governor shares less power)

Appointment Power*

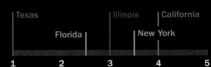

Texas | Florida (2) | Illinois | California | New York (4)

1   2   3   4   5

(1 = weakest—other state officials have some appointment power; 5 = highest—governor's appointees need no other approval)

*Appointment power is measured in the areas of K–12 education, health, highways and transportation, public utilities regulation, and welfare.

SOURCES: U.S. Census Bureau, "Florida Passes New York to Become the Nation's Third Most Populous State, Census Bureau Reports," December 23, 2014, www.census.gov; Audrey Wall, "Table 4.4, The Governors: Powers," Book of the States 2016, knowledgecenter.csg.org; Thad Beyle and Margaret Ferguson, "Governors and the Executive Branch," in *Politics in the American States*, ed. Virginia Gray and Russell L. Hanson (Washington, DC: CQ Press, 2008), pp. 212–213.

Several institutional factors help to determine whether a state has a powerful governor. Powerful governors will often have full responsibility for budget making. They will also often have line-item veto powers on all bills, the ability to order governmental reorganizations, and no requirement to share their power with separately elected executive officials. Powerful governors are not restricted on the number of terms they may serve and they have broad appointment powers. How does the power of the Texas governor compare to other states'?

CRITICAL THINKING

- Compared with those of other large-population states, are the institutional powers of the Texas governor high or low? Explain your answer based on the data in this graphic.

- Would Texas government be more efficient and more responsive to public needs if it had a stronger governor? What enhancements in the powers of Texas governors would be most beneficial to the management of state government?

showed that he averaged only 21 hours per week on state business and took six three-day weekends.[12] Governor Abbott's schedule does not seem particularly grueling either. Of course, his formal schedule excludes phone calls and impromptu meetings as well as preparation time for meetings, but the schedule suggests the demands of the office are not stressful. On Monday, January 26, 2015, for example, Abbott's schedule started at 10 AM with a meeting with deputies and senior staff. From 11:30 AM to 1:00 PM, he had a working lunch and from 2:00 PM to 4:00 PM, he had a budget meeting. From 4:00 PM to 4:30 PM, he had an interview with reporters from radio station KTRH and, at least according to his formal schedule, his workday ended. The following day was not any busier. From 3:00 PM to 4:00 PM, he had a budget meeting and briefing; at 4:30 PM, he met with state senator Charles Perry. Then his scheduled day ended with a meeting from 5:00 PM to 5:30 PM with Senator Perry and Representative Cecil Bell.[13]

Qualifications

Only three formal constitutional qualifications are required to become governor of Texas. Article 4 of the Texas Constitution requires the governor to (1) be at least 30 years of age, (2) be a U.S. citizen, and (3) live in Texas five years immediately before election. Texas governors have tended to be male, white, conservative, either personally wealthy or with access to wealth, Protestant, and middle-aged, and they have had considerable prior political experience.

Women compose more than 50 percent of the population of the United States and Texas, but only two women—Miriam Ferguson (1925–27, 1933–35) and Ann Richards (1991–95)—have served as governor of Texas.

William Clements's victory over John Hill in the gubernatorial campaign of 1978 was the first time since Reconstruction that a Republican had won the office. George W. Bush was the second Republican elected governor and the first individual elected for two consecutive four-year terms.

Access to money is important because running for governor is inordinately expensive. A campaign for the governorship can cost tens of millions of dollars, and few Texans have or can raise that kind of money. The 2010 gubernatorial campaign set a record, costing about $91 million when all primary and general election candidates are considered. Tony Sanchez, the Democratic nominee for governor in 2002, spent over $66 million in that campaign, a record for an individual candidate. About $60 million of those funds came from his family's fortune in a losing effort for the governor's mansion.

Sam Kinch, a former editor of *Texas Weekly*, suggests that prior political experience is an important consideration in selecting a governor. Kinch maintains that although experience may not mean that someone will be a better governor, it does mean he or she is more likely to know how to handle the pressures of the office.[14]

Election and Term of Office

Before 1974, Texas governors served two-year terms, with most being elected to a maximum of two consecutive two-year terms. As Table 8.1 shows, there have been exceptions, such as Coke Stevenson, Price Daniel, and John Connally, who each served

Rick Perry's 14-year tenure as Texas's governor was the longest in the state's history. Here, Perry celebrates at the victory party for his successor, Greg Abbott.

TABLE 8.1

Governors of Texas and Their Terms of Office since 1874

Richard Coke	1874–76	Miriam Ferguson	1933–35
Richard B. Hubbard	1876–79	James V. Allred	1935–39
Oran M. Roberts	1879–83	W. Lee O'Daniel	1939–41
John Ireland	1883–87	Coke Stevenson	1941–47
Lawrence S. Ross	1887–91	Beauford H. Jester	1947–49**
James S. Hogg	1891–95	Allan Shivers	1949–57
Charles A. Culberson	1895–99	Price Daniel	1957–63
Joseph D. Sayers	1899–1903	John Connally	1963–69
S. W. T. Lanham	1903–07	Preston Smith	1969–73
Thomas M. Campbell	1907–11	Dolph Briscoe	1973–79[†]
Oscar B. Colquitt	1911–15	William Clements	1979–83
James E. Ferguson	1915–17*	Mark White	1983–87
William P. Hobby	1917–21	William Clements	1987–91
Pat M. Neff	1921–25	Ann Richards	1991–95
Miriam Ferguson	1925–27	George W. Bush	1995–2000[††]
Dan Moody	1927–31	Rick Perry	2000–2015
Ross Sterling	1931–33	Greg Abbott	2015–

*Impeached.
**Died in office.
[†]Term changed to four years with the 1974 general election.
[††]Resigned to become president of the United States.
SOURCE: Dallas Morning News, *Texas Almanac and State Industrial Guide 1998–99* (Dallas: A. H. Belo, 1999).

for six years, or Allan Shivers, who served for eight years. In 1972, Texas voters adopted a constitutional amendment changing the governor's term to four years. In 1974, Dolph Briscoe was the first governor elected to a four-year term of office. Rick Perry served as governor from 2000 through 2014, the longest tenure for a Texas governor.

Gubernatorial elections are held in off-years (years in which a president is not elected) to minimize the effect of presidential elections on the selection of the Texas governor. The Texas legislature, controlled at the time by Democrats, designed the off-year system to eliminate the possibility that a popular Republican presidential candidate would bring votes to a Republican candidate for governor. Likewise, party leaders wanted to negate the chances of an unpopular Democratic presidential candidate costing a Democratic gubernatorial candidate votes in the general election. Unfortunately, because of this timing, voter turnout in gubernatorial contests is relatively low.

Campaigns

Just as with campaigns for president, Texas gubernatorial campaigns have become very lengthy affairs. Greg Abbott, for example, announced he would campaign for governor in July 2013 and Wendy Davis, Abbott's Democratic opponent, announced her campaign in early October 2013. The election for governor was not until November 2014, and even before their formal campaign announcements, both candidates, especially Abbott, were amassing campaign funds. Candidates must win their party's primary election in March; then they continue campaigning until the November general election. Successful candidates spend thousands of hours and millions of dollars campaigning. The money goes to pay staff salaries and for travel, opinion polls, telephone banks, direct mailings, and advertisements in print, broadcast, and digital media. Texas is so large that statewide candidates must purchase print, television, radio, and digital advertisements in numerous media outlets.

In the 2010 Republican primary, Kay Bailey Hutchison spent over $14 million in her losing battle against Rick Perry. Perry spent nearly $13 million in the primary. Overall, Perry spent about $39 million and Bill White, the Democratic candidate, spent about $26 million in their campaigns. That is $14.37 for every vote Perry received and $12.48 for every vote White received. High-priced campaigns illustrate that successful candidates need personal wealth or access to wealth. Greg Abbott spent $47.4 million and Wendy Davis spent about $4 million. Abbott spent $16.96 for every vote he received in the general election and Davis spent $2.20.

Public debates give Texans the chance to see gubernatorial candidates face off over key campaign issues. In September 2014, Wendy Davis and Greg Abbott held their first debate in Edinburg in the Rio Grande Valley.

Who Elected Governor Greg Abbott in 2014?

Greg Abbott's support was widespread across the state. He had decisive support in nonborder rural counties. Although not winning in all, he polled well in urban counties. He received surprising support from Latino voters, winning 44 percent statewide.

2014 Election Results, by County

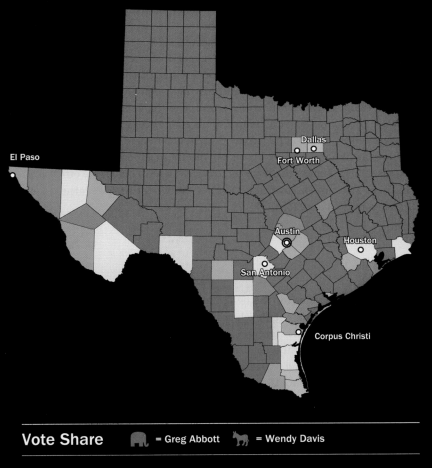

Margin of victory

Greg Abbott (R)
- > 30%
- 20–29%
- 10–19%
- 0.1–9%

Wendy Davis (D)
- > 30%
- 20–29%
- 10–19%
- 0.1–9%

Vote Share

= Greg Abbott   = Wendy Davis

	Greg Abbott	Wendy Davis
Urban and suburban	55%	45%
Rural and small town	77%	23%

SOURCE: CNN Election Center, www.cnn.com/election/2014/results/state/TX/governor (accessed 11/28/14).

QUANTITATIVE REASONING

- Wendy Davis's strengths were along the Texas border with Mexico and in some of the urban counties, whereas Abbott's strongest support was in rural Texas and suburban counties. What do you think caused these differences in support for Davis and Abbott?

- Given the election results, which parts of the state are likely to benefit the most from Governor Abbott's policies?

Removal of a Governor

impeachment the formal
charge by the House of Representatives that leads to a trial
in the Senate and the possible
removal of a state official

In Texas, the only constitutional method of removing a governor from office is by **impeachment** and conviction. "To impeach" means to accuse or to indict, and impeachment is similar to a true bill (indictment) by a grand jury. The Texas Constitution notes that the governor may be impeached but does not give any grounds for impeachment. Possible justifications for impeachment are failure to perform the duties of governor, gross incompetence, and official misconduct.

Impeachment begins in the Texas House of Representatives. A majority vote of the Texas House is required to impeach or to bring charges. If the House votes for impeachment, the trial takes place in the Texas Senate. One or more members of the Texas House prosecute the case, and the chief justice of the Supreme Court of Texas presides over the impeachment proceedings. A two-thirds vote of the senators present and voting is necessary to convict. If convicted, the governor is removed from office and disqualified from holding any other state office.

Any member of the executive or judicial branch may be impeached. Once the House votes for impeachment charges against an official, that individual is suspended from office and cannot exercise any of his or her duties. Governor James Ferguson was the only Texas governor to be impeached and convicted. He had sought to remove several members of the faculty at the University of Texas at Austin whom he opposed and, when he failed to remove them, he vetoed practically the entire University of Texas appropriation. That led to investigations and his impeachment. The Texas house voted 21 articles of impeachment against Ferguson, and the Texas Senate convicted him on 10 articles. Three charges were related to his actions regarding the University of Texas, five were related to misapplication of funds, one related to his failure to enforce banking laws, and one was over his secret receipt of $156,500 in cash. Ferguson dealt with his inability under the terms of impeachment to hold state office again by running his wife, Miriam, for governor.[15] She served two terms as governor—from 1925 to 1927 and from 1933 to 1935.

Succession

The Texas Constitution provides for the lieutenant governor to become governor if the office becomes vacant through impeachment and conviction, death, resignation, or the governor's absence from the state.

In December 2000 a succession occurred when Governor George W. Bush became president-elect of the United States and resigned as governor. Lieutenant Governor Rick Perry immediately took the oath to become governor of Texas. The only time a Texas governor died in office was when Governor Beaufort Jester suffered a fatal heart attack on July 11, 1949, and Lieutenant Governor Allan Shivers became governor and, like Perry, was able to win later election to that office.

Should the governor leave the bounds of the state, the lieutenant governor becomes acting governor. If the governor is impeached, the lieutenant governor serves as acting governor before and during the trial. While serving as acting governor, the lieutenant governor earns the governor's daily salary, which is far better than the $20 earned as lieutenant governor. (However, a governor who is absent from the state still earns the same daily salary.)

Constitutionally, the governor's office is weak enough that when the governor is out of state, his absence does not seem to affect state operations. Former lieutenant governor Bill Hobby noted that about the only way he knew when he was acting governor was by a note his secretary left on his daily calendar.[16] In the first three months of 2000, Rick Perry, then lieutenant governor, served as acting governor more days than George W. Bush was in the state to serve as governor. Perry's press secretary commented that the added duties of being acting governor were not very noticeable and that those duties made little difference in Perry's schedule.[17] State government takes little notice of the governor's absences. Former Speaker of the Texas House Pete Laney has said that the governor's office is "holding court and cutting ribbons" and in 2000 commented on Governor Bush's out-of-state campaigning by saying, "I guess we've been doing pretty well without [a governor]."[18]

Compensation

The governor's salary is set by the legislature. Texas pays its governor $150,000 annually. In addition to this salary, the governor receives use of an official mansion near the capitol grounds. Governors and the legislature often squabble about the amount of money needed for upkeep of the mansion and its grounds. The governor also receives use of a vehicle, a state-owned aircraft, and a personal staff.

Staff

The governor's staff consists of nearly 300 individuals. The staff is divided into several divisions. The Executive Office has overall responsibility for staff management and has primary contact with the governor. The highest-level person on the staff is chief of staff, who is responsible for the management of the entire staff. Governor Abbott's chief of staff is Daniel Hodge, who has long-standing ties to him. Hodge had been the first assistant attorney general when Abbott was attorney general. He was the manager of more than 4,000 employees under Abbott in the attorney general's office. Hodge was then in charge of the transition team that managed the change from the Perry to the Abbott administration. Trusted top-level managers are necessary for a governor to successfully manage the people, issues, and policies involving state government. Under Hodge's supervision are staff offices that deal with such matters as scheduling for the governor, with political matters relating to the First Lady, with appointments to offices, legislative matters, budget, policy, and constituent communications.[19]

The staff keeps the governor informed about issues and problems facing the state, and it may suggest courses of action. In addition, during a four-year term, a governor makes about 3,000 appointments to various state posts. It is impossible for a governor to be acquainted personally with each appointee. Some of the staff find qualified individuals for each post and recommend them to the governor. Other staff members track legislation. They talk with legislators, especially key people such as committee chairpersons. The staff lets the governor know when his or her personal touch might make a difference in the outcome of legislation. For each bill that passes the legislature, a staff member prepares a summary of the bill with a recommendation that the governor sign or veto the bill.

Recent governors have used their staffs to be more accessible to the public. Governor Abbott, like his immediate predecessors, encourages this public accessibility through the Office of Constituent Communications, which reviews and responds to all communications to the governor.

Executive Powers of the Governor

Texas has a board or agency form of government. Over 400 state boards, commissions, and agencies make up the executive branch of Texas government. Agencies may be as obscure as the Texas Funeral Commission or the State Preservation Board or as well known as the Public Utilities Commission of Texas or the Texas Department of Human Services, but each is important to its constituents. These multimember boards are the policy-making bodies for their agencies. They employ and oversee the people who operate the agencies on a daily basis.

appointment the power of the chief executive, whether the president of the United States or the governor of a state, to appoint persons to office

patronage the resources available to higher officials, usually opportunities to make political appointments to offices and to confer grants, licenses, or special favors to supporters

Appointment Power The governor's power of **appointment** is the most significant executive power. It allows a degree of control over 410 governmental entities, including a wide range of agencies, commissions, and boards, as shown in Table 8.2. Governor Perry's long tenure allowed him to appoint every member of these boards, and through these appointments he was able to exert control throughout state government.

The power of appointment enables the governor to exercise the power of **patronage**. It permits the governor to reward supporters by appointing them to office. About half of the first 58 appointees of Governor Abbott's were campaign donors. If one examines contributions to Abbott going back to 2000, one of his appointees to the Texas Historical Commission had contributed about $700,000 to him. An appointee to the Texas A&M System Board of Regents and an appointee to the Texas Higher Education Coordinating Board had each contributed about $500,000. A person he reappointed to the University of Texas System Board of Regents contributed $246,000.[20] Most of the offices pay fairly small salaries, but they do offer supporters some prestige. The governor can also use the appointment power to repay political favors by appointing friends and associates of legislators to office as well as to garner political IOUs from politicians. It may be that the reason Abbott made his controversial appointment of Donna Bahorich (see "Appointment Controversies," below) to chair the State Board of Education was because Bahorich had managed Lieutenant Governor Dan Patrick's first run for the Texas Senate and such an appointment probably would have pleased Patrick.

Most important, a governor can use the appointment power to influence agency policy. Of course, large donors generally share the same views as the governor, so an appointment of a large donor can also be a way to influence agency policy in the direction sought by the governor. Sometimes a governor needs to appoint people who are highly competent who can solve agency problems. When Abbott talked Deputy Executive Commissioner Chris Traylor out of retirement to chair the Health and Human

TABLE 8.2

The Governor's Appointment Power

The following are examples of some of the entities in Texas, in just four policy areas, where the governor has the power to appoint members. This power can provide the governor with significant influence over policy in these areas.

WATER

Angelina and Neches River Authority, Upper, Lower Central Colorado River Authority, Brazos River Authority, Canadian River Compact Commissioner, Board of Pilot Commissioners for Galveston County Ports, Guadalupe-Blanco River Authority, Upper Guadalupe River Authority, Gulf of Mexico Fishery Management Council, Gulf States Marine Fisheries Commission, Lavaca-Navidad River Authority, Nueces River Authority, Red River Authority and Red River Compact, Sabine River Authority and Sabine River Compact, San Antonio River Authority, San Jacinto River Authority, Trinity River Authority, Sulphur River Basin Authority, Western StatesWater Council, Evergreen Underground Water Conservation District, and Drought Preparedness Council

HEALTH

Aging and Disability Services Council, Texas Council on Alzheimer's Disease and Related Disorders, Texas Council on Autism and Pervasive Developmental Disorders, Chronic Kidney Disease Task Force, Texas Council for Developmental Disabilities, Health Professions Council, Oversight Committee of the Cancer Prevention and Research Institute, Council on Cardiovascular Disease and Stroke, and Sickle Cell Disease Advisory Committee

LAW ENFORCEMENT

Automobile Burglary and Theft Prevention Authority, Border Security Council, Task Force to Reduce Child Abuse and Neglect, Crime Stoppers Council, Crime Victims' Institute Advisory Council, Texas Board of Criminal Justice, Homeland Security Council, Commission on Jail Standards, Juvenile Justice Advisory Board, Juvenile Probation Commission, and Commission on Law Enforcement Officer Standards and Education

PROFESSIONAL LICENSING

Texas Optometry Board, Board of Orthotics and Prosthetics, Board of Nursing, Board of Occupational Therapy Examiners, Board for the Licensure of Professional Medical Physicists, Medical Board, Board of Examiners of Marriage and Family Therapists, Board of Examiners in the Fitting and Dispensing of Hearing Instruments, Board of Podiatric Medical Examiners, Physician Assistant Board, Board of Plumbing Examiners, Board of Physical Therapy Examiners, Board of Pharmacy, Board of Veterinary Medical Examiners, Appraiser Licensing and Certification Board, Board of Architectural Examiners, Board of Chiropractic Examiners, Board of Dental Examiners, State Board of Examiners of Dietitians, and State Board for Educator Certification

Services Commission, it was clear that Abbott needed the widely respected Traylor to lead the commission, troubled with problems with questionable contracts, out of its difficulties.[21] To a great degree, the effectiveness of a governor's use of the appointment power will determine the governor's success in office.

In some cases, the governor shares appointment power with others. For example, the State Commission on Judicial Conduct regulates the ethics and behavior of Texas judges. It is governed by a 13-member commission. Six of the commission members, appointed by the Texas Supreme Court, are judges representing various court levels. Two members, appointed by the state bar, are non-attorneys and non-judges. The governor appoints five citizen members. The Texas Ethics Commission promotes ethics rules for state officials, and the commission is where campaign finance data are reported. The commission has eight members—four appointed by the governor, two appointed by the lieutenant governor, and two by the Speaker of the Texas House of Representatives. Some of the entities to which the governor makes appointments are advisory as opposed to policy-making. For example, the governor appoints the three-member Firefighters' Star of Texas Award Advisory Committee, which considers for an award firefighters killed or seriously injured in the line of duty.

Some of these entities are both advisory and appointed by several different officers. For example, the Oil-Field Cleanup Fund Advisory Committee has 10 members. One member is appointed by the lieutenant governor, one by the presiding officer of the house committee with primary jurisdiction over energy resources, one by the lieutenant governor from the academic field of geology or economics, one by the Speaker of the Texas House of Representatives from the field of geology or economics, one by the governor, and one by the executive officer (or the officer's designee) of the Texas Oil and Gas Association, the Texas Independent Producers and Royalty Owners Association, the Panhandle Producers and Royalty Owners Association, the Permian Basin Producers Association, and the Alliance of Energy Producers. The committee meets with the Railroad Commission about oilfield cleanup issues and reports to the governor, the lieutenant governor, and the Speaker about any problems in the administration of oilfield cleanup funds and about any recommendations for legislation dealing with oilfield cleanup. Oilfield cleanup is not a top priority for most Texans, but it is a vital issue for oil producers and royalty owners. Such commissions provide input to state government for specialized issues. There are a number of these rather obscure advisory committees where the governor has an appointive role. For example, there is the Parental Rights Advisory Panel, the Nursing Facility Administrators Advisory Committee, the Advisory Committee to the Texas Board of Criminal Justice on Offenders with Medical or Mental Impairments, the Texas Academy of Mathematics and Science Advisory Board, the Governor's Advisory Council on Physical Fitness, the Preservation Trust Fund Advisory Board, the Real Estate Research Advisory Committee, and numerous other such groups.

The governor also makes appointments to many commissions that have major policy impact. Examples include the governing boards of Texas public universities that have considerable influence over the governance and policies of universities. The governor appoints all members to the boards of regents. Additionally, the governor appoints all of the nine members to the Texas Higher Education Coordinating Board, which oversees all public postsecondary education in the state including determining when public colleges and universities start or continue offering degrees, or what core class requirements all students in state colleges or universities must take. Another major commission is the Parks and Wildlife Commission. Appointed by the governor, the commissioners run an agency responsible for the management and conservation of the state's natural resources, with particular responsibility to provide for hunting, fishing, and outdoor recreation for Texans. The governor appoints the three members of the Alcoholic Beverage Commission, which is responsible for the regulation of all aspects of alcoholic beverages within the state and which collects $200 million a year in taxes and fees on alcohol. Many of the bodies over which the governor has supervision through the appointment process deal with water (its conservation, use, control, and navigation), health and aging, law enforcement, and professional licensing.

To a great extent, Texas government is run through these many boards and commissions. These boards have three main purposes: (1) they provide the broad policy guidance and advice for the operation of Texas's executive branch; (2) they provide a place where interests can influence the executive branch; (3) they can provide important patronage to the governor where political friends and supporters can be rewarded with positions of influence, honor, and sometimes income.

Appointment Controversies A governor must exert some care in appointments. Failure to appoint responsible individuals can lead to serious political problems. In 2007 there was a scandal within the Texas Youth Commission, which has authority over institutionalized juveniles. It became clear that not only was there a widespread pattern of physical and sexual abuse of juveniles in the facilities, but authorities tried to cover up the abuse. As a result, Governor Perry's appointees had to resign from the commission, and it was necessary to reorganize the agency.

In the early stages of his administration, Greg Abbott ran into intense criticism for appointing Donna Bahorich as chair of the State Board of Education. Even some fellow Republicans were shocked when Abbott appointed Bahorich as chair of the State Board of Education, which makes policy and standards for the state's public schools, because Bahorich had home-schooled her three sons prior to sending them to private schools. They never attended public school. Thomas Ratliff, a Republican member of the board, said, "When 94 percent of our students in Texas attend public schools, I think it ought to be a baseline requirement that the chair of the State Board of Education have at least some experience in that realm, as a parent, teacher, something."[22] (As we discussed, Bahorich's appointment was perhaps an act of political patronage; Bahorich managed now lieutenant governor Dan Patrick's first campaign for the Texas Senate.) Of course, a governor makes so many appointments that some are

Donna Bahorich was a controversial Abbott appointee to chair the State Board of Education, since her three children had never attended public schools.

bound to provoke criticism, but a governor must be careful that the appointments do not prove damaging to his political support.

The Senate's Role in Gubernatorial Appointments

The governor appoints people to office, but the Texas Senate must also confirm them. However, because the Senate may not meet for almost two years, the appointee takes office immediately and does not wait for Senate confirmation. This doesn't mean that the governor ignores how he or she thinks the Senate will react to appointees. Consider the appointment of Eleanor Kitzman as Texas insurance commissioner. Insurance commissioner is a particularly important office in Texas, since it is a single appointed office rather than a board or commission and the commissioner has regulatory authority over insurance companies that operate in Texas. Kitzman had great problems with the legislature. She was criticized for being too favorable to insurance companies. What seemed to sink her chances for approval by the Senate, however, was when Kitzman, who never blocked any large insurance premium hikes while she was commissioner, withheld insurance company profit data from the legislature. If it had not been clear before the data were withheld, it was certainly clear afterward that Kitzman would not be confirmed. Governor Perry did not even submit her name to the Senate Nominations Committee and the Senate did not vote on her nomination, which meant that she had to leave office at the end of the regular legislative session.[23]

An important limitation on the power of the governor to appoint persons to office is the informal requirement that the individual's state senator must approve the appointment. This is known as **senatorial courtesy** and applies regardless of the party affiliation of the governor, senator, or appointee. Usually, if the appointee's senator concurs in the appointment, the remainder of the Senate will agree. However, if the appointee's senator opposes the appointment, the remainder of the Senate will also oppose the appointment.

The process for removing an appointee is also complicated. With the approval of two-thirds of the Texas Senate, a governor can remove his or her appointee who refuses to resign. This complex procedure for the termination of members of boards and commissions, along with the practice of senatorial courtesy, can be a significant limitation on the governor's power to influence the policies of state agencies. Chairs of boards, however, serve at the pleasure of the governor and so can easily be removed if they do something that displeases the governor.

Budgetary Power

Officially, the Texas governor is the state's chief budget officer. As such, governors submit an **executive budget** to the legislature. This budget suggests a plan for revenue and expenditure for Texas, but more important, it indicates the governor's priorities for the state in the next biennium.

In 1949, in an effort to gain more control over the state's budget, the legislature established the Legislative Budget Board (LBB), which is responsible for preparing a **legislative budget**. Thus, two budgets are prepared and submitted to the legislature: an executive budget by the governor and a legislative budget by the LBB. As a creation of the legislature, the LBB's budget proposal receives more consideration by the House and Senate than the governor's recommendations, and in recent years the governor's budget has fallen into disuse. Legend has it that the governor's budget has been used as a doorstop and a paperweight, and one diminutive legislator used two copies as a booster in his office chair. In 1989, Governor Clements recognized the

senatorial courtesy the practice whereby the president, before formally nominating a person for a federal judgeship, seeks the indication that senators from the candidate's own state support the nomination; in Texas, the practice whereby the governor seeks the indication that the senator from the candidate's home district supports the nomination

executive budget the state budget prepared and submitted by the governor to the legislature, which indicates the governor's spending priorities. The executive budget is overshadowed in terms of importance by the legislative budget

legislative budget the state budget that is prepared and submitted by the Legislative Budget Board (LBB) and that is fully considered by the House and Senate

futility of submitting an executive budget and simply endorsed the recommendations of the LBB. Ann Richards followed Clements's precedent, but Governor George Bush took a more active role in budget preparation and Governor Perry was very involved in dealing with the state's 2011 budgetary shortfall. Governor Abbott also has shown involvement in budgetary policy making.

The governor has some control over the final appropriations bill through the use of the line-item veto. However, the governor must have the support of the legislative board to impound funds or transfer funds from one agency to another if circumstances change from the time the money was appropriated. There is one exception to the constraint on gubernatorial power to transfer funds. Under a 1993 law, the governor can declare an emergency and bypass the other legislative members of the LBB. In 2014, Governor Perry declared an emergency and shifted $38.7 million from a Department of Public Safety fund to pay for the National Guard to patrol the Texas-Mexico border. Overall, the budgetary process does not provide the governor acting alone with a highly effective means of controlling state agencies.

Military and Police Power

The governor is commander in chief of the state's National Guard units when they are not under presidential orders. These units are headed by the adjutant general, who is appointed by the governor. The governor can declare martial law, which suspends most civil authority and imposes military rule over an area. Martial law can be declared in the event of a riot, a flood, a hurricane, a tornado, or another disaster to protect lives and property. In Texas, law enforcement and police power are primarily a local responsibility, and the governor has few responsibilities in this area. The governor appoints, with Senate approval, the three-member Public Safety Commission that directs the work of the Department of Public Safety (DPS). The DPS is responsible for highway traffic enforcement (highway patrol), drivers' licensing, motor vehicle inspection, truck weighing stations, and the Texas Rangers (an elite, highly trained force of about 150 officers with 58 support staff). When circumstances warrant, the governor can assume command of the Rangers. If there is evidence of ongoing violence or corruption, the governor can use informal powers, the prestige of the governor's office, and appeals to the media to compel appropriate action from local law enforcement officials.

It is not often that the governor uses his or her military and police powers, but when he or she does, it usually makes news. Governor Perry ordered Texas National Guard troops to patrol the Texas-Mexico border in the summer of 2014 because of a surge of undocumented immigrants. Governor Abbott also used his military powers as governor to extend their service on the border. Additionally, Abbott used his powers over state police forces to order the DPS to team with the Texas Department of Parks and Wildlife to increase boat patrols on the Rio Grande as part of his border security efforts.[24]

In what must be the most bizarre use of the governor's military power in modern times, Governor Abbott directed the Texas State Guard to monitor a U.S. military exercise (code-named Jade Helm 15). Prodded by conspiracy theories hatched by talk radio hosts, people became convinced the military exercise meant a federal takeover of Texas or at least martial law and the confiscation of Texans' guns. Abbott received hundreds of letters and emails from people who demanded

Opposition to a U.S. military exercise code-named Jade Helm 15 led Governor Abbott to order the Texas National Guard to monitor the military exercise. Opponents of Jade Helm 15 believed the exercise would lead to martial law and confiscation of guns.

action from the governor. The effect of Abbott's order was a strong political backlash from those who thought he disrespected the military and embarrassed himself and the state.[25]

Legislative Powers of the Governor

The governor's legislative powers include message power, power of the veto, and the authority to call special sessions and set their agendas. If a governor uses these powers effectively, he or she can have considerable control over the state's legislative business, but they do not enhance his or her ability to control the executive branch of state government.

Message Power Any communication between the governor and the legislature is part of the message power. Early in each regular session, the governor delivers a State of the State message. In this speech to a joint session of the legislature, the governor explains his or her plan for the state in the coming two years. The governor may propose specific programs or simply set general goals for the state. The speech is covered by most news media and is often broadcast on public television and radio stations, analyzed on blogs, and discussed on social media.

If the governor submits an executive budget, he or she may address the legislature on the important items in the proposed plan of spending and revenue. At the very least, the budget proposal is forwarded to the legislature with a letter briefly explaining the budget.

Lobbying by governors is part of the message power. Governors try to pass or defeat bills important to them. Governor Abbott, for example, emphasized transportation funding, governmental ethics legislation, border security, early education funding, and higher education research funding in his State of the State address. He then worked with the legislature to try to ensure legislation would be passed regarding these issues. Representative Dennis Bonnen, a sponsor of border security legislation, said that Abbott had "been very wise to engage early and engage often so we can make sure we're all working together." Senator Van Taylor, a sponsor of ethics reform, said that he talked almost daily with Abbott's office about the issue. Abbott pushed this agenda by meeting with small groups of lawmakers at the governor's mansion, sometimes dining with them as well. At the same time, Abbott's legislative team met with top staff people on both the Democratic and the Republican side regarding Abbott's program.[26]

veto the governor's power to turn down legislation; can be overridden by a two-thirds vote of both the House and Senate

Veto Power Governors of Texas can sign or **veto** legislation—but in most cases they sign legislation. After becoming governor in 2000, Rick Perry vetoed 301 bills.[27] In his first legislative session, Greg Abbott vetoed 44 bills. Abbott signed about 1,300 bills, which means the veto was exercised in only about 3 percent of the cases where a bill was presented to the governor for signature.[28] In modern times, vetoes are simply not overridden by the legislature. The Legislative Reference Library found that from 1876, the starting year for the current Texas Constitution, to 2013, there had been only 26 legislative overrides of vetoes. Ten of those overrides occurred in 1941 during the administration of Governor W. Lee (Pappy) O'Daniel. No veto override has occurred since 1979.[29]

When the governor vetoes a bill after the legislature adjourns, it is called a **post-adjournment veto** (or strong veto). This veto is absolute, because the legislature that passed the vetoed bills no longer exists. As a result, if the governor decides to veto a bill, it stays vetoed.

Texas governors possess the **line-item veto**, which is the ability to veto individual parts of an appropriations bill. The governor signs the bill but strikes out particular lines in the bill. Items struck from the bill do not become law, but the remainder of the appropriations bill does.

The line-item veto allows Texas governors considerable control over appropriations to state agencies, and this power can be used by the governor to reduce state expenditures or to punish agencies or programs disfavored by the governor.[30] It is one important power of the governor that is greater than that of the president of the United States, who does not have the power to issue a line-item veto because the U.S. Supreme Court has held that such a power violates separation of powers in the U.S. Constitution.

In 2013, Governor Perry used the line-item veto to eliminate about $7.5 million in state funding for the prosecutors who investigate public corruption cases in the state capital. Perry claimed that the investigative unit had "lost the public confidence" as a result of the DWI conviction and unruly behavior while arrested of the Democratic district attorney of Travis County, Rosemary Lehmberg. The funding veto jeopardized the jobs of 35 employees and threatened about 400 cases being investigated. Critics of the veto claimed the veto was an effort to stop the continuing investigation into corruption in the Cancer Prevention and Research Institute that could prove embarrassing to Governor Perry. There was also a belief that this veto was a partisan move on Perry's part, since Travis County is heavily Democratic and the district attorney is and will likely continue to be a Democrat. Republicans preferred that public corruption cases be handled by district attorneys in the home county of the case where many of the district attorneys would likely be Republican. Regardless, Perry's veto had negative consequences for him and his presidential prospects. He tried to force the district attorney to resign by threatening veto of funding for her office and, when she did not resign, he carried out his threat. A grand jury believed this action by Perry was criminal and indicted him on a coercion of a public servant charge and an abuse of official capacity charge.[31] After much legal wrangling, both charges against Perry were dismissed prior to trial.

Generally, line-item vetoes do not have such severe consequences on the governor. Governor Abbott issued two line-item vetoes out of his 44 vetoes in the 2015 legislative session. One of those involved a line-item veto of numerous items in the general appropriations bill that ranged from relatively small amounts such as a $193,000 appropriation for the Texas Education Agency to pay membership fees in the Southern Regional Education Board to a $132,000,000 appropriation to replace a state government building. His second line-item veto was $500,000 in planning costs for a new Department of Motor Vehicles facility that he had line-item vetoed in the general appropriations bill.[32] Still, Abbott faced an unusual challenge to some of his vetoes. The Legislative Budget Board Director, Ursula Parks, wrote State Comptroller Glenn Hegar arguing that Abbott had not actually vetoed actual appropriations under the line-item veto, but he had vetoed items that were legislative statements of intent, direction, or conditions on the use of funds. Abbott's office responded that if an appropriation was labeled something else like a rider, or strategy,

post-adjournment veto a veto of a bill that occurs after the legislature adjourns, thus preventing the legislature from overriding it

line-item veto the power of the executive to veto specific provisions (lines) of an appropriations bill passed by the legislature

direction, goal, statement of intent, or anything else, it was still an appropriation that could be vetoed. An opinion was sought by the comptroller from the Office of the Attorney General, which agreed with Abbott's position. Abbott had earlier unsuccessfully sought expanded veto powers, and this dispute was seen as a legislative effort to rebuke Abbott, since the Legislative Budget Board is co-chaired by the Speaker of the Texas House and the lieutenant governor.[33]

Special Sessions Special sessions of the Texas legislature are called by the governor, last for no more than 30 days, and may consider only those items placed on the agenda by the governor. **Special sessions** are called to address critical problems as defined by the governor. The nature of special sessions allows the legislature to focus attention on specific issues.

From 1989 through 2013 the legislature met in 22 special sessions. These sessions considered the complicated and divisive issues of reform of workers' compensation laws, public school finance, reapportionment, and voter identification. The sessions ranged from 30 days to 2 days, with six of the sessions occurring in 1989–90 and five occurring from 2005 through 2011.[34] In 2013 three special sessions were called, two lasting 30 days and one lasting seven days. The issues involved redistricting, sentencing, transportation, and abortion regulation, which received the most attention.

Judicial Powers of the Governor

Texas elects each of its appellate and district court judges, but when vacancies occur because of the death, resignation, or retirement of the incumbent or as a result of creation of new courts, the governor is responsible for appointing individuals to fill these vacancies. The governor also fills vacancies (before an election) in the office of district attorney.

Once appointed to office, judges tend to remain in office. More than 95 percent of incumbents win re-election. Through this power to appoint judges, the governor has considerable influence over the Texas judicial system.

The governor has limited powers to issue clemencies for people convicted of crimes. Clemency normally includes the power to issue pardons, grant paroles, and issue reprieves. The governor's power in this area is severely limited because of abuses of previous governors. Pardons can be granted only on the recommendation of the Board of Pardons and Paroles. Governors have the ability to grant each person condemned to death one 30-day reprieve. Additional reprieves and any other act of clemency must be recommended by the Board of Pardons and Paroles.

There is a tradition for Texas governors to issue pardons just before Christmas Day. Governor Abbott, in 2015, issued only four pardons, all for relatively minor offenses. In one case a person was sentenced in 1969 to a $150 fine for unlawfully carrying a weapon; in another case a person was sentenced to 13 months of community supervision for theft of property; in the third case, in 1999 a person was fined $150 for a worthless check; and in the fourth case, a person was sentenced in 2001 for 12 months of community supervision for unlawfully carrying a weapon. Interestingly, in none of these cases did the pardon release a person from imprisonment. Rather it cleared their record of a crime from years in the past. The use of the pardoning power by governors has been criticized by criminal justice experts because governors usually issue pardons as did Abbott for minor crimes where the pardon has little impact on the life of the individual. If pardons are to have any real value, these experts argue, they should be issued for reformed felons who cannot join the free world because of the felony on their record.[35]

The Plural Executive

 Identify the other elected officials who make up Texas's plural executive

When Texans drafted a constitution in 1876, they chose to limit executive power and disperse it through several elected officials called the **plural executive**. Texans elect six of the seven people who make up the plural executive: the governor, lieutenant governor, attorney general, comptroller of public accounts, commissioner of the General Land Office, and commissioner of agriculture (see Tables 8.3 and 8.4). The governor appoints the seventh person, the secretary of state. With the exception of the commissioner of agriculture, whose office is created by statute, these offices are established by Article 3, Section 1, of the Texas Constitution. Except for the lieutenant governor, who receives the same salary as a legislator, salaries of members of the plural executive are set by the legislature.

The Railroad Commission of Texas and the State Board of Education assume considerable executive authority in the state, although these offices are not formally part of the executive branch established under Article 4 of the Texas Constitution. Instead the Railroad Commission of Texas is created by the legislature under statutory law authority granted under Article 10, Section 2, of the Texas Constitution. The State Board of Education, in contrast, is created under Article 7, Section 8. This is

plural executive an executive branch in which power is fragmented because the election of statewide officeholders is independent of the election of the governor

TABLE 8.3

Elected Officials* in Texas with Executive Responsibilities

SINGLE-ELECTED EXECUTIVES	MULTIELECTED EXECUTIVES
Governor	Railroad Commission (3 members)
Lieutenant governor	State Board of Education (15 members)
Attorney general	
Land commissioner	
Agriculture commissioner	
Comptroller	

*All officials listed above are elected statewide except the State Board of Education, whose members are elected from single-member districts.

TABLE 8.4

Executive Officeholders Elected Statewide, 2017

Governor	Greg Abbott (R)
Lieutenant governor	Dan Patrick (R)
Attorney general	Ken Paxton (R)
Comptroller of public accounts	Glenn Hegar (R)
Commissioner of the General Land Office	George P. Bush (R)
Commissioner of agriculture	Sid Miller (R)
Railroad commissioners	Ryan Sitton (R) Wayne Christian (R) Christi Craddick (R)
Secretary of State (appointed)	Carlos Cascos (R)

important because the constitution allows the legislature to decide in both cases whether these offices will be appointed or elective, how large the commission or board will be, and how long terms of office will be.

If the legislature wanted to change the way that the commissioner of agriculture, the Railroad Commission, or the Board of Education is selected, all it would have to do is pass a new law. To change the other executive offices' term or authority would demand a constitutional amendment. The ultimate result of all these constitutional nuances is vast fragmentation of responsibility for public policy in the state.

Elections are partisan, and each member of the plural executive may choose to operate independently of the others. At times, members of the plural executive may be in competition with each other, often because of conflicting personal ambitions. That occurred when John Hill was attorney general and sought to take the governorship from Dolph Briscoe, and when Mark White was attorney general and sought the governorship from Bill Clements. Because of the difficulty of defeating incumbents, however, it is far more likely that members of the plural executive will wait for a vacancy in a more prestigious office before seeking that higher office. Champions of the plural executive believe that it limits the power of executive officials and makes these officers more accountable to the public. Opponents assert the plural executive is inefficient and does not promote good government. The governor is a member of the plural executive, but this multipart executive limits the governor's control of the executive branch because he or she has little authority over this group.

One can get a sense of the importance of the various positions in the plural executive simply by looking at the campaign contributions received by winning candidates for these offices in the 2014 elections. Table 8.5 shows the contributions received by both the Democratic and the Republican nominees in 2014.

Two things are especially notable about these figures. One is the enormous amounts of money that are contributed to candidates. The Republican candidate for land commissioner, George P. Bush, had nearly $5.3 million in contributions, which is an extraordinary sum for this office. George P. Bush is son of former Florida governor and 2016 presidential candidate Jeb Bush and the grandson of former president George H. W. Bush, and is viewed as an up-and-coming Republican star. These factors no doubt explain his remarkable success at fund-raising. George P. Bush may be a bit of an outlier, but it is clear that large sums are being given to candidates to these offices.

The other thing that stands out about Table 8.5 is how lopsided the contributions are in favor of the Republican candidates. There were no incumbents running for these offices, so none of this vast difference in contributions between Democrats and Republicans can be explained as a fund-raising advantage caused by the incumbency of the candidate. Part of the reason for the large sums contributed to Republican candidates for these offices is that some faced significant primary opposition. That was

TABLE 8.5

Campaign Contributions in 2014 for Statewide Elective Offices

OFFICE	WINNING CANDIDATE	CONTRIBUTIONS TO WINNER ($)	LOSING CANDIDATE	CONTRIBUTIONS TO LOSER ($)
Governor	Greg Abbott (R)	$47,436,720	Wendy Davis (D)	$4,034,095
Lieutenant governor	Dan Patrick (R)	18,262,478	Leticia Van de Putte (D)	8,263,861
Attorney general	Ken Paxton (R)	8,335,845	Sam Houston (D)	596,153
Comptroller	Glenn Hegar (R)	5,047,564	Mike Collier (D)	1,561,942
Agriculture commissioner	Sid Miller (R)	837,917	Jim Hogan (D)	0
Land commissioner	George Bush (R)	5,292,154	John Cook (D)	77,246
Railroad commissioner*	Ryan Sitton (R)	4,070,984	Steve Brown (D)	73,789

*There was an election for one position on the Railroad Commission.
SOURCE: National Institute on Money in State Politics.

certainly true in the Republican primary for lieutenant governor, attorney general, and agriculture commissioner as well as the railroad commissioner race, but hard-fought primaries are a sign that the Republican nomination is the path to general election victory. It is a sign of the strength of the Republican Party and the weakness of the Democratic Party in Texas elections that Republican candidates raise so much more money for their campaigns than do Democratic candidates.

Lieutenant Governor

The **lieutenant governor** has executive responsibilities, such as serving as acting governor when the governor is out of state and succeeding a governor who resigns, is incapacitated, or is impeached. The real power of the office of lieutenant governor, however, is derived from its place in the legislative process.

According to the Texas Constitution, the lieutenant governor is the "Constitutional President of the Senate" and has the right to debate and vote on all issues when the Senate sits as a "Committee of the Whole." The Texas Constitution also grants the lieutenant governor the power to cast a deciding vote in the Senate when there is a tie. Like the Speaker of the House, the lieutenant governor signs all bills and resolutions. The constitution names the lieutenant governor to the Legislative Redistricting Board, a five-member committee that apportions the state into senatorial and house districts if the legislature fails to do so following a census. Other powers of the lieutenant governor are derived from various statutes passed by the legislature. For example, the lieutenant governor is chair of the Legislative Budget Board and is a member of a number of other boards and committees, including the Legislative Audit Committee, the Legislative Education Board, the Cash Management Committee, and the Bond Review Board.

lieutenant governor the second-highest elected official in the state and president of the state Senate

In 2014, Texans elected conservative state senator Dan Patrick to the powerful position of lieutenant governor. Here, Patrick presides over a session in the Senate that took up a bill to restrict access to abortions.

The Texas Constitution grants the Senate the power to make its own rules, and lieutenant governors traditionally have been granted significant legislative power by the Senate itself. The Senate rules empower the lieutenant governor to decide all parliamentary questions and to use discretion in following Senate procedural rules. The lieutenant governor is also empowered to set up standing and special committees and to appoint committee members and chairs of the committees. The Senate rules, and not just the Texas Constitution, make the lieutenant governor one of the most powerful political leaders in the state. New Senate rules passed by a future Senate could, of course, substantially alter the power possessed by the lieutenant governor.

Political Style of Lieutenant Governors

Bob Bullock served as lieutenant governor of Texas from 1991 to 1999. A force in Texas politics for over 40 years, he was one of the strongest and most effective lieutenant governors Texas politics had ever seen. He took a bluff, rough, tough, head-knocking approach to leadership. He was feared and respected by friends and foes alike. Although a Democrat, Bullock worked closely with Republicans and appointed several to be chairs of major committees. His relationship with Republican governor George W. Bush was remarkably close and cooperative. Oddly, his relationship with Bush was far closer than with Bush's predecessor, Democrat Ann Richards. Bullock's base of support was broad. He has support from Democratic loyalists, from the business community, and from trial lawyers. His politics were flexible—he went from supporting a state income tax to supporting a constitutional amendment that would make an income tax unlikely in Texas. His focus was on economic development matters rather than a political social agenda. His mantra was that all he wanted was what was good for Texas.

In 2014, Texas elected a Tea Party–backed conservative Republican, Dan Patrick, as lieutenant governor. Patrick was a Houston AM radio talk show host, and he parlayed his talk show skills and his audience support into a state senate seat in 2006. In 2013 he was chosen by *Texas Monthly* as one of the worst Texas legislators. *Texas Monthly* claimed he was both a bully and an ideologue who treated the committee he chaired, the Education Committee, as if it were part of his radio show. He lectured other legislators, interrupted witnesses, and assumed those who disagreed with his bills did not understand them. The only opinion that mattered, *Texas Monthly* claimed, was Patrick's.[36] Still, he ran (and won) an extraordinary race against three Republicans in the primary and against a very capable Democratic opponent in the general election.

Patrick's goals were to pursue a political agenda reflective of his Tea Party/religious right support. This represents a different political faction and a different political orientation from the business interest support of previous lieutenant governors. Patrick changed the rules of the state senate to make it easier for votes to be taken on bills opposed by the Democratic minority, and he sought to lessen the power of Democrats over committees by exercising his power to appoint committee chairs. He sought to restrict abortion as much as possible and has worked to control the border and to promote gun rights. His plan for the 2017 legislative session is to continue to promote gun rights, to promote religious liberty, to promote free political speech, to prevent public funds from being used to process union dues, and to weaken the influence of the federal Environmental Protection Agency.[37]

Attorney General

The **attorney general** (AG) is elected to a four-year term and acts as the chief lawyer for the state of Texas. The AG is, in effect, head of Texas's civil law firm. Currently, the Texas AG oversees the work of over 700 lawyers.

attorney general elected state official who serves as the state's chief civil lawyer

The AG's office is concerned primarily with civil matters. When a lawsuit is filed against the state or by the state, the AG manages the legal activities surrounding that lawsuit. Any time a state agency needs legal representation, the AG's office represents the agency. In any lawsuit to which Texas is a party, the AG's office has full responsibility to resolve the case and can litigate, compromise, settle, or choose not to pursue the suit.

One of the more important powers of the AG's office comes from the opinion process. Any agency of state or local government can ask the AG's office for an advisory opinion on the legality of an action. The AG's office will rule on the question, and the ruling has the force of law unless overturned by a court or the legislature.

The AG's office has little responsibility in criminal law but may appoint a special prosecutor if a local district attorney asks the AG for assistance. This can happen when there is a potential conflict of interest—for example, if the district attorney is a friend of or works with a local official who is under criminal investigation. In one recent case, lawyers from the AG's office prosecuted a state district judge in Collin County on bribery charges. Generally, criminal cases in Texas are prosecuted by district or county attorneys elected in each county. The county is usually responsible for the costs of the trial and for all appeals in state court. If a criminal case is appealed to the federal courts, the AG's office assumes responsibility.[38]

Probably the most controversial and criticized aspect of the work of the AG's office is child support collection. Almost one-half of the AG's 4,000 employees are involved in collecting child support. However, this program is the subject of intense criticism because much child support remains uncollected.

In 2014 Ken Paxton was elected attorney general. Paxton had served in the Texas House from 2002 to 2012 and then was elected to the Texas senate. He was elected with the support of the Tea Party in 2014 when the former attorney general, Greg Abbott, ran for and was elected governor. Taking a page from Abbott's political playbook as attorney general, Paxton has placed great emphasis on suing the federal government. In his biography on the attorney general's website, it is noted, "In his first year in office, General Paxton hit the ground running, filing eight lawsuits against the federal government to protect Texas sovereignty on environmental issues, health care, religious freedom and immigration."[39] Though the Texas attorney general had battled in the past with the federal government over integration and offshore oil ownership, especially in the 1950s, Abbott and Paxton appear to have been the most litigious of Texas attorneys general when it comes to suits against the Obama administration.

The General Land Office is influential in large part because it awards oil and gas exploration rights for publicly owned lands. Land Commissioner George P. Bush was elected in 2014 and has sought to change how the GLO operates. Here, Bush meets with San Antonio mayor Ivy Taylor at an event announcing the receipt of funds for preservation of the Alamo, which is now under GLO supervision.

land commissioner elected state official who is the manager of most publicly owned lands

A cloud has remained over Paxton for much of his administration as attorney general because he has been charged with two first degree felonies involving securities fraud and one third degree felony involving failure to register as a securities agent. These charges stem from his time in the legislature in 2011–2012. He has pled not guilty to these charges. He was also under investigation for a land sale in McKinney, Texas, that involved him, Collin County district attorney Greg Willis, and eight others. The group bought 35 acres of undeveloped land for $700,000, got a zoning change on the land, and sold half of the land at a price of $1,000,000 for construction of the Collin County Central Appraisal District building. A grand jury decided in the spring of 2016 not to pursue charges in this matter. Attorney General Paxton was under a disciplinary investigation by the State Bar of Texas for an opinion he gave where it is alleged that he violated the rules of professional conduct by stating that county clerks could opt out of issuing marriage licenses to same-sex couples if they had religious objections to issuing the licenses. The State Bar did not ultimately discipline Paxton, and Paxton claimed that all the charges against him were politically motivated.[40]

Commissioner of the General Land Office

The General Land Office (GLO) is the oldest state agency in Texas. Historically the **land commissioner** gave away land. Today, the GLO is the land manager for most publicly owned lands in Texas. Texas owns or has mineral interest in 13 million acres of land in the state, plus all submerged lands up to 10.35 miles into the Gulf of Mexico. All but 28 of Texas's 254 counties have some of these public lands.

The GLO also awards grazing and oil and gas exploration rights on this land. Thousands of producing oil and gas wells are found on state-owned land and are managed by the GLO. These responsibilities make the office of land commissioner quite influential. A significant portion of royalties on oil and natural gas produced by these wells goes to the Permanent School Fund and the Permanent University Fund.

The commissioner also manages the Veterans' Land Program, through which the state makes low-cost loans to Texas veterans. The program includes loans for land, housing, and home improvements. Recently, the GLO was given authority over some environmental matters. The land commissioner is responsible for environmental quality on public lands and waters, especially along the Texas coast. All of Texas's Gulf Coast beaches are publicly owned and under the jurisdiction of the GLO.

George P. Bush, the son of former Florida governor Jeb Bush and nephew of President George W. Bush, was elected commissioner of the GLO in 2014 and is generally believed to have sought the position as a stepping-stone to higher political office. However, he has made it clear that he intends to take an active and aggressive role in running and changing the GLO. He has terminated two top-level GLO officials, and a third has resigned. In the wake of critical reports from the state auditor that found problems with the GLO's contracting process and internal audits that have found numerous problems, Bush has undertaken a complete restructuring of the organization.

The GLO has 21 major divisions, which Bush is changing out of concern that many of them have become centers of power and control for managers who do not work well with other divisions. His top aide has warned employees that there will no longer be "kingdoms" within the agency and that staff should not expect to "sit on laurels" or "count on connections" to get by.

The GLO has traditionally been the state agency where things get done. When other parts of the government fail to do something, often the work is transferred to the GLO to fix the problem. Recently, for example, the GLO took over the management of the Alamo when there were claims of mismanagement by the Daughters of the Republic of Texas. Bush, to the chagrin of Jerry Patterson, who was his predecessor and was commissioner of the GLO for 12 years, believes that his role as commissioner is to bring major changes to the organization.[41]

Agriculture Commissioner

The **agriculture commissioner** is primarily responsible for enforcing agricultural laws. These include administration of animal quarantine laws, inspection of food, and enforcement of disease- and pest-control programs. Enforcement of the state's laws helps to ensure that Texas's farm products are of high quality and disease free.

agriculture commissioner elected state official who is primarily responsible for enforcing agricultural laws

The Department of Agriculture checks weights and measures. Each year a representative of the department checks each motor fuel pump to make sure that it dispenses the correct amount of fuel. Scales used by grocery stores and markets are checked to guarantee that they weigh products correctly.

Farming and ranching are big business in Texas. Although a large number of small family farms exist in the state, large corporate farms increasingly dominate Texas agriculture. These large agribusinesses are greatly affected by the decisions of the commissioner. Such decisions can increase or decrease the cost of production. Changes in production costs affect the profit margins of these agribusinesses and ultimately the price consumers pay for food products.

The new agriculture commissioner, Sid Miller, was elected in 2014 and has promised that his agency will employ 26 more consumer protection inspectors and aggressively prosecute consumer protection violations. At the same time, he had run into trouble with the state legislature for his intense lobbying of them in behalf of his agency, for his extravagant proposal to renovate his office, for $413,700 in bonuses given to 146 of his employees, for using state funds for personal travel, and for employing an ex-felon who continued to have private clients while working for the agency. Miller was under criminal investigation for using state funds to travel to a rodeo and to obtain an injection for pain treatment.

Publicity seems to be a primary goal of Miller's administration. For his first official act as commissioner, he held a press conference where he granted full amnesty to cupcakes. He said he wished to reassure Texans that it was legal to bring cupcakes and other sweets to school and that he would protect that right. He then took a large bite of a cupcake and said, "Let them eat cake." He also sent a cupcake to each member of the House and Senate. Miller's search for publicity has not decreased. He, for example, has threatened to slap anyone who tells him "Happy Holidays" rather than "Merry Christmas"; has advocated dropping nuclear bombs on "the Muslim world"; and has

Commissioner of Agriculture Sid Miller bites into a cupcake at a press conference where he granted full amnesty to cupcakes in order to assure Texans that it was legal to bring sweets to school.

spoken in favor of deep fryers and soda machines in public schools. Borrowing a political page from Governor Abbott and Attorney General Paxton, he has joined with Paxton in a suit against the federal Environmental Protection Agency and has argued, "Drought, hurricanes and tornadoes are not the biggest threats facing Texas, rather it is an overzealous federal government."[42] After the 2016 elections, Miller was mentioned as a possible nominee for secretary of agriculture in the Trump administration.

Comptroller of Public Accounts

comptroller elected state official who directs the collection of taxes and other revenues and estimates revenues for the budgeting process

The **comptroller** is a powerful state official because he or she directs the collection of tax and nontax revenues and issues an evaluation and estimate of anticipated state revenues before each legislative session. Tax collection is the most visible function of the comptroller. The taxes collected by the comptroller include the general sales tax, severance tax on natural resources, business franchise tax, motor fuel tax, inheritance tax, most occupational taxes, and many minor taxes.

Although collecting billions in revenue is important, estimating revenues provides the comptroller with more power. These estimates, issued monthly during legislative sessions, are vital to the appropriations process because the legislature is prohibited from spending more than the comptroller estimates will be available. Final passage of any appropriations bill is contingent on the comptroller's certifying that revenues will be available to cover the monies spent in the appropriation. Because most bills require the expenditure of monies, this certification function provides the comptroller with significant power over the legislative process. If the comptroller is unable to certify that monies are available to pay for the appropriation, the legislature must reduce the appropriation or increase revenues. More than just an auditor, accountant, and tax collector, the comptroller is a key figure in the appropriations process.

In 1996 the office of state treasurer was eliminated, and the comptroller of public accounts assumed the duties of that office. Since then, the comptroller of public accounts has been the official custodian of state funds and is responsible for the safety of the state's money and for investing that money. To ensure the safety of Texas's money, funds are deposited only in financial institutions designated by the State Depository Board as eligible to receive state monies. Deposits are required to earn as much money as possible. The more money earned as interest on deposits, the fewer tax dollars are needed.

An interesting responsibility of the comptroller is returning abandoned money and property to their rightful owners. In October of each year, the comptroller publishes a list of individuals with unclaimed property. One list included $117,000 in a forgotten savings account, a certificate of deposit for $104,000, gold coins, diamond rings, and rare baseball trading cards. Money or property that remains unclaimed goes to the state.

In 2014, Glenn Hegar was elected comptroller. Hegar is a former state senator from Katy who campaigned for this office, which largely involves economic and revenue forecasting and tax collections, as being the "pro–Second Amendment," "pro-taxpayer," and "pro-life" candidate. Hegar faces an unenviable task in that he must estimate what effect the dramatic decline in oil prices will have on tax revenues and on the Texas economy in general. Inaccurate estimates could force unnecessary budget cuts or bring about tax increases, and yet it is unclear how extensive or how long the decline in oil prices will last.

SOCIAL RESPONSIBILITY: GET INVOLVED

- The commissioner of agriculture, the land commissioner, the state comptroller, and the attorney general each head agencies that have significant responsibility for the operation of state government. To what extent is the public aware of these agencies and the major role they play in government?

- Do you think that activities of these agencies should be better known? What could the agencies do to be more transparent? What could the people do to gather more information?

Secretary of State

Strangely given Texas's fragmentation of power, the governor does appoint the Texas **secretary of state**, even though this office is an elective one in 37 other states. Though once considered a "glorified keeper of certain state records," the secretary of state is now an important officer.[43] The secretary of state has myriad responsibilities, and the appointment of a secretary of state is one of the governor's most important tasks.

As Texas's chief election official, the secretary of state conducts voter registration drives. His or her office works with organizations such as the League of Women Voters to increase the number of registered voters. The secretary of state's office also collects election-night returns from county judges and county clerks and makes the results available to the media. This service provides media and voters with a convenient method of receiving the latest official election returns in Texas.

All debt and Uniform Commercial Code filings are placed with the secretary of state's office. When any individual borrows money from a financial institution, a copy of the loan agreement is placed in the secretary of state's office.

secretary of state state official, appointed by the governor, whose primary responsibility is administering elections

Accountability of the Plural Executive

Except for the secretary of state, each member of the plural executive is directly accountable to the people of Texas through elections. The plural executive is accountable to the legislature in three ways: the budgetary process, Sunset Review, and the impeachment process.

The legislature can demonstrate its satisfaction, or lack thereof, with an agency of the plural executive by the amount of money it appropriates to that agency. A significant increase in appropriations indicates an agency in good standing with the legislature, whereas little or no increase in funds indicates legislative displeasure. Sunset Review can lead to reforms of an agency and even its elimination.

The Texas Constitution, not the legislature, creates most of the plural executive. Impeachment and conviction are the ultimate check on an elected official. The Texas House of Representatives can impeach an official for such things as criminal activity or gross malfeasance in office. The Texas Senate then tries the official. If convicted by the Senate, the official is removed from office.

The Plural Executive and the Governor

The plural executive dilutes the ability of the governor to control state government. The governor appoints the secretary of state but has no control over other members of the plural executive. Officials are elected independently, and they do not run as a slate. They do not answer to the governor, and they do not serve as a cabinet. They tend to operate their offices as independent fiefdoms, and they jealously guard their turf. The plural executive can make state government appear as if it is going in several different directions at once. This is especially true when members of the plural executive are political rivals. For example, widely publicized tensions between Governor Rick Perry and Comptroller Carole Strayhorn led to Strayhorn's unsuccessful campaign as an independent against Perry in 2006.

Boards, Commissions, and Regulatory Agencies

Explain the roles played by boards, commissions, and regulatory agencies

bureaucracy the complex structure of offices, tasks, rules, and principles of organization that are employed by all large-scale institutions to coordinate the work of their personnel

The state **bureaucracy** in Texas has numerous state boards, commissions, councils, and committees as well as major agencies within the plural executive that have administrative or advisory functions. In addition to the governmental bodies under the direct control of the single executives who are part of the elected plural executive,

A Plural or Single Executive?

The Texas executive branch is similar to the federal executive branch. The governor, like the president, is the chief executive. The governor is the commander-in-chief of military forces in the state, has the power to appoint people to various administrative offices, and is responsible for making sure that the laws are faithfully executed. But unlike the president and vice president, who run on the same ticket, the governor and lieutenant governor are elected separately. Moreover, the governor of Texas does not have a cabinet that he appoints and controls. The secretary of state is appointed by the governor, but the comptroller of public accounts, the attorney general, the land commissioner, and the agriculture commissioner (a statutory, not constitutional, office) are all elected separately. We call this a plural executive system because executive power is divided among different officeholders. Current Governor Greg Abbott (at right, seated on the left), Attorney General Ken Paxton (center), and Lieutenant Governor Dan Patrick (right) are just a few of the people that today comprise Texas's plural executive.

Many other states follow the federal model or single executive model, so that the governor and lieutenant governor are elected to office together. The governor then appoints all of the relevant officeholders to run the executive branch. In these instances, the attorney general, the secretary of state, the agriculture commissioner, and all other "cabinet" officials are appointed by the governor and serve at his or her pleasure.

Advocates of the plural executive model argue that a decentralized system of power within the executive branch helps guard against abuses of power. The Texas Constitution intentionally provides for a weak governorship, and the plural executive is one way to guarantee this. If the attorney general and other statewide officials are not beholden to the governor, they will not necessarily support the governor's agenda. Supporters of the Texas model also argue that it is more democratic in that the electorate has a larger role to play in the selection of executive officers.

Opponents of the plural executive model argue that the problem is that the office of the governor is too weak. The plural executive makes it difficult for the governor to govern effectively and creates a counterproductive tug of war among all of the separately elected officials. In the federal model, the president can decide who is best suited for a particular role and delegate power accordingly. The Texas governor, on the other hand, cannot give orders to the lieutenant governor or the attorney general, thus making it more difficult to run the state in a responsible manner.

In Texas's recent past, Republican governor George W. Bush had to work alongside Democratic lieutenant governor Bob Bullock in order to pass his legislative agenda. Some observers saw this as a positive effect of the plural executive, because it required compromise for the good of the state. Opponents of the plural executive might have seen this as a negative effect, because it undermined the power of the governor to implement his agenda. Each form of governance has its benefits and its costs for democracy.

COMMUNICATING EFFECTIVELY: YOUR VOICE

- Is the plural executive more democratic than the single executive model? Does it lead to more efficient and accountable government? Why or why not?

- If you were to design a state executive branch, how would you decide whether to have a plural executive or a single executive? What are the arguments for and against each model?

there are also bodies (1) run by multimember boards appointed by the governor and confirmed by the Senate; (2) with single executives appointed by the governor and confirmed by the Senate; (3) run by boards appointed by several persons within the plural executive or even by legislative officers, and confirmed by the Senate; and (4) run by multimember boards elected by the people. Overall, the state bureaucracy employed 315,961 in 2015,[44] up over 15 percent from 2004.[45]

Governor Perry's lengthy service gave him enormous influence throughout state government, as he is the only Texas governor in modern history to have made every appointment in state government that a governor can make—and he also made numerous appointments to vacancies in office such as the Texas appellate courts and scores of district judgeships. State law usually sets the terms of persons on state boards at four or six years. As a result, each new governor spends a great deal of time replacing holdover appointments from previous governors. With Perry's lengthy tenure as governor, however, those holdover appointments are long gone. The result, according to former state representative and author Brian McCall, is that "in this regard, [Perry] is by far the most powerful governor in Texas history. No governor has been able to do what he has done."[46] Perry placed many of his closest advisers in key positions, which has spread not only his personal influence but also his personal political philosophy of a pro-business state government.

Multimember Appointed Boards

As we have discussed, most boards and commissions in Texas are headed by members appointed by the governor and confirmed by the Senate. Some commissioners are appointed by a variety of other people, including the lieutenant governor, the Speaker of the House, or leaders of select professional organizations like the state bar or state medical association. Multimember commissions with heads appointed by the gov-

The Department of Parks and Wildlife is an agency in the Texas executive branch and is led by a board appointed by the governor. The department manages natural resources and fishing, hunting, and outdoor recreation in the state. Here, an employee measures fish caught near Corpus Christi.

ernor include innocuous agencies, such as the Bandera County River Authority, the State Seed and Plant Board, the Caddo Lake Compact Commission, and the Texas Funeral Commission. There are also better-known agencies, such as the Texas Alcoholic Beverage Commission, the Department of Parks and Wildlife, the Texas Youth Commission, and the Texas Department of Corrections. Except in the case of a major controversy, such as the sexual abuse scandal that embroiled the Texas Youth Commission in 2007, these agencies work in anonymity, although several of them have a direct effect on the lives of Texans. One such example is the Public Utilities Commission.

Public Utilities Commission (PUC) More than most other agencies, the Public Utilities Commission (PUC) has a direct effect on consumers' pocketbooks. Before 1975 cities in Texas set utility rates. The PUC was established in 1975, in part to protect consumers and to curb the rate at which utility costs were increasing. The commission is responsible for setting all local telephone and some electric rates.

Local telephone rates vary from one part of Texas to another, but all rates in a service area are the same. The commission also determines the maximum charge for pay telephones and approves additional services such as caller ID, call waiting, and call forwarding. The PUC promulgates rules that govern public utilities such as one that prohibits an individual's local service from being disconnected for nonpayment of long-distance bills. Another regulation by the PUC establishes a "no call" list for phone numbers of Texas residents who do not wish to receive telemarketing calls from companies that do not have a business relationship with the phone customer.

With the introduction of retail competition to the electric industry, the PUC has had a major role in providing information to consumers and in setting requirements for providers of electric services. The PUC maintains a website, www.powertochoose .org/, that allows electric customers to compare the costs of electricity from the various electric service providers.

Appointed Single Executives

The Texas Department of Insurance Whereas the PUC is run by a multimember body appointed by the governor and confirmed by the Texas Senate, the Texas Department of Insurance is run by one commissioner appointed by the governor for a two-year term and confirmed by the Senate. The purpose of the Department of Insurance is to regulate the insurance market in Texas, a complicated task that affects most Texans.

In the early 2000s, Texas was faced with huge increases in the cost of homeowners' insurance brought on at least in part by major increases in insurance claims, most notably for mold damage. From the first quarter of 2000 to the fourth quarter of 2001, the number of mold claims increased from 1,050 to 14,706. Additionally, the costs of these claims increased significantly to the point that insurance payments became greater than insurance premiums. And with a declining economy during this period, insurance companies were no longer making substantial profits on their investment of insurance premiums. Homeowners' premiums increased rapidly. Between 2001 and 2002 homeowners' premiums rose 21.8 percent. Some companies chose not to write any new homeowners' policies; other companies simply pulled out of the Texas market. In 1997, 166 companies were writing homeowners' policies in Texas; by 2003 only 101 companies were writing such policies.[47]

In response, the Texas Department of Insurance began to deregulate insurance coverage so that, for example, policies could be written that charged more for complete mold coverage, less for reduced mold coverage, and significantly less for no mold coverage.

The legislature also stepped into the homeowners' insurance cost issue, which by 2002–03 was reaching crisis proportions. One effect of the legislature's involvement was a "file and use" regulatory system that was implemented at the end of 2004. This system allowed insurers to institute new rates immediately after filing them with the Texas Department of Insurance. The commissioner of insurance can then disapprove of the new rates and may force the company to issue rebates to policyholders.[48] Thus, the commissioner of insurance appears to wield great power over insurance rates but only after those rates have gone into effect.

Although insurance companies advocate less regulation, consumer groups argue that the insurance commissioner has inadequate powers to deal with insurance companies. Indeed, it is doubtful that the commissioner has sufficient power to force an uncooperative insurer to comply with his or her decisions. The commissioner is also faced with the seemingly intractable problem of keeping rates low and coverage available in hurricane-prone areas to which more and more people are moving.

Multimember Elected Boards

Members of two state agencies are elected by the voters: the Railroad Commission of Texas and the State Board of Education. The Railroad Commission has 3 members elected statewide to six-year terms of office. One of the 3 members is elected every two years. The Board of Education is a 15-member board elected to four-year terms from single-member districts.

Railroad Commission of Texas (RRC)

At one time, the Railroad Commission of Texas (RRC) was one of the most powerful state agencies in the nation. It regulated intrastate railroads, trucks, and bus transportation and supervised the oil and natural gas industry in Texas. For most of the RRC's existence, regulation of the oil and gas industry was the RRC's primary focus.

Today, the RRC is a shadow of its former self. Court decisions, deregulation of the transportation industry, other state and federal legislation, and the decline in the nation's dependence on Texas's crude oil production have diminished the commission's power. In 2005 the RRC's limited authority over railroads was transferred to the Texas Department of Transportation, so the RRC now has no authority over what was once its major reason for existence. During the RRC's heyday when Texas was a major oil producer, the commission limited production to conserve oil and to maintain prices. Because it restricted oil production, the RRC was one of the most economically significant governmental bodies on the national and international stage. As oil production shifted to the Middle East, the RRC became the model for OPEC, the Organization of Petroleum Exporting Countries, which also seeks to limit oil production to maintain prices. At one time, members of the Texas RRC wielded such vast economic power that they were among the state's most influential politicians. Renewed energy production in Texas as a result of fracking and horizontal drilling appears to be increasing the importance of the RRC, although it will never again be a major decision-making body for world oil and gas prices. There are now simply too many major oil and gas fields outside of Texas.

State Board of Education (SBOE)

The State Board of Education (SBOE) sets policy for public education (pre-kindergarten to 12th grade programs supported by the state government) in Texas. The education bureaucracy that enforces the SBOE's rules and regulations is called the Texas Education Agency (TEA). Together these two bodies control public education in Texas by determining licensing requirements for public school teachers, setting minimum high school graduation criteria for recommended or advanced curriculums, establishing standards for accreditation of public schools, and selecting public school textbooks.

Texas spends millions of dollars each year purchasing textbooks, and the state furnishes these books without charge to students. Books must meet stringent criteria, and because the state buys so many textbooks, publishers print books especially for students in Texas. Often states that spend less money on textbooks than Texas must purchase those originally printed for Texas.

The commissioner of education is appointed by the governor from a list of candidates submitted by the SBOE. He or she is administrative head of the TEA and serves as adviser to the SBOE. The commissioner of education is at the apex of the public education bureaucracy in Texas.

The SBOE is composed of 15 members. Because the board is elected from single-member districts, Democrats continue to be elected. Also, SBOE district lines are drawn in such a way that it is rare for a seat on the board to flop from one party to the other. In 2014, for example, there were seven seats up for election. In six of those seats an incumbent was running; only one seat was an open seat. Three of the incumbents were Democrats, and three were Republicans; they all won re-election. A Democrat won the open seat and had no Republican opponent.

In the 2016 elections, three Republican incumbents were re-elected and a Republican won an open seat. Democratic and Republican incumbents are generally able to win re-election with little in campaign contributions compared with other elected executive offices—probably because these offices are low visibility and each board member's district is one-fifteenth the size of the entire state.

In recent years, the Texas SBOE has become an ideological battleground. In 2009 these battles led the board to review how evolution was taught. In what was a partial defeat for the social conservatives, no longer would teachers be required to teach "strengths and weaknesses" of evolution, although they would be encouraged to teach "all sides."

Other battles have broken out over other aspects of educational policy. For example, in late 2015 a Facebook posting that went viral brought the SBOE process for reviewing textbooks to widespread attention and led to a major effort to change the textbook review process. Roni Dean-Burren, the mother of a 9th grader, posted what her son's geography text said about the Atlantic slave trade. The text said that the slave trade between the 1500s and 1800s "brought millions of workers from Africa to the southern United States to work on agricultural plantations." One might conclude from this text that the slaves brought from Africa were plantation employees, and the publisher quickly apologized and promised to correct the terminology. The remaining issue was whether the process for reviewing textbooks was adequate, however. The existing process had led to numerous ideological struggles within the board

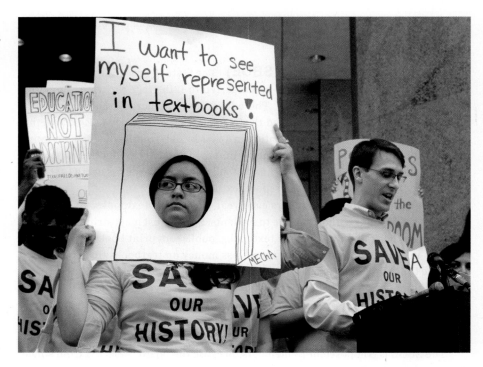

The State Board of Education sets policy for public education, from pre-kindergarten through 12th grade. In recent years, some of the board's decisions concerning curriculums and textbooks have generated controversy.

over proper treatment of religion, the Civil War, and even climate change. Under that process, the board relies on citizen review panels that review texts. The members are nominated by board members. Others can also review the texts and can testify about their objections for language or interpretations of the texts during board meetings. In the aftermath of the outcry over the use of the word "workers" rather than "slaves," a motion was made to let university experts fact check textbooks. That motion failed by an 8–7 vote. However, another motion passed unanimously: in the future, review panels should have at least a majority of people "with sufficient content expertise and experience" to make judgments about textbooks. Whether this new policy reduces the ideological battles and factual errors in texts remains to be seen.[49]

An SBOE candidate in the 2015 run-off Republican primary made some particularly provocative statements that suggest possible future intense ideological battles over educational policy. Mary Lou Bruner stated that she believed President Obama had been a male prostitute in New York, that humans and dinosaurs existed together, that health classes should avoid discussions of sexuality, and that Democrats had John F. Kennedy killed because he was too conservative, among numerous other unusual comments. Her statements were so bizarre that even though she almost won the Republican nomination without a runoff, once her statements were widely publicized she suffered an overwhelming defeat in the runoff primary.

Although many Texas voters may not be aware of them, the battles fought within the SBOE have wide-reaching effects. They affect not only the education of Texas schoolchildren but also that of children across the nation. Because the state's textbook market is so large, the content of the textbooks used in Texas sets the tone for textbook content in other states that are less populous and therefore have smaller markets for texts.[50]

Making Agencies Accountable

In a democracy, elected officials are ultimately responsible to the voters. Appointed officials are indirectly accountable to the people through the elected officials who appoint them. Both are responsible to legislatures that determine responsibilities and appropriate money to carry out those responsibilities. In Texas, the plural executive is responsible to the legislature for its biennial funding and to the voters for re-election. The myriad state agencies look to the legislature for funding, and once every 12 years they must justify their existence to the **Sunset Advisory Commission (SAC)**.

The 12-member SAC has 5 members from the Texas Senate and 1 public member appointed by the lieutenant governor. Five members from the Texas House and 1 public member are appointed by the Speaker of the Texas House.

The Sunset Review Act created the SAC in 1977. The act established specific criteria to be considered in evaluating the continuing need for an agency. One of several laws enacted in the mid-1970s to bring more openness and accountability to Texas government, the Sunset process establishes a date on which an agency is abolished unless the legislature passes a bill for the agency to continue in operation.

During its Sunset review, an agency must, among other things, document its efficiency, the extent to which it meets legislative mandates, and its promptness and effectiveness in handling complaints, and it must establish the continuing need for its services. The review process is lengthy, lasting almost two years.

After a thorough study of an agency, the SAC recommends one of three actions to the legislature: (1) the agency continues as is, with no change in its organization or functions; (2) the agency continues but with changes (reorganization, a new focus for the agency, or merger with other agencies); or (3) the agency is abolished.

If option 1 or 2 is recommended, specific action by the legislature is required before the date of the agency's abolition. Option 1 requires specific legislation to re-create the agency in its existing form. Option 2 requires the legislature to recreate the agency with some or all of the changes recommended by the SAC. If the legislature agrees the agency should be abolished, no action is necessary. It will expire at the Sunset deadline; the sun sets and the agency is no more.

Each state agency has been through the Sunset process. The legislature has allowed the sun to set on more than 37 agencies or programs, and 46 agencies or programs have been merged with existing bodies. Since its beginning the legislature has accepted 80 percent of recommendations of the SAC and the agency claims to have saved Texas taxpayers $980 million.[51]

Sunset Advisory Commission (SAC) a commission created in 1975 for the purpose of reviewing the effectiveness of state agencies

The Executive Branch and the Future of Texas

At the national level, the president is elected, through the Electoral College, by the people as a whole. The president is the spokesperson for the nation in the world and is the commander in chief of the armed forces. When there is a national crisis, the people look to the president for leadership. Throughout the twentieth century, the power and authority of the presidency increased significantly, often at the expense of Congress. American democracy has become an executive-led system, with a weak Congress and a partially demobilized electorate.

Such is not the case in Texas. The fear of a strong executive who could ignore the wishes of either the legislature or the people, as was the case during Reconstruction in Texas, led in 1876 to a constitution that created a plural executive. The governor is the chief executive officer in the state, elected directly by the popular vote of all the people of Texas. People turn to the governor for leadership and direction during times of crisis. But compared with that of the president, the power of the Texas governor is more limited. Many key executive officials, including the lieutenant governor, the attorney general, the comptroller, and the land commissioner, are elected—like the governor—directly by the people. These members of the plural executive, along with other popularly elected statewide boards and commissions, possess power and authority that under other constitutional arrangements the governor might possess. As has been noted throughout this chapter, Governor Perry's ability to accumulate power in the governor's office is unprecedented in recent history. That his successors will be able to wield the limited powers of the governor as efficiently is by no means certain.

Greg Abbott would have to serve many more years in office before he could amass the power of Rick Perry. At the moment, with the exception of some members of the Railroad Commission, all statewide elected executive officers are rookies in their positions, having been in their current office only since January 2015. Some, like Greg Abbott, have years of experience in other statewide offices—he has been a Texas Supreme Court justice as well as an attorney general, but he is still new to his role as governor. All these officials are going through a learning phase and adapting to their new positions. Greg Abbott is trying to follow in the footsteps of an exceptionally powerful Texas governor. Land Commissioner George P. Bush, though likely destined for higher office, seems to be settling into a role as an internal reformer of his agency. Agriculture Commissioner Sid Miller seems to be the political publicity hound of the group. Lieutenant Governor Dan Patrick is pushing hard to be the Tea Party leader in state politics. Comptroller Glenn Hegar is simply trying to cope with the massive effects of the drop in the price of oil on state revenues and the state economy, while Attorney General Ken Paxton is just trying to survive his indictments and other investigations. The mix of these competing roles, ambitions, and personal goals is what makes the plural executive of Texas so tumultuous.

There is no likelihood that the plural executive structure will see structural change. Nor is it likely that the Democratic Party will be able to successfully challenge anytime in the near future the Republican Party's control of these positions. Still, the differences in the values, abilities, ambitions, and goals of these members of the plural executive will provide the fodder for the policies and controversies of the future.

Use 📖 INQUIZITIVE to help you study and master this material.

The Governor

> • Describe the powers of the Texas governor and the limits of the governor's power (pp. 249–67)

Although the Texas governor is considered weak compared with governors of other states, the power of appointing members to boards made Governor Rick Perry the most powerful governor in state history largely because of his long tenure. Among the executive powers the governor possesses are appointment, budgetary, military, and police powers. Among his legislative powers are message and veto powers and the ability to call special sessions of the legislature.

Key Terms

impeachment (p. 256)
appointment (p. 258)
patronage (p. 258)
senatorial courtesy (p. 262)
executive budget (p. 262)
legislative budget (p. 262)
veto (p. 264)
post-adjournment veto (p. 265)
line-item veto (p. 265)
special session (p. 266)

Practice Quiz

1. Which of the following is *not* necessary to become governor of Texas?
   a) A governor must be at least 30 years of age.
   b) A governor must have lived in Texas for at least five years.
   c) A governor must be a U.S. citizen.
   d) A governor must be a lawyer.
   e) A governor must have substantial campaign funding.

2. The election for governor of Texas is held in an off-year in order to
   a) increase voter participation in elections in odd-numbered years.
   b) influence the presidential vote in Texas.
   c) decrease the likelihood of voter fraud.
   d) give governors an opportunity to campaign for presidential candidates.
   e) prevent the presidential vote in Texas from influencing the election of state officials.

3. The only constitutional method of removing the governor is
   a) *quo warranto* proceedings.
   b) *ex post facto* removal.
   c) a vote of no confidence.
   d) impeachment.
   e) impeachment and conviction.

4. The governor's most effective power in controlling the executive branch of state government is the power
   a) of the veto.
   b) of appointment.
   c) of removal.
   d) of judicial review.
   e) to create a state budget.

5. The governor's veto is absolute when it is a
   a) line-item veto.
   b) special veto.
   c) budgetary veto.
   d) post-adjournment veto.
   e) select veto.

6. The governor can grant
   a) pardons.
   b) suspended sentences.
   c) probation.
   d) retrials.
   e) parole.

The Plural Executive

Unlike the president of the United States, the governor of Texas does not appoint a cabinet. Voters in Texas elect the lieutenant governor and other major statewide offices in separate elections. This disperses power within the executive branch, which means that executive officers must compromise not only with the legislature but also within the executive branch.

Key Terms
plural executive (p. 267)
lieutenant governor (p. 269)
attorney general (p. 271)
land commissioner (p. 272)
agriculture commissioner (p. 273)
comptroller (p. 274)
secretary of state (p. 275)

Practice Quiz
7. Which member of the plural executive is appointed?
   a) secretary of state
   b) land commissioner
   c) lieutenant governor
   d) comptroller of public accounts
   e) attorney general

8. The attorney general is
   a) part of the governor's cabinet.
   b) elected independently of the governor.
   c) appointed by the Texas Supreme Court.
   d) the governor's lawyer.
   e) chosen by the State Bar of Texas.

9. The land commissioner
   a) records all property deeds.
   b) administers state land.
   c) surveys property in Texas.
   d) is appointed by the state senate.
   e) administers Big Bend National Park.

10. Members of the plural executive are accountable to the
    a) voters and the governor.
    b) legislature and voters.
    c) constitution.
    d) state supreme court.
    e) legislature.

Boards, Commissions, and Regulatory Agencies

The governor's most important power is the ability to appoint people to boards, commissions, councils, committees, and regulatory agencies. Such institutions have important powers to interpret state regulations and make a difference in the lives of everyday Texans.

Key Terms
bureaucracy (p. 276)
Sunset Advisory Commission (SAC) (p. 283)

Practice Quiz
11. The Public Utilities Commission
    a) regulates some electric rates.
    b) regulates local phone rates.
    c) maintains a website so consumers can compare electric rates.
    d) maintains a "do not call" registry.
    e) All of the above are features of the Public Utilities Commission.

12. The Texas Department of Insurance
    a) has limited power to regulate insurance rates.
    b) collects the penalties for not buying health insurance under Obamacare.

c) sells insurance for mold coverage.

d) is run by a five-member elected board.

e) All of the above are features of the Texas Department of Insurance.

13. The Railroad Commission of Texas

a) is responsible for the safety of the state's railroads.

b) issues bonds to support the state's transportation needs.

c) regulates oil and gas production in Texas.

d) approves mergers of railroads.

e) is the most powerful agency in the state.

14. The State Board of Education

a) has a major role in determining the books used in Texas public schools.

b) is appointed by the legislature.

c) reviews applications to state colleges and universities.

d) is responsible for school property tax rates.

e) governs local boards of education.

15. Which agency investigates the performance of state agencies and recommends whether an agency should be abolished, continued as is, or continued with changes?

a) Legislative Budget Board

b) Legislative Research Bureau

c) Texas Research League

d) Public Utilities Commission

e) Sunset Advisory Commission

The mass shootings at Waco have led to the indictments of scores of bikers. In the process, there have also been serious questions of fairness raised in the mass arrests and bail hearings of those bikers.

The Judiciary

WHY THE JUDICIARY MATTERS On May 17, 2015, there was a gun battle at the Twin Peaks restaurant in Waco, Texas, that left 9 people dead and 18 others wounded. The shootout involved rival biker gangs, and there is no doubt that some of the bikers were armed and dangerous—police claim they recovered over 300 weapons in and near Twin Peaks. What happened next, however, raises serious questions about the functioning of the Texas judicial system.

Well over a year after the shootings, it is still unclear how many of the numerous shots were fired by police (the police chief claims 12 shots) and whether some of the victims may have been shot by police. Although the police claim the shooting began in the restaurant and moved outside, the Associated Press claimed that restaurant video showed the shooting began outside the restaurant where the police were.

Police swept up the bikers in a massive arrest of over 170 people. Justice of the Peace W. H. "Pete" Peterson set $1,000,000 bonds for 174 bikers, explaining, "I think it is important to send a message. . . . We had nine people killed in our community. These people just came in, and most of them were from out of town. Very few of them were from in town." District judges Matt Johnson and Ralph Strother approved the bonds and ordered no other judge could rule on motions to reduce the bonds.

A bond of $1,000,000 is exceptionally large. Bond in Harris County for noncapital murder is usually $50,000. The problem of a $1,000,000 bond is that bond is supposed to be set to insure the appearance of the suspect at trial, not to "send a message." Many of the bikers were incarcerated for weeks while awaiting a bond reduction hearing. Of course, during that time taxpayers were paying the cost of their incarceration and the suspects were unable to work or provide for families. Eventually most of the suspects got their bonds reduced to somewhere between $20,000 and $50,000. Interestingly, many of the bikers appear to have had nothing to do with the shootings and were not outlaws. A check by the Associated Press found that two-thirds of the bikers had no prior criminal convictions.

In November 2015, a grand jury in Waco indicted 106 persons including 9 who were not arrested in the initial mass arrests at the Twin Peaks restaurant. Still other bikers were indicted in March 2016. All were indicted for engaging in organized criminal activity. The charge of engaging in organized criminal activity carries a penalty of 15 years to life imprisonment—a range of punishment so substantial that defendants will have a huge incentive to plea bargain and perhaps provide evidence against those bikers responsible for the killings. A Waco police detective was the foreman of the grand jury. He had been in law enforcement 34 years and a member of the Waco police department for 26 years. In response to concerns of a conflict of interest in having a Waco officer as foreman of the grand jury, Judge Ralph Strother, who presided over the grand jury, stated, "Who would know the law better than an officer?"

An article in the *Houston Press* stated, "In the coming years, the Waco authorities' handling of the Twin Peaks biker gang shootout will become a textbook example of how not to handle an emergency situation."[1] Is this treatment of the bikers an exceptional case brought about by incredible violence in a small city? Or is this treatment of the bikers more characteristic of how the criminal justice process operates in the state? Would this crisis in Waco have been handled with greater attention to due process of law if Justice of the Peace Peterson had been a lawyer (he was not)? Would there have been greater attention to due process if the district attorney and the judges were appointed rather than elected?

CHAPTER GOALS

- Describe how the Texas court system is organized (pp. 291–96)

- Explain the legal process and the differences between criminal and civil law (pp. 296–99)

- Evaluate the process for selecting judges in Texas (pp. 299–312)

- Assess the impact of recent changes related to tort reform, regulation of lawyers, and disciplining judges (pp. 312–17)

Court Structure

Describe how the Texas court system is organized

Like the federal courts, the state and local courts in Texas are responsible for securing liberty and equality under the law. However, the democratic mechanisms put into place in Texas to select judges and to hold them accountable for their actions are quite different from those at the national level. Federal judges are appointed by the president and confirmed by the Senate. They have lifetime appointments. This means that federal judges, subject to good behavior in office, are free from the ebb and flow of democratic politics. They do not have to cater to public opinion and are empowered to interpret the law as they see fit, without fear of reprisal at the polls. In Texas, however, judges are elected to office. Although they may initially be appointed to their offices, sooner or later they are responsible to the people for their decisions in office. Election of judges brings not only the people but also interest groups into the selection and retention of judges. The influence of special interest money in judicial campaigns raises important questions about the relationship between the rule of law and the nature of democratic politics.

Texas has a large and complex court structure consisting of a hodgepodge of courts with overlapping jurisdiction (see Figure 9.1). Additionally, some courts have specialized jurisdiction, whereas others have broad authority to handle a variety of cases. At the highest level for civil cases is the **Texas Supreme Court**, which consists of nine justices, including a chief justice. This court hears civil and juvenile cases only, and at the state level it has final appellate jurisdiction. The only requirements for being a Texas Supreme Court justice are that one must be a citizen of the United States and of Texas, be at least 35 years of age and under 74 years, and have been either a practicing lawyer or judge for at least 10 years. The term of a justice is six years, with at least three justices being elected every two years. Justices on the Texas Supreme Court are paid $168,000 a year; the chief justice receives $2,500 a year more. Texas Supreme Court justices are elected to six-year terms.

The **Texas Court of Criminal Appeals** is the highest appeals court in the state for criminal cases. This court also has nine judges, including a presiding judge. The pay, terms, and qualifications of Court of Criminal Appeals judges are the same as for the Texas Supreme Court. Perhaps the most important task of the Court of Criminal Appeals is its jurisdiction over automatic appeals in death penalty cases.

Both the Texas Supreme Court and the Court of Criminal Appeals have appellate jurisdiction. This means that they have the authority to review the decisions of lower courts to determine whether legal principles and court procedures were followed correctly. This authority also provides the power to order that a case be retried if mistakes were made. Texas has 14 other appellate courts, located in various parts

Texas Supreme Court the highest civil court in Texas; consists of nine justices and has final state appellate authority over civil cases

Texas Court of Criminal Appeals the highest criminal court in Texas; consists of nine justices and has final state appellate authority over criminal cases

The Texas Supreme Court is the highest civil court in Texas. The court consists of nine justices (pictured here as of 2016).

FIGURE 9.1

The Structure of the Texas Court System

SOURCE: Texas Office of Court Administration.

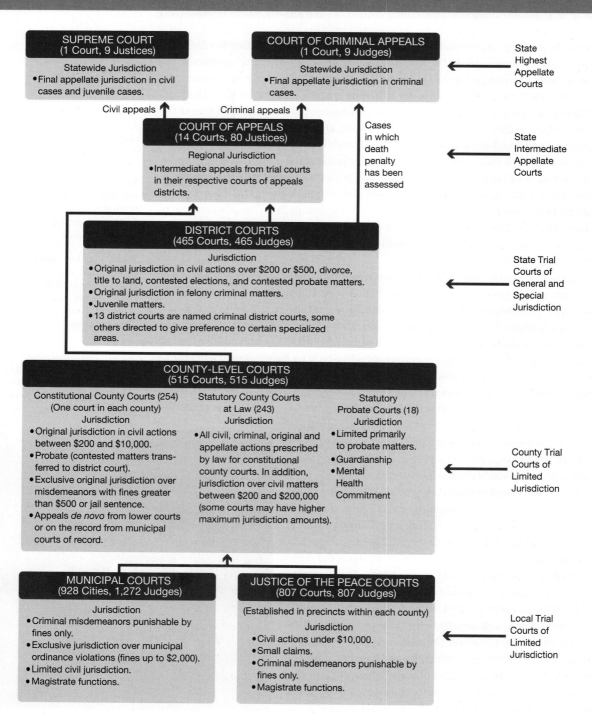

SUPREME COURT
(1 Court, 9 Justices)
Statewide Jurisdiction
• Final appellate jurisdiction in civil cases and juvenile cases.

COURT OF CRIMINAL APPEALS
(1 Court, 9 Judges)
Statewide Jurisdiction
• Final appellate jurisdiction in criminal cases.

State Highest Appellate Courts

Civil appeals   Criminal appeals

COURT OF APPEALS
(14 Courts, 80 Justices)
Regional Jurisdiction
• Intermediate appeals from trial courts in their respective courts of appeals districts.

Cases in which death penalty has been assessed

State Intermediate Appellate Courts

DISTRICT COURTS
(465 Courts, 465 Judges)
Jurisdiction
• Original jurisdiction in civil actions over $200 or $500, divorce, title to land, contested elections, and contested probate matters.
• Original jurisdiction in felony criminal matters.
• Juvenile matters.
• 13 district courts are named criminal district courts, some others directed to give preference to certain specialized areas.

State Trial Courts of General and Special Jurisdiction

COUNTY-LEVEL COURTS
(515 Courts, 515 Judges)

Constitutional County Courts (254)
(One court in each county)
Jurisdiction
• Original jurisdiction in civil actions between $200 and $10,000.
• Probate (contested matters transferred to district court).
• Exclusive original jurisdiction over misdemeanors with fines greater than $500 or jail sentence.
• Appeals de novo from lower courts or on the record from municipal courts of record.

Statutory County Courts at Law (243)
Jurisdiction
• All civil, criminal, original and appellate actions prescribed by law for constitutional county courts. In addition, jurisdiction over civil matters between $200 and $200,000 (some courts may have higher maximum jurisdiction amounts).

Statutory Probate Courts (18)
Jurisdiction
• Limited primarily to probate matters.
• Guardianship
• Mental Health Commitment

County Trial Courts of Limited Jurisdiction

MUNICIPAL COURTS
(928 Cities, 1,272 Judges)
Jurisdiction
• Criminal misdemeanors punishable by fines only.
• Exclusive jurisdiction over municipal ordinance violations (fines up to $2,000).
• Limited civil jurisdiction.
• Magistrate functions.

JUSTICE OF THE PEACE COURTS
(807 Courts, 807 Judges)
(Established in precincts within each county)
Jurisdiction
• Civil actions under $10,000.
• Small claims.
• Criminal misdemeanors punishable by fines only.
• Magistrate functions.

Local Trial Courts of Limited Jurisdiction

of the state, which have both criminal and civil jurisdiction. These courts are intermediate appellate courts and hear appeals from the trial courts. Usually, before the Texas Supreme Court or the Court of Criminal Appeals hears a case, the initial appeal has been heard by one of the **courts of appeal**. These courts have jurisdiction in various regions of the state for civil, juvenile, and criminal cases. Presently, there are 80 judges who serve on the 14 courts of appeal, which range in size from 3 to 13 judges. Although there are occasions when every judge on a court of appeal will hear a case, mostly appeals at this level are heard by panels of three judges. The requirements for a court of appeal justice are the same as those for justices of the higher courts. Courts of appeal justices are paid $154,000 a year, and the chief justice of each of the courts of appeal receives an additional $2,500.

The major trial courts in Texas are the **district courts**. Each county has at least one district court, although rural parts of Texas may have several counties that are served by one district court. Urban counties have many district courts. Harris County (Houston), for example, has 60 district courts and Dallas County has 39. District courts usually have general jurisdiction, meaning that they hear a broad range of civil and criminal cases. However, in urban counties, some district courts with specialized jurisdiction hear only civil, criminal, juvenile, or family law matters. Those district courts having general jurisdiction would hear felony criminal cases, divorces, land disputes, election contests, and civil lawsuits. District court judges receive $140,000 a year, and they may receive up to $18,000 in additional salary a year from county supplement payments to the state salary. All state judges from district judges through Texas Supreme Court and Court of Criminal Appeals judges also receive longevity pay of 3.1 percent of their monthly salary for each year of service after 16 years of service. Currently, there are 465 district judges, 9 state supreme court judges, 9 court of criminal appeals judges, and 80 courts of appeal judges.

Texas is unusual in having the office of **county judge** in each of its 254 counties. Not only does the county judge preside over the county commissioners' court and thus have responsibilities for administration of county government, but the county judge also presides over the county court. Often these **county courts** have jurisdiction over uncontested probate cases and over the more serious misdemeanor criminal offenses involving fines greater than $500 or a jail sentence, as well as over civil cases where the amounts in dispute are relatively small, generally in the $200 to $10,000 range. The county court may also hear appeals from municipal courts or from justice of the peace courts. Thus, the county judge combines political-administrative functions with some judicial functions. However, in the more populated counties, there are county courts at law and sometimes probate courts. As a result, in the larger counties most, and sometimes all, of the county judges' judicial duties are now performed by other courts.

In larger counties, there are **statutory county courts at law**. Since the county courts at law were created by statute, often at widely different times, the jurisdiction of these courts varies significantly. Usually, the county courts at law hear appeals from justices of the peace and from municipal courts. In civil cases, they usually hear cases involving sums that would generally be greater than would be heard by a justice of the peace court. Typically, county courts at law hear civil cases involving less than $200,000. In comparison to the district courts, the county courts at law would hear less serious criminal offenses.

courts of appeal the 14 intermediate-level appellate courts that hear appeals from district and county courts to determine whether the decisions of these lower courts followed legal principles and court procedures

district courts the major trial courts in Texas, which usually have general jurisdiction over a broad range of civil and criminal cases

county judge the person in each of Texas's 254 counties who presides over the county court and the county commissioners' court, with responsibility for the administration of county government; some county judges carry out judicial responsibilities

county courts the courts that exist in some counties that are presided over by county judges

statutory county courts at law courts that tend to hear less serious cases than those heard by district courts

Some of the county courts at law have specialized jurisdiction; most commonly these are in the most urban counties, where some of the courts will have only civil jurisdiction and others only criminal jurisdiction. Currently there are 243 county court at law judges.

In the most urban areas of the state, the legislature has created courts known as **statutory probate courts**. These courts are highly specialized, as their primary activity involves probate matters that relate to the disposition of property of deceased persons. They may also deal with matters relating to guardianship of people unable to handle their own affairs, and they may handle mental-health commitments. In other parts of the state, depending on the statute, probate matters may be heard by the county court, the county court at law, or the district court. Currently, there are 18 statutory probate court judges.

Each county in Texas has between one and eight justice of the peace precincts, depending on population, although large urban counties have more than one judge in each precinct. Harris County, for example, has two in each of eight precincts. Within each precinct are **justice of the peace courts**. There are 807 justice of the peace courts in Texas. These courts hear class C misdemeanors, which are less serious crimes usually involving traffic offenses. They also have jurisdiction over minor civil matters. In the past, the courts functioned as small claims courts. Unfortunately, the courts used formal rules of evidence, which gave a great advantage to parties represented by lawyers. As a result of a law passed in 2011, however, while suits must be for less than $10,000, the suits can be handled more informally. Rules governing suits now may not be "so complex that a reasonable person without legal training would have difficulty understanding or applying the rules."[2] Justices may issue search and arrest warrants. In counties without medical examiners, they may fulfill the administrative functions of coroners.

Justices of the peace mostly handle traffic misdemeanors. Of the more than 2.3 million cases disposed of by justice of the peace courts from September 2014 through August 2015, almost 1.5 million were traffic and parking cases. In contrast, justice of the peace courts heard only about 378,000 civil cases.[3]

statutory probate courts
specialized courts whose jurisdiction is limited to probate and guardianship matters

justice of the peace courts
local trial courts with limited jurisdiction over small claims and very minor criminal misdemeanors

Justices of the peace have faced considerable criticism in recent years. Professor Barbara Kirby found that between 2008 and 2014, 28 percent to 62 percent of the disciplinary actions imposed on judges for inappropriate or unethical behavior by the State Commission on Judicial Conduct were on justices of the peace. Yet justices of the peace only constituted about 22 percent of the judges under the purview of the commission. Kirby found that between December 2002 and April 2015, 50 Texas judges had been suspended from their duties by the commission—one of the most severe punishments imposed. Of those 50 judges, 21 were justices of the peace and 19 of those justices did not have a law degree. One of the most common sanctions imposed on justices of the peace by the commission is a requirement that justices undergo additional education because, the commission explained, "Legal and procedural issues are often complex, so it is not surprising that some judges, particularly non-lawyer judges, take judicial action that may exceed their authority or that is contrary to procedural rules."[4] Only about 10 percent of the justices of the peace in Texas are lawyers, and the lack of justices' legal credentials has led to considerable debate in the state.[5] The office has its origins in medieval England and has existed in Texas since 1837, even before statehood. In the days of the frontier, justices of the peace provided legal authority where no other existed. The initial idea was that a justice of the peace would be a respected person in the community who was chosen for ability, judgment, and integrity. Today, as the former Texas state bar president Frank Newton has pointed out, "in almost every large metropolitan area, there are some JPs [justices of the peace] who do virtually nothing and sort of get lost in the shuffle. People don't tend to get all excited about JP elections. Most people don't know what a JP does. JP is not a very prestigious job."[6]

Municipal courts have been created by the legislature in each of the incorporated cities of the state. There are 928 cities and towns in Texas that have these courts;

municipal courts local trial courts with limited jurisdiction over violations of city ordinances and very minor criminal misdemeanors

The boxes of evidence that the State of Texas prepared for the trial against tobacco companies in 1997 occupied an entire gym in Texarkana. In a civil case, the plaintiff bears the burden of proof and must demonstrate that the defendant is more than not likely responsible for the harm suffered by the plaintiff.

larger cities have multiple courts. There are 1,272 municipal court judges in the state. Municipal courts have jurisdiction over violations of city **ordinances** and, concurrent with justice of the peace courts, have jurisdiction over class C misdemeanors, for which the punishment for conviction is a fine. Municipal judges may issue search and arrest warrants, but they have only limited civil jurisdiction.[7] Municipal courts, like justice of the peace courts, function primarily as traffic courts. From September 2013 through August 2014, municipal courts disposed of slightly fewer than 6.2 million cases. About 4.5 million of these cases were traffic and parking cases.[8]

Great controversy has erupted in the city of Dallas, where the city council has demanded that municipal judges get tougher with offenders or lose their judicial appointments. In particular, city officials have claimed that the judges give too many trial postponements, set fines too low, and don't hold accused violators accountable for ignoring citations.[9]

The Legal Process

Explain the legal process and the differences between criminal and civil law

Just as the Texas Supreme Court hears civil cases and the Texas Court of Criminal Appeals hears criminal cases, it is useful to think of the law as divided into these parts. **Civil law** involves a dispute, usually between private individuals, over relationships, obligations, and responsibility. Though there are exceptions with a violation of the civil law, the remedy is often for the offending party to pay compensation to the injured party.

In contrast, **criminal law** involves the violation of concepts of right and wrong as defined by criminal statutes. In criminal law, the state accuses individuals of violations, and if found guilty, the violator is subject to punishment. In some cases, that punishment may involve loss of liberty or even loss of life.

In civil law, an aggrieved person will usually obtain a lawyer and file a petition that details the **complaint** against the person accused of causing the harm. The petition is filed with the clerk of court, who issues a citation against the defendant. The defendant will usually file an **answer** explaining why the allegations are not valid. Depending on the issue, the amounts of money that may be awarded as damages, and the probability of success, the aggrieved person may be able to obtain the services of a lawyer on a **contingent fee** basis. This means that the lawyer will not charge the individual if the case is lost but will obtain a portion of the damages awarded if the case is won. It is not unusual for such contingent fee arrangements to involve one-third or more of the damages award plus expenses. Lawyers who handle cases on contingent fee agreements often handle personal-injury cases and are known as trial lawyers. Traditionally, these lawyers will contribute money to judicial candidates who are sympathetic to plaintiffs. They make money only if they win, so they have a strong economic

ordinance a regulation enacted by a city government in each of Texas's incorporated cities and towns

civil law a branch of law that deals with disputes, usually between private individuals over relationships, obligations, and responsibility

criminal law the branch of law that regulates the conduct of individuals, defines crimes, and specifies punishment for criminal acts

complaint the presentation of a grievance by the plaintiff in a civil case

answer the presentation of a defendant's defense against an allegation in a civil case

contingent fee a fee paid to the lawyer in a civil case which is contingent on winning the case

interest in supporting judicial candidates who are sympathetic to plaintiffs and to the awarding of large damages.

The person being sued either will have to hire an attorney on his or her own or, if insured, will be represented by an attorney paid for by the insurance company. Fee arrangements vary for civil defense lawyers, but often they are paid by the hour, in which case they get paid whether they win or lose. Their economic incentives to contribute money to judicial campaigns may be different from the incentives trial lawyers have, but civil defense lawyers do contribute large sums to judicial campaigns in order to elect judges who support their views on **tort** law.

The court to which a civil case is taken depends on the type of case and the amount of money involved. Most commonly, a civil case will be settled, meaning the dispute is resolved without going to court. Settlements may, however, occur during trial, sometimes immediately before a jury renders its decision. If a case is not settled and goes to trial, it may be heard either by a judge or, if requested by either side, by a jury. Although civil jury cases do not have to be unanimous in Texas, the burden of proof is on the plaintiff. The standard of proof that the plaintiff must meet is **preponderance of the evidence**. That means that the plaintiff must show that it is more likely than not that the defendant is the cause of the harm suffered by the plaintiff.

Civil cases may involve tiny amounts of damages or they may involve billions of dollars, which have the potential of breaking huge corporations, such as happened in the 1980s when Pennzoil successfully sued Texaco in a dispute over the takeover of the Getty Oil Company.[10]

Civil case verdicts may, of course, be appealed. Appeals are usually from the trial court to the intermediate court of appeal and perhaps further to the state supreme court. Given the cost of appeals and the delay that is involved, it is not unusual for some settlement to be reached after the verdict but before the case goes through the appellate process. For example, a plaintiff might agree to settle for much less than the verdict in the case to avoid the expense and delay of further appeals.

Litigating a civil case is time consuming and expensive. As a result, in Texas and in other states, it is increasingly common to try to negotiate a settlement through mediation or arbitration. With arbitration, the parties to the dispute agree to present their case to a decision maker and to be bound by the decision. With mediation, the parties to the dispute try to reach a compromise resolution of the problem without going to trial. Generally, lawyers are used in mediations and arbitrations that have significant financial value, although persons assisting the parties in mediations and arbitrations do not necessarily have to be lawyers. Mediation is especially popular in civil disputes because the parties to the dispute are reaching the agreement and are not forced into a particular decision as they would be with arbitration. Mediation is also a very flexible process for resolving disputes where resolutions of disputes are contractual agreements between the opposing parties. To resolve the dispute they may agree to any legal remedy. One of the most unusual such remedies for a dispute occurred a number of years ago when Southwest Airlines and Stevens Aviation had a dispute over which company could use the slogan "Plane Smart." The two sides initially agreed to determine which company would use the slogan by having an arm-wrestling match between Southwest's and Stevens Aviation's company chairmen. Lawyers later worked out another agreement, but the company chairmen went ahead and held their arm-wrestling event.

tort a civil wrong that causes harm to another; it is remedied by awarding economic damages to the injured party

preponderance of the evidence the standard of proof in a civil jury case, by which the plaintiff must show that the defendant is more likely than not the cause of the harm suffered by the plaintiff

In criminal cases, the state alleges a violation of a criminal law and is usually represented in court by a prosecutor. Some prosecutors are career prosecutors with vast trial experience. These people will often prosecute the most difficult and complex cases, such as felonies and **capital cases**. However, because the pay of prosecutors is often much lower than that of private lawyers who do litigation in the private sector, it is common for most prosecutors to be quite young and inexperienced. Once they gain trial experience, prosecutors commonly move into the private sector.

Defendants may hire criminal defense attorneys, who usually charge a flat fee to handle the case. Criminal defense lawyers, of course, do not work on a contingent fee basis. Since most criminal defendants are found guilty, criminal defense lawyers often prefer to obtain as much of their fee as possible in advance of the verdict.

Some parts of Texas have public defender offices where salaried lawyers provide at least some adult criminal defense services for low-income persons in a county. Bexar County has established the first public defender office for indigent criminal appeals. Travis County has a public defender office representing only poor people with mental impairments.[11] A public defender office represents indigents in capital cases in west Texas.[12]

In Texas, poor criminal defendants are more commonly represented by court-appointed lawyers. These are lawyers appointed by the judge to represent a defendant. Usually, these government-paid fees are less than would be charged to nonindigent defendants. Thus, some lawyers are reluctant to fulfill court appointments; others may not put the time and energy into a court-appointed case that they would if they were privately paid; others take court appointments because they have a limited number of paying clients; and still others take court appointments to gain experience. Concern over the poor quality of legal representation provided indigent criminal defendants, especially in capital cases, led to legislation in 2001 to increase the pay and qualifications of court-appointed lawyers.

Serious crimes are **felonies**. In those cases, and potentially for lesser offenses known as **misdemeanors**, prior to the trial there will be an indictment by a grand jury. In Texas, a **grand jury** consists of 12 persons and two alternates who sit for two to six months. Depending on the county, a grand jury may meet only once or twice, or it may meet several times a week. Until recently most Texas grand jurors were chosen by a commissioner system. A district judge would appoint several grand jury commissioners, who then selected 15 to 20 citizens of the county. The first 12 who are qualified become the grand jury.[13] New legislation now requires that grand juries be selected randomly from a pool of qualified citizens.

Grand juries can inquire into any criminal matter but usually spend most of their time on felony crimes. They work in secret and rely heavily on the information provided by the prosecutor, though in some cases grand juries will work quite independently of the prosecutor. These grand juries are called runaway grand juries because the prosecutor has lost control of them, but such cases are very rare. If nine of the grand jurors decide a trial is warranted, they will indict a suspect. An **indictment** is also known as a "true bill." On the other hand, sometimes a grand jury does not believe a trial is warranted. In those cases, the grand jury issues a "no bill" decision.

Although a suspect has the right to trial by jury, he or she may waive that right and undergo a **bench trial** before the judge only. Most commonly, the suspect will engage in a **plea bargain**. With plea bargaining, a suspect agrees to plead guilty in exchange for a lighter sentence than might be imposed if the suspect were found guilty at trial. Approximately 97 percent of criminal convictions in Texas are the result of plea bargains.[14]

---

capital case a criminal case in which the death penalty is a possible punishment

felony a serious criminal offense, punishable by a prison sentence or a fine; a capital felony is possibly punishable by death

misdemeanor a minor criminal offense, usually punishable by a fine or a jail sentence

grand jury jury that determines whether sufficient evidence is available to justify a trial; grand juries do not rule on the accused's guilt or innocence

indictment a written statement issued by a grand jury that charges a suspect with a crime and states that a trial is warranted

bench trial a trial held without a jury and before only a judge

plea bargain negotiated agreement in a criminal case in which a defendant agrees to plead guilty in return for the state's agreement to reduce the severity of the criminal charge or prison sentence the defendant is facing

If the suspect does choose trial by jury, felony juries will have 12 members; misdemeanor juries will have 6 members. There must be a unanimous verdict of guilty or not guilty. If the jurors are not unanimous, the result is a hung jury and a mistrial is declared. The prosecutor may then choose to retry the suspect. In addition to the requirement of unanimity in jury decisions, another important difference between civil and criminal cases is the standard of proof. In criminal cases, rather than the standard of preponderance of the evidence, the standard is **beyond a reasonable doubt**. This means that the prosecutor must prove the charges against the defendant, and they must be proven to a very high standard so that a reasonable doubt of innocence does not exist.

beyond a reasonable doubt
the legal standard in criminal cases, which requires the prosecution to prove that a reasonable doubt of innocence does not exist

If a guilty verdict is returned, there will be a separate hearing on the sentence, which in Texas is sometimes also determined by the jury. At the sentencing hearing, factors such as prior record and background will be considered, even though these factors could not be considered at the trial portion of the proceeding.

Of course a defendant may also appeal a verdict. Usually, the appeals are by a convicted defendant who alleges that an error in the trial may have affected the case's outcome. In rare cases, a prosecutor may also appeal. For the most part, however, criminal defendants will appeal their convictions to an intermediate appeals court and perhaps further to the Texas Court of Criminal Appeals. In capital cases, however, the appeal will be directly to the Texas Court of Criminal Appeals.

Judicial Politics

 Evaluate the process for selecting judges in Texas

Although there are still generalist lawyers who handle all sorts of cases, much of the practice of law is very specialized. Thus, in the civil process, trial lawyers and civil defense lawyers tend to back opposing candidates for judgeships. It is not unusual for trial lawyers to support one candidate, often the Democrat, who is more likely to be the more liberal, or pro-plaintiff, candidate, and for the civil defense lawyers to support the Republican, who is more likely to be the conservative, or pro-defendant, candidate. The civil defense lawyers will often align themselves with business groups and with professional groups, such as medical doctors, to support judges inclined to favor the civil defense side.

Likewise, in the criminal process, it is sometimes possible to see criminal defense lawyers backing one candidate and prosecutors backing the other. Some prosecutors' offices are quite political, and the prosecutors will publicly support pro-prosecution judicial candidates. They will often be aligned with victims' rights groups. Criminal defense lawyers, on the other hand, will often back one of their own in contested criminal court races.

One big difference in the campaigns of civil court judges versus criminal court judges is the amount of money involved. Enormous amounts can be involved in civil cases, and so it is worth lots of money to trial lawyers and civil defense interests to elect candidates favorable to their point of view. On the other hand, with the exception of a relatively few highly paid criminal defense lawyers, the practice of criminal law is not very lucrative. Prosecutors are on salary, and usually the salaries are not large. Criminal defense lawyers often represent clients with little money. And most criminal cases are plea-bargained. The economic incentives to contribute large sums to criminal court races don't exist. The result is that a strong candidate for the Texas Supreme Court may raise in the neighborhood of $1,000,000 for a campaign, whereas a strong candidate for the Texas Court of Criminal Appeals may raise $100,000. However, as Texas has become predominantly Republican at the statewide level, hard-fought contests between Democrats and Republicans for the Texas Supreme Court and the Texas Court of Criminal Appeals have become rare.

Initial Appointment of Judges by the Governor

A notable aspect of the Texas judiciary is that with the exception of municipal judges, who tend to be appointed by local governments, all judges are elected in partisan elections. Still, because the governor appoints district and appellate judges to the bench to fill vacancies prior to an election or to fill judgeships on new courts, large percentages of judges initially get on the bench through appointment. Although there has been some controversy over the relatively small number of appointments of minorities made by some governors, gubernatorial appointment has generated little additional controversy.[15] Table 9.1 shows the percentage of district and appellate judges who have initially gained their seats through appointment by the governor. Currently, about 55 percent of appellate judges and 37 percent of the trial judges initially got on the bench through appointment. Still, the controversial issue in Texas judicial politics deals with how the remaining judges obtained their seats and how all judges retain their seats if they wish to remain in office. That controversy involves the partisan election of judges in Texas.

TABLE 9.1

Percentage of Judges Obtaining Their Position Initially through Appointment

YEAR	TRIAL COURTS*	APPELLATE COURTS**
1962	57%	50%
1984	67	51
1998	46	40
2001	34	38
2003	43	43
2006	43	50
2009	36	51
2011	37	52
2012	38	55
2014	37	55

* Trial courts are the district and criminal district courts.
** Appellate courts are the Texas Supreme Court, the Court of Criminal Appeals, and the courts of appeal.
SOURCES: Anthony Champagne, "The Selection and Retention of Judges in Texas," 40 *Southwestern Law Journal* 66 (May 1986); Texas Office of Court Administration, "Profile of Appellate and Trial Judges" as of September 1, 1998, 2001, 2003, 2006, 2009, March 1, 2011, September 1, 2012, 2014.

The Elections Become Highly Partisan

Until 1978 the selection of judges in partisan elections did not create much concern. They were low-key, sleepy affairs. Texas was overwhelmingly a Democratic state, and judges were elected as Democrats. The only real competition occurred in the Democratic primary, and with the political advantage of incumbency, judges were rarely defeated even in the primary. Competition in judicial races occurred in those relatively rare cases where there was an open seat in which no incumbent sought office. One journalist aptly described the judicial elections of that era in this way:

Is justice for sale in Texas? Because statewide judicial races are expensive, candidates for judgeships have been forced to raise considerable amounts of money. This, in turn, has led to criticism that judicial decisions are, in effect, being bought.

Justices' names seldom appeared in the press and were known only to the legal community. Most justices had been judges in the lower courts; a few had served in the Legislature. At election time, sitting justices almost never drew opposition. Some justices resigned before the end of their terms, enabling their replacements to be named by the governor and to run as incumbents. In the event that an open seat was actually contested, the decisive factor in the race was the State Bar poll, which was the key to newspaper endorsements and the support of courthouse politicians.[16]

Beginning in 1978, however, changes began to occur in Texas judicial politics. William Clements, the first Republican governor since Reconstruction, was elected. The governor has the power to appoint judges to the district and higher courts when new courts have been created or when a judicial vacancy occurs as a result of death, resignation, or retirement. Unlike the previous Democratic governors who appointed members of the Democratic Party, Clements began appointing Republicans. With that advantage of incumbency and with the increasing popularity of the Republican party label, some of the Republican judges began to win re-election.

Helped by the popularity of Ronald Reagan in Texas, other Republicans began seeking judicial offices and winning. Thus, by the early 1980s, in statewide elections and in several counties in Texas, competition began to appear in judicial races. With that competition, incumbent judges began to be defeated. Sensing the growth of Republican strength, a number of Democratic judges changed to a Republican Party affiliation.

Judicial elections became more expensive because judicial candidates needed money to run meaningful campaigns. In particular, campaigns that used television advertising became very expensive because of high media costs.

- Why do you think so few people vote in judicial elections in Texas? Would the outcome of these elections change if more people voted in judicial elections?

- What would you advise candidates to do in order to get more people interested in judicial races?

Judicial candidates needed money because judicial races tend to have low-visibility campaigns in which voters are unaware of the candidates. The races tend to be overshadowed by higher-visibility races, such as the race for governor or U.S. senator. Money was needed to give judicial candidates some degree of name visibility by voters. However, in general, Texas voters do not give much money to judicial campaigns. Instead, it is lawyers and interest groups who tend to be donors in judicial races.[17] Thus, by the early 1980s, there was a new and expensive competitiveness in Texas judicial politics that in turn fed a demand for judicial reforms in the way Texas judges were selected.

Issues Involving the Texas Judiciary and Proposed Reforms

There have been numerous efforts to reform the Texas judiciary. In general, reformers are concerned with (1) changing the system for selecting judges, (2) increasing minority representation on the bench, or (3) restructuring the judiciary to make it more rational and efficient.

Changing the System for Selecting Judges One reform movement has focused on changing the method by which judges are selected in Texas. This group of reformers has been concerned with the low visibility of judicial races in Texas so that voters are rarely aware of the qualifications and abilities of judicial candidates. As a result, voters rely on party labels when electing judges. At other times, reformers claim, voters rely on the attractiveness of judicial candidates' names in voting, since they lack knowledge of judicial candidates. Still another problem pointed out by judicial reformers is that in urban counties there are so many candidates on the ballot that it is impossible for voters to make informed decisions. While more campaign funding will lead to more campaign advertising and greater visibility of judicial candidates, reformers are concerned that campaign contributions to judicial candidates come from individuals and interest groups concerned with the outcomes of court cases so that campaign contributions can interfere with the neutrality of judges.

merit selection a judicial reform under which judges would be nominated by a blue-ribbon committee, would be appointed by the governor, and, after a brief period in office, would run in a retention election

retention election an election in which voters decide whether to keep an incumbent in office by voting "yes" or "no" to retain the incumbent and where there is no opposing candidate

For decades there have been efforts to change the system of selecting judges in Texas. Some states elect judges in nonpartisan elections where judicial candidates run for office without a party label; in some, judges are appointed by the executive; in a couple of states the legislature elects judges. By far the most frequently proposed reform has been to switch to **merit selection** of judges. Under this system a blue-ribbon commission solicits interest in a vacant judicial seat and screens possible candidates for that seat. The commission then recommends from three to five persons to the governor who they believe are highly qualified for the position, and the governor appoints one of those recommended to the vacancy subject to state senate confirmation. After serving as a judge for about one year, the appointed judge runs in a **retention election** where the judge has no opponent but voters decide if they wish to retain the judge

Elected or Appointed Judges?

In Texas members of the Texas Supreme Court and the Court of Criminal Appeals, as well as all lower state courts, are elected to their posts in partisan elections. Texas is one of only eight states that elect judges in partisan elections. Other states use a variety of selection systems ranging from gubernatorial appointment to legislative selection to nonpartisan election. Many "good government" advocates support merit selection, which several states employ and which has been suggested many times as a possible alternative to the current system in Texas. Merit selection involves a commission that vets potential judges based on their character and temperament. A list of approved judicial nominees is then presented to the governor, who appoints one as judge. After a period of time, that judge runs in a retention election. The judge does not face an opponent, but the ballot question asks voters whether the judge should be retained in office.

Former Texas Supreme Court justice Wallace Jefferson has been a major advocate of merit selection. He has pointed out that there are so many judges that voters cannot make an informed decision. As a result, voting for judges is heavily based on party label and on the attractiveness of candidates' names—things that Jefferson points out are not good indicators of judicial competence. Partisan elections make little sense, according to Jefferson, when judges have so little to do with politics. He notes that what they do is "mundane, if nonetheless important. They probate wills and apportion divorcing spouses' assets. They determine child support and custody. They oversee trials and changes of pleas in criminal cases. They police discovery and preside over settlement conferences." Yet in every election, Jefferson argues, judges are swept out of office because of partisan voting, rather than decisions about judicial competence. Because of these concerns, Jefferson argues that the current system of selecting judges is one "in which an overwhelmed electorate ineffectually uses partisanship and name recognition as a proxy" for competence and integrity. "The result is the loss of good judges and a decrease in public confidence. Reform," Jefferson insists, "beginning with merit selection followed by retention elections, is imperative."[a]

In response to Jefferson, Houston lawyer David Butts pointed out that Texas already has a system where judges are appointed. The governor appoints judges to district and higher-level courts when new courts are created or when there are vacancies to fill. In fact, Governor Perry appointed more judges than any other previous governor, and that included seven of the nine justices currently on the Texas Supreme Court. That appointment process is a political process, as was pointed out by a study of Perry's appointments that was done by the *Austin American-Statesman*. The study found that Perry "appointed reliably like-minded people—donors to his campaigns, one-time staffers in his office, former lobbyists—to dozens of boards, commissions and judgeships." If there is judicial reform, Butts argued, it should begin with restricting the governor's ability to appoint anyone he chooses. Butts noted that reformers always propose merit selection as a way to take politics out of judicial selection, but, he wrote, "the only politics that are restricted from the selection of our judges are the voters'. The governor, the Legislature, the elite group of lawyers on the selection committee, and the special interest groups will continue to influence and decide who those select candidates are and who is chosen." In reference to retention elections, Butts noted evidence from retention elections in California, Wisconsin, and Iowa where judges were defeated because their decisions angered "deep-pocket special interests or ideological fault lines" and thus became as subject to defeat as if they were in a partisan election. There will always be politics in a selection system, claimed Butts, and Texans should "trust the voters with the final say. Voters will not always make the best choice, but they usually get it right."[b]

COMMUNICATING EFFECTIVELY: YOUR VOICE

- Should judges be elected or appointed? Is merit selection an effective compromise?

- Should the selection system vary according to type of judge?

in office. Thereafter the judge would continue to run for reelection in a retention election. Retention elections can be expensive campaigns, such as occurred in Tennessee in 2014, but in general retention elections are very low-budget affairs. There have been variations on this merit selection plan proposed from time to time, but this description provides the basic framework of the merit selection proposals in Texas. The result of adopting merit selection, in the view of its advocates, is a far greater likelihood that judges will be highly competent and will have little need to depend on lawyers and interest groups for funding to remain in office.

Reformers advocate this plan because they believe voters lack sufficient knowledge of judicial candidates and rely too heavily on the party label in casting their ballots. As a result, they vote for the party rather than for the best-qualified person to be a judge. As the Republican Party has become increasingly dominant in statewide races, it is the Republican label, rather than the qualifications or experience of judicial candidates, that has determined the outcome of judicial races. In 2016, for example, 65 percent of Harris County voters cast a straight-party ballot, which meant that they voted the party label rather than for the individual candidate. In the 10 largest counties in Texas, 64 percent of the ballots cast in 2016 were straight ticket.[18]

In the absence of voter awareness of judicial candidates, reformers are also concerned that voters will rely on irrelevant factors such as the perceived attractiveness of a candidate's name when they vote for judges. In 2008 there was heavy voting for Democrats in Harris County because of the popularity of presidential candidate Barack Obama. So many voters voted straight Democratic that all but four Republican judges were voted out of office. Interestingly, the four Republican judges who survived were all challenged by Democrats with unusual names. As a result, the incumbent Republican judge Sharon McCally was able to defeat the Democratic challenger Ashish Mahendru; Republican judge Mark Kent Ellis defeated Democrat Mekisha Murray; Judge Patricia Kerrigan, a Republican, defeated the Democrat Andres Pereira; and Judge Joseph Halback defeated his Democratic challenger, Goodwille Pierre.[19]

In the 2016 Republican Supreme Court primary, incumbent justice Paul Green was challenged by Rick Green. Paul Green has been an appellate court justice for 21 years and was a trial lawyer for 17 years. Rick Green has never been a judge, never tried a case, and never appealed a case. He has previously served in the Texas House, where he used his capitol office to film infomercials. He also lobbied successfully to get a convicted swindler out of prison after 3 years of a 16-year sentence. The swindler had earlier given Rick Green a $400,000 loan. Rick Green received 6 months' probation for hitting the Democrat who took his House seat. Paul Green did win the Republican primary with 52 percent of the vote, but the closeness of the vote showed that Paul Green's concern about voter confusion over similar names was a real one. Another example of voter confusion over names occurred in the Republican primary race for a Place 5 (appellate courts have multiple members, and judicial candidates run for specific seats or places on those courts) on the Court of Criminal Appeals. No incumbent was running for re-election and there were four candidates including one, Sid Harle, with stellar credentials—he had been a criminal defense attorney, a Bexar County prosecutor, and a longtime trial judge who had presided over more capital murder cases than any other judge in Texas, and he was a former chair of the State Commission on Judicial Conduct. His three opponents had no judicial experience and

In 2012, Democrat Keith Hampton ran against Sharon Keller for presiding judge of the Court of Criminal Appeals. Although he ran a fairly strong campaign, Hampton faced a major difficulty because Texas has more Republican voters than Democratic voters, and voters tend to follow party labels in judicial races. Keller defeated Hampton 55.5 percent to 41.2 percent in the general election.

one had civil rather than criminal law experience. Harle finished fourth in the race with only about 18.5 percent of the vote. The candidate with the highest percentage of votes had limited criminal trial and appellate experience over an 18-year career and did not run an active campaign. He ran not as Richard Walker, but used his middle name, Scott, on the ballot—which happens to be the name of the highly visible Republican governor of Wisconsin.[20] Walker later overwhelmingly won the Republican runoff primary and won in the general election.

The sheer number of candidates for judicial offices also leads to voter confusion and a lack of voter awareness of judicial candidates. Even voters who try to make a serious effort to learn about judicial candidates can have a hard time. In Harris County, for example, voters are faced with ballots loaded with so many judicial candidates that it becomes nearly impossible to be an informed voter. In 2016, in Harris County, voters were faced with casting ballots for 31 judges as well as 13 nonjudicial offices.[21]

Of special concern to reformers has been the role of money in judicial campaigns because of a concern that campaign funds create problems for the integrity of the judicial branch and for the appearance of fairness in judicial decision making. Contributions for judicial races in Texas can sometimes amount to several hundred thousand dollars, especially for hotly contested district court races or appellate races. In general, however, the most expensive races are for the Texas Supreme Court.

When races are contested between Democratic and Republican candidates, a candidate can raise well over $1 million. However, hard-fought races are now rare, as these statewide elections have moved into the Republican column. Because these are statewide races and because this court sets the tone of tort law (civil lawsuits over harm to another) throughout the state, a great deal of money is needed and a great deal can be raised. One million dollars may seem like a small sum for a statewide race in Texas considering that in his 2014 campaign for governor, Greg Abbott alone raised over $47.4 million and even the winning candidate for railroad commissioner, Ryan

TABLE 9.2

State Supreme Court Elections in 2013–2014 with More Than $1,000,000 in Contributions

STATE	SYSTEM OF SELECTION	SEATS UP FOR ELECTION	TOTAL CONTRIBUTIONS
Michigan	Partisan	3	$9,518,353
North Carolina	Nonpartisan	4	$6,005,984
Texas	Partisan	4	$3,664,248
Illinois	Partisan	1	$3,352,951
Ohio	Partisan	2	$3,261,542
Tennessee	Retention	3	$2,515,396
Wisconsin	Nonpartisan	1	$1,831,678
Montana	Nonpartisan	2	$1,503,522

SOURCE: Scott Greytak, Alicia Bannon, Allyse Falce, and Linda Casey, "Bankrolling the Bench: The New Politics of Judicial Elections, 2013–14," p. 9, brennancenter.org.

Sitton, raised over $4 million.[22] Judicial candidates, however, unlike other elected officials are supposed to be neutral decision makers not reflecting the values of particular interests in the state. Winning Texas Supreme Court candidates overwhelmingly get their contributions from the oil and gas industry, lawyers and lobbyists, and the finance sector. In terms of state supreme court races throughout the country, Table 9.2 shows there were eight states where total contributions to supreme court candidates amounted to $1 million or more. Texas was the third-ranking state in terms of total contributions to supreme court candidates. While not all of these eight highest contribution states had partisan election of judges, four of the states did have a partisan election system and only one of the states, Tennessee, had a retention election system.[23]

As Texas's statewide elections have become overwhelmingly Republican, the amounts contributed to supreme court candidates have dropped precipitously. In 1988, when Texas Supreme Court races were still competitive between Democrats and Republicans, contributions for supreme court candidates came to over $11.4 million with one candidate alone receiving over $2 million in contributions.[24] By 2014, far less money was contributed or needed by Republican candidates, since they faced no serious threat by Democratic opponents. The Democratic candidate for the chief justice position against Republican incumbent Nathan Hecht could only raise $17,650. Hecht, on the other hand, raised $1,459,497.[25] To the extent that there is any real battle for a position on the Texas Supreme Court, it is now within the Republican primary. In 2016 all three of the incumbent Republican justices faced primary opponents, and all three incumbents were re-elected.

In spite of decades-long efforts to change Texas from partisan election to merit selection, the attempts at such a comprehensive reform have failed. The only successful reform has been one dealing with judicial campaign finance. That law is the **Judicial Campaign Fairness Act**. Texas is the only state with a campaign finance regulation of this type. Among the most important aspects of compliance with the act are campaign contribution limitations. For example, statewide judicial candidates limit themselves to contributions of no more than $5,000 from any individual in any election. Additionally, statewide candidates can receive no more than $30,000 per election from any law firm. Although the amounts of money that can be donated are still quite high, there has been a significant reduction from contribution amounts in the 1980s when, prior to the act, some donors would give candidates $25,000, $50,000, and even more in campaign contributions. A recent strengthening of campaign contribution limits requires that if a judge receives campaign contributions from a party to a lawsuit, or if the party's lawyer made contributions in excess of the limits in the Judicial Campaign Fairness Act, the judge shall recuse him- or herself from the case.[26]

At least for the time being, it seems likely that not much will change in the way Texas selects its judges. Restructuring the system would be a major change, and such changes are always difficult to initiate. Changing might upset many voters, who like being able to vote for judges, and it would surely upset the political parties, which like having large numbers of judicial candidates running under their party label. It might also upset lawyers accustomed to the traditional ways of selecting judges and even judges who have benefited from the present system.

In looking at the experience of other states, it seems clear that each state has developed a judicial selection system to reflect its own political objectives. While systems of judicial selections can roughly be classified as merit selection, partisan election, nonpartisan election, gubernatorial appointment, and selection by the legislature, states have great variations in selection systems within these broad categories. Illinois, for example, has partisan election of judges for its initial selection of judges and then has retention elections for subsequent elections. Missouri has merit selection for some courts and partisan election for other courts. New Mexico has merit selection for initial selection of judges. That judge then serves until the next general election, when he or she must run in a partisan election. The winning candidate serves the remainder of the term, at which time the judge runs in a retention election for another term. In order to be retained, the judge must receive at least a 57 percent affirmative vote. If the judge is not retained, the nominating commission presents another list to the governor, who then appoints a new judge. Governors appoint judges in California, but a commission has the power to veto that appointment. When it comes down to the details of selecting judges in states, there are almost as many ways to select judges as there are states. (See the Texas and the Nation graphic in this chapter.)

Increasing Minority Representation on the Bench
A second group of reformers has been interested in increasing the numbers of African Americans and Latinos on the bench. In 1985, Professor Paul Brest wrote about the characteristics of judges, "Judges are far from a representative cross-section of American society. They are overwhelmingly Anglo, male, well educated, and upper or upper middle class. They are also members of the legal profession. . . . Women, Blacks, and Hispanics are only the groups most notoriously under-represented on the judiciary."[27] What Brest wrote

Judicial Campaign Fairness Act a judicial reform that places limits on judicial campaign contributions

in 1985 is still true in Texas and throughout the nation. Although African Americans and Hispanics make up about 50 percent of the Texas population, relatively few Texas judges belong to these groups.

Minority groups have been concerned that countywide and larger partisan judicial races make it difficult for minorities to get elected to judgeships—and that Texas judges do not reflect the diversity of the state. The lack of diversity on the bench creates significant problems for the legitimacy of the courts and for the proper functioning of those courts within a diverse population. Professor Sherrilyn Ifill has argued that diversity among judges is necessary for impartiality in judicial decision making, public confidence in the court system, and the perception that society as a whole is represented on the bench. Ifill wrote, "First, the creation of a racially diverse bench can introduce traditionally excluded perspectives and values into judicial decision-making. The interplay of diverse views and perspectives can enrich judicial decision-making. . . . Second, racial diversity on the bench also encourages judicial impartiality, by ensuring that a single set of values or views do not dominate judicial decision making."[28]

Although women do not make up 50 percent of the judiciary as they do of the population, there is a higher proportion of women in the Texas judiciary than of minorities. Women were at one time a great rarity on the bench. In 1970 only 1 percent of the nation's judiciary was female. As late as 1979 only 4 percent of the nation's judges were women.[29] In Texas, the first woman to serve as a state judge was Sarah Hughes, who was appointed in 1935 and who served as a district judge until 1961, when she was appointed to the federal bench. Famous for a number of her decisions, including one that forced Dallas County to build a new jail, she is probably best known as the judge who swore in Lyndon Johnson as president after the assassination of John F. Kennedy. In 2014, however, 42 percent of appellate judges in Texas were women, and 31 percent of trial judges were women. In contrast, only 2 percent of appellate judges and 4 percent of trial judges are African American and only 13 percent of appellate judges and 17 percent of trial judges are Latino.[30]

Different interpretations have been offered for the low numbers of minorities on the bench. The lack of racial and ethnic diversity on the bench is a nationwide problem. Ninety-two percent of the state judges in the nation are white.[31] Civil rights groups in several states with elective judiciaries, including Texas, have argued that white voters dominate countywide and larger districts and will vote against minority judicial candidates. Civil rights organizations representing Latinos and African Americans have argued that for minorities to get elected to office, there must be smaller judicial districts where minority voters make up the majority. One problem with dividing judicial districts into areas smaller than counties is that Latino and African American organizations have been unable to agree on the appropriate method of creating smaller districts. Both groups have sought to divide counties in different ways to reflect their group's respective interests. Additionally, the business community in Texas has been opposed to smaller judicial districts out of fear that it will lead to the election of judges

PERSONAL RESPONSIBILITY: WHAT WOULD YOU DO?

- Few minorities hold judicial office in Texas. Although African Americans and Latinos make up about 50 percent of the Texas population, relatively few Texas judges belong to these groups. Offer at least three suggestions, including alternative election methods, to increase the number of minorities holding judicial office in Texas.

Comparing How Texas Selects Its Judges to the Rest of the Country

Method of Initial Selection for State's Highest Court Judges

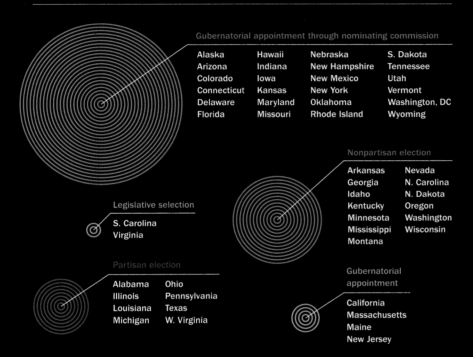

Gubernatorial appointment through nominating commission

Alaska	Hawaii	Nebraska	S. Dakota
Arizona	Indiana	New Hampshire	Tennessee
Colorado	Iowa	New Mexico	Utah
Connecticut	Kansas	New York	Vermont
Delaware	Maryland	Oklahoma	Washington, DC
Florida	Missouri	Rhode Island	Wyoming

Nonpartisan election

Arkansas	Nevada
Georgia	N. Carolina
Idaho	N. Dakota
Kentucky	Oregon
Minnesota	Washington
Mississippi	Wisconsin
Montana	

Legislative selection

S. Carolina
Virginia

Partisan election

Alabama	Ohio
Illinois	Pennsylvania
Louisiana	Texas
Michigan	W. Virginia

Gubernatorial appointment

California
Massachusetts
Maine
New Jersey

Texas is one of eight states that choose their state judges through partisan elections. Voters generally decide for whom to vote based on party affiliation. With so many offices on the ballot, it is simply easier for voters to use their party affiliation as a shortcut. Not all states select judges this way. Most states employ a merit selection method through nominating commissions that make recommendations to the governor. Other states have judges selected by the governor without nominating commissions. Thirteen states elect their judges in nonpartisan elections, meaning that the role of political parties in judicial elections is minimized. The state legislature chooses judges in the remaining two states.

Judicial Selection Methods: A Regional View

- Gubernatorial appointment through nominating commission
- Gubernatorial appointment
- Partisan election
- Nonpartisan election
- Legislative selection

SOURCES: American Judicature Society, Judicial Selection in the States, www.judicial selection.us/ and IAALS, the Institute for the Advancement of the American Legal System at the University of Denver published in "Selection and Retention of State Judges," *Texas Bar Journal* (February 2016): 92–97.

CRITICAL THINKING

- What are the advantages of nonpartisan elections to select judges? Which method of selection do you think is the best and why?

- Are there regional patterns in how judges are selected? If so, why do you think that is?

who will have a narrow constituency that might not reflect the interests of a sufficiently diverse community.

An alternative perspective is that minority candidates in Texas, like minority voters, tend to be Democrats at a time when Republicans increasingly are winning judicial races. Thus, minorities do not get elected to judicial office because they run as Democrats.[32] Still another argument is that there are few minority judges because there are few minority lawyers and, with the exception of county judges and justices of the peace, judges in Texas must be lawyers.

Restructuring the Texas Judiciary to Make It More Rational and Efficient
Texas judges may be elected, but Texas judges do not represent an electorate like legislators or county commissioners do. As a result, Texas judges are not subject to redistricting according to the one person–one vote standards used in districting officials in legislative bodies. The result is that Texas judicial districts are a hodgepodge of jurisdictions. Things have not changed much since a 1993 report that criticized the structure of the Texas courts. That report stated,

> The framers of our current Constitution deliberately designed a system to "localize justice," establishing a multiplicity of largely autonomous conveniently located courts across the state. With the passage of time, the organization of the courts has become more, not less, cumbersome. A case may frequently be eligible for filing in more than one court, either because of overlapping geographical boundaries or overlapping subject matter jurisdiction. Courts with the same name may have different responsibilities and similar places may have quite dissimilar court structures.[33]

In 2009, Rick Perry appointed Eva Guzman—the first Latina woman to serve on the Texas Supreme Court—to fill a vacancy on the court. Guzman was elected to a full term in the 2010 election.

As a state bar commission pointed out, the idea behind having justice of the peace courts, statutory county courts, constitutional county courts, and district courts was that each level of court was supposed to have its own jurisdiction that was to be consistent across each tier of courts. That has not happened because these courts have developed into a "patchwork array of courts."[34]

One illustration of this cumbersome court structure can be found in the district court structure in Anderson County in east Texas. There are four district courts in Anderson County. One of those courts also has jurisdiction in Henderson and Houston counties; one of them also has jurisdiction in Freestone, Leon, and Limestone counties; one has jurisdiction in Houston County; and the fourth has jurisdiction in Cherokee County. Bastrop County has three district courts—two of them have jurisdiction only in Bastrop County, but the third court has jurisdiction in Bastrop, Burleson, Lee, and Washington counties.

The appellate courts in Texas are also plagued by a cumbersome structure, especially in the ten counties in the Houston area. That is because these ten counties are served by two courts of appeal—the 1st and the 14th Courts of Appeal. The two appellate courts have overlapping jurisdictions and cases are randomly assigned between the two courts. The result is that at times the two courts render opposing decisions in cases that rely on the same facts. If there is a conflict in the decisions of the two courts, then there is no precedent that prevails that lower courts and lawyers in the ten-county area can rely on. This leads to a lack of certainty and predictability. One justice described the effect of this appellate court structure as "practicing law on a guess and a gamble."[35]

These structural problems in the Texas judicial system are primarily a concern of the Texas legal community. While reforms have addressed some of the problems in

Who Are Texas's Judges?

○ By race ● White ● African American ● Latino ● Other

○ By gender ● Male ● Female

Trial Courts

Trial courts include district courts, county courts at law, and probate courts

Total judges reporting race or ethnicity:
684

Total judges reporting gender:
711

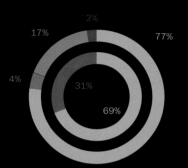

2%
17%
77%
4%
31%
69%

Appellate Courts

Appellate courts include the state Supreme Court, courts of appeal, and Court of Criminal Appeals

Total judges reporting race or ethnicity:
96

Total judges reporting gender:
97

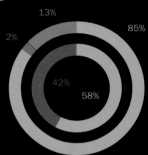

13%
2%
85%
42%
58%

Texas Lawyers, 2015

Total lawyers reporting race or ethnicity:
83,645

Total lawyers reporting gender:
87,957

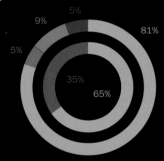

5%
9%
81%
5%
35%
65%

Texas Population, 2015

Total population:
27,469,114

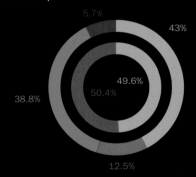

5.7%
43%
49.6%
50.4%
38.8%
12.5%

Although the proportion of women and of Latino and African American judges is roughly representative of the proportion of women, Latino, and African American lawyers, the composition of the Texas judiciary is very unrepresentative of the Texas population as a whole. Should there be a rough proportionality between the racial/ethnic/gender composition of the judiciary and Texas as a whole?

QUANTITATIVE REASONING

- Are there more or fewer minority judges in Texas than in the state population overall? (Texas is 12.5 percent African American and 38.8 percent Latino.)

- What are some of the factors that might lead to an increase in the representation of minorities in the state's courts?

SOURCES: Texas Office of Court Administration, Profile of Appellate and Trial Judges as of September 1, 2014; State Bar of Texas, State Bar of Texas Membership: Attorney Statistical Profile (2015–16); U.S. Census.

the design of the Texas court system such as the passage of a law in 2011 that allows justice of the peace courts to handle small claims with less formal rules of procedure, changes are rare and piecemeal rather than comprehensive.

Issues in the Texas Court System Today

Assess the impact of recent changes related to tort reform, regulation of lawyers, and disciplining judges

One of the most important issues in Texas has been tort reform, which is the effort to change the system for awarding damages in lawsuits where harm is claimed. Tort reform has had important effects on the Texas judiciary.

Civil Cases and Tort Reform

Figure 9.2 shows the numbers of civil cases disposed of by the appellate courts and the trial courts in 2014–15. The Texas county court system and especially the district courts are handling huge caseloads. While the caseload of the Texas Supreme Court is quite low, it sets the tone for civil cases throughout the state. Most important of those types of cases, because of the large amounts of money involved, is tort law. Tort law refers to civil cases in which one person has been harmed by the actions of another. For example, medical malpractice cases are a common type of tort case. In the early to mid-1980s, the court tended to be sympathetic to the plaintiffs' positions in tort cases. That is, the court tended to support the side in a case that was suing businesses, professionals, and insurance companies. However, in 1988 more justices began to be elected who favored the defendants in civil lawsuits. One reason for this change was that in 1988 Republican justices began to be elected, and they were more conservative than many of the previous justices, who were Democrats. Interest groups that were harmed by the pro-plaintiff tendencies of the court began to organize, raise and spend money, and elect justices more sympathetic to their perspective. Today the Texas Supreme Court is quite favorable to defendants in civil cases, in part because it is now an all-Republican and conservative court. Additionally, during Governor Perry's administration a number of laws were passed, most notably involving medical malpractice lawsuits, that make it much harder for the plaintiff to prevail over the defendant in a lawsuit.[36]

The Regulation of the Legal Profession

Lawyers occupy a crucial role in the legal process. In order to practice law, one must be a licensed lawyer, and in order to be licensed in Texas, it is generally necessary

FIGURE 9.2

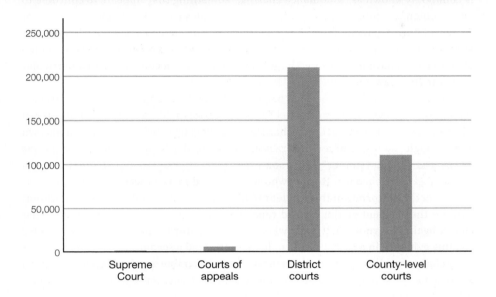

Civil Cases Disposed of by Texas Courts, September 1, 2014–August 31, 2015

SOURCE: Texas Office of Court Administration, 2015 Annual Statistical Report.

to complete a Juris Doctor (JD) degree at a law school accredited by the American Bar Association. Usually this degree takes three years beyond the bachelor's degree if the law student attends full-time. After completing law school, it is necessary for a prospective lawyer to take the state bar exam. After passing the Texas state bar, one may be sworn in as a lawyer in Texas. Texas has an integrated bar, which means that all licensed lawyers in the state must join and pay dues to the State Bar of Texas. That agency, which is under the administrative control of the Supreme Court of Texas, offers a variety of services to lawyers such as insurance plans, a journal, and professional meetings. Since lawyers must undergo continuing education, the state bar authorizes continuing education credit for a number of educational programs. The State Bar of Texas is unusual in that it is not only a professional organization of lawyers but also an agency of government that is charged with enforcing ethical standards for the profession. Lawyers can be disciplined for a variety of infractions ranging from serious criminal behavior, to failing to keep a client informed of the status of a legal matter, to failure to promptly pay out funds from a legal settlement. The state bar may also enforce rules against illegal efforts to generate litigation. Perhaps the most important task of the state bar is to enforce the ethical standards of the profession. In 2014–15 the state bar exercised that enforcement power by disbarring 28 Texas lawyers, obtaining the resignations from legal practice from 19, suspending the legal practice of 111, publicly reprimanding 32, and privately reprimanding 65 lawyers. The bar also has a program known as the grievance referral program where lawyers with problems such as substance abuse or mental health problems will be referred for assistance in dealing with those problems rather than face more severe sanctions. In 2014–15, 63 lawyers were referred for assistance.[37]

Illegal generation of litigation is commonly known as barratry, and the state legislature has become so concerned about lawyers' inappropriately generating legal business that in 2011 it passed new legislation that allows for a penalty of up to $10,000 and the recovery of attorney's fees. The goal of the new legislation was to prevent what is commonly known as "ambulance chasing," something that appears to continue to be a problem in spite of long-standing state bar rules against it. Some of the horror stories of barratry include people being solicited to sign contracts with lawyers for lawsuits at home, in hospitals, and even during funerals. At times the relatives of accident victims have been offered large payments to sign a contract with a particular lawyer to file a lawsuit.[38]

Barratry as a problem became particularly visible in 2012 when state representative Ronald Reynolds was arrested for barratry. Reynolds, who was a supporter of the new barratry law in 2011, was charged with illegally soliciting clients on his own and through the office of a chiropractor. The alleged scheme to solicit clients was discovered when a "runner"—a person used by an attorney to solicit clients for the attorney—approached an attorney who was involved in a car accident. The "runner" tried to get the attorney in the accident to hire Representative Reynolds to represent her, but the accident victim instead reported that solicitation to authorities.[39] That charge against Reynolds fell apart when an investigator in the case was arrested for stealing evidence in a case. But Reynolds was arrested a second time on another barratry charge for allegedly paying a man who would examine accident reports and then approach and persuade accident victims to sign contracts for legal representation.[40] Altogether eight lawyers were arrested in that barratry case, and seven of the lawyers made plea arrangements. Reynolds was the only lawyer who went to trial, and he was convicted on five counts of barratry and sentenced to one year in jail. Reynolds is currently released on bail while appealing his conviction.[41]

In 2014 there were almost 85,000 active lawyers in Texas and nearly 1.27 million active lawyers in the United States. In Texas, 31.5 active lawyers exist for every

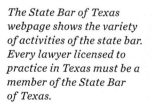

The State Bar of Texas webpage shows the variety of activities of the state bar. Every lawyer licensed to practice in Texas must be a member of the State Bar of Texas.

10,000 people, and in the United States as a whole 39.7 active lawyers exist for every 10,000 people.[42] With the decline in the number of legal jobs during the Great Recession, both in Texas and nationally, there is much discussion about whether there are too many lawyers, although it seems likely that the demand for lawyers will increase with an improvement in the economy. Of course, lawyers trained in out-of-state law schools may take the bar exam and be licensed in Texas, but the state has a substantial number of law schools: the University of Texas, the University of Houston, Texas Tech, Texas Southern, St. Mary's, South Texas, Southern Methodist University, Baylor, and Texas A&M. A new law school in Dallas, the University of North Texas College of Law, opened in 2014. In spite of the weakened job market for lawyers, Texas has law schools aplenty.

The legal process in Texas relies on lawyers. Constitutional county court judges are not required to be lawyers, and justices of the peace do not have to be lawyers, but all other judges must be "learned in the law," a term found in the Texas Constitution whose meaning has come to require a law degree. Even justice of the peace courts, which in theory are informal courts where people can easily resolve their minor criminal and civil issues, often have rules of operation that would be confusing to non-lawyers. The Texas Rules of Civil Procedure and Evidence, for example, apply to civil cases in justice of the peace courts, although not when justices of the peace sit as judges in small claims courts, a distinction that itself is confusing to non-lawyers—and much of the litigation in justice of the peace courts involves lawyers who, for example, are representing businesses trying to collect debts or apartment complexes trying to evict a tenant. Of course, in civil and criminal litigation, it is possible for a layperson to pursue a case without a lawyer, but it is generally recognized that non-lawyers are at a significant disadvantage if they are without legal help in either a civil or a criminal proceeding.

State representative Ronald Reynolds supported the new barratry law in Texas only to find himself in trouble for allegedly violating that law.

Judicial Conduct

The State Commission on Judicial Conduct was created by a constitutional amendment in 1965. It is charged with investigating allegations of judicial misconduct and disability and is charged with discipline of judges. There are 13 members on the commission and they serve six-year terms. Members of the commission are unpaid. The commission also has a staff of 14. In 2015 the commission's budget was slightly over $982,000, mostly for staff salaries. The commission is an unusual hybrid agency in that two attorney members are appointed by the state bar and the six judicial members are appointed by the Supreme Court of Texas, with one of the judicial members being an appellate judge, one a county court at law judge, one a constitutional county judge, one a district judge, one a justice of the peace, and one a municipal judge. There are five citizen members who can neither be lawyers nor be judges who are appointed by the governor. The state senate confirms the commission members.

In dealing with disciplinary issues involving Texas judges, the commission relies on complaints from the public, from attorneys, and from members of the judiciary. In 2015 the commission disposed of 1,242 cases, but some of the cases were immediately dismissed for failure of the complaint to allege misconduct. A common complaint is that the person disagrees with the judge's decision, but of course this is not a violation of the Code of Judicial Conduct, which is the ethical code promulgated by the Supreme Court of Texas that is enforced by the commission along with certain legislative requirements on judges. Indeed, one of the problems of the commission is that it is responsible for enforcing requirements that the Supreme Court of Texas places on judges and laws passed by the legislature that affect judges. Potentially, there could be a conflict between the Texas Supreme Court rules and the legislatively imposed requirements, in which case it would be unclear what the commission should do. Still another problem with the commission is that because it deals with ethical issues of judges, its decision making is done behind closed doors and thus the commission lacks openness and transparency in decision making. Still, other than impeachment by the legislature or criminal prosecution of judges, both rare and extreme measures, the commission is the only mechanism for regulating ethical and legal conduct of Texas judges.[43]

In 2015 the commission imposed 96 sanctions on judges that included five judges who were suspended from their judicial duties. In 14 disciplinary actions, the commission accepted the resignations of judges who chose to resign rather than to be sanctioned. The commission can recommend public censure or removal of a judge or the judge's involuntary retirement to a seven-judge review tribunal that is composed of the chief justice of Texas and six appellate judges. The review tribunal's decision can be appealed by the affected judge to the Supreme Court of Texas. No such case occurred in 2015. Other decisions of the commission can be appealed by the affected judge to a court of review consisting of three appellate judges. Two such cases occurred in 2015.

Many of the disciplinary actions of the commission involve private sanctions of the judge. In 2015, 28 sanctions were of a private nature and consisted of the commission providing a private admonition, warning, or reprimand to the judge (admonitions are less severe sanctions than are warnings, which are less severe than are reprimands). In 13 of the private sanction cases, judges were ordered to obtain additional training. In 49 cases, sanctions were made public. Seven were public admonitions, 1 was a warning, 25 were reprimands, and 16 were public sanctions with an order for continuing education of the judge. Public reprimands do have especially serious consequences for judges, as often when judges retire they become visiting judges, where they are paid to hear cases when sitting judges are on vacation or where dockets are overloaded, and they also continue to be paid retirement income. Judges who receive a public reprimand are not allowed to serve as visiting judges. Additionally, public sanctions may be used by the judge's opponent if the judge chooses to run for re-election.

Many of the sanctions are against justices of the peace—32 percent of the 96 sanctions in 2015 were against justices of the peace. However, in 2015 an unusually large number of sanctions were against district judges. Although district judges are only 13 percent of the total number of judges in the state, 32 percent of the sanctions were against them.[44]

Two sanctions in 2015 received considerable media attention. One was the sanction against the only appellate justice disciplined in 2015. Justice Nora Longoria of the 13th Court of Appeals was stopped by McAllen police for speeding. It became clear that she had been drinking, and she was emotional and uncooperative with the police.

Among other things, she demanded to see the police supervisor, and she told the police she was a judge and showed identification to them showing she was a judge. She was charged with DWI. At trial she pled no contest to the speeding charge and was fined $500. The DWI charge was dismissed. However, dash cam footage of the police stop was released by McAllen police, and it became a popular item on social media and portrayed Justice Longoria very negatively. The commission provided a public admonition to Justice Longoria.[45] District Judge Carter Tinsley Schildknecht received a public admonition and an order for additional education because in a private conversation with District Attorney Michael Munk's secretary, she referred to the district attorney as a "New York Jew." When she later tried to explain her statement to Mr. Munk, she said to the effect, "When I tell people why you are different and have different thoughts, I explain because you are from New York and because you are Jewish." In the same month, July 2014, she, with no breaks, held a 19-hour marathon court session that dealt with probation revocations where the session did not end until 4 AM. She also instructed her bailiff not to allow District Attorney Munk in the courtroom on another occasion. Finally, she told an assistant district attorney who had a beard to the effect, "You look like a Muslim, and I wouldn't hire you with it [the beard]."[46]

Justice Nora Longoria of the 13th Court of Appeals received a public admonition from the State Commission on Judicial Conduct due to her behavior during a traffic stop by McAllen police.

The most widely publicized disciplinary case against a judge in recent years was the one against the presiding judge of the Texas Court of Criminal Appeals, Sharon Keller. In 2007, Judge Keller refused to keep the clerk's office at the court open beyond 5 PM to receive an appeal from death row inmate Michael Richard. As a result, Richard was executed later that evening. Although Keller received a public warning as a disciplinary action by the State Commission on Judicial Conduct, she was successful in her litigation against the discipline by arguing that a warning cannot be a penalty following a formal proceeding against a judge.[47] Re-elected to another six-year term in 2012 with 55.49 percent of the vote, she remains the presiding judge of the court.

★ ★

The Judiciary and the Future of Texas

Texas elects its judges in partisan judicial elections. For many years, when the Democratic Party was dominant, Texas judicial elections were staid, low-budget, noncompetitive events. However, with the growth of the Republican Party, judicial elections became highly political, and large amounts of money have been raised for judicial candidates, especially in Texas Supreme Court races. Often these judicial races pitted business interests against candidates backed by the plaintiffs' bar because the Texas Supreme Court sets the tone of tort law in the state. These elections have calmed down in recent years as the Democratic Party has weakened, and at least in statewide races judicial elections have become less competitive.

There have been problems in Texas judicial races, in large part because voters often don't know much about judicial candidates. As a result, voters often decide on the basis of the candidate's party affiliation or the candidate's name appeal.

Numerous efforts have been undertaken to change the way judges are selected in Texas. There have been efforts to change the system of selection to merit selection. Minority groups have pushed to reduce the size of judicial districts in order to increase the election of minority judges. However, no major change has so far been successful. No majority coalition can agree on appropriate changes in the judicial selection system, and significant opposition to change comes from groups such as the political parties and business interests. Additionally, Texans seem satisfied with the current system of selection and seem to prefer to elect their judges. Recent injustices in the Texas criminal system do raise questions about how the system can be improved. One might speculate that a criminal justice system in which both judges and prosecutors are elected creates political pressures to gain convictions at all costs.

Because the Texas court system affects the liberty and especially the pocketbooks of Texans, it will continue to be an area of concern and controversy. And the most controversial area of Texas justice will continue to be the process by which judges are selected. Nevertheless, change in the Texas judiciary does not appear to be likely. Efforts to change the Texas judicial system have been ongoing for decades with no result, and there seems no reason to believe change will occur in the near future. Even more minor changes in the judiciary, such as redistricting trial courts, seem to be a low priority in Texas. It is likely that the judiciary will continue "as is," at least for the next several years, with overlapping jurisdictions and a mishmash of courts. The only likely changes appear to be increases in the numbers of trial court judges as the population of Texas continues to increase.

STUDY GUIDE

Use **INQUIZITIVE** to help you study and master this material.

Court Structure

- Describe how the Texas court system is organized (pp. 291–96)

The appellate court system in Texas is divided into civil and criminal tracks with the Texas Supreme Court being the highest state-level court for civil cases and the Texas Criminal Court of Appeals being the highest for criminal cases. Texas has an intermediate appellate court system and trial courts that range from district courts for the most important criminal and civil cases, to county courts for less important criminal and civil cases, to justice of the peace and municipal courts for settling the lowest level of conflicts.

Key Terms
Texas Supreme Court (p. 291)
Texas Court of Criminal Appeals (p. 291)
courts of appeal (p. 293)
district courts (p. 293)
county judge (p. 293)
county courts (p. 293)
statutory county courts at law (p. 293)
statutory probate courts (p. 294)
justice of the peace courts (p. 294)
municipal courts (p. 295)
ordinance (p. 296)

Practice Quiz
1. The highest criminal court in the state of Texas is the
   a) Texas Supreme Court.
   b) Texas Court of Appeals.
   c) Texas Court of Criminal Appeals.
   d) county court.
   e) district court.

2. The major trial courts in Texas are the
   a) courts of appeal.
   b) justice of the peace courts.
   c) district courts.
   d) municipal courts.
   e) county courts.

3. Which of the following positions in the judiciary are filled primarily by non-lawyers?
   a) Texas Supreme Court justices
   b) district judges
   c) justices of the peace
   d) Texas Criminal Court of Appeals justices
   e) probate judges

The Legal Process

- Explain the legal process and the differences between criminal and civil law (pp. 296–99)

Civil law is dramatically different from criminal law, with the burden of proof relying on different standards. Plaintiffs are the initiators of legal actions in civil cases. Defendants in civil cases respond to accusations made against them. Civil cases may lead to trial or dismissal by a judge. They may also be resolved by a settlement between the parties. The state is a prosecutor in a criminal case, and the accused individual is the defendant. Criminal cases can result in a trial, a dismissal, or a plea bargain.

Key Terms

civil law (p. 296)
criminal law (p. 296)
complaint (p. 296)
answer (p. 296)
contingent fee (p. 296)
tort (p. 297)
preponderance of the evidence (p. 297)
capital case (p. 298)
felony (p. 298)
misdemeanor (p. 298)

grand jury (p. 298)
indictment (p. 298)
bench trial (p. 298)
plea bargain (p. 298)
beyond a reasonable doubt (p. 299)

Practice Quiz

4. Grand juries
   a) determine the guilt of defendants.
   b) decide whether a trial of an accused is warranted.
   c) agree to plea bargains.
   d) recommend that defendants undergo bench trials.
   e) hear appeals of convictions.

5. On conviction, the criminal's punishment is determined
   a) by the grand jury.
   b) in a separate hearing by the jury or judge that determined the person's guilt.
   c) by the prosecuting attorney.
   d) by the prosecuting and defense attorneys.
   e) by the Texas Court of Criminal Appeals.

Judicial Politics

- Evaluate the process for selecting judges in Texas (pp. 299–312)

Unlike federal judges, Texas judges are elected in partisan elections. Partisan elections make judges accountable to voters, but critics claim that unqualified judges are elected solely because of their party labels. These critics advocate alternatives for choosing judges such as merit selection. Minorities are not proportionately represented, possibly in part because most judges are elected from large districts that are non-minority.

Key Terms

merit selection (p. 302)
retention election (p. 302)
Judicial Campaign Fairness Act (p. 307)

Practice Quiz

6. Civil defense lawyers often align themselves with
   a) business and professional groups.
   b) the grand jury.
   c) groups that support workers.
   d) judges supported by the Democratic Party.
   e) labor groups.

7. Texas's movement from being a Democratic to a Republican state led to
   a) defeats of large numbers of incumbent judges.
   b) party switching by incumbent judges.
   c) large campaign contributions to judges.
   d) election of more Republican judges.
   e) all of the above

8. In Texas, which event marked the rise of the Republican Party and partisan judicial elections?
   a) the election of President Ronald Reagan
   b) the impeachment of William Jefferson Clinton
   c) the appointment of Tom Phillips as chief justice of the United States
   d) the election of Bill Clements as governor of Texas
   e) the Shivercrat movement

9. How likely is Texas to change its method of selecting judicial candidates?
   a) Texas is scheduled to change to the Missouri Plan in January 2016.

b) extremely likely in the next two decades
c) likely in the next decade
d) a 50–50 chance change will soon occur
e) unlikely

10. Which of the following sets campaign contribution limits for judicial candidates in Texas?
    a) Judicial Campaign Fairness Act
    b) Judicial Campaign Law
    c) Equal Justice Act
    d) Code of Judicial Conduct
    e) Federal Rules of Civil Procedure

11. Which of the following groups has the largest number of judges?
    a) African Americans
    b) American Indians
    c) Asian Americans
    d) Latinos
    e) women

Issues in the Texas Court System Today

- Assess the impact of recent changes related to tort reform, regulation of lawyers, and disciplining judges (pp. 312–17)

Texas courts make decisions affecting Texans on a variety of issues, including the ultimate penalty of death and tort cases such as medical malpractice.

Practice Quiz
12. Philosophically, in the past few years, Texas courts became
    a) more pro-defendant in civil cases.
    b) more liberal.
    c) more pro-defendant in criminal cases.
    d) more conservative.
    e) hostile to tort reform.

13. All lawyers who regularly practice in Texas
    a) must be members of the State Bar of Texas.
    b) must have graduated from a Texas law school.
    c) must appear in court at least twice a year.
    d) must volunteer to sit on grand juries.
    e) do not need any additional training once they have a law license.

14. The State Commission on Judicial Conduct
    a) screens judicial candidates to determine if they are qualified to be judges.
    b) offers continuing education courses for judges.
    c) investigates complaints of ethical violations by judges.
    d) recommends trial judges for promotion to appellate courts.
    e) makes rules governing the conduct of judges.

Sometimes the decisions of local governments can have dire consequences. Fifteen people, including 12 firefighters, died in an explosion and fire at a fertilizer plant in West, Texas. West had no fire code, and thus the plant was not required to install sprinklers. This photo shows the memorial service for the firefighters.

Local Government

WHY LOCAL GOVERNMENT MATTERS On April 17, 2013, the tiny town of West, Texas, was rocked by an explosion at the local fertilizer plant. There were 15 fatalities, 260 injuries, insurance-related losses of $230 million, and federal disaster aid of $16 million. One hundred fifty buildings were damaged or destroyed. Among the major buildings so damaged that they had to be demolished were an intermediate school, a high school, a twenty-two-unit apartment complex, and a 145-bed nursing home. There are estimates that $40,000 worth of sprinklers would have prevented the explosion, but the town did not have a fire code that mandated them. Under state law, both the city and the county could adopt a fire code, but they chose not to do so. Less than one week before the West explosion, state representative Walter Price (R-Amarillo) testified before the County Affairs Committee that all Texas counties should be authorized to have a fire code. The proposal was opposed on the grounds that a fire code would require property owners to retrofit their buildings to comply with the code.

Only 15 counties in Texas have adopted a fire code, although 81 are allowed by state law to do so. Texas is one of just a handful of states with no statewide fire code. And there are many counties that cannot impose a fire code even if they chose to do so. For a county to have a fire code, state law requires that they have a population of more than 250,000 or that they touch a county of that size. One hundred seventy-three counties do not meet that requirement, and 85 percent of those counties do not have a full-time professional fire department anywhere in the county, although 21 of those counties do have special districts called emergency service districts that provide some fire protection. Still, Victoria County has approximately 39 million pounds of poisonous chemicals within its borders and 11 million pounds of flammable chemicals; Parmer County has 10 companies within its borders that have 2.3 million pounds of toxic anhydrous ammonia; Jasper County has a paper mill containing 83,280 pounds of chlorine dioxide. None of these counties are allowed by law to have a fire code.

On January 28, 2016, the United States Chemical Safety Board, an independent federal agency that investigates chemical accidents, issued its report on the West disaster. Most disturbing was that the board found there were 19 facilities in Texas that stored more than 10,000 pounds of fertilizer-grade ammonium nitrate (the chemical that caused the West explosion) that were located within a half mile of a school, hospital, or nursing home. The board noted that these 19 facilities raised "concerns that an incident with offsite consequences of this magnitude could happen again." In the opinion of the board, there was much blame to go around: the national government had an outdated patchwork of regulations dealing with ammonium nitrate fertilizer; the state insurance code provided no additional protections; and the city had allowed schools, apartments, and a nursing home to be built close to the facility. In the time since the explosion, the board noted that there had only been limited improvements in the rules for storage of this fertilizer, and it singled out the new Texas law that allowed the state fire marshal to inspect businesses that store ammonium nitrate but rely on the state chemist for enforcement as an inadequate law.[1]

Local government is generally praised for being closer to the people it serves and, therefore, being more responsive to those people than the state or national government can be. The problem is sometimes local governments do not have the power or the ability to provide adequate services for their citizens. The disaster in West raises the question of whether local governments are doing a basic job—protecting the people they serve.

CHAPTER GOALS

- Explain the importance, role, and structure of county government in Texas (pp. 325–33)
- Describe the major types of city government in Texas (pp. 333–44)
- Examine the role of special districts in Texas government (pp. 344–52)
- Examine the financial problems facing local government (pp. 352–55)

County Government in Texas

Explain the importance, role, and structure of county government in Texas

Local government institutions play a major role in Texas. There are more than 4,800 general-purpose local governments, an average of about 19 per county.[2] Local government is everywhere in Texas, providing water, electricity, and sewer services, as well as police protection and public education.

All but two states have governmental units known as counties (or parishes), but Texas has 254 counties, more than any other state.[3] County government in Texas is primarily a way of governing rural areas. Because Texas is so vast, with huge areas that are sparsely populated, county government remains an important aspect of local government. As was discussed in Chapter 2, the Texas Constitution places numerous restrictions on government, and numerous provisions of the constitution place restrictions on counties. Indeed, in Texas, counties have very constricted governmental powers. Unlike city governments, county governments usually do not have powers to legislate. Because they lack much of the power of self-government, they often function primarily as an administrative arm of the state government.

Texas counties have their origins in the "municipality or ayuntamiento," which was the local governmental unit under Spanish and Mexican rule. These municipalities were large and included settlements and surrounding rural territories. In 1835, Texas was divided into 3 departments and 23 municipalities. With the Republic of 1836, the 23 municipalities became counties. By the time Texas became a state in 1845, there were 36 counties, and when Texas entered the Confederacy in 1861, there were 122 counties. The number of counties increased steadily until 1921, when the 254th county was created. The underlying goal of the proliferation of counties was that any citizen could travel to the county seat—on horseback, of course—and return home in a day. Given the sparse population of west Texas, in particular, that initial plan for county organization was eventually rejected, but it does show that Texans believed that the local center of government, the county seat, should be accessible to the people.[4]

What Are the Functions of County Government?

The main functions of Texas county government are construction and maintenance of county roads and bridges; law enforcement; dispute resolution; record keeping; and administration of social services. Like most other aspects of county government in Texas, these five primary functions are performed with great variation among the counties.

County road and bridge construction and maintenance have traditionally been such important functions of the commissioners' court that often county commissioners are called "road commissioners." County commissioners maintain more than one-half of the roads in the state.[5] There are roughly 134,000 miles of rural roadways and 17,000 rural bridges in Texas. Maintenance of these roads and bridges is a major

Counties have control over law-enforcement budgets, but sheriffs often decide how the money gets spent. Pictured here is the Montgomery County Sheriff's Department's $220,000 drone that quickly crashed because it was too heavy to fly.

cost for county government.[6] For example, a 20-foot-wide asphalt road for lightweight traffic costs a county $45,000 per mile to resurface; a road of the same width for heavy trucks costs about $100,000 per mile.[7] Although a 1947 law allowed counties to place the road system under the authority of a county engineer, in most counties roads and bridges remain one of the most important responsibilities of the commissioners.

Law enforcement is another important responsibility of county government. This job is undertaken by constables and by the sheriff. The sheriff is the chief law-enforcement officer within county government. In rural counties with few city police departments, the sheriff may be the major law-enforcement official in the county. In addition to law enforcement and the provision of deputies for the district and county courts, sheriffs are responsible for the county jail and the safety of prisoners. In many counties, operating a county jail is an expensive and major undertaking. On December 1, 2015, for example, Harris County was guarding and supervising 8,687 inmates in its county jail and Dallas County had 5,234 inmates in its jail. On the other hand, 23 counties had no jails. Crockett County had room for 13 inmates in its jail but had only 1 inmate. Overall, there were 61,995 inmates in Texas county jails.[8]

Although the law-enforcement budget is approved by the county commissioners' court, sheriffs often have considerable influence in county government and develop their own law-enforcement styles. The sheriff of Montgomery County was the first sheriff in Texas to have an aerial drone at a cost of $220,000 until it rose into the air about 18 feet, went out of control, and crashed into the Sheriff's Department's SWAT team armored vehicle.[9]

Traditionally in Texas, the office of constable has been an elective office with limited duties. Constables have served civil court papers and have provided bailiffs for justices of the peace. However, some constables have transformed their offices into full-fledged police departments. Some constables' offices have traffic enforcement roles; some enforce truancy laws; some even have formed heavily armed, tactical units that patrol high-crime areas. Since constables are elected officials, they are not subject to much oversight by other public officials and they tend to function as law enforcement fiefdoms in larger counties in Texas.

County attorneys and **district attorneys** also perform a law-enforcement role by prosecuting criminal cases. Usually, the district attorneys prosecute the more serious criminal cases in the district courts, whereas the county attorneys prosecute the lesser criminal cases in the county courts. In more urban counties, the offices of county attorney and district attorney may be combined into one office that is usually called the office of criminal district attorney.

Record-keeping is an important function of county government. **County clerks** keep vital statistics for the county and issue licenses; they maintain records for the commissioners' court and the county courts. Most important, the county clerk is responsible for records relating to property transactions. Sometimes the county clerk maintains election and voting records. If there is a **district clerk**, he or she maintains records for the district courts, though in small counties this office is combined with the office of the county clerk. Tax records are maintained by the **county tax assessor-collector**, who also collects taxes, though in the smaller counties the sheriff often performs this job. Although constitutional amendments have eliminated the office of

county attorney county official who prosecutes lesser criminal cases in the county court

district attorney public official who prosecutes the more serious criminal cases in the district court

county clerk public official who is the main record-keeper of the county

district clerk public official who is the main record-keeper of district court documents

county tax assessor-collector public official who maintains the county tax records and collects the taxes owed to the county

county treasurer in many counties, where the office does exist, the treasurer is responsible for receiving and expending county funds. The **county auditor** now does much of the work of the county treasurer. There are now 200 county auditors in Texas. Auditors are not elected; they are appointed by the county's district judges. Not only do they audit the county's funds, but in large counties they will often prepare the county budget for the commissioners' court.

Counties also have an important role in dispute resolution through their court systems. Civil law is a way to resolve disputes between people, and the justice of the peace court and the county and district courts deal with large numbers of civil disputes as well as criminal matters. County and district attorneys may also represent the interests of the county or state in disputes that involve governmental interests.

Finally, counties may perform a social service function. The social services provided vary from county to county. However, the most important social services involve emergency welfare assistance to individuals. This may include the provision of food, housing, rental assistance, or shelter to needy individuals. Larger counties have health departments to work on the prevention and control of communicable diseases. Some counties operate mental health services. Some counties provide parks, airports, fire protection, and sanitation facilities. One of the most important social services provided by counties is indigent health care.

county auditor public official, appointed by the district judges, who receives and disburses county funds; in large counties, this official also prepares the county budget

Numerous County Offices: Checks and Balances or Built-In Problems?

As with the state government, one of the characteristics of county government in Texas is a multiplicity of elected governmental officials. Some argue that the large number of public officials at the county level is desirable because it creates a strong system of checks and balances, allowing no one official to dominate county government.[10] However, that system of checks and balances comes at a high price. There are problems of coordination of governmental activity, much as at the state level. One of the most important bodies of county elected officials is the **county commissioners' court**, which is the main governing unit in the county. Although the commissioners' court is not really a judicial court, it may have gotten its name from the Republic of Texas Constitution (1836–45), in which the county governing unit consisted of the chief justice of the county court and the justices of the peace within the county.[11]

The current structure of the county commissioners' court, shown in Figure 10.1, consists of a **county judge** and four commissioners. The county judge is elected countywide and serves for four years. He or she presides over the meetings of the commissioners' court and has administrative powers as well as judicial powers in rural counties. In those counties, the county judge hears minor criminal cases and handles some civil matters such as probate matters. In larger counties, the county judge is an administrator only, with the judicial duties of the office removed by the creation of judgeships, such as probate judgeships and county-court-at-law judgeships.

Each commissioners' court also has four **county commissioners**; each of these officials is elected from a precinct that encompasses roughly one-fourth of the population of the county. In the late 1960s one of the great issues in constitutional law

county commissioners' court the main governing body of each county; has the authority to set the county tax rate and budget

county judge the person in each of Texas's 254 counties who presides over the constitutional county court and county commissioners' court, with responsibility for the administration of county government; some county judges carry out judicial responsibilities

county commissioner government official (four per county) on the county commissioners' court whose main duty is the construction and maintenance of roads and bridges

FIGURE 10.1

The County Commissioners' Court

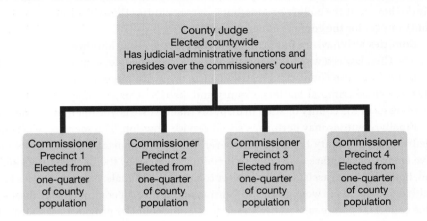

County Judge
Elected countywide
Has judicial-administrative functions and
presides over the commissioners' court

| Commissioner Precinct 1 Elected from one-quarter of county population | Commissioner Precinct 2 Elected from one-quarter of county population | Commissioner Precinct 3 Elected from one-quarter of county population | Commissioner Precinct 4 Elected from one-quarter of county population |

involved the issue of malapportionment, the allegation that election districts did not represent equal population groupings. The malapportionment of Texas's county commissioners' courts became an important case before the U.S. Supreme Court because those precincts tended to be drawn to represent fairly equal land areas rather than equal population groupings. In *Avery v. Midland County* (1968), the U.S. Supreme Court held that the principle of "one person–one vote" applies to commissioners' courts just as it applies to legislative districts. The result was that commissioners' precincts must now be drawn to reflect equal population groupings within counties.[12]

The main duty of county commissioners is the construction and maintenance of county roads and bridges; usually each commissioner provides for roadwork within his or her precinct. That aspect of a commissioner's work is, of course, very important to rural residents; it can be politically controversial and has sometimes been tinged with corruption.[13]

The commissioners' court also sets the county tax rate and the county budget. Related to its taxing and budgeting powers is its power to make contracts and pay bills. Perhaps the most important expenditure of most county commissioners' courts, other than road and bridge expenditures, is the cost of building and maintaining county jails. Health care for people in poverty can be a significant cost for counties as well, along with, in some cases, fire protection and sanitation. Some counties also have costs associated with the maintenance of libraries and hospitals and costs for emergency welfare expenditures, such as those brought on by natural disasters or fires. The commissioners' court can appoint certain county officials, and it can hire personnel as well as fill vacancies in county offices. It also administers elections in the county.

However, as noted earlier, there are numerous elected officials in Texas counties, each with an independent power base. It seems nearly inevitable that tensions would develop between the budgetary powers of the commissioners' courts and the needs and desires of other elected county officials. Such disputes among county officials can be mundane, as was the battle between Titus County commissioners and the county attorney over whether the commission could ban the county attorney's dog from the courthouse.[14] The disputes can also be far more serious and acrimonious, such as the litigation going on between the Galveston County commissioners and the Galveston County district judges over the firing of the county court administrator by the commissioners over the opposition of the judges.[15]

As Table 10.1 shows, other officeholders are elected at the county level and still others at the precinct level of the county. There is some variation in the numbers of officeholders, depending on the county. For example, larger counties will have more justices of the peace and more **constables** than smaller ones. In some counties, constables serve legal papers, while in others, constables also have a law-enforcement role with the authority to patrol, give tickets, and make arrests. Some counties use constables to check on truants from school, having found a niche area that others in law enforcement do not seem to want.

constable precinct-level county official involved with serving legal papers and, in some counties, enforcing the law

Larger counties may have probate judges, numerous district judges, and county-court-at-law judges. Smaller counties may not have probate judges or even county-court-at-law judges. Some of the smaller counties may share district judges and district attorneys with other counties. Laws setting up different offices often vary from county to county as well. As a result, some counties have county attorneys and district attorneys; others have criminal district attorneys that combine the county attorney and district attorney offices. Some counties have county clerks and district clerks; smaller counties may combine the offices in one person. Some counties have county treasurers; others do not have such an office.

TABLE 10.1

Countywide and Precinct-Level Elected Officials

COUNTYWIDE OFFICIALS	PRECINCT-LEVEL OFFICIALS
County judge	County commissioners
Possibly county court-at-law judges, possibly probate judges, and district judges	Justices of the peace
County and district attorney or criminal district attorney	Constables
Sheriff	
County and district clerk or district clerk	
Possibly county treasurer	
Tax assessor-collector	
Possibly county surveyor	

The county commissioners' court is the main governing unit at the county level, with control over the county budget and projects such as road construction. Here, Denton County commissioner Andy Eads appears with Texas Motor Speedway president Eddie Gossage at the groundbreaking for a highway extension near the speedway.

The Challenges of County Government

Are Some Counties Too Small? The reason for the variation in offices is not simply that laws were passed at different times, thus sacrificing uniformity among counties. It is also the case that Texas is a large, diverse state with great variation among its counties. The result is great variation in the numbers of government officials, the duties of officials, and the services provided by the different county governments. Brewster County has a population of only 9,173, but it covers a territory of 6,193 square miles, about the size of Connecticut and Rhode Island combined. Rockwall County, in contrast, has only 149 square miles and a population of 87,809. Although Harris County has a population of 4,441,370, Loving County has a population of only 86, yet Loving County covers a huge land area—nearly 677 square miles.[16] Most employed residents of Loving County work for the Loving County government. The fact that the county government is the major employer in the county may be the main justification for Loving County's continuing existence as a governmental unit— although people with taxable property may also prefer the Loving County tax structure to that of another governmental unit.[17]

A small population may create a sense of community and closeness to local government, but it can place a huge strain on county resources when unusual events occur such as an expensive capital murder trial or a natural disaster. Presidio County has a population of 6,976 and has suffered from flooding and a bad economy. As a result, it had insufficient money to pay bills. Several Presidio County phone lines were disconnected because of lack of payment. The county had to cut its budget by 30 percent and had to raise taxes in order to continue functioning.[18]

Polk County in east Texas (2014 population of about 46,079) estimated that it had unanticipated costs of $200,000 when the U.S. Supreme Court overturned the sentence of Johnny Paul Penry, who was convicted in the stabbing death of a woman in 1979, and sent the case back for another trial. Even with $100,000 in aid from the state to help pay the bill, the costs of one trial tremendously burdened Polk County.[19] An even more severe situation faced tiny Franklin County (2014 population of 10,600) in 2007, when it needed to come up with a minimum of $250,000 for a murder trial.[20] Since capital murder cases were so rare in the county, the commissioners had no money at all budgeted for such a purpose. For small counties such as Polk and Franklin, expenses like these require either major cuts in other budget items or tax increases.

Very small counties in the Big Bend area of Texas are discovering that they cannot afford to prosecute the drug violations that are too small for the federal government to prosecute. In counties that have Border Patrol checkpoints, relatively minor drug cases have been prosecuted at the county level rather than by the federal government, although the federal government has provided some aid for funding these prosecutions. But Hudspeth County (2014 population of 3,211) has discovered that for every dollar it gets for handling federal border crimes and seized assets, it costs the county $2 to detain, process, and prosecute the offenders. As Hudspeth County is the site of a border checkpoint, the cost has gotten so substantial that the county has chosen to no longer prosecute the federal drug cases sent to it. Brooks County (2014 population of 7,194) had previously stopped taking the federal drug cases from its Border Patrol checkpoint because the county found the costs too great, and Kenedy County (2014 population of 400) has recently made the same decision. Part of the problem is that the federal government has decided to reimburse local authorities only for prosecution costs and not for detention costs. For small-population counties like Hudspeth County, that imposed too great a financial burden, since detention is the most expensive item in the county budget.[21]

According to the 2010 census, 137 Texas counties have populations of fewer than 20,000. One study confirmed fears that Texas has wide variations in its counties'

Agents and drug-sniffing dogs at the U.S. Customs and Border Protection checkpoint in Hudspeth County, 85 miles east of El Paso. Smaller counties on the U.S.–Texas border, like Hudspeth, have found prosecuting smaller drug violations too costly.

application of capital punishment, in part because of the costs of death penalty cases to smaller counties. Between 1976, when the U.S. Supreme Court reinstated capital punishment, and July 2011, Texas sent just over 1,060 inmates to death row. Only four of the state's most heavily populated counties—Harris, Bexar, Dallas, and Tarrant—accounted for 534 of these death sentences. By itself, Harris County, the county with the largest population, accounted for 280, or 28 percent, of the death sentences. In contrast, 135 Texas counties with relatively small populations had not sent an inmate to death row in 1976–2011.[22]

Counties exist as they do for a variety of reasons. The original goal of making county seats easily accessible by horseback is, of course, no longer pertinent. Other reasons are political. For example, wealthy landowners may have urged the legislature to create counties so that they could control county government and hence the amount of property taxes they might pay. Still, we must wonder if so many small counties are needed. Even moderate-size counties by Texas standards may be too small to function adequately in unusual situations. It would take a state constitutional amendment to merge counties so that many counties could have a sufficient population to function efficiently and to have a tax base to adequately deliver services. In modern times there is arguably no practical reason for Texas to have so many counties. Nevertheless, the issue of county mergers is not one that is on the political agenda and would likely be controversial because of traditional loyalties to a county, because county office holders would fear losing their jobs, and since a vote in a populous county is less influential than a vote in a small county, voters might feel they would lose control over county government.

Accountability of County Officials County officials are made accountable to the public through elections. If county government acts in ways that displease the public, county elected officials who are in charge of operating county government can be defeated for office and new officials can be elected who are more responsive to the wishes of the voters. Thus, generally every four year the voters get a chance to review county officials and make a judgment about their competence, efficiency, and ability and determine whether those officials should hold office for another four years. One question is whether having elections every four years is a sufficient mechanism to ensure the accountability of officials. In cases of inefficiency or incompetence, the only alternative to elections for the removal of county officials is a rarely used and generally unsuccessful judicial proceeding against an official believed incapable of performing duties.

One example of the problems of accountability of county officials involves Susan Hawk, the district attorney of Dallas County. She was a political superstar. Hawk had been a highly successful assistant district attorney in Dallas County beginning at the age of 24. At 32, she was elected a state district judge, and in 2014 she resigned from the bench to run against incumbent Democrat Craig Watkins for district attorney. Hawk was the only Republican who won a county-wide race in Dallas County in 2014. As the newly elected district attorney, Hawk was responsible for running an office with 260 assistant district attorneys and 190 support staff.

Even during her campaign, however, she began to have problems due to severe depression and an addiction to prescription pain medications. She became suicidal and paranoid and went into a rehabilitation facility, claiming she was going to have back surgery. As district attorney, her paranoia continued and she became manic and forgetful, sometimes making impulsive decisions. She fired top assistant district attorneys, including people who were close associates. By the summer of 2015, she was again suicidal and was planning her resignation when she obtained treatment. After Hawk fired a lawyer who oversaw the budget, the lawyer claimed Hawk had repeatedly tried to misuse public funds. A removal suit was filed against Hawk, but in early 2016 the suit was dismissed.[23] Hawk's mental health problems were not controlled, however, and she was frequently in treatment. Finally, in September 2016 she resigned, waiting just long enough to prevent an election for her replacement who in Democratic Dallas County would most likely have been a Democrat. Instead, her replacement will be appointed by Republican governor Greg Abbott.

The descent of Susan Hawk into depression, drug abuse, and paranoia is a tragedy, but in the process of trying to gain self-control, Hawk damaged the careers of several employees in the district attorney's office and introduced considerable confusion and chaos in the office. Hawk's story may be the most dramatic, but numerous examples of local governmental officials can be identified that raise concerns about possible lack of accountability. Dallas County Commissioner John Wiley Price, for example, is facing an 11-count indictment on corruption charges where he is alleged to have received $950,000 in payments in money, cars, and land.[24] Travis County district attorney Rosemary Lehmberg was arrested and convicted on a drunk driving charge.[25] Houston Community College Trustee Dave Wilson won his office with a questionable campaign that suggested to his heavily African American constituents that he was black. Wilson is white, but his campaign leaflets did not show his picture, but featured pictures of African Americans that were taken off the Internet beside the request, "Please vote for our friend and neighbor Dave Wilson." One leaflet said Wilson was endorsed by Ron Wilson—it turns out that Ron Wilson was his cousin in Iowa rather than the former African American state representative.[26]

Local officials are supposed to be closest to the electorate, and therefore voters are supposed to be more aware of the strengths and flaws of these officials. But is this actually the case? Do voters have sufficient awareness of local officials when they elect them, and are future elections a sufficient control over the behavior of those officials once they are in office?

City Government in Texas

 Describe the major types of city government in Texas

As of the 2010 census, there were 1,221 municipalities in Texas, ranging in size from 27 residents in Corral City to nearly 2.1 million in Houston (see Table 10.2). Like county governments, municipal governments are creations of the state of Texas. In the early years of the Republic of Texas, the Texas Congress was responsible for enacting laws that incorporated cities. The number of urban areas grew in the state in the late

TABLE 10.2

Municipal Entities in Texas

POPULATION	NUMBER OF MUNICIPALITIES
100,000 or more	28
50,000–99,999	30
10,000–49,999	157
5,000–9,999	115
Fewer than 5,000	891
Total	1,221

SOURCE: Calculated from texasalmanac.com.

home-rule charter the rules under which a city operates; local governments have considerable independent governing power under these charters

nineteenth and early twentieth centuries, making the management of local affairs a growing burden on the state legislature. In 1912 the legislature passed the Home-Rule Charter Amendments that enabled cities of more than 5,000 inhabitants to adopt home-rule charters.

Home-rule charters essentially lay down the rules under which a city will operate.[27] They provide for the form of government that operates in the city and specify the number of members serving on the city's governing body. They also may grant the governing body the power to annex land adjacent to the city as well as to set property tax rates up to $2.50 per $100 valuation. Home-rule cities are also constitutionally authorized to borrow money in ways not available to smaller municipal entities. Home-rule charters must be consistent with the state constitution and any other relevant statutory provisions. For example, the state has mandated that most city elections take place on a date provided by the Texas Election Code. City elections must be conducted under the general guidelines set by the state. Nevertheless, home rule in Texas has delegated enormous power to local city governments. According to a report by the Advisory Commission on Intergovernmental Relations, the Texas Constitution leaves cities more "home rule" than does any other state. There are now 335 home-rule cities in Texas.[28] Table 10.3 lists the 10 largest of these. In contrast, California has only 121 home-rule cities and Illinois has only 209.

While home-rule cities have substantial power to act independently of state control, the city of Denton, Texas, discovered that there are limits on local control when home rule comes in conflict with the oil industry and with state government. In

TABLE 10.3

Texas's Largest Home-Rule Cities

NAME	2014 POPULATION ESTIMATES	FORM OF GOVERNMENT	FIRST CHARTER	PRESENT FORM ADOPTED
Houston	2,239,558	Mayor-council	1905	1994
San Antonio	1,436,697	Council-manager	1914	1951
Dallas	1,281,047	Council-manager	1889	1907
Austin	912,791	Council-manager	1919	1994
Fort Worth	812,238	Council-manager	1924	1985
El Paso	679,036	Council-manager	1873	2004
Arlington	383,204	Council-manager	1920	1990
Corpus Christi	320,434	Council-manager	1926	1993
Plano	278,480	Council-manager	1961	1993
Laredo	252,309	Council-manager	1848	1911

SOURCES: Compiled from *Texas Almanac 2006–2007* (Dallas: Dallas Morning News, 2006), 340–64; *Texas Almanac 2008–2009* (Dallas: Dallas Morning News, 2008), 8; Texas State Data Center; www.citypopulation.de; City Charter of the City of Laredo as Amended (2010); City of El Paso website; U.S. Census Bureau, "State and County QuickFacts."

2014, Denton, Texas, was the home of 277 gas wells. Concerned about the effects of the fracking drilling technique used for gas production, nearly 59 percent of the voters in Denton passed an ordinance banning further fracking in the city. Immediately the petroleum industry sued the city over the ban, and the industry was joined in opposition to the ban by the Texas General Land Office. Within a year, Denton's city council was forced to repeal the ban when the legislature passed a law prohibiting cities from adopting such bans and when faced by more litigation from the oil and gas industry. In the brief lifetime of the Denton anti-fracking law, the city spent over $842,000 trying to defend the ordinance.[29]

Cities and towns of fewer than 5,000 people are chartered by general statute, as was the case for all cities and towns prior to the 1912 home-rule amendments. These "general-law" cities and towns may act or organize themselves only as explicitly permitted by statutory law passed by the state legislature. The constitution also limits what they can do. For example, general-law cities may levy, assess, and collect taxes as authorized by statute. But the constitution sets a maximum property tax rate of $1.50 per $100 valuation, compared with $2.50 per $100 valuation for home-rule cities.

Politics at the local level is often politics at its most basic. Unlike in presidential elections, in which the issues may well involve questions of war and peace, or state elections, which may involve issues such as whether a state should have an income tax, in local elections the most pressing issue may well be potholes in the city streets. Although pothole repair may not seem earthshaking in the hierarchy of political concerns, it is exactly such an issue that most directly and routinely affects most people's lives, and thus it becomes a prime issue for discussion among candidates. As mundane as such concerns are, these are the fundamental issues in most local elections because they reflect the needs and expectations that residents have of local government.

Forms of Government in Texas Cities

Texas home-rule cities have had three major forms of city government: the mayor-council form, the commissioner form, and the council-manager form. The **mayor-council form of government** is the oldest. It consists of an elected mayor and city council. The mayor is usually elected from the city in an **at-large election**. The council may be elected either at large or from a series of **single-member districts**, or a mixture of the two. In the mayor-council form of government, the mayor is the chief executive officer of the city. He or she presides over council meetings and has a variety of appointment powers. The city council, meanwhile, serves as the legislative body in the city, passing local laws and watching over the executive departments.

There have been both strong mayor–council systems and weak ones, depending on the powers given to the mayor by the city charter or state statute. In the *strong mayor–council* variation, various executive powers, such as appointive and removal powers to boards and departments or veto powers, are concentrated in the office of mayor. These powers enable the mayor to establish effective control over various executive departments in the city and to control the legislative agenda of the city council. In the *weak mayor–council* variation, these executive powers are much more limited, fragmenting power between the mayor and other elected or appointed

mayor-council form of government a form of city government in which the mayor is the chief executive and the city council is the legislative body; in the *strong mayor–council* variation, the mayor's powers enable him or her to control executive departments and the agenda of the city council; in the *weak mayor–council* variation, the mayor's power is more limited

at-large election an election in which officials are selected by voters of the entire geographical area, rather than from smaller districts within that area

single-member district an electorate that elects only one representative for each district

officials. Strong-mayor systems reflect a perspective that a strong executive should be in charge of city government. Additionally, supporters of strong mayors believed that city government would operate more efficiently with a strong executive in charge. In contrast, with a weak-mayor system, power is more diffuse, with city council members retaining a great deal of power and therefore giving a greater voice to the various constituencies represented by council members.[30]

In the 1990s the mayor-council form of government was the dominant form of government in most of the incorporated cities in Texas, particularly among general-law cities. However, among home-rule cities the mayor-council government was not popular. According to a 1995 survey of 284 home-rule cities conducted by the *Texas Almanac*, only 31 had adopted the mayor-council form of government.

A second form of city government is the **commissioner form of government**. Under the commissioner system, the city is run by a small commission, composed of between five and seven members generally elected at large. The commission acts in both a legislative and an executive capacity. As a group, commissioners enact laws for the city. Each commissioner is in charge of one of a variety of departments. One commissioner is also designated as the mayor to preside at meetings.

The commission plan was developed as a response to the devastating hurricane that hit Galveston in 1900, claiming an estimated 6,000 lives. In the aftermath of the hurricane, wealthy business leaders known as the Deep Water Committee became convinced that the incumbent city council was incapable of bringing about economic recovery for the city. They proposed as an alternative that the governor appoint a commission to govern the city during rebuilding, but opponents of the plan argued that appointed government was undemocratic and so the plan was modified so that two of the five commissioners would be elected. There were still court challenges to the idea of appointed commissioners, and in response, the state legislature made all five commissioners elected. The commission plan, which came to be known as the "Texas Idea," reflected a desire to bring good business practices to city government that would somehow escape the squabbles and inefficiency of traditional local government found in the mayor-council form. It was believed that commissioners with direct responsibility for operation of various departments of government would bring professional management to government.[31]

The commission plan was adopted by Houston in 1905 and by a number of other Texas cities in 1907, including Dallas, Fort Worth, and El Paso. Progressives across the country supported the plan and other reform principles often integrated with it, including nonpartisan elections, merit selection of employees, and such direct democracy techniques as the initiative, referendum, and recall. At its peak in 1918 the commission form was used by approximately 500 cities across the country and 75 cities in Texas. Following World War I, the number of commission-form cities decreased. By 2000 no city in Texas had a pure commission form of government, although 26 still claimed to have some variation of a commission-manager form of government.[32] In practice, none of the "commissioners" in these cities exercised executive control over specific city departments as envisioned in the original commission system. Instead, they functioned more like council members under the council-manager form of city government.[33]

Essentially the "Texas Idea" led to the third form of city government found in Texas, which is the **council-manager form of government**. The city manager replaced the commissioners because a single city manager provided the professional

---

commissioner form of government a form of city government in which the city is run by a small group of elected commissioners who act in both legislative and executive capacities

---

council-manager form of government a form of city government in which public policies are developed by the city council and executive and administrative functions are assigned to a professional city manager

The commissioner form of government was developed as a response to the devastating hurricane that hit Galveston in 1900.

management of city government without the squabbles and jurisdictional disputes that naturally occurred with the multiple managers of the various departments of government in the commission system.[34] As originally envisioned, a city council elected in at-large elections was to be the policy-making body. Council members generally received little or no pay and were intended to be publicly motivated citizens interested in serving the public good, rather than professional politicians. A mayor was selected from among the council members. The city manager was to be a professional public manager who served as the chief executive and administrative official in the city. As in the commissioner form of government, the goal of the council-manager form of government was twofold: to free local government from the seamier side of politics and to bring administrative expertise to local government.

In 1913, Amarillo was the first city to abandon the commissioner form of government for the council-manager system. In 1914, Taylor and Denton followed suit. By 1947 there were 47 council-manager systems in Texas. By the mid-1990s, 251 of the home-rule cities had council-manager systems. Across the United States, it has become the most popular form of government for cities of over 10,000 residents.[35]

Today, council-manager systems vary across the state in a number of ways. The desire for professional administration of local government remains high. Most city managers have graduate degrees and are paid high salaries like other executive officers in the private sector. But a desire for more political accountability through traditional democratic processes has introduced some changes. The growing ethnic and racial diversity of some Texas cities has forced many political leaders to question the wisdom of freeing local government too much from democratic controls. In most cities, mayors now are elected at large from the population as a whole, rather than only from the council. Many cities also elect council members from single-member districts rather than only from at-large districts. Many see at-large districts as undercutting minority representation by diluting minority votes. Only when Dallas moved from an at-large council to a council elected from single-member districts in 1991 did minorities come to play a major role in the decision-making processes of city government. But most cities and towns under the council-manager system continue to view local political offices as part-time jobs. Mayoral and council salaries remain low, although a few cities, such as Austin, offer considerably higher salaries. The demand for more democratic accountability in local government will likely continue to lead to more changes in the council-manager system of government across Texas. Balancing an efficient city government run by professionals with democratic political processes will continue to be a problem as Texas's metropolitan areas grow and diversify in the early twenty-first century.

A Tale of Five Cities

Houston Houston is the largest city in Texas, with over 2.2 million people. It has a strong mayor–council form of government. There are 16 elected officials in the city serving concurrent four-year terms, including a mayor, a controller, and 16 council members. The mayor serves as the chief executive official in the city and is the city's chief administrator and official representative. Much of the mayor's power stems from the authority to appoint department heads and people serving on advisory boards, subject to council approval. The mayor also presides over the city council with voting privileges. The 16-member council is a legislative body composed of five at-large seats and eleven single-member district seats.

Unlike in most other cities, the city controller in Houston is an elected official.[36] The city controller is the city's chief financial officer. Besides investing city funds, conducting internal audits of city departments, and operating the city's financial management system, the controller is also responsible for certifying the availability of funds for city council initiatives. In the end, the office of the controller is both a professional position and a political position. Not surprisingly, the controller often comes into conflict with the mayor and the council over important policy issues.

Although local politics in Houston is nominally nonpartisan, in recent years it has taken on a partisan flavor. Houston's current mayor is Sylvester Turner, who serves as executive officer of the city. He is a well-known Democrat who had previously served in the Texas legislature for 26 years and had major responsibilities for the state's budget while in that position. Turner had unsuccessfully sought the mayor's office in 1991 and in 2003. He is the second African American to serve as Houston's mayor.

San Antonio San Antonio has overtaken Dallas as the second-largest city in Texas. San Antonio has a council-manager form of government. The council is composed of members elected from 10 single-member districts on a nonpartisan basis. The mayor, Ivy R. Taylor, is the 11th member of the council and is selected at large. All members of the council serve for two-year terms and until May 2015 received largely honorific salaries. Until an election in May that amended the city charter, the mayor's salary was a paltry $4,040 per year and other council members were paid $20 per meeting, not to exceed $1,040 per year. Recognizing that service as an elected official in the

Houston's "Bathroom Ordinance"

Texas municipal governments may pass local laws known as ordinances which govern behavior within the city limits. These ordinances are numerous and vary somewhat from city to city. Rarely do these ordinances generate much controversy, because their scope tends to be limited. For example, because of the great noise produced by large trucks that use a braking system known as "jake brakes," many cities ban the use of this type of braking within the city limits. Other types of ordinances include animal control laws such as Baytown's ban on keeping or maintaining hogs in the city limits or Tomball's requirement that tow trucks only charge fees approved by the city council for tows where the vehicle owner does not consent to the tow.

Houston, however, held a referendum on an antidiscrimination ordinance in November 2015 that gained national attention and was one of the most bitter and costly local elections in Texas history. Texas is one of 28 states with no statewide laws prohibiting discrimination based on sexual orientation or gender identity. In the absence of a state law, Houston's proposed ordinance would have prohibited bias in city housing, employment, city contracting, and business services for a number of classifications including race, age, sexual orientation, and gender identity. The core of the political argument surrounding the ordinance was the ban on discrimination based on sexual orientation and gender identity.

Opponents reframed the political debate from one of civil rights for gay and transgendered persons to a claim that the law would allow sexual predators in women's bathrooms. Signs reading, "No Men in Women's Bathrooms" were displayed outside polling places and television ads showed a young girl being followed into a bathroom stall by an older man.[a] Opponents of the ordinance included Governor Greg Abbott and Lieutenant Governor Dan Patrick, who used the bathroom argument to support their position. Megachurches from the Houston area and former Houston Astros star Lance Berkman were strong opponents of the ordinance as well.[b] Governor Abbott attempted to tie the issue into presidential politics when he tweeted, "HOUSTON: Vote Texas values, not Hillary Clinton values. Vote NO on City of Houston Proposition 1. No men in women's bathrooms."

Supporters of the ordinance included Houston's then-mayor Annise Parker, who had been elected as the first openly gay mayor of a U.S. city and who argued that passage of the ordinance would show that "Houston does not discriminate."[c] Groups such as Equality Texas, the ACLU, and the Human Rights Campaign also strongly supported the ordinance. Actress Sally Field was a well-

known celebrity supporter of the ordinance. Hillary Clinton, President Obama, Vice President Biden, actors Eva Longoria, Jesse Tyler Ferguson, and Matthew Morrison, and football player Michael Sam used social media to show their support for the ordinance. Matt Bomer, another actor, released a video calling on Houstonians to vote "yes," saying, "I was raised with the belief that everyone deserves to be treated equally. These are the same values I grew up with in Houston and they're the same values that I try to teach my kids."[d]

The ordinance, however, failed overwhelmingly by a 61 percent to 39 percent margin in November 2015.

COMMUNICATING EFFECTIVELY: YOUR VOICE

- Should cities' lawmaking powers be limited to local concerns such as traffic or animal control issues, rather than broader issues such as antidiscrimination laws?

- Why do you think the Houston bathroom ordinance failed? What arguments do you think the "pro" side should have made in order to persuade more people?

Pictured here are the mayors of Texas's two largest cities. Sylvester Turner (left) is the current mayor of Houston. Prior to being elected mayor in the closest mayoral election in Houston history, he served in the Texas State House from 1989 to 2016. San Antonio mayor Ivy R. Taylor (right) was chosen in a special election by the city council in 2014 to replace former mayor Julian Castro, who was appointed to the position of secretary of Housing and Urban Development in the Obama administration.

second-largest city in Texas had become a full-time job, salaries for council members were raised to $45,722 a year and the salary for the mayor was raised to $61,725 a year. This charter amendment was approved by 54.8 percent of the voters. Members are subject to recall if 10 percent of the qualified voters in a district sign a petition of recall and a recall election is successful. The city charter also provides for initiatives and referendums that emerge from the voters.

The city manager in San Antonio serves at the pleasure of the council as the chief executive and administrative official in the city. He or she has wide-ranging appointment and removal authority over officers and employees in the administrative service of the city. The current city manager is Sheryl Sculley. Prior to becoming city manager, she was assistant city manager of Phoenix. She supervises the activities of all city departments, a budget of $2.4 billion, and 12,000 employees. Indicative of the city manager's central role in running the city is her salary, which in 2015 was $400,000 plus a $65,000 bonus.

Dallas Dallas also operates under a council-manager form of government. For years, city politics had been dominated by the white business community. At-large nonpartisan elections tended to elect a council that was relatively united in its understanding of the problems facing the city and its vision of where the city should go. A bitter struggle in the late 1980s and early 1990s over rewriting the city charter divided the city along racial lines. The new charter, which went into effect in 1991, called for a 14-member council elected from single-member districts and a mayor elected at large. Members are limited to serving four 2-year terms consecutively. Under the new charter, membership on the council was transformed as a significant number of African Americans and Latinos were elected to the council.

As in other council-manager systems, the power of the mayor in Dallas is weak. The mayor—currently Mike Rawlings—presides over council meetings, creates council committees, and appoints members, chairs, and co-chairs. In many ways, however,

the mayor is only first among equals on the council. The council as a whole is the legislative body for the city, approving budgets, determining the tax rate, and appointing key public officials, including the city manager, city attorney, city auditor, city secretary, municipal court judges, and various citizen boards and commissions. The city manager serves at the will of the council and is removable by a two-thirds vote of the council. As in San Antonio, the city manager's powers in Dallas are great. As the chief administrative officer, the city manager has the power to appoint and remove all heads of departments and subordinate officers and employees in the city, subject to civil service provisions. Despite the attempt to remove the city manager from the pressures of political life in Dallas, recent city managers have found themselves forced to accommodate the reality of an increasingly politicized city council. The political pressures emerging from Dallas's single-member district council may ultimately compel the city to reexamine the wisdom of retaining a council-manager system. As Dallas learned in the 1990s, efficient government and democratic governance are not as easy to balance as advocates of the council-manager system once thought.

One illustration of the push for change is that in 2001–02, each of the three major candidates for mayor suggested that the structure of city government needed reexamining. One of the mayoral candidates publicly commented on the need for more power to be in the hands of the mayor. A city council member argued that council members have so little power to set spending priorities or influence city staff that individual citizens do not see city government as a way to influence their lives. There has even been some discussion of the value of partisan elections in city races.

Austin Austin is the 11th most populous city in the United States and the 4th most populous city in Texas. It is the county seat of Travis County and is the state capital.

Austin's mayor, Democrat Steve Adler, speaks at a celebration of same-sex marriage rights at a church in Austin.

In the November 2012 elections, Austinites adopted a plan by more than a 60 percent margin to change the method for selecting members of the city council. The system had been a mayor and a six-member city council. All seven of the officials were elected citywide. A city manager then served as chief administrative officer of the city. Austin continues to have a city manager; however, as of 2014 only the mayor is elected citywide. The 10 city council members are elected from single-member districts. Until this change, Austin was unusual in that it was the largest city in the United States that lacked a city council where at least some of the members were elected from geographic districts.[37]

Over the past 40 years, Austin voters had rejected district plans six times. This time, however, there was a strong grassroots movement favoring the 10-district plan with support from a broad coalition of groups such as the Travis County Republican Party and Hispanic groups. One important reason for the success of the proposal was that the issue appeared on the November ballot when there was a larger and more diverse group of voters than in the prior six elections. Past district plans were submitted in elections when turnout was less than the November turnout.

A peculiar characteristic of the election was that another proposal was on the ballot, which had been submitted by the mayor and city council, that provided for eight city council seats to be elected through single-member districts, with the mayor and two other council seats to be elected citywide. Critics of that proposal claimed that the city council put that proposal on the ballot to confuse voters and keep the status quo by dooming both plans to failure. That proposal also gained a majority of the voters with about 51 percent approving. However, since the 10-district plan got about 60 percent of the vote, it was the proposal that was implemented.

The proposal required that the districts be drawn by a commission of citizens chosen through an application process that was overseen by the city auditor. The first elections under the new system were in 2014.[38]

El Paso El Paso, located in the far western part of the state, has a council-manager form of government with eight city council members chosen by single-member districts and a mayor who is elected at large. The mayor and council are elected in nonpartisan elections. The city manager, Tommy Gonzalez, reports to the elected mayor and city council.

Home to over 679,000 people, El Paso is on the border with Mexico, which makes the city a center for international trade. The military is also important to the El Paso economy because of the presence of Fort Bliss. El Paso has only a tiny African American population. In 2010 only 3.4 percent of the city's population was African American—far smaller than the proportion of African Americans statewide. However, 80.7 percent of the city's population is Latino, far larger than the overall proportion of Latinos in Texas.

The main problem facing El Paso is its poverty. The U.S. Census reports that 21.5 percent of its population is in poverty compared with 17.2 percent of the state as a whole. Median household income is $42,037 compared with $52,576 in Texas as a whole. The per capita income in El Paso is $20,050 compared with $26,513 statewide.[39]

Who Governs Texas's Cities?

Racial and Ethnic Composition of Texas's Major Cities and Their City Councils

● White ● African American ● Latino ● Other

Houston

City pop. — 25.6% 23.7% 43.8% 6.8%

Council — 56% 25% 12.5% 6.3%

Houston has an African American mayor and 16 city council members, 5 of whom are elected at large and 11 elected in single-member districts. Four of the five at-large members of the council are white.

San Antonio

City pop. — 26.6% 6.9% 63.2% 3.4%

Council — 30% 10% 60%

San Antonio has an African American mayor and a city council of 10 elected from single-member districts.

Dallas

City pop. — 28.8% 25% 42.4% 3.6%

Council — 57% 29% 14%

Dallas has a white mayor and 14 council members elected from single-member districts.

Austin

City pop. — 48.7% 8.1% 35.1% 7.3%

Council — 60% 10% 30%

Austin has a white mayor and 10 council members elected from single-member districts.

El Paso

City pop. — 14.2% 3.4% 80.7% 2%

Council — 25% 12.5% 62.5%

El Paso has a Latino mayor, and its eight city council members are elected from single-member districts.

Representation is an important issue at all levels of government. Who's in power can have a profound impact on what policies are enacted. A snapshot of representation at the municipal level raises critical questions: Can a community be properly represented when its elected officials do not reflect the racial and ethnic characteristics of the community? For example, does it make a difference that the city of Dallas city council is 14 percent Latino while the Dallas population is 42.4 percent Latino? Whom are the elected officials representing? Is it the population as a whole or the people who vote?

QUANTITATIVE REASONING

- Of these major Texas cities, which city council best reflects the racial/ethnic composition of its population? Which council diverges most from its city's racial/ethnic composition?

- Do you think it is important that the city councils do reflect the racial/ethnic composition of their communities? Why or why not?

SOURCES: Data for city councils are from 2016, taken from each city's website; city populations are from 2014 Census data.

Poverty and unemployment plague El Paso, and the city is trying to attract more jobs by developing the downtown area.

What El Paso desperately needs are well-paying jobs. This explains the strong efforts being made by city government to attract business to El Paso and to make it easier to conduct business in the city.

Special Districts

Examine the role of special districts in Texas government

special district a unit of local government that performs a single service, such as education or sanitation, within a limited geographic area

A **special district** is a unit of local government that performs a single service in a limited geographic area. These governments can solve problems that cross borders of existing units of government. Special districts can be created to serve an entire county, part of a county, all of two or more counties, or parts of two or more counties. The number of special districts has increased dramatically in the last 50 years. In the United States, the number increased by 400 percent.[40] In Texas, the number increased by more than 600 percent.[41] By the year 2002 there were more special districts than any other form of local government. There are now 2,309 special districts in Texas, not including school districts.[42]

Districts can be created to do almost anything that is legal. Some districts are formed to provide hospital care, others to furnish pure water to communities, still others to provide mosquito control—Texas has 13 mosquito control special districts[43]—navigation, flood control, sanitation, drainage, fire protection, ambulance services, and law enforcement. Some special districts can be very large—one, for example,

How Extensive Are Texas's Local Governments?

Number of Local Governments in Each State, 2012

Number of local governments

	Number of local governments (per 100,000 people)
6,963	Illinois 54
5,147	Texas 20
4,425	California 12
3,842	Ohio 33
3,453	New York 18

	Total local govs.	Per 100K people		Total local govs.	Per 100K people		Total local govs.	Per 100K people		Total local govs.	Per 100K people		Total local govs.	Per 100K people
IL	6,963	54	CO	2,905	56	AK	1,556	53	TN	916	14	UT	622	22
TX	5,147	20	MI	2,875	29	OR	1,542	40	NM	863	41	NH	541	41
PA	4,897	38	IN	2,709	41	GA	1,378	14	MA	857	13	LA	529	12
CA	4,425	12	ND	2,685	384	NJ	1,344	15	ME	840	63	VA	518	6
OH	3,842	33	NE	2,581	139	KY	1,338	31	WY	805	140	MD	347	6
KS	3,826	133	SD	1,983	238	MT	1,265	126	VT	738	118	DE	339	37
MO	3,768	63	IA	1,947	63	AL	1,208	25	SC	678	14	NV	191	7
MN	3,672	68	WA	1,900	28	ID	1,168	73	AZ	674	10	AK	177	24
NY	3,453	18	OK	1,852	49	MS	983	33	WV	659	36	RI	133	13
WI	3,128	55	FL	1,650	9	NC	973	10	CT	643	18	HI	21	2

Local governments include county governments, school board districts, special districts, and municipal utility districts. One would expect that Texas's political culture would lead it to have fewer local governments than other states with traditions of more governmental involvement. Is this the case?

NOTE: Different sources provide different numbers of local governments, but Texas does have somewhat more than 4,800 local governments.

SOURCE: Governing, "Number of Local Governments by State." www.governing.com (accessed 7/21/16).

CRITICAL THINKING

- What are some of the characteristics of states with large numbers of local governments?
- Does the picture change when we factor in population? Which states have larger numbers of local governments per capita? What might explain these differences?

manages Houston's two hospitals for the poor and uninsured and collects well over $500 million in property taxes every year. On the other hand, the North Fort Worth Water Control and Improvement District No. 1 collected a total of $85 in property taxes from its constituents.[44]

Types of Special Districts

school district a specific type of special district that provides public education in a designated area

There are two types of special districts in Texas. The first is the **school district**, which consists of independent school districts in the state. These districts offer public education from pre-kindergarten through 12th grade. Almost all school districts offer the full range of educational opportunities; however, some small, rural schools provide education only through the 8th grade. Others limit their programs to the 6th grade, and still others end with the 4th grade. Those with limited offerings contract with nearby districts to complete the education of their students.

nonschool special district any special district other than a school district; examples include municipal utility districts (MUDs) and hospital districts

The second classification of special districts is the **nonschool special district**. Everything except the school districts is included in this category. Municipal utility districts, economic development corporations, hospital districts, and fire-prevention districts are the most common examples.

In addition to county taxes, for example, a property owner in Upshur County, Texas, will pay taxes to two special districts—the Union Grove Independent School District and the Emergency Services District No. 1 (fire protection). A property owner in Hopkins County, Texas, will pay to the Sulphur Springs Independent School District and to the Hopkins County Hospital District. A property owner in Collin County, Texas, will pay taxes to the Plano Independent School District and to the Collin College special district. One property owner in Houston pays taxes to the Houston Independent School District, the Harris County Department of Education, the Harris County Flood Control District, the Port of Houston Authority, the Harris County Hospital District, the Lone Star College System, Emergency Service District No. 13 (fire protection), and Emergency Service District No. 11 (EMS).

School Districts

Every inch of land in Texas is part of a school district, and the state contains 1,265 school districts. Some districts in east and west Texas cover an entire county. In metropolitan counties, there may be a dozen or more districts. Each is governed by an elected board of trustees composed of five to nine members. The board employs a superintendent to oversee the daily operation of the district. On the recommendation of the superintendent, the trustees

- set overall policy for the school district.
- adopt the budget for the district.
- set the tax rate for the district. (The maximum tax rate for a district is $1.04 for each $100 the property is worth. A rate higher than $1.04 requires voter approval.)
- select textbooks for classroom use.

- hire principals, faculty, and support staff.
- set the school calendar.
- determine salaries and benefits for employees.

Educating millions of students is a daunting task. By localizing public education, the state places much of the burden on the local school districts. This allows local residents to participate in governing the school districts. Unfortunately, few people vote in the elections to select members of the board of trustees. Even fewer individuals attend meetings of the school board.

Nonschool Special Districts

There are a vast number of types of special districts. Larger counties tend to have many different special districts. Dallas County, for example, has 13 nonschool special districts. Harris County is the record-holder for special districts in Texas. It contains a total of 436 nonschool special districts. Some of the most common are as follows.[45]

Municipal Utility Districts Municipal utility districts (MUDs) offer electricity, water, sewer, and sanitation services outside the city limits. These governments might offer all utility services or only one or two, depending on the needs of the special district. Though MUDs are located throughout Texas, the vast majority are found in the Houston greater metropolitan area.

MUDs can be a financial blessing for developers. Entrepreneurs who build housing additions outside the city limits must furnish utilities to the homes they build, but few developers can afford to do this over a long period of time.

Banks and finance companies, legislators, and land developers maintain a warm and snug relationship with each other. Banks and finance companies willingly lend land developers millions of dollars to establish residential subdivisions, build new homes, and run water and sewer services to these houses. When a few houses are sold, the developer asks the residents to establish a MUD. Enabling the legislation is seldom a problem because of the close relationship between developers and local legislators.

Once the MUD is up and running, the board of directors sets a tax rate and determines how much to charge residents for its services. One of its first activities is to borrow money by issuing bonds (interest-bearing financial instruments that are sold in financial markets to fund government projects). The bond proceeds are used to purchase the utilities from the developer, often at a premium. Using the proceeds from the sale of the utilities, the developer is able to repay loans. By establishing the MUD, residents agree to pay a property tax to retire the bonded indebtedness. In addition to the property tax, residents pay a monthly fee for the water, sewer, and sanitation services.

Community College Districts Community college districts are classified as nonschool special districts because they do not offer public education from prekindergarten through 12th grade. Community colleges offer postsecondary academic and vocational programs. They are governed by an elected board of regents. Residents of the district pay a property tax to the district. In return, residents pay lower tuition. The board employs a president or chancellor, who operates the college on a daily basis.

municipal utility district (MUD) a special district that offers services such as electricity, water, sewage, and sanitation outside the city limits

The regents set policy on the recommendation of the president or chancellor. Among the regents' responsibilities are to

- set overall policy for the district.
- set the tax rate.
- set the cost of tuition and fees.
- build new buildings and repair older ones.
- hire teachers, counselors, administrators, and nonprofessional staff.
- set the school calendar.
- determine salaries and benefits for employees.

Hospital, Emergency Services, and Flood Control Districts

A number of counties have hospital districts that serve the poor and uninsured. These districts may collect payments from patients and government programs such as Medicaid for medical services, although it is necessary to supplement the costs of indigent medical care through the creation of hospital districts with taxing authority. Emergency services districts provide fire and ambulance services to areas not served otherwise. The districts can be of varying size—Harris County has more than 30 emergency services districts, though most counties in Texas would contain only one or two such districts. A rural county, Delta County, for example, has only one emergency services district.[46] Flooding is seldom confined to a single county. Flood control districts are established to solve a multicounty problem.

Creating, Governing, and Paying for a Special District

Special districts are created by voters of the area to be served. Creating a special district requires

- a petition signed by the residents of the area to be served, requesting the legislature to authorize an election to create a special district.
- enabling legislation in the form of a law that authorizes a special election to create the district.
- a majority positive vote of those voting in the special election.

Most special districts are governed by boards elected by the voters of the district. The board of a school district is called the board of trustees, the governing board of a community college is often called the board of regents, and the governing boards of other special districts are usually known as boards of directors. Each board is the policy-making group for its district. The directors set the tax rate and establish rules and policy for the operation of the district. The district often employs an individual who runs the district on a day-to-day basis. **Property taxes** are the primary source of revenue for special districts. This was not always the case. In 1949 school districts received 80 percent of their income from the state, and the school district furnished 20 percent of necessary funds, primarily from property taxes. Today, property taxes constitute as much as 90 percent of revenues for some districts. The second-largest source of income is **user fees**. State and federal aid furnish the remainder of special district funding.

Property tax rates and actual user fees are set by governing boards. User fees are raised from providing goods and services. Water districts, for example, sell water, sewer, and possibly sanitation services.

property tax a tax based on an assessment of the value of one's property, which is used to fund the services provided by local governments, such as education

user fee a fee paid for public goods and services, such as water or sewage service

Hospital districts set fees for room occupancy, medicine dispensed, use of surgical suites, X-rays taken and evaluated, nursing and laboratory service, and myriad other charges. The board of trustees of a school district sets the local property rate for taxes, which fund pre-kindergarten through 12th grade education. Tuition paid by in-district and out-of-district students, building fees, student fees, and technology and lab fees are determined by the board of regents of a community college district.

Problems with Special Districts

Hidden Governments Everyone in Texas lives in at least one special district, their school district. Most people live in several, have the opportunity to vote for people to represent them on the governing board of each district, and pay property taxes to these agencies of government. Yet few people are aware these agencies exist, thus their reputation as "**hidden governments.**"

Special districts provide needed services in specific geographic areas. Existing governments may lack authority to provide the service or the necessary funds to finance the project. In theory, special districts are an example of democracy at work. Districts are created by a vote of the residents of the area to be served, and the districts' governing boards are elected by the voters. Board meetings, at which decisions on policy, taxing, and fees are made, are open for attendance by any interested residents. However, fewer than 10 percent of eligible voters cast ballots in special district elections, and fewer than 1 percent of district residents ever attend a board meeting.

hidden government a term that refers to special districts of which many citizens are unaware

Abuses of Power There is a potential for abuse in the creation of special districts. Many special districts were originally authorized by the Texas legislature to develop the economies of poor, rural counties. More recently, however, developers of large tracts of land began creating these districts to place the burden of developing the property's infrastructure on future owners of the property. In order to comply with the law, all the developers must do is create the district and hold an election where at least one short-term resident must vote. These short-term residents then approve bonds in the millions of dollars that must be paid for with the taxation of future homes and property owners. In the 1980s this kind of special district creation in Harris County led to defaults on bond issues after a housing bust.

In 2001 a major investigation of special districts created by developers in Dallas found unusual and questionable practices. Some developers drew district boundaries to exclude existing residents of an area. The developers then moved people into rent-free mobile homes shortly before the special district election. These newly established "residents" were the only ones eligible to vote in the election. After the election, the voters for the new district would often move away after approving large bond sales for the construction of roads, water lines, and sewers. Future homeowners in the area were then expected to pay for the bonds with property taxes on their homes. The investigation found that sometimes a single voter—and always fewer than 10 voters—approved the bonded indebtedness that helped the developers create an infrastructure for their properties. In the Lantana subdivision near Flower Mound, for example, a family of three voted to authorize $277 million in bond sales by two water districts. That bond proposition rivals the biggest bond proposals by the city of Dallas.[47]

The creation of special districts by real estate developers has sometimes been controversial. Recent investigations have charged developers with abusing the process in order to circumvent inconvenient laws and to give the developers greater control over taxes and other government functions in the district.

Similar schemes have been especially prevalent in Travis, Harris, and Denton counties. In 2006 developers in Denton County housed six people at below-market rents on property to be developed. These temporary residents were thus eligible to vote in a special tax-district election that would affect the taxation of thousands of future homeowners.[48]

In 2010 two voters in the Four Seasons Ranch Municipal Utility District No. 1 approved $292.5 million in bonds, including $138.5 million in bonds for water, sewer, and storm sewer systems and $154 million in roads. Recent special district elections near the Four Seasons Ranch district in Denton and Collin counties have authorized close to $1 billion in public debt.[49] One danger is that development will not proceed as planned in the areas covered by these special districts and the result will be either exceptionally high charges to existing homeowners to cover the debt of these special districts or bankruptcy of the special districts where the holders of the bonds lose all or part of their investment. One such example occurred in the Grimes County Municipal Utility District No. 1, which defaulted on its $1.86 million water and sewer revenue bonds. The district could not hope to make payments on the bonds when it ended up providing services to only three customers.[50]

PERSONAL RESPONSIBILITY: WHAT WOULD YOU DO?

- Why are there so many special districts in Texas? Do you feel cities and counties should do the jobs that special districts do? Why don't they?

- Do you think cities and counties should more closely monitor the activities of special districts? Who do you think should be in charge of that oversight?

The pervasiveness of special districts is shown by one study of Texas special districts that addresses water issues. The study found that about 1,000 MUDs were engaged in supplying water; 48 special districts existed to deal with water drainage issues; 66 special districts existed solely to supply fresh water. Others had these purposes: 91 to conserve groundwater, 25 for irrigation, 46 to improve levees, 42 to manage municipal water, 26 to deal with navigation, 31 to deal with rivers. Fifty-five special utility districts dealt with general water issues; 221 were water control and improvement districts; and 18 were water improvement districts. Of course, this hodgepodge of special districts dealing with all aspects of water makes a coherent approach to statewide water policy virtually impossible.[51]

Special districts are among the least-studied areas of Texas politics, but their use as an instrument of private gain and their use by developers as a way to minimize their financial risks suggest the need for much greater scrutiny. Of course, developers may defend this system as a way to improve property and enhance the tax base of communities. On the other hand, the extent of enlistment of governmental taxing powers with little public scrutiny or accountability is disturbing. And if the huge bond issues floated by these entities default, thousands of people could suffer the financial consequences.

Councils of Government (COGs)

The Regional Planning Act of 1965 initially provided for the creation of regional **councils of government (COGs)** to promote coordination and planning across all local governments in a particular region. Councils of government are not special districts, as they do not tax or impose user fees. Still, they play an important role at the local level in providing planning and coordination across numerous local government boundaries. Projects such as major water, airport, or highway projects involve many local governments, and councils are necessary to work across these many local entities.

There are 24 regional councils in Texas today, each with its own bylaws or articles of agreement. The governing body of a regional council must consist of at least two-thirds of local elected officials of cities and counties and may include citizen members and representatives of other groups. Figure 10.2 provides a map and listing of the 24 regional COGs in Texas.

council of government (COG)
a regional planning board composed of local elected officials and some private citizens from the same area

FIGURE 10.2

Regional Councils of Government in Texas

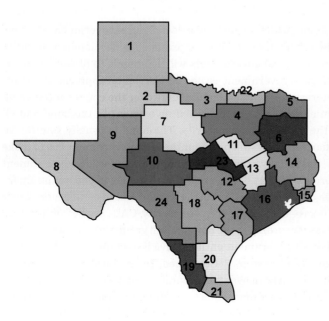

Region Name	Number
Alamo Area Council of Governments	18
Ark-Tex Council of Governments	5
Brazos Valley Council of Governments	13
Capital Area Council of Governments	12
Central Texas Council of Governments	23
Coastal Bend Council of Governments	20
Concho Valley Council of Governments	10
Deep East Texas Council of Governments	14
East Texas Council of Governments	6
Golden Crescent Regional Planning Commission	17
Heart of Texas Council of Governments	11
Houston-Galveston Area Council	16
Lower Rio Grande Valley Development Council	21
Middle Rio Grande Development Council	24
Nortex Regional Planning Commission	3
North Central Texas Council of Governments	4
Panhandle Regional Planning Commission	1
Permian Basin Regional Planning Commission	9
Rio Grande Council of Governments	8
South East Texas Regional Planning Commission	15
South Plains Association of Governments	2
South Texas Development Council	19
Texoma Council of Governments	22
West Central Texas Council of Governments	7

The basic responsibilities of regional councils include planning for the economic development of an area, helping local governments carry out regional projects, contracting with local governments to provide certain services, and reviewing applications for state and federal financial assistance. Originally, COGs focused considerable attention on meeting federal mandates for water and sewer provision, open space, and housing planning. More recently, activities have focused on comprehensive planning and service delivery in such policy areas as aging, employment and training, criminal justice, economic development, environmental quality, and transportation.[52]

Financial Issues Facing Local Government

 Examine the financial problems facing local government

As noted earlier, there are many different forms of local government in Texas, including county governments, municipal governments, school districts, and special districts. These governments manage money through special financial mechanisms based on their ability to tax. Among these financial mechanisms are capital appreciation bonds and local government pensions. Both raise important opportunities and problems for local government.

Capital Appreciation Bonds

capital appreciation bond (CAB) a long-term, high-interest-paying bond that pays off both principal and interest in one lump sum when the bond reaches maturity

A **capital appreciation bond (CAB)** is a method by which local governments borrow money. Its main use is by school districts to raise revenue for development in times of rapid population growth.[53] Local governments will sell bonds to obtain funds for projects, but unlike traditional government-issued bonds, capital appreciation bonds do not make periodic interest payments to bondholders over the course of the bond; instead, the local government pays back the initial investment in the bond and all accrued interest when the bond reaches maturity. The bond is usually sold for an amount that is far less than the lump sum payment the local government has to make when the bond matures. Essentially, this type of bond is a way for local government to get money now for a promise to pay back a great deal of money in one lump sum far into the future. This type of bond has been causing a great deal of controversy, especially in California and Texas—but despite the controversy, CABs are becoming more and more common in Texas. According to the nonpartisan group California Watch, "in Texas, 590 districts and other government entities have issued these bonds over the past six years—more than any other state."[54] Combined, Texas's local governments issued more than $2.3 billion in CABs in over 700 separate issuances between 2007 and 2011—debts that will eventually cost more than $20 billion to repay.[55] The per capita debt of Texas's state government ranks 45th in the nation. However, when local debt is taken into consideration, it jumps to the 15th highest.[56]

CABs are extremely long-term bonds. In many cases they do not have to be paid by the local government until 40 years after they are issued.[57] During this entire time period, the issuer does not have to pay a dime to investors—meaning that local government officials can promise new education facilities to voters without raising taxes.[58] CABs also tend to pay high interest to bond investors.

An analysis of the numbers provided by the *Austin American-Statesman* shows that Texas municipalities will owe, on average, nearly $9 for every $1 they have borrowed using CABs.[59] In extreme cases, the ratio of money owed to money borrowed can reach 35 to 1.[60] As with most municipal bonds, the interest accrued by capital appreciation bonds is tax exempt. Essentially what this all means is that the debt burden facing local government is considerably more than is found on the books.

The dilemma of entities that use these bonds is well illustrated by the Anna Independent School District in Collin County. State law caps the school district tax rate on property, which is the primary funding source for public schools. Anna was undergoing tremendous growth as it was a rural school district that was becoming a suburban school district as the Dallas metropolitan area grew to the north. In 2002–03, Anna Independent School District had about 1,000 students; in 2012–13, it had about 2,500 students. By issuing CABs, Anna could build schools for its rapid growth, but regular interest payments over the course of the bond are not required as they would be by traditional bonds. Additionally CABs do not count against the state cap on property taxes until the payment is due many years later. The state cap requires that when school bonds are issued, they must be paid back at a tax rate that is not greater than 50 cents per $100 of assessed property value. In 2008, Anna had reached the 50-cent limit, which offered no additional bond funding unless CABs were used. When these bonds are repaid, Anna's taxpayers will have to pay back about five times the amount borrowed, but in the meantime Anna's schools can deal with the district's burgeoning growth.[61]

Over the next 40 years, California municipalities will have to pay back a combined $36 billion of CAB debt—on average 3.89 times as much as they borrowed.[62] The California State Assembly recently passed a measure placing new restrictions on CABs, including a maximum length of 25 years on the bond and a requirement that the debt owed can be no more than four times the amount borrowed.[63] In Michigan, legislators have already taken more direct measures—they banned CABs outright in 1994.[64] Texas has not passed restriction on these bonds, and under the current bond financing structure CABs may be the only way that school districts can obtain the funding to pay for rapid growth, but the incautious use of CABs could have dire consequences for local government finances.

Local Government Pensions

Another area of concern with local government involves the cost and financial health of pension plans. Several municipal bankruptcies throughout the United States in the summer of 2012 brought attention to the instability of a number of state and local public pension plans. California cities have been particularly hard hit by the cost of local pensions. For example, in 2012, San Bernardino, California, failed to make a payment on $1 million in bonds that it had issued to support pensions. Two California cities claimed that their local employee pension costs were a major factor in their declarations of bankruptcy.[65]

Texas has 81 different local governmental pension plans that cover nearly 184,000 persons and that have net assets of over $28 billion. Unfortunately, not all these pension plans have sufficient funds to meet their obligations to pay retirees.

Houston's city workers have three major pension systems—the Houston Police Officers Pension System, the Houston Firefighters' Relief and Retirement Fund, and the Houston Municipal Employees Pension System. Houston expects its contributions to pensions will rise to 17.1 percent of all city expenditures by 2017.[66] The city's pension costs in 2015 for the Firefighters' Relief and Retirement Fund were 34 percent of the Fire Department's annual payroll.[67] Bill King, the second-place finisher for mayor of Houston in the 2015 election, claimed that if the problem with Houston's city employee pensions was not fixed, "it's game over" for city finances.[68]

Fort Worth's Employees' Retirement Fund began having serious funding issues in the 1990s when the city's contributions to the fund were decreased while plan benefits were increased. Additionally, investment returns to the fund were wiped out in the 2008 Great Recession. In 2011, Fort Worth's pension problems led to a reduction in benefits for new hires other than public safety workers that included increases in the minimum retirement age, reduction of the multiplier used to calculate benefits, elimination of cost-of-living adjustments, and removal of overtime earnings from benefit calculations. In spite of these reductions, Fort Worth's funding of its pension system remains inadequate.[69]

Probably the most extreme example in Texas of a failing pension system is the Dallas Police and Fire Pension System. Its problems are so severe that Dallas is considering immediate and drastic reforms to the system. Due to overly generous benefits and remarkably poor management, pension benefits for Dallas police officers and firefighters are at risk. According to one accounting of the fund, it has $3 billion in assets and $8 billion in liabilities and will be broke in 15 years. One reason is that pensioners in the fund get an automatic 4 percent cost of living increase. Given low inflation and the fund's low returns on investments, such an increase is not sustainable. Another problem with the fund is the **deferred retirement option plan (DROP)**. Dallas police and firefighter base salaries are low in comparison to those of Fort Worth and neighboring suburbs, and since police and firefighters can retire after 20 years of service, the DROP plan was created in 1993 to discourage them from leaving employment after only two decades. Under the plan, if a 20-year veteran chose to stop contributing to the pension plan and entered DROP, it was as if the police officer or firefighter had retired, but that person could continue working. Instead of receiving pension checks, the checks would be deposited in a DROP account which then paid between 8 percent and 10 percent interest. As a result, the average DROP account has $422,000 in it; 1 person has $3 million in their account; 13 others have over $2 million in their accounts, and 283 have more than $1 million. That return on their

deferred retirement option plan (DROP) retirement plan in which local government employees who are eligible to retire have their retirement benefits deposited in an account in which the benefits draw interest until actual retirement. Some of these plans pay high interest and cost-of-living adjustments and may be coupled with very early retirement ages

SOCIAL RESPONSIBILITY: GET INVOLVED

- What are the tradeoffs in local governments' cutting back pension benefits to their employees?
- Should taxes be raised in order to fully fund these pension plans? Why or why not?

contributions of 8 percent to 10 percent cannot be sustained in an era of low interest rates, and the fund has a $415 million loss that has required at least a temporary halt to adding new veteran employees to the fund.

One of the problems is that fund managers appeared to try to maximize returns on their investments by investing in speculative real estate deals such as an investment of $34 million in some Arizona desert land that later sold for $7.5 million. Managers also overvalued real estate, and made rosy assumptions such as 8.5 percent yearly returns on investment. Last year investment returns actually were 2 percent after expenses.

Taxpayers in Dallas already contribute $100 million per year to the pension fund. It will be difficult to get them to contribute much more, although the alternative has to be pension reductions for police and firefighters. In the meantime, the credit rating for Dallas bonds has been reduced in part because of concerns about the problems with the police and firefighter pension fund. A lower credit rating for bonds issued by a governmental entity means that the entity has to pay a higher interest rate to borrowers.[70]

The Dallas pension problem is so severe that in the November 2016 election 69 percent of Dallas voters approved changes that should reduce the pensions' liabilities by $2.15 billion over the next 30 years. Voters usually tend to be uninterested in and unaware of problems associated with government employee pension plans, but the effects on a government's financial stability and tax system can be enormous.

Future Pension Policy

Pensions have a huge effect on state, county, and local governments. And for some local governments, employee pensions have already become unmanageable. Some pension plans have recognized that their plans were no longer economically viable and have instituted significant plan changes. Table 10.4 identifies the types of changes that are occurring in some pension plans.

One example of significant pension plan changes is the El Paso city retirement plan. El Paso increased the age of retirement, increased the years of service required to receive a pension, and changed the formula for calculating pension amounts to be less favorable to the employee. As an example, prior to the pension changes, assume an El Paso city employee chose to retire at age 60 with 25 years and 5 months of service with the city and that the employee's final wages were $2,000 per month. That employee's pension would be $1,270.85 per month. Under the new plan, that employee would receive $1,143.76. Thus, under the new plan, the employee's pension would be $127.09 a month less, a 10 percent reduction in the employee's pension.[71] For that employee, this no doubt seems a drastic cut in retirement pay, but such changes make pension systems viable.

The complex financial issues involved with providing pensions to local government workers may seem tiresome to students of politics. But they cut to the core of the problems facing government officials in the early twenty-first century. If local governments in Texas are to thrive in the coming decades, they must not be burdened with debts that cannot be paid.

TABLE 10.4

Options for Fully Funding Texas Public Employee Pension Plans

Increases in employee contributions to pensions

Increases in employer contributions to pensions

Formula for calculation of pension that is less favorable to employee

More years of employment required in calculation of pension

Increased retirement eligibility ages

SOURCE: State Pension Review Board, "2013 Guide to Public Retirement Systems in Texas" (2013).

★ ★

Local Government and the Future of Texas

In this chapter, we have investigated the role of local government in Texas government and politics. In many ways, local government affects the average citizen's life much more than either the federal or the state government. Local government generally works well in Texas in providing basic services. It picks up the trash, provides water, provides fire and police protection, and maintains local roads. However, in some ways local government may not be functioning as well as we might hope. As Texas has become more diverse and as Latinos and African Americans have gained political power, there is a greater demand for democratic responsiveness from local government. That demand is most clearly seen in the movement away from at-large city councils and toward single-member city council districts. But is local government sufficiently responsive? Special districts have been described as "hidden governments," suggesting a real lack of democratic accountability for their actions. It is unclear that there is sufficient democratic accountability even for high-level county officials such as district attorneys and county officials. As Texas looks to the future, the issue of expanding democratic accountability in local government looms as increasingly important.

One issue, currently far from the minds of Texas policy makers, is the way local government is structured in Texas. Should real estate developers support a handful of persons in a special district to incur millions in debt for that district and for future residents of that district? In terms of county governments, does Texas need 254 counties? Many of these counties are too small to deal with important concerns such as supporting the costs of a capital punishment trial. Though consolidation of governments in Texas and greater regulation of special districts are matters that are not currently on the state's political agenda, demands for a more transparent and efficient government should lead to consideration of such issues.

Finally, there are potential financial disasters facing local governments in their pension systems and in their method of borrowing money. These financial problems must be dealt with in the near future to avoid financial calamity at the local level in the next few decades. Financial mechanisms must be dealt with to fund the infrastructure needed for the growth of Texas other than risky capital appreciation bonds. And many local pensions are costing local governments more of their resources while the ability of those funds to pay the pensions promised to employees is becoming less likely. For Texas's urban centers, the crisis in local pension funds will become increasingly apparent and, as time goes by, harder to resolve. Most likely, however, this pension crisis cannot be resolved only with a tax increase. It will require pension reductions and ultimately a rethinking of how local employees receive support in retirement.

STUDY GUIDE

Use 🐰 INQUIZITIVE to help you study and master this material.

County Government in Texas

- Explain the importance, role, and structure of county government in Texas (pp. 325–33)

There are more counties in Texas than in any other state. County governance in Texas affects the lives of everyday Texans in ways ranging from hospital care to trash pickup.

Key Terms

county attorney (p. 326)
district attorney (p. 326)
county clerk (p. 326)
district clerk (p. 326)
county tax assessor-collector (p. 326)
county auditor (p. 327)
county commissioners' court (p. 327)
county judge (p. 327)
county commissioner (p. 327)
constable (p. 329)

Practice Quiz

1. Which of the following is *not* a type of local government found in Texas?
   a) city
   b) council of government
   c) county
   d) special district
   e) municipal

2. The basic governing body of a county is known as
   a) a council of government.
   b) a county council.
   c) a city-manager government.
   d) a county commissioners' court.
   e) a county governing committee.

3. How many counties are there in Texas?
   a) 25
   b) 56
   c) 110
   d) 254
   e) 500

4. All county commissioners' precincts must be equal in population according to
   a) Article 1 of the Texas Constitution.
   b) the Civil Rights Act of 1964.
   c) the Voting Rights Act of 1975.
   d) *Avery v. Midland County.*
   e) *Marbury v. Madison.*

5. A county judge
   a) only hears appellate cases from JP courts.
   b) is an appointive position from the governor.
   c) presides over the constitutional county court and the county commissioners' court.
   d) implements all the decisions of the Supreme Court affecting the county.
   e) judges juvenile cases.

6. Which county officials are responsible for the jail and the safety of the prisoners?
   a) sheriff
   b) county council
   c) county commissioners' court
   d) council of mayors
   e) city manager

City Government in Texas

• Describe the major types of city government in Texas (pp. 333–44)

Municipalities in Texas vary in terms of how they are governed. Some cities have strong mayors who run the city, while other cities have weak mayors where the day-to-day running of the city is delegated to city managers. Mayors and city councils often decide issues that directly affect the lives of everyday people.

Key Terms

home-rule charter (p. 334)
mayor-council form of government (p. 335)
at-large election (p. 335)
single-member district (p. 335)
commissioner form of government (p. 336)
council-manager form of government (p. 336)

Practice Quiz

7. To adopt a home-rule charter, a city must have a minimum population of
   a) 201.
   b) 5,000.
   c) 10,000.
   d) 50,000.
   e) There is no minimum.

8. The two legal classifications of Texas cities are
   a) local and regional.
   b) general law and home rule.
   c) tax and nontax.
   d) charter and noncharter.
   e) big and small.

9. The form of city government that allows the mayor to establish control over most of the city's government is called the
   a) commissioner form of city government.
   b) council-manager form of city government.
   c) council of government form of city government.
   d) strong mayor–council form of city government.
   e) none of the above

10. A city controller
    a) works directly for the governor.
    b) controls and manages the election in a city.
    c) is a city's chief elected official who presides over the city council.
    d) is independent of all political control in a small statutory city.
    e) is a city's chief financial officer.

Special Districts

• Examine the role of special districts in Texas government (pp. 344–52)

Special districts often span different cities and counties. They are tasked with operating such things as school districts or water utility districts. They have the authority to levy property taxes to fund the operation of services essential to the lives of many residents.

Key Terms

special district (p. 344)
school district (p. 346)
nonschool special district (p. 346)
municipal utility district (MUD) (p. 347)
property tax (p. 348)
user fee (p. 348)
hidden government (p. 349)
council of government (COG) (p. 351)

Practice Quiz

11. Which local government provides a single service not provided by any other local government?
    a) special district
    b) council of government
    c) police district
    d) city
    e) county

12. What are the two types of special districts found in Texas?
- **a)** school and nonschool
- **b)** home rule and general law
- **c)** tax and nontax
- **d)** statutory and constitutional
- **e)** none of the above

13. A special district
- **a)** must be limited to under 150,000 people.
- **b)** covers the entire state to provide a particular service.
- **c)** is a unit of local government that provides a special service to a limited geographic area.
- **d)** temporarily combines two congressional districts.
- **e)** none of the above

14. A MUD
- **a)** serves the needs of developers.
- **b)** is generally opposed by banks and real estate developers as being too expensive.
- **c)** provides ambulance service inside a city's geographic limits.
- **d)** delegates the setting of tax rates in a particular geographic area to the state legislature.
- **e)** provides funding for special districts.

15. Comprehensive planning and service delivery in a specific geographic area are the function of a
- **a)** special district.
- **b)** council of government.
- **c)** city.
- **d)** county.
- **e)** town.

Financial Issues Facing Local Government

- Examine the financial problems facing local government (pp. 352–55)

Local government in Texas is facing a looming financial crisis as a result of widespread issuance of capital appreciation bonds, which allow funds to be raised in the present while interest and payments on the principal are paid far into the future, and the liabilities imposed on local government by generous retirement plans for governmental employees.

Key Terms
capital appreciation bond (CAB) (p. 352)
deferred retirement option plan (DROP) (p. 354)

Practice Quiz
16. Capital appreciation bonds
- **a)** are long-term bonds on which local governments pay back principal and interest on a yearly basis.
- **b)** are short-term bonds on which local governments borrow money for emergencies.
- **c)** are bonds on which interest is paid quarterly by local governments but the principal is not paid back for 40 years.
- **d)** are bonds on which principal and interest are not paid back until the end of a lengthy term while local governments can use the borrowed money immediately.
- **e)** create such long-term financial risks that they are illegal in Texas.

17. Some governmental employee retirement plans in Texas
- **a)** impose huge financial liabilities on government.
- **b)** need to be increased to support needy retired employees.
- **c)** have not kept up with inflation.
- **d)** will soon be merged into the Social Security retirement program.
- **e)** are so minimal that it is hard to recruit employees at the local level.

In 2010 students at UT Austin protested against cuts in education spending and increases in tuition. As lawmakers work to balance the state budget, the decisions they make about taxes and spending affect all Texans.

STOP THE CUTS

Public Finance

WHY PUBLIC FINANCE MATTERS For college students, the state budget might appear to be pretty far removed from everyday life and things like attending class, preparing for an exam, or getting everything in order for a timely graduation. But like it or not, the budgetary decisions made by legislators every two years affect students where they matter most: in the pocketbook.

In 2003 state political leaders found themselves staring at a $10 billion shortfall in the upcoming budget period. Mandated by the state constitution to maintain a balanced budget, they needed to find new ways to close the budget gap without raising taxes. One method was to cut higher education funding.

Prior to 2003 tuition and fee rates for state universities had been set by the state legislature, and in Texas they tended to be low when compared to tuition in other states. Costs ranged from $2,870 per year at Texas A&M at Texarkana to $4,912 per year at the University of Texas (UT) at Austin. General revenues funded a large portion of the state university's education budget. In 2003, as a trade-off for a 2 percent cut in the higher education budget, the legislature gave the regents of the various state schools the authority to raise tuition to make up the difference.[1]

Tuition skyrocketed across the country in the first decade of the twenty-first century. Texas was not spared these inflationary pressures. Tuition and fees for Texas A&M at Texarkana rose 132 percent between 2003 and 2016 to $6,649 per year. At UT Austin, they rose 100 percent to $10,570 per year. The average tuition and fees for a four-year public university in Texas in 2016 reached $8,670. Although this was below the national average, higher education had become an expensive commodity in Texas.[2]

As universities and colleges lined up in 2015 and 2016 to present a new round of tuition increases, many lawmakers expressed serious concerns about the wisdom of the 2003 decision to give over control of tuition and fees to the universities. Spiraling student debt coupled to higher tuition and fees was making it difficult for Texans to attend college. Moreover, state leaders believed that college spending was out of control. If universities could not hold the line on costs, then perhaps the legislature would have to take action.

University leaders across the state did not take the challenge to their control over tuition and fees lightly. Supporting continued deregulation, Deputy Chancellor David E. Daniel of the University of Texas System argued that each university or university system was better equipped to make decisions about tuition and fees than the legislature. Others argued that the universities had kept increases in tuition and fees lower than the legislature had.[3]

Constituent pressure to keep higher education prices down likely will continue over the next few years. But three factors related to public finance will work against a return to highly regulated tuition and fees. First, state political leaders want costs held down, but few appear to want to return all decision making about tuition back to the legislature. Deregulation, after all, freed the legislature from having to choose between higher costs and lower quality. Second, most political leaders also recognize that if Texas wants to build high-quality universities, someone has to pay for them. But the third factor may be the most important. Over the past 25 years, the legislature has been unwilling to allocate more general revenue monies directly to fund higher education, even in an era of rapidly escalated costs in the industry. Appropriated dollars per student have actually fallen approximately 15 percent since the Great Recession in 2008. Until the state is willing to invest more in higher education or is willing to accept lower-quality institutions of higher education, tuition, fees and public discontent will continue to rise.[4]

The debate over tuition and fees is one example of how matters of public finance lie at the heart of Texas government. Passing a balanced budget is the most important task presented to the state legislature during its regular session every two years. Priorities must be identified and money must be allocated across a wide range of governmental activities through a variety of financial mechanisms. Difficult decisions must be made about how to fund governmental activities through increased taxes and fees. Understanding public policy demands a mastery of public finance. That is the subject of this chapter.

CHAPTER GOALS

- Explain the purpose of the state budget and what is typically included (pp. 363–64)

- Describe the general pattern of state spending in Texas and where state revenue comes from (pp. 365–73)

- Describe how the money in the budget is organized into specific funds (pp. 374–78)

- Outline the constitutional provisions that affect how the state budget is made (pp. 378–83)

- Identify the major steps and players in making the state budget (pp. 383–87)

- Analyze major budget crises in Texas (pp. 387–92)

What Is the Budget?

Explain the purpose of the state budget and what is typically included

One of the most distinguishing characteristics about public finance in Texas is that the state constitution mandates that the legislature operate within a "balanced budget." On its face, the idea of a balanced budget is straightforward. A balanced budget would exist whenever the projected income from tax revenues is equal to or exceeds the projected expenditure. But public finance is a complicated business. There are actually a number of different ways to talk about the funds that constitute the "budget." One way to look at them is to divide them into the following five broad budgetary categories.[5]

- The **General Revenues Fund budget** is the state's primary operating fund. It is the place where most state taxes and fees flow. It also includes three educational funds. Expenditures may be made directly from the nondedicated funds and may be transferred to special funds or accounts for allocation.
- The **General Revenue–Dedicated Funds budget** includes over 200 funds dedicated to specific purposes. This budget includes such funds as the State Parks Account and the college operating accounts (which hold tuition funds). Generally speaking, the legislature can appropriate money from these accounts only for their dedicated purposes. The balances in this budget are used to certify that the constitutional pay-as-you-go limits (discussed below) are being met.
- The **Federal Funds budget** includes all grants, payments, and reimbursements received from the federal government by state agencies and institutions, including the Medicaid program, Title 1 Grants to Local Educational Agencies, transportation grants, and the Children's Health Insurance Program.
- The **Other Funds budget** consists of all other funds flowing into the state treasury not included in the other methods of financing. These include, among other funds, the State Highway Fund, the Texas Mobility Fund, the Property Tax Relief Fund, and the Economic Stabilization Fund.
- The **All Funds budget** is the aggregate of all of the above budgets, referring to all spending that goes through agencies, including federal and state programs.

Appropriations from these funds for the period 2016–17 are shown in Table 11.1.

Some important things must be noted about this complicated system of public financing through these various budgets. First, the state budget involves huge amounts of money (see Table 11.2). Second, much of this money lies outside the direct control of the legislature. Trust funds and other dedicated funds exist for particular purposes

General Revenues Fund budget budget for a nondedicated revenue account that functions as the state's primary operating fund

General Revenue–Dedicated Funds budget budget composed of funds for dedicated revenues that target money for specific purposes

Federal Funds budget state budget that includes all grants, payments, and reimbursements received from the federal government by state agencies and institutions

Other Funds budget budget consisting of all other funds flowing into the state treasury that are not included in other state budgets; this includes the Texas Highway Fund, various trust funds operated by the state, and certain revenues held for local higher education accounts

All Funds budget budget that aggregates all monies flowing into the state treasury and all state spending

TABLE 11.1

Texas Budgetary Funds Appropriated, 2016–17 (in billions of dollars)

General Revenues Fund budget	$106.0
General Revenue–Dedicated Funds budget	7.8
Federal Funds budget	68.0
Other Funds budget	27.3
All Funds budget	209.1

SOURCE: Legislative Budget Board, *Fiscal Size-Up: 2016–17 Biennium* (May 2016), pp. 3–8.

and are hard to manipulate for other budgetary purposes. Legislators seeking to balance the budget are often left with relatively few places to cut expenditures. Given its large proportion of the General Revenues Fund budget, education is often at the top of the list. Third, federal expenditures have a very important role in shaping the overall direction of the state budget. The bulk of federal funds expenditures is in two areas: health and human services, and education. Strings are often attached to these monies. If legislators want federal dollars, they must spend state dollars first. Figure 11.1 highlights the increasingly important role that federal dollars have played in spending patterns in Texas. Expenditures from the All Funds budget (which takes into account federal spending) have exploded recently. The pressure to maximize federal dollars flowing into Texas is one legislative goal. But legislators also desire to minimize state spending and not raise taxes.

TABLE 11.2

Summary of All Funds State Budget Allocation by Biennium (in millions of dollars)

ALL FUNCTIONS	2014–15	2016–17*	PERCENTAGE CHANGE
Article I: General Government	$5,321.5	$6,252.6	17.5%
Article II: Health and Human Services	74,751.5	77,199.8	3.3
Article III: Agencies of Education	74,724.5	78,570.1	5.1
Public Education	56,171.9	58,556.2	4.2
Higher Education	18,552.6	20,013.9	7.9
Article IV: The Judiciary	764.5	807.8	5.7
Article V: Public Safety and Criminal Justice	11,869.0	12,432.6	4.7
Article VI: Natural Resources	6,933.5	4,367.5	–37.0
Article VII: Business and Economic Development	27,429.5	27,762.2	1.2
Article VIII: Regulatory	1,132.6	934.2	–17.5
Article IX: General Provisions	0.0	390.2	N/A
Article X: The Legislature	374.0	386.1	3.2
Total, all articles	**$203,300.5**	**$209,103.0**	**2.9%**

*Appropriated.
SOURCE: Legislative Budget Board, *Fiscal Size-Up: 2016–17 Biennium* (May 2016), p. 2.

Spending and Revenue in Texas

 Describe the general pattern of state spending in Texas and where state revenue comes from

Texas has a reputation of being a "low service, low tax" state that seeks to maintain a favorable environment for business. In this section, we will look at the general pattern of state spending in Texas, as well as taxes and other sources of revenue in the state.

Trends in State Spending

For the most part, Texas's reputation as a low-spending state is well earned. On a variety of measures, Texas spends less than other states. A 2014 Texas Legislative Budget Board study found that among the 50 states, Texas ranked 46th on per capita state government expenditures, with $4,916 spent per person. On a per capita basis, Texas ranks 27th in educational spending, 44th in highway spending, 25th in hospital spending, and 41st in public welfare spending.[6] Conversely, Texas ranked high when compared with other states on the per capita federal dollars flowing into the state. In 2012, Texas took in $10,647 per capita from the federal government, ranking it 11th among the states, above the national state average of $8,844.[7]

The trend in overall spending reveals a similar story, particularly in recent years (see Figure 11.1). In unadjusted dollars (that is, dollars spent not taking into account inflation or population increases), state spending (General Revenue Funds) in Texas rose from a little over $40 billion in the 1996–97 biennium to over $106.0 billion in the

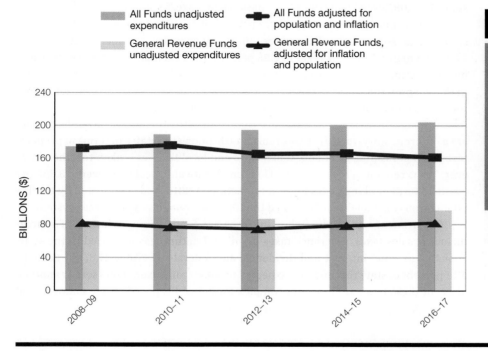

FIGURE 11.1

Trends in State Government Expenditures

*Appropriated.

SOURCE: Texas Legislative Budget Board, Fiscal Size-Up: 2016–17 Biennium (May 2016), p. 26.

2016–17 biennium. However, in real per capita dollars (that is, dollars spent controlling for inflation and population increases), state spending hovered around $40 billion.[8]

When considering state and federal spending in Texas together (see the All Funds State Budget in Figure 11.1), the story is a little bit different. Unadjusted spending for all funds (state and federal) in Texas rose from around $80 billion in 1996–97 to over $209 billion in 2016–17. But in real per capita dollars, spending in the same periods rose much more modestly. There was an increase in the federal monies available to the state due to the Great Recession in 2008 for a few years. But real federal dollars per capita declined during the 2012–13 biennium and the 2016–17 biennium. In fact, real per capita state and federal monies spent in Texas fell from $172.1 billion in 2008–09 to $161.3 billion in 2016–17. Still, though the federal government has backed away from its 2008 efforts, a lot of federal money continues to flow into Texas.[9]

Revenue in Texas

Spending is only part of Texas's "low service, low tax" reputation. The taxes that fund government are the other dimension. It is difficult to measure the state tax burden Texans face compared with that of citizens in other states. There are a variety of taxes that individuals can pay to the state government, including state income taxes, general state sales taxes, specific state sales taxes, local sales taxes, and property taxes. Moreover, some state taxes can be lower in one state than another but be offset by higher local taxes.

After the legislature passes the biennial state budget, the state comptroller certifies the budget, confirming that it is within current revenue estimates for the period. Here, state comptroller Glenn Hegar certifies the 2016–17 budget.

Two measures are often used to compare tax burdens across states: state tax revenue per $1,000 of personal income and per capita state tax revenues. On both measures, Texas's low tax reputation seems to be well earned. In 2012, Texans paid $44.97 in state taxes for each $1,000 of personal income, ranking it 46th among the 50 states. This was well below the $59.29 national average in terms of per capita state tax revenue. A study by the Tax Foundation found that for 2014 per capita state taxes in Texas stood at $2,085, well below the $2,677 national average.[10]

Texas is one of seven states that still do not have a personal income tax. Two states, Tennessee and New Hampshire, only tax income from dividends and interest. There is a high sales tax in Texas of 6.25 percent, the 13th highest in the nation. Combined state and local sales taxes in the state can reach 8.25 percent. As we will see later in this chapter, there are a variety of other specific sales taxes that bring revenue into the state to fund government, including cigarettes, alcohol, and gasoline.

Although Texas state taxes are low compared with other states' taxes, local taxes are a different story. In 2011, Texas ranked 14th among the states in terms of property taxes paid per capita, at $1,560. When state and local taxes are taken together, however, Texas remains a low-tax state. Combined state and local taxes were $3,863 per capita in 2013, ranking Texas 30th in the nation. A 2016 study conducted by the Tax Foundation concluded that Texas had the 10th most business-friendly tax system.[11]

Government and public policy in Texas are funded from a variety of sources including sales taxes, severance taxes on oil and natural gas produced in the state, licensing income, interest and dividends, and federal aid (Table 11.3). In 2016–17, 47.6 percent of state revenues are expected to come from taxes of one sort or another. Many of these taxes are based on complex formulas. People often are unaware that they are paying them. But they are important sources of state revenue.

TABLE 11.3

State Revenue Biennial Comparison, by Source, 2014–15 and 2016–17 Bienniums (in millions of dollars)

REVENUE	2014–15	2016–17*	PERCENTAGE CHANGE
Tax collections	$102,675.6	$101,884.2	–0.8%
Federal receipts	70,967.0	72,798.7	2.6
Licenses, fees, fines, and penalties	18,146.7	16,579.3	–8.6
Interest and investment income	2,856.7	2,784.9	–2.5
Lottery	3,771.6	3,796.1	0.6
Land income	3,411.2	2,033.8	–40.4
Other revenue sources	12,541.6	14,120.3	12.6
Total, net revenue	**$214,370.5**	**$213,997.3**	**–0.2%**

*Estimated.
SOURCE: Texas Legislative Budget Board, *Fiscal Size-Up: 2016–17 Biennium* (May 2016), p. 33.

Sales Tax The most important single tax financing Texas government is the sales tax. Today, the sales tax in Texas is 6.25 percent of the retail sales price of tangible personal property and selected services. Together, county, city, and metropolitan transit authorities are allowed to impose an additional 2 percent sales tax. For the 2016–17 biennium the sales tax is expected to account for 58.8 percent of the total tax collections in the state (see Figure 11.2).

Oil Production and Regulation Taxes The oil severance tax (a tax incurred when oil is removed or severed within a taxing jurisdiction) is 4.6 percent of the market value of oil produced in the state. (There is also an oil regulation tax of three-sixteenths of one cent per barrel of oil produced in Texas.) The tax revenue from oil production fluctuates with the price of oil and the volume of oil produced in Texas. In fiscal year 2014, 903.0 million barrels were produced in Texas for an average price of $96.56 per barrel. In fiscal year 2015, production rose to 1,085.9 million barrels, while the average price fell to $59.97 per barrel. Oil production taxes are expected to fall significantly from $6.8 billion in 2014–15 to $3.9 billion in the 2016–17 biennium as a result of the continuing fall in the price of oil. Fracking and horizontal drilling, new technologies lying behind Texas's latest oil boom, likely rescued the state budget during the 2014–15 biennium. Unstable prices and uncertain tax revenues beginning in 2016 are posing new challenges to officials trying to project revenues from oil taxes.

Natural Gas Production Tax There is a 7.5 percent tax on the market value of all natural gas produced in the state. As with the oil tax, the tax raised from natural gas depends on the price and the amount produced. Revenues from natural gas have fluctuated considerably over time. They fell significantly from $734 million, or

Gas prices have fluctuated widely in recent years. In early 2016, regular gas prices fell below $1.50 a gallon for a time. A couple of years before, however, the price of gas fluctuated around a much higher price: $3.50 a gallon. The state of Texas collects a tax of 20 cents per gallon on motor fuels. The federal government collects an additional 18.4 cents per gallon, but Texans still pay less tax on gasoline than residents of many other states.

6.9 percent of state revenues, in 1980 to $489 million, or a little more than 1 percent of state revenues, in 1997. For the 2014–15 biennium, $3.2 billion flowed into the state treasury from the natural gas tax. That amount is projected to fall to $1.9 billion in the 2016–17 biennium, a decrease of 39.8 percent.

Motor Fuels Tax The motor fuels tax in Texas is 20 cents per gallon of gasoline and diesel fuel. There is a 15-cents-per-gallon tax on liquefied gas. In 2016–17 the motor fuels tax is projected to generate approximately $7.1 billion, or 6.9 percent of all state revenues, far below the historical average of 10 to 12 percent.

The revenues flowing from the motor fuels tax are "dedicated" monies. This means that the tax revenues can only be used for purposes specified by the legislature. About three-quarters of these monies are appropriated to the Texas Department of Transportation and the Texas Department of Public Safety and are dedicated to the construction, maintenance, and policing of public roads. Most of the remaining one-quarter of the revenues are dedicated to public education.

Motor Vehicle Sales and Rentals and Manufactured Home Sales Tax There is a 6.25 percent tax on the sales price of all motor vehicles in the

FIGURE 11.2

State Tax Revenue Sources, 2016–17 Biennium

*Percentages calculated based on constitutionally and statutorily dedicated tax revenues and appropriations in the 2014–15 General Appropriations Act, as modified by other legislation.

SOURCE: Legislative Budget Board, *Fiscal Size-Up: 2016–17 Biennium* (May 2016), p. 33.

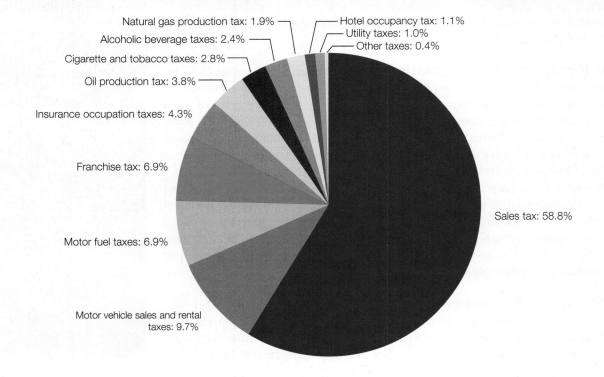

Natural gas production tax: 1.9%
Alcoholic beverage taxes: 2.4%
Cigarette and tobacco taxes: 2.8%
Oil production tax: 3.8%
Insurance occupation taxes: 4.3%
Franchise tax: 6.9%
Motor fuel taxes: 6.9%
Motor vehicle sales and rental taxes: 9.7%
Hotel occupancy tax: 1.1%
Utility taxes: 1.0%
Other taxes: 0.4%
Sales tax: 58.8%

Who Pays the Highest State Taxes?

Texas is one of a handful of states that do not tax income, which means that Texans pay income taxes only to the federal government. Where does the state get its money? Through a variety of taxes including sales, property, severance, and franchise taxes, the state is able to fund roads, schools, prisons, and other needs. Critics of this approach argue that states without income taxes fail to distribute tax burdens fairly and that they underfund essential government services. Proponents argue that businesses are attracted to Texas because it does not tax personal income.

Top State Income Tax Rates, 2016

- No income tax
- 2.9–4.7%
- 4.8–6.2%
- 6.3–7.8%
- 7.9–9.4%
- 9.5–13.3%

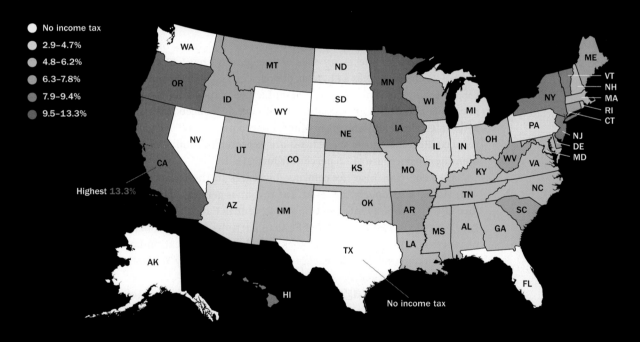

Highest 13.3%

No income tax

Number of States in Each Tax Bracket

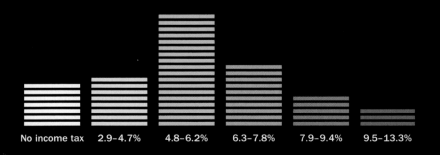

No income tax 2.9–4.7% 4.8–6.2% 6.3–7.8% 7.9–9.4% 9.5–13.3%

SOURCE: Tax Foundation, taxfoundation.org (accessed 6/13/16).

CRITICAL THINKING

- Which states have the highest income tax rates? Which have the lowest? What might explain this?

- What are the advantages and disadvantages to having no state income tax in Texas?

state. There is also a 10 percent tax on all rental vehicles up to 30 days and 6.25 percent thereafter. Newly manufactured homes are also taxed at 5 percent of 65 percent of the sale price. Because of the effects of the economic slowdown brought on by the Great Recession, motor vehicle sales and rental taxes declined by 5.6 percent in the 2010–11 biennium to $5.6 billion. The economic recovery since then increased the revenues from these taxes up to $8.7 billion in 2014–15. For the 2016–17 biennium, it is projected that tax revenues from this source will increase $9.9 billion.

Franchise Tax The so-called franchise tax is imposed on all corporations in Texas. Prior to 2008 the tax was imposed on taxable capital and on earned surplus. Most businesses pay a tax rate of 1 percent on their taxable margin, although a lower rate is available to businesses primarily in retail or wholesale trade. Some reforms aimed at small businesses were introduced into the franchise tax during the 2013 legislative session. The goals of the legislature in reworking the franchise tax were to make it more difficult for corporations to escape the tax and to offset some of the costs of property tax reform. Of the $4.7 billion collected under the franchise tax in fiscal year 2015, $2.9 billion were allocated to the General Revenue Fund and $1.8 billion to the Property Tax Relief Fund.[12]

Tobacco Taxes Texas imposes a variety of taxes on cigarettes and tobacco products. For example, every pack of 20 cigarettes has a $1.41 tax per pack and every pack of 25 cigarettes has a $1.76 tax per pack included in the purchase price. The tax on tobacco products is based on the manufacturer's listed net weight. This tax was $1.22 per ounce in 2013. Approximately 87 percent of tobacco taxes are derived from cigarette sales, the remainder from other tobacco products like cigars, snuff, and chewing tobacco. Revenues from these taxes are expected to total $2.8 billion for the 2016–17 biennium, a decrease of 1.5 percent from 2014–15.

Like the franchise tax reforms, increases in the tobacco taxes passed in 2006 were linked to property tax relief. Tax revenues generated by the tax rate in place before 2007 go directly into the General Revenues Fund. The excess above this amount goes into the Property Tax Relief Fund. A portion of the other tax increase on tobacco products put into effect in 2007 goes to a Physician Education Loan Repayment program. The remainder of the excess goes into the Property Tax Relief Fund.

Alcoholic Beverage Taxes As with tobacco, a variety of taxes are imposed on alcoholic beverages. Some of these were increased during the 2013 legislative session. This tax took in $2.2 billion in the 2014–15 biennium and is expected to rise to $2.4 billion in the 2016–17 biennium.

Insurance Occupation Taxes A complex schedule of tax rates is applied to insurance premiums. For example, life, health, and accident insurance is taxed at the rate of 1.75 percent on gross premium receipts. In the 2016–17 biennium, insurance premium taxes are expected to be $4.4 billion, up from $4.0 billion in the 2014–15 biennium.

Utility Taxes Utility tax revenue flows from three sources in Texas. First, there is a tax on gas, electric, and water utility gross receipts. Rates vary from 0.581 percent to 1.997 percent based on the size of the city population. There are also taxes imposed on the gross receipts of public utilities and a gas utility pipeline tax. In 2016–17, it is estimated that the utility tax will take in $970.7 million, representing a 1.2 percent increase from the 2014–15 biennium.

Hotel and Motel Tax This state tax is 6 percent of the hotel and motel occupancy bill paid by the occupant. This tax revenue fell during the Great Recession but has rebounded along with increased tourism during the economic recovery over the past four years. It is expected to generate $1.1 billion in the 2016–17 biennium, a 12 percent increase from the previous biennium.

Inheritance Tax Federal tax reforms in 2001 effectively eliminated the Texas inheritance tax by 2005. The law was scheduled to expire in 2012 along with other portions of the Bush tax cuts. The federal law was extended in 2011, meaning that there would be no inheritance tax collected in Texas for the 2014–15 or 2016–17 bienniums.

Other Taxes There are a small number of other taxes on such items as attorney services, cement, sulfur, coin-operated machines, and bingo rental receipts that are expected to generate $357.9 million for the 2016–17 biennium.

The Question of the Income Tax in Texas

Many commentators have complained that the tax system in Texas is too **regressive**.[13] By this they mean that the tax burden in the state falls more heavily on lower-income individuals. Sales and use taxes such as those found in Texas are generally considered to be regressive. Property taxes on individuals and businesses are generally considered to be somewhat regressive. Poor homeowners and renters generally pay more of their income in property taxes than do the wealthy.

regressive tax type of tax where the tax burden falls more heavily on lower-income individuals

progressive tax type of tax where the tax burden falls more heavily on upper-income individuals

There have been occasional calls for the institution of a state income tax in Texas. Supporters argue that not only is the income tax a more reliable source of revenue for the state, it can also be made fairer. Unlike sales and use taxes, which are applied equally to everyone whatever their income, income taxes can be made **progressive**. With a progressive income tax, people with lower income pay a lower tax rate than people with higher income. Progressive income taxes thus place a higher tax burden on the rich than on the poor. A 2015 study conducted by the Institute on Taxation and Economic Policy found that among the states Texas had the third most unfair tax system in the nation. The study estimated that in Texas people with incomes at the bottom 20 percent paid 12.5 percent of their income in state and local taxes, while those with incomes in the upper 1 percent paid only 2.9 percent of their income in taxes.[14]

SOCIAL RESPONSIBILITY: GET INVOLVED

- Do you think sales and use taxes are a fair way for the state to generate revenue? Why or why not?

- If you were writing a letter to the editor on behalf of a group advocating for poor Texans, how would you argue that the state change tax policy to help your supporters?

Few politicians have ever been willing to support an income tax. One of the attractive features of Texas to business has always been the absence of an income tax. It was not until the late 1980s and early 1990s that the first serious attempt to put a state income tax in place was undertaken. Responding to mounting budgetary pressures, the retiring lieutenant governor, Bill Hobby, came out in favor of an income tax in late 1989. Bob Bullock, Hobby's successor, announced in early 1991 that he would actively campaign for an income tax. A blue-ribbon panel chaired by former governor John Connally was charged with looking into new revenue sources for the state. The committee ended up recommending to the legislature both a corporate and a personal income tax, but not without generating an enormous amount of controversy.[15]

Chairman Connally himself opposed the income-tax recommendations, as did Governor Ann Richards. By the 1993 legislative session, Lieutenant Governor Bullock was backing off. Bullock proposed a constitutional amendment requiring voter approval of any personal income tax. Moreover, the amendment specified that funds raised under the personal income tax be used to support public education. The amendment quickly passed the 73rd legislature and was overwhelmingly approved by voters on November 2, 1993. As this amendment effectively gave the electorate a veto over any proposal for an income tax, it is unlikely that Texans will have a personal income tax in the foreseeable future.

Other State Revenue

matching funds federal monies going to a state based on state spending for a program

The largest source of revenue for Texas is the federal government (see Table 11.4). Historically, Texas spends relatively little, compared with other states, for state-federal programs. As a result, the federal grants and **matching funds** (federal monies going to a state based on state spending for a program) also have been relatively low. Nevertheless, federal aid to Texas skyrocketed in the 1980s because of the expansion of transportation and human services programs. For the 2016–17 biennium, federal funds account for $72.8 billion, about 34.0 percent of the total state revenue, up 2.6 percent from 2014–15. Much of the increase in these federal funds in recent years can be attributed to Medicaid, a state-federal program providing funds to finance health care delivery to the poor.[16]

In addition to federal monies, there are a number of other revenue sources, as shown in Table 11.5, including licenses, fees and fines, the sales of goods and services provided by the state, and land income. Two other sources in recent years have had a major impact on monies flowing into the state budget. A state lottery was passed by the state legislature and approved by the voters in 1991. Although the lottery was passed by voters overwhelmingly, attitudes about the appropriateness of using gambling as a source of state revenues are mixed. Some argue that the lottery unfairly takes money from people who can least afford it by fooling them into thinking that they too can strike it rich if only they have a little luck. Large numbers of people from all social classes continue to play the lottery. A 2015 study found that 28.7 percent of Texans claimed that they had played a lottery game in the previous year. The median monthly dollar amount spent on any

TABLE 11.4

Estimated State Revenue Collections, 2016–17 Biennium
Total: $213,997.3 Million

Federal funds	34.0%
Sales tax	28.0
Other receipts	10.6
Motor vehicle sales and rental tax	4.6
Licenses, fees, fines, penalties	7.7
Other taxes	5.7
Franchise tax	3.3
Motor fuels tax	3.3
Severance tax	2.7

TABLE 11.5

Tax Collections Biennial Comparison by Source, 2014–15 and 2016–17 (in billions of dollars)

	2014–15	2016–17*	PERCENTAGE CHANGE
Sales tax	$56.3	$59.8	6.2%
Oil production taxes	6.7	3.9	−42.7
Natural gas production tax	3.2	1.9	−40.6
Motor fuels tax	6.7	7.1	6.0
Motor vehicle sales and rental taxes	8.7	9.8	12.6
Franchise tax	9.3	7.1	−23.6
Cigarette and tobacco taxes	2.8	1.8	−0.6
Alcoholic beverages taxes	2.2	2.4	10.0
Insurance occupation taxes	4.0	4.4	10.0
Utility taxes	1.0	1.0	0
Hotel occupancy tax	1.0	1.1	10.0
Inheritance tax	0.0	0.0	0
Other taxes	0.5	0.35	−3.0
Total tax collections	$102.67	$101.88	−0.8%

NOTE: Biennial change and percentage change have been calculated on actual amounts before rounding in all tables and graphics in this chapter. Totals may not sum as a result of rounding.
*Estimated.
SOURCE: Legislative Budget Board, *Fiscal Size-Up: 2016–17 Biennium* (May 2016), p. 34.

lottery game was $10. In fiscal year 2015, lottery ticket sales totaled $4.5 billion, up 3 percent from fiscal year 2014. Payouts to winners totaled $2.9 billion. After administrative expenses were paid, $1.153 billion was transferred to the Foundation School Account, $11.7 million was transferred to the Texas Veterans Commission, and $73.0 million of unclaimed prizes was transferred to the state. It is projected that over $2.7 billion will be available to transfer to the Foundation School Account in the 2016–17 biennium.[17]

A second major source of nontax revenue is a result of the settlement the state reached with tobacco companies in 1998. Under the settlement, Texas would receive over $17.3 billion over the next 25 years and an additional $580 million every year thereafter from the tobacco industry. The largest payment—$3.3 billion—came up front, while the remainder was to be spread out over the remaining 25 years. Nationwide, states received a total of $246 billion in the final settlement reached with the tobacco industry. The Texas Comptroller's Office projects that Texas tobacco settlement receipts will total $942.0 million in 2016–17, down from the $986 million received in 2014–15. This drop is the result of a projected decline in cigarette sales.[18]

State Funds

Describe how the money in the budget is organized into specific funds

Money comes into state coffers from a variety of sources and is dispersed to a wide range of activities. But money spent by the state doesn't just flow into and out of one pot. There are, in fact, 400 funds in the state treasury whose monies are directed to a wide variety of functions. Understanding how money flows into and out of these funds lies at the heart of mastering the state budget. We examine some of the most important funds here.

As previously mentioned, the **General Revenue Fund** consists of two parts: nondedicated general revenue and general revenue–dedicated accounts. The nondedicated revenue is the state's primary operating fund and is the place where most state taxes and fees flow. In 1991, 200 special funds were brought into the General Revenue–Dedicated Funds account as part of a budget reform and consolidation package. Expenditures may be made directly from the nondedicated funds and may be transferred to special funds or accounts for allocation.

The **Permanent School Fund (PSF)** was created in 1854 with a $2 million appropriation by the legislature to fund primary and secondary schools. The Constitution of 1876, along with subsequent acts, stipulated that certain lands and sales from these lands would constitute the PSF. The second-largest educational endowment in the country, the PSF is managed primarily by the state board of education. The fund distributes money to school districts across the state based on attendance and guarantees bonds issued by local school boards, enabling them to get lower interest rates in the bond markets. At the end of 2013 the fund was guaranteeing about $55.2 billion in school district bonds across the state.

The value of this fund has fluctuated throughout the turbulent first decade of the twenty-first century, dropping to a little over $20 billion in 2009. At the end of fiscal year 2015, the fund balance had recovered to $33.8 billion. The fund provided $838.7 million to help fund public education in 2015.[19]

The **Available School Fund (ASF)** is a dedicated fund established by the constitution for the support of public education in the state. The ASF is funded through distributions of the Permanent School Fund (mentioned above) and 25 percent of the state's motor fuels tax. The ASF also provides funds for another fund, the Instructional Materials Fund, that funds state purchases of instructional materials. Revenue flowing into the ASF for the 2016–17 biennium from the motor fuels tax and PSF together is projected to be $3.84 billion.

The **State Highway Fund** comes from a variety of sources, including motor vehicle registration fees, the federal highway fund, and the sales tax on motor lubricants. A significant portion of the motor fuels tax initially is deposited in the General Revenue Fund and then is allocated to the State Highway Fund. The purposes of the State Highway Fund are constructing, maintaining, and policing roadways in Texas and acquiring rights of way. Constitutional amendments passed in 2014 and 2015 provide for diverting billions of dollars into the State Highway Fund from the Economic Stabilization Fund (see next entry) and states sales and use taxes. Excluding federal revenue

---

General Revenue Fund the state's primary operating fund

Permanent School Fund (PSF) fund created in 1854 that provides monies for primary and secondary schools

Available School Fund (ASF) dedicated fund established by the constitution for the support of public education in the state

State Highway Fund fund that supports the construction, maintenance, and policing of roadways and acquires rights of way; funded through a variety of taxes such as motor vehicle registration fees, the federal highway fund, and the sales tax on motor lubricants

Who Pays the Most State Taxes in Texas?

Taxes as a Percentage of Income in Texas, 2015*

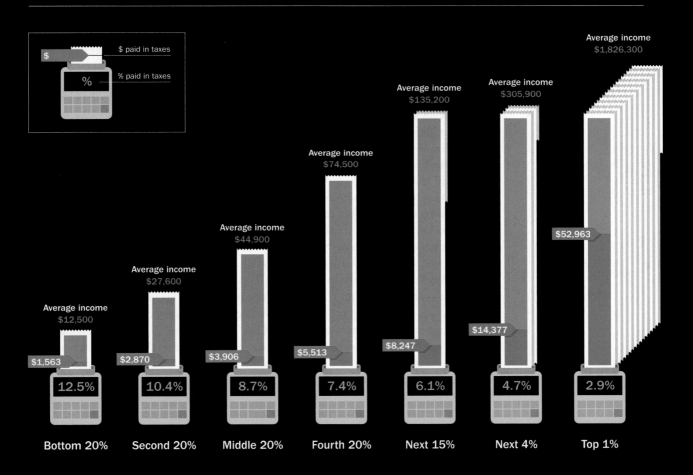

$ paid in taxes

% paid in taxes

Average income $12,500	Average income $27,600	Average income $44,900	Average income $74,500	Average income $135,200	Average income $305,900	Average income $1,826,300
$1,563	$2,870	$3,906	$5,513	$8,247	$14,377	$52,963
12.5%	10.4%	8.7%	7.4%	6.1%	4.7%	2.9%
Bottom 20%	Second 20%	Middle 20%	Fourth 20%	Next 15%	Next 4%	Top 1%

Texas has no state income tax, which does keep overall individual tax rates down. However, this means that the state's revenues rely heavily on sales and property taxes. These taxes are regressive—those with less income pay a higher share of their income in taxes; those with higher incomes pay a lower share of their income in taxes.

QUANTITATIVE REASONING

- Which group pays the highest percentage of its income in taxes in Texas?
- How would the proportions paid in taxes change across all incomes if a progressive state income tax was instituted?

*Based on family income for non-elderly taxpayers.

SOURCE: Institute for Taxation and Economic Policy, www.itep.org (accessed 6/13/16).

and bond proceeds, over $11.4 billion is allocated from this fund in the 2016–17 biennium, with the bulk of the monies going to the Texas Department of Transportation.[20]

The **Economic Stabilization Fund (ESF)**, commonly known as the Rainy Day Fund, was established through constitutional amendment in 1988 to provide relief during times of financial distress. The fund is generated by a formula involving the base year of 1987. If collections from oil and gas taxes exceed the 1987 base year amount, 75 percent is transferred to the fund. Transfers are made in February by the comptroller. Half of any "unencumbered" general revenue, that is, revenue not already targeted for a specific purpose, also goes into the fund. The legislature has the authority to contribute additional funds but never has.

Under certain extraordinary circumstances, ESF monies can be appropriated only with a three-fifths vote of members of both houses of the legislature. These circumstances include when a budget deficit develops in a biennium or the comptroller estimates that revenue will decline from one biennium to the next. Money can also be appropriated from this fund for other purposes at any time with the support of two-thirds of present members in each house.

Few thought that large sums would accumulate in the fund. The first transfer of funds from oil and gas tax revenues of $18.5 million took place in 1990. The ESF account balance was kept below $100 million until 2001, when deposits transferred into the account exceeded $700 million. In 2003 the ESF was depleted to help solve the impending $10 billion budget shortfall. In 2003 and 2005 the legislature appropriated ESF monies to a variety of agencies, including the Teachers' Retirement System, various health and human service agencies, the governor's office, and the Texas Education Agency. Rising tax revenues from oil and gas production in the first decade of the twenty-first century flooded the ESF with funds. In 2014 and 2015, constitutional amendments passed that transferred rainy day funds to supporting water and transportation funding initiatives in the state. By the end of fiscal year 2015 the Texas Rainy Day Fund had grown to over $8.5 billion and is projected to increase to $10.4 billion by the end of the 2016–17 biennium (see Table 11.6). This fund contains more cash than similar funds in any other state. Only Alaska, also awash in oil and gas revenues, had a fund whose size approached that of the Texas Rainy Day Fund. The debate over whether or how to use the Rainy Day Fund to close the budget shortfall was a major issue during the 2011 and 2013 legislative sessions, and likely will be so again whenever the economy falters and the state revenues decline.[21]

To appreciate the importance of the operations of Texas's 400 funds and the complexity that they introduce into the budgetary process, one need only look at a few funds lying at the heart of higher education. Legislative goals are met through the creation of these funds and the allocation and reallocation of funds to and from them. Some funds, such as the Permanent University Trust Fund or the Higher Education Fund, were established to channel money directly to certain institutions of higher education. Others, like the National Research University Fund, operate in order to encourage universities to behave in certain ways and to achieve a specific set of legislative objectives.

The **Permanent University Trust Fund (PUF)** contributes to the support of most institutions in the University of Texas (UT) and Texas A&M University systems. Originally established in 1876 by a land grant of 1 million acres, the fund contains approximately 2.1 million acres in 24 west Texas counties. Under provisions in the state constitution, all surface lease income goes into the Available University Fund (AUF),

Economic Stabilization Fund (ESF) fund established by constitutional amendment in 1988 to provide funds for the state during times of financial stress, commonly known as the Rainy Day Fund

Permanent University Trust Fund (PUF) fund established in 1876 and funded from the proceeds from land owned by the state; monies go to various universities in the University of Texas (UT) and Texas A&M systems

TABLE 11.6

Economic Stabilization Fund History, Fiscal Years 2004 to 2017 (in billions of dollars)

BIENNIUM	REVENUES	EXPENDITURES	ENDING BALANCE
2002–03	$0.8	$0.4	$0.4
2004–05	1.0	1.5	–0.1
2006–07	2.5	1.2	1.2
2008–09	5.5	0.1	6.7
2010–11	1.5	3.2	5.0
2012–13	3.0	1.9	6.2
2014–15	4.3	2.0	8.5
2016–17*	1.9	0.0	10.4

*Projected estimates.
Note: These are reported figures. Columns and rows may not add due to rounding.
SOURCE: Comptroller of Public Accounts, 2015 Certification Revenue Estimate. See also Texas Legislative Budget Board, *Fiscal Size-Up: 2016–17 Biennium*, p. 43.

a fund set up to distribute PUF monies. Mineral income and the proceeds from the sale of PUF lands go into PUF and are invested. In 1999 an amendment to the constitution authorized the UT Board of Regents to channel investment income into the AUF. Two-thirds of the monies going to AUF go to the UT system; one-third goes to the Texas A&M system. The first obligation of any income earned by PUF is to pay the debt service on outstanding PUF bonds. The estimated market value of the PUF on December 31, 2015 was $17.4 billion.[22]

The **Higher Education Fund (HEF)** was established by a constitutional amendment for universities that did not have access to PUF monies. It is funded through the General Revenue Fund. Appropriations for the HEF are projected to be $656.3 million for the 2016–17 biennium. An advisory committee made up of member institutions provides input to the Texas Higher Education Coordinating Board, which in turn makes recommendations to the legislature for budgetary allocation to each school out of the HEF.

Higher Education Fund (HEF) state higher education fund for universities not having access to PUF monies

The **National Research University Fund (NRUF)** was established through a 2009 constitutional amendment to provide a source of funding for universities seeking to achieve national prominence as research institutions. Under the amendment, money was transferred from the HEF to the NRUF. UT Austin and Texas A&M are already considered to be national research institutions and therefore do not qualify for this fund. Eligibility criteria as well as distribution rules were established in 2011 by the legislature. An institution must be identified as an emerging research university by the Higher Education Coordinating Board and must expend at least $45 million in specifically defined types of research. In addition, universities must meet at least four of the following criteria to qualify: (1) maintain an endowment of at least $400 million in the two preceding academic years; (2) produce 200 Ph.D. degrees during the previous two years; (3) have a freshman class of high academic achievement;

National Research University Fund (NRUF) fund established in 2009 to provide funding to universities seeking to achieve national prominence as research institutions

(4) be designated as a member of the Association of Research Libraries, have a Phi Beta Kappa Chapter, or be a member of Phi Kappa Phi; (5) have a certain number of tenured faculty who have demonstrated excellence by winning a Nobel Prize or other prestigious fellowships, or have been elected to one of the National Academies; and (6) have a demonstrable excellence in graduate education. In 2015, the value of the fund was over $630 million.

In 2011 seven universities were designated as emerging research universities, each of which could have access to these funds if certain criteria were met. They were Texas Tech University, the University of Texas at Arlington, the University of Texas at Dallas, the University of Texas at El Paso, the University of Texas at San Antonio, the University of Houston, and the University of North Texas. In January 2012, Texas Tech and the University of Houston were identified by the Coordinating Board as being eligible to receive some of these NRUF monies subject to meeting a state audit. Appropriations from the fund are estimated to total $61.1 million for the 2016–17 biennium.[23]

The Texas Constitution and the Budget

 Outline the constitutional provisions that affect how the state budget is made

A number of constitutional factors affect the way the budget is made in Texas. Probably the biggest constraint on the budgetary process has to do with time limits. As noted in Figure 11.3, the legislature is compelled to write a two-year, or biennial, budget because of the constitutional provision that the legislature may meet in regular session only once every two years. One of the effects of this restricted time frame is to force government agencies to project their budgetary needs well in advance of any clear understanding of the particular problems they may be facing during the biennium. In addition, the legislature can meet for only 140 days in regular session. This seriously limits the amount of time that the legislature can spend analyzing the budget or developing innovative responses to pressing matters of public importance.

Another important factor is that a large portion of the biennial budget is dedicated for special purposes by federal law or by the Texas Constitution or state statute. These dedicated funds include federal monies earmarked for financing health care for the poor (Medicaid), as well as state funds for highways, education, teachers' retirement, and numerous other purposes. The purpose of dedicated funds is not difficult to understand. Supporters of particular programs want to create a stable revenue source for priority programs. But in protecting their own programs, supporters encourage other interests to do likewise, with the result that the legislature loses control of a large portion of the budget.

Finally, a number of specific constitutional provisions constrain the legislature's control of the budget.[24] Two of these—the Pay-as-You-Go Limit and the Spending Limit—limit the appropriations process in very specific ways.

What to Do with a Budget Surplus

Unlike the federal government, Texas state government cannot approve a budget deficit and must pass a balanced budget every two years. This is a complicated process full of uncertainty. Projecting expenditures in programs like Medicaid, public education, and higher education is difficult. Predicting future tax revenues is even more problematic. An unexpected recession or bust in oil price can drive revenues down significantly, throwing the projected state budget into a deficit that must be resolved before it can be passed. And the reverse can be true: an unexpected economic boom or surge in oil prices can drive up revenues unexpectedly, creating an unexpected surplus.

Not surprisingly, the politics of budget surpluses are quite different from those involving deficits. In the 2015 legislative session, state lawmakers faced a budget surplus. Previous comptroller Susan Combs had underestimated the revenues flowing into state coffers for the 2014–15 biennium by $11.3 billion, the worst estimate in 40 years of budgeting.[a]

The budgetary windfall led to a lively debate about what to do with the surplus funds. On the one hand, some policy makers, such as Chuck DeVore of the Texas Public Policy Foundation, a conservative think tank in the state, argued that the surplus means that Texas taxpayers have overpaid the state and they should receive refunds.

On the other hand, Dick Lavine and Eva DeLuna Castro of the Center for Public Policy Priorities, a progressive think tank in Austin, argued that cuts to education and health care from the last session should be restored so that the state can better prepare for an uncertain economic future.

DeVore countered that education money is spent not on the classroom but on bureaucratic overhead, and he pointed to the fact that the student-teacher ratio in Texas is better than the national average. He also contended that as the legislature spends more on new programs, a sense of entitlement will develop, making it difficult to make cuts later on during times of economic difficulty. Lavine and Castro, in turn, responded that Texas was simply not spending enough in real dollars given the state's rapid growth. With new residents on highways, in classrooms, and in hospitals, the state needs to maintain these public goods for future generations. Spending the same amount of money as we did when the state's population was smaller will not lead to a prosperous state.

After considerable wrangling over the best level of funding for existing programs, the legislature passed a

two-year budget that represented a 3.6 percent increase from the previous budget. Funding increased for education and border security. The final budget left a surplus of $6.4 billion and did not touch the estimated $11 billion in the Rainy Day Fund. Most importantly for conservative Republicans, property and franchise taxes were cut by $3.8 billion.[b]

COMMUNICATING EFFECTIVELY: YOUR VOICE

- How should policy makers deal with a projected budgetary surplus? Should taxes be cut or spending increased? If the latter, where should it be increased first?

- Suppose your state representative thought that taxes should be reduced but you think spending for public education should be increased. What argument would you make to try to bring your representative around on the issue?

FIGURE 11.3

Texas Biennial Budget Cycle

SOURCE: Senate Research Center, *Budget 101: A Guide to the Budget Process in Texas* (January 2011), p. 5.

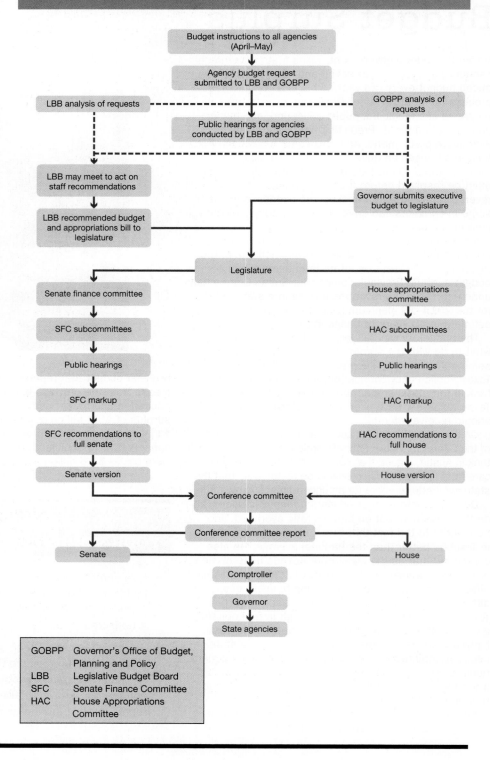

GOBPP	Governor's Office of Budget, Planning and Policy
LBB	Legislative Budget Board
SFC	Senate Finance Committee
HAC	House Appropriations Committee

The Pay-as-You-Go Limit Article 3, Section 49a (Pay-as-You-Go Limit), of the Texas Constitution requires the state to maintain a balanced budget. Under this provision, the General Revenue Fund Budget is not allowed to exceed the projected available revenue. All bills that get as far as **appropriations** in the legislative process must be sent to the comptroller of public accounts so the comptroller can certify that the bills are within available budget limit projections. One of the most important consequences of the pay-as-you-go limit is to put the comptroller at the heart of the budget process.[25]

The Spending Limit, or, The Limit on the Growth of Certain Appropriations Article 8, Section 22, which was passed in 1978, specifies that the growth in appropriations cannot be more than the growth of the state's economy, not counting dedicated spending as specified in the state constitution. This means that when the state's economy shrinks, appropriations also have to shrink. The Legislative Budget Board (LBB) is responsible for determining what the proper financial figures are to meet this mandate. Under Texas law, the LBB determines this by dividing the estimated total state personal income for the next biennium by the estimated total state personal income for the current biennium. The LBB may adopt "a more comprehensive definition of the rate of growth" if the alternative definition is approved by a special committee composed of the governor, the Speaker of the House, and the comptroller.[26]

One might think that there would be times that the LBB would be reluctant to perform its constitutional duties. Adopting particularly dismal projections derived from the growth formula hardly makes one popular politically. But there are checks in place to make sure that the projections are made and the limit on growth is delivered in a timely fashion to the legislature. Under law, the LBB is prohibited from distributing the budget or the appropriations bill to either the legislature or the governor until this limit on the rate of growth of appropriations has been adopted. If the LBB fails to adopt a growth limit (and a spending limit), the rate of growth in the state's economy is treated as if it were zero. State revenues not dedicated by the Texas Constitution to particular functions must remain at the same level as in the previous biennium.

For 2016–17, these two spending limits worked in the following way (see Table 11.7). The Comptroller calculated the available revenue to be $110.1 billion, $4.1 billion above General Revenue Funds appropriations. Meanwhile, the LBB calculated that the spending limit was $94.6 billion, $1.7 billion above the biennial appropriations funded with state tax revenues not dedicated by the constitution. Because it was lower, the legislature had to adapt the CBB's spending limits.[27]

Along with the Pay-as-You-Go Limit and the Spending Limit, three other constitutional provisions affect the budgeting process.

The Welfare Spending Limit Article 3, Section 51a, provides that the amount of money the state pays for assistance to or on behalf of needy dependent children and their caretakers shall not exceed 1 percent

Article 3, Section 49a (Pay-as-You-Go Limit) portion of the Texas Constitution that requires the state to maintain a balanced budget

appropriations authorization by the legislature to a government agency or body to spend up to a particular amount of money

PERSONAL RESPONSIBILITY: WHAT WOULD YOU DO?

- Though the Texas Constitution mandates that the state maintain a balanced budget, there are times when an unexpected shortfall hits the state. If you were a state legislator facing that situation, what would you do—argue that Texas should run a budget deficit, or cut services?

- Do you think the federal government should maintain a balanced budget, no matter what the circumstances? If not, why should Texas and the federal government act differently?

TABLE 11.7

Two Ways to Calculate the Constitutional Spending Limit

Pay-as-You-Go Limit

2016–17 General Revenue Funds appropriations	$106.0 billion
2016–17 Comptroller projection for revenue	$110.1 billion
Remaining spending authority	$4.1 billion

Spending Limit

2014–15 appropriations (not dedicated)	$84.7 billion
LBB adopted growth rate	11.7%
2016–17 spending authority	$94.6 billion
2016–17 appropriations (not dedicated)	$92.8 billion
Remaining spending authority	$1.7 billion

of the state budget in any biennium. This article sets a constitutional limit on the amount of money that the state may pay out to welfare beneficiaries under the Temporary Assistance for Needy Families program (TANF). The total state budget appropriated by the 83rd legislature was $209.4 billion, instituting a welfare spending limit of over $2 billion. State funds appropriated for TANF, however, were only $96.5 million, far below the 1 percent limit. State expenditures on Medicaid are not included in this spending limit.[28]

Limitation on Debt Payable from the General Revenue Fund
The state constitution also limits the amount of debt the state can incur. Under a 1997 amendment to Article 3, Section 49j, the legislature cannot authorize additional debt if the resulting **debt service** is greater than 5 percent of the average General Revenue Fund revenue for the three preceding fiscal years (this excludes dedicated spending). Basically, Texas state debt cannot be more than 5 percent of state revenue.

> **debt service** money spent by the state to pay off debt; includes interest and principal payments

One of the consequences of this constitutional debt limit is that compared with other states (as well as with the federal government), the Texas debt burden is relatively low. A 2015 Tax Foundation study calculated that Texas's per capita debt burden was $1,509. This contrasted with per capita debts of $6,935 in New York, $4,997 in Illinois, and $4,944 in California. Texas's per capita state debt was ranked 45th out of the 50 states.[29]

Budget-Execution Authority
Under a constitutional amendment passed in 1985 (now Article 16, Section 69), the legislature was empowered to establish rules for the expenditure of funds by state agencies. Today this means that between legislative sessions, the governor or the LBB may propose (1) that an agency stop spending money appropriated to it in the budget, (2) that money be transferred from one

agency to another, or (3) that the purpose for an appropriation to a particular agency be changed. If the governor proposes the changes, the LBB must approve or amend the proposal. If the LBB proposes the changes, the governor must approve or amend the proposal.

The Budgetary Process

Identify the major steps and players in making the state budget

In theory, Texas has a "dual-budget" system. This means that responsibility for preparing an initial draft of the budget is shared by the governor through the Governor's Office of Budget, Planning, and Policy (GOBPP) and the legislature through the LBB. In practice, the budget is primarily the responsibility of the legislature.

The GOBPP is responsible for advising the governor, the chief planning officer of the state, regarding fiscal matters. It prepares the governor's budget recommendations for the legislature, monitors state appropriations and operations, provides analysis on fiscal and economic matters, coordinates federal programs in the state, and assists in the operations of various regional and state planning councils.

Before 1949 there was little coordination in public budgeting. Financial procedures varied, and state agencies were funded by individual appropriations. In 1949 a law was enacted to establish the 10-member LBB, whose primary job would be to recommend appropriations for all agencies of state government. The board is chaired by the lieutenant governor. The vice chair is the Speaker of the House. Other members include the chairs of the House Appropriations Committee, the House Committee on Ways and Means, the Senate Finance Committee, and the Senate State Affairs Committee. Two additional members from the Senate and the House are chosen by the lieutenant governor and the Speaker, respectively.

The LBB appoints a budget director, who brings together budgeting requests from the various state agencies and prepares appropriations bills for them. The LBB is also responsible for evaluating agency programs and developing estimates of the probable costs of implementing legislation introduced in a legislative session. The LBB's draft budget, not the governor's, is the basis for final legislation. Table 11.8 summarizes the duties of key players in the budgetary process.

Preparing and implementing a budget are complex matters. The budgetary process involves two stages. In the first stage, the LBB develops a draft budget based on requests supplied by state agencies. This draft budget follows a series of steps. First, strategic plans are developed by each agency. A strategic plan includes (1) a mission statement, (2) a statement about the goals of the agency, (3) a discussion of the population served by the agency, (4) an explanation of the means that will be used to achieve these goals, and (5) an identification of the measures to be used to assess the agency's success in meeting these goals. This information provides the basis for LBB funding recommendations for each agency. In the spring or early summer prior to the legislative session, the LBB sends out detailed Legislative Appropriation Request (LAR) instructions to the agencies. Hearings are then held by the LBB and the GOBPP with

TABLE 11.8

Key Players in the Budgetary Process

The Legislative Budget Board (LBB)

1. adopts a constitutional spending limit

2. prepares a general appropriations bill

3. prepares agency performance reports

4. guides, reviews, and finalizes agency strategic plans

5. prepares fiscal notes regarding costs and impacts of proposed legislation

6. engages in "budget execution actions" in conjunction with the governor by transferring money from one assigned purpose to another purpose or to another agency

The governor and the Governor's Office of Budget, Planning, and Policy (GOBPP)

1. develop a strategic plan for the state

2. help to develop agency Legislative Appropriation Requests (LARs)

3. hold LAR hearings, often in conjunction with the legislature

4. deliver a governor's appropriations budget and a general appropriations bill at the beginning of the legislative session

5. exercise a line-item veto after an appropriations bill is passed by the legislature

6. engage in "budget execution actions" in conjunction with the LBB by transferring money from one assigned purpose to another purpose or to another agency

The comptroller of public accounts

1. submits a statement regarding the estimated anticipated revenues for the coming biennium

2. certifies that an appropriations bill is in balance with projected state revenues

3. collects state taxes

4. tracks 600+ separate revenue and spending funds and makes sure that agencies stay within their budgets

The state auditor's office develops independent audits of state agencies, including institutions of higher education. These audits are used to evaluate agencies.

each agency where the agency's strategic plan and LAR are discussed. LARs become the starting point for the appropriations bill that is prepared by the LBB. *Legislative Budget Estimates* is a publication of the LBB that contains information on the proposed appropriations bill, including expenditures for previous bienniums and proposed expenditures for the next biennium.[30]

While the draft budgets are being prepared, the comptroller's office prepares the Biennial Revenue Estimate (BRE). The BRE is a detailed forecast of the total revenue that the state is expected to take in over the next biennium. The Texas Constitution requires that the BRE contain "an itemized estimate of the anticipated revenue . . . to be credited during the succeeding biennium." The BRE includes other information to assist legislators in the budget process, including (1) statements about the anticipated revenue from different sources, (2) an analysis of the economic outlook facing Texas and the nation, and (3) a detailed accounting of the funds in the state treasury. The comptroller effectively sets a ceiling on what the state legislature may spend. Although the legislature can override the comptroller's estimates with a four-fifths vote of each house, this has never happened. The BRE is updated by the comptroller when economic conditions change significantly and for special sessions of the legislature.

The difficulty of making accurate projections about tax revenue over the next biennium has been a concern in recent years. A study conducted by the Comptroller's Office in 2015 highlighted how frequently actual biennial tax revenues undershot or overshot Comptroller projections. Interestingly, the study found that over the past 40 years overestimations of tax revenue were a result of an unexpected recession or a "precipitous" decline in energy prices. Underestimates of tax collections were associated with soaring energy prices, the implementation of new technologies in the oil and gas industry (such as fracking), and boom periods in the economy that led to higher employment rates and an expansion of the housing market. One thing was clear from the study: making accurate predictions about tax collections over a two-year period was difficult, if not impossible.[31]

The second stage of the budget process involves the legislative process. By the seventh day of each regular session, appropriations bills are submitted by the LBB to the House Appropriations Committee and the Senate Finance Committee. Traditionally, the bills are introduced to these committees by their respective chairs, although any member may do so. The bills then work their way through the committee system of each house separately and are subject to hearings, debates, and revisions. This process of drafting the bill is referred to as a "markup." Final versions of the budget are prepared by the House Appropriations Committee and the Senate Finance Committee. Each house then votes on the bill. Differences between the two versions of the bill are reconciled in a conference committee.

The conference committee is composed of representatives from the Senate and the House. Senate members are selected by the lieutenant governor or the president pro tempore of the Senate. The senator sponsoring the bill, traditionally the chairman of the Senate Finance Committee, appoints the chair of the Senate conferees. At least two members from the Senate Finance Committee must sit on the conference committee. The Speaker of the House appoints all conferees from the House as well as the chair of the House conferees. Traditionally, Senate and House representatives alternate each session in chairing the conference committee.

Specific rules govern how disagreements between the Senate and House versions of the appropriations bills are to be handled.[32]

- Items that appear in both versions of the bill must be included in the final conference committee report.
- Items that appear in both versions of the bill with identical amounts allocated to them may not be changed by the committee.

- Items that appear in both versions of the bill with differing amounts allocated to them cannot be eliminated. The committee has the discretion to fund these items at a level not larger than the larger allocation or smaller than the smaller allocation.
- Items that appear in one version of the bill but not the other can be included or eliminated from the final bill subject to the discretion of the committee. However, no more money may be allocated to that item than is found in the original version of the bill.
- Items found in neither version of the bill may not be included in the final conference report. However, the conference committee has the discretion to propose the appropriation of money for bills that already have been passed by the legislature.

While constraining the discretionary authority of the committee to a degree, these rules still leave considerable room for political maneuvering on the part of the committee. Membership on this important committee is a highly prized commodity. Once the bill passes the conference committee, it is returned to both houses for final passage.

Under Article 3, Section 49a, of the Texas Constitution, the comptroller has the formal authority to "certify" the budget. This means that the comptroller confirms that the comptroller's office has analyzed the budget and concluded that it is within the current revenue estimates. For all intents and purposes, the budget is being declared balanced. If the general appropriations bill is not certified by the comptroller, it is returned to the house in which it originated. The legislature must then either decrease expenditures or raise revenues to make up the difference. According to provisions set out in Article 3, Section 49a, under conditions of "imperative public necessity" the legislature may with a four-fifths vote in each house decide to spend in excess of anticipated revenue.

After certification, the budget moves on to the governor, who can sign, not sign, or veto the entire bill or exercise the line-item veto. With the line-item veto, in particular, the governor has the power to unravel some of the compromises that legislators may have forged to get the bill through the committee system. The line-item veto also potentially gives the governor enormous power to limit expenditures in certain targeted areas. Of course, line-item vetoes exercised too vigorously in one session can come back to haunt the governor's legislative agenda in the next session.

The appropriations bill takes effect on September 1 in odd-numbered years. All agencies are bound by it. Monitoring agency compliance with the budget is the job of the LBB and the state auditor's office. The governor and LBB have the authority to execute the budget. This includes the power to shift funds between agency programs or between agencies if necessary when the legislature is not in session. This power to execute the budget is an important one. It has been a tool used by the governor and LBB to cope with the unanticipated shortfalls in the state budget by ordering state agencies to cut their expenditures in the middle of a biennium.

As noted in the chapter on the executive power, the governor is able to move funds from one account to another without permission of the LBB if he declares an emergency. Such a situation has only occurred once—in the summer of 2014—when Governor Perry declared an emergency and transferred funds to pay for the deployment of

National Guard troops along the border with Mexico to cope with illegal immigration into Texas.

Budget Crises in Twenty-First-Century Texas

 Analyze major budget crises in Texas

The Great Recession of 2008 plunged Texas into an intense budgetary crisis. The 2011 legislative session was a particularly difficult one.[33] From the outset, legislators knew that difficult budgetary choices would have to be faced. For two years, Texas had dodged the worst effects of the Great Recession. But in 2011 hard decisions were going to have to be made to balance the budget.

Two factors had delayed the full impact of the recession upon the Texas budget. First, LBB projections in January 2009 for tax revenues for the 2010–11 biennium grossly underestimated the impact that the recession would have upon tax revenues. The projection had anticipated a surplus of $2.1 billion in General Revenues and $3 billion set aside for property tax relief from the previous budget, making the 2010–11 financial outlook appear to be quite secure. But in reality the surpluses had evaporated, revealing the budget to be far too optimistic and exposing policy makers to some difficult decisions. Second, Texas had been initially protected from the worst of the recession by an infusion of federal funding. In an effort to fight the recession at the national level, the federal government instituted a surge of deficit spending under the American Recovery and Reinvestment Act passed in February 2009. This enabled the 2009 Texas legislature to appropriate $6.4 billion in federal funds to cover a projected General Revenues Fund gap and maintain educational and health and human services programs sponsored with the federal government. By the end of the 2010–11 biennium, the federal dollars coming into the state rose to $8 billion, largely as a result of higher-than-expected caseloads for Medicaid, as well as an expansion of that program through federal legislation.

The pressures on the budget continued unabated through 2009 and 2010. One of the chief effects of the Great Recession across the country was the sharp contraction in real estate prices.[34] Low interest rates supported by Federal Reserve policy along with loose credit standards had led to a "bubble" in real estate that had pushed up property values through the early years of the twenty-first century. The real estate bubble popped in 2008, bringing many banks to their knees as the value of their portfolios plunged with collapsing real estate prices. Banks turned to Washington for assistance and were ultimately bailed out by a massive intrusion of the federal government into the banking system.

Although Texas escaped the worst of the real estate collapse, largely because the real estate bubble had been more muted in Texas than elsewhere, credit tightened and property values declined across the state through 2007, 2008, and 2009. As property values declined, so did property tax revenues. What had been a banking crisis at the national level became a funding crisis at the state and local levels, particularly for schools, community colleges, and health districts where funding was based largely on property taxes. In addition, sales tax receipts in Texas fell for the first time in 2009 since 2003. Sales tax receipts fell each month from February 2009 to April 2010 in Texas.

By January 2011 the comptroller projected a $4.3 billion shortfall in general tax revenues against projected expenses for fiscal year 2011, the second year of the previous biennium. The deficit projections for the 2012–13 biennium were even worse, putting the shortfall in general tax revenue at around $17 billion. Taking into account increasing demands for Medicaid and school district funding put the general revenue shortfall for the coming biennium somewhere between $24 and $27 billion.

The Great Recession was not the only cause of the financial shortfall. There were also long-term structural problems facing the budget brought on by property tax reform. In 2006 the legislature required schools to reduce their school property tax rates by one-third. The reasons were complicated. The Texas Supreme Court had ruled in *West Orange Cove ISD v. Neeley* that school districts needed to have some "meaningful discretion" in the setting of property tax rates.[35] If all property tax rates were set at the maximum allowed under law, a situation found in many districts, the court concluded that a statewide property tax essentially would have been put into place, and this was a violation of the state constitution prohibiting such a statewide property tax. Lowering property tax rates was thus one way to bring the existing property tax into compliance with the court's ruling.

A key component of the 2008 financial crisis was home foreclosures like this one in San Antonio. This crisis put intense strains on the Texas state budget.

Pressures to balance Texas's state budget often create difficult and controversial choices for legislators, like how much funding to provide for public schools.

Lowering property tax rates, however, would have serious funding implications for public schools. In an effort to replace lost property tax revenues and maintain funding levels at the schools, the legislature also increased the state corporate franchise tax and the cigarette tax. The LBB calculated that lost revenue from the property tax cut would be $14.2 billion for the next 2014–15 biennium. Tax increases would bring in $8.3 billion. From the outset, there was thus a projected shortfall of $5.9 billion for the next 2013–14 biennium. Proponents argued that this shortfall would evaporate as new tax collections grew. Unfortunately, these optimistic predictions were wrong. The new taxes actually brought in $3.78 billion less than projected for 2008–09 and $5.13 billion less than anticipated for 2010–11. Thus, there was a structural deficit built into the budget from the property tax relief of $9.16 billion for 2008–09 and $9.95 billion for 2010–11.

The initial response of state leaders to the impending fiscal shortfall was a call for immediate spending cuts in the current fiscal year. In January 2010 the governor, lieutenant governor, and Speaker of the House asked all state agencies and institutions of higher education to plan to reduce spending by 10 percent in fiscal year 2010 and 5 percent for fiscal year 2011. In December 2010 there was an additional 2.5 percent cut in spending. State leaders also drew upon the Economic Stabilization Fund (the Rainy Day Fund). Under a supplemental appropriations bill in 2011, the 2011 budget deficit thus was closed, $1.2 billion coming from reduced spending and $3.2 billion coming from the Rainy Day Fund.

But the bigger problem lay with the multibillion-dollar shortfall for the next biennium. Legislators had to agree exactly on what the deficit was, finally concluding that it was approximately $22.6 billion. How was this to be addressed? Conservative Republicans led by Governor Perry and Tea Party supporters rejected the idea that new taxes might be a solution. Instead they looked to spending cuts, payment deferments, and various "revenue enhancements" that would bring the budget back into balance. It took a special session of the legislature in June 2011 to finally pass the bill that brought the budget for 2012–13 back into balance. There were a few financial tricks used to balance the budget. For example, some taxpayers were required to speed up payments of various sales, alcohol, and motor fuels taxes so that the revenues would be received during this biennium rather than the next. The transfer of motor fuels tax receipts from the General Revenue Fund to the State Highway Fund was delayed, keeping money in this biennium. Payments to school districts for August 2013 were also deferred to September 2013, pushing another set of expenditures into the next biennium. Such budgetary sleights of hand can be done only once. But the hope was that the worst of the crisis would have passed by the time that these tactics became an issue in a future biennium.

The most important initiatives taken up to address the budget shortfall were spending cuts. Entitlement funding to public schools in the state was cut by $4 billion for the 2012–13 biennium. In addition, five months of the two-year Medicaid budget, approximately $4.3 billion, was not funded. On the face of it, one might think that a partially unfunded Medicaid proposal would not pass constitutional muster. But key legislators and the comptroller agreed to cover these unfunded Medicaid expenditures with either unexpected revenues or the remaining $7 billion in the Rainy Day Fund. They also agreed that this would meet the balanced budget requirement. Medicaid also underwent $1.8 billion in "cost containment savings." Ultimately, a total of $5 billion in new revenues was put into place along with $17.6 billion in cuts in expenditures.

On paper at least, the budget deficit had been addressed and political leaders had met their constitutional duties to balance the budget. Sales tax receipts began to recover from the depths of the recession throughout 2011 and into 2012. In June 2012, Comptroller Susan Combs reported that sales tax receipts were up 7 percent over the previous year and had increased every month for 12 months. The Texas economy was outperforming that of much of the nation, but not enough to cover a projected $4 billion budget shortfall for the 2012–13 biennium. There were also a number of school financing lawsuits in court that could potentially cost the state over $4 billion. In addition, state leaders had to figure out how to cover the onetime school payment delay and the Medicaid underfunding in the 2012–13 budget. But the biggest threat to a balanced budget did not lie in school funding or even in sales tax receipts. President Obama's federal reforms to health care presented new short-term and long-term spending commitments that could pose new and unanticipated challenges to the Texas budget in coming years.

Looking Beyond the Budget Crisis of 2011

The regular 2013 and 2015 legislative sessions were smooth regarding budget matters, at least when compared to the 2011 session. Collegiality on budget matters was largely the result of Republican control of all branches of government coupled to a

Public finance deeply affects the trade-offs in Texas's public policy. In 2013 the legislature compromised on a bill that would continue to fund highway construction (like this one in Sebastian) while still balancing the state budget.

burgeoning state economy fueled by expanding job opportunities, rising housing prices, increased exports, and a resurgent oil and gas industry. Rosy budget projections for the next biennium offered legislators some wiggle room to do what they did best: cut taxes and increase spending on popular programs.

During the 2013 session some modifications to the franchise tax were passed by the legislature, including modest tax cuts contingent upon the comptroller's certifying that the state will receive enough revenue to offset the proposed cuts. Also, a constitutional amendment was proposed during the regular session and passed by the voters in November 2013, providing the establishment of two new funds: the State Water Implementation Fund for Texas (SWIFT) and the State Water Implementation Revenue Fund for Texas (SWIRFT). The amendment also provided for a onetime transfer of Rainy Day Fund monies to support the financing of water supply projects in Texas through these funds.

Perhaps the most controversial budget issue dealt with by the legislature during the 2013 and 2015 sessions centered upon transportation policy. How was the legislature going to pay for improving and expanding state highways, a cost that some experts put at up to $4 billion? Failing to pass a bill during the regular session and the first two special sessions in the summer of 2013, legislators finally brokered a compromise in the third special session. The financial mechanism that was established says much about the byzantine way in which budgetary matters often operate in the state. Under current law, 75 percent of funds raised above 1987 tax collection levels (which were $531.9 million for oil and $599.8 million for gas) was transferred from the General Revenue Fund to the Rainy Day Fund. The legislature sought to change this by proposing an amendment to the constitution (Article 3, Section 49g) taken before the voters on November 4, 2014. The amendment allowed half of this money (that is, half of the 75 percent above the 1987 levels) to still go to the Rainy Day Fund, but the other half would go to the State Highway Fund. There would be two provisos: first, certain statutory defined requirements would have to be met regarding the minimum funding of the Rainy Day Fund; second, the proposals for transferring money to the State Highway Fund would sunset in 2025. The amendment passed in November 2014 with 79.8 percent of the vote in favor. A second constitutional amendment involving transportation was passed following the 2015 session in November. This amendment dedicated some taxes collected on car sales to the State Highway Fund. Like the 2014 amendment, the 2015 amendment included a complicated formula for distributing the funds to the State Highway Fund and a sunset provision limiting the collections to 10 years.

Public Finance and the Future of Texas

Public finance in Texas will continue to be a troubling issue for political leaders in Texas in the future. Revenues from the sales tax, severance taxes, and local property taxes are increasing once again. Confidence has grown among policy makers that the worst of the Great Recession is behind Texas. Despite this newfound optimism, state and local political leaders remain cautious in their projections about the future. There still remains uncertainty about the future course of the national and international economies. Texas's economy is tied inextricably to the booms and busts of the U.S. economy as well as the world economy. Moreover, the revenue mechanisms that support policy initiatives in Texas are sensitive and can move down quickly when the national and international economies falter. A declining economy can cut back on consumer spending, which affects the sales tax revenue. Falling housing prices can adversely affect property revenue. Falling prices for oil and natural gas can cut into severance revenues and undercut the revenue flowing into the Rainy Day Fund. Such are the rules that govern public finance in Texas in the early twenty-first century.

State budgetary policy ultimately depends on the successful implementation of a national recovery policy that works. Few leaders in the state, particularly Tea Party Republicans, are confident about the current direction of national economic policy. A looming national deficit with no solution in sight may lead to calls in Washington to push more responsibilities (and costs) onto the backs of the states, further exacerbating Texas's budgetary problems.

Four factors will continue to dominate public finance in Texas over the next biennium. First, economic conditions look favorable in the short run, assuring the state a healthy flow of revenues from its complex structure of state and local taxes. Second, there will be increased demands from the federal government for paying for expanded federal initiatives in health care (see Chapter 12).

Third, increased population will lead to increased demands on state agencies for services ranging from health care to roads, to water, and to public education. All other things being equal, a larger population demands more from government, and that costs money. Fourth, there is a growing antigovernment feeling among portions of the population in Texas that state government is too big already. For Tea Partyers and other conservative Republicans, "No new taxes" is a successful mantra for winning office. Whether it will be a successful one for legislating and leading is another question. Navigating a passage between the rock of intensifying demands for expanded services and the hard place of "No new taxes" may be the most difficult problem legislators face in the foreseeable future.

Use ⚛ INQUIZITIVE to help you study and master this material.

What Is the Budget?

• Explain the purpose of the state budget and what is typically included (pp. 363–64)

Texas is required to operate within a balanced budget. The budget can be considered in light of five revenue streams: the General Revenues Fund budget, the General Revenue–Dedicated Funds budget, the Federal Funds budget, the Other Funds budget, and the All Funds budget.

Key Terms
General Revenues Fund budget (p. 363)
General Revenue–Dedicated Funds budget (p. 363)
Federal Funds budget (p. 363)
Other Funds budget (p. 363)
All Funds budget (p. 363)

Practice Quiz
1. The Texas Constitution requires that the Texas budget must be
   a) balanced.
   b) approved by the governor's cabinet.
   c) funded only from sales taxes.
   d) approved by the governor, the legislature, and the state treasurer.
   e) funded only from federal grants.

2. Federal expenditures primarily affect the state budget in which two areas?
   a) energy and law enforcement
   b) health and human services and education
   c) business development and highways
   d) interstate highways and airports
   e) Medicare and transportation

Spending and Revenue in Texas

• Describe the general pattern of state spending in Texas and where state revenue comes from (pp. 365–73)

Texas spends less than the national average in a variety of policy areas, including education and highway spending. Although Texas does not have an income tax, it has one of the highest sales taxes in the nation. However, the per capita revenue from those sales taxes is among the lowest in the nation. Property taxes in Texas are among the highest in the nation. Among other important state taxes are the natural gas production tax and the oil production and regulation tax. Although a controversial issue in the past, a state income tax has little support either in the legislature or in the population as a whole. Texas also has on average fewer state employees per capita than other states.

Key Terms
regressive tax (p. 371)
progressive tax (p. 371)
matching funds (p. 372)

Practice Quiz
3. Texas has the reputation for being
   a) a low-service, low-tax state.
   b) a high-service, high-tax state.
   c) a low-service, high-tax state.
   d) a high-service, low-tax state.
   e) an average-service, average-tax state.

4. One major revenue source for Texas is the sales tax, which is
   a) 8.25 percent for state government and 2.25 percent for local government.
   b) 4.25 percent for state government and 2 percent for local government.
   c) 6.25 percent for state government and 2 percent for local government.
   d) 5 percent for state government and 1.25 percent for local government.
   e) none of the above

5. A Texas personal income tax
   a) used to exist but was repealed because of new taxes on oil production.
   b) would have to be approved by the voters, and the revenues from it would have to support public education.
   c) would have to be passed through a constitutional amendment.
   d) could only be imposed on incomes greater than $250,000 per year.
   e) would be unlikely to raise much revenue.

State Funds

• Describe how the money in the budget is organized into specific funds (pp. 374–78)

Money flows into and out of a variety of over 400 different funds controlled by the state. Among the most important are the General Revenue Fund, the Permanent School Fund, the State Highway Fund, and the Economic Stabilization Fund (the Rainy Day Fund). The existence of these funds makes budgeting a complicated process.

Key Terms
General Revenue Fund (p. 374)
Permanent School Fund (PSF) (p. 374)
Available School Fund (ASF) (p. 374)
State Highway Fund (p. 374)
Economic Stabilization Fund (ESF) (p. 376)
Permanent University Trust Fund (PUF) (p. 376)
Higher Education Fund (HEF) (p. 377)
National Research University Fund (NRUF) (p. 377)

Practice Quiz
6. The Rainy Day Fund
   a) provides funds for flood victims.
   b) was designed to provide funding for the state during times of financial distress.
   c) contains only a small amount of state funds.
   d) is used to promote oil and gas development.
   e) can only be spent by the Texas comptroller.

7. The National Research University Fund
   a) pays for university-level research at all state universities.
   b) provides the funding for the University of Texas at Austin.
   c) funds Texas universities seeking national prominence as research institutions.
   d) only provides funds to universities with Nobel Prize winners.
   e) will not provide funds if more than 20 percent of students fail to graduate in four years.

The Texas Constitution and the Budget

> • Outline the constitutional provisions that affect how the state budget is made (pp. 378–83)

There are many constitutional restrictions on the budget, including the requirement of a biennial budget, a pay-as-you-go limit, a welfare spending limit, a limit on the growth of some appropriations, rules on the spending of funds by state agencies, and limitations on debt payable from the general revenue fund. These restrictions play important roles in shaping the budget policy-making process.

Key Terms

Article 3, Section 49a (Pay-as-You-Go Limit) (p. 381)
appropriations (p. 381)
debt service (p. 382)

Practice Quiz

8. Which of the following is *not* a constitutional constraint on the budgetary process in Texas?
   a) the annual budget
   b) a welfare spending limit
   c) a pay-as-you-go limit
   d) a limitation on the debt payable from the General Revenue Fund
   e) All are constitutional limits.

9. What is meant by "the budget-execution authority"?
   a) the power to execute the laws of the land
   b) the legislature's power to establish rules for the expenditure of funds by state agencies
   c) the governor's power to veto the budget
   d) the LBB's power to create the budget for the judiciary in Texas
   e) none of the above

The Budgetary Process

> • Identify the major steps and players in making the state budget (pp. 383–87)

In theory, Texas has a dual budget system with budgeting shared by the governor and the legislature. In reality, the budget is the responsibility of the legislature. There are a series of steps that the budget must go through to be passed by the legislature. Among the most important is the requirement that the Texas comptroller certify the budget as being balanced.

Practice Quiz

10. Who is the chief planning officer of the state of Texas?
    a) the lieutenant governor
    b) the Speaker of the House
    c) the comptroller
    d) the governor
    e) the state treasurer

11. The principal job of the Legislative Budget Board is
    a) to keep track of the expenses of the executive.
    b) to monitor the operations of the House.
    c) to raise taxes.
    d) to recommend appropriations for all agencies of state government.
    e) to conduct audits of state expenditures.

Budget Crises in Twenty-First-Century Texas

• Analyze major budget crises in Texas (pp. 387–92)

Texas has experienced a number of budgetary crises in the early years of the twenty-first century. Budgetary problems were exacerbated by property tax reforms and the Great Recession, which led to serious declines in revenue while the demands for services were increasing.

Practice Quiz

12. Which factors lie behind the budget crisis of 2011?
 a) the Great Recession and property tax reform
 b) declining oil and gas prices
 c) a burdensome income tax being implemented for the first time
 d) bipartisan government
 e) Obamacare

13. Which solution was put into place to address the budget crisis of 2011?
 a) instituting a state income tax
 b) speeding up the payments of various taxes on alcohol and motor fuels
 c) increasing the state sales tax
 d) allocating more money to elementary and secondary education
 e) increasing gasoline taxes

Toll roads play an important role in transportation policy in Texas today. While toll roads get people to their destination quickly, they can be expensive. Increasing toll costs have led many people to argue that a new approach is needed to address the state's transportation problems. The problem is that raising taxes to pay for "freeways" is almost as unpopular as increasing toll fees.

Public Policy

WHY PUBLIC POLICY MATTERS Toll fatigue. It is not a term that you will find in any dictionary, but it is one that policy makers and politicians today ignore at their own risk. Simply put, toll fatigue refers to the idea that people are becoming tired of toll roads in their everyday lives. They are tired of spending money each time they get on a new road to go to work or visit friends. They are tired of hearing about new plans by the state to use the power of eminent domain to seize private property for the public good and then to charge a toll for the right to travel on so-called public roads. They are tired of hearing about private investors with cozy relationships to politicians who might make fortunes by financing private toll roads in the state.[1]

Throughout the twentieth century, roads were largely "free" in Texas. People could travel from place to place in Texas on roads without paying a fee to use them. The building and upkeep of the roads was the responsibility of state and local government. Roads were paid for through a variety of taxes such as the state motor fuel tax. Chronic budget problems in the late twentieth and early twenty-first centuries undermined this arrangement. A significant portion of gasoline tax dollars was siphoned away from road building to another area of pressing concern: public education. This reallocation may have succeeded in getting more money to public education, but it also gave rise to a shortfall in funds dedicated to roads.

In order to address the burgeoning transportation demands of Texas's big urban areas, like Houston and Dallas–Fort Worth, politicians over the last 20 years have turned to toll roads as a way to fund, build, and maintain a new system of roads without raising taxes. By 2016, 25 toll roads were operating in the state. Rapidly growing metropolitan areas like Houston, Dallas–Fort Worth, and Austin had come to rely upon them heavily. It was difficult in moving around parts of these areas without getting on a toll road. Other areas like El Paso and San Antonio were seeing toll roads as a solution to their immediate transportation problems.[2]

Antitax, small-government Republicans initially saw two advantages to toll roads in the early twenty-first century: first, toll roads addressed a problem with a solution that was off-budget. Money would be borrowed and paid for through planned fees without raising formal state expenditures. Second, the toll road policy enabled legislatures to get access to funding without raising the gasoline tax, which is widely assumed to be unpopular with voters. Of course, from the perspective of drivers, the toll or fee functioned like a gasoline tax in that it had to be paid if they wanted to drive on the road. The toll road solution to building new roads spoke to the truth of an old joke: When is a tax not a tax? Answer: when it's a fee.

Governor Rick Perry proposed to build a massive 4,000-mile Trans-Texas Corridor connecting private toll roads, railroad tracks, and utility lines across the state, but opposition built throughout the state and the issue died in 2012. Since then, opposition to toll roads has expanded. In 2014, the Republican state convention replaced language in the state platform supporting "the legitimate construction of toll roads in Texas" with language opposing the use of public monies to subsidize private toll road projects. During the 2015 legislative session legislators failed to pass a new "comprehensive development agreement" that would authorize new toll projects in the state, and they passed a bill that blocked the state from borrowing money for toll road projects as it had in the past from the State Mobility Fund, a rotating fund used to fund highway projects. The legislature also asked for a report on what it would cost to eliminate toll roads in the state. A preliminary version of the report released in March 2016 reached the sobering conclusion that it would cost the state up to $40 billion to make Texas toll free.[3]

Toll fatigue is part of everyday life in Texas and is likely not to go away in the near future. Toll roads are but one policy that affects your life. Public policy is everywhere. Public policy is where the topics we have covered in the text—including the constitution, federalism, interest groups, elections, the legislature, and the courts—all come together. Public policy is where Texas addresses problems from the past and marks a new path into the future.

CHAPTERGOALS

- Describe the key steps and concepts in the policy-making process (pp. 401–4)

- Describe the major issues that have shaped education policy in Texas (pp. 404–16)

- Describe the state's role in addressing poverty and how it is affected by national policies (pp. 416–22)

- Explain why Medicaid in particular and health care policy in general have been so controversial in Texas (pp. 422–32)

- Consider the growing importance of policies related to water supplies in Texas (pp. 432–37)

The Policy-Making Process

In broadest terms, public policy refers to the outputs of governmental institutions. More narrowly, public policy can be defined as the expressed goals of a governmental body backed by incentives or sanctions.[4] Public policies can be found in laws passed by legislative bodies as well as in the rules, regulations, and orders from properly authorized public agencies. The incentives or sanctions can include a wide range of actions from subsidies encouraging individuals to act in a certain way to monetary penalties or admonitions to severe criminal penalties that punish people for engaging in particular actions.

One way that political scientists have approached the study of public policy is by focusing attention upon the different stages of the policy-making process, the political and administrative process through which governmental goals are identified, formulated, articulated into law, and evaluated.[5] The idea that there are stages of the policy-making process is not so much a step-by-step description or explicit roadmap of how public policy is made within institutions such as a legislature or a bureaucracy. Public policy is not made in a simple linear way. The real world of policy making is, in fact, much messier. In the real world, stages in the policy-making process may overlap or even collapse into one another. Nevertheless, the idea that there are stages of the policy-making process has proven to be a useful analytical framework for understanding the various factors that go into the making of public policy.

Problem Identification

The first stage is problem identification. Here, society at large and actors in the political system develop an understanding of how we must think about and address a particular problem. Roger Cobb and Charles Elder refer to this set of ideas as a "systemic agenda" where all issues are "commonly perceived by members of the political community as meriting public attention and as involving matters within the legitimate jurisdiction of existing governmental authority."[6] This systemic agenda is used by citizens and policy makers as a conceptual framework to understand the nature of public problems and to shape and direct the way policy makers will develop public policy aimed at them. For example, if we view the problem of poverty being fundamentally one of limited income, we might conclude that the best solution is increasing welfare payments to the poor. However, if we consider the problem of poverty to be behavior that causes people to be poor such as unwillingness to work or poor job skills, we might conclude that policies directed toward encouraging work or subsidizing education are better courses of action. In the problem identification stage, our ideology—that is, our ideas, concepts, and visions about the way society works—plays a major role in defining public-policy making.

Policy Formulation

Policy formulation is the second stage of the policy-making process. Here, the more general ideas that we have about social and political problems become clarified and strategies for dealing with these specifically defined problems are developed. Policy formulation involves the detailed procedures in passing legislation as well as in making administrative rules and regulations. Here, a kind of agenda setting—institutional agenda setting—takes place. As we noted in our earlier discussion of interest groups, one of the goals of interest groups is to gain access to policy discussions inside legislatures and agencies. Access provides interest groups with the opportunity to help set the institutional agenda in the policy formulation stage. Setting the agenda on what problems will be discussed, how these problems will be understood, and what concrete measures will be taken to address them lies at the heart of all policy formulation.

Implementation The third stage in the policy-making process is implementation. At this stage, the goals of public policy along with the incentives or sanctions to support them are put into effect by a particular government agency. Identifying the appropriate agency to implement a program is crucial at this stage. Similarly, budgetary policy plays a major role in the implementation stage and can determine the success or failure of a particular public policy. A well-formulated public policy can be dashed by poorly executed or poorly funded implementation.

Evaluation The fourth stage of the policy-making process is evaluation. At a certain point all public policies must be evaluated for their effectiveness. In the best of all possible worlds, good evaluation procedures would assess the stated goals of a particular policy against the actual outcomes of the implemented policy. Good evaluation would lead to a rethinking of the public policy in light of the problems being addressed and the solutions being formulated to address the problem. Similarly, good evaluation could lead to a rethinking of the strategies being used and the resources being committed to implementing the policy. Closing the loop between problem identification and program evaluation is one of the most difficult problems facing policy makers.

Some political scientists identify policy legitimation as another stage in the policy-making process. Legitimation—the establishment and recognition in the political community of the legality and constitutionality of a particular policy initiative—is probably better understood not as a separate stage but as something that takes place throughout the entire policy-making process. Legitimation can include a wide range of activities: open discussions of a problem in the press, committee investigations and oversight investigations, following the appropriate rules for passing a bill in the legislature or making a rule in an administrative agency, and judicial review of the policy. Establishing the legitimacy of a public policy throughout the various stages of the policy-making process is an essential part of any democratic political system.

Rationality in Policy Making

rationality the idea in public-policy making that we have clearly identified goals and that we seek to achieve these goals in an optimal or efficient manner

An often-stated goal of policy makers is to make public policy more rational and more efficient. **Rationality**, in this regard, generally refers to the idea that we have clearly identified the goals that we wish to achieve and have formulated and implemented policies that address these problems in an optimal or efficient manner. Optimality or efficiency refers to the idea that policy will be developed that will maximize the outputs of government with a minimum commitment of resources. Given this commitment to rationality in policy making, people are often surprised by how irrational and

As shown here, education policy involves the four key stages in the policy-making process. Clockwise from top left: A policy issue like school funding is identified. Politicians, like former state senator Wendy Davis, who filibustered a bill to lower school funding, create policies to address the issue. Bureaucrats implement policy changes (for example, adding more computers in classrooms). Finally, policies are evaluated and changes are considered. Here, the Texas Education Commissioner Michael Morath visits a middle school classroom in Dallas.

inefficient public policy can seem in a democracy. Part of the problem lies in the fact that the policy-making process is highly complex. Writing reports, holding committee hearings, and passing legislation often involve political compromises that muddy the waters of policy making. Vagueness in the problem identification stage along with compromises made among competing parties in the policy formulation stage can work against the development of rational and efficient solutions to problems.

There are additional factors that tend to work against rationality and efficiency in the making of public policy. The first is the fact that governments tend to work incrementally. Neither legislators nor government agencies begin their work on a particular problem from ground zero every year. Year in and year out, there is a general agreement among policy makers on the nature of a public problem and on how it should be addressed. Unless measures are taken to compel agencies to reassess what they are doing and why, programs, policies, and budgets tend to grow incrementally from one policy cycle to another. And even when such measures are taken, as in the Sunset process, as discussed in Chapter 8, or major changes are initiated in the fundamental direction of public policy, incrementalism governs the decision-making process.

A second factor that tends to work against rational and efficient government is that policy makers and other politically active individuals may not behave strictly rationally or efficiently. The economist Herbert Simon has argued that individual rationality is limited by a number of factors, including the expense of getting information about a problem, the cognitive limitations of the human mind, and the time constraints that all individuals face in making a decision.[7] Policy makers' rationality may

bounded rationality the idea in policy making that decision makers may seek satisfactory solutions to problems that are not necessarily optimal or efficient

be a "**bounded rationality**." Rather than seeking to rationally understand everything that is involved in a particular policy problem or optimize every action taken to address this problem, they may actually simply seek to "satisfice." Essentially, satisficing means to reach a decision that is satisfactory rather than optimal to the individual. From the perspective of the policy process as a whole, satisficing by many individuals and groups can lead to less-than-rational and less-than-efficient public policy.

To appreciate the intricacies of policy making, we will turn to a discussion of four policy areas shaping political life in Texas: education, welfare, health care, and water.

Education Policy

 Describe the major issues that have shaped education policy in Texas

Education policy is a complex field. There is no one education "problem" that has been identified to drive education policy, nor is there just one formulated solution to this problem. Education policy in Texas involves a large number of overlapping problems, each of which spawns a variety of solutions.

Education is big business in Texas. For the 2016–17 biennium, an estimated $41.3 billion in state General Revenue Funds went to public education. Local property taxes contributed over $51 billion in revenue to local school districts. The federal government contributed an estimated $10.2 billion to fund a variety of programs including Child Nutrition Grants, No Child Left Behind Grants, disabilities funding, and other formula grants.[8]

There are 1,219 regular school districts in Texas with 8,646 public schools. Approximately 5.2 million students were enrolled in public schools in Texas in 2015, second only to California. Enrollments increased by 15.7 percent between 2005 and 2015, the fastest of the top 15 most populous states. The student-teacher ratio of 15.6 students per teacher compares favorably with the national average of 15.9 students per teacher. But expenditures in Texas of $8,681 per student is far below the national average of $11,355. Texas ranked 45th in per capita student expenditure in 2013, a fall from 24th in 1998.[9]

Along with the regular school districts there are over 195 charter schools operating 613 open-enrollment charter school campuses. Although funded with public monies, charter schools have been set up as an alternative to traditional public schools, often because the public schools have failed to meet the needs of certain groups of students. Charter schools are in many ways more flexible than public schools, but they must meet the standards set by the state for public schools. In 2014–15, there were 227,826 students attending charter schools.[10]

Eight hundred and twenty-five state school districts and charters had fewer than 1,600 students in 2014. A large number of these school districts were small and in rural areas. Eighteen school districts enrolled over 50,000—62 percent of all students in the state. The largest school districts are in Houston (211,552), Dallas (159,713), Cypress-

Texas has a large and compli-cated public school system fraught with nearly constant public-policy battles, including that over the level of funding for public schools.

Fairbanks in Harris County (111,440), and Northside in Bexar County (102,129).[11] Over 294,000 students graduated from Texas high schools in 2014.[12]

State school districts employ over 342,000 teachers. According to a *Texas Tribune* study, salaries ranged from a beginners' salary of $44,540 to $59,787 for teachers with 20+ years' experience. Not surprisingly, there was considerable variation across different school districts. The race and ethnicity of teachers differ considerably from those of the student body in Texas: 61.4 percent of teachers are white, 25.6 percent are Latino, and 9.9 percent are African American. The districts also employ almost 26,000 administrators and almost 70,000 professional support staff (such as counselors, librarians, and nurses). On top of that, they employ another 235,000 educational aides and auxiliary staff. Total staffing in elementary and secondary schools in Texas exceeds 674,000 people.[13]

The challenges facing educational policy in Texas are great, but a few stand out. First, there is the above-noted low level of public spending per pupil. Second, the demographics are increasingly minority and disadvantaged.[14] In 2015, 52 percent of students in Texas were Hispanic, 28.9 percent were white, 12.6 percent were African American, and 4.0 percent were Asian or Pacific Islander. Of these students, 18.2 percent had "limited English proficiency." In addition, 58.8 percent were considered to be "economically disadvantaged" (meaning they were poor), and 51.2 percent were consider to be "at risk" (meaning that given their circumstances, they are more likely to fail academically). Not surprisingly, these demographic characteristics often lead to lower performance on national and state tests. Third, there are high dropout rates in Texas. For example, the dropout rate for students in the 2013 graduating cohort was 6.6 percent (21,686 students).[15] Dropout rates, particularly among Latinos and African Americans, affect other state and federal efforts to address the problem of poverty. To understand how policy makers are dealing with these challenges, we must look deeper into the making of educational policy since the founding of the state.

The Roots of Education Policy in Texas

The debate over public education in Texas extends back to the break with Mexico. One of the indictments of the Mexican regime contained in the Texas Declaration of Independence was that the government had failed to establish a public system of education. Later, the Constitution of the Republic of Texas required a public system of education, but a bill actually establishing a public school system did not pass the legislature until 1854.

Public education was to be financed with a special school fund that would use $2 million of the $10 million given to Texas by the U.S. government on Texas's admission to the Union to settle outstanding land claims in parts of what are now New Mexico, Colorado, and Oklahoma. Unfortunately, the fund was used for a variety of other purposes in the following years, including the purchase of railroad stock and the building of prisons. When Democrats returned to power following Reconstruction, an effort was made to protect the fund and commit its use solely to education. Under the Constitution of 1876, the Special School Fund became the Permanent School Fund, and restrictions were placed on how the money could be used and invested.[16] The Constitution of 1876 also had provisions to support public education through one-quarter of the occupation tax, a $1 poll tax, and local taxation.

Throughout much of the late nineteenth and early twentieth centuries, public education remained largely a local affair. Schools were funded by local taxes, and decisions such as what to teach and how long the school year would be were made at the local level. Many of the school systems were chronically short of funds, facing such problems as a shortage of supplies and textbooks, inadequate facilities, and poorly trained teachers. In 1949 the state legislature tried to address some of these problems by passing the **Gilmer-Aikin Laws**, under which school districts were consolidated into 2,900 administrative units, state equalization funding was provided to supplement local taxes, teachers' salaries were raised, and a minimum 175 teaching days school year was established. In addition, the laws established the Texas Education Agency (TEA), originally known as the State Department of Education, to supervise public education in the state.

The Gilmer-Aikin Laws also established bureaucratic institutions responsible for public education in the state. Previously, public education had been run by a state board of education, whose 9 members were appointed by the governor for six-year terms, and an elected state superintendent of public instruction. This was replaced by an elected 21-member board. The State Board of Education became the policy-making body for public education in the state, selecting budgets, establishing regulations for school accreditation, executing contracts for the purchase of textbooks, and investing in the Permanent School Fund. The board also had the power to appoint a commissioner of education, subject to confirmation by the Texas Senate. The commissioner of education served a four-year term and became the chief executive officer for the TEA. The TEA was responsible for setting standards for public schools, for supervising the public schools of the state, and for handling federal funds related to public education. For the next 50 years, educational policy in the state would work through the institutional framework established by the Gilmer-Aikin Laws.[17]

Gilmer-Aikin Laws education reform legislation passed in 1949 that supplemented local funding of education with public monies, raised teachers' salaries, mandated a minimum length for the school year, and provided for more state supervision of public education

Since 1949 the State Board of Education has undergone occasional restructuring. Membership was expanded to 24 in 1973 and to 27 in 1981. Following a special legislative session, the board became a 15-member appointed body in 1984. But in 1988 it reverted to an elected body composed of 15 members serving four-year terms.

Three specific problems have been identified by policy makers as playing a major role in educational policy over the last 50 years: desegregation, equity in funding, and the search for educational excellence. Each has its own set of policy formulations, implementation procedures, and evaluative processes.

Desegregation

Few problems have troubled educational policy in Texas as much as desegregation. Few have given rise to such controversial policy formulations or implementations.

Segregation of the races was provided for under the Texas Constitution of 1876. In *Plessy v. Ferguson* (1896), the U.S. Supreme Court upheld the validity of state-imposed racial segregation through the now-infamous "separate but equal" doctrine. In Texas, as elsewhere across the South, segregated schools may have been separate, but they were far from equal. In the 1920s and '30s, for example, the length of the school term for black schools was only about four days shorter than that for white schools, but Texas spent an average of $3.39 less per student (about one-third less) on the education of African American students than on white students.[18]

The U.S. Supreme Court overturned *Plessy v. Ferguson* in the 1954 case *Brown v. Board of Education*, ruling that state-imposed segregation in schools violated the equal protection clause of the Fourteenth Amendment. School districts were ordered to desegregate their school systems "with all deliberate speed." In some cases, "all deliberate speed" was rapid. The San Antonio school district, for example, became one of the first school districts in the nation to comply with the Supreme Court's order. Other school districts in the state, such as Houston's, were much slower in implementing the Court's desegregation ruling.

The desegregation of public schools was hampered further by political opposition at both the local and state levels. In 1957 the Texas legislature passed laws encouraging school districts to resist federally ordered desegregation, although then-governor Price Daniel, Sr., chose to ignore such laws.[19] By the late 1960s legally segregated schools were largely a thing of the past. Nevertheless, de facto segregation remained a problem, particularly in urban areas with large minority populations. As in many other urban areas across the country, a large number of middle- and upper-income whites in Texas abandoned urban public school systems for suburban public schools or private schools.

Equity in the Public School System

Federal court cases such as *Brown v. Board of Education* played a major role in shaping educational policy regarding the desegregation of schools. Two other important court cases have affected education policy and politics in Texas over the last 30 years: *San Antonio v. Rodríguez* and *Edgewood ISD v. Kirby.* These cases forced policy makers to look at the problems of education in a new light and to formulate new solutions to address these problems.

San Antonio v. Rodríguez

San Antonio v. Rodríguez was a landmark case involving the constitutionality of using property taxes to fund public schools.[20] At the heart of the case lay the question of the equitable funding of public schools. Lawyers for Rodríguez and seven other children in the poor Edgewood independent school district (ISD) in the San Antonio area argued that the current system of financing public schools in Texas was unfair. The Edgewood school district had one of the highest property tax rates in the country, but it could raise only $37 per pupil. Meanwhile the neighboring school district of Alamo Heights was able to raise $413 per pupil with a much lower property tax rate. The difference was that the value of the property subject to taxation in Alamo Heights far exceeded that in Edgewood. Equalizing educational funding would require Edgewood to tax at the rate of $5.76 per $100 of property value, while Alamo Heights could tax at a rate of $0.68 per $100 of property value.

A three-judge federal district court was impaneled to hear the case in January 1969. The district court initially delayed action, giving the 1971 Texas legislature time to address the funding issue. When the legislature failed to act during its regular session, the court took action. On December 23, 1971, it ruled that the Texas school finance system was unconstitutional under the **equal protection clause** of the Fourteenth Amendment to the U.S. Constitution. However, on appeal to the U.S. Supreme Court, the decision was overturned. On March 21, 1973, the Supreme Court ruled 5–4 that states such as Texas were not required to subsidize poorer school districts under the equal protection clause of the U.S. Constitution. The question of equity in public school funding would have to be addressed later in terms of Texas's state constitution and in Texas courts.

Edgewood ISD v. Kirby

The second landmark case involving the financing of public schools was *Edgewood ISD v. Kirby*. Unlike *Rodríguez*, *Edgewood* considered whether the system of funding public schools through local property taxes fulfilled the Texas State Constitution's provisions on education. Much of the litigation over the next few years would center on Article 7, Section 1, of the 1876 Constitution, which read:

> A general diffusion of knowledge being essential to the preservation of the liberties and rights of the people, it shall be the duty of the Legislature of the State to establish and make suitable provision for the support and maintenance of an efficient system of free public schools.

A key constitutional issue would be exactly what constituted a "general diffusion of knowledge" and an "efficient system of free public schools."

On behalf of the Edgewood ISD, the Mexican American Legal Defense and Education Fund (MALDEF) sued William Kirby, the state commissioner of education, on May 23, 1984. Initially, only 8 districts were represented in the case. By the time the case was finally decided, 67 other school districts had joined the original plaintiffs. The plaintiffs argued that the state's reliance on local property taxes to fund public education discriminated against poor children by denying them equal opportunities

equal protection clause
provision in the Fourteenth Amendment of the U.S. Constitution guaranteeing citizens the "equal protection of the laws"; this clause has been the basis for the civil rights of African Americans, women, and other groups

Who Attends Public School in Texas?

Two factors have played a role in shaping the demographics of the children attending Texas urban public schools since *Brown v. Board of Education*. First, the state has become more diverse, with a growing Latino presence in large urban areas. Second, while African American attendance has remained steady, white attendance has not. In major cities like Houston and Dallas, whites have moved to suburban school districts, leaving the largest urban school districts to serve minority populations, particularly Latinos. While Texas schools are legally desegregated, there is de facto segregation in public education across much of the state.

Demographics of Selected Houston-Area School Districts, 2014–2015

District	White	African Am.	Latino	Other	Total students
1. Aldine	1.9%	24.5%	71.3%	2.3%	69,533
2. Alief	3.7%	29.6%	52.6%	14.2%	47,174
3. Channelview	8.5%	11.8%	77.2%	1.7%	9,130
4. Cypress–Fairbanks	27.5%	16.5%	44.0%	11.3%	112,640
5. Friendswood	73.8%	2.0%	15.5%	8.4%	6,087
6. Houston	8.3%	24.9%	62.1%	5.7%	214,462
7. Huffman	77.0%	2.0%	19.0%	2.8%	3,381
8. Spring	10.2%	39.9%	43.1%	5.5%	36,781

Percentage of White Students in Houston-Area School Districts

Under 5% | 5.1–10.0% | 10.1–25.0% | 25.1–50.0% | Above 50.0%

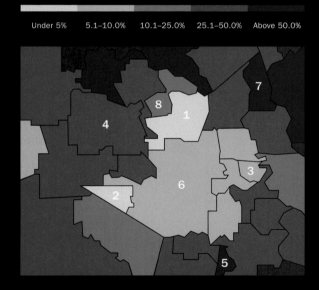

Public School Enrollment by Race vs. Texas State Population, 2014–2015

Latino

Enrollment 52.0%
State population 38.8%

African American
Enrollment 12.6%
State population 12.5%

White

Enrollment 29.0%
State population 43.0%

Other

Enrollment 6.4%
State population 5.7%

SOURCES: schools.texastribune.org/districts; Texas Education Agency, Enrollment Trends, tea.texas.gov.

in education. One month after the original case was filed, the legislature passed House Bill 72, a modest reform measure that increased state aid to poor districts. In 1985 plaintiffs filed an amended lawsuit, arguing that the legislature's action was far from satisfactory.

The amended case was heard early in 1987 by a state district judge, who ruled on April 29, 1987 in favor of the plaintiffs, calling for the institution of a new system of public school funding by September 1989.

The decision was reversed on appeal to the state appeals court in late 1988. But in a 9–0 decision, the Texas Supreme Court held that the funding system was, indeed, in violation of the state constitution. The court held that education was a fundamental right under the Texas Constitution and that the "glaring disparities" between rich and poor schools violated the efficiency clause of the constitution. In its ruling, the court did not demand "absolute equality" in per pupil spending. But it did require a standard of "substantially equal access to similar revenues per pupil at similar levels of tax effort."[21] It ordered the legislature to implement an equitable system by the 1990–91 school year.

The Texas Supreme Court's ruling touched off a political firestorm that swept through Texas politics throughout the 1990s and into the first 16 years of the twenty-first century. Over the years, various courts held various funding provisions of public education to be unconstitutional. The legislature responded with various funding plans for public education. One was dubbed the "Robin Hood" plan because it transferred funds from rich to poor districts.

In November 2005 the Texas Supreme Court upheld a lower court ruling that the school districts lacked "meaningful discretion" in setting local maintenance and operation tax rates. In the court's opinion, too many districts were being forced to set tax rates at the maximum $1.50 per $100 valuation. Essentially, this meant that the school system was being financed by an unconstitutional state property tax. The court gave the legislature until June 1, 2006, to address the matter or the court would enjoin the state from distributing funding to the public school system.

It took three special sessions of the state legislature to craft a compromise and finally put constitutional concerns over the financing of public schools brought on by Robin Hood to rest. The final proposal cut property taxes by one-third and replaced lost revenues with money raised statewide by an expanded business tax and a new $1-per-pack tax on cigarettes. General revenue monies are now used to address some of the inequities of the property tax system.[22] Unfortunately, the compromise generated, at least in the short run, as many problems as it solved.

The Great Recession of 2008–09 brought a budget crisis to the 2011 legislative session that shook educational policy in Texas to its core. One of the principal ways that the 2011 legislature balanced the budget without raising taxes was by making severe cuts to the tune of $5.6 billion in elementary and secondary education funding. The cuts not only jeopardized many of the reform initiatives of the previous 20 years but raised fundamental questions about fairness that had been resolved with the Edgewood decisions. Approximately $3.4 billion in educational funds from the state were restored during the 2013 legislative session, but many educational reformers believed that was not enough. School districts went to court arguing that the state was no longer meeting the demands for a fair and equitable school system laid down by the Texas Supreme Court. Judge John Dietz had ruled in February 2013 during the leg-

standards losing state funds; a longer school year—from 175 to 180 days; and a professional career ladder for teachers, tying pay raises to performance.[28] In early July 1984 many of the reform proposals were put into place in a 266-page education reform bill, along with the necessary accompanying tax increases.

The so-called Perot reforms were but the first round in the debate over excellence and accountability in the public school system. A second round opened during the 1995 legislative session. As in the past, there was strong business and bipartisan support for reforms that supported increased accountability through testing. There were some important differences in the reform package finally signed by Republican governor George W. Bush. The Perot reforms had generally centralized control over education policy in the state. The Bush reforms, in contrast, gave more discretion to local school districts to achieve the educational goals the state was mandating. Some of the reforms put through were symbolic. The controversial "No Pass, No Play" rule was relaxed, cutting the period of nonparticipation from six to three weeks and lifting a ban on practicing while on scholastic probation. But other changes were more substantive. Local control of public schools was increased by limiting the power of the TEA. Local voters were empowered to adopt home charters that could free their school districts from many state requirements, including class-size caps at lower grades. The 1995 reforms also enabled students under certain circumstances to transfer from low-performing schools to high-performing schools in their districts, thus promoting competition among the schools by holding the schools accountable for the performance of their students.[29]

Testing has remained a controversial issue in Texas schools. Some say frequent testing will raise standards and student performance, while others say that it will lead to "teaching to the test."

One of the most controversial aspects of the reform movement in public education in Texas was the development of statewide assessment standards. "Testing," as assessment came to be known, was first instituted in 1986 with the Texas Educational Assessment of Minimal Skills (TEAMS) exams. TEAMS sought to certify that students from all districts met certain minimum academic expectations. Students had to pass TEAMS to be eligible to receive a high school diploma. TEAMS was replaced with the Texas Assessment of Academic Skills (TAAS) test in 1990, which focused on minimum academic skills in reading, writing, and math at grade 10. The implementation of Texas Assessment of Knowledge and Skills (TAKS) in 2003 pushed statewide testing across the state-mandated curriculum, requiring students to pass exit-level tests in English, math, science, and social studies. TAKS, in turn, was replaced by the State of Texas Assessments of Academic Readiness (STAAR), 15 end-of-course exams across the curriculum for grades 9 through 12 beginning in 2011. The idea was to have passing standards increased with subsequent administrations of the exam. Schools would be held accountable for their student performances. In the process, it was hoped that public education in Texas would ratchet upward in quality.

Unfortunately, high-minded expectations about reforming public schools through intensified testing and accountability were dashed as failure rates stayed stubbornly high. In 2012 the TEA reported passing rates on five of the STAAR end-of-course exams ranged from 87 percent in biology to 55 percent in English writing. Although failing students were allowed to retake the test, fears began to mount about the impact that failure rates would have on retention and graduation rates. In addition, a storm brewed up out of the classrooms as teachers and administrators complained about the growing need to teach to the test.[30]

Support among business and political elites for an expanded, intensified set of tests to reform public education collapsed during the 2013 legislative session. As we discussed in the introduction to Chapter 6, new groups with different interests emerged to challenge the consensus around accountability and testing that had driven educational reform policy for 25 years. Under House Bill 5, the state legislature cut the number of required end-of-course tests from 15 to 5. The idea of testing to promote academic excellence was not being abandoned completely, but it no longer held center stage for reformers. As state senator Dan Patrick, the chair of the Senate Public Education Committee, noted, "By the elimination of 15 [tests] to 5 . . . that could save 40 or more days of testing, give teachers more time to teach, be innovative and creative."[31]

Education Policy in a New Era

One might have hoped that the educational reforms of the past 25 years would have ushered in an era of rising educational attainment in Texas in the first decade of the twenty-first century. Such was hardly the case. New problems have been identified by policy makers in recent years that have led to new initiatives to overhaul education in the state. Despite the efforts of policy makers, teachers' salaries and overall state and local spending on public education remained low compared with those in other states, as did graduation rates. In 2015 the average SAT scores in Texas were 470 in reading and 486 in math, compared with a national average of 495 in reading and 511 in math.[32] These scores represented a slight but ongoing drop in Texas test scores in the first decade of the twenty-first century.

Although the dropout rate in grades 7 through 12 has been declining since the 1990s, it remained high among minorities. For a few years at the turn of the century, scores on standardized tests such as the TAAS test improved across the state, sparking calls for the development of new assessment tests to hold teachers and schools more accountable. But with the implementation of more rigorous STAAR assessments, overall student performance stayed flat or fell on various tests. More disturbingly, there appeared to be a growing "achievement gap" where minorities and at-risk students failed at higher rates than whites in consecutive iterations of the tests.[33]

Vouchers and Charter Schools The perceived failure of educational reform efforts based on the ideas of testing and accountability led some to advocate new ideas in public education. One new idea—actually an old idea from the early '60s—being offered up by conservatives, particularly in the Tea Party wing of the Republican Party, is vouchers. The basic idea of vouchers is simple. Increase competition in the school system by letting funding follow the students. If the public school doesn't work, let parents and students opt out and take their funding with them.[34] Among the recurring criticisms of voucher-based reform is that middle- and upper-middle-income students will leave poorer students behind in poorly funded public schools.

An alternative to vouchers has been available to some in Texas through open-enrollment charter schools. Like vouchers, the idea of charter schools is to make more options available to parents and students, particularly in places where schools are under performing. As part of a larger reform package, in 1995 the legislature authorized the establishment of charter schools, which would be given increased flexibility to deliver education to student populations with special needs. Working under their own charter and granted freedom to manage their own schools, charter schools operate under the TEA and receive their own accountability ranking based on test scores. While they receive state monies, as of 2014 charter schools do not receive local tax revenue or, in most cases, funding for facilities. Charter schools are able to receive privately raised funds. In 2014–15, 195 charters had been awarded in Texas, with 613 charter schools in operation. An estimated 227,827 students attended charter schools, with approximately 105,000 on waiting lists.

The criticisms of charter schools resemble, in some ways, the criticism of vouchers. Opponents fear that charter schools will drain money from public schools. While serving the needs of their specially identified student bodies, they will distract attention away from the needs of other, possibly more needy groups. In addition, there is some concern that charter schools will not be able to meet the challenges of educating youth any better than traditional public schools. In 2016 some larger public school districts began to challenge the wisdom of diverting public monies to charter schools. For example, Michael Hinojosa, superintendent of the Dallas Independent School District (DISD), charged that DISD had acted "fat, dumb, and happy" as it watched students move to Dallas-area charter schools. In 2016, DISD enrollment had dropped by 2,000 students, costing DISD over $10 million in state funding. Significantly, about half of those students were kindergarteners attending charter schools. In Hinojosa's mind, DISD had to respond to the challenges posed by an aggressive charter school movement.[35]

SOCIAL RESPONSIBILITY: GET INVOLVED

- Do you think that Texas should increase investment in charter schools, provide increased funding for vouchers that can be used for private schools, or increase funding for traditional public schools? Why?

- Think about your high school experience. What was good about it? What could be better? Draft an email to your state representative explaining how you would like to see your high school improved. If you are arguing for spending more money on teachers, sports, the arts, or other programs, where would you suggest policy makers save money to compensate?

Increased Funding A third alternative to current education policy is rather simple: spend more money, a lot more money. Here, the idea is that Texas schools fail us because they are woefully underfunded. Salaries of teachers are too low, and state regulations of the curriculum and classroom are too great. Get the best teachers to be in the classroom and the problem of public education will be able to right itself. Vouchers and charter schools are seen as threats to this alternative.

New interest groups have emerged over the last two sessions of the Texas legislature to champion approaches to educational reform far different from the business-led bipartisan efforts of the Bush and Perry years that championed testing and accountability. Groups like Texans for Educational Reform, Texans Deserve Great Schools, and Raise Your Hand Texas will change the direction of the debate on education policy in the future.[36]

Interestingly, the public appears to be in favor of increased expenditures going to public education, but it splits along partisan lines. A poll conducted by the University of Texas in 2014 found that 74 percent of Texans believed that increasing pay to teachers would be an effective way of improving public education in Texas, including 87 percent of Democrats and 65 percent of Republicans. Even 52 percent of self-identified Tea Partiers supported increased pay to teachers as a way to improve public education. But when respondents were asked if increasing overall funding would be effective, a different story emerged. Eighty-nine percent of Democrats agreed that increased overall funding would improve public education, but only 51 percent of Republicans did. One of the problems facing policy makers in the future will be formulating reform proposals amid a divided electorate.[37]

Welfare Policy

Describe the state's role in addressing poverty and how it is affected by national policies

One long-term policy issue has been how to provide for the basic needs of poor people in Texas. This issue raises fundamental questions about the state's role in helping people in poverty and the extent to which national policies determine the state's response to the needs of poor people. Welfare policy is a clear example of how changes in problem identification and formulation can lead to an overhaul in policy implementation and evaluation.

Poverty in Texas

Poverty has never been a popular subject in Texas. The idea that some individuals have trouble taking care of themselves or meeting the basic needs of their families seems to fly in the face of Texas's individualistic culture. In light of the booming Texas economy, many policy makers may have hoped that the poverty problem would go away. It hasn't. Between 1990 and 1999 the percentage of Texans living in poverty fell from 15.9 percent to 15.0 percent, but it rose again during the Great Recession. In 2014, 17.2 percent of Texans lived below the poverty line. The five counties of more than 10,000 residents with the highest percentage of people living in poverty were along the border: Willacy County (38.8 percent), Starr County (35.4 percent), Cameron County (34.5 percent), Hidalgo County (33.5 percent), and Zapata County (32.6 percent). The counties with the lowest were three in the Dallas–Fort Worth area, Rockwall County (6.8 percent), Collin County (7 percent) and Denton County (8.7 percent); one north of Austin, Williamson County (7.8 percent); and one north of San Antonio, Kendall County (8.3 percent). In addition, in March 2016, a total of 4,065,627 people (approximately 14.7 percent of all residents of Texas) were enrolled in Medicaid, the federally financed, state-operated program providing medical services to low-income people. Poverty remains one of the most intractable problems facing the state.[38]

Policy makers define poverty in very specific terms. Poverty is the condition under which individuals or families do not have the resources to meet their basic needs, including food, shelter, health care, transportation, and clothing. The U.S. Department of Health and Human Services developed a "poverty index" in 1964 and revised it in

1969 and 1980. The index calculates the consumption requirements of families based on their size and composition. The poverty index is adjusted every year to account for the rate of inflation. Although there is considerable controversy as to whether it adequately measures the minimal needs of a family, the poverty index is the generally accepted standard against which poverty is measured.

In 2016 the federal poverty guideline was $11,880 a year for one person and $4,140 a year for each additional person in the family. Over 23 percent of Latinos, 22 percent of African Americans, and 10 percent of whites in Texas are poor. Of those over age 65 in Texas, 11 percent are poor compared with 10 percent in the nation as a whole. Poverty among children under age 18 is much higher in Texas (24 percent) than in the United States as a whole (21 percent).[39]

Though poverty in Texas afflicts many different social groups, Latinos currently make up the majority of Texans living below the poverty line. The border counties in Texas are by far the poorest in the state.

Texas uses these federal poverty guidelines to determine eligibility for a variety of social programs. For example, a family of three is eligible for reduced-price school meals if the family is at no more than 185 percent of the poverty level. A family of three is eligible for free school meals and food stamps (the Supplemental Nutritional Assistance Program or SNAP) if the family is at no more than 130 percent of the poverty level.

Since 2003 the Texas Health and Human Services Commission (HHS) has been responsible for overseeing the Department of Family and Protective Services, the Department of Assistive and Rehabilitative Services, the Department of Aging and Disability Services, and the Department of State Health Services (see Table 12.1). HHS is responsible for coordinating, determining eligibility for, and administering the major welfare and antipoverty programs in Texas, including Temporary Assistance to Needy Families (TANF), a welfare program for families with dependent children; Medicaid, a state-federal program providing health coverage to the poor; SNAP; and other programs to address family violence, provide disaster relief, and settle refugees. The appropriated budget for HHS programs in 2016–17 is almost $77.2 billion, 36.9 percent of all state appropriations. HHS agencies employ almost 56,000 state workers at more than 1,000 locations.[40]

Poverty is a complicated policy issue in Texas. There are more than 200 programs administered by HHS that are aimed at different problems related to poverty. We will

TABLE 12.1

Agency Budgets for the 2016–17 Biennium, All Funds

Health and Human Services Commission: $56.6 billion

Department of Aging and Disability Services: $8.8 billion

Department of Assistive and Rehabilitative Services: $7.0 billion

Department of Family and Protective Services: $3.5 billion

Department of State Health Services: $6.5 billion

TOTAL: $76.4 billion

SOURCE: Texas Legislative Budget Board, *Fiscal Size-Up: 2016–17 Biennium*, p. 161.

now focus attention on two of the most important initiatives aimed at addressing poverty in Texas: welfare and health care financing. Understanding how these programs evolved over time and the reforms that were put into place over the past 20 years will shed considerable light on public-policy making in the state.

Welfare in Texas, 1935–96

New Deal President Franklin Delano Roosevelt's 1930s programs to stimulate the national economy and provide relief to victims of the Great Depression

Aid to Families with Dependent Children (AFDC) a federally and state-financed program for children living with parents or relatives who fell below state standards of need; replaced in 1996 by TANF

Medicaid a federal and state program financing medical services to low-income people

The Texas Department of Public Welfare was established in 1939 during the New Deal. This photo shows farmers receiving support from the government at the time.

The origins of modern welfare policy lie in President Franklin Delano Roosevelt's **New Deal**.[41] Prior to the 1930s welfare was considered to be a state and local responsibility. The Great Depression overwhelmed many state and local welfare arrangements, causing the federal government to expand its role in addressing the needs of the poor and the unemployed. The Social Security Act of 1935 transformed the way in which welfare policy was implemented in the United States. Along with two social insurance programs (Old Age Insurance and Unemployment Insurance), the Social Security Act established a number of state-federal public assistance programs: Aid for Dependent Children (ADC, later **Aid to Families with Dependent Children or AFDC**), Old Age Assistance (OAA), and Aid for the Blind (AB). States administered and determined the benefit levels for these programs. In exchange for federal assistance in funding, state programs had to meet certain minimum federal guidelines.

The Department of Public Welfare was established in Texas in 1939 to run the state's various public assistance programs. It was to be supervised by a state board of welfare, composed of three members appointed by the governor for six-year terms. The board appointed an executive director who, in turn, was the chief administrative officer of the department.[42]

Through the early 1960s the basic strategy adopted by welfare-policy makers in Texas was to minimize the cost to the state while maximizing federal dollars. Some programs were expanded during these years. In 1950, ADC became AFDC as mothers were included in the program. Other new social-service programs were also added. Much of the initiative for the expansion of welfare came from the federal government. One of the major issues in Texas was the problem of the constitutional ceiling on welfare spending. This had to be raised from $35 million in 1945 to $52 million in 1961, and again to $60 million in 1963.[43]

Welfare policy in Texas was transformed fundamentally in the 1960s. Federal court decisions between 1968 and 1971 effectively ended a series of policies such as bans on men in the houses of mothers receiving welfare and residency requirements, both of which had been used by states to keep welfare rolls low. In 1965, Congress established **Medicaid**, a state-federal program to finance health care for the poor. President Lyndon Johnson's "War on Poverty" also expanded the number of social service programs available to the poor. Increasingly, it was argued, the solution to alleviating poverty was through expanded federal control over welfare programs.

In 1965 the Department of Public Welfare was authorized to work with the federal government's new antipoverty programs. The welfare ceiling was raised to $80 million in 1969. Among the welfare programs administered by the department were four public assistance programs: AFDC, Aid for the Blind, Aid to the Permanently and Totally Disabled, and Old Age Assistance. The latter three programs were taken over by the federal government in 1972 in the form of the new national **Supplemental Security Income (SSI)** program to provide assistance to individuals in need who have disabilities or are aged. Along with these programs, the department ran the Texas Medical Assistance Program (Medicaid), the national food stamp program, and a series of social-service programs.

In 1977 the Department of Public Welfare became the Department of Human Resources. It was renamed again in 1985 as the Texas Department of Human Services and then as the Health and Human Services Commission in 2003. The name reflected an ongoing desire on the part of policy makers to think of the agency less as a welfare agency and more as a service agency to the poor. By 1980 the department was reorganized to focus on the major client groups it served: families with children and aged and disabled people. In 1981 the constitutional ceiling on welfare spending was replaced with a more flexible standard. Instead of having a flat cap of $80 million, welfare expenditures could not exceed 1 percent of the total state budget.

Between 1967 and 1973 participation rates and welfare expenditures in Texas exploded. The number of children on AFDC during this time rose from 79,914 to 325,244, while the number of families on AFDC went from 23,509 to 120,254. Rates leveled off in the late 1970s, but they began to push upward again in the 1980s. Liberal attempts to reform welfare by nationalizing AFDC (turning the state-federal program into a national program like SSI) failed throughout the 1970s. Conservative attempts to compel welfare recipients to participate in job-training programs, such as the Work Incentive Program of 1967, had limited success. A frustrating political stalemate set in. Few were happy with welfare policy as then conducted. But no consensus had emerged as to what would be a better alternative. Meanwhile, welfare rolls expanded and expenditures continued to increase in both Texas and the nation.

> **Supplemental Security Income (SSI)** a national welfare program passed in 1972 that provides assistance to low-income elderly or disabled individuals; replaced the federal-state programs that had offered assistance to the blind, the permanently and totally disabled, and the aged

In 2012, 3.6 million Texans participated in the food stamps program (now called SNAP), which allows low-income people to buy groceries with a special debit card. SNAP benefits are paid by the federal government, but the state and federal governments share administrative costs.

The Idea of Dependency and Welfare Reform in the 1990s

By the mid-1980s a new critique of welfare programs had begun to emerge. This led to a new understanding of what the problem of poverty was and how solutions might be developed to address it. At its heart lay the idea that the well-intentioned policies of the 1960s had backfired, creating a dysfunctional underclass of people dependent on welfare. Welfare programs such as AFDC may have helped people financially in the short run, but in the long run they had robbed people of the character traits and the moral values that would enable them to succeed in a market economy.[44] Observers believed that the skyrocketing rate of children born to poor, unwed mothers was in part the result of a perverse set of incentives created by welfare programs. Under the existing welfare system, at least to a point, the more children one had, the higher the welfare payment. Because some states like Texas did not provide welfare to families with fathers in the home, fathers were actually being encouraged to abandon their families so that the families might qualify for welfare. According to critics, the poor needed encouragement and proper incentives to become independent workers rather than have a permanent source of income from the state.

At the national level, the deadlock over welfare reform was broken with the passage of the Family Support Act in 1988. In the attempt to stem the rising tide of illegitimacy rates and single-parent families among the poor, the act mandated two-parent coverage for all state AFDC programs. It also established a number of new "workfare" programs whose goals were to get people off welfare and into the workforce. New standards were also developed requiring parents to participate in these workfare programs or lose their benefits.[45]

Much hyperbole surrounded the passage of the Family Support Act. Although the act did break new ground in formulating programs to help people make the transition from welfare to work, it also was an important expansion of the existing AFDC system. Far from declining, welfare roll expansion continued in the early 1990s. In Texas, this expansion was especially rapid. By 1994 approximately 786,400 people were receiving AFDC in Texas. Total federal and state expenditures rose from $188.3 million in 1984 to $544.9 million in 1994. Food stamp costs also rose rapidly during this period, from $664.9 million to $2.2 billion. But AFDC and food stamps were only part of the problem. Medicaid was escalating at a rate of more than 20 percent a year. During the 1994–95 biennium, $18.6 billion in state and federal funds was being spent on Medicaid. Texas's share was 13 percent of the state budget, or $6.7 billion. Escalating costs of AFDC, food stamps, and Medicaid provided the backdrop to the welfare reforms that would be put into place by Texas policy makers in 1995.

Growing discontent over welfare policy across the country encouraged many states like Texas to seek waivers from federal regulations so that they too might experiment with welfare reform.[46] Some states sought to modify AFDC rules to eliminate some of the perverse incentive structures in the welfare system. Other states set caps on benefits and how long one could continue to receive welfare. Welfare became a state issue during the 1994 elections. As governor of Texas, George W. Bush echoed the ideas of conservative critics of the welfare system, arguing that the existing system was robbing people of their independence. Among the changes that he called for were

- strengthening child-support procedures and penalties
- imposing a two-year limit on benefits for recipients able to work
- requiring individuals receiving welfare to accept a state-sponsored job if after two years they were unable to find work
- creating new child-care and job-training programs
- requiring unwed mothers to live with their parents or grandparents
- moving family support systems from the state to the local level

Data released by the comptroller's office lent support to the Bush contention that there were serious problems with the existing system of welfare in Texas. Over one-quarter of all welfare recipients in 1993 were "long-term" recipients who had remained on the rolls for five years or more. The publication of *A Partnership for Independence: Welfare Reform in Texas*, by the office of the comptroller, John Sharp, a Democrat, helped to set the legislative agenda for the debate over welfare policy. Agreeing with other critics across the nation who were unhappy with the current state of welfare policy, the report documented how welfare often failed to help those most in need or to encourage those dependent on welfare to become independent of government largesse. Among the report's 100 proposals were many of the reforms that had been implemented by conservative reformers in other states or by the Bush gubernatorial administration.

A bipartisan legislative coalition ultimately supported major welfare reform in Texas. On May 26, 1995, the vote on House Bill 1863 was 128 to 9 in the House and 30 to 1 in the Senate. The law provided a number of "carrot and stick" incentives that sought to mold the character of welfare recipients in positive ways and wean them off welfare. Among the carrots were expanded education and job-training programs, as well as a select number of pilot studies involving transitional child care and medical benefits. Among the sticks were a limitation on benefits to 36 months, alimony for ex-spouses who couldn't support themselves, and the institution of a five-year ban on reapplying for benefits once benefits ran out. To implement the state reforms, Texas secured a waiver from the federal government that freed the state from various federal regulations regarding welfare programs. In granting the waivers to Texas and other states, the Clinton administration hoped to stimulate innovative reforms that might be duplicated elsewhere.

Texas was ahead of the welfare reform curve in 1995. In 1996, President Bill Clinton signed into law the most important reform in federal welfare policy since the New Deal. The Personal Responsibility and Work Opportunity Reconciliation Act essentially rethought the assumptions that had guided the expansion of welfare programs for 60 years. Under the legislation, AFDC, JOBS (a work-related training program), and the Emergency Assistance Program were combined into one block grant titled **Temporary Assistance for Needy Families (TANF)**. As with the welfare reforms instituted in Texas and in other states across the country, the primary purpose of TANF was to make families self-sufficient by ending the cycle of dependency on government benefits. States such as Texas were given great flexibility in setting benefit levels, eligibility requirements, and other program details.

Today in Texas, TANF provides temporary financial assistance to families with needy children when one or both of the parents are missing or disabled.[47] The TANF program provides a onetime $1,000 payment to individuals in certain crisis situations. To qualify, a recipient's income must be below 17 percent of the poverty income limit based on family size. In addition, the combined equity of the family may not exceed $2,000 ($3,000 for the elderly and disabled). People participating in TANF receive a monthly assistance payment based on the size of their family. They cannot receive benefits for more than 36 months. They are also eligible for Medicaid benefits, food stamps, and child day-care services. Unless legally exempt, recipients are also required to participate in an employment services program.

The maximum monthly grant available to a household of three under TANF is low, only $285 a month. For the 2016–17 biennium TANF expenditures will be $131.8 million in the all funds budget, including $101.8 million in General Revenue Funds and $30 million in federal funds.

Temporary Assistance for Needy Families (TANF) a welfare program passed in 1996 to provide temporary assistance to families with needy children; replacing the AFDC program, TANF sought to make poor families self-sufficient and to give states greater flexibility in setting benefit levels, eligibility requirements, and other program details

Evaluating Welfare Reforms

The welfare reforms in Texas have been evaluated along two dimensions. First, they are measured in terms of the number of people receiving welfare assistance from the state. Success is determined by the degree to which the reforms help lower the number of welfare recipients in Texas. If the reforms do not decrease the welfare rolls, they likely will be considered a failure. A second measure of success is the degree to which the reforms help take people off welfare and move them into the workforce as productive, independent members of society.

Judged by changes in the number of people on welfare, the reforms appear to be a success. The average monthly number of people on welfare in Texas rose from a little more than half a million in 1989 to a peak of more than three-quarters of a million in 1994 but then began to fall in 1995. Time limits and work requirements were put into place by the state legislature in 1995, one year before similar measures were passed nationally by the U.S. Congress. The decline in the number of people on welfare continued over the next decade, falling to 155,895 people in 2006 and to approximately 75,000 in 2016.[48]

By a second measure—the number of people moving from welfare to work—indications are that the welfare reforms of 1995 are more mixed in their success. Studies by the Center for Public Priorities in Austin over the past decade have found that caseloads on TANF may have fallen, but child poverty was on the rise. Moreover, there were indications that people leaving the welfare rolls were not necessarily transitioning to work. Such problems were likely exacerbated by the economic downturn of the Great Recession that began in 2008. Welfare reform in the 1990s took place under conditions of a booming economy and a rising demand for all types of labor. Jobs seemed to be available for people who were willing and able to work. But how will the new welfare policies respond to the economic problems of the early decades of the twenty-first century? Now that labor markets have tightened and jobs are difficult to find, will Texas policy makers be satisfied with the welfare reforms in place? Will policy makers be willing to offer more or longer "temporary assistance" to the poor if job markets become too tight and too many people lose eligibility for TANF? These are questions that policy makers concerned with welfare reform will have to consider one day. Only then will we be able to have a more accurate evaluation of the welfare reforms of the mid-1990s.

Medicaid and Health Care Policy

 Explain why Medicaid in particular and health care policy in general have been so controversial in Texas

Health insurance is a major policy problem facing Texas. People get health insurance from a variety of sources, including Medicare (a federal program for the elderly), health insurance through an employer, individual insurance policies, and Medicaid (a state-federal program for the poor). The Affordable Care Act (Obamacare) requires individuals to prove that they are insured when they file their federal income taxes

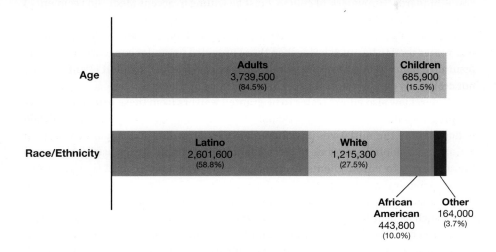

FIGURE 12.1

Texas's Uninsured Population by Age Group and Race/Ethnicity (Estimated)

SOURCE: Texas Health and Human Services Commission, *Texas Medicaid and CHIP in Perspective*, 9th ed. (February 2015), and Henry J. Kaiser Family Foundation, kff.org.

or they will incur a tax penalty. Despite efforts to get people medical insurance, the number of uninsured in Texas remains stubbornly high. In 2014 an estimated 17 percent of Texans were uninsured. This contrasted with 10 percent of the U.S. population that was uninsured. This number was the highest percentage in the nation. Figure 12.1 shows the breakdown of this uninsured population by age group. Approximately 1.2 million children under age 18 (16.3 percent) were without insurance, far below the national average of 9.8 percent.[49]

Medicaid

Other than health insurance programs established for state employees, Texas's principal policy initiative regarding health care and health insurance is Medicaid, a health financing program closely linked to poverty programs. Medicaid, which provides for the health care of poor people, particularly poor children, is an especially costly program for the state. The caseload for Medicaid has exploded in recent years, pushed up by the Great Recession. Between 2003 and 2013, the caseload grew from 3.36 million recipients to 4.67 million. For the 2016–17 biennium a total of $61.2 billion of state and federal funds will be appropriated to Medicaid client services programs in Texas. General Revenue Funds from the state increased by $1.9 billion from the previous biennium. The program's costs have risen more quickly than the rate of inflation, which makes Medicaid increasingly burdensome for the state budget. Funding Medicaid is a major issue in the broader debate over the state and national governments' roles in providing health care.[50]

Medicaid is a state-federal program that was established under the Social Security Amendments of 1965 as Title XIX of the Social Security Act. The Social Security Act requires that Texas and other states follow certain principles and meet certain standards if they are to receive federal funds. First, Medicaid services must be available on a statewide basis. Second, the same level of service must be available to all clients throughout the state. Children are entitled to a broader range of services than adults. Third, participants must be allowed to use any health provider who meets program standards. (Providers, of course, must be willing to accept Medicaid recipients.) Fourth, the amount, duration, and scope of medical services must be "sufficiently reasonable." Exactly what this constitutes is a problem, and Medicaid reimbursement rates tend to be much lower than those provided for under conventional private insurance plans. While Texas may limit the services provided to adult clients, it may not arbitrarily deny services for specific conditions or illnesses.

Federal law also allows states to be granted waivers from these principles to create programs directed toward particular clients. In this approach, federal Medicaid policy mirrors the initiatives in welfare policy by providing states more freedom of action in developing programs to serve clients. For example, Texas has been granted the authority to enroll clients in managed care programs. In traditional fee-for-service programs a doctor or a hospital provides a service directly to the patient and is paid a fee for that service. In the managed care organization (MCO) model, programs such as health maintenance organizations or doctor-hospital networks act as an intermediary between the patient and the doctor, and negotiate discounted fees for medical services. In addition, MCOs reimburse their member health care providers with a monthly payment, which is known as a capitation payment because it has a limit or "cap" based on medical expenses calculated for the average patient. The State of Texas Access Reform program (STAR) is the managed care program where the Health and Human Services Commission contracts with MCOs to provide health care in various areas to poor populations in Texas.

Another model, found primarily in rural areas in Texas, is now referred to as traditional Medicaid. It is a noncapitated program enabling Medicaid recipients to receive medical home services from a primary care provider. As a noncapitated plan, it does not contain any average dollar amount per patient per month set by the state to pay for the cost of health care service. Primary care providers receive fee-for-service reimbursement and a small monthly management fee directly from the state. A recent initiative, Medicaid Rural Area STAR, has been implemented to provide managed care to clients in 164 mostly rural counties. The goal is to move rural clients away from traditional fee-for-service delivery as much as possible.

Managed care programs in Texas Medicaid have been growing in popularity since the early 1990s and became an essential part of cost containment measures instituted by the legislature over the next 20 years. In 1994, 2.9 percent of Texas Medicaid recipients were in state-sponsored managed care programs. By 2004 this participation had risen to 41.44 percent. By 2014 almost 82 percent of Medicaid recipients were in managed care programs.[51]

Medicaid Participation The initial goal of Medicaid in 1965 was to pay the medical bills of low-income individuals on public assistance. Over the last five decades, Medicaid has grown from a narrowly defined program targeting people on public assistance to a large, complex insurance program serving a variety of special groups. In the late 1980s and early 1990s Medicaid was expanded to include older adults not fully covered by Medicare (a federal medical insurance program funded through payroll taxes for persons age 65 and older), people with disabilities, and pregnant women. Individuals participating in TANF and SSI automatically qualify for Medicaid, as do others who meet these other criteria.

A variety of factors can affect an individual's eligibility to participate in Medicaid. People can go on and off Medicaid given their changing eligibility status. For example, eligibility can change when a parent or caregiver has a change in income or when a child is born. Eligibility also can change when a child reaches a certain age. For these reasons, there is significant fluctuation in Medicaid enrollment from month to month. However, one fact is strikingly clear: participation rates have gone up significantly in the first decade of the twenty-first century. Between 2001 and 2009 the average monthly Medicaid enrollment in Texas rose from 1.87 million people to 3.1 million.

The increase in participation is not caused by a rise in participation through Texas's principal public assistance program, the TANF program. As the number of monthly caseloads grew between 2001 and 2009 for Medicaid, the number of those eligible through the TANF actually decreased from approximately 500,000 to less than 350,000 in 2009 and to 75,000 in 2016. Although Medicaid and public assistance are still joined together, the close link between them that existed at the founding of Medicaid has largely been severed.

Figure 12.2 shows participation in Medicaid by gender, age, and ethnicity. Seventy-one percent of those on Medicaid are under the age of 20. Over 54 percent on Medicaid rolls are Latino, 22 percent are white, and 17 percent are African American.

FIGURE 12.2

Texas Medicaid Recipients by Gender, Age, and Race/Ethnicity (Estimated)

SOURCE: Texas Health and Human Services Commission, Texas Medicaid and CHIP, The "Pink Book," February 2015, Chap. 5, pp. 5–14 to 5–15. Note that total numbers fluctuate month by month on total number of clients.

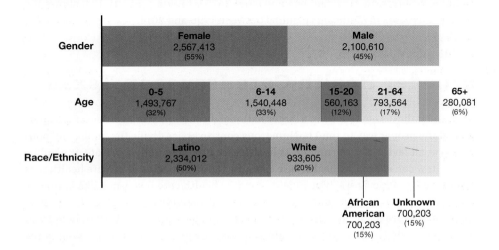

Administration and Financing of Medicaid in Texas In Texas, Medicaid is administered through the Texas Health and Human Services Commission. At the federal level, the Centers for Medicare and Medicaid in the Department of Health and Human Services monitor Texas's Medicaid program and establish basic services, delivery, quality, funding, and eligibility standards. Through Medicaid, Texas and the federal government together pay for a variety of health care services for a number of low-income populations. The acute health care services paid for include physicians' bills, inpatient care in a hospital and outpatient care, and pharmacy, lab, and X-ray services. Medicaid also provides for selected long-term and support services, including home- and community-based services for the disabled, home-health and personal care, and nursing services.

The federal portion of the program is determined every year by comparing average state per capita income to the average national per capita income. Each state thus has its own FMAP (the federal medical assistance percentage). Poorer states receive more federal assistance for the program than richer states. In 2017 the FMAP for Texas was 56.18 percent, which means that 43.82 percent of all Medicaid expenditures were state funded.[52]

A related program to Medicaid is the Children's Health Insurance Program (CHIP), which provides coverage for children in families with incomes too high to qualify for Medicaid. Established in 1997 under Title XXI of the Social Security Act, CHIP is administered like Medicaid through the Centers for Medicare and Medicaid Services in the U.S. Department of Health and Human Services. The 2010 federal allocation to Texas for CHIP was more than $925 million. The average monthly caseload for CHIP was 497,666 in 2002. After falling to 312,101 in 2007 before the Great Recession, enrollment in CHIP has fluctuated between 500,000 in early 2010 and 600,000 in early 2013. Participation numbers were falling throughout the first half of 2014 as the economy continued to improve, dropping below 500,000 in April 2014. The bulk of the increase in Medicaid caseload in the 2014–15 biennium mentioned in Chapter 11 will come because of the transfer of children from CHIP to Medicaid under the Affordable Care Act.

Medicaid and CHIP expenditures have become an increasing part of both the national and state budgets. In 1996 the total Medicaid budget of both federal and state dollars was $8.2 billion. By 2014, this had risen to $32.2 billion in Texas. By 2014 federal expenditures on Medicaid encompassed $475.9 billion.[53] Figure 12.3 shows the average increases in Medicaid spending between 1990 and 2014.

Broader Health Care Issues in Texas

Medicaid policy is embedded in a larger national discussion over health care in America and the proper way to fund it. Numerous controversies divide the public and politicians at all levels of government. Is health care fundamentally a private or a public issue? How can exploding health care costs, including the costs of private health care insurance like Blue Cross/Blue Shield or public health care insurance like Medicare and Medicaid, be brought under control? Should individuals be compelled to purchase health care insurance? How much and what kind of insurance? Who should foot the bill for individuals who cannot afford to pay for private insurance? What is the

FIGURE 12.3

Percentage of Medicaid Expenditures in Texas State Budget
SOURCE: Texas Health and Human Services Commission, *Texas Medicaid and CHIP in Perspective*, 10th ed., February 2015, Chap. 8.

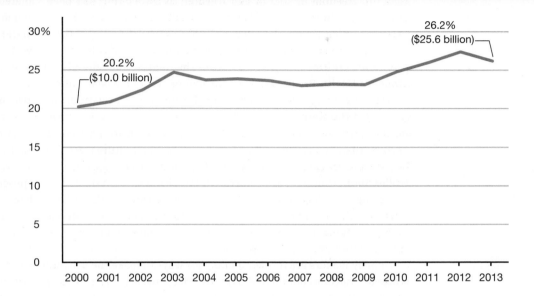

proper role for the state and federal governments in the delivery of health care across the nation?

As in other state-federal programs, federal money for Medicaid is accompanied by federal rules and regulations with which the state must comply in order to maintain this funding. This sometimes breeds tremendous political controversy between the state and the federal government. One such controversy broke out in early 2012 over provisions relating to Texas's Medicaid Women's Health Program.[54]

The Medicaid Women's Health Program in Texas serves more than 100,000 women and is funded by $35 million from federal funds and $7 million from state funds. Through subsidized clinics located across the state, the program helps pay for birth control, health screening, and family exams for a select group of women on Medicaid. Planned Parenthood offers these services as well as abortion services at its various clinics across the state. Conservatives in Texas, including Governor Perry, were unhappy with any state monies being used to subsidize groups supporting abortion and moved to cut program funds from going to these clinics. But federal regulations clearly state that patients in the program, not state officials, decide where money from the program is spent.

By March 2012 an impasse had been reached. On one side were Governor Perry and the Republican-dominated state legislature, who ordered an end to Medicaid funding of Planned Parenthood clinics. On the other side were the federal government and supporters of Planned Parenthood, who insisted on strictly following federal rules and guidelines. Interestingly, some moderate Republicans, like Senator Kay Bailey Hutcheson, broke with the governor and backed Planned Parenthood in the dispute. By early March 2012 all federal funding of the Texas Women's Health Program had been pulled. Governor Perry claimed that he would find new funding for the program at the state level that would exclude Planned Parenthood.

In early May 2012 the issue became even more complicated. Eight Planned Parenthood clinics that did not provide abortion services sued the state, claiming their rights to freedom of speech and freedom of association had been violated. A federal appeals court ruled on August 22, 2012 that Texas could ban Planned Parenthood from receiving funds. Texas solicitor general Jonathan Mitchell reiterated the state's opposition to providing taxpayer money "to entities that affiliate with abortion-promoting entities."[55] The conflict over the funding and administration of the Texas Women's Health Program signals the emergence of a new set of conflicts over Medicaid in Texas and a new round in the debate over the relationship between the national and the state government in the federal system. Cost, however, is the single most important issue confronting policy makers regarding Medicaid in Texas. Now encompassing more than 25 percent of state expenditures, Medicaid in Texas as in other states threatens to overwhelm the budget. In the spring of 2012, Texas comptroller Susan Combs began referring to Medicaid as "The Big Red," the program that was going to push an otherwise healthy state budget into the red. She claimed that by 2023 "Big Red is going to be over a third of state spending."[56] Medicaid expenditures, many mandated by the federal government, would begin to crowd out other forms of spending from the state budget.

Policy makers are forever looking for ways to make the program less costly. Two strategies have predominated over the past 20 years: first, to bring more efficiency into the program by expanding managed care initiatives across the state, and second, to institute cost controls and cutbacks to providers. Both efforts have had limited success, and at the same time have sparked concern over the quality of care being offered to Medicaid participants across the state. As cost containment efforts intensify, Texas policy makers inside and outside the legislature will be compelled to increase their monitoring of the delivery of the program.

The Affordable Care Act

In March 2010, Congress passed two bills, the Patient Protection and Affordable Care Act and the Health Care and Reconciliation Act of 2010, which together became known as the Affordable Care Act (ACA), often referred to as Obamacare. The passage of the ACA transformed the debate over health care policy in the United States. Passed on a party line vote by Congress, the legislation requires individuals not covered by existing plans to pursue health insurance or pay a penalty. Along with this "individual mandate," as the mandatory coverage came to be called, the act also increased coverage for preexisting conditions and expanded medical insurance to an estimated 30 million people.[57]

When fully implemented, the ACA was expected to bring significant change to the health insurance market in Texas as well as to Texas's Medicaid program.[58] Initial estimates in 2012 projected that under the ACA, insurance coverage in Texas will rise to 91 percent, with almost 40 percent of the remaining uninsured being undocumented persons. The expansion of Medicaid in Texas would be funded through a complicated set of subsidies based on family income. For the first three years of the

Abortion Policy in Texas

Abortion laws are among the most contentious public policies in the United States. In 1973, the U.S. Supreme Court ruled that a woman's right to privacy extended to her decision to have an abortion. This right was balanced, however, by the state's interest in guaranteeing safe and effective medical regulations. The balance has led to considerable controversy over the last 40 years as many state legislatures tried to limit the opportunities for women to have an abortion. Texas passed legislation in 2013 that effectively would have shuttered three-fourths of the abortion clinics in Texas. These laws, requiring abortion facilities to be like surgical facilities and requiring doctors providing abortion to have admitting privileges at a nearby hospital, were invalidated by the U.S. Supreme Court in 2016. In the decision *Whole Woman's Health v. Hellerstedt*, the Court reaffirmed a woman's right to abortion services without facing an undue burden imposed by the state.

Significantly, *Whole Woman's Health v. Hellerstedt* has not rejected all state regulations of abortion procedures. Earlier, in 2011, the Texas legislature passed and the courts upheld a law requiring doctors who perform abortions to provide a sonogram to women before carrying out the procedure.

The law requires doctors to provide with the sonogram "a simultaneous verbal explanation of the results of the live, real-time sonogram images, including a medical description of the dimensions of the embryo or fetus, the presence of cardiac activity, and the presence of arms, legs, external members, and internal organs." Doctors are also required to make the fetus's heartbeat audible to the woman. Pregnant women affected by the law may choose not to view the sonogram, listen to the doctor's explanations, or listen to the heartbeat. However, doctors who refuse to comply with the law are subject to losing their licenses to practice medicine. Doctors are not required to perform the sonogram procedure for women who were impregnated as a result of rape or incest.

Proponents of Texas's law argue that because abortion involves a nascent human life, efforts to make women think twice about going forward with an abortion should be implemented. They believe that the state has a compelling interest to protect the lives of what they consider to be human beings in the earliest stages of development. Supporters emphasize that women can still go forward with a legal abortion if they so choose, but they should have full and complete information about the consequences of the decision they are making. Elizabeth Graham, the director of Texas Right to Life, adds, "This paternalistic attitude, that we're saddling women with too much information, really does an injustice . . . It underestimates the capability of women to make a decision with more information, not less."[a]

Opponents of the law argue that abortion is a constitutional right that has been protected by the Supreme Court and that, through forcing women to take the extra step of having a sonogram, the state is making it more difficult for women to exercise this right. They cite the Court's argument that no abortion law can place an undue burden on women who choose to obtain an abortion, and they note that the law makes women come into a medical office twice—once for the sonogram and again for the abortion after the 24-hour waiting period. In particular, opponents argue that vaginal ultrasounds invade a woman's privacy, as they necessarily involve an invasive procedure that women should not be required to endure. Jenni Beaver, assistant director at the Southwestern Women's Surgery Center in Dallas, argues that the sonogram law "treats women as if they are stupid and don't know what is in their uterus . . . The law just creates hoops and barriers and drives up the cost for the women. And we have not had anyone decide not to have an abortion because of a sonogram."[b]

COMMUNICATING EFFECTIVELY: YOUR VOICE

- Do you believe abortions should be curtailed in Texas, and if so, is the sonogram law an effective way to achieve this goal?

- Do you believe that the sonogram policy presents an "undue burden" on the right of a woman to choose to have an abortion? Why or why not?

expansion (2014–16), the federal government would cover all costs for newly eligible participants in Medicaid and CHIP. Thereafter, the percentage would slowly decline, committing Texas to a larger portion of the funding. The long-term effect of the ACA for Texas would be a budgetary one. Increased expenditures on Medicaid and health care in Texas are all but inevitable.

The ACA sparked a national controversy. A majority of the states (including Texas) and a number of private individuals and groups challenged the constitutionality of the act in court, focusing on the mandatory coverage provisions. For three days in March 2012 the U.S. Supreme Court held oral argument on the case, *National Federation of Independent Business v. Sebelius.* A complicated decision was delivered by a divided Court on June 28, 2012. Four liberal justices believed that most features of the ACA were constitutional. Four conservative justices countered that they were not. Representing the decisive vote, Chief Justice Roberts rejected the idea that people could be mandated or forced to buy insurance under Congress's power to regulate commerce, but he nevertheless concluded that a tax penalizing people who did not get medical insurance met constitutional muster. Regarding the expansion of Medicaid, he supported a conservative position, arguing that states could not be bullied into expanding medical insurance coverage for poorer segments of the population. Chief Justice Roberts wrote that for federalism to thrive, states had to have a meaningful and real choice as to whether or not they would participate in federally sponsored programs.

The complicated U.S. Supreme Court decision opened the door for a new round of political posturing around the health care issue in Texas. Governor Perry announced that Texas would refuse to participate in the expanded Medicaid program, giving up millions of federal dollars for not having to incur new financial responsibilities at the state level. The state legislature, supporting Governor Perry, has refused to expand Medicaid in Texas. An estimate by the Kaiser Family Foundation in 2014 concluded that over 1 million uninsured adults in Texas, 17 percent of the uninsured in the state, would not be brought under the ACA provisions to expand Medicaid because of Texas's actions (or inactions).[59] Perry also decided that the state would not go into the business of designing an insurance exchange in the state. Texas would let the federal government sell federally designed insurance policies in the state on its own.

As if things weren't complicated enough in the emerging discussion over what to do about Medicaid and health care coverage in Texas, a 2012 survey was released by the Texas Medical Association that found only 31 percent of Texas doctors were accepting new patients who relied on Medicaid for insurance coverage, down from 42 percent in 2012 and 67 percent in 2000. Low payment and excessive red tape were cited as the reasons for the declining acceptance of Medicaid as a form of medical insurance.[60] Further complicating matters, officials from the Texas Health and Human Services Commission released a new estimate of the costs of the ACA in Texas based upon new, more conservative assumptions about how quickly newly eligible people might apply to participate in the program. The new estimates were 42 percent less than the original ones. In July 2012 state officials believed that if Texas opted into the new ACA Medicaid programs, by 2023 the state would spend $15.6 billion of state money and bring in $100.1 billion of federal money. Despite these projections, neither the Health and Human Services commissioner Tom Suehs nor Governor Perry believed that Texas should opt into the new ACA programs. Before Texas should participate in an expanded program, they believed the act should be "fixed" by Congress.[61]

What Are the Trade-Offs in Texas Public Policy?

The contemporary Texas government tends to pass conservative policies (low taxes and lower levels of social services). The figures below show these policies compared with those of other states. Texas collects the sixth-lowest share of taxes of any state. But when government lacks revenue, it cannot spend money to address social problems, such as providing health insurance to those who cannot afford it.

State Taxes (as a percentage of state income)

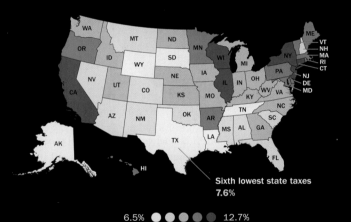

Sixth lowest state taxes
7.6%

6.5% ●●●●● 12.7%

Percentage without Health Insurance

Highest % uninsured
19.1%

3.3% ●●●●● 19.1%

State Taxes Compared with Percent Uninsured*

	Low tax rank	Uninsured rank		Low tax rank	Uninsured rank		Low tax rank	Uninsured rank
Alaska	1	2	North Dakota	18	40	Delaware	35	42
South Dakota	2	28	Georgia	19	4	Hawaii	36	48
Wyoming	3	18	Iowa	20	46	Maine	37	27
Tennessee	4	18	Nebraska	21	29	Pennsylvania	38	36
Louisiana	5	7	Idaho	22	11	Massachusetts	39	50
Texas	6	1	Missouri	23	22	Oregon	40	29
New Hampshire	7	32	Virginia	24	23	Vermont	41	49
Nevada	8	6	Washington	25	32	Minnesota	42	47
South Carolina	9	11	Michigan	26	36	Rhode Island	43	43
Mississippi	10	8	Indiana	27	20	Maryland	44	40
Oklahoma	11	5	Kansas	28	26	California	45	16
Alabama	12	17	Kentucky	29	36	Illinois	46	29
Montana	13	10	Utah	30	15	Wisconsin	47	44
New Mexico	14	8	North Carolina	31	14	New Jersey	48	23
Arizona	15	11	Ohio	32	39	Connecticut	49	45
Colorado	16	25	West Virginia	33	35	New York	50	34
Florida	17	3	Arkansas	34	21			

SOURCES: Tax Data: 2012 tax data from TaxFoundation.org (accessed 7/7/16). Uninsured Data: 2014 uninsured data from U.S. Census Bureau, Current Population Survey, Annual Social and Economic Supplements, www.census.gov (accessed 7/7/16).

*States with the same percentage of uninsured individuals are given the same rank.

CRITICAL THINKING

- What appears to be the relationship between state taxes and insurance rates in a state?

- When Obamacare is fully implemented, will the numbers of uninsured change? Why or why not?

FIGURE 12.4

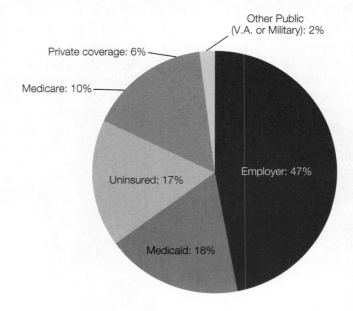

Where Do Texans Get Their Insurance? (2014)
SOURCE: Henry J. Kaiser Family Foundation, kff.org.

As of the end of 2016 the ACA was still in effect, but it is unclear what that will mean for poorer Texans over the long run. Health insurance coverage overall has increased in Texas 20 percent since 2013 (see Figure 12.4). But according to a 2015 study by the Episcopal Health Foundation, Texas continues to lag behind others states in Affordable Care Act coverage. Nearly half of those with an income under $27,000 are still uninsured. Texas's refusal to participate in the optional state-federal expansion of Medicaid has effectively denied insurance coverage to many poor people.[62] And then there is the issue of undocumented workers in Texas who compose a growing portion of uninsured individuals. The election of Donald Trump to the presidency has raised even more questions about the future of the ACA and health care in Texas. One thing is clear: few individuals are willing to argue that Texas has solved the problem of providing health care to the poor.

Water Policy

Consider the growing importance of policies related to water supplies in Texas

Water is the life blood of Texas. Access to plentiful water supplies over the past 100 years has been a necessary condition for a thriving economy and an expanding urban population in Texas. Approximately 59 percent of the water used in Texas comes from aquifers (underground pools of water), the vast majority of which (60 percent) is used in irrigation, particularly in the arid Panhandle region (Figure 12.5). The remainder comes from surface sources, including rivers and reservoirs. Twenty-seven percent of the state's water use is in municipal areas. Individual cities rely on various amounts of aquifer and surface water, but overall, aquifers are the source for more than one-third of the water consumed by metropolitan areas.

Texas's water consumption is projected to increase by 82 percent, from about 18 million acre-feet per year in 2010 to about 22 million acre-feet per year in 2060.[63] An acre-foot is a volume measurement used by water planners. It comprises an acre of area (43,560 square feet) one foot deep.[64] At the same time, existing supplies under current systems of production and conservation are expected to decrease by 10 percent, largely as a result of the depletion of the Ogallala Aquifer in the Texas Panhandle and reduced reliance on the Gulf Coast Aquifer. By 2060 experts project that an additional 8.3 million acre-feet per year will be needed for the state to continue to thrive.

Formulating a coherent water policy in Texas to address these and other issues is difficult for many reasons. As noted in Chapter 1, Texas is a large state with a diverse climate. The water-related issues along the Gulf Coast in southeast Texas near Houston, which is subtropical and humid, are quite different from those in the high plains Panhandle, which is semiarid savanna, or in the El Paso desert. For example, along the southeastern border with Louisiana, average annual rainfall is more than 80 inches per year, while near El Paso it is only 10 inches per year.[65] There are 15 major river basins and 8 coastal basins across the state, as well as 9 major and 21 minor aquifers.

FIGURE 12.5

Water Usage by Sector

About 8.42 million acre-feet of water used in Texas (62 percent) came from groundwater sources. About 5.27 million acre-feet (38 percent) came from surface water sources. These two charts illustrate how these waters were used in various activities in Texas.

SOURCE: Texas Water Development Board.

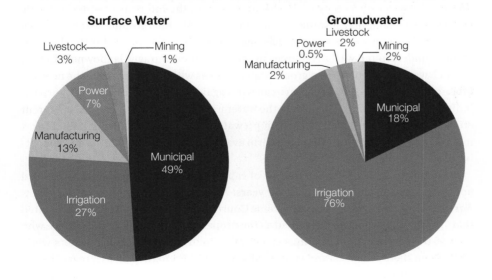

Surface Water
- Livestock 3%
- Mining 1%
- Power 7%
- Manufacturing 13%
- Municipal 49%
- Irrigation 27%

Groundwater
- Livestock 2%
- Power 0.5%
- Mining 2%
- Manufacturing 2%
- Municipal 18%
- Irrigation 76%

Water policy is further complicated by the fact that various regions of the state have periodically experienced severe droughts and devastating floods. Throughout the twentieth century, reservoirs have been built to more effectively distribute water during times of shortage and to control flooding. In 1913, when the Texas Board of Water Engineers was established, there were only 8 major reservoirs in the state. By 1950 the number of major reservoirs had grown to 53. Today there are 188.[66]

Water Law in Texas

Underlying water policy in Texas is a complicated system of private property rights derived from three sources: Spanish law, traditional English common law, and statutory law. Texas law recognizes several legal classes of water rights for surface water and groundwater that are governed by different rules. Historically, these variations in the law have made the forging of water policy an arduous and at times a politically charged matter.

In 1967 the law covering surface water and relatively well-defined underground streams was clarified when the state legislature passed the Water Rights Adjudication Act. This legislation essentially merged the various water rights doctrines dating back to the nineteenth century into a unified water permit system. It requires individuals seeking water rights to file a claim with the Texas Commission on Environmental Quality (originally called the Texas Water Commission) before using the water. A complex administrative and judicial process was put into place that essentially grants water rights holders certificates of adjudicated water rights. The ability of the state to control and manage surface water use thus was greatly expanded by the 1967 act.[67]

Groundwater law, that is, law regarding water flowing, or "percolating," underground, differs significantly from surface water law.[68] In *Houston and Texas Central Railroad Company v. East* (1904), the Texas Supreme Court adopted a strict common law notion of property law for percolating underground water called the **law of capture**. This standard is also found in Texas oil and gas law. Essentially, the law says that the first person to "capture" the water by pumping it out of the ground and using it owns the water. Landowners have the right to capture as much groundwater that is under their property as they wish without regard to the interests of other property owners whose land may also lie on top of the pool of underground water. The rule of capture in water property rights has one important consequence for the development of underground water resources in the state. It encourages landowners to take as much water as possible from groundwater sources without considering the needs of other consumers. The law of capture can work against conservation efforts of private individuals who are trying to protect the water under their lands. It can also undercut efforts of planning authorities to develop a water plan for a particular area that takes into account the short-term and long-term availability of water as well as the competing uses for available water.

Finding a balance between the law of capture and the need to plan has troubled policy makers for much of the last 60 years. *Houston and Texas Central Railroad v. East* was reaffirmed by the Texas Supreme Court in 1955. In its ruling, the court stated that "percolating waters are regarded as the property of the owner of the surface who may, in the absence of malice, intercept, impede and appropriate such waters while they are on their premises, and make whatever use of them they please, regardless of the fact that use cuts off the flow of such waters to adjoining land and deprives the ad-

law of capture the idea that the first person to "capture" water or oil by pumping it out of the ground and using it owns that water or oil

joining owner of their use." Nevertheless, the court also accepted the state's authority to regulate groundwater. In 1949 the state legislature passed the Texas Groundwater Act, which created water districts to manage groundwater supply.

Today there are 99 groundwater districts in Texas with varying powers. The smallest district is the Red Sands Groundwater Conservation District in Hidalgo County, covering 31 square miles. The largest is the High Plains Underground Water District, covering 12,000 square miles over the Ogallala Aquifer. Generally, the groundwater districts are able to develop regulations to protect the water supply provided by groundwater sources, including rules that may restrict pumping, require well permits, delineate well-spacing, and establish rates of water usage. The rules and regulations generated by these groundwater districts, however, can come into direct conflict with the law of capture, as we will see in the next section.[69]

Planning Authorities and Water Policy

The history of water planning in Texas stretches back to the early twentieth century. A constitutional amendment in 1904 paved the way for the development of various agencies and authorities concerned with water planning. Among the most important innovations put into place by the state legislature in the early 1900s were drainage districts (1905); conservation and reclamation districts, later referred to as river authorities (1917); and water and control improvement districts (1925).

From 1950 to 1956 Texas experienced its worst drought in history. Every major urban area experienced the effect of the drought, many turning to emergency supplies and to rationing. In 1957 the drought was ended by heavy rains that resulted in the massive flooding of every major river and tributary in the state. Two hundred fifty-three of Texas's counties were declared disaster areas. Estimates were that the drought had cost the state hundreds of millions of dollars. Damages from flooding were calculated to cost another $120 million. Calls for a more permanent planning and policy agency to direct and coordinate water policy came from all over the state.[70]

New agencies were established by the state in the 1960s to address various water issues. In 1977 the three major state water agencies—the Texas Water Development Board (TWDB), the Texas Water Rights Commission, and the Water Quality Board—were combined into the Texas Department of Water Resources, whose job was to develop Texas's water resources, maintain the quality of water, and assure an equitable distribution of water rights. Sunset legislation in 1985 reorganized this single agency into two new agencies: a new Texas Water Commission and a new version of the TWDB. Today, the TWDB is the state's primary water planning and financing agency. Enforcement of the state's environmental regulations regarding water is the job of the Texas Commission on Environmental Quality, an agency that resulted from the 1993 consolidation of the Texas Water Commission with the Texas Air Control Board.[71]

The TWDB is composed of a six-member board serving six-year terms with overlapping membership. Each member comes from a different part of the state. The TWDB has had a number of important responsibilities, including the following:

- Supporting the development of 16 regional water plans
- Developing a state water plan every five years

- Providing financial assistance to local governments for (1) water supply and waste management projects, (2) flood protection and control projects, (3) agricultural water conservation projects, and (4) the creation of groundwater districts
- Administering the Texas Water Bank, which facilitates the transfer, sale, and lease of water and water rights throughout the state
- Administering the Texas Water Trust, which holds water rights for environmental flow maintenance purposes
- Data collection for the state's freshwater needs[72]

A number of strategies for meeting the short- and long-term water needs in the state were articulated in the 2012 State Water Plan. Two elements of the plan stand out. First, there is a notable focus on the importance of conservation. Policy makers agree that in the future water must be used more efficiently in Texas. One of the most important policies is a conservation strategy throughout all regions that seeks a more efficient use of current water supplies. Second, there is an emphasis on the importance of expanding and developing available surface water throughout Texas. The plan calls for the building of 26 new major reservoirs by 2060 and new pipeline infrastructure from existing sources to new points of use. Such projects represent an important shift in existing water policy in some planning areas, as they shift the focus of water policy from flood control or hydroelectric power generation to the provision of water.

Groundwater strategies include the expansion of production by drilling more wells or building treatment plants for water quality. Conservation efforts also play a major part in groundwater initiatives, as some of the aquifers are experiencing overuse. The TWDB estimates that total groundwater supplies available to Texans will decline by 30 percent between 2010 and 2060. The Ogallala Aquifer (which runs from the Texas high plains up through western Kansas and into Nebraska) and the Edwards Aquifer (which runs along the Balcones fault line near San Antonio) are estimated to decline by 50 percent by 2060.

The total capital needs of funding these future initiatives proposed by regional water planning groups are estimated to be $53 billion, along with annual operating and maintenance costs. But cost is not the only challenge facing water policy makers. Some environmental groups in the state are opposed to the further expansion of the state reservoir system, arguing that the costs to the ecosystem of the state far outweigh the advantages provided by more water. On the other hand, some property owners, particularly in west Texas, are opposed to any new conservation restrictions or penalties put upon them by the state. Texas water law itself may be one of the most intractable problems that water planners may have to face in coming years.

On February 24, 2012, the Texas Supreme Court ruled on the case *The Edwards Aquifer Authority v. Burrell Day and Joel McDaniel*, which has important implications for future attempts to regulate water usage in Texas, particularly in those areas that rely heavily upon aquifers. The case involved two farmers who had applied to the Edwards Aquifer Authority for permission to pump 700 acre-feet per year of water to irrigate their 350-acre ranch in Van Ormy, a small town south of San Antonio. The farmers argued that they had rights to water from the aquifer based on their ownership of land above it. Maintaining that the farmers were unable to prove "historical use" of water from the aquifer, the authority granted them a permit for pumping only 14 acre-feet.

Writing for the 9–0 court majority, Justice Hecht ruled that using "historical use" as a criterion for granting a permit to pump water was a departure from the Texas Water Code. "Unquestionably," Hecht wrote, "the state is empowered to regulate groundwater production . . . [but] groundwater in place is owned by the landowner on the basis of oil and gas law."[73] Texas regulatory authorities thus had the power to reasonably regulate the use of water drawn from an aquifer in the public interest, but they may have to pay property owners with a stake in that water any damages that are incurred by the regulation.

The ruling sparked a firestorm of controversy among interested parties. Landowners celebrated the decision as vindication of their ownership of water under their lands. In contrast, state planning authorities and environmentalists were aghast at the implications that the case could have for their attempts to efficiently allocate and conserve water in Texas. The Texas Supreme Court's ruling raised an important question regarding water policy in Texas: Which policy-making body would dominate water policy in the foreseeable future in Texas? Would it be the courts working through judicial interpretations of the applicability of water property law? Or would it be the regulatory bodies whose job was to plan and to allocate water based on their assessment of available water supplies and the competing needs for water? Developing regulatory rules for the use of aquifer water that both protect property rights and promote the public interest through reasonable and efficient regulations will be a challenge facing these policy makers in years to come.[74]

A major step toward planning for water in the future took place in 2013, when voters approved a constitutional amendment to create a $2.0 billion water fund. The bulk of the monies being directed to water policy came from a onetime transfer of money from the Rainy Day Fund to the State Water Implementation Fund for Texas (SWIFT). Proponents claimed that the two accounts could fund over $25 billion in water development projects over the next 50 years.

The basic idea behind this water initiative is that SWIFT projects would generate revenue that would go into another account (the State Water Implementation Revenue Fund for Texas or SWIRFT) that could be used to fund more water projects. Proposals for projects to be funded by SWIFT and SWIRFT would come from regional water planning groups and could include such things as building new reservoirs, fixing pipes, and groundwater development. A number of provisos were attached to the legislation that put forward the constitutional amendment: 20 percent of the funds had to be directed to conservation and 10 percent would have to serve rural areas. Interestingly, concerns were raised about the fact that the agency managing the program, the TWDB, might be too close to the governor given that the board would be appointed by him or her. The authorizing legislation thus established a separate committee to oversee how SWIFT and SWIRFT funds are managed. The committee would be appointed by the Speaker of the House and the lieutenant governor and be composed of the comptroller, three state representatives, and three state senators. Planning for Texas's water future did not mean that traditional concerns over too much executive power in public policy matters would be ignored.[75]

The drought of 2011 was the worst in the history of Texas. The drought extended into 2012, 2013, and 2014, threatening the state's prosperity, causing dust storms in the Texas panhandle (top), and drying lake beds throughout the state. Many of the state's cities were put on various levels of water emergencies that restricted use. Some smaller towns saw their water supplies drift down to 60 days and less.

Public Policy and the Future of Texas

In this chapter, we examined various aspects of public-policy making in Texas. We focused particular attention on the complex issues that have driven the various stages of the policy-making process in public education, welfare, health care, and water policy. Looking at these matters with a critical eye to the future demands that we pay attention to a number of key political questions: How are problems identified by policy makers and the public at large? What kinds of solutions are formulated to address these problems? Who benefits by a particular public policy? Who pays for the policy? What ideas are used to justify or legitimate a particular program? How are programs evaluated? How do particular public policies evolve and change over time to address new problems? How do they alter the relationship between individual citizens and the government that represents them in Austin?

In earlier chapters, we saw how the high-tech revolution transformed Texas's economy in the 1980s and '90s. We also traced how social and political changes have restructured the political party system in the state and the increasing power of the Republican Party. In this chapter, we have seen how many of these shifts resulted in important changes in public policy in the twentieth and twenty-first centuries. These policy changes are occurring as the Texas political economy moves from an oil, cattle, and cotton economy into an era of computers, high technology, and globalization.

What will be the future of public policy in the areas of education, welfare, health care, and water policy? What issues will be seen as problems? What policies will be formulated to address these problems? How will those new policies be implemented, evaluated, and legitimated?

Funding and fairness issues will be dominated by the legislature now that the courts have pulled out of the business of figuring out what was meant in the constitution by "efficiency." Charter schools likely will continue to expand, challenging the dominance of the traditional public schools. Poverty policy will continue to be the poor child of public policy as the state continues to find ways to reform welfare by ending dependency and by putting people back to work. Water policy will build upon the initiatives made possible for the billion-dollar water fund.

The wild card for the state may be health care policy. Will the state ever accept the expansion of Medicaid and insurance services provided under the Affordable Care Act? What will be done to address the continuing problem of the uninsured? Must the poor be allowed to fend for themselves, even those who are too young to do much fending? There is a chance that the state will punt on these issues, leaving segments of the poor and uninsured exposed. It is ironic that a state proud of its entrepreneurial energies is having so much trouble coping with the challenges of health care in an age of high-tech innovation and globalization.

STUDY GUIDE

Use **INQUIZITIVE** to help you study and master this material.

The Policy-Making Process

> • Describe the key steps and concepts in the policy-making process (pp. 401–4)

Public policies are the outcomes of governmental institutions. There are a number of stages in the policy-making process. One stage is problem identification, where political actors and society at large develop an understanding of a problem and how that problem can be addressed. The second stage in the process is policy formulation, where strategies for dealing with specifically defined problems are developed. The third stage is policy implementation, where the goals of public policy along with sanctions to support them are put into effect by a particular government agency. A fourth stage of the process is evaluation, where efforts are made to evaluate the effectiveness of a policy. Some political scientists argue that still another stage in the process is policy legitimation, where the legality of a particular policy initiative is determined.

Key Terms
rationality (p. 402)
bounded rationality (p. 404)

Practice Quiz
1. *Satisficing* means that decision makers are seeking
   a) the optimal means of solving a problem.
   b) a satisfactory way for solving a problem.
   c) policies that will satisfy voters.
   d) the easiest policies to adopt.
   e) policies that satisfy the courts.

2. Among the factors that work against rationality and efficiency in the making of public policies is that
   a) politicians are more interested in votes than in effective policies.
   b) administrators of policies often seek the easiest way of administering laws rather than the most efficient ways.
   c) governments work incrementally.
   d) rational and efficient policies are often difficult to legitimate to a broader public.
   e) all of the above

3. An example of policy legitimation is when
   a) the courts uphold the constitutionality of a law.
   b) the governor vetoes a particular bill.
   c) the governor appoints an official to run a bureaucracy.
   d) political scientists research the effectiveness of a law.
   e) the legislature does not repeal a law during the legislative session following its passage.

Education Policy

• Describe the major issues that have shaped education policy in Texas (pp. 404–16)

One of the most important functions of state government is providing and funding public education. Under the Gilmer-Aikin Laws, Texas extended its control over financing and administering public education through local school districts. As in many southern states, segregation of public schools was a major problem that was not dealt with until federal courts forced Texas to desegregate in the 1950s and '60s. Equity in the funding of public education remains a major issue in Texas. State courts continue to play an important role in addressing the equity issue. Concerns over excellence and accountability in public education persist today.

Key Terms
Gilmer-Aikin Laws (p. 406)
equal protection clause (p. 408)

Practice Quiz
4. The Gilmer-Aikin Laws
   a) regulate schools in the Gilmer-Aikin ISD.
   b) were major educational reforms passed in 1949.
   c) established an office of elected state superintendent of public instruction.
   d) allowed for homeschooling of children.
   e) required that money raised from the poll tax be spent on public education.

5. State courts tried to address the issue of equity in the funding of public schools
   a) in the case of *Edgewood ISD v. Kirby*.
   b) in the case of *Brown v. Board of Education*.
   c) in the case of *San Antonio v. Rodríguez*.
   d) by appointing Ross Perot to recommend changes to the property tax in Texas.
   e) by abolishing the office of the State Board of Education.

6. Among the reforms in public education in Texas to improve the quality of education was
   a) "No Pass, No Play."
   b) "No Play, No Pass."
   c) a shorter school year.
   d) more flexible standards for accrediting schools.
   e) tying teacher pay raises to student grades.

Welfare Policy

- Describe the state's role in addressing poverty and how it is affected by national policies (pp. 416–22)

Texas has large numbers of people living in poverty who have received governmental assistance since the New Deal when the Social Security Act of 1935 was passed. Texas's most important welfare program was AFDC. President Lyndon Johnson's War on Poverty expanded social welfare programs for the poor in the 1960s. But compared with other states, welfare benefits remained low in Texas. Concerns over the problem of welfare dependency led to major reforms at the national level in 1996 when AFDC was replaced with TANF. Since these reforms, welfare rolls have declined, although poverty has remained a chronic problem among a significant portion of the Texas population.

Key Terms
New Deal (p. 418)
Aid to Families with Dependent Children (AFDC) (p. 418)
Medicaid (p. 418)
Supplemental Security Income (SSI) (p. 419)
Temporary Assistance for Needy Families (TANF) (p. 421)

Practice Quiz
7. Poverty among those over age 65 and those under age 18 in Texas
   a) is almost nonexistent because of the welfare reforms of the 1990s.
   b) is at a level above the national average.
   c) is at a level below the national average.

   d) was largely eliminated by the Social Security Act of 1935.
   e) was largely eliminated by Lyndon Johnson's "War on Poverty."

8. The welfare reforms of the 1990s
   a) resulted from a belief that the welfare policies of the 1960s had failed.
   b) led to a 36-month limitation on welfare benefits in Texas.
   c) led to a five-year ban on reapplying for benefits once benefits ran out.
   d) expanded education and job-training programs.
   e) all of the above

9. Two presidents who had major roles in welfare policy are
   a) Franklin Delano Roosevelt and Lyndon B. Johnson.
   b) Dwight Eisenhower and Herbert Hoover.
   c) Harry Truman and John F. Kennedy.
   d) Woodrow Wilson and Franklin Delano Roosevelt.
   e) Lyndon B. Johnson and George H. W. Bush.

Medicaid and Health Care Policy

• Explain why Medicaid in particular and health care policy in general have been so controversial in Texas (pp. 422–32)

One major welfare program that has become increasingly costly is Medicaid, a state-federal program that finances health care for the poor. Reforms instituted under the Obama administration have significantly expanded health care coverage for the poor. Texas, however, is not participating in that expansion. The rising cost of Medicaid is seen by many conservatives to be a growing threat to the financial integrity of the state's budget.

Practice Quiz

10. Which of the following statements is *true* about Medicaid in Texas?
  a) Medicaid is a program that was part of the New Deal.
  b) Texas policy makers make all the major decisions regarding the principles and standards directing Medicaid in Texas. There is no federal oversight.
  c) Texas can apply for a waiver with the federal government, enabling it to create programs directed toward particular clients.
  d) Medicaid employs doctors and nurses as members of the Department of Health and Human Services hired to provide medical care to the poor.
  e) Medicaid is funded entirely by the state.

11. Managed care programs
  a) are not found in the Texas Medicaid program.
  b) provide medical care to an increasing number of Medicaid clients in Texas.
  c) provide medical care to a small number of Medicaid clients in Texas.
  d) provide direct fee-for-service care for Medicaid recipients.
  e) have declined in popularity since the 1990s.

12. The Affordable Care Act
  a) was part of the War on Poverty.
  b) merged Medicare and Medicaid into a single program.
  c) will increase health insurance coverage to millions of Texans.
  d) was declared unconstitutional by the Texas Supreme Court.
  e) originated in the Texas legislature.

Water Policy

- Consider the growing importance of policies related to water supplies in Texas (pp. 432–37)

A looming threat to Texas's further economic development is access to freshwater. Over the next 50 years, water consumption is expected to vastly increase while existing supplies may decrease. Current water law in Texas adds complexity to the development of rational water policies for the state.

Key Terms
law of capture (p. 434)

Practice Quiz
13. Which of the following is *true*?
   a) Texas water consumption will decrease as the population expands.
   b) The idea of planning for future water provision has been rejected by the Texas state legislature as being too socialistic.
   c) Water law in Texas distinguishes between surface water and groundwater.
   d) Providing water in Texas is primarily a federal responsibility.
   e) Current state water policies do not emphasize conservation.

14. The law of capture concerns
   a) property rights in underground percolating water.
   b) the right of the state to regulate rivers and estuaries.
   c) political control of the legislature by a particular policy interest.
   d) the Corps of Engineers' various attempts to direct the flow of the Rio Grande.
   e) the federal government's ability to override Texas water laws.

15. Which of the following is *true*?
   a) The Texas Supreme Court rejects the idea that the state can regulate *surface* water.
   b) Texas is empowered by the state constitution to seize without compensation an individual's right to use underground water.
   c) Aquifers provide a negligible supply of water to Texas.
   d) Attempts to regulate groundwater access frequently come into conflict with property rights.
   e) The Water Rights Adjudication Act of 1967 prohibits the state from regulating surface water permits.

In 2011, Michael Morton was released from prison based on new DNA testing in his case. He served nearly 25 years in prison before another man was arrested for the crime. DNA evidence has revealed a series of wrongful convictions, raising questions about criminal justice in Texas.

13

Crime and Corrections Policy

WHY CORRECTIONS POLICY MATTERS On August 13, 1986, Christine Morton was beaten to death at her home in Austin. Her husband, Michael Morton, was charged with the murder and was prosecuted by Williamson County district attorney Ken Anderson. Michael received a life sentence for the murder, though he persisted in claiming his innocence and argued that some unknown intruder must have killed his wife after he had gone to work. The day after the murder, Christine's brother had found a bloodstained blue bandana near the crime scene, and he had turned it over to detectives. In 2005, Michael asked for DNA testing on several items including the blue bandana.

John Bradley, the district attorney at the time, and known as a tough prosecutor, opposed the requests for DNA testing, claiming there was no way the testing would lead to some "mystery killer." Michael Morton's lawyers were, argued Bradley, "grasping at straws." Morton's lawyers suspected that key evidence had been withheld in the case, and so they sought investigative materials in Morton's case. Bradley opposed those requests as well. In 2008, Bradley was forced to turn over the investigative materials, and Morton's defense lawyers discovered that Eric Morton, who was three years old at the time of his mother's murder, had seen the murder and described the killer as a "monster" who had red gloves and a big mustache. He also had said that the killer was not his father.

Defense lawyers discovered other information as well from the newly released files of the case. Police reports noted that there was a check to Christine that was cashed with a forged signature after her death, and there were reports of fraudulent use of her credit card after her death. There were also neighbors' statements to police that a man was seen parked in a green van near the Morton home on several occasions before the murder. Contrary to a legal requirement that prosecutors share exculpatory materials, this information had not been provided to the defense lawyers.

Then, in 2010, DNA testing on the blue bandana was allowed. DNA was found on the bandana to belong to the victim, Christine, and to a man whose DNA was in a national database as a result of an arrest in California. That man was Mark Alan Norwood. On October 4, 2011, Michael Morton was released from prison—he had been convicted in 1987. Mark Alan Norwood was convicted of the murder of Christine Morton on March 27, 2013. He is believed to have murdered another woman in 1988.

District Attorney Bradley was defeated for re-election in the Republican primary in 2012. His opponent, Williamson County Attorney Jana Duty, won with 55 percent of the vote and hammered

Bradley for blocking the postconviction DNA testing for Morton. Bradley's resistance to that testing meant that Morton spent six additional years in prison.[1] Judge Ken Anderson was sentenced to 10 days in jail, a $500 fine, and 500 hours of community service for criminal contempt in telling the Morton trial judge that he had no evidence favorable to Morton.[2] He has also lost his judgeship and law license. Morton is free and will receive financial restitution from the state for the quarter century that he spent in prison for a murder he did not commit. He was present when the Texas legislature passed a bill, the Michael Morton Act, which establishes a uniform policy for district attorneys to make material that can help defendants' cases available to defense attorneys.[3]

The Morton case highlights several aspects of the criminal justice system in Texas and raises questions about how it works. It is within the criminal justice process that the power of the state is greatest—the criminal law can take away an individual's liberty and even life. Texas has long been the poster child for its harshness in criminal punishment. No state executes more prisoners than Texas, which has the largest correctional population in the United States with 699,300 people in prison or jail or on probation or parole. The next largest correctional population is California's, whose population is about 11.8 million larger than Texas's and whose correctional population is 589,600. To give a sense of the importance of criminal corrections to an understanding of Texas politics and policy, although Texas has 8.5 percent of the nation's population, it has 10.2 percent of its correctional population. At any point in time, 2.6 percent of all Texans are in prison or jail or on probation or parole, including 4.2 percent of all Texans between the ages of 18 and 65.[4] In this chapter we will look both at the basics of the criminal justice system and at recent issues related to criminal justice in Texas.

CHAPTER GOALS

- Identify the major classifications of crime under Texas law and the types of punishments that may be imposed (pp. 447–49)

- Outline the procedural steps that occur after a person is arrested (pp. 449–55)

- Describe prisons and corrections policy in Texas (pp. 455–67)

- Explain why Texas's criminal justice system is often controversial (pp. 468–73)

- Consider recent proposals to improve Texas's criminal justice system (pp. 473–77)

Categorizing Crime in Texas

Identify the major classifications of crime under Texas law and the types of punishments that may be imposed

Crimes, of course, have different levels of seriousness, and punishments vary according to the legislature's classification of the seriousness of the crime. In the Texas criminal justice system, crimes are classified as felonies or misdemeanors. Table 13.1 shows the punishment range for the various classifications of crime in Texas.

Felonies and Misdemeanors

A **felony** is a serious criminal offense that subjects a person to state prison punishment. Fines can be up to $10,000, and prison punishment can range from six months to the death penalty. The right to vote, to have a gun, or to have certain occupational licenses can also be taken away, although in Texas voting rights for felons are restored after the sentence has been fully discharged. The most serious felony is capital murder, for which the penalty can be death or life imprisonment without parole. There are degrees of felonies, with stricter sentences attached to more serious crimes.

Misdemeanors are less serious crimes, for which the fine is $4,000 or less and the sentence is up to one year in the county jail. No rights such as the right to vote, the right to possess a weapon, or the rights to have some occupational licenses are lost as a result of a misdemeanor conviction. There are three classes of misdemeanors, again with stricter sentences attached to more serious crimes (see Table 13.1).

> **felony** a serious criminal offense, punishable by a prison sentence or a fine. A capital felony is punishable by death or a life sentence

> **misdemeanor** a minor criminal offense usually punishable by a small fine or short jail sentence

Punishing Crime

In some cases, the judge may allow **probation**, or community supervision, rather than a jail or prison sentence, especially if it is the defendant's first conviction. Probation is a suspension of the jail or prison sentence with the understanding that the defendant will meet certain requirements that are imposed by the court. These requirements usually include reporting to a probation officer on a regular basis, holding a steady job, paying fines or restitution, and abstaining from alcohol or drug use. Generally, community supervision can run up to 2 years for misdemeanors and up to 10 years for felonies, although if a probationer is compliant with the rules of community supervision, it is possible to obtain early release from probation after serving one-third of the term.[5]

Violation of probation requirements can result in being sent to jail or prison to serve out the sentence behind bars. Often prosecutors know that people with lengthy probation sentences will find it difficult to comply with all of the requirements. So, in cases where they believe it will be difficult to get a conviction, they might agree to a plea bargain allowing community supervision for a long period. They expect that the defendant will violate probation and spend time in jail or prison.

> **probation** punishment where an offender is not imprisoned but remains in the community under specified rules and under the supervision of a probation officer

TABLE 13.1

Classification of Crimes

FELONY CRIMES	EXAMPLES	PENALTIES*
Capital murder		Death or life without parole
First degree	Aggravated (using a weapon) assault on a public servant, aggravated kidnapping, aggravated sexual assault, arson of a habitation	5 to 99 years in state prison; fine up to $10,000
Second degree	Arson, bigamy, bribery, robbery, sexual assault, manslaughter, possession of 50 to 2,000 pounds of marijuana	2 to 20 years in state prison; fine up to $10,000
Third degree	Stalking conviction, third driving while intoxicated (DWI) charge, third offense of violation of a protective order	2 to 10 years in state prison; fine up to $10,000
State jail	Burglary of a building, DWI with a child as a passenger, forgery of a check, possession of less than one gram of a controlled substance	180 days to 2 years in a state jail; fine up to $10,000

MISDEMEANOR CRIMES	EXAMPLES	PENALTIES*
Class A	Burglary of a vehicle, second DWI offense, public lewdness, possession of two to four ounces of marijuana	No more than 1 year in county jail; fine up to $4,000
Class B	Prostitution, terrorist threats, first DWI charge, criminal trespass, possession of two ounces or less of marijuana	No more than 180 days in county jail; fine up to $2,000
Class C	Public intoxication, disorderly conduct, minor's possession of alcohol	Fine up to $500

*In many cases, probation is a possible substitute for serving jail or prison time. If jail or prison time is imposed, it is possible to obtain parole or early release.

SOURCES: "Texas Criminal Laws & Penalties," Texas Criminal Defense Lawyer; Fred Dahr, "Crimes and Punishment in Texas State Court," texasdefenselaw.com.

parole the conditional release of an offender who has served some prison time, under specified rules and under the supervision of a parole officer

People who are sentenced to prison may be released on **parole** after a period of time behind bars. This decision to grant parole is made by the Texas Board of Pardons and Paroles. The agency is composed of a chair and six board members. Members of the board serve six-year staggered terms. The board makes recommendations about state prisoners' sentences, clemency, parole, and supervision. In order for the governor to alter a prisoner's sentence, a majority of the board must support the change. The board also determines which prisoners are to be released on parole, determines conditions of parole, determines revocation of parole, and recommends clemency matters to the governor.

People serving time for capital crimes are not eligible for parole, and generally those convicted of other violent crimes must serve at least half their sentence before being considered for parole. People convicted of nonviolent crimes must serve at least one-fourth of their sentences or 15 years, whichever is less, before being considered for parole. A complex formula is used by the Board of Pardons and Paroles that considers the crime, when it was committed, the time served, and the behavior of the inmate, so that no simple rule generally applies to offenders. If a prisoner is granted parole, he or she must comply with the requirements imposed on the parole or, like probation violators, he or she can be sent to prison for the remainder of the sentence.[6]

There are also sentencing enhancements that increase sentences or increase the classification of the crime in certain circumstances. Previous convictions can be used to enhance the punishment for a crime. For example, a DWI offense is a class B misdemeanor, but a second DWI is a class A misdemeanor, and a third DWI is a third degree felony. That means, of course, that a second or third DWI conviction will result in more serious penalties than will the first DWI offense.

Texas enhances sentences for repeat felony offenders as well. If a person who commits a third degree felony has a prior felony conviction, that person is sentenced for a second degree felony. Similarly, a second degree felony is punished as a first degree felony if the person had a prior felony conviction. A person convicted of a third felony can be sentenced to life imprisonment based on a **"three strikes" provision** in the penal code, and in some cases, such as sexual assault cases, two felony convictions are sufficient for life imprisonment.

"three strikes" provision a law that allows persons convicted of three felonies (or in some cases two felonies) to be sentenced to life imprisonment

The Criminal Justice Process

Outline the procedural steps that occur after a person is arrested

There are several procedural steps that occur after a person is arrested and prior to the determination of guilt or innocence. In Texas, as in most other states, this process may take months or even years. The major procedural steps are listed below.

After being charged, a defendant may be released on bail. If the individual does not have enough money to post bail, he or she may make arrangements with a bail bondsman, who posts bail in exchange for a nonrefundable payment.

Arraignment and Posting Bail

Generally, when a person is arrested for a felony or misdemeanor and jailed rather than ticketed, he or she will be arraigned before a judge. At the arraignment, the charges will be explained to the accused, and he or she will be reminded of the due process rights—such as the right to remain silent and the right to an attorney. Generally, bail will be set at this point. In some cases, a date will be determined for the judge to review the charges against the defendant.

After being charged, a defendant may be released on bail until the trial. **Bail** is money that is provided by the defendant to assure his or her appearance in court. Usually, if a defendant does not show up for trial, the bail is forfeited. If the defendant appears as required, the bail money is returned. An individual may put up the entire sum for bail in order to be released from prison pending trial. Often, however, bail is more than the accused can pay, and so he or she will arrange with a bail bondsman to pay the bail in exchange for a nonrefundable payment that is often 10 percent of the amount but can be higher. If a person cannot provide bail on the person's own or cannot pay a bondsman, the accused possibly can be released on personal recognizance, which is the accused's promise to appear. This process is most likely if the accused has ties in the community such as a family or employment and does not have a criminal record. If an accused person cannot provide bail or be released without bail, he or she usually will be held in jail pending the trial.

bail payment of money to the state as an assurance that an accused person who is released from jail pending trial will appear for trial; if the accused does not appear, the bail is forfeited

Grand Jury Indictment

Although the procedure can vary, generally after arraignment, a felony case will be presented to a **grand jury**, which consists of 12 persons who will hear the case to determine if there is sufficient evidence to hold the accused for trial. Grand juries do not find people guilty of a crime, but instead will vote a "true bill," meaning that they find probable cause that an accused person has committed the crime, or they will return a "no bill," meaning that they did not find probable cause. A person would, of course, be held for trial only if a grand jury voted a "true bill." A grand jury indictment is far from conviction, as all a grand jury determines is the existence of probable cause and usually the grand jury's decision is based only on a presentation made by the prosecutor. In a trial, to find a person guilty, there must be a finding of guilt "beyond a reasonable doubt," which is a demanding standard of proof for a prosecutor. At a trial the defense is also heard and has the opportunity to cross-examine witnesses and present the defense's version of events. The major criticism of the grand jury is that it usually hears only what the prosecutor chooses to let it hear and that it serves as a "rubber stamp" for the prosecutor's decision.

grand jury jury that determines whether sufficient evidence is available to justify a trial; grand juries do not rule on the accused's guilt or innocence

Pretrial Hearings

After indictment for a felony, there will likely be a number of pretrial hearings in which the accused will formally plead guilty or not guilty, the trial is scheduled, and various motions may be presented such as motions to move the trial or motions to exclude certain evidence. These hearings vary in length but in most cases are quite brief. In a criminal trial, a common motion is one to exclude certain evidence on the grounds that the evidence was seized in violation of the Fourth Amendment to the U.S. Constitution, meaning that it was illegally seized. In these instances, the judge examines the facts of the seizure and determines whether the evidence was legally seized and therefore can be used at trial.

Although plea bargaining can occur even during a trial and even after a finding of guilt but before sentencing, the prosecution and the defense will often discuss a punishment in exchange for a guilty plea and reach an agreement before the trial.

Trial and Sentencing

If the case does go to trial, a defendant may waive the right to a jury trial and have the determination of guilt made by a judge. A jury trial may be waived in cases where a judge is perceived as more inclined to be favorable to the defendant because of past decisions by the judge or because the crime is believed to be one that would inflame the emotions of jurors, resulting in less favorable treatment. A defendant may also have a jury trial but waive the right to sentencing by a jury so that the judge determines the sentence if there is a guilty verdict. In Texas, felony juries are composed of 12 people and misdemeanor juries are composed of 6. Decisions by criminal juries must be unanimous, and for both felonies and misdemeanors the standard of proof is "beyond a reasonable doubt." If the jury's decision in either a felony or misdemeanor case is not unanimous, the case results in a mistrial, and the prosecutor must decide whether to retry the defendant.

If the defendant is acquitted (found not guilty), the defendant is, of course, set free. If the defendant is found guilty, there will be a jail or prison sentence or probation and/or a fine. A defendant may appeal a determination of guilt, meaning that the defendant asks a higher court to reconsider the lower court's decision. Very minor criminal cases that are heard by municipal courts or by justice of the peace courts can be appealed to the county courts. More serious misdemeanors and felonies, however, are heard by county or district courts, and appeals from county courts or district courts will be to one of the 14 courts of appeal in Texas. An appeal beyond the Texas courts of appeal will be to the highest criminal court in Texas, the Texas Court of Criminal Appeals. Death penalty cases are directly appealed to the Texas Court of Criminal Appeals. In rare events where a question of U.S. constitutional or statutory law is raised, it may also be possible to appeal to the federal courts.

Does the Criminal Justice System Create Criminals?

In some cases, the requirements of the Texas criminal justice system can be quite burdensome on individuals. For some people, complying with the rules of the process can be difficult and even financially impossible. One common crime in Texas, especially among younger offenders, is possession of less than two ounces of marijuana. Although a few Texas counties treat this crime as the equivalent of a traffic offense where the police officer tickets the offender, in other Texas counties offenders will be taken to a local jail to be held until the bond hearing and until they can make bail.

Commonly, the bail on such a charge would be $500, which means that the full $500 will have to be posted with the county, or a bail bondsman will have to be retained for roughly a $50 nonrefundable fee. After bail is posted, the defendant will eventually have to go to trial in a county-court-at-law. Some defendants hire an attorney, which may cost $1,000 to $3,000 for the entire process in this type of case; others may appear in court without an attorney. It would not be unusual for a first offense to result in at least a $500 fine plus court costs, a sentence of 30 hours of community service, a sentence of 15 hours in an approved drug education course, and nine months' probation where the defendant would pay a fee for each visit to the probation officer and any drug testing required by the probation officer. After court costs, probation costs, and the fine, the offender will probably have spent about $1,000 to $1,200, plus legal fees.

While on probation, the offender will not be allowed to use drugs or alcohol and will be subject to testing. There will be a required visit with a drug counselor and regular trips to a probation officer. Travel will be restricted. If the offender is in compliance, he or she will probably get early release from probation. If not, probation could be full length and jail time is possible. Additionally, because this is a drug case, the driver's license of the offender will be suspended for six months. If driving is necessary for the offender, in order to be in compliance, the offender must go to court and obtain an occupational driver's license in order to drive to and from work or care for family matters. Filing this paperwork can easily cost nearly $300 not counting possible attorney's fees. Additionally, the offender will have to purchase an SR-22 automobile insurance policy for two years in order to drive legally. This is a high-risk insurance policy in which the insurance company reports directly to the state that the offender has automobile insurance coverage. This type of insurance can cost twice as much as a regular insurance policy. Thus, an arrest for possession of a marijuana cigarette can easily cost more than $5,000 to $7,000 overall in fines, court costs, insurance charges, probation fees, and attorney costs, not to mention time in jail after arrest and, if the marijuana was found in the offender's vehicle, towing and impoundment charges. Failure to comply with all probation requirements can lead to violation of probation and other criminal charges such as driving with a suspended license or driving without proper insurance.

The structure of the criminal justice process even for minor crimes such as a class B misdemeanor may deter future crimes because of the severity of punishment, but the cost and penalty structure also seems to encourage failure and further criminality by the offender.

Crime and Texas District Attorneys

county attorney an elected official in some counties who prosecutes misdemeanor cases

district attorney public official who prosecutes the more serious criminal cases in the district court

Ordinarily when we think of the criminal justice system, we think of the police who make arrests and the Texas criminal courts that adjudicate those criminal cases. The most important actors in the Texas criminal justice system, however, are probably the prosecuting attorneys. Some counties have an elected county attorney whose office represents the state in misdemeanor criminal cases. The county attorney usually provides legal advice to the county commissioners as well, although generally the **county attorney** does not represent the county in civil cases. Counties with elected county attorneys also have elected **district attorneys**. They represent the state in felony cases. There are counties that have merged the offices of county and district attorney into a combined office that represents the state in both misdemeanor and felony cases. Of-

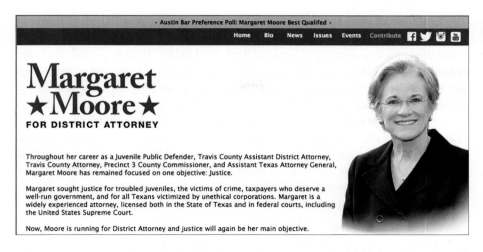

Margaret Moore's campaign website shows how candidates for district attorney must emphasize how they are "tough on crime." Moore was elected Travis County district attorney in 2016.

ten, when the offices of county and district attorney are merged, the combined office is called the office of the criminal district attorney.[7]

In urban counties in Texas, the office of the district attorney is huge, encompassing several hundred lawyers, investigators, and support staff. In 2016, the Harris County district attorney's office employed 310 prosecutors and had a total of about 700 employees. In most rural counties, the district attorney's office may be composed of only one or two lawyers. The head of every district attorney's office in Texas is an elected officer who runs under a party label. The term of office is four years. And as the chief prosecuting officer of the county or district, the district attorney has the responsibility for criminal prosecutions within the district attorney's jurisdiction. This means that the district attorneys generally campaign as officials who are "tough on crime," and they brag about high conviction rates. If they appear too lenient or their conviction rates are too low, political opponents will emerge who will accuse them of not doing their job appropriately. Because prosecutors often deal with people who have committed terrible crimes, they often see the worst aspects of humanity, and this also may lead to a "tough on crime" approach.

Prosecutors must maintain high conviction rates in order to keep their positions. One way that high conviction rates are maintained is through plea bargaining. In a **plea bargain**, a prosecutor will meet with the accused or his lawyer and offer a sentence in exchange for a plea of guilty. The prosecutor's offer might involve reducing the charge, dropping some of the charges, or recommending a lighter sentence than the defendant might get at trial if found guilty. Plea bargaining is not only necessary politically for an elected district attorney to maintain high conviction rates but also crucial in managing the limited resources of the prosecutor's office and the courts. Prosecuting a case that goes to trial after a defendant pleads not guilty can cost thousands and even hundreds of thousands of dollars and uses up the time of employees. If plea bargaining were suddenly abandoned in Texas, the criminal justice system would quickly come to a halt as a result of a massive overflow of trials. There is often an incentive for defense lawyers to plea bargain as well. In many cases, defense lawyers can generate more income by representing numerous defendants (who often have limited resources) in plea negotiations than they can generate in a few time-consuming trials. And, of course, plea bargains can benefit defendants, even innocent defendants, in that they get an assured sentence that may be less than they would receive if they went to trial and were found guilty and sentenced by either a judge or a jury.

plea bargain a negotiated agreement in a criminal case in which a defendant agrees to plead guilty in return for the state's agreement to reduce the severity of the criminal charge or prison sentence the defendant is facing

In almost all cases that involve plea bargaining, the judge with jurisdiction over the case will agree with the bargain made by the district attorney's office. For one thing, plea bargains reduce the crowded dockets of judges. Without a trial, the judge cannot be aware of the strengths and weaknesses of the state's case and so will generally recognize that the district attorney is in a far better position to determine the appropriate sentence.

The district attorney has prosecutorial discretion, which includes the power to charge or not charge a person with a crime. Even when a case is presented before a grand jury to determine if a criminal indictment should be issued, the grand jury is dependent on the prosecutor to present the evidence that may lead to an indictment, and a prosecutor has great discretion in choosing to go before a grand jury and in deciding to accept or not accept the decision of a particular grand jury.

Crime and Criminal Defense

Persons accused of crime may represent themselves or may retain a criminal defense lawyer to represent them. Since the famous Supreme Court case *Gideon v. Wainwright*, persons too poor to hire a lawyer have had a constitutional right to have an attorney appointed to represent them in serious cases. In Texas, that representation will generally be provided by **assigned counsel**—that is, the judge will appoint a lawyer to represent people who cannot afford one. However, in some counties in at least some types of cases, a **public defender** will represent an indigent. A public defender is a lawyer who is paid a salary by the government to represent people who cannot afford a lawyer. With assigned counsel, usually judges appoint a private attorney on a case-by-case basis for a fee that varies according to the county and the legal service performed. One concern with the assigned counsel system is that the fee paid by counties may be so small that the assigned attorneys do not do an adequate job in representing their clients. The issue of the quality of representation provided to indigents in Texas, however, is an important one because large numbers of cases are tried and substantial amounts of money are spent in providing this representation. Table 13.2 specifies the 2014 costs of indigent defense in the state and the numbers of cases involving poor people whose lawyers are paid by the state.

With the use of assigned counsel, different counties have different fees that they pay lawyers. Some of those fees seem remarkably inadequate. As examples, Bexar County pays appointed counsel $75 an hour for trial work involving a state jail felony, $100 an hour for a second degree felony, and $125 an hour for a first degree felony. The first chair—the lead defense attorney—in a capital case in Bexar County gets $150 an hour for trial time. Harris County pays $300 a day for trial work in a state jail felony, $400 a day for a second degree felony, and $500 a day for a first degree felony. In capital cases the first chair is paid $150 an hour. Hunt County pays $100 an hour, but in a capital case, the lead lawyer gets $110 an hour.[8]

Public defenders are far rarer in Texas than are assigned counsel. However, there is a public defender program available for capital cases that is statewide and serves participating small and midsize counties. Altogether there are 19 other public defender offices in

assigned counsel private lawyers appointed by judges to provide legal representation for indigent defendants in serious criminal cases. The lawyer's fee is determined by and paid by the county

public defender salaried lawyer who is funded by the government or by grants who represents indigents in Texas in some counties or for some types of cases

TABLE 13.2

Indigent Defense in Texas, 2014

State costs of indigent legal services	$229,943,369
Number of noncapital felony trials	192,261
Number of misdemeanor trials	223,045
Juvenile hearings	45,340
Appeals	3,023
Capital cases	474

SOURCE: Texas Indigent Defense Commission, "Indigent Defense Data for Texas."

Texas. Most of these offices are regional or county-wide in scope and many have specialized caseloads such as mentally ill defendants, rural areas, appeals, or juvenile defendants. Interestingly, the public defender program for capital cases has been evaluated by comparing the program with assigned counsel in capital cases. Several interesting findings emerged from the study. For one thing, in rural areas of the state, there are few lawyers qualified to handle capital cases. In an area of Texas spanning over 80,000 square miles, for example, there are only 13 private lawyers qualified for capital cases. For such an area, death penalty specialists who are public defenders are particularly useful. Additionally, death penalty public defenders have the necessary support team that would be difficult to organize in the more rural and isolated parts of the state. For many smaller counties, the cost of death penalty cases is prohibitive—defense costs alone often exceed $100,000. Participating in a public defender program with death penalty specialists can greatly reduce costs for these counties. The public defenders were also more likely than assigned counsel to avoid a death penalty and were more likely than assigned counsel to get better dispositions for their clients overall.[9] Death penalty work is very specialized and complex, but the success of public defender programs over assigned counsel in death penalty cases suggests that an expansion of public defender programs in other areas may be beneficial to indigent defendants.

Crime, Corrections, and the Texas Prison System

Describe prisons and corrections policy in Texas

It has long been claimed that Texas does things in a big way. That is certainly true of its levels of crime and the way it deals with criminals. As of August 31, 2014, there were 150,361 offenders incarcerated in the state's prisons, state jails, and substance abuse facilities.[10] These numbers exclude those incarcerated in municipal and county facilities. In 2014 the average cost per day for each bed in the state's correctional facilities was about $55. It costs about thirty-six times more to imprison someone than to place that person on probation and costs about fourteen times more to keep him or her in prison rather than on parole.[11]

History of the Prison System

Shortly after Texas joined the Union, construction was authorized for a state penitentiary in Huntsville. The 225-cell facility opened in 1849. It confined prisoners in single cells at night and congregated inmates during the day to work in silence. From 1870 to 1883 the entire prison system was leased to private contractors who used the labor of inmates in exchange for providing maintenance and security for prisoners. After 1883 convicts in the Texas prison system were leased to railroads, planters, and others who provided the prisoners with food and clothing and paid a stipend to the state. These leasing arrangements were abandoned in 1910 as a result of scandals and abuses of the system.[12]

Although Texas moved to a state-run system, abuses continued. In 1924 an investigation of the system found cruel and brutal treatment of prisoners, inefficient management, and inadequate care of inmates. That investigation led to the creation of a state prison board, which supervised the work of a general prison manager. Still, however, the abuses continued. By the mid-1940s the Texas prison system was considered one of the worst in the United States. In 1974 the Joint Committee on Prison Reform submitted findings to the legislature that were very critical of the Texas prison system. The committee found fault with numerous aspects of the prison system's operation—from living and working conditions for inmates to classification of inmates to medical care to staff training. Still, no significant reforms were made to the system.[13]

The event that had the most dramatic effect on the operation of the Texas prison system in modern times was a federal court case, *Ruiz v. Estelle*.[14] Lawsuits filed by prisoners are nothing new. During the tenure of W. J. Estelle, Jr., the prison director from 1973 to 1983 and the defendant in the *Ruiz* case, prisoners filed 19,696 cases in the federal courts in Texas, a caseload amounting to about 20 percent of the federal court docket in Texas during that period.[15] However, the *Ruiz* case was exceptional. It was a class-action suit on behalf of inmates that began in 1972, and it focused on issues of crowding in the system, security and supervision, health care, discipline, and access to the courts. In 1980 the federal court concluded that inmates' constitutionally guaranteed rights had been violated. Texas joined several other states in having its prison system declared unconstitutional.

The result was the appointment by the court of a special master, a court officer, to oversee the Texas prison system to eliminate the constitutional problems such as

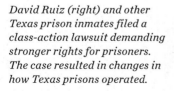

David Ruiz (right) and other Texas prison inmates filed a class-action lawsuit demanding stronger rights for prisoners. The case resulted in changes in how Texas prisons operated.

Who Is in Prison in Texas?

Prison Population in Texas by Race, 2014*

■ % of Texas population   ■ % of Prison population

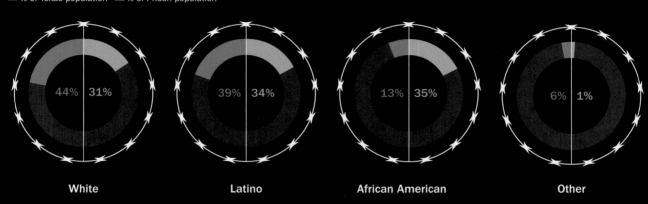

White	Latino	African American	Other
44% 31%	39% 34%	13% 35%	6% 1%

Death Row Population in Texas, 2016*

% of Texas population   % of death row population   Total death row inmates

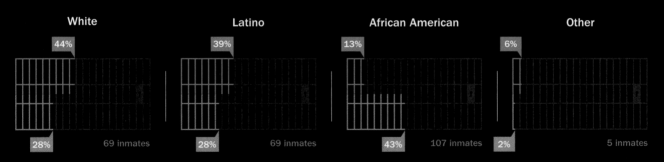

White	Latino	African American	Other
44%	39%	13%	6%
28% — 69 inmates	28% — 69 inmates	43% — 107 inmates	2% — 5 inmates

While Texas does not lead the nation in its incarceration rate, it is still the seventh highest in the United States. A disproportionately high number of African American men, for example, are serving in the state's prisons compared with their percentage of the population in the state. In fact, 7 out of every 10 prisoners in Texas are either African American or Latino.

*May not add to 100 percent due to rounding.

SOURCES: Texas Department of Criminal Justice, "Demographic Highlights–August 31, 2014," Fiscal Year 2014 Statistical Report, www.tdcj.state.tx.us; Texas Department of Criminal Justice, "Gender and Racial Statistics of Death Row Offenders," www.tdcj.state.tx.us; U.S. Census Bureau, "Quick Facts," quickfacts.census.gov.

QUANTITATIVE REASONING

- The Texas population is 39 percent Latino, 13 percent African American, and 44 percent white. According to the data shown here, how does the Texas prison population compare?

- What might help explain the racial/ethnic makeup of the prison population in Texas?

overcrowding, improper supervision of inmates, and improper care of inmates. There was a massive reform of the system, one that had to be imposed by the federal courts, because the state seemed unwilling or unable to reform its own prison system. Federal court supervision of the prison system ended in 2002.

For a long time, many in Texas government were resistant to federal court supervision of the prison system, arguing, for example, that the *Ruiz* decision involved federal court judicial activism and interfered with the rights of the state. In order to reduce the overcrowding in state prisons to comply with *Ruiz*, the state also encouraged the early release of prisoners, some of whom reentered society and committed more crimes. *Ruiz* did, however, help turn the criminal justice system into a major public policy issue in Texas.

The Prison System Today

The Texas prison system is operated by the Texas Department of Criminal Justice. This agency is run by a nine-member board appointed by the governor, and board members serve staggered six-year terms. The board hires an executive director to lead the sprawling agency, and it is responsible for developing the rules and regulations that govern the entire state prison system.[16]

There have been dramatic increases in the costs of prison construction and prison maintenance in Texas over time. Operating costs of Texas prisons rose from $147 million in 1982 to $609 million in 1990 to nearly $1.5 billion in 1996 and over $2.8 billion in 2008. In 2014 the total operating budget for the Texas Department of Criminal Justice was $3.2 billion. Despite a steady increase in prison operating costs, prison construction costs have varied from year to year. In 1982, $126 million was spent on prison construction, but in 1990 only $24 million was spent. The greatest period of prison construction was from 1991 through 1995. During those years, nearly $1.4 billion was spent on prison construction. In the wake of estimates in 2007 that Texas would need 17,000 new prison beds costing $1 billion by 2012, the Texas legislature increased the capacity of prison alternatives such as drug treatment and halfway homes, much cheaper alternatives to prison.[17]

Until 2007, when the Texas legislature began to seriously address alternatives to imprisonment, the state government had significantly increased the incarceration of offenders by building more prisons. In 2011, however, for the first time in Texas history, the state actually closed a prison—the century-old Central Unit in Sugarland. State leaders also announced plans to close three juvenile detention centers with its move toward rehabilitation, crime prevention, and cost-cutting. Two other prisons closed on August 31, 2013, the Dawson State Jail and the Mineral Wells Pre-Parole Transfer Facility.[18]

From 1976 to 1990 the rate of property crime in Texas rose 38 percent, and the violent crime rate rose 113 percent. During the same time period, prison expansion did not keep up with the increase in the crime rate. Instead, generous early-release policies were used to move prisoners out of jail to allow room for newly convicted inmates. With prison expansion, however, early-release policies were reduced. In 1990, for example, 38,000 prisoners were given early release from prison; however, even with a much larger prison population in 1997, only slightly more than 28,000 prisoners were given early release.[19] The steady lengthening of sentences is shown

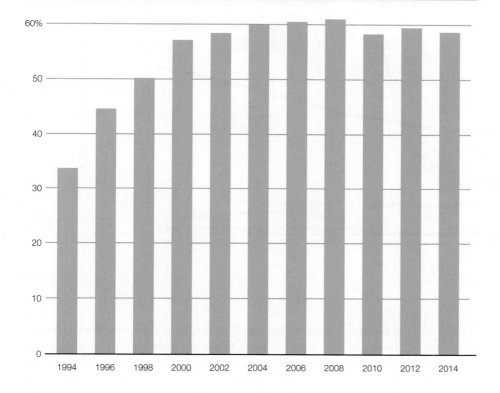

in Figure 13.1. In 1994 prisoners on average were released after serving one-third of their sentences. In 2014 prisoners were serving about 58.1 percent of their sentences before being released. Inmates at state jails served on average 99.4 percent of their sentences.[20]

As shown in Figure 13.2, the Texas prison population reached its peak in 2000 and then dropped off in later years. In 1980, at the time of the *Ruiz* case, the Texas prison population consisted of fewer than 30,000 inmates. A decade later, in 1990, there were slightly more than 49,000 inmates in Texas prisons. Only seven years later, in 1997, there were almost 130,000 inmates in state prisons. In 2000 the number of inmates in state prisons had jumped to over 150,000, dropping back to about 145,000 in 2002, to 139,316 in 2010, and to 136,460 in 2014.[21]

For much of the 1980s the rates of violent and property crime in Texas were especially high.[22] By the mid-1990s, however, those rates had dropped. Some observers

FIGURE 13.2

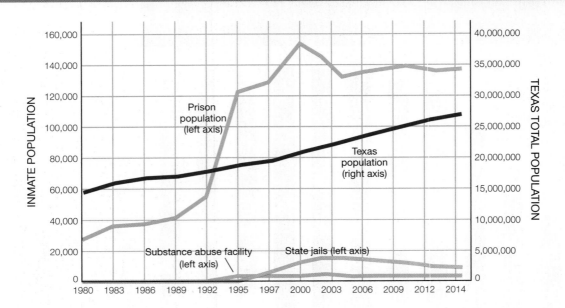

Texas Inmate Population, 1980–2014

SOURCE: Associated Texans against Crime Annual Report, 1998; Texas Department of Criminal Justice, "Fiscal Year 2004 Statistics"; Criminal Justice Policy Council, "Texas Department of Criminal Justice State Incarcerated Population, Fiscal Years 1988–2002"; Texas Department of Criminal Justice, 2006, 2008, 2010, 2012, and 2014 Statistical Report; and Texas State Library and Archives Commission, "United States and Texas Populations, 1850–2015."

argued that the reduction in the crime rate is caused by the increased incarceration of offenders. There may also be other causes, however. Other analysts have suggested demographic change determines the size of the prison population. The most prison-prone group in society is males between the ages of 20 and 29. If that demographic group is large, then we would expect the prison population to also be large.[23] Indeed, 93.5 percent of Texas prisoners are male, and the average age of prisoners is 38.6 years.[24] Of course, changes in laws and treatment practices also affect the crime rate and the incarceration rate. Long sentences for habitual criminals, for example, are relatively new, as are long sentences for the use of a firearm in the commission of a crime.[25] The number of prison inmates per 100,000 total population in Texas in 2014 was 584. Only six states, including Louisiana with an astounding incarceration rate of 816 per 100,000, beat the Texas per capita incarceration rate. (See the "Texas and the Nation" graphic.) Texas had 8.14 percent of the nation's total state prison population in 2014. Neither the national government nor any other state had more inmates in its prison system than Texas.[26] In spite of its high rate of incarceration, Texas ranked high in crime. A study of crime rates nationwide found that Texas in 2014 ranked 40 in the United States in crime where a ranking of 1 is the least crime and 50 is the greatest crime ranking.[27]

How Does Criminal Justice in Texas Compare with Other States?

Incarceration Rate, 2014 per 100,000 residents

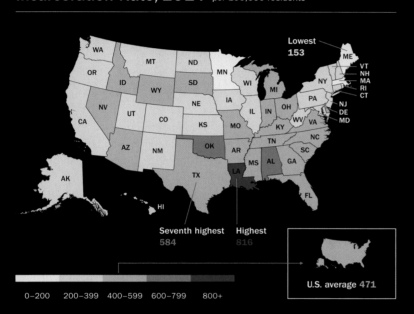

Lowest
153

Seventh highest
584

Highest
816

U.S. average 471

0–200   200–399   400–599   600–799   800+

The Texas criminal justice system is known for high incarceration rates. In 2014, 584 out of every 100,000 Texans were sentenced to time in prison, and rates in other recent years are similar. Texas is also known for its harsh punishment of criminals, especially the use of the death penalty. Since the U.S. Supreme Court reinstated the death penalty in 1976, Texas has executed 531 people: four times more than any other state.

SOURCES: Incarceration rate: E. Ann Carson, "Prisoners in 2014," Bureau of Justice Statistics, September 2015. Total executions: Death Penalty Information Center, "Facts about the Death Penalty," January 7, 2016.

Total Executions, 1976–2015

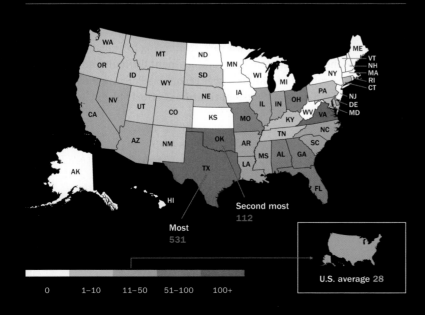

Second most
112

Most
531

U.S. average 28

0   1–10   11–50   51–100   100+

CRITICAL THINKING

- Which elements of Texas political culture or public opinion may contribute to the willingness to use the death penalty and to have high incarceration rates?

- Examine the regional patterns on the two maps. Do certain regions of the country have higher incarceration rates and death penalty usage? What do you think explains these regional patterns?

FIGURE 13.3

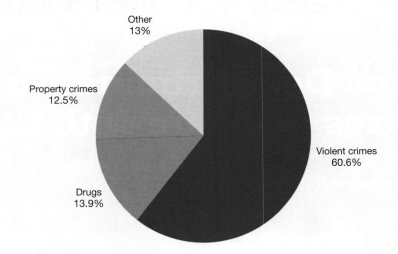

Prison Population by Offense, 2014

SOURCE: Texas Department of Criminal Justice, FY 2014 Statistical Report.

As Figure 13.3 shows, Texas imprisons mostly violent offenders. In 2014, 60.6 percent of Texas prison inmates had been convicted of violent offenses and 12.5 percent had been convicted of property offenses. Nearly 14 percent of the inmate population was convicted of drug offenses.[28] Whether imprisonment for drug offenses is an appropriate remedy for the drug problem has been debated, but it is interesting to note that almost 14 percent of people in Texas prisons are there because of drugs.

It is especially difficult for felons to gain legitimate employment after their release—so much so that the federal government offers a large tax credit to employers who will give jobs to people who have been convicted of a felony and have served their sentence. This difficulty in finding legal employment makes it more likely that former prisoners will commit further crimes. Another problem that inmates face once they leave prison is that the average sentence in a Texas prison is 19.2 years. After serving substantial time in prison, it is hard to readjust to life in the free world, and support structures such as family members have often died or removed the inmate from their lives. Still another difficulty is that 44.3 percent of inmates in Texas prisons do not have a high school diploma or GED and their average educational achievement is slightly more than eight years.[29] That lack of education makes adjustment to life and legitimate employment outside of prison an extremely difficult experience. Still another issue that creates problems for felons who are attempting to adjust to life in the free world is drug and alcohol addiction, making employment difficult and encouraging criminal behavior. The problem of addiction was recognized during Governor Ann Richards's administration, and drug and alcohol treatment efforts begun at that time have continued and expanded.

The Death Penalty

Texas is one of 31 states that have the death penalty. Of the 19 states that do not impose the death penalty, four have banned it since 2010. There are 2,959 people on death

Cite and Release: Necessary Cost-Savings or Soft on Crime?

Eight states have legalized the recreational use of marijuana: Alaska, Oregon, Colorado, Washington, California, Nevada, Massachusetts, and Maine. In contrast, possession of less than two ounces of marijuana in Texas is a class B misdemeanor and possession of two to four ounces of marijuana is a class A misdemeanor. The maximum punishment for a class B is 180 days in the county jail and a $2,000 fine, and for a class A is a year in the county jail and a $4,000 fine. Such punishments are unlikely—far more likely is a substantial fine and probation. However, until 2007, a person arrested with less than four ounces of marijuana would be taken to jail, would be booked, and would likely spend hours in jail until he or she could post bond (and far longer in jail awaiting trial if unable to post bond). To ease jail crowding and to free police officers to deal with more egregious offenses, in 2007 the Texas legislature gave police the option to cite an offender for possession of less than four ounces of marijuana. A person arrested for possession could be released with a citation much like a traffic ticket. The person would have to appear in court and would be subject to criminal punishment, but would not be arrested, be booked, and spend time in jail until bail was paid.

The theory behind this change was that jail space would not be taken up by minor offenders, police resources would be saved (police in the City of Dallas make 100 to 120 arrests per month for small amounts of marijuana), and the county would save money (on average it costs taxpayers $120 to arrest and book someone in an urban Texas county, and it costs taxpayers about $63 a day to keep a prisoner in jail).[a]

Despite these benefits, most counties in Texas were unwilling to use this cite and release option. By 2016, only Hays, Williamson, and Travis counties were frequently using cite and release.[b]

Collin County district attorney Greg Davis said Collin County did not use cite and release because "it may . . . lead some people to believe that drug use is not more serious than double parking."[c] Prosecutors also claimed they lacked a system for dealing with misdemeanor tickets. Another concern was that without a booking process where all ten fingerprints are taken, police would have difficulty establishing a person's identity and it would be easier for an offender to avoid showing up for trial.

Supporters of cite and release, however, note the savings in police time and jail space. They point out

that the offender is still subject to criminal punishment. Additionally, they point to a study of Hays County where 95 percent of those cited and released did show up for trial.[d]

In 2016 the city of Dallas seriously considered an experiment with a cite and release program, though the idea was ultimately rejected.[e] Other police departments are looking into beginning cite and release as well.

COMMUNICATING EFFECTIVELY: YOUR VOICE

- Why is there sudden interest in cite and release, which has been allowed since 2007?

- Consider the advantages and disadvantages of cite and release programs. If you could voice your opinion on this issue to local law enforcement, what would you say? What arguments would you use to support your opinion?

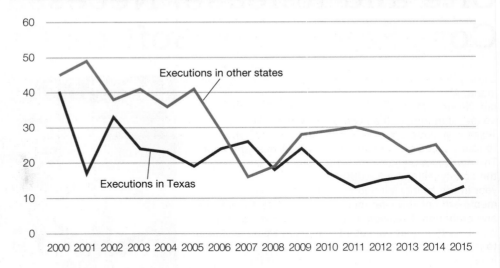

FIGURE 13.4

Executions in Texas Compared with Other States

Executions in other states

Executions in Texas

row throughout the nation, although five states have over 60 percent of death row inmates—California with 743, Florida with 399, Texas with 263, and Alabama with 196. Although the number of executions nationally has declined dramatically since 2000, a number of states such as Texas still retain the death penalty and carry out executions. In Texas, one is subject to the death penalty for the murder of a public safety officer, fireman, or correctional employee; murder during commission of a kidnapping, burglary, robbery, aggravated rape, or arson; murder for hire; multiple murders; murder during a prison escape; murder by a prison inmate serving a life sentence; or murder of a child under the age of 6. Texas executed 531 people from 1976 through 2015.[30]

As Figure 13.4 shows, though Texas has led the nation in the number of executions since the death penalty was reinstated by the Supreme Court, there has been a decline in the imposition of the death penalty in Texas as well as states other than Texas. National polling data do show an increase in opposition to the death penalty—from 28 percent in 2000 to 37 percent in 2015. Perhaps because 240 people in Texas prisons have been exonerated since 1989 and 13 death row inmates have been exonerated since 1973, there has been a reduction in the number of executions in Texas.[31] More important is that death penalty cases have become very expensive and time-consuming for the state; imposition of a life without parole sentence is far less costly, while ensuring that the defendant will not pose a future danger to the public.

Political scientists Paul Brace and Brent Boyea found that judges tend to affirm death penalty sentences in states where judges are elected and where there is strong public support for the death penalty.[32] This may explain why Texas appellate courts are so supportive of the death sentences imposed by juries at the trial court level. Texas judges are elected, and polls show strong public support in Texas for the death penalty.

One 2012 Texas poll, for example, showed that 73 percent of Texas voters either somewhat or strongly supported the death penalty and only 21 percent were opposed.[33]

A stay on death row can be a lengthy one, even in Texas. The average time spent on death row prior to execution is 10.87 years, although the time varies considerably. One inmate under a death sentence waived his appeals and spent only 252 days on death row prior to execution. On the other hand, David Lee Powell spent 31 years on death row prior to being executed in 2010.[34] A death sentence carried out in February 1998, however, initiated the greatest controversy over the death penalty. The case of Karla Faye Tucker, a convicted ax murderer, generated national demands for clemency. Tucker was widely believed to have undergone a religious conversion after her 1983 conviction. She was also attractive and articulate and was the first woman in modern times condemned to be executed in Texas. Supporters of her execution argued that her gender, appearance, articulateness, and possible religious conversion were irrelevant to the fact that she was a convicted murderer who should be treated like others in similar situations.

In 1998, Karla Faye Tucker became the first woman executed in Texas since 1863. She was convicted of murder in 1983.

One of the issues involving the death penalty is whether all offenders are treated in the same way. There is a racial and ethnic disparity such that minorities, especially African Americans, are disproportionately represented on death row. As of November 2015, 107 death-row inmates were African American, 69 were Hispanic, 71 were white, and 5 were classified as "other."[35]

From 1977 to 2015, 231 whites have been executed, 197 African Americans, 99 Hispanics, and 4 of "other" racial and ethnic groups.[36] It may be that there is a bias in the criminal justice system such that minorities are disproportionately subject to the death penalty, although a counterargument is that the murder rate is higher among minorities. When the issue of whether there was racial bias in the imposition of the death penalty was presented to the U.S. Supreme Court, the Court refused to strike down the death penalty on the basis of statistical generalizations—essentially saying that there had to be evidence of racial bias in the imposition of the death penalty in the specific case presented to the Court.[37]

The Texas Board of Pardons and Paroles votes on clemency for death-row inmates. The board was originally considered to be a remedy for possible corruption in clemency granted by the governor. Prior to 1936 the governor essentially had unlimited power to grant clemency. This power was often abused, especially by Governor Miriam Ferguson, who granted 4,000 requests for commutations of sentences in 1922 alone. It was widely believed that payments were made for many of these acts of executive clemency. In reaction, a constitutional amendment was passed in 1936 that charged the board with giving the governor recommendations on clemency.

SOCIAL RESPONSIBILITY: GET INVOLVED

- A disproportionate number of African Americans have been executed in Texas since 1977. Does this mean there is inherent bias in the death penalty system? Why or why not?

- Do you agree with the Supreme Court that statistical generalizations should not be used to argue against the death penalty? If so, what kind of evidence would provide stronger arguments?

Without such a recommendation, the governor can only grant a single 30-day reprieve. No other state so limits the powers of the governor.

In August 2007 the board recommended commutation of Kenneth Foster's sentence to be executed—only seven hours before Foster was scheduled to die. Governor Perry commuted Foster's sentence to life imprisonment about one hour later.[38] Foster's much-publicized case seemed to challenge two aspects of the death penalty in Texas: (1) Foster had been tried simultaneously with the other capital defendants rather than in a separate trial, and (2) he was the getaway driver in the crime and not the actual shooter in the robbery and murder. Simultaneous trials with other defendants in murder cases can be a huge disadvantage for a defendant like Foster, who was not the shooter but who is being tried with the shooter. Texas also has the law of parties—a person involved in a crime that leads to a murder is guilty of murder even though that person is not actually the person who committed the murder.

Kenneth Foster's father and wife celebrate after hearing that Governor Perry had commuted Foster's sentence only hours before Foster was to receive the death penalty. Foster was convicted of murder despite only driving the getaway car.

Self-Defense and Concealed/Open Carry of Handguns

In any examination of crime in Texas, the enormous concern of Texans with self-defense cannot be ignored. One of the most controversial issues in the state over the past few years has dealt with concealed and open carry of handguns, most recently the issue of concealed carry of handguns on college campuses. Advocates of concealed and open carry argue that the U.S. Constitution's Second Amendment provides them with a constitutional right to bear arms. Article 1, Section 28, of the Texas Constitution provides a similar right with the caveat that carrying arms is subject to state regulation. It states:

> Every citizen shall have the right to keep and bear arms in lawful defense of himself or the state; but the Legislature shall have the power, by law, to regulate the wearing of arms with a view to prevent crime.

To a large degree the wording in the Texas Constitution sums up the long-standing political debate over bearing arms: does carrying firearms provide protection against crime, or does it lead to crime?

In 1871, during Reconstruction, Texas passed legislation against concealed and open carry, and that law was not substantially changed until 1995. There were unsuccessful attempts to change the ban on carrying handguns in every regular legislative session beginning in 1983. In 1995 the Texas legislature passed its first concealed carry bill that was signed by Governor George W. Bush in fulfillment of a campaign promise. While the law was slightly changed in later legislative sessions, major battles erupted over concealed carry in the 2011 legislative session, where concealed carry of handguns on college campuses became a major issue and where there clearly were enough votes to pass the bill. However, the bill failed because of a parliamentary challenge. The other major controversy in 2011 was over whether employees could secure firearms in their vehicles parked in company-owned parking lots. Legislation was passed and signed into law that prohibited employers from banning guns secured in vehicles in parking lots.[39]

In the 2015 legislative session the issue became open carry of firearms. That bill passed amid the further expression of concern that such a law would increase violence and lead to intimidation of others. Under the 2015 provision, the handgun must be in a hip or shoulder holster, but the gun no longer needs to be concealed. A concealed handgun license is still required, which means the license holder must be 21, must pass a criminal and psychological record check, and must have classroom and shooting training.[40]

A February 2015 University of Texas/Texas Tribune poll found that 10 percent of Texans thought carrying guns should always be allowed without a license, 22 percent of Texans thought carrying guns either concealed or open should be allowed with a license, 45 percent thought only concealed carry should be allowed with a license, and 23 percent thought carrying guns in public should never be allowed. Clearly public support for open carry is considerably less than support for concealed carry, but both the House and the Senate considered open carry legislation to be a top priority in the 2017 legislative session.[41]

The most controversial aspect of Texas handgun legislation has probably been campus carry, which went into effect August 1, 2016, and required public universities to allow concealed handgun license holders to carry, with some restricted locations, on college campuses. Some faculty, especially at the University of Texas at Austin campus, expressed concern that campus carry would lead to campus violence. At least one senior professor resigned over campus carry, and three professors filed a lawsuit in an unsuccessful effort to stop it. Public opinion about campus carry has been only slightly favorable. One February 2015 poll found that 47 percent of Texans favored campus carry, 45 percent opposed, and 8 percent did not know.[42]

To date, however, campus carry, concealed carry, and open carry have not led to the violence their opponents predicted. Open carry has proven rare in the state's urban centers, and the number of students who can carry handguns on campus is limited by the requirement that concealed carry license holders be 21. The greatest problems have been in determining the specific locations where bans on carrying handguns can be legally implemented. There were problems during the shootings of Dallas police officers on July 7, 2016, where there was difficulty in distinguishing demonstrators who were carrying long guns from the shooter, but carrying a long gun in Texas has long been lawful and has never been part of the debate over concealed carry, open carry, or campus carry of handguns.

What is clear is that Texas's handgun legislation has led to a large number of concealed carry licenses being issued. As of December 31, 2015, there were 937,419 active concealed carry license holders in Texas.[43]

The Integrity of the Texas Criminal Justice System

Explain why Texas's criminal justice system is often controversial

In recent years, numerous controversial issues and cases have raised questions about how criminal justice works in Texas. Earlier in the chapter we discussed concerns with prosecutorial abuses of power and with the difficulty some people may have in complying with the rules of the criminal justice process. Here, we consider whether aggressive use of the death penalty, wrongful convictions, and flawed evidence procedures are compromising the integrity of the criminal justice system. At the end of this section, we consider some of the reforms that have been attempted and proposed as ways to address concerns about criminal justice in Texas.

How Fair Is the Criminal Justice System?

Ideally, the criminal justice system should hold the guilty accountable and protect the innocent from punishment. That has not always been the case in Texas. There seem to be problems with fairness in the implementation of the death penalty, and there are a number of cases where overzealous police and prosecutors have punished innocent parties. The question is how common are those abuses and what, if anything, can be done about them.

Problems with Police Procedures and Evidence The Sandra Bland case is probably the most recent and most highly publicized case that involved questionable police practices in Texas. In 2015, Bland, from Naperville, Illinois, returned to her alma mater at Prairie View A&M to start a new job working with the university's alumni association. A Texas Department of Public Safety (DPS) trooper stopped Bland for failing to signal a lane change. The encounter escalated when Bland refused a request to extinguish her cigarette and the trooper threatened to use a Taser on her. The trooper claimed Bland was combative and uncooperative and that he removed her from her car to conduct a safer traffic investigation. He then arrested her for assaulting a public servant. She was taken to the Waller County, Texas, jail where she remained because she was unable to pay the $500 bail. After being in the jail for three days, Bland was found dead in her cell. A medical examiner ruled the death a suicide. While an investigation of her death led to no criminal charges at the jail, the trooper was indicted for perjury and was terminated from his position. DPS claimed the trooper had violated its courtesy policy, had prolonged the stop beyond the time reasonably necessary, and had failed to follow procedure for interviewing traffic violators. The key question was, of course, how a simple traffic stop could possibly escalate into a death in a county jail. Bland was African American, and there were questions

Sandra Bland was stopped for a minor traffic violation that escalated and led to her being jailed. Bland subsequently died in the county jail, which led to a national outcry. In response to national attention over Sandra Bland's case, major political figures such as Lieutenant Governor Dan Patrick spoke to the press about her death.

about whether her race played a role in her treatment. Additionally, there were questions about how frequently simple police stops unnecessarily escalated, particularly in the absence of police dashboard camera video coverage.[44]

In September 2016, Sandra Bland's family agreed to a settlement in a civil suit where they would be paid $100,000 by the Department of Public Safety and $1.8 million by Waller County. Additionally, Waller County agreed to provide emergency nurses on all shifts at the jail, to use electronic sensors to insure timely cell checks, and to seek state funds for jail improvements.

While the Bland case raises questions about police procedures, there are other concerns about the handling of criminal cases within Texas courts. Texas is the home of more verified wrongful convictions than any other state.[45] Concerns about wrongful convictions are often related to the methods police and prosecutors use to convict suspects. An exceptionally large number of wrongful convictions have come from Dallas County. One reason for the large number of DNA exonerations in Dallas County is simply that Dallas County has a policy of preserving physical evidence for lengthy periods of time, but others point to a pattern of convictions based on eyewitness identification with little or questionable forensic evidence. Many of the wrongfully convicted were prosecuted during the administration of District Attorney Henry Wade, whose office was known for high conviction rates. Critics claimed his office prized those high conviction rates above all else.[46]

Immediately after he became Dallas County district attorney in 2007, Craig Watkins did something no other Texas district attorney had ever done: he created a Conviction Integrity Unit in his office to investigate postconviction claims of actual innocence, to identify valid claims, and to then take appropriate action. Interestingly, with the exception of one case, every exoneration case that was investigated by the Conviction Integrity Unit involved mistaken eyewitness identification. At some point before their trial testimony, each eyewitness became certain that the innocent man was the criminal. In most cases, the innocent man was in the photo spread or the police lineup even though there was no specific reason to believe that he was the criminal. Being wrongly chosen in the lineup or photo spread by the eyewitness became the evidence against the innocent man. In many case, that was the only evidence against the innocent man, and in every case it was the most compelling evidence against him. That has led to a suggestion that there needs to be some minimum threshold of probability that those displayed in the photo spread or the lineup actually committed the crime. Additionally, it has been suggested that pretrial identification procedures be done in a way recognized by scientific best practices rather than in a haphazard, potentially unreliable way.[47] For example, with photo spreads, eyewitnesses are provided six photographs and asked if they recognize anyone in the photographs. However, sometimes those in the photographs are wearing distinguishing clothing or they are smiling or posed differently. One case examined by the Innocence Project of Texas, an organization that works on claims of innocence of those who have been imprisoned, involved a photo spread of six persons. A rape victim had told the police that the rapist was wearing a blue windbreaker. Only one person in the photo spread was wearing a blue windbreaker.

There have also been problems with the handling of evidence sent to state and local crime labs. In 2002 the Houston Police Department Crime Laboratory was closed. An independent audit of the lab's DNA section had identified enormous problems. Analysts did not know how to do their jobs, and supervisors were also incompetent. There was no quality control system, and there were few standardized procedures. Other sections of the lab had problems as well, but the most serious were in the DNA section. Harris County sends more people to death row than any other county in America, and it had done thousands of other tests in non-death-penalty cases. One of the first retests of the lab's work showed that a man who had been convicted of rape in 1998 at the age of 16 and had been given a 25-year sentence largely on the basis of DNA evidence was actually innocent. The problem with the lab was that as DNA technology changed, the analysts got no training in new methods, were overworked, and were following procedures inconsistently. Additionally, the lab was never inspected by an outside agency and did not seek accreditation. Nor were judges, prosecutors, and defense attorneys able to spot the lab's sloppy work—they had not kept up with DNA technology either. The lab's facilities were not conducive to good forensic science. The roof leaked over the DNA section of the crime lab, and the leaks were never patched. In 2001, when Tropical Storm Allison hit Houston, water poured through the roof, and DNA evidence in three dozen murder and rape cases was soaked. Bloody water was seen seeping out of evidence boxes.[48] DNA is often seen as the definitive proof of guilt or innocence in many serious crimes, but it is hardly definitive when the facilities are defective and the analysts are incompetent.

Johnny Pinchback celebrates after being freed from prison after serving 27 years. In 1984, Pinchback was convicted of aggravated sexual assault of two teenage girls, but DNA evidence cleared him in 2011. At the time, Pinchback was the 22nd person to be exonerated through DNA testing in Dallas County since 2001.

The Willingham Case The case of Cameron Todd Willingham raises serious questions about whether questionable evidence led to the execution of an innocent man for the arson murders of his three children. In 1991, Willingham's three girls were killed in a fire at their home shortly before Christmas. Willingham was convicted of starting the fire that killed them. Even though he was offered a plea bargain of a life sentence, he refused the plea, claiming that he was innocent. Willingham was executed in 2004. His conviction was largely based on expert testimony that the fire was arson. To a great extent, that testimony was based on the opinion that the fire had burned so hot that a fire accelerant must have been used to start the fire. Additionally, forensic tests had found evidence of an accelerant on the front porch of the house. However, before Willingham was executed, a noted arson expert examined the case and prepared a report that showed that the fire patterns relied upon by the forensic experts who testified for the prosecution could have occurred without the presence of an accelerant and that the prosecution experts were relying on outdated information about the behavior of fire to reach their conclusions. That report was submitted to the Board of Pardons and Paroles, but the board rejected the plea for clemency.

After Willingham's execution, reporters for the *Chicago Tribune* investigated the case and asked three fire experts to examine the evidence. They concluded that the fire was not arson. Later, the Innocence Project of Texas asked four fire experts to review the Willingham case. They all agreed that the fire was not arson.

In 2005, Texas created a commission, the Texas Forensic Science Commission, to investigate claims of error or misconduct by forensic scientists. A fire scientist was hired by the commission to investigate the Willingham case, and he too concluded there was no evidence that the fire was arson.[49] In September 2009, 48 hours prior to the review of the report by the Texas Forensic Science Commission, Governor Perry replaced the head of the commission and two of its members. The meeting of the commission was canceled as a result. Earlier, Governor Perry had expressed confidence in Willingham's guilt, called the critics of the original arson investigation "supposed experts," and said that he had not "seen anything that would cause me to think that the decision [to execute Willingham] was not correct."[50] The commission, however, did not drop the Willingham case, which remained under its review.

In July 2011, then attorney general Greg Abbott issued a ruling that restricted the further investigation of the Willingham case after a new commission chair showed greater interest in investigating the case. Nevertheless, cases of persons now in prison on arson charges are being reviewed by the Innocence Project to determine if their imprisonment resulted from bad arson science.[51]

The Tulia Drug Arrests Other widely publicized matters have also contributed to the questions raised about the adequacy of the Texas criminal justice system in protecting the innocent. One of those matters in particular became a national scandal—drug arrests in 1999 in Tulia, Texas. An undercover narcotics officer was responsible for the arrests of 47 persons in Tulia; 38 of them were black and made up about 20 percent of the black adults in the town. The defendants were zealously prosecuted. Though they were charged with possessing only small amounts of cocaine, the defendants, including those with no prior records, received long sentences—including one as long as 361 years. The undercover officer was supported by local authorities even as questions about his veracity mounted, and he was even named Officer of the Year in Texas. Doubts about the arrests and convictions, however, did not die. The officer

Billy Wafer stands along Main Street in Tulia, Texas. Wafer was part of a large group of black Tulia residents who were arrested and imprisoned in a highly questionable 1999 drug sting. All of the people arrested were either pardoned or had their sentences greatly reduced.

never wore a wire, never videotaped his alleged drug buys, and was never observed by another officer. Indeed, most of his alleged drug buys had no corroboration at all.

Two and a half years after the last trials of the Tulia defendants, the undercover officer had been fired from two later narcotics assignments. It became clear that he had no undercover narcotics experience prior to coming to Tulia and that he had left jobs as a deputy sheriff in two other towns, leaving behind significant unpaid debts. One of the sheriffs who had employed him had filed criminal charges against him, which meant that he was indicted while working undercover in Tulia. Accusations were also made against him that he had racist attitudes as well as difficulties with telling the truth.

It eventually became clear that the Tulia drug busts were a massive miscarriage of justice. Thirty-five of the 47 defendants were pardoned by the governor; 9 had their charges dismissed prior to trial or were placed on deferred adjudication. One was a juvenile at the time of his alleged crime and so will not have an adult criminal record. The remaining 2 were sent to prison on probation violations. The disturbing factor is that without the efforts of a small number of concerned citizens, lawyers, and the press, this gross abuse of the criminal justice process would have remained undetected and unresolved.[52]

Nor was the Tulia affair the only major problem with drug arrests. In 2001 the Dallas Police Department agreed to pay an informant $1,000 per kilogram of confiscated drugs. Although the informant did know actual drug dealers, he realized they were dangerous, so he found harmless persons—Mexican immigrants and legal residents—on whom he could plant drugs. Apparently the informant also realized he could make more money with less risk if he passed off gypsum as cocaine. (Gypsum is a substance found in billiard-cue chalk.) Convictions on dozens of drug cases were obtained without even testing to see if the seized material contained real drugs. The informant was the Dallas Police Department's highest paid in 2001, earning more than $210,000 for the seizure of nearly 1,000 pounds of cocaine and amphetamines that turned out to be fake drugs. Twenty fake drug cases were multikilo seizures, and two were the largest busts in the history of the Dallas police. Yet nothing seemed to arouse the suspicions of the police about the arrests. This scandal reached deep into the police department, where there was a lack of supervision of undercover officers and an extreme push for numbers in terms of amounts of drugs seized and number of arrests. The implausibility of some of the arrests is amazing: a lone mechanic working under his car, with no guns or cash seized; a drug buy on credit, according to the uncorroborated word of a confidential informant; and a seizure of 25 kilos of fake cocaine, for example. Nor did the district attorney's office escape blame: its policy was not to test seized drugs unless plea bargains failed and a case went to trial. When more than 80 of the drug cases were dismissed, Dallas district attorney Bill Hill went on television and insisted that many of those who were released were guilty. Were it not for the efforts of some criminal defense attorneys who were suspicious of the drug seizures, the Dallas Police Department might well still be seizing huge quantities of gypsum and paying its informant, and Texas might be sending innocent men and women to prison.[53]

Reforms

Consider recent proposals to improve
Texas's criminal justice system

Improvements in the Texas criminal justice system have occurred. Texas is no longer handling its crime problem solely by incarceration. The number of drug treatment programs has increased, and there is greater emphasis on imprisonment as a last response to criminal behavior and more emphasis on community supervision such as requiring increased reporting to probation officers, community service, electronic monitoring of offenders, or mandatory treatment for alcohol or drug addiction as a first response. The result has been a decline in prison construction and even the beginning of prison closings. Efforts are being made to compensate those who are wrongfully convicted. Texas has one of the most generous compensation systems in the nation for the wrongfully convicted. If a wrongfully convicted person waives his or her right to sue the state and is not convicted of further felonies after exoneration, he or she will receive a lump sum payment of $80,000 for each year wrongfully served in prison as well as an additional yearly payment during his or her lifetime that can amount to as much as $80,000 per year.

Some police departments are modifying their procedures for obtaining eyewitness evidence. For example, the Dallas Police Department has changed the way lineups are conducted so that the police officer administering the photographic lineup does not know who the actual suspect is, thus avoiding the police officer providing

Does Texas's criminal justice system need to be reformed? Some observers feel that, beyond problems with wrongful convictions, the emphasis on imprisonment and the large number of inmates in Texas are major concerns, though incarceration rates are declining.

cues to the witness as to which photo to pick. Additionally, photos are now shown by many police departments sequentially rather than as a group. Research has shown that this helps prevent witnesses from comparing the photos and choosing the photo that most closely resembles the suspect rather than picking the suspect's picture. Prosecutors often call on scientific experts, such as arson investigators, to help prove their cases. However, fields such as arson science are rapidly evolving, and sometimes the scientific theories that were once used to convict defendants in the past have now been debunked. For example, certain indicators that were once considered signs of arson are now known to appear in accidental fires.[54] A new Texas law makes it much easier for an inmate to challenge a conviction if it was based on bad science. The Texas Forensic Science Commission has recommended that testimony that connects bite marks to a specific defendant's teeth is junk science and should not be used as evidence against a defendant.

As noted in the introduction, the Michael Morton Act has established a uniform system for district attorneys to provide exculpatory evidence to defense attorneys. Some Texas district attorneys, most notably the district attorneys in Dallas County, have recognized the problem of wrongful conviction and have appointed prosecutors who review claims of wrongful convictions and who take a cooperative approach toward lawyers working with various innocence projects that exist to provide legal representation to people who claim they have been wrongfully convicted. In early 2016 the Harris County district attorney announced major programs to divert first time felony drug offenders into treatment programs rather than jail; to divert class B theft offenders to treatment programs; and to provide treatment rather than jail for the mentally ill.[55] It is a recognition that not all crimes are best handled by jailing the offenders.

For the first time in Texas, prosecutors are suffering significant consequences for actions that deny rights to defendants. Michael Morton's prosecutor lost his law license and served brief jail time for his actions in the Michael Morton case where he failed to turn over exculpatory evidence to the defense. Since then the former district attorney of Burleson County has failed in his effort to retain his law license. He had used false testimony and withheld evidence from the defense in a case where the defendant was sent to death row and later exonerated.

The Politics of Criminal Justice Reform

In addition to the county level, reforms are also occurring at the state level. In the 2013 legislative session, state senator Rodney Ellis (D-Houston) was the senate sponsor of House bill 166, which would create a commission whose members would be appointed by the governor. The commission would investigate wrongful convictions, identify the causes of wrongful convictions, and determine if there was any evidence of ethical violations by lawyers and judges that led to those convictions. Related commission bills had failed in legislative sessions going back to 2007. This time, however, Ellis thought he had the votes to get the bill out of the Senate Criminal Justice Committee.

The Criminal Justice Committee was chaired by state senator John Whitmire (D-Houston), like Ellis a criminal justice reformer and a supporter of the bill. There was only one major opponent of the bill on the committee, state senator Joan Huffman (R-Houston), vice chair of the committee, formerly chief felony prosecutor for the Harris County district attorney, and formerly a criminal court judge. She did not believe the commission was necessary, and she had made no secret of her opposition to the bill. During hearings on the bill, Whitmire had to leave the room to attend to other business and Huffman became chair. The witness testifying in favor of the bill was Cory Sessions, who worked with the Innocence Project of Texas and was the brother of Tim Cole, who had been wrongfully convicted of being a serial rapist at Texas Tech University and who had died in prison. When Huffman voiced opposition to the bill, Sessions exploded, "The attitude you have is deplorable. I am sickened. . . . I am pissed off." Sessions informed Huffman that she should "get another job," and as he stormed out of the hearing room and slammed the door, he audibly said the word "bitch." It was not, to say the least, the ideal lobbying effort on behalf of the bill. When Whitmire returned to the hearing room, he was amazed at how things had deteriorated. He was unable to soothe Huffman, who insisted that Sessions was unprofessional and disrespectful. Ellis no longer had the votes to get the bill out of committee. The House sponsor of the bill, state representative Ruth Jones McClendon (D–San Antonio), also a major criminal justice reformer, tried to save the bill by a hardball approach—placing parliamentary objections in the House against Senator Huffman's bills and thus stopping those bills from passage. It was to no avail. The bill was dead.

In the 2015 legislative session, McClendon, as she had in 2013, got support for the bill from Jeff Leach, a Republican from Plano who was one of the most conservative members of the House. Leach worked with McClendon because he saw the bill not as a liberal-conservative issue, but as an issue of justice. McClendon, coping with lung cancer and retiring from the House, also treated the bill as a bipartisan one. With Leach as her ally and with lobbying efforts by Cory Sessions and several men who had been exonerated, the bill passed the House by a vote of 138 to 5. When McClendon, obviously ill from the effects of her cancer treatments, addressed the House after the bill's passage, a remarkable thing happened: the chamber broke out in bipartisan cheering.

The Senate was to prove more difficult. Whitmire, a strong supporter of the bill, was still the chair of the Criminal Justice Committee. However, the bill was referred to the State Affairs Committee chaired by Senator Huffman. There had been other developments, though, since 2013. In 2014 a monument to Tim Cole was unveiled in Lubbock, and Sessions made sure that leading Republicans were invited. Among those attending were Governor Rick Perry, future governor Greg Abbott, and future lieutenant governor Dan Patrick—a state senator who had joined with Huffman in 2013 to kill the bill. Sessions claimed that he intended the attendance of these Republican leaders to be a message to Huffman to not block the bill in 2015. Sessions was able to get statements of support for the bill from Abbott and Patrick. Patrick's support, given his opposition to the bill in 2013, was particularly surprising, but he told Ellis that he would be an "unlikely ally," and prior to the final senate vote on the bill, he told Ellis his reasoning: "Senator, I can't think of a worse thing than to be in jail and to be innocent."

Huffman, of course, as chair of the State Affairs Committee, could have killed the bill, but this time she and other Republicans negotiated with Ellis to modify the bill in a way that satisfied their concerns. Additionally, in the hearings on the bill in 2015, Sessions kept silent and let his relatives testify for the bill. Huffman backed the modified bill, which then sailed through the Senate with a vote of 31 to 0.

It was not everything the sponsors of the bill, including McClendon, wanted. Rather than no bill at all, however, McClendon supported the Senate revisions in the House, and the new law created the Timothy Cole Exoneration Review Commission. Instead of a 9-member commission, the new commission would have a somewhat more cumbersome 11 members. It would only be able to review exonerations since January 1, 2010, and the commission will be dissolved on December 1, 2016—but it was a start.

It took years of dedicated lobbying—along with a huge lobbying misstep, cultivation of top state leaders, and dedicated legislative sponsors—to pass the bill. Most importantly, however, the bill was passed because it was framed not as a partisan issue, but as an issue of justice for all.[56]

It was not the only major criminal justice reform passed by the legislature in 2015. Senator Whitmire successfully sponsored a bill that eased criminal proceedings for misdemeanors committed by children—a bill that passed unanimously in the Senate and with only three nay votes in the House. Whitmire was also successful in sponsoring a bill that ensured that juveniles convicted of felonies would be sent to correctional facilities near their homes. That bill also unanimously passed the Senate and had only seven nay votes in the House. Representative Rafael Anchia (D-Dallas) in the House and Senator Rodney Ellis in the Senate sponsored a bill that received unanimous support in both the House and Senate that provided that annuity payments to those who were wrongfully imprisoned could be passed on to a surviving spouse. Senator Ellis sponsored a bill that got unanimous support in the Senate and only two nay votes in the House that provided that prisoners could get DNA testing if there was evidence that likely contained biological material. One of the more controversial and major reforms was sponsored by Senator Whitmire. That legislation involved a major reform in the selection of grand jurors. Texas was the last state to have what was commonly called the "pick-a-pal" system for selecting grand jurors or the "key man" system. With this selection method, a district judge appoints commissioners who select persons to serve on grand juries. One problem with such a system is that those chosen for grand juries tend to be unrepresentative of the community. For example, a police officer is foreman of the grand jury that heard cases in the Waco biker shoot-out that, among other things, involved charges that police may have shot several of the bikers and that there were violations of due process in holding the bikers and setting their bail. The new grand jury selection system will select 12 grand jurors along with 4 alternates in a random selection process like the selection of trial juries. The reform proved controversial because the Senate version of the bill had a clause that would require district judges to "consider the county's demographics related to race, ethnicity, sex, and age" when grand juries were empaneled. The House completely rejected such language. However, the conference committee was able to come up with language satisfactory to both the House and Senate: jurors were to be "randomly selected from a fair cross section of the population of the area served by the court." The new grand jury selection law passed the Senate with only 5 nay votes and passed the House with 57 nay votes.[57]

PERSONAL RESPONSIBILITY: WHAT WOULD YOU DO?

- Are wrongful convictions inevitable? Overall, is the Texas criminal justice process working as it should?

- Do you think the reforms discussed here will make a difference in the fairness of the Texas criminal justice system? What are some other changes you think need to be made?

By avoiding a direct challenge to the death penalty, which is a highly visible, controversial, and somewhat partisan issue, criminal justice reformers have recently been remarkably successful in their efforts to bring about reforms in the criminal justice system.[58] In part, this may be because many criminal justice reforms involve fundamental issues of justice rather than partisanship; many of the reforms are important changes in the system but are low-visibility and low-controversy matters; and, in a state that has developed a rather notorious record for wrongful imprisonment such as the highly visible Michael Morton case, these reforms are ways political leaders can respond to public concerns about the fairness of the criminal justice system.

Criminal Justice and the Future of Texas

Perhaps the criminal justice system in Texas works well. Overall, the previous examples may be exceptions to the rule. However, the documented problems with evidence, the Willingham case, the Tulia drug arrests, and the Michael Morton case discussed in the introduction to this chapter do raise questions about whether the criminal justice system in Texas is working as well as it should.

One of the issues facing Texas is the fairness of the process toward those accused of crime. Will Texas, for example, decide that there needs to be greater quality in the representation of people accused of crime so that the problems in the system can be identified and resolved before a person is convicted and imprisoned for a lengthy period? Former Dallas County district attorney Craig Watkins received national acclaim by offering a new perspective on the role of a district attorney. Watkins saw the role of a prosecutor as not only convicting the guilty but also protecting the innocent charged with crime.

While Texas remains the major death penalty state and the state that has the most offenders within its criminal justice system, it is notable that Texas's correctional policies are changing. Texas is imposing the death penalty far less often than in the past—in large part because of a new alternative life without parole punishment. Will Texas continue to reduce the imposition of the death penalty in the state? Imposition of the death penalty has been reduced, and other criminal justice reforms have been approved, but politically the death penalty remains unassailable. Texans want it as potential punishment, and it is a useful tool for prosecutors to obtain guilty pleas by offering high prison sentences in exchange for removing the death penalty as a sentencing option. Texas is also sending fewer people to prison than in earlier years. Alternative punishments, such as community supervision, are becoming more common. The state is recognizing the strong connection between alcohol and drug addiction and crime and more resources are being expended in addiction treatment programs. Texas is recognizing that the cost of imprisoning offenders is enormous and that there are alternatives to prison, especially for nonviolent offenders. Today, the old Texas corrections model of "lock 'em up" seems to be replaced by a somewhat more economically efficient approach to corrections where nonviolent offenders are often given alternatives to prison. The issue of the future will be whether Texas will continue pursuing alternatives to prison for offenders. Finally, many states are reducing the penalties for some crimes such as possession of small amounts of marijuana. Will Texas join the national movement toward decriminalization? Crime and corrections have always been a major issue in Texas politics, and Texas appears to be on the cusp of major changes in this area.

Use ⚙ INQUIZITIVE to help you study and master this material.

Categorizing Crime in Texas

- Identify the major classifications of crime under Texas law and the types of punishments that may be imposed (pp. 447–49)

Crimes are categorized along a number of dimensions. The more serious crimes are felonies. The less serious crimes are misdemeanors. Within each classification are various degrees of crime based upon the severity of the offenses. The more serious the crime, the greater are the penalties.

Key Terms

felony (p. 447)
misdemeanor (p. 447)
probation (p. 447)
parole (p. 448)
"three strikes" provision (p. 449)

Practice Quiz

1. The most serious crimes are classified as
   a) felonies.
   b) misdemeanors.
   c) trial-eligible crimes.
   d) grand jury felonies.
   e) county-court-at-law crimes.

2. Probation refers to
   a) a judge's initial term in office.
   b) a suspension of the jail or prison sentence.
   c) a court in the local state court system.
   d) release into the community after time in prison.
   e) failure to pay bail.

3. Which of the following is true?
   a) Parole is granted by the governor.
   b) Members of the Texas Board of Pardons and Paroles are chosen by the legislature every two years.
   c) People convicted of capital crimes are not eligible for parole.
   d) The death penalty is required in all serious felonies.
   e) Texas does not enhance the sentence of repeat felony offenders.

The Criminal Justice Process

- Outline the procedural steps that occur after a person is arrested (pp. 449–55)

There are a number of stages in the criminal justice process, including arrest, arraignment, possible posting of bail, possible grand jury indictment, pretrial hearings, and either plea bargaining or trial. If a person is found guilty, he or she will be sentenced, after which there may be appeals. Within this process, the most important actor is probably the district attorney, who is the key decision maker with regard to charging a suspect,

presenting evidence to a grand jury, plea bargaining, or recommending a sentence to a jury or judge.

Key Terms

bail (p. 450)
grand jury (p. 450)
county attorney (p. 452)
district attorney (p. 452)
plea bargain (p. 453)
assigned counsel (p. 454)
public defender (p. 454)

Practice Quiz

4. Grand juries
 a) review all decisions made by a trial judge.
 b) determine if witnesses are telling the truth by voting "true bills" or "false bills."
 c) determine if there is probable cause to prosecute an individual for a crime.
 d) hear trials involving the death penalty.
 e) hear trials in district court.

5. District attorneys may have the most important roles in the criminal justice process because
 a) they have the power to charge people with crimes.
 b) they have the power to plea bargain with defendants.
 c) they usually make the only presentation before grand juries.
 d) all of the above
 e) none of the above

6. Which of the following statements about plea bargaining is true?
 a) Plea bargaining threatens to overwhelm the limited resources of a prosecutor's office.
 b) Plea bargaining does not benefit defendants.
 c) Plea bargains are made by defendants with district attorneys and agreed to by a judge.
 d) Most Texas district attorneys oppose plea bargaining.
 e) Most Texas criminal defense attorneys oppose plea bargaining.

7. Indigent defendants charged with serious crimes in Texas
 a) must represent themselves.
 b) are represented by private attorneys pro bono as part of their ethical obligation to help others.
 c) most commonly are represented by public defenders.
 d) most commonly are represented by judicially appointed private attorneys.
 e) are usually represented by legal clinics at law schools.

Crime, Corrections, and the Texas Prison System

• Describe prisons and corrections policy in Texas (pp. 455–67)

The Texas prison system is one of the largest in the nation. A major federal court decision (*Ruiz v. Estelle*) found serious overcrowding in the prison system. A series of reforms have been implemented to address the concerns raised by the decision. There has been an effort to lessen the number of people in prison through community supervision. While Texas remains the death penalty capital of the United States, fewer death penalties have been imposed recently than in earlier years.

Practice Quiz

8. The Texas prison system
 a) was vastly affected by a federal court decision, *Ruiz v. Estelle*, that declared that the overcrowded system was unconstitutional.
 b) holds mostly persons convicted of violent crimes.
 c) is a very costly way of dealing with crime as opposed to community supervision such as drug and alcohol programs and probation and parole.
 d) is beginning to contract in size after a long period of expansion.
 e) All of the above are true of the Texas prison system.

9. The Texas Department of Criminal Justice
 a) is run by a nine-member board appointed by the governor.
 b) is run by an elected body.
 c) runs the court system for felony murder.
 d) establishes sentencing guidelines for crimes.
 e) grants probation to those convicted of crimes.

10. The death penalty
 a) is imposed in Texas for all murders.
 b) has been imposed less frequently since Texas allowed juries to sentence a defendant to life without parole.
 c) is carried out in the county where the crime occurred.
 d) is carried out with an electric chair.
 e) cannot be carried out without approval by the Texas Board of Pardons and Parole.

The Integrity of the Texas Criminal Justice System

- Explain why Texas's criminal justice system is often controversial (pp. 468–73)

Texas has had a significant number of people who have been wrongfully convicted. Numerous recent cases in which convictions were overturned have raised questions about the criminal justice system in Texas.

Practice Quiz

11. People have been wrongfully convicted in Texas because of
    a) police misconduct.
    b) bad or outdated forensic science.
    c) mistaken identifications.
    d) prosecutorial misconduct.
    e) All of the above are reasons for wrongful convictions.

12. An advance in which technology has conclusively proved the innocence of a large number of convicted people is
    a) drug testing.
    b) ballistics testing.
    c) DNA analysis.
    d) fire science.
    e) fingerprinting.

Reforms

- Consider recent proposals to improve Texas's criminal justice system (pp. 473–77)

Recent reforms that have been enacted may help reduce the number of wrongful convictions in Texas and improve the fairness of the criminal justice system. Reforms also may rely more on rehabilitation programs and less on incarceration as a solution to crime.

Practice Quiz

13. Reforms in the criminal justice process include
    a) financial compensation for people wrongfully convicted.
    b) changes to suspect lineups so that the police officer in charge of the lineup does not know who the actual suspect is.
    c) expanding drug treatment programs.
    d) showing photos in photo identifications to witnesses sequentially rather than at the same time to reduce the danger of witnesses comparing photos and choosing the one that best fits their memory of the assailant.
    e) All of the above are reforms to the criminal justice process.

14. Probation costs are
    a) about the same as prison costs.
    b) 10 percent higher than prison costs.
    c) considerably less than prison costs.
    d) extremely expensive due to costs of drug treatments.
    e) double the cost of prison.

Appendix

Here we include a series of documents that capture the nature of philosophical and practical problems the people of Texas confronted during their lengthy founding period. For each text we provide short introductions to guide the reader from the Texas Revolution, through statehood and the Civil War, to the Constitution of 1876. Copies of the various constitutions of Texas are available online at www.tarlton.law.utexas.edu/constitutions.

The Declaration of Independence (1836)

The Texas Declaration of Independence was the product of the Convention of 1836.[1] Drawing upon John Locke's Two Treatises of Government (1689) and Thomas Jefferson's Declaration of Independence (1776) for inspiration, it lays out an explanation of the nature of government, lists the grievances that Texas's people hold against the Mexican government, and declares independence and the establishment of a new "free, sovereign, and independent Republic." Note the appeals to "the first law of nature, the right to self-preservation," "the inherent and inalienable right of the People to appeal to first principles," and the "sacred obligation" that people have to their posterity to create a government that will "secure their future wealth and happiness." In addition to presenting the Texas Constitution of 1836, the Texas Declaration of Independence *lays down the republican principles that would define government and politics in Texas from 1836 to 1845, when Texas joined the United States of America.*

To the Public.

The undersigned, Plenipotentiaries from the Republic of Texas to the United States of America, respectfully present to the American People the unanimous DECLARATION OF INDEPENDENCE, made by the People of Texas in General

[1] "Unanimous Declaration of Independence, by the Delegates of the People of Texas," *Laws of the Republic of Texas, in Two Volumes* (Houston: Printed at the Office of the Telegraph, 1838), 1:3–4; Thomas W. Streeter, *Bibliography of Texas, 1795–1845* (5 vols.; Cambridge, MA: Harvard University Press, 1955–60). Errors in the original document are retained.

Convention, on the 2d day of March, 1836; and, also, the CONSTITUTION framed by the same body.

Robert Hamilton,
GEO. C. CHILDRESS.
WASHINGTON CITY, May 22, 1836.

Unanimous Declaration of Independence, by the Delegates of the People of Texas.

In General Convention, at the town of Washington, on the 2d day of March, 1836.

When a Government has ceased to protect the lives, liberty, and property of the People from whom its legitimate powers are derived, and for the advancement of whose happiness it was instituted, and so far from being a guarantee for the enjoyment of their inestimable and inalienable rights, becomes an instrument in the hands of evil rules for their oppression: when the Federal Republican Constitution of their country, which they have sworn to support, no longer has a substantial existence, and the whole nature of their Government has been forcibly changed, without their consent, from a restricted Federative Republic, composed of sovereign States, to a consolidated central military despotism, in which every interest is disregarded but that of the army and the priesthood, both the eternal enemies of civil liberty, the ever-ready minions of power, and the usual instruments of tyrants: when, long after the spirit of the constitution has departed, moderation is at length so far lost by those in power, that even the semblance of freedom is removed, and the forms themselves of the Constitution discontinued; and so far from their petitions and remonstrances being regarded, the agents who bear them are thrown into dungeons and mercenary armies sent forth to force a new Government upon them at the point of the bayonet.

When, in consequence of such acts of malfeasance and abdication on the part of the Government, anarchy prevails, and civil society is dissolved into its original elements: in such a crisis, the first law of nature, the right of self-preservation, the inherent and inalienable right of the People to appeal to first principles, and take their political affairs into their own hands in extreme cases enjoins it as a right towards themselves, and a sacred obligation to their posterity, to abolish such Government, and create another in its stead, calculated to rescue them from impending dangers, and to secure their future welfare and happiness.

Nations, as well as individuals, are amenable for their acts to the public opinion of mankind. A statement of a part of our grievances is therefore submitted to an impartial world, in justification of the hazardous but unavoidable step now taken, of severing our political connexion with the Mexican People, and assuming an independent attitude among the nations of the earth.

The Mexican Government, by its colonization laws, invited and induced the Anglo-American population of Texas to colonize its wilderness, under the pledged faith of a written constitution, that they should continue to enjoy that constitutional liberty and republican Government to which they had been habituated in the land of their birth, the United States of America.

In this expectation they have been cruelly disappointed, inasmuch as the Mexican nation has acquiesced in the late changes made in the Government by General Antonio Lopez de Santa Ana, who, having overturned the Constitution of his country, now offers us the cruel alternative, either to abandon our homes, acquired by so many privations, or submit to the most intolerable of all tyranny, the combined despotism of the sword and the priesthood.

It hath sacrificed our welfare to the State of Coahuila, by which our interests have been continually depressed, through a jealous and partial course of legislation, carried on at a far-distant seat of Government, by a hostile majority, in an unknown tongue; and this too notwithstanding we have petitioned in the humblest terms for the establishment of a separate State Government, and have, in accordance with the provisions of the National Constitution, presented to the General Congress a Republican Constitution, which was, without just cause, contemptuously rejected.

It incarcerated in a dungeon, for a long time, one of our citizens, for no other cause but a zealous endeavor to procure the acceptance of our Constitution and the establishment of a State Government.

It has failed and refused to secure, on a firm basis, the right of trial by jury, that palladium of civil liberty and only safe guarantee for the life, liberty, and property of the citizen.

It has failed to establish any public system of education, although possessed of almost boundless resources, (the public domain,) and although it is an axiom in political science that, unless a People are educated and enlightened, it is idle to expect the continuance of civil liberty, or the capacity for self-government.

It has suffered the military commandants stationed among us to exercise arbitrary acts of oppression and tyranny, thus trampling upon the most sacred rights of the citizen, and rendering the military superior to the civil power.

It has dissolved by force of arms the State Congress of Coahuila and Texas, and obliged our Representatives to fly for their lives from the seat of Government, thus depriving us of the fundamental political right of representation.

It has demanded the surrender of a number of our citizens, and ordered military detachments to seize and carry them into the interior for trial; in contempt of the civil authorities, and in defiance of the laws and the Constitution.

It has made piratical attacks upon our commerce by commissioning foreign desperadoes, and authorizing them to seize our vessels and convey the property of our citizens to far-distant ports for confiscation.

It denies us the right of worshipping the Almighty according to dictates of our own conscience, by the support of a national religion calculated to promote the temporal interests of its human functionaries rather than the glory of the true and living God.

It has demanded us to deliver up our arms, which are essential for our defence, the rightful property of freemen, and formidable only to tyrannical Governments.

It has invaded our country, both by sea and by land, with intent to lay waste our territory, and drive us from our homes; and has now a large mercenary army advancing, to carry on against us a war of extermination.

It has, through its emissaries, incited the merciless savage, with the tomahawk and scalping-knife, to massacre the inhabitants of our defenceless frontiers.

It has been, during the whole time of our connexion with it, the contemptible sport and victim of successive military revolutions, and hath continually exhibited every characteristic of a weak, corrupt, and tyrannical government.

These and other grievances were patiently borne by the People of Texas, until they reached that point at which forbearance ceases to be a virtue. They then took up arms in defence of the National Constitution. They appealed to their Mexican brethren for assistance. Their appeal has been made in vain: though months have elapsed, no sympathetic response has yet been heard from the interior. They are, therefore, forced to the melancholy conclusion that the Mexican People have acquiesced in the destruction of their liberty, and the substitution therefor of a military despotism; that they are unfit to be free, and incapable of self-government.

The necessity of self-preservation, therefore, now decrees our eternal political separation.

We, therefore, the Delegates, with plenary powers, of the People of Texas, in solemn Convention assembled, appealing to a candid world for the necessities of our condition, do hereby resolve and DECLARE that our political connexion with the Mexican nation has forever ended, and that the People of Texas do now constitute a FREE, SOVEREIGN, AND INDEPENDENT REPUBLIC, and are fully invested with all the rights and attributes which properly belong to independent States; and, conscious of the rectitude of our intentions, we fearlessly and confidently commit the issue to the decision of the Supreme Arbiter of the destinies of nations.

RICHARD ELLIS,
President.

C. B. Stewart,
Thomas Barnett, of Austin,
James Collinsworth,
Edwin Waller,
Asa Brigham
J. S. D. Byrom, of Brazoria,
Francisco Ruis,
Antonio Navaro,
Jesse B. Badgett, of Bexar,
Wm. D. Lacy,
Wm. Menifee, of Colorado,
James Gains,
M. B. Menard,
A. B. Hardin, of Liberty,
Baily Hardiman, of Matagorda,
J. W. Bunton,
Thos. J. Gazeley,

R. M. Coleman, of Mina,
Robert Potter,
Thos. J. Rusk,
Charles S. Taylor,
Jno. S. Roberts, of Nacogdoches
Robert Hamilton,
Collin McKinnee,
Alb. H. Lattimer, of Red River,
Martin Palmer,
W. Clark, jr., of Sabine,
John Fisher,
Matt. Caldwell, of Gonzales,
Wm. Motley, of Goliad,
L. de Zavala, of Harrisburg,
S. C. Robertson,
Geo. C. Childress, of Milam,
Steph. H. Everett,

Geo. W. Smith, of Jasper,
Elijah Stapp, of Jackson,
Claiborne West,
Wm. B. Scates, of Jefferson,
E. O. Legrand,
S. W. Blount, of San Augustine,
Syd. O. Bennington,
W. C. Crawford, of Shelby,
J. Power,
Sam. Houston,
David Thomas,
Edward Conrad, of Refugio,
John Turner, of San Patricio,
B. Briggs Goodrich,
G. W. Barnett,
James G. Swisher,
Jesse Grimes, of Washington.

Ordinance of Annexation Approved by the Texas Convention on July 4, 1845

The independent Republic of Texas ceased to exist in 1845 following the implementation of a new state constitution and Texas's formal admission into the Union as a state. Resolutions passed by the U.S. Congress stated the conditions under which Texas was to be admitted into the Union.[2] Note that the resolutions demand a republican form of government be adopted by the people through a constitutional convention (via a new constitution) and that the existing government consent to this action. Passage of this ordinance by the convention is an expression of the consent of the people of Texas to this new political configuration.

An Ordinance
Whereas,

the Congress of the United States of America has passed resolutions providing for the annexation of Texas to that Union, which resolutions were offered by the President of the United States on the first day of March, 1845; and

Whereas,

the President of the United States has submitted to Texas the first and second sections of said resolutions, as the basis upon which Texas may be admitted as one of the States of the said Union; and

Whereas,

the existing Government of the Republic of Texas, has assented to the proposals thus made,—the terms and conditions of which are as follows:

"Joint Resolutions for annexing Texas to the United States.

Resolved by the Senate and House of Representatives of the United States of America in Congress assembled, That Congress doth consent that the territory properly included within and rightfully belonging to the Republic of Texas, may be erected into a new State to be called the State of Texas, with a republican form of government adopted by the people of said Republic, by deputies in convention assembled, with the consent of the existing Government in order that the same may by admitted as one of the States of this Union.

2nd. And be it further resolved, That the foregoing consent of Congress is given upon the following conditions, to wit: First, said state to be formed, subject to the adjustment by this government of all questions of boundary that may arise with other governments,—and the Constitution thereof, with the proper evidence of its adoption by the people of said Republic of Texas, shall be transmitted to the President of the United States, to be laid before Congress for its final action on, or before the first day of January, one thousand eight hundred and forty-six. Second, said state when admitted into the Union, after ceding to the United States all public edifices, fortifications, barracks, ports and harbors, navy and navy yards, docks, magazines and armaments, and all other means pertaining to the public defense, belonging to the said Republic of Texas, shall retain funds, debts, taxes and dues of every kind which may belong to, or be due and owing to the said Republic; and shall also retain all the vacant and unappropriated lands lying within its limits, to be applied to the payment of the debts and liabilities of said Republic of Texas, and the residue of said lands, after discharging said debts and liabilities, to be disposed of as said State may direct; but in no event are said debts and liabilities to become a charge upon the Government of the United States. Third—New States of convenient size not exceeding four in number, in addition to said State of Texas and having sufficient population, may, hereafter by the consent of said State, be formed out of the territory thereof, which shall be entitled to admission under the provisions of the Federal Constitution; and such states as may be formed out of the territory lying south of thirty-six degrees thirty minutes north latitude, commonly known as the Missouri Compromise Line, shall be admitted into the Union, with or without slavery, as the people of each State, asking admission shall desire; and in such State or States as shall be formed out of said territory, north of said Missouri compromise Line, slavery, or involuntary servitude (except for crime) shall be prohibited."

Now in order to manifest the assent of the people of this Republic, as required in the above recited portions of said

---

[2] *Journals of the Constitution Convention of Texas, 1845* (Austin: Miner and Cruger, Printers to the Constitution, 1845), 367–70.

resolutions, we the deputies of the people of Texas, in convention assembled, in their name and by their authority, do ordain and declare, that we assent to and accept the proposals, conditions and guarantees, contained in the first and second sections of the Resolution of the Congress of the United States aforesaid.

In testimony whereof, we have hereunto subscribed our names.

THOMAS J. RUSK
President

followed by 61 signatures

Attest
JAMES H. RAYMOND
Secretary of the Convention

Sam Houston's Address on Secession (1860) and Declaration of Causes (1861)

Texas joined the Union in 1845 and left it in 1861. Following the lead of other southern states after the election of Lincoln, Texas called a Secession Convention that met in January 1861. Despite the efforts of Governor Sam Houston to keep Texas in the Union, the convention passed an Ordinance of Secession *on February 1 and a* Declaration of Causes *on February 2, 1861.*[3] *Texas joined the Confederacy as a state on March 1, 1861. Following a four-year conflict, as a practical matter the war ended in April 1865 with the surrender of Lee's Army of Northern Virginia. The last battle of the war (the Battle of Palmito Ranch) was fought May 12–13, 1865, near Brownsville.*

Sam Houston's address captures the minority pro-Union position in Texas. A disciple of Andrew Jackson who rigorously opposed the attempts of South Carolina to reject the dominance of the national government during the Nullification Debates of the 1830s, Houston argued that leaving the Union was a dangerous action for the South. Note that Houston does not reject slavery as an institution but argues that the best way to defend Texans and Texas's interests is within the existing constitutional structure.

The Declaration of Causes *presents the pro-secession argument in Texas, the one that ultimately carried the day. Note this document expresses the fear that southern proslavery states will become a minority in the Union. It also rejects the northern abolitionist contention that there is a "higher law" operating above the U.S. Constitution.*

From Sam Houston's Address on Secession, Austin, Texas, 1860

. . . [I]n 1836, I volunteered to aid in transplanting American liberty to this soil, it was with the belief that the Constitution and the Union were to be perpetual blessings to the human race,—that the success of the experiment of our fathers was beyond dispute, and that whether under the banner of the Lone Star or that many-starred banner of the Union, I could point to the land of Washington, Jefferson, and Jackson, as the land blest beyond all other lands, where freedom would be eternal and Union unbroken. . . . Power, wealth, expansion, victory, have followed in its path, and yet the aegis of the Union has been broad enough to encompass all. Is not this worth perpetuating? Will you exchange this for all the

[3] Edwin Anderson Alderman, *Library of Southern History*, ed. Joel Chandler Harris (Atlanta: Martin and Hoyt, 1909).

hazards, the anarchy and carnage of civil war? Do you believe that it will be disservered and no shock felt in society? You are asked to plunge into a revolution; but are you told how to get out of it? Not so; but it is to be a leap in the dark—a leap into an abyss, whose horrors would even fright the mad spirits of disunion who tempt you on.

. . . What is there that is free that we have not? Are our rights invaded and no Government ready to protect them? No! Are our institutions wrested from us and others foreign to our taste forced upon us? No! Is the right of free speech, a free press, or free suffrage taken from us? No! Has our property been taken from us and the Government failed to interpose when called upon? No, none of these! The rights of the States and the rights of individuals are still maintained. We have yet the Constitution, we have yet a judiciary, which has never been appealed to in vain—we have yet just laws and officers to administer them; and an army and navy, ready to maintain any and every constitutional right of the citizen. Whence then this clamor about disunion? Whence this cry of protection to property or disunion, when even the very loudest in the cry, declared under their Senatorial oaths, but a few months since, that no protection was necessary? Are we to sell reality for a phantom?

There is no longer a holy ground upon which the footsteps of the demagogue may not fall. One by one the sacred things placed by patriotic hands upon the altar of our liberties, have been torn down. The Declaration of our Independence is jeered at. The farewell counsels of Washington are derided. The charm of those historic names which make glorious our past has been broken, and now the Union is no longer held sacred, but made secondary to the success of party and the adoption of abstractions. We hear of secession—"peaceable secession." We are to believe that this people, whose progressive civilization has known no obstacles, but has already driven back one race and is fast Americanizing another, who have conquered armies and navies,—whose career has been onward and never has receded, be the step right or wrong, is at last quietly and calmly to be denationalized, to be rent into fragments, sanctioned by the Constitution, and there not only be none of the incidents of revolution, but amid peace and happiness we are to have freedom from abolition clamor, security to the institution of slavery, and a career of glory under a Southern Confederacy, which we can never attain in our present condition! When we deny the right of a State to secede, we are pointed to the resolves of chivalric

South Carolina and other States; and are told, "Let them go out and you can not whip them back." My friends, there will be no necessity of whipping them back. They will soon whip themselves, and will not be worth whipping back. Deprived of the protection of the Union, of the aegis of the Constitution, they would soon dwindle into petty States, to be again rent in twain by dissensions or through the ambition of selfish chieftains, and would become a prey to foreign powers. They gravely talk of holding treaties with Great Britain and other foreign powers, and the great advantages which would arise to the South from separation are discussed. Treaties with Great Britain! Alliance with foreign powers! Have these men forgotten history? Look at Spanish America! Look at the condition of every petty State, which by alliance with Great Britain is subject to continual aggression! And yet, after picturing the rise and progress of Abolitionism, tracing it to the Wilberforce movement in England, and British influence in the North, showing that British gold has sustained and encouraged Northern fanaticism, we are told to be heedless of the consequences of disunion, for the advantages of British alliance would far over-estimate the loss of the Union!

. . . It is but natural that we all should desire the defeat of the Black Republican candidates. As Southern men, the fact that their party is based upon the one idea of opposition to our institutions, is enough to demand our efforts against them; but we have a broader, a more national cause of opposition to them. Their party is sectional. It is at war with those principles of equality and nationality upon which the Government is formed, and as much the foe of the Northern as of the Southern man. Its mission is to engender strife, to foster hatred between brethren, and to encourage the formation here of Southern sectional parties equally dangerous to Southern and Northern rights. The conservative energies of the country are called upon to take a stand now against the Northern sectional party, because its strength betokens success. Defeat and overthrow it, and the defeat and overthrow of Southern sectionalism is easy.

I come not here to speak in behalf of a united South against Lincoln. I appeal to the nation. I ask not the defeat of sectionalism by sectionalism, but by nationality. These men who talk of a united South, know well that it begets a united North. Talk of frightening the North into measures by threats of dissolving the Union! It is child's play and folly. It is all the Black Republican leaders want. American blood, North nor South, has not yet become so ignoble as to be chilled by threats. Strife begets strife, threat begets threat, and taunt begets taunt, and these disunionists know it. American blood brooks no such restraints as these men would put upon it. I would blush with shame for America, if I could believe that one vast portion of my countrymen had sunk so low that childish threats would intimidate them. . . .

The error has been that the South has met sectionalism by sectionalism. We want a Union basis, one broad enough to comprehend the good and true friends of the Constitution at the North. To hear Southern disunionists talk, you would think the majority of the Northern people were in this Black Republican party; but it is not so. They are in a minority, and it but needs a patriotic movement like that supported by the conservatives of Texas, to unite the divided opposition to that party there and overthrow it. . . .

I came not here to vindicate candidates or denounce them. They stand upon their records. If they are national, approve them; if they are sectional, condemn. Judge them by the principles they announce. Let past differences be forgotten in the determination to unite against sectionalism. I have differed with all three of the candidates; but whenever I see a man at this crisis coming boldly up to the defense of the Constitution of the country, and ready to maintain the Union against its foes, I will not permit old scores to prejudice me against him. Hence I am ready to vote the Union ticket, and if all the candidates occupy this national ground, my vote may be transferred to either of them. This is the way to put Mr. Lincoln down. Put him down constitutionally, by rallying the conservative forces and sacrificing men for the sake of principles.

But if, through division in the ranks of those opposed to Mr. Lincoln, he should be elected, we have no excuse for dissolving the Union. The Union is worth more than Mr. Lincoln, and if the battle is to be fought for the Constitution, let us fight it in the Union and for the sake of the Union. With a majority of the people in favor of the Constitution, shall we desert the Government and leave it in the hands of the minority? A new obligation will be imposed upon us, to guard the Constitution and to see that no infraction of it is attempted or permitted. If Mr. Lincoln administers the Government in accordance with the Constitution, our rights must be respected. If he does not, the Constitution has provided a remedy.

No tyrant or usurper can ever invade our rights so long as we are united. Let Mr. Lincoln attempt it, and his party will scatter like chaff before the storm of popular indignation which will burst forth from one end of the country to the other. Secession or revolution will not be justified until legal and constitutional means of redress have been tried, and I can not believe that the time will ever come when these will prove inadequate. . . .

Declaration of Causes: February 2, 1861[4]
A declaration of the causes which impel the State
of Texas to secede from the Federal Union.

The government of the United States, by certain joint resolutions, bearing date the 1st day of March, in the year A.D. 1845, proposed to the Republic of Texas, then a free, sovereign and independent nation, the annexation of the latter to the former as one of the co-equal States thereof,

The people of Texas, by deputies in convention assembled, on the fourth day of July of the same year, assented to and accepted said proposals and formed a constitution for the proposed State, upon which on the 29th day of December in the same year, said State was formally admitted into the Confederated Union.

Texas abandoned her separate national existence and consented to become one of the Confederated States to promote her welfare, insure domestic tranquility [*sic*] and secure more substantially the blessings of peace and liberty to her people. She was received into the confederacy with her own constitution, under the guarantee of the federal constitution and the compact of annexation, that she should enjoy these blessings. She was received as a commonwealth holding, maintaining and protecting the institution known as negro slavery—the servitude of the African to the white race within her limits—a relation that had existed from the first settlement of her wilderness by the white race, and which her people intended should exist in all future time. Her institutions and geographical position established the strongest ties between her and other slave-holding States of the confederacy. Those ties have been strengthened by association. But what has been the course of the government of the United States, and of the people and authorities of the non-slave-holding States, since our connection with them?

The controlling majority of the Federal Government, under various pretences and disguises, has so administered the same as to exclude the citizens of the Southern States, unless under odious and unconstitutional restrictions, from all the immense territory owned in common by all the States on the Pacific Ocean, for the avowed purpose of acquiring sufficient power in the common government to use it as a means of destroying the institutions of Texas and her sister slave-holding States.

By the disloyalty of the Northern States and their citizens and the imbecility of the Federal Government, infamous combinations of incendiaries and outlaws have been permitted in those States and the common territory of Kansas to trample upon the federal laws, to war upon the lives and property of Southern citizens in that territory, and finally, by violence and mob law, to usurp the possession of the same as exclusively the property of the Northern States.

The Federal Government, while but partially under the control of these our unnatural and sectional enemies, has for years almost entirely failed to protect the lives and property of the people of Texas against the Indian savages on our border, and more recently against the murderous forays of banditti from the neighboring territory of Mexico; and when our State government has expended large amounts for such purpose, the Federal Government has refused reimbursement therefor, thus rendering our condition more insecure and harrassing [*sic*] than it was during the existence of the Republic of Texas.

These and other wrongs we have patiently borne in the vain hope that a returning sense of justice and humanity would induce a different course of administration.

When we advert to the course of individual non-slave-holding States, and that [of] a majority of their citizens, our grievances assume far greater magnitude.

The States of Maine, Vermont, New Hampshire, Connecticut, Rhode Island, Massachusetts, New York, Pennsylvania, Ohio, Wisconsin, Michigan and Iowa, by solemn legislative enactments, have deliberately, directly or indirectly violated the 3rd clause of the 2nd section of the 4th article of the federal constitution, and laws passed in pursuance thereof; thereby annulling a material provision of the compact, designed by its framers to perpetuate amity between the members of the confederacy and to secure the rights of the slaveholding States in their domestic institutions—a provision founded in justice and wisdom, and without the enforcement of which the compact fails to accomplish the object of its creation. Some of those States have imposed high fines and degrading penalties upon any of their citizens or officers who may carry out in good faith that provision of the compact, or the federal laws enacted in accordance therewith.

In all the non-slave-holding States, in violation of that good faith and comity which should exist between entirely distinct nations, the people have formed themselves into a great sectional party, now strong enough in numbers to control the affairs of each of those States, based upon the unnatural feeling of hostility to these Southern States and their beneficent and patriarchal system of African slavery,

[4] Ernest William Winkler, ed., *Journal of the Secession Convention of Texas 1861, Edited from the Original in the Department of State by Ernest William Winkler, State Librarian* (Austin: Texas Library and Historical Commission, 1912), 61–65.

proclaiming the debasing doctrine of the equality of all men, irrespective of race or color—a doctrine at war with nature, in opposition to the experience of mankind, and in violation of the plainest revelations of the Divine Law. They demand the abolition of negro slavery throughout the confederacy, the recognition of political equality between the white and the negro races, and avow their determination to press on their crusade against us, so long as a negro slave remains in these States.

For years past this abolition organization has been actively sowing the seeds of discord through the Union, and has rendered the federal congress the arena for spreading firebrands and hatred between the slave-holding and non-slaveholding States.

By consolidating their strength, they have placed the slave-holding States in a hopeless minority in the federal congress, and rendered representation of no avail in protecting Southern rights against their exactions and encroachments.

They have proclaimed, and at the ballot box sustained, the revolutionary doctrine that there is a "higher law" than the constitution and laws of our Federal Union, and virtually that they will disregard their oaths and trample upon our rights.

They have for years past encouraged and sustained lawless organizations to steal our slaves and prevent their recapture, and have repeatedly murdered Southern citizens while lawfully seeking their rendition.

They have invaded Southern soil and murdered unoffending citizens, and through the press their leading men and a fanatical pulpit have bestowed praise upon the actors and assassins in these crimes, while the governors of several of their States have refused to deliver parties implicated and indicted for participation in such offences, upon the legal demands of the States aggrieved.

They have, through the mails and hired emissaries, sent seditious pamphlets and papers among us to stir up servile insurrection and bring blood and carnage to our firesides.

They have sent hired emissaries among us to burn our towns and distribute arms and poison to our slaves for the same purpose.

They have impoverished the slave-holding States by unequal and partial legislation, thereby enriching themselves by draining our substance.

They have refused to vote appropriations for protecting Texas against ruthless savages, for the sole reason that she is a slave-holding State.

And, finally, by the combined sectional vote of the seventeen non-slave-holding States, they have elected as president and vice-president of the whole confederacy two men whose chief claims to such high positions are their approval of these long continued wrongs, and their pledges to continue them to the final consummation of these schemes for the ruin of the slave-holding States.

In view of these and many other facts, it is meet that our own views should be distinctly proclaimed.

We hold as undeniable truths that the governments of the various States, and of the confederacy itself, were established exclusively by the white race, for themselves and their posterity; that the African race had no agency in their establishment; that they were rightfully held and regarded as an inferior and dependent race, and in that condition only could their existence in this country be rendered beneficial or tolerable.

That in this free government all white men are and of right ought to be entitled to equal civil and political rights; that the servitude of the African race, as existing in these States, is mutually beneficial to both bond and free, and is abundantly authorized and justified by the experience of mankind, and the revealed will of the Almighty Creator, as recognized by all Christian nations; while the destruction of the existing relations between the two races, as advocated by our sectional enemies, would bring inevitable calamities upon both and desolation upon the fifteen slave-holding States.

By the secession of six of the slave-holding States, and the certainty that others will speedily do likewise, Texas has no alternative but to remain in an isolated connection with the North, or unite her destinies with the South.

For these and other reasons, solemnly asserting that the federal constitution has been violated and virtually abrogated by the several States named, seeing that the federal government is now passing under the control of our enemies to be diverted from the exalted objects of its creation to those of oppression and wrong, and realizing that our own State can no longer look for protection, but to God and her own sons—We the delegates of the people of Texas, in Convention assembled, have passed an ordinance dissolving all political connection with the government of the United States of America and the people thereof and confidently appeal to the intelligence and patriotism of the freemen of Texas to ratify the same at the ballot box, on the 23rd day of the present month.

Adopted in Convention on the 2nd day of Feby, in the year of our Lord one thousand eight hundred and sixty-one and of the independence of Texas the twenty-fifth.

Ordinance of Secession Null (1866) and Texas v. White et al. (1869)

Once the South and Texas had been defeated in the Civil War, the question arose as to the constitutional status of the secessionist states, including Texas. From the perspective of law and constitutional thought, had the southern states ever left the Union? Were the actions of state governments under the Confederacy legal or not? Two documents help clarify this issue.[5]

The ordinance declaring secession null and void answers these questions directly. By the expressed declaration of the Texas people in convention, the ordinance proclaims the 1861 act of secession to be null and void. Texas may have been in rebellion, but it never left the Union. Actions by the Confederate state of Texas thus were not legal.

The Texas v. White et al. *case answers this question further by exploring the legality of specific actions of the Confederate legislature in Texas. In 1850, Congress authorized $10 million in bonds to Texas. In 1862 the Confederate legislature authorized using the bonds for war supplies. In 1866, after the war, the Reconstruction government of Texas tried to reclaim the bonds on the grounds that the Confederate state government had illegally sold the bonds. Note the constitutional theory about the nature of the Union and the rebellion that is developed in the Chief Justice's opinion. The union established under the Articles of Convention and the U.S. Constitution is "perpetual" and "indissoluble." Once Texas joined the Union, Texas and Texans became part of this Union. Texas may have been in rebellion against the Union, but it had never left the Union. The actions of the Confederate government, like the act of secession, were thus null and void. The bonds thus had not been legally sold.*

An Ordinance, Declaring the Ordinance of Secession Null and Void (*March 15, 1866*)

Be it ordained by the people of Texas in Convention assembled, That we acknowledge the supremacy of the Constitution of the United States, and the laws passed in pursuance thereof; and that an Ordinance adopted by a former Convention of the people of Texas on the 1st day of February, A.D. 1861, entitled "An Ordinance to Dissolve the Union between the State of Texas and the other States, united under the compact styled 'Constitution of the United States of America,'" be and the same is hereby declared null and void; and the right heretofore claimed by the State of Texas to secede from the Union, is hereby distinctly renounced. Passed 15th March, 1866.

From TEXAS v. WHITE ET AL. (*1869*)
Supreme Court of United States.

The CHIEF JUSTICE delivered the opinion of the court.

. . . If, therefore, it is true that the State of Texas was not at the time of filing this bill, or is not now, one of the United States, we have no jurisdiction of this suit, and it is our duty to dismiss it.

We are very sensible of the magnitude and importance of this question, of the interest it excites, and of the difficulty, not to say impossibility, of so disposing of it as to satisfy the conflicting judgments of men equally enlightened, equally upright, and equally patriotic. But we meet it in the case, and we must determine it in the exercise of our best judgment, under the guidance of the Constitution alone. . . .

. . . [T]he word . . . [*state* is] used in the clause which provides that the United States shall guarantee to every State in the Union a republican form of government, and shall protect each of them against invasion. . . .

The Republic of Texas was admitted into the Union, as a State, on the 27th of December, 1845. By this act the new State, and the people of the new State, were invested with all the rights, and became subject to all the responsibilities and duties of the original States under the Constitution.

From the date of admission, until 1861, the State was represented in the Congress of the United States by her senators and representatives, and her relations as a member of the Union remained unimpaired. In that year, acting upon the theory that the rights of a State under the Constitution might be renounced, and her obligations thrown off at pleasure, Texas undertook to sever the bond thus formed, and to break up her constitutional relations with the United States. . . .

The governor and secretary of state, refusing to comply, were summarily ejected from office.

The members of the legislature, which had also adjourned and reassembled on the 18th of March, were more compliant. They took the oath, and proceeded on the 8th of

---

[5] The Constitution of the State of Texas, as Amended by the Delegates in Convention Assembled, Austin, 1866 (Austin: Printed at the Southern Intelligencer Office, 1866), 32.

April to provide by law for the choice of electors of president and vice-president of the Confederate States.

The representatives of the State in the Congress of the United States were withdrawn, and as soon as the seceded States became organized under a constitution, Texas sent senators and representatives to the Confederate Congress.

In all respects, so far as the object could be accomplished by ordinances of the convention, by acts of the legislature, and by votes of the citizens, the relations of Texas to the Union were broken up, and new relations to a new government were established for them.

The position thus assumed could only be maintained by arms, and Texas accordingly took part, with the other Confederate States, in the war of the rebellion, which these events made inevitable. During the whole of that war there was no governor, or judge, or any other State officer in Texas, who recognized the National authority. Nor was any officer of the United States permitted to exercise any authority whatever under the National government within the limits of the State, except under the immediate protection of the National military forces.

Did Texas, in consequence of these acts, cease to be a State? Or, if not, did the State cease to be a member of the Union? . . .

The Union of the States never was a purely artificial and arbitrary relation. It began among the Colonies, and grew out of common origin, mutual sympathies, kindred principles, similar interests, and geographical relations. It was confirmed and strengthened by the necessities of war, and received definite form, and character, and sanction from the Articles of Confederation. By these the Union was solemnly declared to "be perpetual." And when these Articles were found to be inadequate to the exigencies of the country, the Constitution was ordained "to form a more perfect Union." It is difficult to convey the idea of indissoluble unity more clearly than by these words. What can be indissoluble if a perpetual Union, made more perfect, is not? . . .

When, therefore, Texas became one of the United States, she entered into an indissoluble relation. All the obligations of perpetual union, and all the guaranties of republican government in the Union, attached at once to the State. The act which consummated her admission into the Union was something more than a compact; it was the incorporation of a new member into the political body. And it was final. The union between Texas and the other States was as complete, as perpetual, and as indissoluble as the union between the original States. There was no place for reconsideration, or revocation, except through revolution, or through consent of the States.

Considered therefore as transactions under the Constitution, the ordinance of secession, adopted by the convention and ratified by a majority of the citizens of Texas, and all the acts of her legislature intended to give effect to that ordinance, were absolutely null. They were utterly without operation in law. The obligations of the State, as a member of the Union, and of every citizen of the State, as a citizen of the United States, remained perfect and unimpaired. It certainly follows that the State did not cease to be a State, nor her citizens to be citizens of the Union. If this were otherwise, the State must have become foreign, and her citizens foreigners. The war must have ceased to be a war for the suppression of rebellion, and must have become a war for conquest and subjugation.

Our conclusion therefore is, that Texas continued to be a State, and a State of the Union, notwithstanding the transactions to which we have referred. And this conclusion, in our judgment, is not in conflict with any act or declaration of any department of the National government, but entirely in accordance with the whole series of such acts and declarations since the first outbreak of the rebellion. . . .

These new relations imposed new duties upon the United States. The first was that of suppressing the rebellion. The next was that of re-establishing the broken relations of the State with the Union. The first of these duties having been performed, the next necessarily engaged the attention of the National government.

The authority for the performance of the first had been found in the power to suppress insurrection and carry on war; for the performance of the second, authority was derived from the obligation of the United States to guarantee to every State in the Union a republican form of government. . . . It follows that the title of the State was not divested by the act of the insurgent government in entering into this contract. . . .

From Governor Richard Coke's Second Inaugural Address (1876)

Following the Civil War, Texas operated under two constitutions (the Constitution of 1866 and 1869). The return to power of the Democratic Party in the elections of 1872 and 1873 effectively ended reconstruction in Texas. A Constitutional Convention dominated by the Democrats in 1875 drafted a new constitution for the state that took effect in 1876.

Governor Richard Coke's second inaugural address in 1876 captures how many people thought of the new constitution. For Coke the 1876 Constitution was not meant to be a reworking of the earlier state constitutions. The people of Texas had become dissatisfied with the power granted to governmental institution over the last decade and were seeking to limit the powers and reach of government. The new constitution was to be unabashedly conservative in design and intent.

After years of trial and struggle, the people of Texas have at length inaugurated a government made in all its parts by themselves. Its faults and errors, as well as its blessings, have no uncertain paternity. The highest exercise of sovereign power of which a State in the American Union is capable, is that through which the people of Texas have swept out of existence the old government and enacted in its stead that which today has been put in operation in all its departments. Thus has a great revolution been accomplished, without violence or disorder, and with no other conflict than the attrition of opposing opinions in the field of argument and discussion, preparatory to the grand arbitrament of the peaceful ballot. . . . This is the sixth time in the history of Texas that this sovereign right has been exercised. . . .

In the more recently framed constitutions we plainly see a wide departure from the beaten track of constitutional structure, and in none of them is this more apparent than in the new Constitution of Texas.

The accepted theory of American constitutional government is that State constitutions are limitations upon, rather than grants of power; and, as a general rule, not without its exceptions, that powers not prohibited exist in State government. Hence, express prohibitions are necessary upon the powers the people would withhold from the State government, and as time and circumstances and experience suggest their wisdom, these restrictions upon the powers of government have multiplied in the more recently created instruments of fundamental law. Many causes have conspired to produce these great changes of constitutional theory, and prominent among them are the enormous amounts of capital concentrated in few hands, operating under charters which perpetuate its power; immense railroad systems, which drive off competition and monopolize the carrying trade of the country; the wonderful growth of towns and cities, whose immediate local governments are peculiarly subject to abuses and malign influences, general extravagance, and frequent corruptions of all departments of government, of late years becoming so alarming—all producing results which necessitate a clearer definition and closer guardianship of the rights of the people; and, for their protection, constitutional barriers not demanded by the conditions of society a quarter of a century ago.—

In this instrument we see mirrored the result of issues made in the politics of the State, in the halls of legislation, and in the primary assemblies of the people during the last decade; and we see faithfully reflected in its restrictions upon the power of government, as in its assertion of powers, the dangers of the past, a recurrence of which is so well guarded against in the future. The instrument presents in its fundamental and leading features a basis on which a government may be reared, eminently conservative of all the purposes for which government is instituted; adapted to a sound and healthy growth and development of the State. It may possibly be, in some respects too restrictive, but when such is the case, the error is on the safe side, and while temporary inconvenience may ensue, no permanent injury will result. . . .

The country and people whose welfare depends upon our deliberations and action need and expect a government light in its burdens, effective in administration, and certain in its securities for person and property. Naught else is necessary to ensure prosperity and continued progress and advancement. With such government the elements of greatness so abundant in the noble State we represent, in the hands of our intelligent adventurous and enterprising people, will combine, and evolve from the womb of the future a destiny of grander proportions than the most gorgeous dream of the enthusiast now pictures. . . .

The Texas Constitution's Bill of Rights (1876 plus amendments)

One of the distinguishing features of the Texas Constitution is a lengthy Bill of Rights. Here the Texas Constitution protects Texans from the actions of state government. Unlike the U.S. Constitution where the Bill of Rights comprising the first ten amendments is located at the end of the document, the Texas Bill of Rights is placed at the beginning as Article 1.

The Texas Bill of Rights articulates a distinctive governing philosophy about the "principles of liberty and free government" that underlies the Texas Constitution. Power comes from the people and Republican government is guaranteed. The people reserve "at all times the inalienable right to alter, reform or abolish their government in such a manner as they may think expedient." Texas is a free and independent state, "subject only to the Constitution of the United States." But the Texas Bill of Rights also declares that the "perpetuity of the Union" depends upon the preservation of unimpaired local self-government. Today such a statement might seem to be uncontroversial. Put in the proper historical context, however, this philosophy signals a rejection of the 1869 Constitution's explicit affirmation of the supremacy of the U.S. Constitution in matters of federalism. Such a philosophy reflects the return to power of traditional secessionist political elites in Texas. This philosophy would dominate (and haunt) Texas politics and government from 1876 until the 1960s when federal civil rights legislation would redefine what local self-government would mean, particularly in regard to the protections afforded minorities by the U.S. Constitution.

Some of the rights in Article 1 echo the protections provided by the U.S. Bill of Rights. Freedom of worship is guaranteed (Sec. 6), as is freedom of speech (Sec. 8), freedom of the press (Sec. 8), freedom of assembly and petition (Sec. 27), and freedom from the quartering of soldiers (Sec. 25). Texans are protected in the Bill of Rights from unreasonable searches and seizures (Sec. 9), and the accused has certain due process rights (for example, Secs. 10, 12, 13, 14, 15, and 19). The Texas Bill of Rights explicitly bans religious tests for public office or appropriations for sectarian purposes (Sec. 7).

Some protections provided by the Texas Bill of Rights seem strange to the modern ear. Monopolies are outlawed (Sec. 26). Primogeniture (limiting the inheritance of land to the first born) and entails (conditions put on the inheritance of land) are forbidden. No one can be found guilty due to corruption of blood (guilt by family association) or be punished in their inheritance by the suicide of a family member.

The Texas Bill of Rights most sharply diverges from the U.S. Bill of Rights in the amendments that have been added over the years. Many of these reflect the ebb and flow of political and cultural concerns in the state. In contrast to the federal government, Texas added an Equal Rights Amendment to the Bill of Rights in 1972, protecting people from discrimination because of sex, race, color, creed, or national origin (Sec. 31). Between 1956 and 2007, complicated provisions were added to the Bill of Rights allowing the denial of bail for multiple convictions (Secs. 11a, 11b, and 11c). Lengthy provisions were added to the Bill of Rights granting rights to crime victims in 1989 (Sec. 30) and providing for compensation for crime victims in 1997 (Sec. 31). Provisions protecting traditional marriage were added in 2005 in Section 32, although these are now inoperable due to a recent Supreme Court ruling. Access to public beaches is guaranteed to individuals in 2009 (Sec. 33) as is the right to hunt, fish, and harvest wildlife by traditional methods such a guns (Sec. 34). In 2009, an amendment was added to the Bill of Rights clarifying when property could be seized by the state under eminent domain. These protections were added to the Bill of Rights largely in response to the furor created by cities taking land from individuals and giving it to others for development projects, like the building of modern sports stadiums.

The extensive list of rights contained in Article 1 of the Texas Constitution shows the ongoing concerns of people and politicians in Texas to limit what government does through constitutional mandate. These rights will likely be expanded in the future.

ARTICLE 1. BILL OF RIGHTS

That the general, great and essential principles of liberty and free government may be recognized and established, we declare:

Sec. 1. FREEDOM AND SOVEREIGNTY OF STATE. Texas is a free and independent State, subject only to the Constitution of the United States, and the maintenance of our free institutions and the perpetuity of the Union depend upon the preservation of the right of local self-government, unimpaired to all the States.

Sec. 2. INHERENT POLITICAL POWER; REPUBLICAN FORM OF GOVERNMENT. All political power is inherent in the people, and all free governments are founded on their authority, and instituted for their benefit. The faith of the people of Texas stands pledged to the preservation of a republican form of government, and, subject to this limitation only, they have at all times the inalienable right to alter, reform or abolish their government in such manner as they may think expedient.

Sec. 3. EQUAL RIGHTS. All free men, when they form a social compact, have equal rights, and no man, or set of men, is entitled to exclusive separate public emoluments, or privileges, but in consideration of public services.

Sec. 3a. EQUALITY UNDER THE LAW. Equality under the law shall not be denied or abridged because of sex, race, color, creed, or national origin. This amendment is self-operative.

(Added Nov. 7, 1972.)

Sec. 4. RELIGIOUS TESTS. No religious test shall ever be required as a qualification to any office, or public trust, in this State; nor shall any one be excluded from holding office on account of his religious sentiments, provided he acknowledge the existence of a Supreme Being.

Sec. 5. WITNESSES NOT DISQUALIFIED BY RELIGIOUS BELIEFS; OATHS AND AFFIRMATIONS. No person shall be disqualified to give evidence in any of the Courts of this State on account of his religious opinions, or for the want of any religious belief, but all oaths or affirmations shall be administered in the mode most binding upon the conscience, and shall be taken subject to the pains and penalties of perjury.

Sec. 6. FREEDOM OF WORSHIP. All men have a natural and indefeasible right to worship Almighty God according to the dictates of their own consciences. No man shall be compelled to attend, erect or support any place of worship, or to maintain any ministry against his consent. No human authority ought, in any case whatever, to control or interfere with the rights of conscience in matters of religion, and no preference shall ever be given by law to any religious society or mode of worship. But it shall be the duty of the Legislature to pass such laws as may be necessary to protect equally every religious denomination in the peaceable enjoyment of its own mode of public worship.

Sec. 7. APPROPRIATIONS FOR SECTARIAN PURPOSES. No money shall be appropriated, or drawn from the Treasury for the benefit of any sect, or religious society, theological or religious seminary; nor shall property belonging to the State be appropriated for any such purposes.

Sec. 8. FREEDOM OF SPEECH AND PRESS; LIBEL. Every person shall be at liberty to speak, write or publish his opinions on any subject, being responsible for the abuse of that privilege; and no law shall ever be passed curtailing the liberty of speech or of the press. In prosecutions for the publication of papers, investigating the conduct of officers, or men in public capacity, or when the matter published is proper for public information, the truth thereof may be given in evidence. And in all indictments for libels, the jury shall have the right to determine the law and the facts, under the direction of the court, as in other cases.

Sec. 9. SEARCHES AND SEIZURES. The people shall be secure in their persons, houses, papers and possessions, from all unreasonable seizures or searches, and no warrant to search any place, or to seize any person or thing, shall issue without describing them as near as may be, nor without probable cause, supported by oath or affirmation.

Sec. 10. RIGHTS OF ACCUSED IN CRIMINAL PROSECUTIONS. In all criminal prosecutions the accused shall have a speedy public trial by an impartial jury. He shall have the right to demand the nature and cause of the accusation against him, and to have a copy thereof. He shall not be compelled to give evidence against himself, and shall have the right of being heard by himself or counsel, or both, shall be confronted by the witnesses against him and shall have compulsory process for obtaining witnesses in his favor, except that when the witness resides out of the State and the offense charged is a violation of any of the anti-trust laws of this State, the defendant and the State shall have the right to produce and have the evidence admitted by deposition, under such rules and laws as the Legislature may hereafter provide; and no person shall be held to answer for a criminal offense, unless on an indictment of a grand jury, except in cases in which the punishment is by fine or imprisonment, otherwise than in the penitentiary, in cases of impeachment, and in cases arising in the army or navy, or in the militia, when in actual service in time of war or public danger.

(Amended Nov. 5, 1918.)

Sec. 11. BAIL. All prisoners shall be bailable by sufficient sureties, unless for capital offenses, when the proof is evident; but this provision shall not be so construed as to prevent bail after indictment found upon examination of the evidence, in such manner as may be prescribed by law.

Sec. 11a. MULTIPLE CONVICTIONS; DENIAL OF BAIL. (a) Any person (1) accused of a felony less than capital in this State, who has been theretofore twice convicted of a felony, the second conviction being subsequent to the first, both in point of time of commission of the offense and conviction therefor, (2) accused of a felony less than capital in this State, committed while on bail for a prior felony for which he has been indicted, (3) accused of a felony less than capital in this State involving the use of a deadly weapon after being convicted of a prior felony, or (4) accused of a violent or sexual offense committed while under the supervision of a criminal justice agency of the State or a political subdivision of the State for a prior felony, after a hearing, and upon evidence substantially showing the guilt of the accused of the offense in (1) or (3) above, of the offense committed while on bail in (2) above, or of the offense in (4) above committed while under the supervision of a criminal justice agency of the State or a political subdivision of the State for a prior felony, may be denied bail pending trial, by a district judge in this State, if said order denying bail pending trial is issued within seven calendar days subsequent to the time of incarceration of the accused; provided, however, that if the accused is not accorded a trial upon the accusation under (1) or (3) above, the accusation and indictment used under (2) above, or the accusation or indictment used under (4) above within sixty (60) days from the time of his incarceration upon the accusation, the order denying bail shall be automatically set aside, unless a continuance is obtained upon the motion or request of the accused; provided, further, that the right of appeal to the Court of Criminal Appeals of this State is expressly accorded the accused for a review of any judgment or order made hereunder, and said appeal shall be given preference by the Court of Criminal Appeals.

(b) In this section:

(1) "Violent offense" means:
(A) murder;
(B) aggravated assault, if the accused used or exhibited a deadly weapon during the commission of the assault;
(C) aggravated kidnapping; or
(D) aggravated robbery.
(2) "Sexual offense" means:
(A) aggravated sexual assault;
(B) sexual assault; or
(C) indecency with a child.

(Added Nov. 6, 1956; amended Nov. 8, 1977; Subsec. (a) amended and (b) added Nov. 2, 1993.)

Sec. 11b. VIOLATION OF CONDITION OF RELEASE PENDING TRIAL; DENIAL OF BAIL. Any person who is accused in this state of a felony or an offense involving family violence, who is released on bail pending trial, and whose bail is subsequently revoked or forfeited for a violation of a condition of release may be denied bail pending trial if a judge or magistrate in this state determines by a preponderance of the evidence at a subsequent hearing that the person violated a condition of release related to the safety of a victim of the alleged offense or to the safety of the community.

(Added Nov. 8, 2005; amended Nov. 6, 2007.)

Sec. 11c. VIOLATION OF AN ORDER FOR EMERGENCY PROTECTION INVOLVING FAMILY VIOLENCE. The legislature by general law may provide that any person who violates an order for emergency protection issued by a judge or magistrate after an arrest for an offense involving family violence or who violates an active protective order rendered by a court in a family violence case, including a temporary ex parte order that has been served on the person, or who engages in conduct that constitutes an offense involving the violation of an order described by this section may be taken into custody and, pending trial or other court proceedings, denied release on bail if following a hearing a judge or magistrate in this state determines by a preponderance of the evidence that the person violated the order or engaged in the conduct constituting the offense.

Sec. 12. HABEAS CORPUS. The writ of habeas corpus is a writ of right, and shall never be suspended. The Legislature shall enact laws to render the remedy speedy and effectual.

Sec. 13. EXCESSIVE BAIL OR FINES; CRUEL AND UNUSUAL PUNISHMENT; REMEDY BY DUE COURSE OF LAW. Excessive bail shall not be required, nor excessive fines imposed, nor cruel or unusual punishment inflicted. All courts shall be open, and every person for an injury done him, in his lands, goods, person or reputation, shall have remedy by due course of law.

Sec. 14. DOUBLE JEOPARDY. No person, for the same offense, shall be twice put in jeopardy of life or liberty; nor shall a person be again put upon trial for the same offense after a verdict of not guilty in a court of competent jurisdiction.

Sec. 15. RIGHT OF TRIAL BY JURY. The right of trial by jury shall remain inviolate. The Legislature shall pass such laws as may be needed to regulate the same, and to maintain its purity and efficiency. Provided, that the Legislature may provide for the temporary commitment, for observation and/or treatment, of mentally ill persons not charged with a criminal offense, for a period of time not to exceed ninety (90) days, by order of the County Court without the necessity of a trial by jury.

(Amended Aug. 24, 1935.)

Sec. 15-a. COMMITMENT OF PERSONS OF UNSOUND MIND. No person shall be committed as a person of unsound mind except on competent medical or psychiatric testimony. The Legislature may enact all laws necessary to provide for the trial, adjudication of insanity and commitment of persons of unsound mind and to provide for a method of appeal from judgments rendered in such cases. Such laws may provide for a waiver of trial by jury, in cases where the person under inquiry has not been charged with the commission of a criminal offense, by the concurrence of the person under inquiry, or his next of kin, and an attorney ad litem appointed by a judge of either the County or Probate Court of the county where the trial is being held, and shall provide for a method of service of notice of such trial upon the person under inquiry and of his right to demand a trial by jury.

(Added Nov. 6, 1956.)

Sec. 16. BILLS OF ATTAINDER; EX POST FACTO OR RETROACTIVE LAWS; IMPAIRING OBLIGATION OF CONTRACTS. No bill of attainder, ex post facto law, retroactive law, or any law impairing the obligation of contracts, shall be made.

Sec. 17. TAKING, DAMAGING, OR DESTROYING PROPERTY FOR PUBLIC USE; SPECIAL PRIVILEGES AND IMMUNITIES; CONTROL OF PRIVILEGES AND FRANCHISES. (a) No person's property shall be taken, damaged, or destroyed for or applied to public use without adequate compensation being made, unless by the consent of such person, and only if the taking, damage, or destruction is for:

  (1) the ownership, use, and enjoyment of the property, notwithstanding an incidental
      use, by:
      (A) the State, a political subdivision of the State, or the public at large; or
      (B) an entity granted the power of eminent domain under law; or

  (2) the elimination of urban blight on a particular parcel of property.

(b) In this section, "public use" does not include the taking of property under Subsection (a) of this section for transfer to a private entity for the primary purpose of economic development or enhancement of tax revenues.

(c) On or after January 1, 2010, the legislature may enact a general, local, or special law granting the power of eminent domain to an entity only on a two-thirds vote of all the members elected to each house.

(d) When a person's property is taken under Subsection (a) of this section, except for the use of the State, compensation as described by Subsection (a) shall be first made, or secured by a deposit of money; and no irrevocable or uncontrollable grant of special privileges or immunities shall be made; but all privileges and franchises granted by the Legislature, or created under its authority, shall be subject to the control thereof.

(Amended Nov. 3, 2009.)

Sec. 18. IMPRISONMENT FOR DEBT. No person shall ever be imprisoned for debt.

Sec. 19. DEPRIVATION OF LIFE, LIBERTY, ETC.; DUE COURSE OF LAW. No citizen of this State shall be deprived of life, liberty, property, privileges or immunities, or in any manner disfranchised, except by the due course of the law of the land.

Sec. 20. OUTLAWRY OR TRANSPORTATION FOR OFFENSE. No citizen shall be outlawed. No person shall be transported out of the State for any offense committed within the same. This section does not prohibit an agreement with another state providing for the confinement of inmates of this State in the penal or correctional facilities of that state.

(Amended Nov. 5, 1985.)

Sec. 21. CORRUPTION OF BLOOD; FORFEITURE; SUICIDES. No conviction shall work corruption of blood, or forfeiture of estate, and the estates of those who destroy their own lives shall descend or vest as in case of natural death.

Sec. 22. TREASON. Treason against the State shall consist only in levying war against it, or adhering to its enemies, giving them aid and comfort; and no person shall be convicted of treason except on the testimony of two witnesses to the same overt act, or on confession in open court.

Sec. 23. RIGHT TO KEEP AND BEAR ARMS. Every citizen shall have the right to keep and bear arms in the lawful defense of himself or the State; but the Legislature shall have power, by law, to regulate the wearing of arms, with a view to prevent crime.

Sec. 24. MILITARY SUBORDINATE TO CIVIL AUTHORITY. The military shall at all times be subordinate to the civil authority.

Sec. 25. QUARTERING SOLDIERS IN HOUSES. No soldier shall in time of peace be quartered in the house of any citizen without the consent of the owner, nor in time of war but in a manner prescribed by law.

Sec. 26. PERPETUITIES AND MONOPOLIES; PRIMOGENITURE OR ENTAILMENTS. Perpetuities and monopolies are contrary to the genius of a free government, and shall never be allowed, nor shall the law of primogeniture or entailments ever be in force in this State.

Sec. 27. RIGHT OF ASSEMBLY; PETITION FOR REDRESS OF GRIEVANCES. The citizens shall have the right, in a peaceable manner, to assemble together for their common good; and apply to those invested with the powers of government for redress of grievances or other purposes, by petition, address or remonstrance.

Sec. 28. SUSPENSION OF LAWS. No power of suspending laws in this State shall be exercised except by the Legislature.

Sec. 29. PROVISIONS OF BILL OF RIGHTS EXCEPTED FROM POWERS OF GOVERNMENT; TO FOREVER REMAIN INVIOLATE. To guard against transgressions of the high powers herein delegated, we declare that everything in this "Bill of Rights" is excepted out of the general powers of government, and shall forever remain inviolate, and all laws contrary thereto, or to the following provisions, shall be void.

Sec. 30. RIGHTS OF CRIME VICTIMS. (a) A crime victim has the following rights:

(1) the right to be treated with fairness and with respect for the victim's dignity and privacy throughout the criminal justice process; and

(2) the right to be reasonably protected from the accused throughout the criminal justice process.

(b) On the request of a crime victim, the crime victim has the following rights:

(1) the right to notification of court proceedings;

(2) the right to be present at all public court proceedings related to the offense, unless the victim is to testify and the court determines that the victim's testimony would be materially affected if the victim hears other testimony at the trial;

(3) the right to confer with a representative of the prosecutor's office;

(4) the right to restitution; and

(5) the right to information about the conviction, sentence, imprisonment, and release of the accused.

(c) The legislature may enact laws to define the term "victim" and to enforce these and other rights of crime victims.

(d) The state, through its prosecuting attorney, has the right to enforce the rights of crime victims.

(e) The legislature may enact laws to provide that a judge, attorney for the state, peace officer, or law enforcement agency is not liable for a failure or inability to provide a right enumerated in this section. The failure or inability of any person to provide a right or service enumerated in this section may not be used by a defendant in a criminal case as a ground for appeal or post-conviction writ of habeas corpus. A victim or guardian or legal representative of a victim has standing to enforce the rights enumerated in this section but does not have standing to participate as a party in a criminal proceeding or to contest the disposition of any charge.

(Added Nov. 7, 1989.)

Sec. 31. COMPENSATION TO VICTIMS OF CRIME FUND; COMPENSATION TO VICTIMS OF CRIME AUXILIARY FUND; USE OF FUND MONEY. (a) The compensation to victims of crime fund created by general law and the compensation to victims of crime auxiliary fund created by general law are each a separate dedicated account in the general revenue fund.

(b) Except as provided by Subsection (c) of this section and subject to legislative appropriation, money deposited to the credit of the compensation to victims of crime fund or the compensation to victims of crime auxiliary fund from any source may be expended as provided by law only for delivering or funding victim-related compensation, services, or assistance.

(c) The legislature may provide by law that money in the compensation to victims of crime fund or in the compensation to victims of crime auxiliary fund may be expended for the purpose of assisting victims of episodes of mass violence if other money appropriated for emergency assistance is depleted.

(Added Nov. 4, 1997.)

Sec. 32. MARRIAGE. (a) Marriage in this state shall consist only of the union of one man and one woman.

(b) This state or a political subdivision of this state may not create or recognize any legal status identical or similar to marriage.

(Added Nov. 8, 2005.)

Sec. 33. ACCESS AND USE OF PUBLIC BEACHES. (a) In this section, "public beach" means a state-owned beach bordering on the seaward shore of the Gulf of Mexico, extending from mean low tide to the landward boundary of state-owned submerged land, and any larger area extending from the line of mean low tide to the line of vegetation bordering on the Gulf of Mexico to which the public has acquired a right of use or easement to or over the area by prescription or dedication or has established and retained a right by virtue of continuous right in the public under Texas common law.

(b) The public, individually and collectively, has an unrestricted right to use and a right of ingress to and egress from a public beach. The right granted by this subsection is dedicated as a permanent easement in favor of the public.

(c) The legislature may enact laws to protect the right of the public to access and use a public beach and to protect the public beach easement from interference and encroachments.

(d) This section does not create a private right of enforcement.

(Added Nov. 3, 2009.)

Sec. 34. RIGHT TO HUNT, FISH, AND HARVEST WILDLIFE. (a) The people have the right to hunt, fish, and harvest wildlife, including by the use of traditional methods, subject to laws or regulations to conserve and manage wildlife and preserve the future of hunting and fishing.

(b) Hunting and fishing are preferred methods of managing and controlling wildlife.

(c) This section does not affect any provision of law relating to trespass, property rights, or eminent domain.

(d) This section does not affect the power of the legislature to authorize a municipality to regulate the discharge of a weapon in a populated area in the interest of public safety.

(Added Nov. 3, 2015.)

Endnotes

CHAPTER 1

1. Alan Rosenthal, "On Analyzing States," in *The Political Life of the American States*, ed. Alan Rosenthal and Maureen Moakley (New York: Praeger, 1984), 11–12.

2. Daniel Elazar, *American Federalism: A View from the States*, 2nd ed. (New York: Crowell, 1971), 84–126. See also John Kincaid, "Introduction," in *Political Culture, Public Policy and the American States*, ed. John Kincaid (Philadelphia: Center for the Study of Federalism, Institute for the Study of Human Issues, 1982), 1–24.

3. Rosenthal, "On Analyzing States," 13.

4. An excellent discussion of the problem of characterizing Texas political culture is found in Chandler Davidson, *Race and Class in Texas Politics* (Princeton, NJ: Princeton University Press, 1990), chap. 2.

5. Texas General Land Office, *History of Texas Public Lands*, pp. 9–17. Austin: Texas General Land Office, revised January 2015.

6. The following is drawn from Texas State Historical Association, *Texas Almanac 2014–2015* (Denton: Texas State Historical Association, 2014), 78–84.

7. See Joseph A. Schumpeter, *Capitalism, Socialism, and Democracy*, 3rd ed. (New York: Harper & Brothers, 1950), chap. 6. For a discussion of the relationship between long-term economic transformation and political change at the national level, see Brian J. L. Berry, Euel Elliott, Edward J. Harpham, and Heja Kim, *The Rhythms of American Politics* (Lanham, MD: University Press of America, 1998).

8. The following is drawn from Karen Gerhardt Britton, Fred C. Elliott, and E. A. Miller, "Cotton Culture," *Handbook of Texas Online*.

9. See Cecil Harper, Jr., and E. Dale Odum, "Farm Tenancy," *Handbook of Texas Online*.

10. See Harper and Odum, "Farm Tenancy"; Texas State Historical Association, *Texas Almanac 2014–2015*, 687.

11. See T. C. Richardson and Harwood P. Hinton, "Ranching," *Handbook of Texas Online*.

12. Texas State Historical Association, *Texas Almanac Online*, "Principal Crops of Texas"; Texas State Historical Association, *Texas Almanac 2014–2015*, 687–88; Southern Plains Regional Office, U.S. Department of Agriculture, National Agriculture Statistics Service, "Texas Cotton Production," Issue No. PR-123-14 (Austin: May 2014).

13. Texas State Historical Association, *Texas Almanac 2014–2015*, 683–84.

14. The following is drawn from Mary G. Ramos, "Oil and Texas: A Cultural History," Dallas Morning News, *Texas Almanac 2000–2001*, 29–35; Roger M. Olien, "Oil and Gas Industry," *Handbook of Texas Online*.

15. Ramos, "Oil and Texas," 31.

16. Olien, "Oil and Gas Industry."

17. See Texas Legislative Budget Board, *Fiscal Size-Up: 2016–17 Biennium* (May 2016), p. 33.

18. Permanent University Fund, "Report on Certain Specified Data as Required by Art. 4413 (34e) of the Civil Statutes" (December 31, 2015), p. 1.

19. Simone Sebastian, "New Data Show 'Meteoric' Rise of Texas Oil," fuelfix.com, December 3, 2013. See James Osborne, "Texas Oil Production Hits 2 Million Barrels a Day, the Most since 1986," *Dallas Morning News*, April 25, 2014. See Texas Railroad Commission, Texas Permian Basin Oil Production 2008 through March 2016. For a more detailed discussion of the new technology of fracking and its impact on the oil boom in Texas and the United States, see Russell Gold, *The Boom: How Fracking Ignited the American Energy Revolution and Changed the World* (New York: Simon & Schuster, 2014).

20. Texas State Historical Association, *Texas Almanac On Line*, "Petroleum Production and Income in Texas." See also BBC News, "Oil Hits $50 a Barrel for the First Time This Year" (May 26, 2016).

21. See Texas Governor, *Manufacturing in Texas* (2013), "Texas Gross State Product Detail—Calendar Years 1990–2040."

22. TechAmerica Foundation, *Tech Trade in the States: A State-by-State Overview of International Trade in Tech Goods* (2014); Texas State Historical Association, *Texas Almanac 2014–15*, 586.

23. Texas Center for Border Economic and Enterprise Development, texascenter.tamiv.edu.

24. Standard and Poor's, "Twenty Years into NAFTA, Mexico and Texas Have Been the Two Main Beneficiaries of Increased Trade" (January 17, 2014).

25. See Robert E. Scott, "NAFTA's Legacy: Growing U.S. Trade Deficits Cost 682,900 Jobs," Economic Policy Institute (December 13, 2013). See also Anil Kumar, "Did NAFTA Spur Texas Exports?" *Southwest Economy* 2 (March–April 2006); U.S. Department of Labor Employment and Training Administration, "Trade Adjustment Assistance: Number of Certified Workers by State"; Robert E. Scott, "Heading South: U.S.-Mexico Trade and Job Displacement after NAFTA," Economic Policy Institute (May 3, 2011).

26. U.S. Census Bureau, "State Exports for Texas 2013" and "State Imports for Texas 2013." See also Texas Economy Online Report from the Office of the Governor, "Overview of the Texas Economy" (June 2014).

27. Daniel Gross, "Lone Star: Why Texas Is Doing So Much Better than the Rest of the Nation," Slate, April 19, 2010.

28. Texas Comptroller of Public Accounts, "Comptroller's Weekly Economic Outlook," *The Texas Economy, Economic Outlook* (May 21, 2014).

29. See Erica Grieder, *Big, Hot, Cheap, and Right: What America Can Learn from the Strange Genius of Texas* (New York: Public Affairs, 2013). Some have argued that Texas characteristics cannot be duplicated by other states. See, for example, Elizabeth McNichol and Nicholas Johnson, "The Texas Economic Model: Hard for Other States to Follow and Not All It Seems," Center for Budget and Economic Priorities (April 3, 2012).

30. Bruce Wright, "Weathering the Storm," *Fiscal Notes*, April 2009; D'Ann Petersen and Laila Assanie, "Texas Dodges Worst of Foreclosure Wars," Federal Reserve of Dallas (Dallas, 2009).

31. See Texas State Library and Archives Commission, "United States and Texas Populations 1850–2012."

32. See census data analysis on www.governing.com, Governing Data, "State Population Estimates: 2013 Births, Deaths, Migration Totals."

33. See Arnoldo De León, "Mexican Americans," *Handbook of Texas Online*.

34. See U.S. Census Bureau, "State & County QuickFacts"; U.S. Census Bureau, 2010 Census; Sharon R. Ennis, Merarys Rios-Vargas, and Nora G. Albert, "The Hispanic Population: 2010," *2010 Census Briefs* (May 2011); Texas State Historical Association, *Texas Almanac 2014–2015*, 15.

35. See National Association of Latino Elected and Appointed Officials (NALEO), "2014 Latino Primary Profile: Texas," NALEO Educational Fund (2014).

36. See W. Marvin Dulaney, "African Americans," *Handbook of Texas Online*; Chandler Davidson, "African Americans and Politics," *Handbook of Texas Online*.

37. See U.S. Census Bureau, "The Asian Population," 2010 Census Briefs.

38. See Texas State Historical Association, *Texas Almanac 2014–2015* for county-by-county data. The Asian population of Texas counties can be found at www.indexmundi.com.

39. U.S. Census Bureau, "Texas."

40. Bruce H. Webster, Jr., and Alemayehu Bishaw, "Income, Earnings, and Poverty Data from the 2006 American Community Survey," American Community Survey Reports, U.S. Census Bureau (August 2007); U.S. Census Bureau, Poverty 2007 and 2008 American Community Surveys (September 2009); U.S. Census Bureau, *Texas QuickFacts: 2009*; Alemayehu Bishaw, "Poverty: 2000–2012," U.S. Census Bureau, American Community Survey Briefs (September 2013).

41. The definition used to measure the urban/rural dichotomy has shifted over time. For a more detailed discussion, see U.S. Census Bureau, "2012 Census Urban Area FAQs."

42. The following is based on David G. McComb, "Urbanization," *Handbook of Texas Online*.

43. The following is drawn from David G. McComb, "Houston, Texas," *Handbook of Texas Online*.

44. Estimates are drawn from the U.S. Census Bureau, "State & County QuickFacts."

45. The following is drawn from Jackie McElhaney and Michael V. Hazel, "Dallas, Texas," *Handbook of Texas Online*.

46. The following is drawn from Janet Schmelzer, "Fort Worth, Texas," *Handbook of Texas Online*.

47. The following is drawn from T. R. Fehrenbach, "San Antonio, Texas," *Handbook of Texas Online*.

48. Estimates are drawn from the U.S. Census Bureau, "State & County QuickFacts."

CHAPTER 2

1. The following is drawn from Proposition 10, Deleting Constitutional References to County Office of Inspector of Hides and Animals; Eric Aasen, "Round 'Em Up: Hide Inspectors Abolished," *Dallas Morning News*, November 8, 2007; John Council, "Richmond Lawyer Has Personal Stake in Hide Inspector Position," *Texas Lawyer*, November 2, 2007; Mark Lisheron, "Prop. 10 Would Abolish Office That No One Holds," *Austin American-Statesman*, October 15, 2007.
2. See Dick Smith, "Inspector of Hides and Animals," *Handbook of Texas Online*.
3. Donald E. Chipman, "Spanish Texas," *Handbook of Texas Online*; Donald E. Chipman, *Spanish Texas, 1519–1821* (Austin: University of Texas Press, 1992).
4. S. S. McKay, "Constitution of 1824," *Handbook of Texas Online*.
5. S. S. McKay, "Constitution of Coahuila and Texas," *Handbook of Texas Online*.
6. See Ralph W. Steen, "Convention of 1836," *Handbook of Texas Online*.
7. The following is drawn from Joe E. Ericson, "Constitution of the Republic of Texas," *Handbook of Texas Online*.
8. Randolph B. Campbell, "Slavery," *Handbook of Texas Online*.
9. For a brief summary of the war, see Eugene C. Barker and James W. Pohl, "Texas Revolution," *Handbook of Texas Online*.
10. S. S. McKay, "Constitution of 1845," *Handbook of Texas Online*.
11. The Texas Ordinance of Secession (February 2, 1861).
12. See Walter L. Buenger, "Secession Convention," *Handbook of Texas Online*; Walter L. Buenger, *Secession and the Union in Texas* (Austin: University of Texas Press, 1984).
13. See Claude Elliott, "Constitutional Convention of 1866," *Handbook of Texas Online*; S. McKay, "Constitution of 1866," *Handbook of Texas Online*; Charles W. Ramsdell, *Reconstruction in Texas* (New York: Columbia University Press, 1970).
14. See S. S. McKay, "Constitution of 1869," *Handbook of Texas Online*; Ramsdell, *Reconstruction in Texas*.
15. See John Walker Mauer, "Constitution Proposed in 1874," *Handbook of Texas Online*; John Walker Mauer, "State Constitutions in a Time of Crisis: The Case of the Texas Constitution of 1876," 68 *Texas Law Review* 1615–46 (June 1990).
16. Texas Legislative Council, *Amendments to the Texas Constitution since 1876* (Austin: March 1912).
17. For a further discussion, see George D. Braden et al., *The Constitution of the State of Texas: An Annotated and Comparative Analysis* (Austin: University of Texas Press, 1977), 707–10.
18. See Sam Kinch, Jr., "Sharpstown Stock-Fraud Scandal," *Handbook of Texas Online*; Charles Deaton, *The Year They Threw the Rascals Out* (Austin: Shoal Creek, 1973).
19. CBSDFW.com, "Texas Voters Approve 7 Constitutional Amendments," November 9, 2011.

CHAPTER 3

1. "Rick Perry: Restore the 10th Amendment, Restore Freedom," Frontpage Mag, December 18, 2014, www.frontpagemag.com/fpm/247758/rick-perry-restore-10th-amendment-restore-freedom-frontpagemagcom.
2. Greg Abbott, "Restoring the Rule of Law with States Leading the Way," January 8, 2016, static.texastribune.org/media/documents/Restoring_The_Rule_Of_Law_01082016.pdf.
3. Edgar Walters, "Abbott Calls on States to Amend U.S. Constitution," *Texas Tribune*, January 8, 2016.
4. This discussion is taken from David Brian Robertson, *Federalism and the Making of America* (New York: Routledge, 2012), 1–3.
5. Robertson, *Federalism and the Making of America*, 20–21.
6. Robertson, *Federalism and the Making of America*, 20–22.
7. Robertson, *Federalism and the Making of America*, 27.
8. Robertson, *Federalism and the Making of America*, 29–30.
9. Robertson, *Federalism and the Making of America*, 31.
10. *McCulloch v. Maryland*, 17 U.S. 316 (1819).
11. *Gibbons v. Ogden*, 22 U.S. 1, 2 (1824).
12. *Gibbons v. Ogden*, 22 U.S. 1, 2 (1824).
13. Robert F. Nagel, *The Implosion of American Federalism* (New York: Oxford University Press, 2001), 5.
14. *Texas v. White*, 74 U.S. 700 (1869).
15. Morton Grodzins, *The American System*, ed. Daniel J. Elazar (Chicago: Rand McNally, 1966).
16. Equal Justice Initiative, "Lynching in America: Confronting the Legacy of Racial Terror," 2015, www.eji.org/files/EJI%20Lynching%20in%20America%20SUMMARY.pdf.

17. *Wickard v. Filburn*, 317 U.S. 111 (1942).
18. "Getting Stuck with the Check," *Bloomberg Businessweek*, www.businessweek.com/stories/1994-05-29/getting-stuck-with-the-check (accessed 3/24/14).
19. Sean Loughlin, "Local Government Fighting Unfunded Federal Mandates," *Herald-Journal*, November 6, 1993.
20. Loughlin, "Local Government Fighting Unfunded Federal Mandates."
21. "State Officials Warn White House against Enforcing New Gun Regulations," FoxNews.com, January 15, 2013, www.foxnews.com/politics/2013/01/15/ore-sheriff-says-wont-enforce-new-gun-laws/ (accessed 3/24/14).
22. Greg Abbott, "Lawsuits against Obama Are Taxpayer Bargain," dallasnews.com, September 25, 2012, www.dallasnews.com/opinion/latest-columns/20120925-greg-abbott-lawsuits-against-obama-are-taxpayer-bargain.ece (accessed 3/24/14).
23. *Printz v. United States*, 521 U.S. 898, 935 (1997).
24. *McDonald v. Chicago*, 561 U.S. 742 (2010).
25. *Sweatt v. Painter*, 339 U.S. 629 (1950).
26. *Brown v. Board of Education of Topeka*, 347 U.S. 483 (1954).
27. *Shelby County, Ala. v. Holder*, Brief of the State of Texas as amicus curiae in support of Petitioner, Supreme Court of the United States (2013), p. 4.
28. *Shelby County, Ala. v. Holder*, Brief of the State of Texas, p. 2.
29. *Shelby County, Ala. v. Holder*, 2013 WL 3184629 (2013).
30. *Veasey v. Abbott*, 796 F.3d 487 (2015).
31. Jill D. Weinberg, "Remaking Lawrence," 98 *Virginia Law Review in Brief* 61, 66 (2012).
32. *San Antonio v. Rodriguez*, 411 U.S. 1 (1973).
33. *Edgewood Independent School District v. Kirby*, 777 S.W.2d 391, 398 (Tex., 1989).
34. Neena Satya, Ryan McCrimmon, and Becca Aaronson, "Texas v. the Feds: A Look at the Lawsuits," *Texas Tribune*, July 31, 2015; Texas Attorney General website, "About Attorney General Ken Paxton," www.texasattorneygeneral.gov/agency/about-texas-attorney-general-ken-paxton (accessed 3/10/16).
35. *United States v. Texas*, 579 U.S.   (2016).
36. Robert Barnes and Juliet Eilperin, "Clash on Immigration Heads to High Court," *Dallas Morning News*, January 20, 2016, pp. 1A, 6A; Amy Howe, "Court Will Review Obama Administration's Immigration Policy: In Plain English," SCOTUSblog, January 19, 2016, www.scotusblog.com/2016/01/court-will-review-obama-administrations-immigration-policy-in-plain-english/.
37. *Evenwel v. Perry*, Western District of Texas, A-14-CV-335-LY-CH-MHS, November 5, 2014; *Evenwel v. Abbott*, Brief for Appellants before the Supreme Court of the United States, #14-940, July 31, 2015.
38. Zachary Roth, "SCOTUS to Hear Case That Could Set Back Latino Voting Power," MSNBC, May 27, 2015, www.msnbc.com/msnbc/scotus-hear-case-could-set-back-latino-voting-power (accessed 3/29/16).

CHAPTER 4

1. Jeffrey M. Jones, "Special Report: Many States Shift Democratic during 2005," Gallup, January 23, 2006, www.gallup.com.
2. Use of party affiliation as an ideological cue is discussed in Philip L. Dubois, *From Ballot to Bench* (Austin: University of Texas Press, 1980).
3. University of Texas/*Texas Tribune*, "Texas Statewide Survey," May 7–13, 2012.
4. University of Texas/*Texas Tribune*, "Texas Statewide Survey," February 15–24, 2013.
5. University of Texas/*Texas Tribune*, "Texas Statewide Survey," 2012.
6. Quoted in Chandler Davidson, *Race and Class in Texas Politics* (Princeton, NJ: Princeton University Press, 1990), 198.
7. Davidson, *Race and Class in Texas Politics*, 24–25.
8. Jones, "Special Report: Many States Shift Democratic during 2005."
9. Jeffrey M. Jones, "Red States Outnumber Blue States for First Time in Gallup Tracking," Gallup, February 3, 2016, www.gallup.com.
10. James R. Soukup, Clifton McClesky, and Harry Holloway, *Party and Factional Division in Texas* (Austin: University of Texas Press, 1964), 22.
11. Mark P. Jones, "Guest Column: The 2013 Texas House from Right to Left," *Texas Tribune*, October 15, 2013.
12. Robert T. Garrett, "2 Major GOP Donors Show Rift in Party," *Dallas Morning News*, February 3, 2006, p. 2A.
13. Robert T. Garrett, "PAC's Late Aid Altered Races," *Dallas Morning News*, March 10, 2006, pp. 1A, 16A.
14. Dante Chinni and James Gimpel, *Our Patchwork Nation: The Surprising Truth about the "Real" America* (New York: Gotham, 2011).
15. Terri Langford, "District Judge Fends off Democratic Rival's Challenge," *Dallas Morning News*, November 9, 2000, p. 36A.

16. Anthony Champagne and Greg Thielemann, "Awareness of Trial Court Judges," *Judicature* 75 (1991): 271–72.

17. Anthony Champagne, "The Selection and Retention of Judges in Texas," 40 *Southwestern Law Journal* 80 (1986).

18. The lone Democratic survivor, Ron Chapman, became an appellate judge. Democratic judges who did not switch to the Republican Party were defeated.

19. Langford, "District Judge Fends off Democratic Rival's Challenge."

20. David Koenig, "Democrats' Dream Team Falters," *Laredo Morning Times*, November 10, 2002, pp. 1A, 19A.

21. Joe Holley, "Texas Dems Still Waiting for Latino Surge," chron.com, April 4, 2010.

22. In 1994 it was estimated that there were between 420,000 and 460,000 illegal immigrants in Texas. Many of those illegal immigrants were Hispanic. See Leon F. Bouvier and John L. Martin, "Shaping Texas: The Effects of Immigration, 1970–2020," Center for Immigration Studies, April 1995. The Federation for American Immigration Reform cites the Immigration and Naturalization Service for a January 2000 estimate that there were 1,041,000 illegal immigrants then in Texas. See its report, "Texas: Illegal Aliens." An April 2006 study by the Pew Hispanic Center estimated that between 1.4 and 1.6 million unauthorized individuals were living in Texas. Pew Hispanic Center, "Estimates of the Unauthorized Migrant Population for States Based on the March 2006 CPS, Fact Sheet: April 26, 2006." Jeff Salamon reports 10.8 million undocumented immigrants in the United States and 1.68 million in Texas. Jeff Salamon, "Everything You Ever Wanted to Know about Illegal Immigration (But Didn't Know Who to Ask)," *Texas Monthly*, November 2010.

23. Pew Research Hispanic Trends Project, "Latinos in the 2012 Election: Texas," October 1, 2012. See also U.S. Census Bureau, "The Diversifying Electorate—Voting Rates by Race and Hispanic Origin in 2012 (and Other Recent Elections)," May 2013.

YOU DECIDE: SHOULD THE TEA PARTY MOVEMENT LAUNCH A THIRD PARTY?

a. Ross Ramsey, "Smaller Parties Refuse to Be Counted Out," *New York Times*, April 6, 2012, p. A19.

CHAPTER 5

1. Wayne Slater, "Strayhorn Gets Democratic Cash," *Dallas Morning News*, January 26, 2006, pp. 1A, 17A.

2. Pete Slover, "Independents' Day Is a Bid for the Ballot," *Dallas Morning News*, March 8, 2006, p. 14A.

3. Sam Acheson, *Joe Bailey: The Last Democrat* (New York: Macmillan, 1932), 354.

4. Joe Robert Baulch, "James B. Wells: State Economic and Political Leader" (Ph.D. diss., Texas Tech University, 1974), 358–59.

5. Sue Tolleson-Rinehart and Jeanie R. Stanley, *Claytie and the Lady: Ann Richards, Gender, and Politics in Texas* (Austin: University of Texas Press, 1994), 18–19.

6. O. Douglas Weeks, "The Texas-Mexican and the Politics of South Texas," *American Political Science Review* 224 (1930): 625–26; Anthony Champagne, "John Nance Garner," in *Masters of the House*, ed. Roger H. Davidson, Susan Webb Hammond, and Raymond W. Smock (Boulder, CO: Westview, 1998), 145–80.

7. *United States v. Texas*, 384 U.S. 155 (1966).

8. *Beare v. Smith*, 321 F. Supp. 1100 (1971).

9. *Kramer v. Union Free School District No. 15*, 395 U.S. 621 (1969); *Hill v. Stone*, 421 U.S. 289 (1975).

10. *Dunn v. Blumstein*, 405 U.S. 330 (1972).

11. *Newberry v. United States*, 256 U.S. 232 (1921).

12. *Nixon v. Herndon*, 273 U.S. 536 (1927).

13. *Nixon v. Condon*, 286 U.S. 73 (1932).

14. *Grovey v. Townsend*, 295 U.S. 45 (1935).

15. *Smith v. Allwright*, 321 U.S. 649 (1944).

16. *Terry v. Adams*, 345 U.S. 461 (1953).

17. Gary Scharrer, "Holder Issues Challenge to Texas on Voter Rights," chron.com, December 13, 2011.

18. National Conference of State Legislatures, "Voter Identification Requirements," April 30, 2014.

19. Texas Secretary of State, "Turnout and Voter Registration Figures, 1970–Current."

20. The motor voter law is a federal statute that requires states to allow voter registration when individuals apply for or renew their driver's licenses.

21. See U.S. Census Bureau, "Voting and Registration in the Election of November 2012—Detailed Tables," and Texas Secretary of State, "Turnout and Voter Registration Figures, 1970–Current." It is important to recognize how easily different studies can produce different registration rates or voting rates for different racial and ethnic groups. The Texas secretary of state's office uses hard data on the number of registered voters and divides by an agreed-upon number of people in the voting-age population given by state and federal demographers. But the secretary of state's office has no information on how people from different racial and ethnic groups actually

voted. The statistics cited here were based upon a survey done after the election asking individuals to self-identify their race or ethnicity, whether or not they were registered to vote, and if they voted. Registration rates and voting rates were built up from the survey rather than being based on hard data provided by outside authorities. Different methodological approaches to the same question can lead to different numbers without any of the numbers being "wrong."

22. University of Texas/*Texas Tribune*, "Texas Statewide Survey," February 2013.

23. University of Texas/*Texas Tribune*, "Texas Statewide Survey," May 11–18, 2011.

24. Thomas R. Patterson, *The American Democracy* (New York: McGraw-Hill, 1999), 188.

25. Kevin Diaz, "Texas Latino Vote Splits," *Houston Chronicle*, November 6, 2014.

26. Julian Aguilar, "Abbott Defends Corruption Remarks, Border Security Plan," *Texas Tribune*, February 10, 2014; Jens Manuel Krogstad and Mark Hugo Lopez, "Hispanic Voters in the 2014 Election," Pew Research Hispanic Trends Project, November 7, 2014.

27. Candidates in Texas Supreme Court races are affected by "friends and neighbors" voting, whereby voters tend to cast ballots for candidates from their home county or from neighboring counties. See Gregory Thielemann, "Local Advantage in Campaign Financing: Friends, Neighbors, and Their Money in Texas Supreme Court Elections," *Journal of Politics* 55 (1993): 472–78.

28. Roy A. Schotland, "Campaign Finance in Judicial Elections," 34 *Loyola of Los Angeles Law Review* 1508–12 (2001).

29. Alexa Ura, "Davis Renews Equal Pay Attack on Abbott," *Texas Tribune*, March 24, 2014.

30. Donald R. Kinder and Lynn M. Sanders, *Divided by Color: Racial Politics and Democratic Ideals* (Chicago: University of Chicago Press, 1996).

31. University of Texas/*Texas Tribune*, "Texas Statewide Survey," February 1–7, 2010.

32. University of Texas/*Texas Tribune*, "Texas Statewide Survey," June 11–22, 2009.

33. University of Texas/*Texas Tribune*, "Texas Statewide Survey," May 14–20, 2010.

34. University of Texas/*Texas Tribune*, "Texas Statewide Survey," May 14–20, 2010.

YOU DECIDE: VOTER IDENTIFICATION LAWS

a. Alexandra Jaffe, "GOP Hits Back at Hillary Clinton on Voting Rights," CNN.com, June 5, 2015.

b. Alyssa Dizon, "Passage of Voter ID Bill Stirs Strong Reaction, Pro and Con," *Lubbock Avalanche-Journal*, May 17, 2011.

CHAPTER 6

1. The above is drawn from Jeffrey Weiss, "How Texas' Testing Bubble Popped," *Dallas Morning News*, March 30, 2014; Jeffrey Weiss, "Looking into the 'Heart of the Vampire,'" *Dallas Morning News*, March 31, 2014; Jeffrey Weiss, "Testing System Shaken to Its Core," *Dallas Morning News*, April 1, 2014; Dax Gonzalez, "Finding the Funding," *Texas Lone Star*, August 2013; see also www.TAMSATX.org.

2. Mancur Olson, *The Logic of Collective Action: Public Goods and the Theory of Groups*, Harvard Economic Studies (Cambridge, MA: Harvard University Press, 1971).

3. James W. Lamare, *Texas Politics: Economics, Power and Policy*, 3rd ed. (St. Paul, MN: West, 1988), 82. See George Norris Green, *The Establishment in Texas Politics: The Primitive Years, 1938–1957* (Norman: University of Oklahoma Press, 1984).

4. Morgan Smith, "Texas Advocacy Group Wields Charter Policy Power," *New York Times*, May 5, 2013.

5. Smith, "Texas Advocacy Group."

6. Texans for Public Justice, "Power Surge: TXU's Patronage Grid Plugs All but Seven Lawmakers," *Lobby Watch*, March 1, 2007.

7. Matt Stiles, "Lobbyist Gives 'Shocking' Gift to Lawmaker," *Texas Tribune*, February 15, 2010.

8. David Rauf, "Lavish Gifts a Perk for Attorney General Greg Abbott," *San Antonio Express News*, 2014.

9. R. G. Ratcliffe, "The Lobby: $1.8 Million Feeding the Legislature," *Texas Monthly*, May 20, 2015.

10. Emily Ramshaw and Marcus Funk, "For Some Dallas-Area Legislators, Donations Fund the Good Life," *Dallas Morning News*, February 1, 2009.

11. Texans for Public Justice, "Special Interests Paid Lobbyists Up to $328 Million in 2013 Session," p. 1.

12. Texans for Public Justice, "Special Interests Paid Lobbyists."

13. Texans for Public Justice, "Special Interests Paid Lobbyists."

14. Texans for Public Justice, "Special Interests Paid Lobbyists."

15. Andy Pierrotti, "Lobbyist's Lavish Party," Kvue.com, February 21, 2013.

16. Texans for Public Justice, "Special Interests Paid Lobbyists," p. 3.

17. Ross Ramsey, "Legislature Is a Training Ground for Lobbyists," *Texas Tribune*, June 10, 2010.

18. Ramsey, "Legislature Is a Training Ground."

19. Texans for Public Justice, "Ten New Lawmaker Retreads Merge into the 2009 Lobby," *Lobby Watch*, May 20, 2009.

20. Texans for Public Justice, "12 Republicans Flip from Legislature to the Lobby," *Lobby Watch*, April 23, 2013.

21. "Rick Perry's Former Staffers Made Millions as Lobbyists," *Huffington Post*, December 19, 2011.

22. "Rick Perry's Former Staffers."

23. Ramsey, "Legislature Is a Training Ground."

24. Texans for Public Justice, "Texas Revolvers: Public Officials Recast as Hired Guns," *Lobby Watch*, February 5, 1999.

25. Tim Eaton, "Greg Abbott looks to 2017 for Ethics Reform," *Austin American Statesman*, June 22, 2015; W. Gardner Selby, "Greg Abbott Strikes Out on His Ethics Campaign Promises," Austin American Statesman Politifact, July 5, 2015.

26. Ed Payne, "Crystal City: All but One Member of City Council Indicted on Corruption Charges," CNN.com, February 5, 2016.

27. Texans for Public Justice, "Special-Interests Spend Up to $180 Million on Lobby Services in 1999 Legislative Session," May 24, 1999.

28. Texans for Public Justice, "Texas PACs: 2014 Election Cycle Spending, Texans for Public Justice."

29. Anthony Champagne, "Campaign Contributions in Texas Supreme Court Races," *Crime, Law and Social Change* 17 (1992): 91–106.

30. Texans for Public Justice, "Texans for Lawsuit Reform Sustains Pricey Primary Hits," *Lobby Watch*, March 5, 2010; Julian Aguilar, "Primary Color: HD-43," *Texas Tribune*, February 26, 2010.

31. Dick Weekley, "A Good Night for Lawsuit Reform in Texas," Texans for Lawsuit Reform PAC.

32. National Institute on Money in State Politics.

33. Kristen Mack, "New Lawmakers Learn to Juggle Hectic Lives; Everybody—Lobbyists, Family—Wants a Moment of Their Time," *Houston Chronicle*, February 6, 2005, p. 1B.

34. Texans for Public Justice, "Texans for Lawsuit Reform."

35. Jason Embry, "Most Powerful Group in Texas Politics Has Wentworth in Its Sights" *Austin American Statesman*, December 7, 2011; John W. Gonzalez, "Campbell Upsets Wentworth for Texas Senate," *San Antonio Express-News*, August 1, 2012.

36. Texans for Public Justice, "Operation Vouchsafe: Dr. Leininger Injects $5 Million into Election; Many Candidates Fail on His Life Support," *Lobby Watch*, n.d.

37. Texans for Public Justice, "Texas PACs: 2012 Election Cycle Spending" (2013), p. 20.

38. Sunset Advisory Commission Staff Report, "Railroad Commission of Texas," November 2012, p. 12.

39. Public Citizen, "Drilling for Dollars: How Big Money Has a Big Influence at the Railroad Commission" (December 2010).

40. Public Citizen, "Drilling for Dollars," p. 4.

41. National Institute on Money in Politics data.

42. Jim Malewitz, "GOP Railroad Commission Hopefuls Split Donations," *Texas Tribune*, February 8, 2016.

43. Sunset Advisory Commission, "Railroad Commission of Texas," p. 2.

44. Brett Shipp, "Attempt to Overhaul Texas Railroad Commission Fails, Again," WFAA.com, May 31, 2013.

45. Emily Ramshaw, "Fighting for Fair Warning—Man Who Lost Wife, Kids in Blaze Seeks Visual Smoke Alarms for Deaf," *Dallas Morning News*, April 17, 2009; "Tragedy Leads to Improved Fire Safety in Texas," National Association of the Deaf, July 1, 2009.

46. Regina Lawrence, Deborah Wise, and Emily Einsohn, *Texas Civic Health Index* (Austin: Annette Strauss Institute for Civic Life, 2013), 5–14.

47. Lawrence, Wise, and Einsohn, *Texas Civic Health Index*, 22.

YOU DECIDE: SHOULD FORMER LEGISLATORS BE LOBBYISTS?

a. Kelley Shannon, "Former Legislators Kicking Off New Careers as Texas Lobbyists." *Dallas Morning News*, March 7, 2013.

b. Ross Ramsey, "Legislature Is a Training Ground for Lobbyists," *Texas Tribune*, June 10, 2010.

c. Randy Lee Loftis, "State of Neglect: Revolving Door Lets Lawmakers Profit from Capitol Floor Time," *Dallas Morning News*, January 6, 2009.

CHAPTER 7

1. "Senate Gives Tentative OK to Guns on Campuses," *Dallas Morning News*, May 20, 2009.

2. "Texas Bill to Allow Guns on Campus Rejected for Violating Constitutional Requirement," *Security Director News*, June 7, 2011.

3. "Texas Legislature Passes Record Number of Pro-Gun Bills but Key Items Remain as 'Unfinished Business,'" NRA-ILA, June 5, 2013.

4. Ann Marie Kilday, "Equal Measure," *Dallas Morning News*, May 24, 2001, p. 31A.

5. Texas Legislature, "Legislative Statistics," July 10, 2013.

6. Anthony Champagne and Rick Collis, "Texas," in *The Political Life of the American States*, ed. Alan Rosenthal and Maureen Moakley (New York: Praeger, 1984), 138.

7. Ross Ramsey, "Will Texas Lawmakers Cut Their Own Benefits?" *Texas Tribune*, March 11, 2011.

8. Ramsey, "Will Texas Lawmakers Cut."

9. "State Rep. Joe Driver of Garland Double-Billed for Travel," *Dallas Morning News*, August 16, 2010; "Garland Republican Joe Driver Pleads Guilty to Double-Dipping on Travel Reimbursements," *Dallas Morning News*, November 22, 2011.

10. Christy Hoppe, "At Home, Collecting Expense Pay," *Dallas Morning News*, June 19, 2013, pp. 1, 2A.

11. LegiScan, "Texas Legislature, 2015–2016, 84th Legislature, in Recess," legiscan.com.

12. Kelley Shannon, "Doctor Twice Honored by the Texas Legislature Registered as Sex Offender," *Sulphur Springs News-Telegram*, June 22, 2007, p. 1.

13. Frank M. Stewart, "Impeachment in Texas," *American Political Science Review* 24, no. 3 (August 1930): 652–58; George D. Braden et al., *The Constitution of the State of Texas: An Annotated and Comparative Analysis* (Austin: University of Texas Press, 1977), 707–18.

14. Karen Brooks, "Craddick's Win May Cost Him," *Dallas Morning News*, May 27, 2007, p. 1.

15. Karen Brooks, "In 1877, Lawmakers Ran Republican Out of the Chair," *Dallas Morning News*, May 27, 2007, p. 26A.

16. Terrence Stutz, "Texas Senate at Odds over Voter ID Legislation, Two-Thirds Rule," *Dallas Morning News*, January 14, 2009.

17. Joe Straus, letter to Sachi Dave, March 12, 2014.

18. Joe Straus, letter to Sachi Dave, March 12, 2014.

19. Mark P. Jones, "Guest Column: The 2013 Texas House, from Right to Left," *Texas Tribune*, October 15, 2013.

20. Paul Burka, "Partisanship Ranking: The Texas Tribune List," *Texas Monthly*, July 17, 2010.

21. Mark Jones, "Guest Column: The 2013 Texas House, from Right to Left," *Texas Tribune*, October 15, 2013.

22. Mark Jones, "Guest Column: The 2013 Texas Senate, from Left to Right," *Texas Tribune*, November 26, 2013.

23. Paul Starr, *Remedy and Reaction: The Peculiar American Struggle over Health Care Reform*, rev. ed. (New Haven, CT: Yale University Press, 2013), 162–63.

24. *Baker v. Carr*, 369 U.S. 186 (1962); *Reynolds v. Sims*, 377 U.S. 533 (1964).

25. *Wesberry v. Sanders*, 376 U.S. 1 (1964).

26. Sam Attlesey, "Panel OKs Map Favoring GOP," *Dallas Morning News*, December 7, 2001.

27. The preceding is drawn from Sam Attlesey, "Taking Stock of the Fallout from Redistricting," *Dallas Morning News*, December 11, 2001; Terrance Stutz, "GOP Expecting to Grab the House," *Dallas Morning News*, January 3, 2002; Sam Attlesey, "Before Election, House Democrats Seeing Losses," *Dallas Morning News*, December 11, 2001.

28. Medill School of Journalism, "On the Docket: *League of United Latin American Citizens, Travis County, Jackson, Eddie and GI Forum of Texas v. Perry, Rick (Texas Gov.)*."

29. *LULAC v. Perry*, 548 U.S. 399 (2006), Appellants' Brief.

30. Medill School of Journalism, "On the Docket."

31. *LULAC v. Perry*, Appellants' Brief.

32. See, generally, Steve Bickerstaff, *Lines in the Sand: Congressional Redistricting in Texas and the Downfall of Tom DeLay* (Austin: University of Texas Press, 2007).

33. "Texas Redistricting Battle Headed Back to Federal Courts," *Lubbock Avalanche-Journal*, June 21, 2013.

YOU DECIDE: A FULL-TIME OR PART-TIME LEGISLATURE?

a. http://triblive.com/x/pittsburghtrib/news/regional/s_504876.html.

b. www.yourhoustonnews.com./archives/with-government-you-get-what-you-pay-for/article_ec96830b-897c-5952-b868-ca1894dd47e9.html.

CHAPTER 8

1. Ross Ramsey, "A Weak Governor System, with a Strong Governor," *Texas Tribune*, July 8, 2013.

2. Brian McCall, *The Power of the Texas Governor: Connally to Bush* (Austin: University of Texas Press, 2009).

3. Bruce Tomaso, "Adios to Memorable Moments, Achievements," *Dallas Morning News*, July 9, 2013, p. 9A.

4. Greg Abbott, "Gov. Greg Abbott: Counting Successes from the Legislative Session," *Dallas Morning News*, June 4, 2015.

5. Politifact Texas, "Tracking the Promises of Greg Abbott."

6. Abbott is quoted in Erica Ritz, "Greg Abbott Warns Feds: 'They Picked on the Wrong State When They

Came to . . . Texas to Try to Take Our Property,'" *The Blaze*, April 28, 2014; Brandi Grissom, "Abbott's Play for National Audience Draws Questions about Higher-Office Plans," *Dallas Morning News*, January 26, 2016.

7. See the superb master's thesis by Tyler Lang Reisinger, "Beyond Beyle: Assessing the Measurements of Institutional and Informal Gubernatorial Powers" (M.A. thesis in Political Science, Virginia Polytechnic Institute and State University, 2008). See also Thad Beyle and Margaret Ferguson, "Governors and the Executive Branch," in *Politics in the American States*, ed. Virginia Gray and Russell L. Hanson (Washington, DC: CQ Press, 2008), 192–228.

8. Council of State Governments, *The Book of the States 2015*.

9. McCall, *Power of the Texas Governor*, 5.

10. McCall, *Power of the Texas Governor*, 131–39.

11. McCall, *Power of the Texas Governor*, 120.

12. Christy Hoppe and Robert T. Garrett, "How Deep Does Governor Dig into Issues?" *Dallas Morning News*, November 27, 2011, pp. 1, 30A.

13. "Abbott Calendar," *Austin-American-Statesman*.

14. Sam Kinch, in *Government by Consent—Texas, A Telecourse* (Dallas: Dallas County Community College District, 1990).

15. Ralph W. Steen, "James Edward Ferguson," *The Handbook of Texas Online*.

16. William P. Hobby, in *Government by Consent—Texas, a Telecourse* (Dallas: Dallas County Community College District, 1990).

17. Christy Hoppe, "Lt. Gov. Rick Perry, Honoring the Economic Generators of Texas Tourism," *Dallas Morning News*, February 28, 2000, p. 13A.

18. Hoppe, "Lt. Gov. Rick Perry."

19. "Governor's Office," *Texas State Directory*; "Governor-Elect Abbott Announces Staff, Outlines Priorities for Session," Abbott Governor,.gregabbott.com.

20. Peggy Fikac, "Abbott Makes Scores of Political Appointments," *Houston Chronicle*, July 4, 2015.

21. Fikac, "Abbott Makes Scores of Political Appointments."

22. Valerie Strauss, "Texas Governor Picks Home-Schooler to Lead State Board of Education," *Washington Post*, June 26, 2015.

23. Tim Eaton, "Insurance Commissioner on Her Way Out," *Austin American-Statesman*, May 24, 2013; "Perry Names Rathgeber Insurance Commissioner," *Texas Tribune*, May 27, 2013; Terrance Stutz, "Exclusive: Texas Insurance Commissioner Withheld Annual Profit Numbers to Boost Confirmation Case, Sources Say," dallasnews.com, May 28, 2013.

24. Julian Aguilar, "Abbott Orders National Guard to Stay in Place on Border," *Texas Tribune*, December 15, 2015.

25. "Abbott Altered His Message on Jade Helm," *Houston Chronicle*, May 28, 2015.

26. Patrick Svitak, "Abbott's Emergency Items: Where Are They Now?," *Texas Tribune*, March 12, 2015.

27. Legislative Library of Texas, "Bill Statistics."

28. Madlin B. Makelburg, "What Actually Passed the Texas Legislature," *Chron*, June 2, 2015.

29. Legislative Reference Library of Texas, "Vetoes Overridden, 1860–2013."

30. Office of Governor Rick Perry, "Governor Perry Signs State Budget That Reduces GR by $1.6 Billion," press release, June 19, 2009.

31. Carrie Dann, "Appeals Court Tosses 1 of 2 Indictments against Rick Perry," MSNBC, July 24, 2015.

32. Legislative Reference Library of Texas, "84th Regular Session (2015)—Governor Greg Abbott."

33. Ursala Parks to Glenn Hegar, "Memorandum: HB1 Veto Proclamation," July 21, 2015; Ross Ramsey, "Legislature Questions Abbott's Budget Vetoes," *Texas Tribune*, July 21, 2015; Office of the Attorney General of Texas, Opinion No. KP-0048, December 21, 2015.

34. Texas Legislative Library, Special Sessions of the Texas Legislature (2010).

35. Brandi Grissom, "Gov. Greg Abbott Pardons Four Texans Who Committed Minor Crimes," *Dallas Morning News,* December 22, 2015.

36. Andrea Valdez, "The Worst: Senator Dan Patrick," *Texas Monthly*, June 13, 2013.

37. Tim Eaton, "Joe Straus Avoids Hot Button Issues, in Contrast to Dan Patrick," *Austin American Statesman*, November 4, 2015.

38. Much of this material on the attorney general's office is taken from the website of the attorney general of Texas.

39. "About Texas Attorney General Ken Paxton," Office of the Attorney General of Texas.

40. Valerie Wigglesworth, "Judge OKs Amended Indictments in AG Ken Paxton's Criminal Case," *Dallas Morning News*, December 21, 2015; Terri Langford, "Investigation Targets Complaint against Paxton over Land Deal," *Texas Tribune*, January 15, 2016; Jordan Rudner, "State Bar Will Investigate Paxton for Conduct after Marriage Ruling," *Texas Tribune*, February 10, 2016.

41. Jim Malewitz and Neena Satija, "Video: George P. Bush Talks about Plan to Shake up Texas General Land Office," *Texas Tribune*, August 17, 2015; "George P. Bush Speaks to Employees in Late July 2015," valleycentral .com.

42. Dan Solomon, "Sid Miller Is Having Quite a Week," *Texas Monthly*, December 17, 2015; Liz Crampton, "Miller Defends Deep Fryers in Agriculture Address," *Texas Tribune*, July 8, 2015; Eva Hershaw, "Agriculture Commissioner Grants Amnesty to Cupcakes," *Texas Tribune*, January 12, 2015.

43. See the discussion of gubernatorial power in Cheryl D. Young and John J. Hindera, "The Texas Governor: Weak or Strong?" in *Texas Politics: A Reader*, ed. Anthony Champagne and Edward J. Harpham (New York: W. W. Norton, 1998), 61.

44. Texas State Auditor's Office, "A Summary Report on Full-Time Equivalent State Employees for Fiscal Year 2015."

45. Texas State Auditor's Office, "A Summary Report on Full-Time Equivalent State Employees for Fiscal Year 2004" and "A Summary Report on Full-Time Equivalent State Employees for Fiscal Year 2013."

46. Christy Hoppe, "Perry's Appointees Give Him Unprecedented Hold on Texas—Longest-Serving Governor Spreads Pro-Business View," *Dallas Morning News*, December 19, 2008.

47. Texas Conservative Coalition, "Senate Bill 14 (78R)."

48. Bill Peacock, "Policy Perspective: Is the Free Market Working for the Texas Homeowners' Insurance Market?" Texas Public Policy Foundation, February 28, 2006.

49. Will Weissert, "Texas Rejects Allowing Academics to Fact-Check Public School Textbooks," *Christian Science Monitor*, November 18, 2015.

50. Russell Shorto, "How Christian Were the Founders?" *New York Times Magazine*, February 14, 2010, p. MM32; Terrence Stutz, "Debate Continues over Social Studies," *Dallas Morning News*, March 11, 2010.

51. Texas Sunset Advisory Commission, "Impact of Sunset Reviews."

CHAPTER 9

1. Conor Friedersdorf, "What Waco Police Still Won't Reveal about the Biker-Gang Shootout," *The Atlantic*, June 4, 2015; Nomaan Merchant, "Charges Filed against 170 Motorcycle Gang Members in Texas," WTOP.com, May 19, 2015; Lana Shadwick, "Attorney Seeks Removal of Waco Twin Peaks Judges Who Set $1 Million Bonds," Associated Press, May 28, 2015; Ed Lavandera and Christopher Lett, "Waco Detective May Hear Biker Shootout Cases as Grand Jury Foreman," *CNN*, July 10, 2015; Emily Schmall, "71 More Could Face Indictment," *Dallas News*, November 12, 2015, p. 3A.

2. Dave Lieber, "Justice May Be Easier to Access," *Dallas Morning News*, August 25, 2013, pp. B1, B6.

3. Texas Office of Court Administration, "2015 Statistical Report for the Texas Judiciary."

4. Barbara Kirby, "Neighborhood Justice: Non-Lawyer Judges, Repeat Players and Institutional Reform in Justice of the Peace Courts" (Ph.D. diss., University of Texas at Dallas, 2015), 70, 71, 74.

5. Kirby, "Neighborhood Justice," 56.

6. Ed Housewright, "Emotional Issues, Historical Pedigree," *Dallas Morning News*, April 9, 2001, p. 10A.

7. Texas Office of Court Administration, "2014 Activity Report for the Texas Judiciary."

8. Texas Office of Court Administration, "2014 Activity Report."

9. Steve Thompson, "Toughen Up, City Officials Tell Judges," *Dallas Morning News*, August 2, 2012, pp. 1B, 7B.

10. Thomas Petzinger, Jr., *Oil and Honor: The Texaco-Pennzoil Wars* (New York: Putnam, 1987).

11. Task Force on Indigent Defense, "Evidence for the Feasibility of Public Defender Offices in Texas" (2006).

12. Mary Alice Robbins, "West Texas Plans Public Defender Office for Capital Cases," *Texas Lawyer* (August 20, 2007): 1, 19; "New Public Defender for Capital Cases," *Tex Parte Blog*, October 16, 2007.

13. Ken Anderson, *Crime in Texas* (Austin: University of Texas Press, 1997), 40.

14. Anderson, *Crime in Texas*, 44. Nationally, 95 percent of felonies are plea-bargained.

15. Of the 79 judicial appointments made by Governor William Clements, only 6 were either African American or Hispanic. In contrast, one-third of Governor Ann Richards's judicial appointees were minorities. See Michael Totty, "Is This Any Way to Choose a Judge?" *Wall Street Journal*, August 3, 1994, pp. T1, T4.

16. Paul Burka, "Heads, We Win, Tails, You Lose," *Texas Monthly* (May 1987), 138, 139.

17. Texans for Public Justice, "Payola Justice: How Texas Supreme Court Justices Raise Money from Court Litigants" (1998).

18. Wallace B. Jefferson, "Reform the Partisan System," 79 *Texas Bar Journal* 90 (2016).

19. Mary Flood and Brian Rogers, "Why Some Harris County Judges Lost Not Entirely Clear," *Houston Chronicle*, November 6, 2008.

20. Chuck Lindell, "Green vs. Green: State Supreme Court GOP Race a Study in Contrasts," *Austin American-Statesman*, February 14, 2016; Rick Carey, "Imperfect Paul Green Is a Better Choice than Rick Green," *mySA*, February 19, 2016; "Editorial: We Recommend Sid Harle in GOP Race for Texas Court of Criminal Appeals Place 5," *Dallas Morning News*, January 17, 2016; Bruce Davidson, "Bad Old Days Return to Criminal Appeals Court Races," *mySA*, December 10, 2015; Scott Walker for Judge website, scottwalkerforjudge.com.

21. "Here's Your 2014 Election Day Guide," *ABC 13 Eyewitness News*.

22. Data are from the National Institute on Money in State Politics.

23. Scott Grestak, Alicia Bannon, Allyse Falce, and Linda Casey, "Bankrolling the Bench: The New Politics of Judicial Elections, 2013–14," p. 9, brennancenter.org.

24. Anthony Champagne, "The Cycle of Judicial Elections: Texas as a Case Study," 29 *Fordham Urban Law Journal* 907, 914 (2004).

25. Data are from the National Institute on Money in State Politics.

26. Daniel Becker and Malia Reddick, *Judicial Selection Reform: Examples from Six States* (Chicago: American Judicature Society, 2003), 1–10.

27. Professors Brest and Ifill are quoted in Kevin R. Johnson and Luis Fuentes-Rohwer, "A Principled Approach to the Quest for Racial Diversity on the Judiciary," 10 *Michigan Journal of Race and Law* 5, 8–9 (2004).

28. Johnson and Fuentes-Rohwer, "Principled Approach."

29. Elliott Slotnik, "Gender, Affirmative Action, and Recruitment to the Federal Bench," 14 *Golden Gate University Law Review* 524 (1984).

30. Texas Office of Court Administration, "Profile of Appellate and Trial Judges, September 1, 2014."

31. Barbara L. Graham, "Toward an Understanding of Judicial Diversity in American Courts," 10 *Michigan Journal of Race and Law* 178 (2004).

32. One report is that 90 percent of African American voters and 60 to 79 percent of Hispanic voters vote Democratic. See Ronald W. Chapman, "Judicial Roulette: Alternatives to Single-Member Districts as a Legal and Political Solution to Voting-Rights Challenges to At-Large Judicial Elections," 48 *SMU Law Review* 182 (1995).

33. Citizens' Commission on the Texas Judicial System, "Report and Recommendations: Into the Twenty-First Century" (1993), p. 3.

34. "Executive Summary: Report of the Court Administration Task Force," 71 *Texas Bar Journal* 888, 889 (2008).

35. Ray Blackwood, "Overlapping Jurisdiction in the Houston-Based Courts of Appeals—Could a Special En Banc Procedure Alleviate Problems?" 26 *Appellate Advocate* 277–81 (2013).

36. David A. Anderson, "Judicial Tort Reform in Texas," 26 *Review of Litigation* 7 (2007).

37. State Bar of Texas Annual Report, 2014–2015.

38. John McCormack, "Barratry Suit Names Corpus Lawyers," *San Antonio Express News*, December 9, 2011.

39. Isiah Carey, "Lawyer Filed Reynolds Barratry Complaint," myfoxhouston.com, April 25, 2012.

40. Kari-Thomas Musselman, "Rep. Ron Reynolds Charged (again) with Barratry, Constituent Calls for Resignation," Burnt Orange Report, April 6, 2013.

41. Ross Ramsey, "State Rep. Reynolds Guilty of Ambulance-Chasing," *Texas Tribune*, November 21, 2015; Kaitlin McCulley, "Rep. Ron Reynolds Out on Bond While Appealing Barratry Conviction," *abc13 Eyewitness News*, November 24, 2015.

42. Matt Leicher, "Lawyers per Capita by State," *The Last Gen X American*, lawschooltuitionbubble.wordpress .com.

43. State Commission on Judicial Conduct, Annual Report for Fiscal Year 2015.

44. State Commission on Judicial Conduct, Annual Report for Fiscal Year 2015.

45. State Commission on Judicial Conduct, "Public Admonition Honorable Nora Longoria Justice, Thirteenth Court of Appeals, Edinburg, Hidalgo County, Texas."

46. Public Admonition and Order of Additional Education Honorable Carter Tinsley Schildknecht 106th District Court Judge, Lamesa, Dawson County, Texas.

47. Ralph Blumenthal, "Texas Judge Draws Outcry for Allowing an Execution," *New York Times*, October 25, 2007; Christy Hoppe, "Criminal Appeals Court Creates Emergency Filing System," *DallasNews.com*, November 6, 2007; "Texas Judge Fosters Tough-on-Crime Reputation," MSNBC, October 23, 2007; State Commission on Judicial Conduct, "Special Master's Findings of Fact, In Re: Honorable Sharon Keller,

Presiding Judge of the Texas Court of Criminal Appeals" (January 20, 2010); "Judge Who Refused Last-Minute Appeal Re-Elected," News 92 FM, November 6, 2012.

YOU DECIDE: ELECTED OR APPOINTED JUDGES?

a. Wallace B. Jefferson, "Reform the Partisan System," 79 *Texas Bar Journal* 90 (2016).

b. David Butts, "A Democratic Process Is the Best Choice," 79 *Texas Bar Journal* 91 (2016).

CHAPTER 10

1. Randy Lee Loftis, "Texas Bans Fire Codes in 70% of Its Counties," *Dallas Morning News*, May 26, 2013, pp. 1, 12A–13A; United States Chemical Safety Board, "West Fertilizer Final Investigative Report," January 28, 2016.

2. Dallas Morning News, *Texas Almanac 2009–2010* (Dallas: Dallas Morning News, 2008), 500; U.S. Census Bureau, *Lists & Structure of Government*; Texas State Historical Society, "Government," *Texas Almanac*. Different sources provide varying numbers regarding municipal governments in Texas.

3. The two states that don't use counties as units of local government are Connecticut and Rhode Island. See Richard L. Cole and Delbert A. Taebel, *Texas: Politics and Public Policy* (Fort Worth: Harcourt Brace Jovanovich, 1987), 151.

4. Texas Association of Counties, "About Counties: County Government."

5. Cole and Taebel, *Texas: Politics and Public Policy*, 155.

6. Lawrence M. Crane, Nat Pinnoi, and Stephen W. Fuller, "Private Demand for Publicly Provided Goods: A Case Study of Rural Roads in Texas," *TAMRC Contemporary Market Issues Report No. CI-1-92* (1992).

7. Texas Association of Counties, "Debate Goes Back and Forth, Just like Overweight Trucks."

8. Texas Commission on Jail Standards, "Abbreviated Population Report," December 1, 2015.

9. Julie Wilson, "Montgomery County Drone Launch a Major Failure," *Liberty Beat*, May 15, 2013.

10. Texas Association of Counties, "About Counties."

11. Cole and Taebel, *Texas: Politics and Public Policy*, 152.

12. *Avery v. Midland County*, 390 U.S. 474 (1968).

13. Anthony Champagne and Rick Collis, "Texas," in *The Political Life of the American States*, ed. Alan Rosenthal and Maureen Moakley (Washington, DC: CQ Press, 1984), 140.

14. Bob Palmer, "AG Supports Commissioners in Courthouse Dog Dispute," *Daily Tribune*, August 29, 2013.

15. Harvey Rice and Emily Foxhall, "Fort Bend Leaders Weigh in on Galveston Co. Political Fight," *Chron.com*, October 14, 2015.

16. These are 2014 Census estimates. U.S. Census Bureau, "State and County Quick Facts."

17. Brenda Rodriguez, "Loving and Losing in West Texas," *Dallas Morning News*, March 14, 2001, p. 21A.

18. Roma Vivas, "Presidio County Officials Tackling Budget Problems," *NewsWest9.com*, undated.

19. Russell Gold, "Counties Struggle with High Cost of Prosecuting Death-Penalty Cases," *Wall Street Journal*, January 9, 2002, p. B1.

20. "Capital Trial Could Be Costly for Franklin Co.," *Sulphur Springs News-Telegram*, June 27, 2007, p. 4.

21. Andrew Becker and G. W. Schultz, "Drug Busts Strain County Budget," *Dallas Morning News*, July 28, 2013, p. 10A.

22. Adam M. Gershowitz, "Statewide Capital Punishment: The Case for Eliminating Counties' Role in the Death Penalty," 63 *Vanderbilt Law Review* 8–9 (2010).

23. Jamie Thompson, "A Woman on the Verge," *D Magazine*, November 2015, pp. 46–51, 161–167; Sarah Mervosh, "Lawsuit to Remove Dallas DA Susan Hawk to Move Forward," *Dallas Morning News*, December 9, 2015; Ken Kalthoff, "Case to Remove Dallas DA Susan Hawk Dismissed," *5NBCDFW.com*, January 8, 2016.

24. Frank Heinz, "John Wiley Price Arrested, Accused of Taking $950,000 in Bribes," *5NBCDFW.com*, January 25, 2014.

25. Jordan Smith, "What Happens Next? As D.A. Rosemary Lehmberg Serves Her Sentence, the County Attorney Takes on the Civil Lawsuit and the Next Steps," *Austin Chronicle*, May 3, 2013.

26. Emily DeProng, "After Shady Campaign, Houston Community College Foe Becomes Trustee," *Texas Observer*, November 12, 2013.

27. Article 11, Section 5, of the Texas Constitution is concerned with home rule. For a further discussion of home rule in Texas, see Terrell Blodgett, *Texas Home Rule Charters* (Austin: Texas Municipal League, 1994); Terrell Blodgett, "Home Rule Charters," *Handbook of Texas Online*.

28. Correspondence with Terrell Blodgett, Wednesday, February 3, 2000; *Texas Almanac 2009–2010*, 500–510; League of California Cities, "Charter Cities; Ballotpedia, "Cities in Illinois."

29. Jim Malewitz, "Dissecting Denton: How a Texas City Banned Fracking," *Texas Tribune*, December 15, 2014; Max B. Baker, "Denton City Council Repeals Fracking Ban, *Ft. Worth Star-Telegram*, June 16, 2015.

30. Colorado Municipal League, "Forms of Municipal Government."

31. The following is drawn from Bradley R. Rice, "Commission Form of City Government," *Handbook of Texas Online*.

32. Dallas Morning News, *Texas Almanac 1996–97* (Dallas: Dallas Morning News, 1995), 513.

33. Correspondence with Terrell Blodgett, Wednesday, February 3, 2000.

34. Rice, "Commission Form of City Government."

35. For a further discussion, see Terrell Blodgett, "Council-Manager Form of City Government," *Handbook of Texas Online*; Blodgett, *Texas Home Rule Charters*.

36. For a history of the Office of Controller in Houston, see the City of Houston Office of the City Controller, "Controller History."

37. PolitiFact Texas, "Austin Group Says Austin Is the Biggest U.S. City Lacking City Council Members Elected from Geographic Districts," August 17, 2012.

38. Sarah Coppola, "Grass-Roots Effort Drove Austin City Council District Plan to Victory, Observers Say," *Austin American-Statesman*, November 7, 2012.

39. Taken from www.elpasotexas.gov and U.S. Census, "State & County QuickFacts."

40. Jack C. Plano and Milton Greenberg, *The American Political Dictionary*, 10th ed. (Fort Worth: Harcourt, Brace, 1997).

41. *Texas Almanac and State Industrial Guide, 2000–2001* (Dallas: Dallas Morning News, 1999), 533; *Statistical Abstract of the United States* (Washington, DC: Bureau of the Census, 1998), 496.

42. Jennifer Peebles, "Growing Governments: How 'Special Districts' Spread across Texas with Limited Oversight and Accountability—but with Plenty of Power to Tax," Texas Watchdog, February 15, 2011; U.S. Census, "Number of Special Districts," Lists and Structure of Governments.

43. Peebles, "Growing Governments."

44. Peebles, "Growing Governments."

45. County Information Program, Texas Association of Counties. Data are for 2010.

46. County Information Program, Texas Association of Counties. Data are for 2010.

47. Brooks Egerton and Reese Dunklin, "Government by Developer," *Dallas Morning News*, June 10, 2001, p. 1A.

48. Peggy Heinkel-Wolfe, "Developers Still Using Renters to Create Special Tax Districts," *Dallas Morning News*, November 1, 2006, p. 1B.

49. Peggy Heinkel-Wolfe, "Bonds Approved with Blessing of 2 Voters," *Dallas Morning News*, November 22, 2010, p. B6.

50. Richard Williamson, "Texas MUD Sinks toward Chap. 9; Others on Solid Ground," *The Bond Buyer*, May 18, 2009.

51. Sara C. Galvan, "Wrestling with MUDs to Pin Down the Truth about Special Districts," 75 *Fordham Law Review* 3041–80 (2007).

52. See Texas Association of Regional Councils, "About TARC."

53. Chuck DeVore, "On Prohibiting the Issuance of Capital Appreciation Bonds: Testimony to the Senate Committee on Intergovernmental Relations," Texas Public Policy Foundation, March 20, 2013.

54. Trey Bundy and Shane Shifflet, "Controversial School Bonds Create 'Debt for the Next Generation,'" 31 California Watch, January 2013.

55. DeVore, "On Prohibiting the Issuance of Capital Appreciation Bonds."

56. Chuck DeVore, "CAB Rides Can Be Extremely Costly," *Austin American-Statesman*, September 11, 2012.

57. James Estes, "Capital Appreciation Bonds: The Creation of a Toxic Waste Dump in Our Schools," Alpha Wealth Management, April 2013.

58. DeVore, "CAB Rides Can Be Extremely Costly."

59. DeVore, "On Prohibiting the Issuance of Capital Appreciation Bonds."

60. Keeley Webster, "Lockyer Challenges Poway CAB Advisors," Bond Buyer, Business (2012).

61. Eva-Marie Ayala, "Anna ISD Used Costly Bonds to Cope," *Dallas Morning News*, June 16, 2013, p. 1.

62. Bundy and Shifflet, "Controversial School Bonds Create 'Debt.'"

63. Allison Fu, "State Assembly Passes Bill Aimed to Curtail School District Debt Burden," *Daily Californian*, April 10, 2013.

64. DeVore, "On Prohibiting the Issuance of Capital Appreciation Bonds."

65. Susan Combs, Texas Comptroller of Public Accounts, "Your Money and Pension Obligations" (2012), 4.

66. Combs, "Your Money and Pension Obligations," 7.

67. Doug Miller, "Mayor Cuts Firefighter Pension Deal; Experts Call It Bad Bargain," KHOU 11 News, March 6, 2015.

68. Joe Martin, "If We Don't Fix Pension Problem, It's Game Over," *Houston Business Journal*, December 9, 2015.

69. Combs, "Your Money and Pension Obligations," 17.

70. This discussion of the Dallas pension crisis is from Tristan Hallman, "Retirees' Rich Perk Cut Off," *Dallas Morning News*, January 15, 2015, pp. 1B, 9B; Tristan Hallman, "Return of Only 2% Seen as Hole Deepens," *Dallas Morning News*, February 20, 2015, pp. 1B, 7B; Robert Wilonsky, "Moody's Lowers City's Bond Rating," *Dallas Morning News*, October 29, 2015, pp. 5A; Robert Wilonsky, "Police-Fire Fund Pursues Ex-Leaders," *Dallas Morning News*, December 3, 2015, pp. 1B, 4B.

71. Comparison of El Paso City Employees' Pension Fund, "Summary Plan Description First Tier for Persons Whose Participation Date Is before September 1, 2011," with "Summary Plan Description Second Tier for Persons Whose Participation Date Is after September 1, 2011."

YOU DECIDE: HOUSTON'S "BATHROOM ORDINANCE"

a. Alexa Ura, "Bathroom Fears Flush Houston Discrimination Ordinance," *Texas Tribune*, November 3, 2015.

b. Manny Fernandez and Mitch Smith, "Houston Voters Reject Broad Anti-Discrimination Ordinance," *New York Times*, November 3, 2015.

c. Justin William Meyer, "Why Houston's Gay Rights Ordinance Failed: Fear of Men in Women's Bathrooms," *Washington Post*, November 4, 2015.

d. Tierney McAfee, "Hillary Clinton, Sally Field, Matt Bomer and More Stars Rally to Fight Anti-Transgender Discrimination," *People*, October 30, 2015.

CHAPTER 11

1. Jeannie Kever, "As Texas Public College Tuition Rises, Legislators Feel the Heat," *Houston Chronicle*, July 10, 2008; Texas Higher Education Coordinating Board, "Tuition Set-Aside-House Bill 3013, 78th Texas Legislature," *Overview* (February 2010).

2. Texas Legislative Budget Board Staff, *Financing Higher Education in Texas: Legislative Primer*, as submitted to the 82nd Texas Legislature (January 2011); Texas Higher Education Board, "Tuition Deregulation," *Overview* (March 2011). See also collegeforalltexans.com and trends.collegeboard.org.

3. See Ryan McCrimmon and Bobby Blanchard, "Deregulating Tuition Slowed Increase, Universities Say," *Texas Tribune*, March 17, 2016; Ross Ramsey, "Analysis: Raising College Tuition, Deflecting the Blame," *Texas Tribune*, February 12, 2016; Lauren McGaughy and J. David McSwane, "Rise in Costs Not as Steep after Legislature Gave Reins to Schools," *Dallas Morning News*. April 10, 2016; Matthew Watkins, "Lt. Gov. Patrick Slams Universities for Tuition Increases," *Texas Tribune*, April 26, 2016.

4. See *Dallas Morning News* editorial, "Tuition Cost Must Ease," April 14, 2016. See also Minjae Park, "UT Regents Back Some Tuition Hikes, New Med Schools," *Texas Tribune*, May 3, 2012; Reeve Hamilton and Morgan Smith, "UT's Reform-Minded Chairman at the Center of Controversy," *Texas Tribune*, May 18, 2012; Reeve Hamilton, "For In-State Students, UT System Keeps Tuition Steady," *Texas Tribune*, May 20, 2014.

5. The following discussion is drawn from Texas Legislative Budget Board, *Fiscal Size-Up: 2016–17 Biennium* (May 2016), pp. 1–8.

6. Texas Legislative Budget Board, *Fiscal Size-Up: 2014–15 Biennium*, February 2014, p. 58.

7. Texas Legislative Budget Board, *Fiscal Size-Up: 2014–15 Biennium*, p. 59.

8. Texas Legislative Budget Board, *Fiscal Size-Up: 2016–17 Biennium*, p. 26.

9. Texas Legislative Budget Board, *Fiscal Size-Up: 2016–17 Biennium*, p. 26. See also data provided by the Federation of Tax Administratorsattaxadmin.org and Texas Public Policy Foundation at texasbudgetsource.com. See also tax burden rankings provided by the Tax Foundation at taxfoundation.org.

10. Tax Foundation, "Facts and Figures: How Does Your State Compare?" (2016).

11. Tax Foundation, "Facts and Figures, "How Does Your State Compare?" (2016).

12. Texas Legislative Budget Board, *Fiscal Size-Up: 2016–17 Biennium*, pp. 35–36.

13. Carl David et al., *Who Pays? A Distributional Analysis of the Tax Systems in All 50 States*, 3rd ed. (Washington, DC: Institute on Taxation and Economic Policy, January 2013), 4, 11–12.

14. Institute on Taxation and Economic Policy, *Who Pays? A Distributional Analysis of the Tax Systems in All 50 States*, 5th ed. (Washington, DC: Institute on Taxation and Economic Policy, January 2015).

15. Clay Robinson, "Bullock Paints a Grim Picture/Says Income Tax Needed to Avert Financial Crisis," *Houston Chronicle*, March 12, 1991; Clay Robinson, "Bullock Plan May Open Door to Tax Battle," *Houston Chronicle*, March 2, 1993.

16. Texas Legislative Budget Board, *Fiscal Size-Up: 2016–17 Biennium*, p. 37.

17. Texas Lottery Commission, "Demographic Survey of Texas Lottery Players 2015," University of Houston, Hobby Center for Public Policy (November 2015).

18. Texas Lottery Commission, "Demographic Survey of Texas Lottery Players 2015." See also James LeBas, "Who Wants to Be a Billionaire? Texas Spending Tobacco Money on Health Care, Endowments," Texas Comptroller of Public Accounts, *Fiscal Notes* (January 2000); Texas House of Representatives, House Research Organization, "State Finance Report No. 82-3" (March 11, 2011).

19. Michael E. McClellan, "Permanent School Fund," *Handbook of Texas Online*; Texas Permanent School Fund, "Comprehensive Annual Financial Report for the Fiscal Year Ending August 31, 2015"; Texas Legislative Budget Board, *Fiscal Size-Up: 2016–17 Biennium*, pp. 235–36.

20. Texas Legislative Budget Board, *Fiscal Size-Up: 2016–17 Biennium*, pp. 483–88.

21. Susan Combs, Texas Comptroller of Public Accounts, "Rainy Day Fund 101," *Fiscal Notes, February 2011*; Texas Legislative Budget Board, *Fiscal Size-Up: 2016–17 Biennium*, p. 42.

22. UTIMCO, "Permanent University Fund," December 31, 2015, p. 1; Texas Legislative Budget Board, *Fiscal Size-Up: 2016–17 Biennium*, pp. 295–96.

23. For the Higher Education Fund, see Texas Legislative Budget Board, *Fiscal Size-Up: 2016–17 Biennium*, p. 303. For the National Research University Fund, see Texas Higher Education Coordinating Board, "National Research University Fund Eligibility: A Report to the Comptroller and the Texas Legislature (March 2016).

24. Texas Legislative Budget Board, *Fiscal Size-Up: 2016–17 Biennium*, pp. 30–32.

25. Texas Legislative Budget Board, *Fiscal Size-Up: 2016–17 Biennium*, p. 30.

26. The following is drawn from Senate Research Center, *Budget 101: A Guide to the Budget Process in Texas* (January 2011), p. 29.

27. Texas Legislative Budget Board, *Fiscal Size-Up: 2016–17 Biennium*, p. 56.

28. Texas Legislative Budget Board, *Fiscal Size-Up: 2016–17 Biennium*, p. 32.

29. Tax Foundation, "Facts & Figures: How Does Your State Compare?" (2015), table 36.

30. See Senate Research Center, *Budget 101*, pp. 24–25.

31. Senate Research Center, *Budget 101*, p. 28; Glenn Hegar, Texas Comptroller of Public Accounts, "40 Years of Comptroller Revenue Estimates (1974–2013)." *Texas Transparency* (2015). Window.texas.gov.

32. See the discussion in Senate Research Center, *Budget 101*, pp. 34–35.

33. The following discussion is drawn from Texas Legislative Budget Board, *Fiscal Size-Up: 2012–13 Biennium*; Texas Legislative Budget Board, *Texas Fact Book 2012* (Austin: State of Texas, 2012). The data for the following are drawn from Texas Legislative Budget Board, *Fiscal Size-Up: 2012–13 Biennium*; Robert T. Garrett, "Tension Rises over Future Cuts," *Dallas Morning News*, February 24, 2012, p. A1; Dave Montgomery and Anna M. Tinsley, "Texas Budget with $15 Billion in Cuts Clears Legislature," *Fort Worth Star-Telegram*, May 28, 2011; Ross Ramsey, "The End Game: Special Session Wraps Up Today," *Texas Tribune*, June 29, 2011. See also Robert T. Garrett, "Many Texas Politicians, Including Perry and White, Talk Little of $21 Billion Budget Gap," *Dallas Morning News*, September 12, 2010; Robert T. Garrett, "Budget Likely to Cut Deep," *Dallas Morning News*, October 24, 2010; Emily Ramshaw, "Legislators Consider Medicaid Withdrawal," *Texas Tribune*, November 7, 2010. See also Eugenio Aleman and Tyler B. Kruse, "Texas Budget: 2012–2013 Biennium," Wells Fargo Securities, June 24, 2011.

34. For a discussion of the factors lying behind the financial collapse and federal responses to it, see Simon Johnson and James Kwak, *13 Banks: The Wall Street Takeover and the Next Financial Meltdown* (New York: Pantheon Books, 2010); Roger Lowenstein, *The End of Wall Street* (New York: Penguin Press, 2010); David Wessel, *In Fed We Trust: Ben Bernanke's War on the Great Panic* (New York: Crown Business, 2009). See Texas Comptroller of Public Accounts, "State Sales Tax Collections to General Revenue," *Window on State Government* (May 2012).

35. This discussion relies heavily upon Dick Lavine, "How to Fill the Hole in the Texas Revenue System," Center for Public Policy Priorities (February 2012).

YOU DECIDE: WHAT TO DO WITH A BUDGET SURPLUS

a. Aman Batheja, "Hegar: 'Moderate Expansion' of Economy Is Expected," *Texas Tribune*, January 12, 2015.

b. Aman Batheja and Julián Aguilar, "Legislature Sends $209.4 Billion Budget to Abbott," *Texas Tribune*, May 29, 2015.

CHAPTER 12

1. See Aman Batheja, "Toll Road Projects in Limbo Following Session," *Texas Tribune*, June 24, 2015.

2. The above paragraphs draw from Texas Legislative Budget Board, *Texas Highway Funding: Legislative Primer* (April 2016); Aman Batheja, "State Invites More Toll Roads amid Signs of Resistance," *Texas Tribune*, September 19, 2014.

3. The above three paragraphs draw upon the following: Aman Batheja, "Tolling Texans: Impact of Trans-Texas Corridor Linger," *Texas Tribune*, December 3, 2012; Phineas Baxandall and Sara E. Smith, "The Trouble with Toll Roads in Texas," Perspectives on Texas, *Texas Tribune*, October 5, 2014; Aman Batheja, "As Perry Exits, Texas Shifting Away from Toll Roads," *Texas Tribune*, July 4, 2014; "Private Tollway Near East Dallas Draws Ire from Record Crowd," *Examiner.com*, September 23, 2014; Ben Wear, "TxDOT Computes a Hefty Price for Buying off Texas Tolls," *Austin American-Statesman*, March 30, 2016; Ross Ramsey, "Analysis: Government Is Expensive, No Matter How You Pay," *Texas Tribune*, April 1, 2016.

4. See Benjamin Ginsberg, Theodore J. Lowi, Margaret Weir, Caroline Tolbert, Anthony Champagne, Edward J. Harpham, et al., *We the People: Texas Edition*, 9th ed. (New York: W. W. Norton, 2012), 643.

5. B. Guy Peters, *American Public Policy: Promise and Performance*, 9th ed. (Washington, DC: CQ Press, 2012), chaps. 2 and 3; Charles O. Jones, *An Introduction to the Study of Public Policy*, 3rd ed. (Monterey, CA: Brooks, Cole, 1984).

6. Roger Cobb and Charles Elder, *Participation in American Politics* (Baltimore: Johns Hopkins University Press, 1983), 85.

7. See Herbert Simon, "Bounded Rationality and Organizational Learning," *Organizational Science* 2, no. 1: 125–34; Kristen Renwick Monroe, *The Economic Approach to Politics: A Critical Reassessment of the Theory of Rational Action* (New York: HarperCollins, 1991).

8. See Texas Legislative Budget Board, *Fiscal Size-Up: 2016–17 Biennium* (Austin: State of Texas, May 2016), pp. 219, 227.

9. See Texas Legislative Budget Board, *Fiscal Size-Up: 2016–17 Biennium*, 238–41. See also schools.texas tribune.org.

10. American Institutes for Research, *Annual Evaluation of Open-Enrollment Charter Schools 2012–13 School Year*, prepared for the Texas Educational Agency, 2014.

11. See "2016 Largest Districts in Texas," https://k12 .niche.com/rankings/public-school-districts/largest -enrollment/s/texas/.

12. See tea.texas.gov/About_TEA/News_and_Multimedia /Press_Releases/2015/Class_of_2014_graduation_rate _sets_new_mark/. See also www.txcharterschools.org /what-is-a-charter-school/charters-in-texas/.

13. See Texas Legislative Budget Board, *2016–17 Biennium*, p. 240. See also https://schools.texastribune.org /states/tx/.

14. Terrance Stutz, "Texas Moves up in Spending per Pupil, Still Ranks in Bottom Third," *Dallas Morning News*, March 18, 2015.

15. See http://tea.texas.gov/Dropout_Information.html.

16. For a discussion of the history of public education in Texas from which the following is drawn, see Max Berger and Lee Wilborn, "Education," *Handbook of Texas Online*; "Public Schools," *Texas Almanac 2000–2001*, Millennium Edition (Dallas: Dallas Morning News, 1999), 533–54. See also Lewis B. Cooper, *The Permanent School Fund of Texas* (Fort Worth: Texas State Teachers Association, 1934); Michael E. McClellan, "Permanent School Fund," *Handbook of Texas Online*.

17. See Oscar Mauzy, "Gilmer-Aikin Laws," *Handbook of Texas Online*; Dick Smith and Richard Allen Burns, "Texas Education Agency," *Handbook of Texas Online*; Berger and Wilborn, "Education."

18. See Anna Victoria Wilson, "Education for African Americans," *Handbook of Texas Online*.

19. Arnoldo De León and Robert A. Calvert, "Segregation," *Handbook of Texas Online*.

20. The following discussion of the *Rodríguez* and *Edgewood* cases is drawn from Texas Legislative Budget Board Staff, "Financing Public Education in Texas: Kindergarten through Grade 12," *Legislative Handbook* (February 1999); Berger and Wilborn, "Education"; Cynthia E. Orozco, "Rodríguez v. San Antonio ISD," *Handbook of Texas Online*; Teresa Palomo Acosta, "Edgewood ISD v. Kirby," *Handbook of Texas Online*.

21. See Texas Legislative Budget Board Staff, "Financing Public Education in Texas: Kindergarten through Grade 12," 26–27.

22. See Texas House of Representatives, House Research Organization, "Focus Report: Schools and Taxes" (May 25, 2007); Jason Embry, "Session Ends with Property Tax Cut," *Austin American-Statesman*, May 26, 2006.

23. Mark Wiggins, "Attorneys, Schools and 83rd Texas Legislature's Impact on Education," www.kvue.com; Morgan Smith, "Texas School Finance Trial Goes for Round Two," *Texas Tribune*, June 19, 2013; Terrance Stutz, "State Seeks to Remove School Finance Judge," *Dallas Morning News*, June 3, 2014, p. 3a.

24. See *Morath et al. v. The Taxpayer and Student Fairness Coalition et al.* Supreme Court of Texas (No. 14-0776). See also Keith Collier, "Texas Supreme Court Upholds School Funding System (May 13, 2016).

25. See Clark D. Thomas, "Education Reform in Texas," in *Texas Politics*, ed. Anthony Champagne and Edward J. Harpham (New York: W. W. Norton, 1998), 213–32.

26. National Commission on Excellence in Education, *A Nation at Risk: The Imperative for Educational Reform* (Washington, DC: Department of Education, 1983).

27. See Thomas, "Education Reform in Texas," 218.

28. See Thomas, "Education Reform in Texas," 221.

29. See Thomas, "Education Reform in Texas," 231; "Public Schools," *Texas Almanac 2000–2001*, Millennium Edition (Dallas: Dallas Morning News, 1999), 533. See also Terrence Stutz, "State's List Cites Sub-par Schools in Transfer Plan," *Dallas Morning News*, December 24, 1999, p. 1.

30. College Board, "Mean 2009 SAT Scores by State" (2009); College Board, "2009 College-Bound Seniors Total Group Profile Report" (2009), p. 3. See also Texas Education Agency, "College Admissions Testing of Graduating Seniors in Texas High Schools, Class of 2010" (October 2011) and Texas Education Agency, "2010 Comprehensive Annual Report on Texas Public Schools" (Austin, 2010). See Joshua Benton, "Legislators Left Unanswered Questions on New State Tests," *Dallas Morning News*, June 11, 2007, p. B1. See also Terrence Stutz, "Failing Tests, Passing Grades," *Dallas Morning News*, March 8, 2012, p. A1.

31. See Kate McGee, "Two Big Education Bills Gain Approval from Texas Legislature," KUTnews.org, May 27, 2013.

32. Terrence Stutz, "SAT Scores in Texas Plummet as More Students Take Exam," *Dallas Morning News*, September 3, 2015.

33. See Legislative Budget Board, Fiscal Note, 83rd Legislative Regular Session (February 19, 2013). See also Texas Education Agency, "Initial STAAR Results Released," News, TEA (June 8, 2012); Jeffrey Weiss and Daniel Lathrop, "Low-Scoring Groups Slipping More," *Dallas Morning News*, June 9, 2014, pp. 1a and 8.

34. See Milton Friedman, *Capitalism and Freedom* (Chicago: University of Chicago Press, 1962).

35. See Tawnell D. Hobbs, "As Charter Schools Rise, Dallas ISD Rues Loss of Students—and Millions in Funding," *Dallas Morning News*, January 21, 2016. See also http://www.txcharterschools.org/what-is-a-charter-school/charters-in-texas/.

36. See the respective websites of these organizations. See also Morgan Smith, "Education Reform Group Mobilizes for 2014 Elections," *Texas Tribune*, January 8, 2014.

37. See Jim Henson and Joshua Blank, "Polling Center: Threading the Needle on Education," *Texas Tribune*, April 10, 2014. See also University of Texas/*Texas Tribune*, "Texas Statewide Survey," February 2014 and earlier surveys.

38. Alexa Ura, "Latest Data Shows Poverty Rate Highest at Border, Lowest in Suburbs," *Texas Tribune*, January 19, 2016. See also Texas Health and Human Services Commission, "Texas Medicaid Enrollment Statistics."

39. See data at Henry J. Kaiser Family Foundation, kff.org.

40. Texas Legislative Budget Board, *Fiscal Size-Up: 2016–17 Biennium*, p. 163.

41. The following is drawn from Edward J. Harpham, "Welfare Reform and the New Paternalism in Texas," in *Texas Politics*, ed. Champagne and Harpham, 233–49.

42. See Vivian Elizabeth Smyrl, "Texas Department of Human Services," *Handbook of Texas Online*.

43. Harpham, "Welfare Reform and the New Paternalism in Texas," 238.

44. See Charles Murray, *Losing Ground: American Social Policy, 1950–1980* (New York: Basic Books, 1984).

45. For a discussion of these programs, see Lawrence Mead, *The New Politics of Poverty: The Nonworking Poor in America* (New York: Basic Books, 1992).

46. The following paragraphs are drawn from Harpham, "Welfare Reform and the New Paternalism in Texas," 244–47.

47. See Texas Legislative Budget Board, *Fiscal Size-Up: 2014–15 Biennium*, 221–22; Texas Health and Human Services Commission, "Temporary Assistance for Needy Families (TANF): Frequently Asked Questions." See also Texas Health and Human Services Commission, "Presentation to the House Select Committee on Human Services: HHSC Overview" (February 12, 2013).

48. Texas Health and Human Services System, *Consolidated Budget, Fiscal Years 2016–17* (October 2014), p. 21.

49. Texas Health and Human Services Commission, *Texas Medicaid and CHIP in Perspective*, 9th ed. (December

2015). Medicaid and the Children's Health Insurance Program (CHIP) information and data for this section are taken from this document and from data for Texas on the Henry Kaiser Family Foundation website, www.statehealthfacts.org.

50. See Texas Legislative Budget Board, *Fiscal Size-Up: 2016–17 Biennium*, p. 165; Texas Health and Human Services, The "Pink Book," February 13, 2015, chap. 5.

51. Texas Health and Human Services Commission, "Chapter 1: Texas Medicaid in Perspective."

52. See Henry J. Kaiser Foundation, "Federal Medical Assistance Percentage for Medicaid," kff.org.

53. See Henry J. Kaiser Family Foundation, "Total Medicaid Spending FY 2014," kff.org.

54. See Louis Radnofsky, "Texas Medicaid Funds Cut over Planned Parenthood," *Wall Street Journal*, March 15, 2012; Emily Ramshaw and Thanh Tan, "The Storm over Women's Health Care Had Been Brewing," *Texas Tribune*, March 23, 2012; Wade Goodwyn, "As Texas Cuts Funds, Planned Parenthood Fights Back," www.npr.com, May 7, 2012; Amanda Peterson Beadle, Thinkprogress.org, March 16, 2012; Sean Walsh, "Hutcheson Backs Planned Parenthood in Funding Dispute," *Dallas Morning News*, March 22, 2012.

55. Moni Basu, "Court Rules Texas Can Ban Planned Parenthood from Health Program," CNN U.S., articles.cnn.com, August 22, 2012; "Judge Says Texas Not Allowed to Cut Funds to Planned Parenthood," foxnews.com, May 4, 2012.

56. See Nancy Flake, "Combs: Texas in Great Shape, but Watch out for Medicaid," *Cyprus Creek Mirror*, May 2, 2012. See also Kristie Avery, "Comptroller Warns of Medicaid Costs," *Texas Gazette*.

57. In the Senate, 58 Democrats and 2 independents voted for the Patient Protection and Affordable Care Act. All 39 Republicans in the Senate were opposed. In the House of Representatives, the final vote was 219 to 212. All supporters of the bill were Democrats, with 34 Democrats and 178 Republicans opposing the bill.

58. See Texas Health and Human Services Commission, *Texas Medicaid*, chap. 3, for a further discussion of the impact of federal health care reforms on Texas.

59. See Kaiser Family Foundation, "How Will the Uninsured in Texas Fare under the Affordable Care Act?" at kff.org/medicaid.

60. "Fewer Texas Doctors Taking Medicaid Patients," *Dallas Morning News*, July 9, 2012.

61. Robert T. Garrett, "State Slashes Health Law Estimate," *Dallas Morning News*, July 13, 2012.

62. See Edgar Walters, "More Have Health Insurance but Texas Lags," *Texas Tribune*, December 18, 2016. See also Episcopal Health Foundation at www.episcopalhealth.org.

63. Peter G. George, Robert E. Mace, and Rima Petrossian, "Aquifers of Texas," Texas Development Board, Report 380 (July 2011).

64. An acre-foot is equal to 325,851.43 U.S. gallons. Planners typically assume that a suburban family will consume an acre-foot of water a year.

65. Texas Water Development Board, "Water for Texas 2012 State Water Plan" (January 2012), p. xii.

66. See Texas Water Development Board, "Water for Texas 2012," pp. 17–18.

67. See Otis W. Templer, "Water Law," *Handbook of Texas Online*; Otis W. Templer, "Water Rights Issues: Texas Water Rights Law; East Meets West," *Journal of Contemporary Water Research and Education* 85 (Spring 1991).

68. The following is drawn largely from Templer, "Water Law" and "Texas Water Rights." See also Terry L. Hadley, "Texas Water Commission," *Handbook of Texas Online*; Laurie E. Jasinski, "Texas Water Development Board," *Handbook of Texas Online*; Texas Water Development Board, "Water for Texas 2012," Executive Summary and chap. 1. See also Texas Water Development Board, "A Texan's Guide to Water and Water Rights Marketing"; Ronald Kaiser, *Handbook of Texas Water Law: Problems and Need Water Monograph No. 87-1* (College Station: Texas Water Resources Institute, Texas A&M University, 1987). We also thank Benedict Voit for his useful summary of water policy issues. See Benedict Voit, "Texas Water Policy for the 21st Century" (unpublished paper, University of Texas at Dallas, April 10, 2008).

69. See Texas Water Development Board, "A Texan's Guide to Water."

70. Texas Water Development Board, "Water for Texas 2012," pp. 15–16.

71. See the historical timeline regarding environmental policy, Texas Commission on Environmental Quality, www.tceq.texas.gov.

72. See Texas Water Development Board, "About the Texas Water Development Board," www.txdb.texas.gov.

73. See Kate Galbraith, "Texas Supreme Court Rules for Landowners in Water Case," *Texas Tribune*, February 24, 2012. See also Forrest Wilder, "The Texas Supreme Court Turns Water into a Landmark Groundwater Decision," *Texas Observer*, February 24, 2012; Chuck Lindell, "Supreme Court Delivers Major Water Ruling on

Water Regulation," *Austin American Statesman*, February 24, 2012.

74. For a good discussion of some of these issues, see a five-part series published by the *Texas Tribune:* Neena Satija, "Beneath the Surface," *Texas Tribune*, November 19, 2013–January 19, 2014.

75. Michael Marks and Terence Henry, "Everything You Need to Know about Proposition 6, Texas' Water Fund," *State Impact: A Reporting Project of NPR Member Stations*, November 4, 2013.

YOU DECIDE: ABORTION POLICY IN TEXAS

a. Emily Ramshaw, "For Abortion Providers, Sonogram Law Is a Complication," *Texas Tribune*, January 29, 2012.

b. McClatchy DC, "Texas Sonogram Law Has Some Patients Unhappy," February 29, 2012.

CHAPTER 13

1. Jordan Smith, "WilCo D.A.: Duty Upsets Bradley," *Austin Chronicle*, June 1, 2012.

2. Claire Osborn, "Ken Anderson Begins Serving Jail Sentence in Michael Morton Case," statesman.com, November 13, 2013.

3. Will Weissert, "Bill Named for Michael Morton Passes House," May 13, 2013, kxan.com; "Perry Set to Sign Michael Morton Act," May 16, 2013, kxan.com.

4. Danielle Kaeble, Lauren Glaze, Anastasios Tsoutis, and Todd Minton, "Correctional Populations in the United States, 2014," Bureau of Justice Statistics Bulletin, December 2015 (Revised January 21, 2016); U.S. Census, "Quick Facts."

5. Fred Dahr, "Crimes and Punishment in Texas State Court," texasdefenselaw.com; Texas Criminal Defense Lawyer, "Texas Criminal Laws and Penalties," mytexas defenselawyer.com.

6. Texas Board of Pardons and Paroles.

7. Information is from the Texas Association of Counties. The term *district attorney* will be used to encompass district attorneys, county attorneys, and criminal district attorneys.

8. Texas Indigent Defense Commission, "Indigent Defense Data for Texas."

9. Dottie Carmichael, "Judgment and Justice" (2013), pp. vii–x, txcourts.gov.

10. Texas Department of Criminal Justice, "Fiscal Year 2014 Statistical Report."

11. Legislative Budget Board, "Criminal Justice Uniform Cost Report: Fiscal Years 2013 and 2014" (2015), p. 1; Texas Criminal Justice Coalition, "Safer, Smarter, and More Cost-Efficient Approaches to Reduce Crime in Texas."

12. Harry Mika and Lawrence J. Redlinger, "Crime and Correction," in *Texas at the Crossroads*, ed. Anthony Champagne and Edward J. Harpham (College Station: Texas A&M University Press, 1987), 245–46.

13. Mika and Redlinger, "Crime and Correction," 245–46.

14. *Ruiz v. Estelle*, 503 F. Supp. 1265 (1980).

15. Mika and Redlinger, "Crime and Correction," 247.

16. Texas Department of Criminal Justice, "Texas Board of Criminal Justice."

17. See Associated Texans against Crime, "Annual Report" (1998); Texas Department of Criminal Justice, "Fiscal Year 2011 Operating Budget and Fiscal Years 2010–2013 Legislative Appropriations Request" (August 16, 2010).

18. Texas Public Policy Foundation, "2015–16 Legislator's Guide to the Issues" (2014), www.texaspolicy.com; Robert Wilonsky, "Texas Department of Criminal Justice Says Dawson State Jail on the Shores of the Trinity River Will Close August 31," *Dallas Morning News*, June 11, 2013.

19. See Associated Texans against Crime, "Annual Report" (1998).

20. Texas Department of Criminal Justice, "Fiscal Year 2014 Statistical Report."

21. Texas Department of Criminal Justice, "Fiscal Year 2014 Statistical Report."

22. Texas Department of Criminal Justice, "Fiscal Year 2006 Statistical Summary" (December 2006).

23. Texas Department of Criminal Justice, "Fiscal Year 2010 Statistical Reports."

24. Texas Department of Criminal Justice, "Fiscal Year 2014 Statistical Report."

25. Texas State Historical Association, *Texas Almanac 2010–2011* (2010), 482.

26. E. Ann Carson, "Prisoners in 2014," *Bureau of Justice Statistics Bulletin*, September 2015.

27. "Texas Crime and Crime Rate," USA.com.

28. Texas Department of Criminal Justice, "Fiscal Year 2014 Statistical Report."

29. Texas Department of Criminal Justice, "Fiscal Year 2014 Statistical Report."

30. Death Penalty Information Center, deathpenalty info.org.

31. Data come from the Death Penalty Information Center Fact Sheet at deathpenaltyinfo.org and the National Registry of Exonerations at www.law.umich.edu.

32. Paul Brace and Brent D. Boyea, "State Public Opinion, the Death Penalty, and the Practice of Electing Judges,"

American Journal of Political Science 52, no. 2 (2008): 360–72.

33. Ross Ramsey, "UT/TT Poll: Texans Stand behind Death Penalty," *Texas Tribune*, May 24, 2012.

34. Texas Department of Criminal Justice, "Executed Offenders."

35. Death Penalty Information Center.

36. Death Penalty Information Center.

37. *McClesky v. Kemp*, 481 U.S. 279 (1987).

38. "Gov. Perry Commutes Sentences of Man Scheduled to Die Thursday," ABC13, August 30, 2007.

39. Larry Arnold, "The History of Concealed Carry, 1976–2011," Texas Concealed Handgun Association.

40. Eric Aasen, "Here's What You Should Know about Open Carry in Texas," KERA, January 5, 2016.

41. Ross Ramsey, "UT/TT Poll: Voters Less Open to Open Carry," *Texas Tribune*, February 24, 2015.

42. Ramsey, "UT/TT Poll."

43. "Active License/Certified Instructor Counts as of December 31, 2015," Texas Department of Public Safety, Regulatory Services Division.

44. The Sandra Bland case received widespread news coverage. See, for example, Dana Ford, "DA: Sandra Bland's Death Being Treated Like Murder Investigation," CNN, July 21, 2015; David Montgomery, "Sandra Bland Was Threatened with Taser, Police Video Shows," *New York Times*, July 21, 2015; "Texas Trooper Indicted over Sandra Bland Arrest Formally Fired," *Chicago Tribune*, March 2, 2016; St. John Berned-Smith, "DPS Director Affirms Firing of Trooper in Sandra Bland Case," *Chron*, March 2, 2016.

45. National Registry of Exonerations, www.law.umich.edu.

46. Steve McGonigle, "Righting Wrongs," *Dallas Morning News*, January 22, 2007, p. 1; Jennifer Emily, "DA: Man Didn't Do '82 Rape," *Dallas Morning News*, September 17, 2007, p. 1B.

47. Mike Ware, "Dallas County Conviction Integrity Unit and the Importance of Getting It Right the First Time," 56 *New York Law School Law Review* 1034–50 (2011–2012).

48. Michael Hall, "Why Can't Steven Phillips Get a DNA Test?" *Texas Monthly*, January 2006.

49. David Grann, "Trial by Fire," *New Yorker*, September 7, 2009.

50. Jeff Carleton, "Cameron Todd Willingham: Texas Governor Dismisses 3 Commission Members Just 48 Hours before Arson Review," *Huffington Post*, September 30, 2009.

51. Allan Turner, "Abbott Ruling Limits Probe of Arson Case," *Houston Chronicle*, July 29, 2011.

52. See Nate Blakeslee, *Tulia: Race, Cocaine, and Corruption in a Small Texas Town* (New York: Public Affairs, 2005).

53. Paul Duggan, " 'Sheetrock Scandal' Hits Dallas Police," *Washington Post*, January 18, 2002, p. 12.

54. Maurice Chammah, "Bill Addresses Changing Science in Criminal Appeals," *Texas Tribune*, February 4, 2013.

55. Brian Rogers, "Harris County Officials Outline Plans to Curb Jail Population," *Houston Chronicle*, January 7, 2016.

56. Enrique Rangel, "Unlikely Allies: Exonerees, Lawmakers Worked Together for Tim Cole Bill," *Lubbock Avalanche-Journal*, June 6, 2015; Brandi Grissom, "Senator Says Innocence Commission Bill Is in Trouble," *Texas Tribune*, May 16, 2013; Editorial, "The Texas Justice League," *Dallas Morning News*, December 27, 2015.

57. Editorial, "Texas Justice League."

58. Editorial, "Texas Justice League."

YOU DECIDE: CITE AND RELEASE: NECESSARY COST-SAVINGS OR SOFT ON CRIME?

a. Daily Texan Editorial Board, "High Time for Texas to Decriminalize Marijuana," January 31, 2014; Texas Criminal Justice Coalition, "Findings Summary: Issues Facing County Jails."

b. Nathan Bernier, "In Austin, 1 in 4 Pot Busts Doesn't Lead to Arrest," KUT.ORG, November 9, 2012; Mikaela Cannizzo, "Cite and Release Policy in Austin to Soon Be Enacted in Other Texas Counties," *Daily Texan*, January 28, 2016.

c. "Marijuana: Despite Law Allowing Ticketing for Pot Possession, Most Texas Counties Still Arrest," StopTheDrugWar.org., January 8, 2008; "Marijuana Ticket Law Only Catching on Near Austin, Texas," *Dallas Morning News*, December 31, 2007.

d. Eric Nicholson, "Dallas County Will Experiment with Not Arresting People Caught with Marijuana," *Dallas Observer*, October 6, 2014.

e. Melissa Repko, "Marijuana Possession Could Lead to Ticket Instead of Arrest under Dallas Pilot Program," *Dallas Morning News*, December 7, 2015.

AnswerKey

CHAPTER 1
1. B
2. A
3. C
4. D
5. B
6. D
7. E
8. A
9. E
10. C
11. B
12. C
13. A
14. A

CHAPTER 2
1. A
2. E
3. D
4. C
5. E
6. D
7. A
8. D
9. D
10. B
11. A
12. A
13. D
14. D
15. D

CHAPTER 3
1. C
2. C
3. A
4. B
5. B
6. A
7. A
8. C
9. A
10. C
11. B
12. A
13. B
14. C
15. E

CHAPTER 4
1. B
2. B
3. A
4. B
5. A
6. A
7. A
8. D
9. C
10. B
11. B
12. A

CHAPTER 5
1. C
2. C
3. D
4. E
5. C
6. C
7. A
8. C
9. A
10. A
11. D
12. A
13. C
14. B

CHAPTER 6
1. B
2. E
3. E
4. E
5. A
6. E
7. A
8. D
9. C
10. C
11. E
12. B
13. D
14. B
15. A

CHAPTER 7
1. A
2. A
3. D
4. B
5. E
6. B
7. C
8. B
9. D
10. D
11. C
12. A
13. D
14. A
15. A
16. D
17. B

CHAPTER 8
1. D
2. E
3. E
4. B
5. D
6. A
7. A
8. B
9. B
10. B
11. E
12. A
13. C
14. A
15. E

CHAPTER 9
1. C
2. C
3. C
4. B
5. B
6. A
7. E
8. D
9. E
10. A
11. E
12. A
13. A
14. C

CHAPTER 10
1. B
2. D
3. D
4. D

5. C
6. A
7. B
8. B
9. D
10. E
11. A
12. A
13. C
14. A
15. B
16. D
17. A

CHAPTER 11
1. A
2. B
3. A
4. C
5. B
6. B

7. C
8. A
9. B
10. D
11. D
12. A
13. B

CHAPTER 12
1. B
2. E
3. A
4. B
5. C
6. A
7. B
8. E
9. A
10. C
11. B
12. C

13. C
14. A
15. D

CHAPTER 13
1. A
2. B
3. C
4. C
5. D
6. C
7. D
8. E
9. A
10. B
11. E
12. C
13. E
14. C

Credits

Bush, Jeb, 268, 272
business
    dominance of in political
        culture, 6–7, 23
    interest groups and,
        185–86, 203–4
    tax system and, 366, 370,
        372
Butt, Charles, 185
Butts, David, 303

C

Caddo Lake Compact Com-
    mission, 279
Calendars Committee, 222
Calhoun, John C., 92
California
    capital appreciation bonds
        and, 352, 353
    death penalty in, 464
    debt service in, 382
    federal funds to, 95
    Great Recession and, 22
    gubernatorial power in,
        251
    home-rule cities in, 334
    judicial appointments in,
        307
    legislature membership
        characteristics, 225
    lobbyists in, 197
    local government of, 345
    pension system of, 353–54
    political culture of, 5
    population of, 33
    prison system of, 446
    public school enrollment
        in, 404
    retention elections in, 303
    voting in election of 2016,
        163
California Watch, 352
Cameron County, 416
campaign contributions and
    spending, 7, 164–65, 165,
    166, 254, 258
    bundling and, 185
    federal laws on, 165

interest groups/lobbies
    and, 184, 187, 193,
    194–99, 195
in judicial elections, 300,
    301–2, 305–7, 306
"late-train," 196
PACs and, 193, 198, 209
plural executive and,
    268–69
for statewide offices
    (2014), 269
campaigns, 143–44, 164–74
    candidates, 164
    gubernatorial, 254
    important issues in, 168–72
    of incumbents vs. chal-
        lengers, 194–96, 196
    judicial, 299–300, 301–2
    media and, 172–73
    political parties and,
        166–67
    strategy in, 167–68
Campbell, Donna, 194, 198
Campbell, Thomas M., 253
Camp Bowie, 35
Canada, 19, 87
Cancer Prevention and Re-
    search Institute of Texas
    (CPRIT), 265

**capital appreciation bond
(CAB), 352–53** a long-term,
high-interest-paying bond
that pays off both principal
and interest in one lump
sum when the bond reaches
maturity

**capital case, 299, 447,
448, 454–55** a criminal case
in which the death penalty is
a possible punishment
    cost of prosecuting, 331,
        332
    defined, 298

capital punishment. See death
    penalty

Carrollton, 35
Carter, Jimmy, 118
Casas, Juan Bautista de las, 48
Casas Revolt, 48
Cascos, Carlo, 268
Castro, Eva DeLuna, 379
Castro, Joaquin, 26, 135
Castro, Julian, 36, 135, 137,
    139, 143

categorical grants, 94
congressionally appropriated
grants to states and localities on the condition that
expenditures be limited to a
problem or group specified
by law

cattle ranching, 10, 12–13, 13,
    35, 134
Center for Public Integrity,
    173
Center for Public Policy Pri-
    orities, 379, 422
Chapman, Ron, 134
charter schools, 404, 412,
    414–15, 438
Chase, Salmon, 91–92

**checks and balances, 45,
52, 54, 63, 182** the constitutional idea that overlapping
power is given to different
branches of government to
limit the concentration of
power in any one branch

Chemical Safety Board,
    United States, 323–24
Chevron, 14, 20
Chicago Tribune, 471
Child Nutrition Grants, 404
Children's Health Insurance
    Program (CHIP), 363,
    426, 430
Childress, George C., 51

child support collection, 271
Chinni, Dante, 134
CHIP. See Children's Health
    Insurance Program
Christian, Wayne, 268
Christman, Cari, 169
chubbing, 224
cite and release policies, 463
Citizens United v. Federal
    Election Commission,
    198
city councils, 342. See also
    council-manager
    form of government;
    mayor-council form of
    government
city government, 333–44
    comparisons of, 338–44
    forms of, 335–38
    number of municipalities,
        325, 333, 334
    size of municipalities, 333,
        334
civic engagement, measures
    of, 202
civil cases, 299, 312, 313

civil law, 296–97, 326 a
branch of law that deals with
disputes, usually between
private individuals over relationships, obligations, and
responsibility

Civil Rights Act of 1964, 27, 152
civil rights legislation, 96, 214
civil rights movement, 27, 122
Civil War, 12, 13, 15, 23, 26, 37,
    46, 48, 57, 64, 91, 99
Clay, Henry, 49
Clear Lake City, 35
clemency, 266–67, 448,
    465–66
Clements, William R., 130, 167,
    252, 262–63, 268, 301
Clinton, Bill, 96, 421
Clinton, Hillary Rodham, 139,
    339

closed primary, 146 a primary election in which only registered members of a particular political party can vote

Coahuila y Tejas, Constitution of (1827), 48–49, 53
Cobb, Roger, 401
Code of Judicial Conduct, 316

coercive federalism, 96–106 federal policies that force states to change their policies to achieve national goals

Coke, Richard, 59, 61, *253*
Cole, Tim, 475, 476
college campuses, concealed weapons issue, 211, *211*, 466–67
colleges and universities. *See* higher education; individual institutions
Collier, Mike, 170, *269*
Collin County, 35, 463
    poverty in, 416
    racial and ethnic composition of, *34*
    special district elections in, 350
Collin County Central Appraisal District building, 272
Colorado, 115, 406, 463
Colquitt, Oscar B., *253*
Combs, Susan, 379, 390, 428

commissioner form of government, 336 a form of city government in which the city is run by a small group of elected commissioners who act in both legislative and executive capacities

committee assignment powers, 232, 233–35

committee chairmanship appointments, 232, *233*, 233–34
Common Cause, 186
Common Core, 227
community college districts, 347–48, 349

complaint, 296 the presentation of a grievance by the plaintiff in a civil case

Compromise of 1850, 8, 54

comptroller, 66, 228, 267, *267*, 274–75, 277, 381, *384*, 385, 386 elected state official who directs the collection of taxes and other revenues and estimates revenues for the budgeting process

concealed/open carry of guns, 211, *211*, 466–67

concurrent resolution, 216–18 a resolution of interest to both chambers of the legislature and which must pass both the House and Senate and generally be signed by the governor

Confederacy, 20, 47, 55–56, 58, 91–92, 160, 325 the Confederate States of America, those southern states that seceded from the United States in late 1860 and 1861 and argued that the power of the states was more important than the power of the central government

Confederation Congress, 88

conference committee, 219, 224–26, 235, 385–86

a joint committee created to work out a compromise on House and Senate versions of a piece of legislation

Conference of Mayors, U.S., 96
Congress, U.S. *See also* House of Representatives, U.S.; Senate, U.S.
    Constitution on, 46
    Democrats in, 118, 130–32
    party polarization in, 114
    reapportionment and, 238
    Texas legislature compared with, 232, 237
Congressional Hispanic Caucus (CHC), 111
Congressional Reconstruction Acts, 57
Connally, John, 250, 252–53, 372
conservation and reclamation districts, 435

consideration by standing committee, 219 the third step in the legislative process, during which a bill is killed, amended, or heard by a standing committee

Consolidated Vultee Aircraft Corporation, 35–37

constable, 326, 329, *329* precinct-level county official involved with serving legal papers and, in some counties, enforcing the law

constituent, 218 a person living in the district from which an official is elected

constitution, 45 the legal structure of a government, which establishes its power

and authority as well as the limits on that power
    defined, 45
    length of, by state, *73*
    role of, 45–47

Constitution, Texas. *See* Texas Constitutions
Constitution, U.S., 182, 218, 249. *See also* individual amendments
    Article I, 46, 64, 66, 90, 91
    Article II, 66
    Article III, 68
    Article IV, 46, 92
    Article VI, 46, 96
    drafting of, 88
    federalism embodied in, 46, 88–90
    flexibility for states under, 103–4
    on impeachment, 69, 70, 219
    Mexican Constitution compared with, 48
    recognized as supreme law of the land, 58, 64
    restrictions on the states, 99
    Texas Constitution compared with, 43, 44, 45–47, 52, 62–64, 65, 68
Constitutional Convention, 88

contingent fee, 296–97 a fee paid to the lawyer in a civil case which is contingent on winning the case

Convention of 1836, 50
Conviction Integrity Unit, 469–70
Cook, John, *269*

cooperative federalism, *93*, 94 a type of federalism existing since the New Deal era in which grants-in-aid have been used to encourage states and localities (without commanding them) to pursue nationally defined goals; also known as *intergovernmental cooperation*

council-manager form of government, *334,* 336–42 a form of city government in which public policies are developed by the city council and executive and administrative functions are assigned to a professional city manager

council of government (COG), *351,* 351–52 a regional planning board composed of local elected officials and some private citizens from the same area

county attorney, 326, 327, 452–54 an elected official in some counties who prosecutes misdemeanor cases; county official who prosecutes lesser criminal cases in the county court

county auditor, 327 public official, appointed by the district judges, who receives and disburses county funds; in large counties, this official also prepares the county budget

county chair, 119 the county party official who heads the county executive committee

county clerk, 326, *329* public official who is the main record-keeper of the county

county commissioner, 325–26, 327–29, *328* government official (four per county) on the county commissioners' court whose main duty is the construction and maintenance of roads and bridges

county commissioners' court, 327–29, *328, 330* the main governing body of each county; has the authority to set the county tax rate and budget

county convention, 119–20 a meeting held by a political party following its precinct conventions, for the purpose of electing delegates to its state convention

county courts, *292,* 293 the courts that exist in some counties that are presided over by county judges

county executive committee, 119 the party group, made up of a party's county chair and precinct chairs, that is responsible for running a county's primary elections and planning county conventions

county judge, 293, 327, 328, *329* the person in each of Texas's 254 counties who presides over the constitutional county court and county commissioners' court, with responsibility for the administration of county government; some county judges carry out judicial responsibilities

county tax assessor-collector, 326, *329* public official who maintains the county tax records and collects the taxes owed to the county

courts of appeal, 291–93, 310, 451 the 14 intermediate-level appellate courts that hear appeals from district and county courts to determine whether the decisions of

these lower courts followed legal principles and court procedures

criminal law, 296 the branch of law that regulates the conduct of individuals, defines crimes, and specifies punishment for criminal acts

Ellis, Rodney, 474, 475, 476

El Paso

    African American population of, 342

    city government of, *334, 336, 342–44, 343*

    early growth of, 32

    Latino population of, 25, 342

    party affiliations in, 134

    pension system of, 355

    population of, *31, 334*

    toll roads of, 399

    water supplies of, 44, 433

El Paso County, *34*

El Paso Times, 172, *172*

Emergency Assistance Program, 421

emergency services districts, 348

EMILY'S LIST, 198

eminent domain, 44, *79,* 399

Empower Texans, 165–66, 198, *199*

empresarios, 23, 50

Environmental Protection Agency, 271, 274

Episcopal Health Foundation, 432

Equality Texas, 339

Equal Justice Initiative, 93

equal protection clause, 77, 99–100, 104, 151, 158, 407, 408 provision in the Fourteenth Amendment of the U.S. Constitution guaranteeing citizens the "equal protection of the laws"; this clause has been the basis for the civil rights of African Americans, women, and other groups

Equal Rights Amendment (proposed), *79,* 104

ESF. *See* Economic and Stabilization Fund

Esso, 14

Estelle, W. J., Jr., 456

Ethiopia, 87

ethnicity. *See* race and ethnicity

European Union, 87

Evans, Ira, 231

Evenwel v. Abbott, 105–6, 159, 238

evolution, teaching of, 133, 281

executions, 317, 446, *461,* 464, *464,* 465, 471. *See also* death penalty

executive branch. *See* Texas executive branch

executive budget, 262–63, 264 the state budget prepared and submitted by the governor to the legislature, which indicates the governor's spending priorities. The executive budget is overshadowed in terms of importance by the legislative budget

executive powers, 258–64

Exxon, 14

ExxonMobil, 14, 20, 184

F

Facebook, 18, 124, 167, 173, 228, 229, 281

Family Support Act, 420

federal funds

    flow of to Texas, *97*

    to Texas *vs.* other states, *95*

Federal Funds budget, 363 state budget that includes all grants, payments, and reimbursements received from the federal government by state agencies and institutions

federalism, 84–109 a system of government in which power is divided, by a constitution, between a central government and regional governments

    coercive, 96–106

    cooperative, *93,* 94

    defined, 46, 87

    dual, 92–93, *93*

    in early America, 90–92

    layer-cake, 93

    marble-cake, *93,* 93–96

    new, 96

    roots of, 87–92

    states' response to, 98–99

Federalist Papers, The, 45, 182

federal medical assistance percentage (FMAP), 426

Federal Reserve System, 20–21, 387

felony, 298, 299, 447, *448,* 449, 450–51, 476 a serious criminal offense, punishable by a prison sentence or a fine. A capital felony is punishable by death or a life sentence

Ferdinand VII, King of Spain, 48

Ferguson, James, 149, *253,* 256

Ferguson, Jesse Tyler, 339

Ferguson, Ma and Pa, 3

Ferguson, Margaret, 249

Ferguson, Miriam, 252, *253,* 256, 465

fertilizer plant explosion, *322,* 323–24

Field, Sally, 339

"15 percent rule," 179

Fifteenth Amendment (U.S. Constitution), 99, 100, 102, 103, 151

"file and use" regulatory system, 280

filibuster, 222–24 a tactic used by members of the

Senate to prevent action on legislation they oppose by continuously holding the floor and speaking until the majority backs down. Once given the floor, senators have unlimited time to speak as long as they follow Senate rules

fire codes, *322,* 323–24

firefighters, 260, *322,* 323–24, 354–55

Firefighters' Star of Texas Award Advisory Committee, 260

"first past the post," 123 an election rule that states that the winner is the candidate who receives a plurality of the votes

flag of Texas, 55, *92*

Flextronics, 18

flood control districts, 348

floods, 434, 435

floor action, 219, 222–24 the fourth step in the legislative process, during which a bill referred by a standing committee is scheduled for floor debate by the Calendars Committee

Flores, Bill, 130

Flores, Gilbert, 155

Florida

    death penalty in, 464

    federal funds to, *95*

    Great Recession and, 22

    legislature membership characteristics, *225*

    lobbyists in, *197*

    population of, *33*

FMAP (federal medical assistance percentage), 426

food stamps program, 419, 420, 421

Fort Bend County, 28

Fort Bliss, 342

Fort Worth. *See also* Dallas-Fort Worth metropolitan area
city government of, *334,* 336
early growth of, 32
Latino population of, 25
pension system of, 354
political economy of, 35–37
population of, 37, *334*

Foster, Kenneth, 466

Foundation School Account, 373

Founding of Texas (era), 47–49, 60

Four Seasons Ranch Municipal Utility District No. 1, 350

Fourteenth Amendment (U.S. Constitution), 46, 58, 103
equal protection clause of, 77, 99–100, 104, 151, 158, 407, 408
ratification of, 91

Fourth Amendment (U.S. Constitution), 451

fracking, *7,* 16, 280, 335, 367, 385

franchise, 148–52. *See also* voting

franchise tax, 370, 389, 391

Franklin County, 331

free rider problem, 182–83 the incentive to benefit from others' work without making a contribution, which leads individuals in a collective action situation to refuse to work together

Friedman, Kinky, 122–23, *123,* 147–48

Frisco, 35

Fulton, Robert, 91

G

Gallup polls, 128

Galveston, 32, 35, 336, *337*

Galveston County, 329

Garcia, Adrian, 111, 199

Garland, 35

Garner, John Nance, 149

gays, 339. *See also* same-sex marriage

gender. *See also* women
Medicaid participation by, 425, *425*
of Texas judges, *311*
of Texas legislature members, 214–16, *215, 225*

gender identity, discrimination based on, 339

general bill, 216 a bill that applies to all people and/or property in the state

General Dynamics, 35

general election, 146 the election in which voters cast ballots to select public officials

General Land Office (GLO), *63, 69, 272,* 272–73, 335

general-law cities and towns, 335, 336

General Revenue-Dedicated Funds budget, 363, 374 budget composed of funds for dedicated revenues that target money for specific purposes

General Revenue Fund, 374 the state's primary operating fund

General Revenues Fund budget, 363, 364, 365, 370, 374, 377, 381, 382, 387, 390, 391, 404, 421,

423 budget for a nondedicated revenue account that functions as the state's primary operating fund

geographic regions of Texas, 7–10, *9*

George Bush Intercontinental Airport, 18

"German counties," 126

Germany, 87

get-out-the-vote initiatives, 193–94

Getty Oil Company, 297

Gibbons, Thomas, 91

Gibbons v. Ogden, 91

Giddings, Helen, *214*

Gideon v. Wainwright, 454

Gilmer-Aikin Laws, 406 education reform legislation passed in 1949 that supplemented local funding of education with public monies, raised teachers' salaries, mandated a minimum length for the school year, and provided for more state supervision of public education

Gimpel, James, 134

GLO. *See* General Land Office

GOBPP. *See* Governor's Office of Budget, Planning, and Policy

Gonzalez, Henry B., 26

Gonzalez, Tommy, 342

Gooden, Lance, 199

Good Society, 5

Google, 18

Gossage, Eddie, *330*

Governor's Advisory Council on Physical Fitness, 260

governorship, 249–67
budgetary authority of, 262–63, 381, 383, *384,* 386–87
campaigns for, 254

compensation of, 257

constitutional provisions for, 55, 58, *59,* 66

election and term of office, 252–53

executive powers of, 258–64

governors since 1874, *253*

judicial powers of, 266–67

legislative powers of, 226–28, 264–66

plural executive and, 267, *267,* 268, 276, 277

power of position, 227, 247–48, *251*

qualifications for office, 252

removal of governor, 256

staff of, 257–58

succession line in, 256–57

Governor's Office of Budget, Planning, and Policy (GOBPP), 383, *384*

Graham, Elizabeth, 429

grand jury, 298, 450, 454, 476 jury that determines whether sufficient evidence is available to justify a trial; grand juries do not rule on the accused's guilt or innocence

Grand Prairie, 35

Grange, 12, 60–61, 120, 183, 184 a militant farmers' movement of the late nineteenth century that fought for improved conditions for farmers

Great Depression, 12, 93–94, 418

Great Plains, 10

Great Recession, 29, 248, 315, 354, 366, 370, 371, 387–88, 390, 392, 416
CHIP enrollment and, 426

higher education funding and, 362

Medicaid enrollment and, 423

school funding and, 410

the "Texas miracle" and, 20–22

welfare caseloads and, 422

Great Society, 94

Green, Gene, 111, 118, *118,* 132

Green, Paul, 304

Green, Rick, 304

Grimes County Municipal Utility District No. 1, 350

Grodzins, Morton, 93

groundwater, *433,* 434–35, 436

Grovey v. Townsend, 151

Guadalupe Hidalgo, Treaty of, 8

Guillen, Ryan, 236

Gulf Coastal Plains, 8–9

Gulf Coast Aquifer, 433

Gulf Oil, 14

gun control/rights, 98, *98,* 99, 132, 139, 169, 211, *211,* 466–67

Gutiérrez, José Ángel, 122

Gutiérrez de Lara, José Bernardo, 48

Guzman, Eva, *310*

H

Halback, Joseph, 304

Hall, Ralph, 130–32

Halliburton Company, 183

Hamilton, Andrew Jackson, 57

Hammond, Bill, 229

Hampton, Keith, *305*

Harle, Sid, 304–5

Harris County, 34, 405

death sentences given in, 332, 470

district attorney's office in, 453

district courts of, 293

drug offenses in, 474

emergency services districts of, 348

jails of, 326

judicial elections in, 304, 305

justice of the peace courts of, 294

nonschool special districts of, 347

oil industry in, 14

party affiliations in, 136

population of, 330

public defenders in, 454

racial and ethnic composition of, *34*

special districts of, 349, 350

voting precincts of, 145

Harris County Republican Party, *120*

Hawk, Susan, 332–33

Hays County, 463

Health Care and Reconciliation Act of 2010, 428

health care policy, 422–32. *See also* Affordable Care Act; Medicaid

health insurance, 422–23, *423, 431,* 432, *432*

Hecht, Nathan, 306, 437

HEF. *See* Higher Education Fund

Hegar, Glenn, 170, 265, *268, 269,* 275, 284, *366*

Heggerty, Pat, 188–89

Herrero, Abel, 185

Hidalgo County, 416, 435

hidden government, 349, 356 a term that refers to special districts of which many citizens are unaware

higher education

funding of, 8, 15, *360,* 361–62, 363, 376–78, 389

gubernatorial appointees and, 260

segregation in, 100

Higher Education Fund (HEF), 376, 377 state higher education fund for universities not having access to PUF monies

High Plains Underground Water District, 435

high-tech industries, 3, 17–18, *18,* 35

highway system. *See* Interstate Highway System

Hill, John, 72, 252, 268

Hinojosa, Michael, 415

Hispanics. *See* Latinos

Hobby, William P., 149, *253*

Hobby, William P., Jr., 72, 257, 372

Hodge, Daniel, 257

Hogan, Jim, *269*

Hogg, James S., *253*

homeowners' insurance, 279–80

Home-Rule Charter Amendments, 334

home-rule charter, *334,* 334–35, 336, 337 the rules under which a city operates; local governments have considerable independent governing power under these charters

horizontal drilling, 16, 280, 367

hospital districts, 348, 349

hotel and motel taxes, 371

House Bill 5, 414

House Bill 72, 410

House Bill 166, 474–76

House Bill 1863, 421

House of Representatives, U.S. *See also* Congress, U.S.

African Americans in, 264

impeachment proceedings and, 69

Latinos in, 26

party composition of Texas delegation, *129*

redistricting and, 238, 240

Republicans in, 129, *130*

housing bubble and bust, 20, 21–22, 349, 387–88

Houston, 143, 144

African American population of, 27, 28, 136

Asian American population of, 28

"bathroom ordinance" of, 339

city government of, *334,* 336, 338, *343*

crime lab scandal in, 470

early growth of, 32

high-tech industries in, 18

judicial districts of, 310

Latino population of, 25

party affiliations in, 118, 134, 137

pension system of, 354

political economy of, 34–35

population of, *31,* 34, 333, *334,* 338

port of, 18

school desegregation in, 407

school districts of, 404

special districts of, 347

toll roads in, 399

voter turnout in, 146

Houston, Sam (attorney general candidate), *269*

Houston, Sam (governor), 3, 34, 53, 55–56

Houston and Texas Central Railroad, 35

Houston and Texas Central Railroad Company v. East, 434

Houston Chronicle, 172, *172*

Houston Newsmakers (television program), 172

Houston Press, 290

Houston Ship Channel, 34

Howard, Donna, 191

Hubbard, Richard B., *253*

Huckabee, Mike, *117*

Joint Committee on Prison Reform, 456

joint committees, *234*

joint resolution, 218 a resolution, commonly a proposed amendment to the Texas Constitution or ratification of an amendment to the U.S. Constitution, that must pass both the House and Senate but that does not require the governor's signature

Jones, Anson, 54
Jones, Elizabeth Ames, 198
Jones, Jesse, 183
Jones, Mark, 132, 236, 237
Jordan, Barbara, 27, 118
judges, 299–312
    alternative means of selection, 302–7
    appointment of, 266, 291, 300, *300,* 301
    county, 293, 327, *328, 329*
    death penalty cases and, 464
    discipline of, 315–17
    election of, 291, 299–307, 317–18
    federal, 291
    judicial districts and, 310–12
    name game and, 304
    selection of in Texas *vs.* other states, *309*
    trial by, 451
judicial branch. *See* Texas judiciary

Judicial Campaign Fairness Act, 307 a judicial reform that places limits on judicial campaign contributions

judicial districts, 310–12

judicial powers, 218, 219 the power of the House to

impeach and of the Senate to convict members of the executive and judicial branches of state government
    of Texas governor, 266–67

Judson, Jeff, 209
juries
    felony, 299, 451
    grand, 298, 450, 454, 476
    misdemeanor, 299, 451
    women on, *79,* 149
Juris Doctor (JD) degree, 313

justice of the peace courts, *292,* 294–95, 312, 315 local trial courts with limited jurisdiction over small claims and very minor criminal misdemeanors

K

Kaiser Family Foundation, 430
Keller, Sharon, 317
Kendall County, 416
Kenedy County, 145, 331
Kennedy, Anthony, 77
Kennedy, John F., 282, 308
Kentucky, 117
Kerrigan, Patricia, 304
"key man" grand juror selection method, 476
Kinch, Sam, 252
Kinder, Donald, 170
King, Bill, 143, 144, 354
King, Ken, 185
King Ranch, *13*
Kirby, Barbara, 295
Kirby, William, 408
Kirk, Ron, 117, 137
Kitzman, Eleanor, 262

L

labor unions, 7, 9

land commissioner, 267, *267,* 272–73, 277 elected state official who is the man-

ager of most publicly owned lands

land grants, 9, 32, 52–53, 376
Land Office, 7
Laney, Pete, 230, 239, 257
Lang, Katie, 77, *78*
Lanham, S. W. T., *253*
LAR (Legislative Appropriation Request), 383

La Raza Unida, 26, 122 political party formed in Texas in order to bring attention to the concerns of Mexican Americans

Laredo, *334*
"late-train" campaign contributions, 196
Latinos, 10, 173, 174, 342
    Abbott criticized by, 167
    in city government, 340
    civil rights movement and, 122
    in Congress, 118
    on death row, *457,* 465
    interest groups and, 186
    Medicaid participation in, 425
    opinions on issues in, 171–72
    party affiliations of, 111–12, 115, 118, 122, 132, 135, 137–38
    political participation and, 25–26, 160–62
    population, 3, *23,* 24–26, *25, 31,* 37–38, 115
    poverty in, 417, *417*
    in prison, *457*
    in public schools, 405, *409*
    redistricting and, 105–6, 158
    in Texas judiciary, 307–10, *311*
    in Texas legislature, 26, *215, 225*

voting and, 25, 102, 103, 118, 136, *136,* 137, 138, 149, 151–52, 160–62, *161*
Latino Victory Project PAC, *26*
Lavine, Dick, 379
lawmaking, 219–30, *220–21*
    committee action, 219, 222
    conference committees, 219, 224–26
    floor action, 219, 222–24
    governor's action, 219, 226–28
    introduction in the House, 219, 222
    referral, 219, 222

law of capture, 434–35 the idea that the first person to "capture" water or oil by pumping it out of the ground and using it owns that water or oil

law of parties, 466
law schools, 313
lawyers. *See* attorneys

layer-cake federalism, 93 a way of describing the system of dual federalism in which there is a division of responsibilities between the state and the national governments

LBB. *See* Legislative Budget Board
Leach, Jeff, 475
League of United Latin American Citizens, 186
League of Women Voters, 160, 275
Lee, Robert E., 57, 91
Legislative Appropriation Request (LAR), 383
Legislative Audit Committee, 269

legislative branch. *See* Congress, U.S.; Texas legislature

legislative budget, 262 the state budget that is prepared and submitted by the Legislative Budget Board (LBB) and that is fully considered by the House and Senate

Legislative Budget Board (LBB), 262–63, 269, 365, 381, 382–84, *384,* 385, 386, 387, 389
Legislative Budget Estimates (LBB publication), 384
Legislative Education Board, 269
legislative powers
    of Texas governor, 226–28, 264–66
    of Texas legislature, 216–18
Legislative Redistricting Board (LRB), 238, 269
Legislative Reference Library, 264
legitimation, 402
Lehmberg, Rosemary, 265, 333
Leininger, James, 198
Lewis, Gib, 190–92
Libertarian Party, 122, 131

lieutenant governor, 230, 269 a statewide elected official who is the presiding officer of the Senate; the lieutenant governor is one of the most important officials in state government and has significant control over legislation in the state Senate; the second-highest elected official in the state and president of the state Senate
    campaigns for, 116, *117*
    constitutional provisions for, 55, 66
    defined, 230, 269

legislative powers and functions of, 230, 231–35
plural executive and, 267, *267,* 269–71, 277
political styles in, 270–71
succession to governorship and, 256–57
term of office, 231

Limestone County, 14

limited government, 63, 217 a principle of constitutional government; a government whose powers are defined and limited by a constitution

Lincoln, Abraham, 55

line-item veto, 57, 226–27, 249, 263, 265–66, 386 the power of the executive to veto specific provisions (lines) of an appropriations bill passed by the legislature

Ling-Temco-Vought (LTV), 35
Livingston, Robert, 91

lobbyist, 185–203 an individual employed by an interest group who tries to influence governmental decisions on behalf of that group
    See also interest groups
    corruption and, 190–92
    defined, 185
    earnings of lobbyists, 188
    expenditures of, 193
    former legislators and, 188–90, 191
    gubernatorial involvement in, 264
    individuals as, 201–3
    legislative agenda influenced by, 229
    number of registered groups, 188, *197*

ordinary citizens and, 192
types of, 185–86

local and consent calendar, 212

local bill, 216 a bill affecting only units of local government, such as a city, county, or special district

local government, 323–59. *See also* city government; county government; special districts
    financial issues facing, 352–55
    state government control of, 89
    Texas Constitution on, *63,* 69
    in Texas *vs.* other states, *345*
local taxes, 366, 406
Locke, John, 51
Logic of Collective Action, The (Olson), 182–83
Longoria, Eva, *26,* 339
Longoria, Nora, 316–17, *317*
lottery, state, 372–74
Louisiana, 114, 115, 117, 136, 139, 433, 460
Loving County, 145, 330
Lozano, Jose Manuel, 138, 198
LRB. *See* Legislative Redistricting Board
Lubbock, 10
Lucio, Eddie, 216
lynchings, 27, 93

M
Madison, James, 45, 90, 182
Magnolia Petroleum, 14
Mahendru, Ashish, 304
Majcher, Dineen, *178,* 179–80, 201
malapportionment, 328
MALDEF. *See* Mexican American Legal Defense and Education Fund

managed care organizations (MCOs), 424
manufactured home sales tax, 368–70

marble-cake federalism, 93, 93–96 a way of describing federalism where the boundaries between the national government and state government have become blurred

marijuana possession, 451–52, 463, 478
markup, 385
marriage
    same-sex, 76–78, *79,* 114, 130, 171, 272
    Texas Constitution on, 43, 171
Marshall, John, 90–91
Marshall, Khambrell, 172
martial law, 250, 263

matching funds, 372 federal monies going to a state based on state spending for a program

mayor-council form of government, *334,* 335–36, 338 a form of city government in which the mayor is the chief executive and the city council is the legislative body; in the *strong mayor–council* variation, the mayor's powers enable him or her to control executive departments and the agenda of the city council; in the *weak mayor–council* variation, the mayor's power is more limited

Mays, Richard, 135
McAllen, *31*
McCall, Brian, 247, 249–50, 278

McCally, Sharon, 304

McClendon, Ruth Jones, 475, 476

McCulloch v. Maryland, 90

McDonald, Craig, 192

McKinney, 35, 272

McNair, Bob, 198

McWilliams, Andrea, 188, *189*

Meadows Foundations, 16

media, 124, 172–73, 228–29

mediation, 297

Medicaid, 348, 363, 372, 378, 379, 382, 387, 388, 416, 417, 419, 421, 422, 423–26, 438 a federal and state program financing medical services to low-income people

    administration and financing of, 426

    Affordable Care Act and, 96, 428–32

    defined, 418

    description of program, 94, 424

    establishment of, 418, 424

    increased demand for, 420, 423

    participants in, 424–25

    spending on, 420, 426, *427,* 428

    Traditional, 424

    underfunding of, 390

Medicaid Rural Area STAR, 424

Medicaid Women's Health Program, 427–28

medical malpractice cases, 193, 198, 312

Medicare, 94, 422, 426

Meier, Bill, 223

merit selection, 302–4, 307 a judicial reform under which judges would be nominated

by a blue-ribbon committee, would be appointed by the governor, and, after a brief period in office, would run in a retention election

Mesquite, 35

message power, 227, 264

mestizos, 24

Metroplex, 35. *See also* Dallas-Fort Worth metropolitan area

Metzger, Bill, 77

Mexican American Legal Defense and Education Fund (MALDEF), 151–52, 186, 408

Mexican Americans, 24–26. *See also* Latinos

Mexican American War, 8

Mexican Revolution, 37

Mexican War of Independence, 48

Mexico, 10, 22, 36, 37

    Constitution of, 48–49, 50

    federalism in, 87

    independence from Spain, 48

    NAFTA and, 18–20

    Texas as part of, 12, 47, 48–49, 325

    Texas independence from, 26, 50–54, 406

Michael Morton Act, 446, 474

Michigan, *306,* 353

Midland County, 129

military bases, 20, *21,* 37, 342

military powers, 263–64

Miller, Sid, *268, 269,* 273–74, *274,* 284

mineral rights, 7–8, 52–53

Mineral Wells Pre-Parole Transfer Facility, 458

minorities. *See also* specific groups

    redistricting and, 240

    in Texas judiciary, 307–10

    in Texas legislature, 214–16

misdemeanor, 298, 299, 447, *448,* 449, 476 a minor criminal offense usually punishable by a small fine or short jail sentence

missions, 32

Mississippi, 98, 115, 152

Missouri, 307

Missouri Compromise, 55

mistrials, 299, 451

Mitchell, Jonathan, 428

Monitor, 167

Montana, 99, *306*

Montgomery County, 326, *326*

Moody, Dan, *253*

Moore, Margaret, *453*

moralistic political culture, 5 the belief that government should be active in promoting the public good and that citizens should participate in politics and civic activities to ensure that good

Morath, Michael, *403*

Morrison, Matthew, 339

Morton, Christine, 445

Morton, Eric, 445

Morton, Michael, *444,* 445–46, 474, 477

"Mothers Against Drunk Testing" (TAMSA), 179–80

motor fuels tax, *367,* 368, 374, 390, 399

motor vehicle sales and rentals tax, 368–70, 392

motor voter law, 153, 173 a national act, passed in 1993, that requires states to allow people to register to vote when applying for a driver's license

MUDs. *See* municipal utility districts

Mulroney, Brian, 19, *19*

multimember appointed boards, 278–79

multimember elected boards, 280–82

municipal courts, *292,* 295–96 local trial courts with limited jurisdiction over violations of city ordinances and very minor criminal misdemeanors

municipal government. *See* city government

municipal utility district (MUD), 347, 350 a special district that offers services such as electricity, water, sewage, and sanitation outside the city limits

Muñiz, Ramsey, 122

Munk, Michael, 317

Muñoz, Henry R., III, *26*

Murray, Mekisha, 304

Mutscher, Gus, 72

N

NAACP. *See* National Association for the Advancement of Colored People

NAFTA. *See* North American Free Trade Agreement

Napoleonic Wars, 48

National Association for the Advancement of Colored People (NAACP), 151, 186

National Association of Counties, 96

National Association of Latino Elected and Appointed Officials, 26

National Bankers Life Insurance Corporation, 72

National Commission on Excellence in Education, 411

powers

  appointment (*see* appointment)

  budgetary, 262–63

  committee assignment, 232, 233–35

  directive and supervisory, 218, 219

  electoral, 218

  executive, 258–64

  investigative, 218–19

  judicial, 218, 219

  legislative, 216–18, 226–28, 264–66

  message, 227, 264

  military and police, 263–64

  nonlegislative, 218–19

precinct, 119, 329, *329* the most basic level of political organization at the local level

precinct chair, 119 the local party official, elected in the party's primary election, who heads the precinct convention and serves on the party's county executive committee

precinct convention, 119–20 a meeting held by a political party to select delegates for the county convention and to submit resolutions to the party's state platform; precinct conventions are held on the day of the party's primary election and are open to anyone who voted in that election

preclearance, 100–103, 158 provision under Section 5 of the Voting Rights Act of 1965 requiring any changes to election procedures or district lines to be approved by the U.S. Department of Justice or the U.S. district court for the District of Columbia

preemption, 96 where the national government imposes its priorities and prevents the state from acting in a particular field

preponderance of the evidence, 297 the standard of proof in a civil jury case, by which the plaintiff must show that the defendant is more likely than not the cause of the harm suffered by the plaintiff

Preservation Trust Fund Advisory Board, 260

presidency, 249, 283–84

Presidential Reconstruction, 57 a reconstruction plan for reintegrating former confederate states back into the Union and freeing the slaves that placed mild demands upon the existing white power structure.

presidential Republicanism, 126 a voting pattern in which conservatives vote Democratic for state offices but Republican for presidential candidates

president pro tempore of the Senate, 231

Presidio County, 330

presidios, 32

pretrial hearings, 450–51

Price, John Wiley, 333

Price, Walter, 323

primary election, 118–19, 254 a ballot vote in which citizens select a party's nominee for the general election

  defined, 145

  importance of Republican, *162,* 162–64

  types of, 145–46

Prinz v. United States, 99

prison system, 446, 455–62. *See also* death penalty

  current conditions in, 458–62

  early release policies of, 458

  history of, 455–58

  operating costs in, 458

  percentage of sentence served in, *459*

  population of, *457, 459*–60, *460, 462*

  in Texas *vs.* other states, *461*

privatization of public property, 7–8 the act(s) by which Texas gave public land owned by the state over to private individuals for cultivation and development

probation, 446, 447, 452 punishment where an offender is not imprisoned but remains in the community under specified rules and under the supervision of a probation officer

progressive tax, 371 type of tax where the tax burden falls more heavily on upper-income individuals

Prohibition (alcohol), *79,* 149, 183

property crime, 458, 459, 462

property rights, water, 434

property tax, 104, 170, *229, 335, 346, 347*–48, *350, 353, 387, 404, 408*–10 a tax based on an assessment of the value of one's property, which is used to fund the services provided by local governments, such as education

  decline in, 388–89

  defined, 348

  reform of, 370, 388–89

  Texas rank in, 366

Property Tax Relief Fund, 363, 370

proportional representation, 123 a multimember district system that allows each political party representation in proportion to its percentage of the total vote

Proposition 1, *76*

Proposition 2 (2005), 76–78

Proposition 2 (2013), 44

Proposition 2 (2015), *76*

Proposition 3, *76*

Proposition 4, 74, *76*

Proposition 5, *76*

Proposition 6, 44, *76*

Proposition 7, 44, 74, *76*

Proposition 8, 74–75

Proposition 12, 78

provincialism, 6, 23 a narrow, limited, and self-interested view of the world often associated with rural values and notions of limited government

PSF. *See* Permanent School Fund

Public Citizen, 186, 200

public defender, 298, 454–55 salaried lawyer who

Speaker of the House, 209, 224–26, 234, 381, 383, 385 the chief presiding officer of the House of Representatives; the Speaker is the most important party and House leader, and can influence the legislative agenda, the fate of individual pieces of legislation, and members' positions within the House
defined, 230
powers and functions of, 230–31, 232–35

special bill, 216 a bill that gives an individual or corporation a special exemption from state law

special district, 344–52, 350 a unit of local government that performs a single service, such as education or sanitation, within a limited geographic area
creating, governing, and paying for, 348–49
defined, 344
number of, 344
problems with, 349–51
types of, 346

special election, 147 an election that is not held on a regularly scheduled basis; in Texas, a special election is called to fill a vacancy in office, to give approval for the state government to borrow money, or to ratify amendments to the Texas Constitution

special prosecutors, 271
Special School Fund, 406

special session, 212–13, 219, 250, 266 a legislative session called by the governor

that addresses an agenda set by him or her and that lasts no longer than 30 days

spending
constitutional limits on, 378, 381, 382
on Medicaid, 426, *427*, 428
trends in, *365*, 365–66
Spindletop, 14
SSI. *See* Supplemental Security Income program
St. Mary's, 315
STAAR. *See* State of Texas Assessments of Academic Readiness
standardized testing. *See* testing
standing committees, 222, 223, 233–34, 234 a permanent committee with the power to propose and write legislation that covers a particular subject, such as finance or agriculture

STAR (State of Texas Access Reform) program, 424
Starr, Paul, 237
Starr County, 30, 416
State Bar of Texas, 313, *314*
State Board of Education (SBOE), 69, 179, 249, 258, 261, *267*, 267–68, 280, 281–82, *282*, 374, 406–7, 412

state chair and **vice chair, 119** the top two state-level leaders in the party

State Commission on Judicial Conduct, 259–60, 295, 315–17

state convention, 120 a party meeting held every two years for the purpose of

nominating candidates for statewide office, adopting a platform, electing the party's leadership, and in presidential election years selecting delegates for the national convention and choosing presidential electors

state executive committee, 119 the committee responsible for governing a party's activities throughout the state

state funds, 374–78
state government. *See also* federalism
constitutional and statutory flexibility for, 103–4
response to federalism, 98–99

State Highway Fund, 363, 374–76, 390, 392 fund that supports the construction, maintenance, and policing of roadways and acquires rights of way; funded through a variety of taxes such as motor vehicle registration fees, the federal highway fund, and the sales tax on motor lubricants

State Mobility Fund, 400
State of Texas Access Reform (STAR) program, 424
State of Texas Assessments of Academic Readiness (STAAR), 413, 414
State of the State address, 227, 250, 264
State of the Union address, 227
State Seed and Plant Board, 279
States' Rights Amendment. *See* Tenth Amendment

State Water Implementation Fund for Texas (SWIFT), 391, 437
State Water Implementation Revenue Fund for Texas (SWIRFT), 391, 437
State Water Plan, 436

statutory county courts at law, 293–94 courts that tend to hear less serious cases than those heard by district courts

statutory probate courts, 294 specialized courts whose jurisdiction is limited to matters of guardianship
"steak men," 199
Steinbeck, John, 3
Stenholm, Charles, 132
Sterling, Ross, *253*
Stevens Aviation, 297
Stevenson, Adlai, 125, 133
Stevenson, Coke, 252–53
Straus, Joe, *42*, 114, 124, 131, 165–66, 170, 198–99, 209–10, *228*, 230, *231*, 235, 241
campaign contributions to, 196
committee chairs during Speakership of, 233, 234, *234*, *235*
conservative criticism of, 231
Strayhorn, Carole Keeton, 122–23, 147–48, 276
strong mayor-council form of government, 335–36, 338
strong veto. *See* post-adjournment veto
Strother, Ralph, 289, 290
suburbs/suburbanization
defined, 30
partisanship and, 134–36
political culture of, 5–6

on redistricting, 158

on teachers' salaries, 405

on the Tea Party movement, 116

Texas Utilities (TXU), 187

Texas v. White et al., 58, 91–92

Texas Veterans Commission, 373

Texas Water Bank, 436

Texas Water Code, 437

Texas Water Commission, 434, 435

Texas Water Development Board (TWDB), 44, 66, 435–36, 437

Texas Water Trust, 436

Texas Weekly, 252

Texas Youth Commission, 261, 279

TEXPAC, 194

textbooks, 281–82

third parties, 120–24

ballot access, 120

campaign contributions and, *165*

Tea Party formation of considered, 131

Thirteenth Amendment (U.S. Constitution), 58, 99

"three strikes" provision, 449 a law that allows persons convicted of three felonies (or in some cases two felonies) to be sentenced to life imprisonment

Thurmond, Strom, 122

Tidelands, 125

timber production, 8

Timothy Cole Advisory Panel on Wrongful Convictions, 476

Title XIX of the Social Security Act, 424

Title XXI of the Social Security Act, 426

Titus County, 329

tobacco company trial, *295*

tobacco settlement funds, 373

tobacco taxes, 370, 389, 410

toll roads, *398, 399*–400

Tomball, 339

tort, 297, 305, 317 a civil wrong that causes harm to another; it is remedied by awarding economic damages to the injured party

tort reform, *79,* 186, 193, 194, 247–48, 312

Tower, John, 129

traditionalistic political culture, 5 the belief that government should be dominated by political elites and guided by tradition

Traditional Medicaid, 424

transgendered persons, 339

Trans-Texas Corridor, 400

Travels with Charley (Steinbeck), 3

Travis County, 118, 158, 265, 333, 341

Asian American population of, 28

racial and ethnic composition of, *34*

special districts of, 350

Traylor, Chris, 258–59

trial lawyers, 296–97

trials, 298–99, 451

true bill (indictment), 256, 298, 450

Truman, Harry, 122, 125

Trump, Donald, 20

Tucker, Karla Faye, 465, *465*

Tulia drug arrests, 471–72, 477

Turner, Jim, 132

Turner, Scott, 209

Turner, Sylvester, 137, 143, 338, *340*

TWDB. *See* Texas Water Development Board

2015 Book of the States, 249

Twenty-Fourth Amendment (U.S. Constitution), 149

Twin Peaks restaurant gun battle. *See* Waco gun battle

Twitter, 124, 167, 173, 228–29

two-thirds rule, 210, 224, 232–33, 241

tyranny, 45, 89–90 according to James Madison, the concentration of power in any one branch of government

U

Unemployment Insurance, 94, 418

unfunded mandates, 96 federal requirements that states or local governments pay the costs of federal policies

unicameral, 49 comprising one body or house, as in a one-house legislature

Uniform Commercial Code, 275

United States v. Texas, 105

University of Houston, 315

University of North Texas, 315, 378

University of Texas, 15, 315, 361, 376–77, 415, 467

University of Texas at Arlington, 378

University of Texas at Austin, 15, 211, 256, *360,* 361, 377, 467

University of Texas at Dallas, 378

University of Texas at El Paso, 378

University of Texas at Houston, 378

University of Texas at San Antonio, 378

University of Texas Law School, 100

University of Texas System Board of Regents, 258, 377

urbanization, 30–38 the process by which people move from rural areas to cities

changes (1850-2010), *30*

defined, 30

Democratic dominance in, 9

district attorney's office in, 453

partisanship and, 134–36

political culture of, 5–6

political economy of, 32–38

population of, 3, 22

user fee, 347 a fee paid for public goods and services, such as water or sewage service

utility taxes, 370–71

V

Valley Forge, *89*

Van de Putte, Leticia, 116, 143–44, *269*

Van Ormy, 436

Veasey v. Abbott, 103

Vela, Filemon, 111

Velasco, Treaty of, 53–54

Veterans' Land Board, 66

Veterans' Land Program, 272

veto, 226–27, *227,* 247, 250, 264–66, 386 according to the Texas Constitution, the governor's power to turn down legislation; can be